T0336855

Broadband Wireless Access Networks for 4G:

Theory, Application, and Experimentation

Raul Aquino Santos
University of Colima, Mexico

Victor Rangel Licea
National Autonomous University of Mexico, Mexico

Arthur Edwards Block
University of Colima, Mexico

A volume in the Advances in Wireless
Technologies and Telecommunication
(AWTT) Book Series

Managing Director:	Lindsay Johnston
Production Manager:	Jennifer Yoder
Development Editor:	Allyson Gard
Acquisitions Editor:	Kayla Wolfe
Typesetter:	Christina Barkanic
Cover Design:	Jason Mull

Published in the United States of America by
Information Science Reference (an imprint of IGI Global)
701 E. Chocolate Avenue
Hershey PA 17033
Tel: 717-533-8845
Fax: 717-533-8661
E-mail: cust@igi-global.com
Web site: http://www.igi-global.com

Library of Congress Cataloging-in-Publication Data

Broadband wireless access networks for 4G : theory, application, and experimentation / Raul Aquino Santos, Victor Rangel Licea, and Arthur Edwards Block, editors.
     pages cm
 Includes bibliographical references and index.
   ISBN 978-1-4666-4888-3 (hardcover) -- ISBN 978-1-4666-4890-6 (print & perpetual access) -- ISBN 978-1-4666-4889-0 (ebook) 1. Wireless communication systems. 2. Broadband communication systems. I. Aquino Santos, Raul, 1965- II. Rangel Licea, Victor, 1972- III. Block, Arthur Edwards, 1957-
  TK5103.2.B.738 2014
  621.3845'6--dc23
                                                2013034982

This book is published in the IGI Global book series Advances in Wireless Technologies and Telecommunication (AWTT) (ISSN: 2327-3305; eISSN: 2327-3313)

British Cataloguing in Publication Data
A Cataloguing in Publication record for this book is available from the British Library.

All work contributed to this book is new, previously-unpublished material. The views expressed in this book are those of the authors, but not necessarily of the publisher.

For electronic access to this publication, please contact: eresources@igi-global.com.

Advances in Wireless Technologies and Telecommunication (AWTT) Book Series

Xiaoge Xu
The University of Nottingham Ningbo, China

ISSN: 2327-3305
EISSN: 2327-3313

MISSION

The wireless computing industry is constantly evolving, redesigning the ways in which individuals share information. Wireless technology and telecommunication remain one of the most important technologies in business organizations. The utilization of these technologies has enhanced business efficiency by enabling dynamic resources in all aspects of society.

The **Advances in Wireless Technologies and Telecommunication Book Series** aims to provide researchers and academic communities with quality research on the concepts and developments in the wireless technology fields. Developers, engineers, students, research strategists, and IT managers will find this series useful to gain insight into next generation wireless technologies and telecommunication.

COVERAGE

- Cellular Networks
- Digital Communication
- Global Telecommunications
- Grid Communications
- Mobile Technology
- Mobile Web Services
- Network Management
- Virtual Network Operations
- Wireless Broadband
- Wireless Sensor Networks

IGI Global is currently accepting manuscripts for publication within this series. To submit a proposal for a volume in this series, please contact our Acquisition Editors at Acquisitions@igi-global.com or visit: http://www.igi-global.com/publish/.

Titles in this Series

For a list of additional titles in this series, please visit: www.igi-global.com

Wireless Communications and Networking Theory and Practice
M.A. Matin (Institut Teknologi Brunei, Brunei Darussalam)
Information Science Reference • copyright 2014 • 387pp • H/C (ISBN: 9781466651708) • US $205.00 (our price)

Broadband Wireless Access Networks for 4G Theory, Application, and Experimentation
Raul Aquino Santos (University of Colima, Mexico) Victor Rangel Licea (National Autonomous University of Mexico, Mexico) and Arthur Edwards-Block (University of Colima, Mexico)
Information Science Reference • copyright 2014 • 289pp • H/C (ISBN: 9781466648883) • US $180.00 (our price)

Multidisciplinary Perspectives on Telecommunications, Wireless Systems, and Mobile Computing
Wen-Chen Hu (University of North Dakota, USA)
Information Science Reference • copyright 2014 • 274pp • H/C (ISBN: 9781466647152) • US $175.00 (our price)

Mobile Networks and Cloud Computing Convergence for Progressive Services and Applications
Joel J.P.C. Rodrigues (Instituto de Telecomunicações, University of Beira Interior, Portugal) Kai Lin (Dalian University of Technology, China) and Jaime Lloret (Polytechnic University of Valencia, Spain)
Information Science Reference • copyright 2014 • 408pp • H/C (ISBN: 9781466647817) • US $180.00 (our price)

Research and Design Innovations for Mobile User Experience
Kerem Rızvanoğlu (Galatasaray University, Turkey) and Görkem Çetin (Turkcell, Turkey)
Information Science Reference • copyright 2014 • 377pp • H/C (ISBN: 9781466644465) • US $190.00 (our price)

Cognitive Radio Technology Applications for Wireless and Mobile Ad Hoc Networks
Natarajan Meghanathan (Jackson State University, USA) and Yenumula B. Reddy (Grambling State University, USA)
Information Science Reference • copyright 2013 • 370pp • H/C (ISBN: 9781466642218) • US $190.00 (our price)

Evolution of Cognitive Networks and Self-Adaptive Communication Systems
Thomas D. Lagkas (University of Western Macedonia, Greece) Panagiotis Sarigiannidis (University of Western Macedonia, Greece) Malamati Louta (University of Western Macedonia, Greece) and Periklis Chatzimisios (Alexander TEI of Thessaloniki, Greece)
Information Science Reference • copyright 2013 • 438pp • H/C (ISBN: 9781466641891) • US $195.00 (our price)

Tools for Mobile Multimedia Programming and Development
D. Tjondronegoro (Queensland University of Technology, Australia)
Information Science Reference • copyright 2013 • 357pp • H/C (ISBN: 9781466640542) • US $190.00 (our price)

DISSEMINATOR OF KNOWLEDGE

www.igi-global.com

701 E. Chocolate Ave., Hershey, PA 17033
Order online at www.igi-global.com or call 717-533-8845 x100
To place a standing order for titles released in this series, contact: cust@igi-global.com
Mon-Fri 8:00 am - 5:00 pm (est) or fax 24 hours a day 717-533-8661

Table of Contents

Section 2
MAC Layer Issues

Section 3
Network Access Issues

Detailed Table of Contents

Section 1
PHY Layer Issues

Chapter 1

Juan Michel García Díaz, University of Colima, Mexico
Laura Victoria Escamilla Del Río, University of Colima, Mexico
Omar Álvarez Cárdenas, University of Colima, Mexico
Margarita Glenda Mayoral Baldivia, University of Colima, Mexico

This chapter presents a theoretical and experimental analysis of the electromagnetic signal propagation between a base station and a subscriber station in an urban setting using the IEEE 802.16d standard and test bed results, which are then compared to Ergeg's (1998) modified version of the Hata-Okomura (1980) mathematical propagation model. The experimental results of the measurements are similar to the model using the type terrain Category B (Suburban). Additionally, under experimental conditions, equipment with technology IEEE 802.16d and IEEE 802.16e were used to analyze delay and throughput while data, voice, and video was transmitted. The tests show that delay is acceptable for Fixed WiMAX, although it is barely adequate for Mobile WiMAX. As far as throughput is concerned, the average rate is adequate to support applications that include data, voice, and video.

Chapter 2

David González González, Universitat Politècnica de Catalunya, Spain
Mario García-Lozano, Universitat Politècnica de Catalunya, Spain
Silvia Ruiz Boqué, Universitat Politècnica de Catalunya, Spain

Interference mitigation has been identified as an important challenge for cellular technologies based on Orthogonal Frequency Division Multiple Access (OFDMA) such as the Long Term Evolution (LTE) system of the Third Generation Partnership Project (3GPP). In this context, Intercell Interference Coordination (ICIC) techniques have received much attention by the research community, as they are a good approach to address this issue. In particular, static solutions enjoy acceptance due to their low complexity and ease of implementation. ICIC mechanisms are not standardized in LTE, which just provides certain support so that every vendor/operator configures its particular ICIC option. Hence, their interworking with other important network functionalities such as Channel State Information (CSI) feedback must be carefully considered. This chapter provides an overview on the relationship between ICIC and CSI in LTE and introduces a novel mechanism to improve such interworking. The novel scheme is feasible and easy-to-implement and it is especially effective for Non-Real Time services. It provides gains in terms of system capacity, cell edge performance, and energy efficiency with respect to 3GPP LTE mechanisms and previous proposals.

Chapter 3

Elias Yaacoub, Qatar Mobility Innovations Center (QMIC), Qatar
Nizar Zorba, Qatar Mobility Innovations Center (QMIC), Qatar
Zaher Dawy, American University of Beirut (AUB), Lebanon

In this chapter, Long Term Evolution (LTE) for public safety is investigated. Particularly, Distributed Antenna Systems (DAS) are studied, and their impact on LTE public safety networks is analyzed. Furthermore, resource allocation algorithms for the purpose of real-time video transmission, in both the Uplink (UL) and Downlink (DL) directions, are proposed, and a proportional fair scheduling algorithm, applicable in both the UL and DL directions, is presented. The proposed algorithms are compared in several scenarios with and without distributed antenna systems. In addition, Quality of Experience (QoE) metrics are used to measure the quality of the video transmissions, and joint uplink/downlink quality metrics, tailored to video transmission over public safety networks, are presented. Simulation results show large enhancements in video quality due to the application of DAS with smart resource allocation in LTE public safety networks.

Chapter 4

Kui Xu, PLA University of Science and Technology, China
Youyun Xu, PLA University of Science and Technology, China
Dongmei Zhang, PLA University of Science and Technology, China
Wenfeng Ma, PLA University of Science and Technology, China

In this chapter, a novel receiver for Hexagonal Multicarrier Transmission (HMT) system based on the maximizing Signal-to-Interference-plus-Noise Ratio (Max-SINR) criterion is proposed. Theoretical analyses show that there is a timing offset between the prototype pulses of the proposed Max-SINR receiver and the traditional projection receiver. Meanwhile, the timing offset should be matched to the channel scattering factor of the Doubly Dispersive (DD) channel. The closed form timing offset expressions of the prototype pulse for Max-SINR HMT receiver over DD channel with different channel scattering functions are derived. Simulation results show that the proposed Max-SINR receiver outperforms traditional projection scheme and obtains an approximation to the theoretical upper bound SINR performance within the full range of channel spread factor. Consistent with the SINR performance improvement, the Bit Error Rate (BER) performance of the HMT system has also been further improved by using the proposed Max-SINR receiver. Meanwhile, the SINR performance of the proposed Max-SINR receiver is robust to the channel delay spread estimation errors.

Future wireless communication systems are expected to offer several gigabits data rate. It can be anticipated that the advanced communication techniques can enhance the capability of mobile terminals to support high data traffic. However, aggressive technique induces high energy consumption for the circuits of terminals, which drain the batteries fast and consequently limit user experience in future wireless networks. In order to solve such a problem, a scheme called collaborative mobile cluster is foreseen as one of the potential solutions to reduce energy consumption per node in a network by exploiting collaboration within a cluster of nearby mobile terminals. This chapter provides a detailed analysis of the energy consumption of a terminal joining the cluster and also analyzes the conditions for energy savings opportunities.

Reducing the energy consumption in wireless networks has become a significant challenge, not only because of its great impact on the global energy crisis, but also because it represents a noteworthy cost for telecommunication operators. The Base Stations (BSs), constituting the main component of wireless infrastructure and the major contributor to the energy consumption of mobile cellular networks, are usually designed and planned to serve their customers during peak times. Therefore, they are more than sufficient when the traffic load is low. In this chapter, the authors propose a number of BSs switching off algorithms as an energy efficient solution to the problem of redundancy of network resources. They demonstrate via analysis and by means of simulations that one can achieve reduction in energy consumption when one switches off the unnecessary BSs. In particular, the authors evaluate the energy that can be saved by progressively turning off BSs during the periods when traffic decreases depending on the traffic load variations and the distance between the BS and their associated User Equipments (UEs). In addition, the authors show how to optimize the energy savings of the network by calculating the most energy-efficient combination of switched off and active BSs.

Carrier Aggregation (CA) is one of the key features in Long Term Evolution-Advanced (LTE-A) to support wider bandwidth than the bandwidth supported by LTE. In this chapter, design and implementation of LTE-A to support greater bandwidth by improving the carrier aggregation technique and deployment scenarios such as intra-band contiguous carrier aggregation, intra-band non-contiguous carrier aggregation, and inter-band non-contiguous carrier aggregation are provided. As a result, this chapter presents the first evolution case of carrier aggregation on LTE-Advanced to support bandwidth up to 120 MHz in contiguous carrier aggregation instead of 100 MHz and 100 MHz in non-contiguous carrier aggregation instead of 80 MHz, where these challenges can provide high peak data rate, low latency, and high spectral efficiency. Although LTE already in its first release provides very high performance, it can also serve as a robust structure for evolving into even higher performance, as prospectively the revolution will go on beyond LTE-A to converge future requirements emerging with increased user expectations.

Chapter 8

Moon Ho Lee, Chonbuk National University, Korea

Md. Abdul Latif Sarker, Chonbuk National University, Korea

Kyeong Jin Kim, Mitsubishi Electronic Research Lab, USA

In this chapter, the authors investigate several fundamental issues that arise in wireless Multiple-Input and Multiple-Output (MIMO) communication over fading channels. Wireless channels are usually recognized as multipath fading channels. There are two basic aspects in wireless communication that practice the problem. Firstly, the matter of fading and secondly the disparity in the wired world. The special kinds of circulant matrices are called circulant Jacket matrices. In this chapter, the authors investigate circulant Jacket matrices in a massive MIMO channel that uses the eigenvector and the eigenvalues of this channel. In summary, they assume a perfect multipath channel with random sequences. For this system, a significant improvement in channel estimation can be seen compared to Maximum Ratio Combining (MRC), Least Squares (LS), and Minimum Mean Square Error (MMSE)-based linear channel estimations.

Chapter 9

Rongrong Qian, Beijing University of Posts and Telecommunications (BUPT), China

Yuan Qi, Beijing University of Posts and Telecommunications (BUPT), China

"Economies of scale" (called scale effect for notational convenience in this work), as a long run concept in microeconomics, refers to reductions in unit cost as the size of a facility and the usage levels of other inputs increase (Wikipedia, 2013). This chapter applies the concept of scale effect in microeconomics to the studies of algorithmic complexity within which the scale effect can be defined as the feature that the unit complexity (i.e., complexity per instance) of the algorithm decreases as the number of instances of algorithm increases while maintaining the performance. In this chapter, the Early-Termination Fixed-Complexity Sphere Detector (ET-FSD) is developed to exploit scale effect for the multiple-antenna system, which has to detect signals of multiple users under the constraint of sum complexity (e.g., the base-station systems always encounter the run-time limit of signal detection of all the users). Based on the study of ET-FSD, future directions of scale effect research for algorithmic complexity issues appearing in wireless access networks are presented as well.

Chapter 10

Hadi Mirzajani, Sahand University of Technology, Iran

Habib Badri Ghavifekr, Sahand University of Technology, Iran

Esmaeil Najafi Aghdam, Sahand University of Technology, Iran

In recent years, Microelectromechanical Systems (MEMS) technology has seen a rapid rate of evolution because of its great potential for advancing new products in a broad range of applications. The RF and microwave devices and components fabricated by this technology offer unsurpassed performance such as near-zero power consumption, high linearity, and cost effectiveness by batch fabrication in respect to their conventional counterparts. This chapter aims to give an in-depth overview of the most recently published methods of designing MEMS-based smart antennas. Before embarking into the different techniques of beam steering, the concept of smart antennas is introduced. Then, some fundamental concepts of MEMS technology such as micromachining technologies (bulk and surface micromachining) are briefly discussed. After that, a number of RF MEMS devices such as switches and phase shifters that have applications in beam steering antennas are introduced and their operating principals are completely explained. Finally, various configurations of MEMS-enabled beam steering antennas are discussed in detail.

Section 2
MAC Layer Issues

Chapter 11

Rohaiza Yusoff, Universiti Teknologi MARA, Malaysia

Mohd Dani Baba, Universiti Teknologi MARA, Malaysia

Muhammad Ibrahim, Universiti Teknologi MARA, Malaysia

This chapter presents some performance issues in Worldwide Interoperability for Microwave Access (WiMAX) network and focus on the capability of non-transparent relay in Mobile Multi-Hop Relay (MMR) WiMAX Network. In this work, an admission control mechanism with hierarchy Quality of Service (QoS) is developed for the relay architecture. An open source-based simulator is used to evaluate the three types of QoS classes, which are Unsolicited Grant Access (UGS), Real Time Polling Service (rtPS), and Non-Real Time Polling Service (nrtPS). Two scenarios of non-transparent relay topologies are set up for different numbers of subscribers with different types of QoS application classes. Three performance metrics, which are bandwidth utilization, number of slots used, and number of admitted service flow, are observed and plotted in graph. The results show the hierarchy-based QoS admission control mechanism can enhance the throughput of provided services by 35% compared to the conventional method without the admission control approach.

Chapter 12

Yasser Sadri, Department of Computer Engineering, Osku Branch, Islamic Azad University, Osku, Iran

Mohammdhossein Norouzibeirami, Department of Computer Engineering, Osku Branch, Islamic Azad University, Osku, Iran

The IEEE 802.16 has defined wireless access systems called WiMAX. These systems provide high-speed communications over long distances. To support multimedia applications, some service classes with Quality of Service (QoS) requirements are defined in IEEE 802.16, but the QoS scheduler is not standardized. The scheduling mechanism has a significant effect on the performance of WiMAX systems for use of bandwidth and radio resources. Some scheduling algorithms have been introduced by researchers. This study focuses on scheduling techniques proposed for WiMAX. The authors analyze a number of WiMAX scheduling algorithms in the Point-to-Multi-Point (PMP) mode and highlight their main points.

Voice over Internet Protocol (VoIP) is one of the fastest growing applications for the Internet today and is a very important service because mobile users can utilize voice services more cheaply compared with most mobile systems. A crucial application over these networks is VoIP over the Worldwide Interoperability for Microwave Access (WiMAX), which is one of the technologies in Broadband Access Networks based on IEEE 802.16 standards. It provides high throughput broadband connections over long distances, which supports Point to Multi-Point (PMP) wireless access. A hurdle, however, is the number of voice connections that can be supported. Since VoIP requires short end-to-end delays, supporting as many VoIP users as possible in a mobile broadband wireless access network, considering limited radio resources, becomes a very important issue. In this chapter, the authors use a theoretical model and an algorithm to evaluate the performance of some of the most important VoIP codecs.

Chapter 14

In this chapter, an intelligent scheduling architecture is presented for the downlink transmission of LTE-Advanced networks to enhance the Quality of Service (QoS) provision to different traffic types while maintaining system level performance such as system throughput and fairness. Hebbian learning process and K-mean clustering algorithm are integrated in the time domain of the proposed scheduling architecture to intelligently allocate the available radio resource to Real Time (RT) and Non-Real Time (NRT) traffic types. The integration of these algorithms allows just enough resource allocation to RT traffic and diverts the remaining resource to NRT traffic to fulfil its minimum throughput requirements. System level simulation is set up for the performance evaluation, and simulation results show that the proposed scheduling architecture reduces average delay, delay violation probability, and average Packet Drop Rate (PDR) of RT traffic while guaranteeing the support of minimum throughput to NRT traffic and maintaining system throughput at good level.

The feedback load is an important parameter with a large impact in Orthogonal Frequency Division Multiple Access (OFDMA) techniques, as a feedback over each one of the subcarriers will induce a non-acceptable signaling load in the system, so that some optimization and feedback reduction strategies are required to meet practical systems demands. The decision over the best strategy for feedback optimization highly depends on the number of available users in the system. The authors obtain the users' effect on the system through a feedback strategy over a subset of the subcarriers showing the best channel conditions, where a closed form expression of the obtained data rate is formulated to exactly indicate the effect of the number of users, the operating SNR, and/or the available number of feedback bits in the system. Quality of Service (QoS) is also obtained using the Symbol Error Rate (SER). The performance of the presented scheme is compared to the one-bit feedback strategy, where interesting conclusions are obtained.

Selection of a MIMO (Multiple Input Multiple Output) antenna to achieve high throughput, minimize errors, and optimize data speed is an important design issue. Radio resource management to provide Quality of Service (QoS) in WiMAX involves dynamic scheduling of resources according to the user's priority, based classes Platinum, Gold, Silver, and Bronze. Mobility and handoff management in WiMAX is another important issue involving location update, signaling traffic and service delay, and call blocking and dropping. This chapter focuses on some issues concerning MIMO configuration to improve transmit diversity, developing an appropriate scheduling algorithm to improve QoS, and presenting a novel mobility management protocol THMIP (Three Level Hierarchical Mobile IP) in IEEE 802.16e environment to reduce signaling cost with respect to QoS parameters like throughput, end-to-end delay, interference, path loss, bit error rate, and Signal-to-Noise Ratio (SNR). For the simulation, the authors use OPNET Modeler and MATLAB.

Section 3
Network Access Issues

4G networks provide bandwidth of up to 1Gbps for a Mobile Node (MN) that is moving at pedestrian speed. On the other hand, it also supports mobile nodes that can move at a speed of 250 km/hr with bandwidths value of 100 Mbps. This sets the premise of a network that supports diverse needs. This goal will be harder to achieve if Network Selection Problems (NSP) are not addressed comprehensively. NSP refers to the selection of target access network selection from a collection of Candidate Networks (CNs) when MNs are moving from one access network into another. The most logical way of achieving this is to select the "best" network. This translates to identifying performance values of the CNs. The analysis in this chapter shows clearly that access network selection done based on limited criteria is detrimental in achieving optimum communication. Instead, this chapter suggests a framework that would be complementary to a 4G network.

Mobile Ad Hoc Networks (MANET) is a peer-to-peer communication technique that can transmit voice or data from one mobile device to another without the support of fixed infrastructures. Multi-hop routing has improved in the last few decades and MANET is considered one of the latest trends in modern cellular communications. Studies have been carried out to find optimum routing techniques for MANET, but the majority of the works are within IEEE 802.11 environments. Long Term Evolution (LTE) series 8, which is an IP-based architecture, can offer the added benefit of co-operative communication and reduced transfer latency. Earlier research articulated a new MANET algorithm called IP Address Associated 4-N Intelligent Routing Algorithm (IPAA4NIR), which provided fast, reliable, and energy-efficient communications. This book chapter incorporates IPAA4NIR with co-operative communications to obtain an optimum routing technique for MANET using LTE cellular networks. The chapter also includes the statistical analysis of the proposed algorithm and simulations using OPNET modeller. A comparison with other prominent algorithms shows the proposed algorithm can use the added features of LTE and provides an optimum communication technique for MANET devices.

Chapter 19

Jan Oppolzer, Czech Technical University in Prague, Czech Republic
Robert Bestak, Czech Technical University in Prague, Czech Republic

In this chapter, the authors deal with a mechanism of Physical Cell Identifier (PCI) assignment for dense femtocell scenarios within LTE/LTE-Advanced networks. After describing the need for femtocells in future Self-Organizing Networks (SONs), the problem is presented. The chapter discusses background information such as related works in this research field and current assignment methods. Subsequently, challenges are defined, and two mechanisms to assign PCIs are proposed. Both the mechanisms are capable of assigning collision-free PCIs and solving any future confusion events that may occur as the network grows in terms of the number of femtocells. To evaluate the algorithms, a model is described and simulation results for two different scenarios are presented.

Preface

Broadband Wireless Access (BWA) networks will revolutionize the way wireless communication is used today for the transmission of mobile, nomadic, and fixed digital applications and services for the next generation of cellular systems. Global trends indicate that Long-Term Evolution LTE (release 8), LTE-Advanced (release 10), and IEEE 802.16-m will emerge as new technologies to provide very high data rates above 300 Mbps, or even exceed 1 Gbps in LTE-Advanced. These new systems are the best BWA technologies that will support the increased demand of fourth generation (4G) traffic, which will include a larger number of subscribers and active simultaneous requested services per a mobile user such as video conferencing and video streaming applications using a very large radio bandwidth.

International Mobile Telecommunications-Advanced (IMT-Advanced) or 4G are mobile systems that extend and improve upon the capabilities of the IMT-2000 family of standards. These systems are expected to provide users with access to a variety of advanced IP-based services and applications, supported by mobile and fixed broadband packet-based networks. The IMT-Advanced systems can support a wide range of data rates, with different Quality of Service (QoS) requirements and proportional-to-user mobility conditions in multi-user environments. According to the IMT-Advanced, only LTE-Advanced and IEEE 802.16-m fulfill the complete set of requirements for 4G.

Long-Term Evolution (release 8) is one of the primary broadband technologies based on Orthogonal Frequency Division Multiplexing (OFDM) in the downlink. Due to its lower peak-to-average power ratio property, Single-Carrier Frequency-Division Multiple Access (SC-FDMA) has been selected as the multiple access scheme in the uplink for next-generation mobile communication systems, which is currently being deployed and commercialized. LTE (release 8), finalized in March 2009, supports peak data rates up to 300 Mbps and 75 Mbps in the downlink and uplink, respectively, using flexible bandwidth operation from 1.4 MHz up to 20 MHz. This standard, which has been deployed in a macro/ microcell layout since 2010, provides improved system capacity and coverage, low latency (under 10ms), multi-antenna support, reduced operating costs, and seamless integration with existing systems. In addition, LTE (release 8), was designed to ensure high performance between 15 and 120 km/h, and is still expected to maintain mobility at speeds of between 120 and 350 km/h (where mobile speeds above 350 km/h are mainly for trains). At full speed range, this standard is expected to support voice and real-time QoS without interruption. Typical performance criterion is uninterrupted operation below 120 km/h for vehicular and pedestrian speeds.

LTE Advanced is the next evolutionary technology from LTE (release 8). The major feature of this system is the support of bandwidth extension via carrier aggregation, which allows deployment bandwidths of up to 100 MHz, enabling peak data rates above 1 Gbps in the downlink and 500 Mbps in the uplink. LTE-Advanced was standardized in the 3GPP specification release 10 (in late 2010) and is designed to meet or exceed the 4G requirements as defined by ITU-R. These requirements are met using the following advanced techniques: 1) carrier aggregation, 2) DL spatial multiplexing using up to eight-layer Multiple-Input Multiple-Output (MIMO), 3) DL intra-cell Coordinated Multipoint (CoMP) transmission and reception, and 4) UL spatial multiplexing using four-layer MIMO. In addition to the improvement in spectral efficiency, a considerable reduction in latency is also targeted, including 1) transition time from idle to connected mode from 100 ms in LTE (release 8) to less than 50 ms in LTE-Advanced and 2) transition from dormant to active from 50 ms in LTE (release 8) to less than 10 ms in LTE-Advanced. In LTE-Advanced, capacity and coverage enhancement can also be achieved using a heterogeneous network (a collection of low-power nodes distributed across a macrocell network). There are several types of low-power nodes such as microcells, picocells, femtocells, and relays. These low-power nodes are deployed in various environments including hot spots, homes, enterprise environments, and low geometry locations in order to increase the overall system capacity and range coverage of the network.

IEEE 802.16m is an enhancement for the existing mobile WiMAX systems (IEEE 802.16e) to meet the requirements of next-generation mobile broadband communication based on IMT-Advanced. This standard is capable of supporting data rates up to 120 Mbps downlink and 60 Mbps uplink, using 4x2 MIMO antennas on a single 20MHz-wide channel. Higher data rates can be obtained with additional spectrum resources or more complex antenna schemes. Actual commercial performance will be considerably less based on spectrum used and other factors. While 802.16m will provide increased performance for users, the main, driving factor for operators adopting the technology will be increased network capacity to accommodate the massive bandwidth increases driven by smartphones, tablets, and other wireless devices. In addition, IEEE 802.16m provides backward compatible with existing WiMAX networks, providing ease-of-mind for operators deploying networks today. Most mobile WiMAX operators can easily convert from IEEE 802.16e to IEEE 802.16m by updating some circuit plate units and software in their bases stations.

OBJECTIVE OF THE BOOK

This book will present a state-of-the-art overview of the recent developments in the area of broadband wireless access networks, including mobile standards LTE (RELEASE 8), LTE-Advanced, and IEEE 802.16m. These standards need to take many features into consideration, due to optimizations at each level, which are complex and challenging to implement. Numerous changes in lower layers (PHY ad MAC) can be expected to support larger bandwidths with more flexible allocations and to make use of further enhanced antenna technologies, coordinated base stations, scheduling, MIMO, and interference management. Recently, relaying is being studied as an enhancement of LTE towards LTE-Advanced, and the IEEE 802.16m standard. The main objective of introducing relaying in LTE-Advanced and IEEE 802.16m is to provide extended network coverage at a low cost.

The consecutive chapters of this book will present topics related to actual broadband wireless technologies that work together to carry out coordinated functions. The chapters will also present new theory and applications devoted to the improvement and development of broadband wireless access networks.

The mission of the book is to gather the knowledge and experience of enthusiastic and expert researchers who work in the area of broadband wireless access networks and transmit their knowledge and enthusiasm in a collaboration that leads to the edition of a book that will be one of the first of its kind, and a primary source of reading for students wishing to become involved in this area of research.

TARGET AUDIENCE

The prospective audience of the book *Broadband Wireless Access Networks for 4G: Theory, Application, and Experimentation* is undergraduate and graduate students interested in broadband wireless access network theory, implementation, and application, as well as professors teaching or researching this area and practitioners in the public and private sectors.

ORGANIZATION OF THE BOOK

Section 1: PHY Layer Issues

Chapter 1 presents a theoretical and experimental analysis of the electromagnetic signal propagation between a base station and a subscriber station in an urban setting using the IEEE 802.16d standard and test bed results, which are then compared to Ergeg's modified version of the Hata-Okomura mathematical propagation model. The experimental results of the measurements are similar to the model using the type terrain Category B (Suburban). Additionally, under experimental conditions, equipment with technology IEEE 802.16d and IEEE 802.16e were used to analyze delay and throughput while data, voice, and video was transmitted. The tests show that delay is acceptable for Fixed WiMAX, although it is barely adequate for Mobile WiMAX. As far as throughput is concerned, the average rate is adequate to support applications that include data, voice, and video.

Chapter 2

Interference mitigation has been identified as an important challenge for cellular technologies based on Orthogonal Frequency Division Multiple Access (OFDMA) such as the Long Term Evolution (LTE) system of the Third Generation Partnership Project (3GPP). In this context, Intercell Interference Coordination (ICIC) techniques have received much attention by the research community, as they are a good approach to address this issue. In particular, static solutions enjoy acceptance due to their low complexity and ease of implementation. ICIC mechanisms are not standardized in LTE, which just provides certain support so that every vendor/operator configures its particular ICIC option. Hence, their interworking with other important network functionalities such as Channel State Information (CSI) feedback must be carefully considered. Chapter 2 provides an overview on the relationship between ICIC and CSI in LTE and introduces a novel mechanism to improve such interworking. The novel scheme is feasible and easy-to-implement and it is especially effective for Non-Real Time services. It provides gains in terms of system capacity, cell edge performance, and energy efficiency with respect to 3GPP LTE mechanisms and previous proposals.

In chapter 3, Long Term Evolution (LTE) for public safety is investigated. Particularly, Distributed Antenna Systems (DAS) are studied, and their impact on LTE public safety networks is analyzed. Furthermore, resource allocation algorithms for the purpose of real-time video transmission, in both the Uplink (UL) and Downlink (DL) directions, are proposed, and a proportional fair scheduling algorithm, applicable in both the UL and DL directions, is presented. The proposed algorithms are compared in several scenarios with and without distributed antenna systems. In addition, Quality of Experience (QoE) metrics are used to measure the quality of the video transmissions, and joint uplink/downlink quality metrics, tailored to video transmission over public safety networks, are presented. Simulation results show large enhancements in video quality due to the application of DAS with smart resource allocation in LTE public safety networks.

In chapter 4, a novel receiver for Hexagonal Multicarrier Transmission (HMT) system based on the maximizing Signal-to-Interference-plus-Noise Ratio (Max-SINR) criterion is proposed. Theoretical analyses show that there is a timing offset between the prototype pulses of the proposed Max-SINR receiver and the traditional projection receiver. Meanwhile, the timing offset should be matched to the channel scattering factor of the Doubly Dispersive (DD) channel. The closed form timing offset expressions of the prototype pulse for Max-SINR HMT receiver over DD channel with different channel scattering functions are derived. Simulation results show that the proposed Max-SINR receiver outperforms traditional projection scheme and obtains an approximation to the theoretical upper bound SINR performance within the full range of channel spread factor. Consistent with the SINR performance improvement, the Bit Error Rate (BER) performance of the HMT system has also been further improved by using the proposed Max-SINR receiver. Meanwhile, the SINR performance of the proposed Max-SINR receiver is robust to the channel delay spread estimation errors.

Future wireless communication systems are expected to offer several gigabits data rate. It can be anticipated that the advanced communication techniques can enhance the capability of mobile terminals to support high data traffic. However, aggressive technique induces high energy consumption for the circuits of terminals, which drain the batteries fast and consequently limit user experience in future wireless networks. In order to solve such a problem, a scheme called collaborative mobile cluster is foreseen as one of the potential solutions to reduce energy consumption per node in a network by exploiting collaboration within a cluster of nearby mobile terminals. Chapter 5 provides a detailed analysis of the energy consumption of a terminal joining the cluster and also analyzes the conditions for energy savings opportunities.

Reducing the energy consumption in wireless networks has become a significant challenge, not only because of its great impact on the global energy crisis, but also because it represents a noteworthy cost for telecommunication operators. The Base Stations (BSs), constituting the main component of wireless infrastructure and the major contributor to the energy consumption of mobile cellular networks, are usually designed and planned to serve their customers during peak times. Therefore, they are more than sufficient when the traffic load is low. In chapter 6, the authors propose a number of BSs switching off algorithms as an energy efficient solution to the problem of redundancy of network resources. They demonstrate via analysis and by means of simulations that one can achieve reduction in energy consumption when one switches off the unnecessary BSs. In particular, the authors evaluate the energy that can be saved by progressively turning off BSs during the periods when traffic decreases depending on the traffic load variations and the distance between the BS and their associated User Equipments (UEs). In addition, the authors show how to optimize the energy savings of the network by calculating the most energy-efficient combination of switched off and active BSs.

Carrier Aggregation (CA) is one of the key features in Long Term Evolution-Advanced (LTE-A) to support wider bandwidth than the bandwidth supported by LTE. In chapter 7, design and implementation of LTE-A to support greater bandwidth by improving the carrier aggregation technique and deployment scenarios such as intra-band contiguous carrier aggregation, intra-band non-contiguous carrier aggregation, and inter-band non-contiguous carrier aggregation are provided. As a result, this chapter presents the first evolution case of carrier aggregation on LTE-Advanced to support bandwidth up to 120 MHz in contiguous carrier aggregation instead of 100 MHz and 100 MHz in non-contiguous carrier aggregation instead of 80 MHz, where these challenges can provide high peak data rate, low latency, and high spectral efficiency. Although LTE already in its first release provides very high performance, it can also serve as a robust structure for evolving into even higher performance, as prospectively the revolution will go on beyond LTE-A to converge future requirements emerging with increased user expectations.

In chapter 8, the authors investigate several fundamental issues that arise in wireless Multiple-Input and Multiple-Output (MIMO) communication over fading channels. Wireless channels are usually recognized as multipath fading channels. There are two basic aspects in wireless communication that practice the problem. Firstly, the matter of fading and secondly the disparity in the wired world. The special kinds of circulant matrices are called circulant Jacket matrices. In this chapter, the authors investigate circulant Jacket matrices in a massive MIMO channel that uses the eigenvector and the eigenvalues of this channel. In summary, they assume a perfect multipath channel with random sequences. For this system, a significant improvement in channel estimation can be seen compared to Maximum Ratio Combining (MRC), Least Squares (LS), and Minimum Mean Square Error (MMSE)-based linear channel estimations.

"Economies of scale" (called scale effect for notational convenience in this work), as a long run concept in microeconomics, refers to reductions in unit cost as the size of a facility and the usage levels of other inputs increase. Chapter 9 applies the concept of scale effect in microeconomics to the studies of algorithmic complexity within which the scale effect can be defined as the feature that the unit complexity (i.e., complexity per instance) of the algorithm decreases as the number of instances of algorithm increases while maintaining the performance. In this chapter, the Early-Termination Fixed-Complexity Sphere Detector (ET-FSD) is developed to exploit scale effect for the multiple-antenna system, which has to detect signals of multiple users under the constraint of sum complexity (e.g., the base-station systems always encounter the run-time limit of signal detection of all the users). Based on the study of ET-FSD, future directions of scale effect research for algorithmic complexity issues appearing in wireless access networks are presented as well.

In recent years, Microelectromechanical Systems (MEMS) technology has seen a rapid rate of evolution because of its great potential for advancing new products in a broad range of applications. The RF and microwave devices and components fabricated by this technology offer unsurpassed performance such as near-zero power consumption, high linearity, and cost effectiveness by batch fabrication in respect to their conventional counterparts. Chapter 10 aims to give an in-depth overview of the most recently published methods of designing MEMS-based smart antennas. Before embarking into the different techniques of beam steering, the concept of smart antennas is introduced. Then, some fundamental concepts of MEMS technology such as micromachining technologies (bulk and surface micromachining) are briefly discussed. After that, a number of RF MEMS devices such as switches and phase shifters that have applications in beam steering antennas are introduced and their operating principals are completely explained. Finally, various configurations of MEMS-enabled beam steering antennas are discussed in detail.

Section 2: MAC Layer Issues

Chapter 11 presents some performance issues in Worldwide Interoperability for Microwave Access (WiMAX) network and focus on the capability of non-transparent relay in Mobile Multi-Hop Relay (MMR) WiMAX Network. In this work, an admission control mechanism with hierarchy Quality of Service (QoS) is developed for the relay architecture. An open source-based simulator is used to evaluate the three types of QoS classes, which are Unsolicited Grant Access (UGS), Real Time Polling Service (rtPS), and Non-Real Time Polling Service (nrtPS). Two scenarios of non-transparent relay topologies are set up for different numbers of subscribers with different types of QoS application classes. Three performance metrics, which are bandwidth utilization, number of slots used, and number of admitted service flow, are observed and plotted in graph. The results show the hierarchy-based QoS admission control mechanism can enhance the throughput of provided services by 35% compared to the conventional method without the admission control approach.

The IEEE 802.16 has defined wireless access systems called WiMAX. These systems provide high-speed communications over long distances. To support multimedia applications, some service classes with Quality of Service (QoS) requirements are defined in IEEE 802.16, but the QoS scheduler is not standardized. The scheduling mechanism has a significant effect on the performance of WiMAX systems for use of bandwidth and radio resources. Some scheduling algorithms have been introduced by researchers. Chapter 12 focuses on scheduling techniques proposed for WiMAX. The authors analyze a number of WiMAX scheduling algorithms in the Point-to-Multi-Point (PMP) mode and highlight their main points.

Voice over Internet Protocol (VoIP) is one of the fastest growing applications for the Internet today and is a very important service because mobile users can utilize voice services more cheaply compared with most mobile systems. A crucial application over these networks is VoIP over the Worldwide Interoperability for Microwave Access (WiMAX), which is one of the technologies in Broadband Access Networks based on IEEE 802.16 standards. It provides high throughput broadband connections over long distances, which supports Point to Multi-Point (PMP) wireless access. A hurdle, however, is the number of voice connections that can be supported. Since VoIP requires short end-to-end delays, supporting as many VoIP users as possible in a mobile broadband wireless access network, considering limited radio resources, becomes a very important issue. In chapter 13, the authors use a theoretical model and an algorithm to evaluate the performance of some of the most important VoIP codecs.

In chapter 14, an intelligent scheduling architecture is presented for the downlink transmission of LTE-Advanced networks to enhance the Quality of Service (QoS) provision to different traffic types while maintaining system level performance such as system throughput and fairness. Hebbian learning process and K-mean clustering algorithm are integrated in the time domain of the proposed scheduling architecture to intelligently allocate the available radio resource to Real Time (RT) and Non-Real Time (NRT) traffic types. The integration of these algorithms allows just enough resource allocation to RT traffic and diverts the remaining resource to NRT traffic to fulfil its minimum throughput requirements. System level simulation is set up for the performance evaluation, and simulation results show that the proposed scheduling architecture reduces average delay, delay violation probability, and average Packet Drop Rate (PDR) of RT traffic while guaranteeing the support of minimum throughput to NRT traffic and maintaining system throughput at good level.

The feedback load is an important parameter with a large impact in Orthogonal Frequency Division Multiple Access (OFDMA) techniques, as a feedback over each one of the subcarriers will induce a non-acceptable signaling load in the system, so that some optimization and feedback reduction strategies are required to meet practical systems demands. The decision over the best strategy for feedback optimization highly depends on the number of available users in the system. The authors in chapter 15 obtain the users' effect on the system through a feedback strategy over a subset of the subcarriers showing the best channel conditions, where a closed form expression of the obtained data rate is formulated to exactly indicate the effect of the number of users, the operating SNR, and/or the available number of feedback bits in the system. Quality of Service (QoS) is also obtained using the Symbol Error Rate (SER). The performance of the presented scheme is compared to the one-bit feedback strategy, where interesting conclusions are obtained.

Selection of a MIMO (Multiple Input Multiple Output) antenna to achieve high throughput, minimize errors, and optimize data speed is an important design issue. Radio resource management to provide Quality of Service (QoS) in WiMAX involves dynamic scheduling of resources according to the user's priority, based classes Platinum, Gold, Silver, and Bronze. Mobility and handoff management in WiMAX is another important issue involving location update, signaling traffic and service delay, and call blocking and dropping. Chapter 16 focuses on some issues concerning MIMO configuration to improve transmit diversity, developing an appropriate scheduling algorithm to improve QoS, and presenting a novel mobility management protocol THMIP (Three Level Hierarchical Mobile IP) in IEEE 802.16e environment to reduce signaling cost with respect to QoS parameters like throughput, end-to-end delay, interference, path loss, bit error rate, and Signal-to-Noise Ratio (SNR). For the simulation, the authors use OPNET Modeler and MATLAB.

Section 3: Network Access Issues

4G networks provide bandwidth of up to 1Gbps for a Mobile Node (MN) that is moving at pedestrian speed. On the other hand, it also supports mobile nodes that can move at a speed of 250 km/hr with bandwidths value of 100 Mbps. This sets the premise of a network that supports diverse needs. This goal will be harder to achieve if Network Selection Problems (NSP) are not addressed comprehensively. NSP refers to the selection of target access network selection from a collection of Candidate Networks (CNs) when MNs are moving from one access network into another. The most logical way of achieving this is to select the "best" network. This translates to identifying performance values of the CNs. The analysis in chapter 17 shows clearly that access network selection done based on limited criteria is detrimental in achieving optimum communication. Instead, this chapter suggests a framework that would be complementary to a 4G network.

Mobile Ad Hoc Networks (MANET) is a peer-to-peer communication technique that can transmit voice or data from one mobile device to another without the support of fixed infrastructures. Multi-hop routing has improved in the last few decades, and MANET is considered one of the latest trends in modern cellular communications. Studies have been carried out to find optimum routing techniques for MANET, but the majority of the works are within IEEE 802.11 environments. Long Term Evolution (LTE) series 8, which is an IP-based architecture, can offer the added benefit of co-operative communication and reduced transfer latency. Earlier research articulated a new MANET algorithm called IP Address Associated 4-N Intelligent Routing Algorithm (IPAA4NIR), which provided fast, reliable, and energy-efficient communications. Chapter 18 incorporates IPAA4NIR with co-operative communications to obtain optimum routing technique for MANET using LTE cellular network. The chapter also includes the statistical analysis of the proposed algorithm and simulations using OPNET modeller. A comparison with other prominent algorithm proves the proposed algorithm can use the added features of LTE and provides an optimum communication technique for MANET devices.

In chapter 19, the authors deal with a mechanism of Physical Cell Identifier (PCI) assignment for dense femtocell scenarios within LTE/LTE-Advanced networks. After describing the need for femtocells in future Self-Organizing Networks (SONs), the problem is presented. The chapter discusses background information such as related works in this research field and current assignment methods. Subsequently, challenges are defined, and two mechanisms to assign PCIs are proposed. Both the mechanisms are capable of assigning collision-free PCIs and solving any future confusion events that may occur as the network grows in terms of the number of femtocells. To evaluate the algorithms, a model is described and simulation results for two different scenarios are presented.

Raul Aquino Santos
University of Colima, Mexico

Victor Rangel Licea
National Autonomous University of Mexico, Mexico

Arthur Edwards Block
University of Colima, Mexico

Acknowledgment

Raul Aquino Santos would like to thank his wife, Tania, for her deep love and for giving him a wonderful family and his lovely daughters, Tania and Dafne, for providing him with many years of happiness. In addition, he would like to thank his parents, Teodoro and Herlinda, for offering him the opportunity to study and to believe in God. Finally, he wants to thank his brother, Carlos, and his sisters, Teresa and Leticia, for their support.

Arthur Edwards Block would like to thank his wife, Marilú, and his two children, David and Elisa, for having given him their unfaltering love and a meaningful purpose in life.

Victor Rangel Licea would like to thank his wife, Adriana, for her immense love, patience, and support, his lovely kids, Mary Fer, Karen, and Miguel, for making his such a proud dad. He wants to thank Raul Aquino for giving him the opportunity to contribute to this book.

This work was supported by DGAPA, National Autonomous University of Mexico (UNAM) under Grant PAPIIT IN 114713 and APIIT IN 108910. Additional support was from CONACYT MEXICO under grant CB2008-105279.

Raul Aquino Santos
University of Colima, Mexico

Victor Rangel Licea
National Autonomous University of Mexico, Mexico

Arthur Edwards Block
University of Colima, Mexico

Section 1
PHY Layer Issues

Chapter 1
Analysis of Propagation Models, Delay, and Throughput for WiMAX in Urban Environments

Juan Michel García Díaz
University of Colima, Mexico

Laura Victoria Escamilla Del Río
University of Colima, Mexico

Omar Álvarez Cárdenas
University of Colima, Mexico

Margarita Glenda Mayoral Baldivia
University of Colima, Mexico

ABSTRACT

This chapter presents a theoretical and experimental analysis of the electromagnetic signal propagation between a base station and a subscriber station in an urban setting using the IEEE 802.16d standard and test bed results, which are then compared to Ergeg's (1998) modified version of the Hata-Okomura (1980) mathematical propagation model. The experimental results of the measurements are similar to the model using the type terrain Category B (Suburban). Additionally, under experimental conditions, equipment with technology IEEE 802.16d and IEEE 802.16e were used to analyze delay and throughput while data, voice, and video was transmitted. The tests show that delay is acceptable for Fixed WiMAX, although it is barely adequate for Mobile WiMAX. As far as throughput is concerned, the average rate is adequate to support applications that include data, voice, and video.

INTRODUCTION

The demand for connectivity and bandwidth have increased, meaning that present physical connections and fixed workstations no longer satisfy the needs of a new generation of users whose online interactions require ever-growing resources. With the rise of wireless technologies, different technologies have been developed to provide connectivity solutions. At a local level, WiFi technology described in the 802.11 standard is preferred because of its characteristics of

DOI: 10.4018/978-1-4666-4888-3.ch001

mobility, bandwidth, and low cost compared to similar technologies. Because WiFi only provides connectivity in a very localized area, WiMAX technology was created to serve larger areas requiring connectivity.

WiMAX is the name by which the new IEEE 802.16 standard is known. It is presented as an alternative and/or extension to other wide band technologies such as ADSL (Asymmetric Digital Subscriber Line), Cable Modem, 2.5 and 3G. It was created to provide voice services and broadband wireless data and enables rapid deployment of telecommunications networks in areas where there is no an adequate physical infrastructure (Etemad & Lai, 2011).

There are currently three different WiMAX systems:

- Fixed (IEEE 802.16-2004).
- Mobile (IEEE 802.16e-2005).
- Mesh (IEEE 802.16-Mesh).

Fixed WiMAX systems have a coverage area of 3.5-7 km. This standard determines the fixed line connections between a base station and one or more subscriber stations, and works through point-to-multipoint links (Zhang & Chen, 2007).

Mobile WiMAX is a broadband wireless access technology which allows the connection of mobile subscriber stations that are found in a wider area coverage than that of the base station (Jau-Yang & Yu-Chen, 2012),which can handle mobile telephone services via IP service or high speed mobile services.

Furthermore, in the Mesh WiMAX mode, the base station provides connections to one or more subscriber stations, although they are not directly connected to the base station. In this scheme, the network base or subscribers are called nodes. The connection between the nodes is measured by the number of hops and the way in which any two nodes maintain a connection. A subscriber node maintains the connection with its parent node at a distance of one hop, both sending and receiving information. This subscriber node can, in turn, become a parent node for other nodes, thus extending the network range (Algamali, Jianxin, & Alhamidi, 2009).

The different WiMAX systems allow network designers to choose the best solution to satisfy the needs of each customer. Some common scenarios using WiMAX networks include:

- Residential Market.
- SOHO Networks.
- Wireless backhaul islands.
- Telecommunications Services on SME (Small and Medium Enterprises).
- Personal Mobile Access.
- Private Networks.

Although WiMAX systems allow connectivity over larger areas, link reliability depends on the characteristics of the devices and the type of area in which they are used. This chapter discusses the versions of fixed WiMAX and mobile WiMAX in an urban setting. Table 1 lists the key features of both IEEE 802.16d and IEEE 802.16e standards. It highlights a data rate of 75 Mbps and a coverage range up to 50 km maximum for a fixed WiMAX system and an 8 km maximum range for a mobile WiMAX system (Rangel Licea, 2009).

Additionally, this paper describes the propagation models applicable to fixed WiMAX for urban environments. It also describes the tests conducted under experimental conditions for both IEEE 802.16d and IEEE 802.16e standards. Furthermore, this chapter presents information about the characteristics of the radios used in the tests performed, detailing the configuration used in each one of them.

IEEE 802.16

The demand for greater bandwidth for both conventional and wireless networks has increased dramatically over the past few years. In the area of

Table 1.Standard comparison 802.16d and 802.16e

Standard	IEEE 802.16d-2004	IEEE802.16e-2005
Frequency Bands	2 GHz - 11 GHz	2 GHz - 11 GHz for Fixed, 2 GHz - 6 GHz for Mobile
FFT	Single carrier, 256 OFDM o 2048 OFDM	Single carrier, 256 OFDM or 128, 512, 1024, 2048 SOFDM
MAC Architecture	Point-to-multipoint, mesh	Point-to-multipoint, mesh
Supported Usage Scenarios	Fixed, Nomadic, Portable	Mobile, Portable, Nomadic, Fixed
Channel Bandwidths	3.5, 7, 10, 20 MHz	5, 7, 8.75, 10, 20 MHz
Bit Rate	1Mbps - 75 Mbps	1Mbps - 75 Mbps
Duplexing	FDD	TDD
Sub-channelization	DL only	DL and UL
Coverage Range	Up to 50 km	Up to 8 km

wireless networks, this growth has forced technology to mature to the point of having to establish its own standards for wireless metropolitan area networks. The IEEE 802.16 standard adopts WiMAX as a trade name, whose acronym comes from *Worldwide Interoperability for Microwave Access* (Hongxia & Jufeng, 2009), which is a broadband wireless technology that provides services in areas without adequate wired infrastructure.

This technology is based on the Orthogonal Frequency Division Multiplexing (OFDM), which allows communication even without direct line of sight (NLOS). WiMAX uses an adaptive modulation mechanism that depends on the signal to noise ratio (SNR). In difficult propagation conditions with high levels of interference or a weak signal at the receiver, the system selects a more robust and slow modulation to ensure transmissions (Milanovic, Rimac-Drlje, & Bejuk, 2007).

Because WiMAX does not use a reserved frequency band, interference can significantly affect its performance. Consequently, it usually provides speeds approaching 15 Mbps and covers a radius of about 20 km under normal conditions. IEEE 802.16 can be configured to work in either point-to-multipoint (PMP) or mesh modes (Zhang & Chen, 2007).

As defined in the standard, a wireless metropolitan area network (MAN) provides access to buildings through exterior antennas communicating with central radio bases (BBS). Due to their characteristics, wireless MAN systems have the ability to cover large geographical areas without investing in costly infrastructure. Even though these systems have been used for several years, the consolidation of the standard constitutes the basis of the success of the industry using second generation of WiMAX equipment.

The IEEE 802.16 standard was adapted in 2001. Subsequent changes to IEEE 802.16 led to the emergence of two new versions; the first, in 2004, called IEEE 802.16d for fixed wireless applications, and the second, in 2005, designated 802.16e for mobile wireless networks (Kassim & Baba, 2011). Both versions provide speeds of up to 75 Mbps.

THE IEEE 802.16D

The IEEE 802.16-2004 standard (approved in June of 2004, replacing the IEEE 802.16a standard) provides a powerful solution for wireless access networks regarding bandwidth, coverage and overall performance. It offers substantially increased bandwidth (up to 75 Mbps per channel of 20 MHz) and incorporates mechanisms to better manage quality of service (QoS). Furthermore, it permits extensive coverage both in line of sight (LOS) and non-line of sight (NLOS) conditions in both free and licensed frequencies (IEEE-1, 2004).

The WiMAX physical layer uses OFDM 256-FFT (Orthogonal Frecuency-Division Multiplexing 256-Fast Fourier Transform). OFDM divides the carrier or information channel into lower speed sub-channels, which are transmitted in parallel. It is this multiplexing technique allows WiMAX to operate in non-line of sight conditions. One advantage of OFDM signals is their ability to operate with propagation delay in NLOS environments and the robustness of the scheme against multipath and interference attenuations (Carmona-Sánchez, 2008)

WiMAX´s physical layer possesses a scalable architecture which permits more robust data rates with the already existing channel bandwidth. This scaling must be done to support dynamic roaming of users who employ different networks which may have different bandwidths. Although scalability is provided by OFDMA, it is the use of multiple antenna-based techniques that provides better overall system capacity and spectral efficiency. Because WiMAX's MAC layer is connection oriented, it can simultaneously support a number of applications, including voice and multimedia services. Because its design supports a large number of users who can employ multiple terminal connections, WiMAX must support QoS requirements for each of its network connections.

The main feature of fixed WiMAX protocols (802.16, 802.16a, 802.16b, 802.16c) is that they replace the IEEE 802.16a standard. This final version supports mandatory and optional elements, transmitting up to 75 Mbps under ideal conditions, but its actual performance may be affected by transmitting only about 40 Mbps (IEEE-2, 2004).

THE IEEE 802.16E

WiFi technology has proven to be a very effective technology. However, it is limited due to bandwidth and coverage area limitations. IEEE 802.16e standard, on the other hand, offers an option that provides much greater mobility, bandwidth and coverage to better meet the increasing demands of wireless technologies, particularly with regards to voice and multimedia applications (Chi-Ming & Shuoh Ren, 2010).

The IEEE 802.16e standard provides users access to wireless mobile broadband services over large metropolitan area networks while effectively providing Quality of Service (QoS) (Daniel, Rohde, Subik, & Wietfeld, 2009). The version of the standard discussed in this chapter provides wireless broadband mobile access and is more commonly known as Mobile WiMAX.

The main new features of IEEE 802.16e vs. the older IEEE 802.16d include its: mobility of subscriber stations (MS-Mobile Station), support for sub-channelization in the Uplink and Downlink, energy saving features, modified physical layer (SOFDMA), use of MIMO and ASS (Adaptive Antenna System) for efficient signal transmission and reception, addition of a privacy sublayer that enhances security and implements multicast and broadcast strategies (Chapa López 2009). Mobile WiMAX uses SOFDMA (Scalable Orthogonal Frequency Division Multiple Access) to support mobility. With the PHY scalable architecture, it supports a wide range of bandwidth because it allows the FFT to vary in size between 128, 512, 1024 and 2048 (Kassim & Baba, 2011).

Consequently, IEEE 802.16e-2005 can consist of both mobile and nomadic stations, as required. Mobile stations receive the service issued by the base station while in constant or intermittent motion. It is important to note that mobile stations always act as subscriber stations ("IEEE Standard for Local and Metropolitan Area Networks Part

16: Air Interface for Fixed and Mobile Broadband Wireless Access Systems Amendment 2: Physical and Medium Access Control Layers for Combined Fixed and Mobile Operation in Licensed Bands and Corrigendum 1," 2006). Furthermore, to better support mobility, especially for higher vehicle speeds, mobile stations must operate at bands below 6 GHz (Suliman, Elhassan, & Ibrahim, 2012).

EQUIPMENT: DESCRIPTION AND CONFIGURATION

The WiMAX wireless communication system can be either fixed (IEEE 802.16d), mobile (IEEE 802.16e) or mesh (IEEE 802.16-mesh). This chapter presents an analysis of fixed and mobile WiMAX. The WiMAX features chosen for study in this chapter are signal strength, delay and throughput. At least one base station and one or more subscriber stations are required to form a WiMAX network. The base station provides the service to the subscriber stations via transmission of electromagnetic waves and the subscriber stations act as receivers.

For evaluation, a network was created with equipment operating under the IEEE 802.16d standard which included a Tranzeo Base Station (BS: Base Station) model TR-WMX-58-pBS-PlusG and a Tranzeo subscriber station (SS: Subscriber Station), model TR-WMX-5-20-W. The BS and the SS were configured to operate at the 5725000 KHz frequency, a 10000 KHz bandwidth, with an Internet exit speed of 3MB/s.

Figure 1 shows a 2.9 km topographical profile of the point-to-point transmission between the BS and the SS of the fixed WiMAX network. In this architecture, the BS (located at point A in Figure 1; also see Figure 2) provides connection to a SS (point B in Figure 1). The distance between these two points is 2.9 Km.

Also, we implemented the network technology using IEEE 802.16e with equipment manufactured by Airspan. The models chosen for this test were the MacroMAXe Air4G-2510M, which served as the base station, and the Mimax-USB-Q1-1, which was used for the two subscriber stations. The BS and the SSs were connected at 2570000 KHz, Channel 0 and 10 000 kHz bandwidth. The Internet exit speed, using IEEE802.16e technology, was 34 Mbps (E3).

The technical specifications of the equipment used IEEE802.16d and IEEE 802.16e technologies as shown in Table 2. The power transmission from the MacroMAXe Air4G-2510M base station is of up to 2 x +36dBm when using the two antennas that can be added, but for the study reported in this chapter, we only used one antenna; therefore, the power transmission was +36dBm.

PROPAGATION MODELS

Empirical propagation models like Okumura-Hata (Hata, 1980; Okumura, Ohmori, Kawano, & Fukuda, 1968), COST 231-Hata (COST-Action-231, 1999), and COST 231 Walfisch-Ikegami (Walfisch & Bertoni, 1988) are designed for very specific

Figure 1.Connection Diagram of fixed WiMAX link

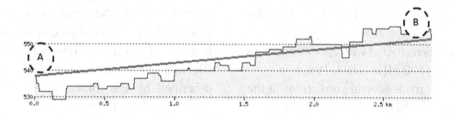

Figure 2. Aerial view of fixed WiMAX link

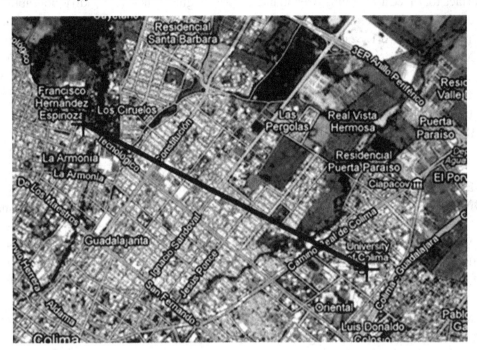

types of communication systems for path loss prediction in frequency bands below 2 GHz (Milanović, Rimac-Drlje, & Majerski, 2010).

Different propagation models have been developed to predict signal strength and path loss power in more recent wireless communications services (designed to operate on higher frequencies, i.e. 2,4 GHz, 35 GHz and 5GHz). One of the most widely used models is the Okumura propagation model.

The Okumura propagation model presents a graphical expression for path loss between the receiving and the transmitting antennas for frequency ranges of between 200 MHz and 1920 MHz (Okumura et al., 1968). The major disadvantage of this model was solved in the Hata model, which offerss a simplification of the Okumura model given by a mathematical expression to predict the median path loss for the 150MHz to 1500 MHz frequency ranges. However, application of the Hata model is restricted with upper frequency ranges of up to 1500 MHz (Hata, 1980).

Erceg (1998) made several corrections to the Hata-Okumura model (Hata, 1980) to better pre-

dict signal strength and path loss for new wireless communications services. As part of his corrections, Erceg (1998) provides three different terrain types to help study electromagnetic propagation in propagation models for Fixed WiMAX users:

- **Category A:** Moderate-to-heavy tree densities (Urban).
- **Category B:** Mostly flat texrain with moderate-to-heavy tree densities, or hilly terrain with light tree densities (Sub-urban).
- **Category C:** Light tree densities (Rural).

This model was extended to compensate for frequencies above 2GHz, receiving antennas with heights above 2 meters and distances between terminal base ranging from 100m to 8km (Erceg V., 1998). Due to the characteristics of the model (antenna height and distance between devices), it is not used to predict signal intensity for WiFi, Bluetooth, Zigbee, etc. Erceg's model is best described by the following equation defining power loss (PL) 1:

Table 2.Technical specifications of equipment used fixed and mobile WiMAX

	Fixed WiMAX		Mobile WiMAX	
	Base Station	**Subscriber Station**	**Base Station**	**Subscriber Station**
Brand	Tranzeo	Tranzeo	Airspan	Airspan
Model	TR-WMX-58-pBS-PlusG	TR-WMX-5-20-W	Air4G- MacroMAXe 2510M	MiMAX-USB-Q1-1
Frequency Range	5150 – 5875 MHz	5150 – 5875 MHz	2.3 -2.7 GHz	Quad Band 2.3-2.4GHz, 2.496-2.69GHz,3.3-3.8GHz, 4.9-5.8GHz
Channel Bandwidth	10 MHz	3.5 MHz, 5 MHz, 7 MHz, 10 MHz	20 MHz, 2x10 MHz, 10 MHz, 5 MHz	10MHz, 8.75MHz, 7MHz, 5MHz
Power Transmission	+20 dBm (max)	+20 dBm (max)	Up to 2 x +36dBm	Up to 22dBm (2.3-2.4GHz, 2.496-2.69GHz, 3.3-3.8GHz) up to 17dBm (4.9-5.8GHz)
Modulation	64-QAM, 16-QAM, QPSK, BPSK	64-QAM, 16-QAM, QPSK, BPSK	512, 1024, 2048 FFT SOFDMA	512, 1024 FFT SOFDMA
Standards	IEEE 802.16d-2004	IEEE 802.16d-2004	IEEE802.16e-2005	IEEE802.16e-2005

$$PL = A + 10\gamma \log_{10}\left(d / d_0\right) + s + Cf + Ch; d > d_0 \qquad (1)$$

where:

- **A:** Path Loss at distance 0.
- γ **:** Path Loss exponent.
- d_0**:** Distance 0, we choose a value of 100m.
- **s:** Shadow fading.
- **Ch y Cf:** Frequency correction factor.

The values used for the case study, and the resulting values are shown in Table 3.

The previous model characterizes three types of topography, which, in this case, is the basis on which to calculate the path loss in the downtown area of the city of Colima, Mexico. For the purposes of this study, the topography is considered "Category A" insofar as the electromagnetic propagation model is concerned. Figure 2 details the physical qualities of the terrain providing an aerial view with the link path superimposed.

Figure 3 provides a comparison between the propagation model of the signal applied to the three types of land mentioned above and experimental measurement of the WiMAX link of this test.

EXPERIMENTAL EVALUATION OF FIXED AND MOBILE WIMAX

WiMAX has been shown to have great potential bandwidth to support the transfer data, voice and video over internet. Besides its expanded bandwidth, it offers the high throughput necessary to support increasingly demanding applications (Ahmad & Habibi, 2008). The main objective of the experimental section of this work is to determine the delay and throughput of wireless communication systems, specifically Fixed WiMAX (FW) and Mobile WiMAX (MW), when transmitting data, voice and video. Ten types of tests were defined, depending on the desired applications, which are listed below:

1. Video conferencing (voice and video) plus Data transfer over Internet (VC + D, Internet).
2. Video conferencing (voice and video) over Internet (VC, Internet).
3. Video conferencing (voice and video) plus Data transfer in Intranet (VC + D, Intranet).
4. Video conferencing (voice and video) in Intranet (VC, Intranet).

Table 3. Numerical values of model parameters

Modeler Parameter	Terrain Category		
	A **(Hilly/Moderate - Heavy Tree Density)**	**B** **(Hilly/Light Tree Density or Flat/Moderate - Heavy Tree Density)**	**C** **(Flat/Light Tree Density)**
A	4.6	4.0	3.6
b (in m^{-1})	0.0075	0.0065	0.0050
c (in m)	12.6	17.1	20.0
σ_γ	0.57	0.75	0.59
μ_σ	10.6	9.6	8.2
σ_σ	2.3	3.0	1.6
Shadow fading standard deviation: $\sigma = \mu_\sigma + z\sigma_\sigma$	9.5029	8.169	7.4368
Channel frequency (GHz)	5.725 GHz		
Wavelength λ (m)	0.051724		
Rx antenna height hss (m)	28m		
BS antenna height h_b(m)	20m		
EIRP[dBm]=Ptx + Gtx -Lc	42dBm		
$\gamma = a - b \times h_b + c / h_b$	5.0077	4.634	4.399
$A = 20\log_{10}\left(4\pi\ d_0\ /\lambda\right)$	87.71		
$s = y\sigma$	-4.532	-3.896	-3.547
$Cf=6\log_{10}(f/1900)$	15.12		
For Cat A and B $Ch=-10.7\log_{10}(h_{ss}/2)$ For Cat C $Ch=-20\log_{10}(h_{ss}/2)$	-12.26		-22.92
PL[dB]	129.025597dB	124.196982dB	110.449577dB
Prx[dBm]= EIRP + Grx – PL	-85.0255971dBm	-80.196982dBm	-66.449577dBm

Figure 3.Comparative results: Experimental vs theoretical model

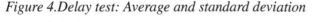

	Model A	Model B	Model C	Experiment
■ dBm	-85.02	-80.19	-66.44	-75.25

5. Call (voice) plus Data transfer over Internet (V + D, Internet).
6. Call (voice) over Internet (V, Internet).
7. Call (voice) plus data transfer in Intranet (V + D, Intranet).
8. Call (Voice) in Intranet (V, Intranet).
9. Internet data transfer (D, Internet).
10. Intranet data transfer (D, Intranet).

To obtain greater insight regarding the behavior of fixed and mobile WiMAX, the mean and standard deviation of delay and throughput were calculated. The experimental results are shown in Figures 4 and 5. Delay is the time necessary for packets to be sent from the sender to the receiver and back to the sender again, measured in milliseconds.

Too much delay can severely affect the performance of applications or even rendering them inoperable. For example, a VoIP application with a delay greater than 150 ms can drastically affect voice quality (Safak & Preveze, 2008). The IEEE 802.16 group has defined that for a VoIP application to offer an acceptable quality service, delay should not be greater than 120 ms; delay of over 150 ms significantly affects voice quality (IEEE_802.16_Working_Group, 2013). In general, a range of 0-150 milliseconds is acceptable for most applications. Delay of 200 ms may be acceptable only for private networks, although 250 ms is considered the absolute limit even for them (Cisco_Systems_White_Paper, 2003).

A ping is the simplest method to measure delay as it sends a packet to the destination node

Figure 4.Delay test: Average and standard deviation

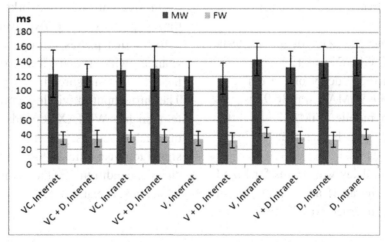

Figure 5.Throughput test: Average and standard deviation

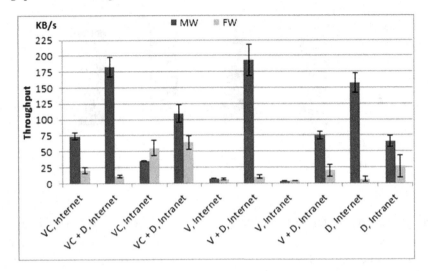

seeking a response. When sending a ping, delay is the elapsed time needed for a source to send the packet and receive the corresponding response. For the tests reported in this chapter, a *.txt* file was sent and received by the source to more easily calculate the average the travel time using the ping command from the MS-DOS console. The instruction used is as follows:

ping IP_Destination_node –t > C:\delay.txt

Figure 4 shows the average delay and standard deviation fixed and mobile WiMAX. The mean and standard deviation were calculated with samples obtained during the performance of each test.

Figure 4 shows that:

- The overall average delay of the ten tests done in fixed WiMAX was 129.5 ms.
- The global average delay of the ten tests made in mobile WiMAX was 36.9 ms.
- The delay in mobile WiMAX was little more than 3 times higher than of Fixed WiMAX.
- The maximum delay was 43 ms for Fixed WiMAX, (V, intranet) and the minimum delay (V + D, internet) was 33 ms.

- The maximum delay was 143 ms for Mobile WiMAX, (V, intranet and D, intranet) and the minimum delay (V + D, internet and V, internet) was 120 ms.
- The average standard deviation of the ten tests shows that the dispersion of the data obtained is approximately 8% in fixed and mobile WIMAX. No significant difference was observed when changing applications in any of experimental tests.
- Delay in Fixed WiMAX was noticeably acceptable (129.5 ms).
- Delay in Mobile WiMAX was barely adequate (36.9 ms).

In communication networks such as WiMAX, throughput is the effective average rate of data delivery that passes through a communication channel, without considering the physical layer headers. It is measured in bits per second (bit/s). The throughput of wireless communication systems such as WiMAX depends on a wide variety of variables such as: packet size, transmission rate, signal to noise ratio, modulation techniques and channel conditions (Zaka, Ahmed, Ibrar-ul-Haq, Irfan Anis, & Faria, 2009).

Five types of tests were conducted over the Internet via Skype 5.11 and the rest were made in Intranet with Microsoft Portrait 2.0. Netlimiter 3 Pro was used to determine the throughput of 33 measurements which measured the upload and download speeds of the application. The sum of the 33 upload and download speeds measured in KB/s provided a statistically accurate average throughput.

Figure 5 shows the consumption of the average throughput for the two wireless communication systems and the corresponding standard deviation. To calculate the average and standard deviation, 33 samples were obtained independently in each test.

An analysis of Figure 5 shows the following:

- The global average consumption of throughput in fixed WiMAX was 22.51 KB/s.
- The overall average consumption of throughput in mobile WiMAX was 90.39 KB/s.
- The test call (voice) consumed the least throughput on the Intranet (V, Intranet), with 4.11 KB / s in Fixed WiMAX and 3.45 KB/s in Mobile WiMAX.
- The maximum throughput consumption in fixed WiMAX was 63.73 KB/s in the test Video conferencing (voice and video), plus data transfer in Intranet (VC + D, Intranet).
- The maximum consumption of throughput in mobile WiMAX was 182.53 KB/s in the test video conferencing (voice and video) plus, data transfer over Internet (VC + D, Internet).
- The dispersion of the data is very high because of the nature of the tests and the internet connection (in tests requiring internet access) of each wireless communication system.
- The average consumption of throughput was higher in 8 of the 10 tests in mobile WiMAX.

- The data dispersion was higher in fixed WiMAX.
- The throughput consumed by wireless WiMAX was three times greater than for fixed.
- The only test in which throughput consumption for fixed WiMAX exceeded that for mobile WiMAX was on videoconferences and calls on the Intranet.

Theoretically, the IEEE 802.16d and IEEE 802.16e standards have transmission rates of up to 75 Mbps and a coverage area of 50 km. In practice, this represents a significant degradation of the field measurements since the quality of service provided by WiMAX depends on factors such as distance, climate and visibility between stations (Parsons & OJA, 2008). Furthermore, if the mobile nodes (specifically in IEEE 802.16e) move at high speeds, WiMAX fails drastically with data rates of less than 1 Mb/s(Ahmad & Habibi, 2008).

CONCLUSION

Because the fixed WiMAX tests were carried out in urban area (Colima, Colima, Mexico), signal strength was predicted by the propagation model employed in 802.16d technology, along with the "Category A" terrain model; although the results of the measurements are closer to those provided by the model using the type terrain Category B, which describes a semi-populated area. This might be the case because the city has few buildings that are over two stories tall and because the measurements were taken along an east-west axis that did not present such great elevation differences. The city also has many public gardens and green areas distributed throughout the city.

The test bed comparison between fixed and mobile WiMAX shows distance, climate and visibility between stations in urban areas makes predicting reception strength almost impossible. Because of this difficulty, predicting the QoS of the WiMAX link is very unpredictable and does not actually correspond to more "ideal" scenarios presented in simulations, although delay and throughput are within the limits necessary to provide QoS for video, voice and data.

REFERENCES

Ahmad, I., & Habibi, D. (2008). *A novel mobile WiMAX solution for higher throughput.* Paper presented at the 16th IEEE International Conference on Networks. New Delhi, India.

Algamali, M. H. M., Jianxin, W., & Alhamidi, R. A. (2009). *Base station scheduler scheme of IEEE 802.16 mesh mode.* Paper presented at the WRI International Conference on Communications and Mobile Computing CMC '09. Yunnan, China.

Carmona-Sánchez, A. (2008). *Planificación mediante ATOLL de red WiMax móvil para los centros de la Universidad de Sevilla. Proyecto de fin de carrera.* Escuela Técnica Superior de Ingenieros, Universidad de Sevilla.

Chapa López, J. (2009). *Análisis del comportamiento dinámico de redes inlámbricas de banda ancha fijas basadas en el estándar IEEE 802.16.* (Master's thesis). Universidad Nacional Autónoma de México, Mexico City, Mexico.

Chi-Ming, L., & Shuoh Ren, T. (2010). *Provisioning an end to end QoS for VoIP over WiMAX network.* Paper presented at the International Computer Symposium (ICS). Taipei, Taiwan.

Cisco Systems. (2003). *Understanding delay in packet voice networks.* Retrieved from http://www.cisco.com/warp/public/788/voip/delaydetails.pdf

COST-Action-231. (1999). *Digital mobile radio towards future generatio systems.* European Communities.

Daniel, K., Rohde, S., Subik, S., & Wietfeld, C. (2009). *Performance evaluation for mobile WiMAX handover with a continuous scanning algorithm.* Paper presented at the IEEE Mobile WiMAX Symposium MWS '09. New York, NY.

Erceg, V. G. L., Tjandra, S., Parkoff, S., Gupta, A., Kulic, B., Julius, A., & Bianchi, R. (1998). *An empirically-based path loss model for wireless channels in suburban environments.* Paper presented at the Global Telecommunications Conference. Sydney, Australia.

Etemad, K., & Lai, M. (2011). *WiMAX technology and network evolution.* New York: Wiley.

Hata, M. (1980). Empirical formula for propagation loss in land mobile radio services. *IEEE Transactions on Vehicular Technology*, 29(3), 317–325. doi:10.1109/T-VT.1980.23859

Hongxia, Z., & Jufeng, D. (2009). *A simple compensation algorithm for VoIP services in IEEE 802.16e system.* Paper presented at 11th International Conference on Advanced Communication Technology. Korea.

IEEE-1. (2006). *IEEE Std 802.16e-2005 and IEEE Std 802.16-2004/Cor 1-2005 (amendment and corrigendum to IEEE Std 802.16-2004).* Retrieved from www.ieee802.org/

IEEE-2. (2004). *EEE Std 802.16-2004 (revision of IEEE Std 802.16-2001).* Retrieved from www.ieee802.org/

IEEE 802.16 Working Group. (2013). *The IEEE 802.16 working group on broadband wireless access standards.* Retrieved from http://www.wirelessman.org/

Jau-Yang, C., & Yu-Chen, L. (2012). Dynamically alternating power saving scheme for IEEE 802.16e mobile broadband wireless access systems. *Journal of Communications and Networks*, 14(2), 179–187. doi:10.1109/JCN.2012.6253066

Kassim, H., & Baba, M. D. (2011). *Performance analysis of fixed and mobile WiMax networks using NCTUns tools*. Paper presented at the Control and System Graduate Research Colloquium (ICSGRC). Malaysia.

Milanovic, J., Rimac-Drlje, S., & Bejuk, K. (2007). *Comparison of propagation models accuracy for WiMAX*. Paper presented at the 4th IEEE International Conference on Electronics, Circuits and Systems. Morocco.

Milanović, J., Rimac-Drlje, S., & Majerski, I. (2010). Radio wave propagation mechanisms and empirical models for fixed wireless access systems. *Tehnički Vjesnik, 17*(1), 43–53.

Okumura, Y., Ohmori, E., Kawano, T., & Fukuda, K. (1968). Field strength and its variability in VHF and UHF land-mobile radio service. *Rev. Elec. Commun. Lab, 16*(9), 825–873.

Parsons, J. J., & Oja, D. (2008). *Conceptos de computación: Nuevas perspectivas*. México: CENGAGE Learning.

Rangel Licea, V. (2009). *Modelado de redes WiMAX*. Retrieved from http://goo.gl/CBNa27

Safak, A., & Preveze, B. (2008). *Analysis of delay factors for voice over WiMAX*. Paper presented at the 23rd International Symposium on Computer and Information Sciences. Turkey.

Suliman, F. E. M., Elhassan, N. M., & Ibrahim, T. A. (2012). *Frequency offset estimation and cell search algorithms for OFDMA based mobile WiMAX*. Paper presented at the 14th International Conference on Advanced Communication Technology (ICACT). Korea.

Walfisch, J., & Bertoni, H. L. (1988). A theoretical model of UHF propagation in urban environments. *IEEE Transactions on Antennas and Propagation, 36*(12), 1788–1796. doi:10.1109/8.14401

Zaka, K., & Ahmed, N. Ibrar-ul-Haq, M., Irfan Anis, M., & Faria, B. (2009). *Performance analysis and throughput optimization in IEEE 802.16 WiMax standard*. Paper presented at the First Asian Himalayas International Conference on Internet. Nepal.

Zhang, Y., & Chen, H. (2007). *Mobile WiMAX: Toward broadband wireless metropolitan area networks*. Boston: Auerbach Publications. doi:10.1201/9780849326400

KEY TERMS AND DEFINITIONS

Bandwidth: Is the amount of data that can be transmitted from the sending node to the destination node in a given time.

Broadband: Having instantaneous bandwidths greater than around 1 MHz and supporting data rates greater than about 1.5 Mb/s.

Base station: Is providing the service to the subscriber stations via transmission of electromagnetic.

Delay: Is the time lapsed at which the sender node packets go to the destination node and back.

Fixed Wireless Access: Wireless access application in which the location of the base station (BS).

Metropolitan Area Network (MAN): Es una red que provee conectividad a un área geográfica de gran tamaño y de tipo urbano.

Mobile Stations: Are able to receive the service that issues the base station while in constant or intermittent motion.

Node: A term associated with a mesh network station. A node, due to the nature of mesh, may behave as a BS, SS, or both, and will generate and forward data to other nodes.

Subscriber Station (SS): A generalized equipment set receive connectivity of service that emits the base station (BS).

Throughput: Is the real rate of data delivery that passes through a medium of communication.

Chapter 2
Aperiodic ICIC–Oriented CSI Reporting for LTE Networks

David González González
Universitat Politècnica de Catalunya, Spain

Mario García-Lozano
Universitat Politècnica de Catalunya, Spain

Silvia Ruiz Boqué
Universitat Politècnica de Catalunya, Spain

ABSTRACT

Interference mitigation has been identified as an important challenge for cellular technologies based on Orthogonal Frequency Division Multiple Access (OFDMA) such as the Long Term Evolution (LTE) system of the Third Generation Partnership Project (3GPP). In this context, Intercell Interference Coordination (ICIC) techniques have received much attention by the research community, as they are a good approach to address this issue. In particular, static solutions enjoy acceptance due to their low complexity and ease of implementation. ICIC mechanisms are not standardized in LTE, which just provides certain support so that every vendor/operator configures its particular ICIC option. Hence, their interworking with other important network functionalities such as Channel State Information (CSI) feedback must be carefully considered. This chapter provides an overview on the relationship between ICIC and CSI in LTE and introduces a novel mechanism to improve such interworking. The novel scheme is feasible and easy-to-implement and it is especially effective for Non-Real Time services. It provides gains in terms of system capacity, cell edge performance, and energy efficiency with respect to 3GPP LTE mechanisms and previous proposals.

I. INTRODUCTION

In the context of modern cellular networks, the demand for new and attractive packet-based services is currently growing faster than ever. Services and applications are increasingly requiring higher levels of Quality of Service (QoS). In this context, the Long Term Evolution (LTE) of the 3rd Generation Partnership Project (3GPP) is foreseen to be a leading system towards the fourth generation (4G). Indeed, LTE-Advanced (LTE release 10) is the 3GPP solution for 4G mobile broadband and was approved by the International Telecommunications Union (ITU) as an Interna-

DOI: 10.4018/978-1-4666-4888-3.ch002

tional Mobile Telecommunications-Advanced (IMT-A) technology in late 2010.

LTE features a packet-optimized Radio Access Technology (RAT) and flat all-IP architecture allowing a reduced number of network elements. It also features flexible bandwidth allocation based on Orthogonal Frequency Division Multiple Access (OFDMA) in the downlink. OFDMA implies intrinsic orthogonality among users in a cell, and so, it provides nearly null intracell interference. However, with a low frequency reuse factor (ideally 1), intercell interference becomes a major concern as users get close to cell edge. Under these circumstances, the QoS remarkably depends on the user position, which yields to the concept of *fairness*.

In the light of this situation, Intercell Interference Coordination (ICIC) has been recognized as a fundamental piece of OFDMA based cellular technologies (Himayat, Talwar, Rao, & Soni, 2010). Broadly speaking, the main target of any ICIC strategy is to determine what resources (bandwidth and power) are available at each cell at any time in order to reduce interference levels and improve fairness among users. Considering the temporality in which resource coordination is performed it is possible to distinguish between static or dynamic ICIC. In particular, static ICIC currently holds certain popularity because of its ease of implementation and distributed operation, being Soft and Fractional Frequency Reuse (SFR and FFR,) the techniques *par excellence*. The reader is referred to (González G, García-Lozano, Ruiz, & Olmos, On the Need for Dynamic Downlink Intercell Interference Coordination for Realistic LTE Deployments, 2012) for a complete review of the state-of-the-art on ICIC. It is worth saying that LTE specifications do not standardize this important functionality, in turn, only certain mechanisms and enablers of potential ICIC strategies are provided.

Whereas ICIC is in charge of determining resources to be used in each cell and groups of users in the mid and long term, scheduling deals

with resource allocation at the very short term scale. In this sense, Channel State Information (CSI) feedback is a key functionality whose role is of utmost importance. Updated and free of errors CSI allows taking opportunistic decisions, and thus, making the most of each user channel conditions. LTE specifications do include several CSI feedback methods comprising periodic and aperiodic mechanisms suitable for Real Time (RT) and Non Real Time (NRT) traffic, respectively. However, such in-built schemes are quite generic and do not take into account the presence of ICIC techniques.

Bearing this context in mind, it is clear that CSI feedback must take into account the resource allocation constraints imposed by ICIC in order to optimize its operation. Both ICIC and CSI feedback have been extensively investigated, however, it is desirable a design in which CSI mechanisms are able to operate efficiently when static ICIC is also employed. As it will be shown later on, this particular interworking deserves special attention as the performance of native LTE CSI reporting schemes is poor in cases where static ICIC policies are applied. Thus, in this chapter an aperiodic CSI feedback scheme, suitable to operate in conjunction with static ICIC is presented. The proposed approach exploits two ideas:

1. Improve accuracy of CSI reports by refining the estimation of the so-called wideband Channel Quality Indicator (CQI). The CQI is a number ranging from 0 to 15 that quantifies the channel quality and refers to a recommended modulation and code rate combination; see Section 7.2.3 in (3GPP Group Radio Access Network, 2010) for details;

2. Reduce required feedback overhead by means of differential encoding.

The new aperiodic scheme, proves to be not only especially useful for bursty traffic patterns but also an excellent companion for static ICIC algorithms as significantly benefits the QoS perceived by cell edge users. The analysis shows that this novel approach outperforms previous proposals in terms of user- and system-oriented performance metrics while it keeps the feedback overhead competitive. The new solution requires no additional capability at User Equipment (UE) and only a very small amount of information needs to be transmitted (occasionally) in the downlink.

The rest of the chapter is organized as follows: the next section introduces the specific problem and provides background for its understanding. Section III presents a review of related works. Next, Section IV contains a description of the operation of different existing CSI feedback schemes and a new proposal that considers the existence of static ICIC mechanisms. After this, the second part of the chapter is devoted to quantitatively comparing these schemes. A detailed description of the system model that has been used for this purpose is presented in Section V. Section VI includes research methodology and overall interworking between CSI and ICIC. Numerical results, complexity, and implementation aspects are discussed in Section VII. Finally, Section VIII closes the chapter with final remarks.

II. BACKGROUND AND PROBLEM STATEMENT

A. Static ICIC

The main target of any ICIC strategy is to reduce intercell interference. Particularly, the focus is usually set on improving the average radio channel quality of cell edge users. This allows a more homogeneous Signal to Interference plus Noise Ratio (SINR) around the cell area and so less variations in the individual Quality of Experience (QoE).

ICIC is typically done by modifying both frequency reuse factor and power allocated to different groups of users. In case this treatment of radio resources is not modified in the mid-term,

the ICIC is said to be *static*. Static proposals are usually based on fractional reuse policies. This means that users are categorized according to their position and higher reuse factors/power levels are used at the outer regions of the cells. To be precise, users are classified as Exteriors (Ext) or Interiors (Int) according to their average radio channel quality, typically expressed as average SINR, $\bar{\gamma}$, which is compared against a threshold γ_{TH}. This value can be chosen according to different criteria, having a paramount importance because of its strong effect on overall network performance (González G, García-Lozano, Ruiz, & Olmos, An Analytical View of Static Intercell Interference Coordination Techniques in OFDMA Networks, 2012).

Figure 1 illustrates the bandwidth/power allocation in SFR and FFR. It can be observed that, in SFR, intercell interference is also interclass. In order to control the amount of interference received by cell edge users, low power is used in the bands to be used by the inner ones. This power is controlled by the parameter α. On the other hand, FFR removes completely interclass interference, i.e., each class has exclusive use of its bandwidth. This way, the performance in terms of throughput and fairness becomes independent of α since the SINR does not depend on the transmitted power as long as the intercell interference level is sufficiently above of the noise power. The bandwidth allocation is controlled by the parameter β.

B. CSI in LTE

In LTE, CSI is expressed in terms of CQIs that are indexes providing estimates of channel quality. Ideally, the SINR at subcarrier level should be known at the base station for every single user m. This metric can be computed as follows:

$$\gamma_m^{n,sc} = \frac{P_{\hat{l}}^{n} \times g_{m,\hat{l}}^{n,sc}}{B_{PRB} \times N_0 + \sum_{l=0,l\neq\hat{l}}^{L-1} P_{\hat{l}}^{n} \times g_{m,l}^{n,sc}} \quad (1)$$

Figure 1. Static ICIC schemes

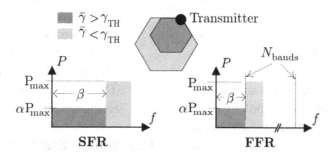

where P_l^n represents the power transmitted by base station l in the Physical Resource Block (PRB) n. In LTE, a PRB is the minimum allocable bandwidth per user (B_{PRB}) and it is composed of 12 subcarriers having the same allocated transmission power (3GPP Group Radio Access Network, 2008). Note that $\hat{l}$ corresponds to the serving cell index of user m. The term $g_{m,l}^{n,sc}$ denotes the channel gain of user m (for subcarrier sc within PRB n) with respect to base station l. N_0 is the power spectral density of the noise and L is the total number of cells in the system. Obviously, transmitting this information through the air interface is prohibitive due to the amount of signaling overhead and required computational cost. Thus, both granularity (frequency domain) and validity (time domain) arise as issues.

CQIs are estimated based on SINR measurements (according to Equation 1) of cell-specific

Reference Signals (RS) that are embedded into the system bandwidth at certain Resource Elements (REs). A RE is the fundamental resource unit within the OFDMA structure of LTE, it comprises one subcarrier during one OFDM symbol (3GPP Group Radio Access Network, 2008). This is depicted in Figure 2a which represents the structure of one PRB having 14 OFDM symbols (normal cyclic prefix configuration). It is a requirement that all RSs are transmitted with constant power within each LTE cell. Moreover, due to their importance, RSs are the highest powered REs within the downlink signal. This is illustrated in Figure 2b, which represents the frequency allocation for interior users, exterior users and RS along with their associated powers.

Note that RSs are always active (even in PRBs that are never used) with the power boost applied to them. This is required to allow better detection as cell-specific RSs are also used for channel

Figure 2. Cell-specific reference signals in LTE

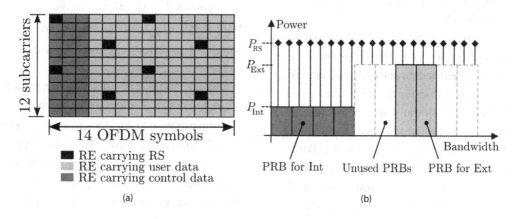

equalization and synchronization. Further details can be found in (3GPP Group Radio Access Network, 2010). From the perspective of CSI estimation, the power offset applied to data REs is not a problem because this power difference is transmitted to users through higher layers signaling as user-specific offsets. Therefore, in order to estimate the quality on a single PRB, the UE has to measure the SINR in the RSs of that PRB and calculate an equivalent effective SINR γ_{eff} from which a CQI is obtained (Olmos, Serra, Ruiz, García-Lozano, & González G, 2009). The process is similar if a CQI needs to be calculated for a set of one or more (contiguous or not) PRBs P. Finally, the equivalent CQI index $\Theta \in \{0\ 1\ 2 \dots 15\}$ corresponding to P is obtained by means of a mapping L as follows:

$$\Theta_P = L\left\{\gamma_{eff}\left(P\right), \varepsilon\right\} \qquad (2)$$

where ε corresponds to the target Block Error Rate (BLER), typically 10% in the first transmission attempt. The mapping L is performed through look-up tables obtained from detailed link level simulations (Brueninghaus, et al., 2005). Summarizing, transmitting information to users in LTE involves the following steps:

1. Measure and report (in CQI format) the quality for an arbitrary set of PRBs (one or more subbands or the whole system bandwidth) by using SINR measurements taken from cell-specific RSs;

2. Based on this information and other aspects such as QoS policies, buffer status and available resources for data and control channels, the scheduler allocates resources for a given set of users. Each transmission has the following attributes: Modulation and Coding Scheme (MCS) index, Transport Block Size (TBS) and Redundancy Version (RV). In case of erroneous transmissions, additional retransmissions are sent following a Hybrid-Automatic Repeat reQuest (HARQ) procedure;

3. At reception, the probability of successfully decoding the information depends on such transmissions attributes and the effective SINR observed in RE carrying user data, see Figure 2a.

C. Problem Statement

In LTE, both periodic and aperiodic CSI reporting schemes (see Section V) are coded differentially with respect to a wideband CQI, Θ_{WB}, representing the average radio channel quality over the whole system bandwidth (3GPP Group Radio Access Network, 2010). In this sense, the highest granularity that can be reported is at subband level, which is a set of contiguous PRBs having a size that depends on the system bandwidth, i.e., N_{PRB}.

Both differential encoding and subband reporting are needed to reduce the uplink CSI feedback overhead over the Physical Uplink Shared Channel (PUSCH) which is, indeed, the same physical channel used to convey users' data in the uplink. Thus, given that (1) Θ_{WB} is computed by considering all RSs in the system bandwidth, and (2) the particular resource allocation used in SFR and FFR, it is clear that Θ_{WB} only provides a very rough estimate of the actual average radio channel quality from the perspective of both set of users (Ext and Int). Since subband CQIs are differentially encoded with respect to Θ_{WB}, in case of static ICIC, Θ_{WB} will be under- and over- estimated for exterior and interior users, respectively.

The aperiodic reporting scheme presented in this chapter aims at alleviating this issue by refining the estimation of Θ_{WB} according to the current classification of each user (Ext or Int). As average radio channel quality depends basically on large scale fading effects, user classification does not change so often, and hence, this fact can be exploited conveniently and resulting in performance improvements.

III. RELATED WORK

The literature about CSI feedback in LTE is extensive since it is (1) a very important aspect affecting the performance of wireless systems (Tse & Viswanath, 2005,) and (2) especially useful in case of multicarrier based access methods (Agarwal, Guo, & Honig, 2010) such as OFDMA. This Section provides an overview of important works, and, in the light of these contributions, put this study in context highlighting both its novelties and relevance.

A. Work within the 3GPP

The work related to CSI feedback is mainly discussed in the meetings of the Technical Specification Group (TSG) Radio Access Network (RAN) specifically by the Working Group 1 (WG1). During the final phase of the standardization of LTE (2007 and 2008), discussions and proposals about CSI feedback were mainly focused on CQI definition, measurement and reporting methodologies (Qualcomm Europe, 2007), (Alcatel-Lucent, 2007), (Nokia Siemens Networks, 2007), (Texas Instruments, 2008), (Texas Instruments, 2008), (Ericsson, 2008). From the very beginning, especial emphasis was placed on the amount of uplink signaling overhead and overall complexity involved in different reporting mechanisms. Subsequent discussions addressed other important aspects such as overhead analysis, feedback compression, CQI computation and interplay with retransmissions (Panasonic, 2009), (NEC Group, 2009), (Alcatel-Lucent, 2009), (Sharp, 2009).

With the advent of LTE-A, during 2010 and 2011, discussions on aperiodic reporting schemes and their adaptation to new features such as Carrier Aggregation and enhanced-ICIC (eICIC) have also taken place (Panasonic, HTC, 2010), (Samsung, 2010), (Motorola, 2010), (Panasonic, HTC, 2010), (Huawei, 2011), (Huawei, HiSilicon, 2011), (Samsung, 2011). More recently, as Coordinated Multipoint (Irmer, et al., 2011) has become a very active research field, further improvements are being discussed in that direction as well (HTC, 2012), (Intel Corporation, 2012), (Hitachi Ltd, 2012), (Qualcomm, 2012).

B. Contributions from the Research Community

CSI feedback is by itself an element that needs to be taken into greater consideration when wireless systems are investigated. However, the way in which this is done is rather diverse and in general depends on the research objectives in each case. Bearing this in mind, it is possible to distinguish among:

- **Group 1:** Works implementing existing reporting mechanisms as a complementary functionality in order to study other aspects, rather than CSI feedback, such as ICIC or scheduling;
- **Group 2:** Studies presenting performance evaluation and/or analysis of one or more existing feedback schemes either analytically or by means of system level simulations; and
- **Group 3:** Contributions introducing new reporting strategies.

Group 1: Modeling CSI Feedback

One common assumption found in the literature is considering full and perfect channel knowledge both in frequency and time domain. In the frequency domain, this implies that channel quality information is available with an arbitrary small resolution, i.e., at subcarrier level, at PRB level or in groups of PRBs. In the time domain, full knowledge implies that channel measurements are available instantaneously to the transmitter. On the other hand, perfect knowledge implies that channel quality estimations are done without errors, which is rather arguable in the radio resource management arena. The performance of procedures that strongly rely on such detailed information could be significantly different if erroneous or delayed channel estimations were considered.

An interesting example is (Kumar, Monghal, Nin, Ordas, Pedersen, & Mogensen, 2009), where the authors proposed a set of interference avoidance schemes for the particular case of light load conditions. In this study, channel information was available for each PRB (full knowledge in the frequency domain) but 2 ms reporting delay was assumed (partial knowledge in the time domain). Measurement error was also introduced as a log-normal random variable, thus imperfect knowledge was assumed. Channel quality information was represented by means of SINR levels with 1 dB resolution to emulate the discrete nature of realistic reporting schemes such as the ones in LTE. This way, the assumptions are perfectly valid for the context of the study since small variations on them would not affect the conclusions qualitatively speaking. The work eventually shows the importance of an accurate and realistic CSI feedback modeling.

Group 2: Performance Analysis of CSI Feedback Strategies

Although analytical treatment is in general advisable, evaluating analytically the performance of CSI feedback schemes in the context of cellular networks requires incurring in analytical approximations and modeling simplifications as it has been pointed out in (Donthi & Mehta, 2011). In this contribution, closed-form expressions measuring the merit of different reporting schemes available in LTE were smartly obtained. Nevertheless, Donthi and Mehta remarked (1) the complementarity nature of their work with respect to the need for detailed/accurate system level simulations, and (2) the fact that their findings should be understood

as independent theoretical references that can provide additional insights in order to improve system optimization. Additional aspects such as the impact of estimation errors were identified as open issues. Given this, the study presented along in this chapter addresses these and other related issues by means of detailed system level simulations. Additional analytical performance assessments have been recently presented in (Hur & Rao, 2012) and (Varanese, Vicario, & Spagnolini, 2012) although for more generic CSI feedback mechanisms.

Group 3: Previous Proposals

One of the first practical CSI feedback schemes was proposed by Su et al. in (Su, Fan, Zheng, & Wang, 2007). Their reporting scheme is mainly based on two ideas: first, only report CQIs for subbands featuring the best channel conditions and, second, using a hierarchical structure to divide the system bandwidth into levels with different granularities. According to (Motorola, 2005), where this structure was initially introduced, by iterating through these levels it is possible to roughly estimate a fading profile of the whole bandwidth. However, this would require certain reporting periodicity that indeed does not exist for several types of services.

Another practical approach was proposed in (Xue, Yin, Yue, & Liu, 2009). In this work, the authors employed a Modified top-M scheme in which UEs only feedback the average channel quality of the best M subbands. In this scheme the value of M depends on traffic load and type. When system load increases, the value of M is decreased in order to keep the uplink overhead mostly constant.

Even though the previous works realistically deal with LTE specifications and its constraints, the vast majority of related works on CSI with limited feedback are proposals mainly oriented to generic OFDMA systems whose LTE feasibility would require important changes in the system design. In practice, new proposals must be, as far as possible, in compliance with the standard. On the other hand, no previous proposal has addressed ICIC aspects explicitly.

Finally, to close this group, a brief overview of other recent generic works (that are not compatible with LTE) is presented. The work in (Mecking, 2002) identifies interesting aspects of the CSI feedback problem: the need for efficient low-rate strategies and the question on how accurate CSI should be to achieve near optimum performance. In this work the system model considers one single access point and flat fading channel. The contribution in (Ouyang & Ying, 2009) extended the analysis to OFDM-based access. This work is important because it introduces a feedback scheme that allocates feedback resources depending on the status of buffers and channel conditions. However, the model used in this study assumes that transmissions are always done with the same MCS and that the number of required subbands per user is constant. These assumptions are hardly justified for complex multiservice modern cellular systems. Recently, a joint feedback-scheduling scheme, similar to (Ouyang & Ying, 2009) was proposed in (Ganapathy & Caramanis, 2012). The authors also highlighted the importance of considering

the impact of CSI feedback on the performance of queuing systems with realistic traffic models. The need for efficient scheduling rules based on queue length information has also been remarked in (Gopalan, Caramanis, & Shakkottai, 2012). Other feedback schemes providing partial CSI for the downlink of generic OFDMA systems include (Chen, Berry, & Honig, 2008), (Agarwal, Majjigi, Han, Vannithamby, & Cioffi, 2008) and (Choi & Bahk, 2008). In order to provide a comparative perspective, Table 1 shows a summary of these contributions highlighting the following important practical aspects:

- **Consideration of CSI Estimation Errors:** Given that channel quality measurements are based on RS, CSI is partial. In addition, this information is subject to other sources of error such as delay processing, quantization and measurement impairments.
- **LTE Feasibility:** Any CSI feedback proposal must be, as far as possible, compliance with technical specifications meaning that only minor changes would be required for implementation.
- **Uplink Capacity:** As mentioned before, the limited capacity of uplink feedback

Table 1. Summary of related work

Ref.	CSI Errors	LTE Feasibility	Uplink Capacity	Overhead Analysis	Realistic Traffic	Model	ICIC
(Xue, Yin, Yue, & Liu, 2009)	✓	✓	✓	X	✓	Multi-cell	X
(Su, Fan, Zheng, & Wang, 2007)	X	✓	✓	✓	X	Multi-cell	X
(Ganapathy & Caramanis, 2012)	X	X	✓	✓	✓	Single-cell	X
(Mecking, 2002)	X	X	✓	✓	X	Single-cell	X
(Ouyang & Ying, 2009)	X	X	✓	X	✓	Single-cell	X
(Gopalan, Caramanis, & Shakkottai, 2012)	X	X	X	X	✓	Single-cell	X
(Agarwal, Majjigi, Han, Vannithamby, & Cioffi, 2008)	X	X	✓	✓	X	Single-cell	X
(Chen, Berry, & Honig, 2008)	X	X	✓	X	X	Single-cell	X
(Choi & Bahk, 2008)	X	X	X	✓	X	Single-cell	X

channels is an important practical constraint in real systems.

- **Overhead Analysis:** Given the previous point, the required uplink overhead is an indicator that must be considered as a performance metric.

- **Realistic Traffic:** Aperiodic feedback schemes are especially useful for NRT traffic patterns where CSI is more likely to be requested on-demand. Considering realistic traffic patterns is required to consistently evaluate the performance of aperiodic reporting schemes.

- **System Model:** This aspect is particularly important in the context of interference limited systems. If only one access point is considered, radio channel quality can be only expressed in terms of SNR instead of SINR and therefore the inherent randomness of intercell interference cannot be taken into account.

- **ICIC Aspects:** As previously indicated, there is a close interaction between CSI and the available resources defined by the ICIC technique. Hence, it is very important to highlight this aspect within the review of related literature.

From Table I, it can be seen that no ICIC-oriented CSI feedback scheme has been investigated so far. Therefore, the technical issue explained in Subsection II-C remains unaddressed. In addition, the lack of a more realistic performance assessment considering a multi-cell environment in which ICI and CSI can be realistically and jointly modeled is notorious. A fair performance assessment must take all the aspects shown in Table 1 into account. Thus, the main contribution of the scheme presented in this chapter can be summarized as follows:

1. A novel aperiodic CSI feedback scheme for LTE aiming at optimizing both user QoS

and system performance when static ICIC is considered. This is done by employing realistic traffic patterns and an independent QoS oriented scheduling policy.

2. The proposed scheme implicitly incorporates all the aspects shown in Table I since channel quality definition and measurement are modeled according to LTE specifications, i.e., CSI is based on CQI reports obtained by means of true RS SINR and subject to delay and measurement errors.

3. Additional notorious aspects include:

   a. The performance of the proposed CSI feedback scheme has been evaluated by considering both FFR and SFR.

   b. The impact of the proposed reporting scheme on user satisfaction ratio is analyzed by means of the *joint system capacity* notion (Marques, Wanstedt, Porto, & Freitas, 2010) which provides better insights of the actual impact on QoS.

   c. Performance comparison includes not only LTE reporting schemes but also previous proposals.

   d. Comparative overhead and complexity analysis is presented together with LTE implementation aspects.

IV. CSI FEEDBACK SCHEMES

In this study, 6 different CSI feedback schemes are considered and subsequently explained. In order to understand the operation of these strategies, some concepts must be introduced in advance:

1. **Active Band (AB):** Portion of the system bandwidth in which a cell is allowed to transmit. In the following, P_{AB}^i represents the set of PRBs belonging to the AB in the ith cell, where N_{AB}^i is the cardinality of that set, i.e., $|P_{AB}^i|$. Note that $N_{AB}^i < N_{PRB}$ for

all i, being N_{PRB} the number of PRBs in the system;

2. **Reserved Band (RB):** $P^{i,j}$ denotes the set of PRBs in the ith cell that are assigned to the user class j ($j \in \{Ext, Int\}$). Thus, $P^i_{AB} = \cup P^{i,j}$ for all j;

3. **Subband (SB):** The system bandwidth is divided in N_{SB} subbands, having $\left\lfloor N_{PRB} / k \right\rfloor$ of them size k and one is of size $N_{PRB} - k \left\lfloor N_{PRB} / k \right\rfloor$. The value of k depends on N_{PRB}. For example, if $N_{PRB}=100$, the standard specifies $k=8$. Further details can be found in (3GPP Group Radio Access Network, 2010).

A. Benchmarks

The different CSI feedback schemes used as benchmarks are explained in the following points. Please note that Δ and δ are the CQI-based CSI report content and uplink signaling overhead, respectively. For the sake of simplicity, the cell indexes are omitted:

1. **IDEAL:** For every single PRB in the AB, a CQI value is estimated by the UE and reported to the serving base station. Thus, an array of CQI values, each encoded with 4 bits, is transmitted. This mechanism allows establishing an upper bound from the performance point of view:

$$\Delta_{IDEAL} = \vec{\Theta} \in \mathbb{R}^{N_{AB}}$$
$$\delta_{IDEAL} = 4 \cdot N_{AB} \ \left[\text{bits}\right]$$

2. **LTE-HLC:** This mechanism is proposed by the 3GPP. One single differential CQI value is reported for each SB in the AB. Two bits differential encoding (with respect to the wideband CQI: Θ_{WB}) is used; details can

be found in (3GPP Group Radio Access Network, 2010):

$$\Delta_{LTE\text{-}HLC} = \left\{\Theta_{WB}, \vec{\Theta} \in \mathbb{R}^{N_{SB}}\right\}$$
$$\delta_{LTE\text{-}HLC} = 4 + 2 \cdot N_{SB} \ \left[\text{bits}\right]$$

3. **LTE-UESEL:** 3GPP proposal also known as Best-M (3GPP Group Radio Access Network, 2010). The UE reports one differential CQI value reflecting the channel quality over the best M SBs. The position of the M selected subbands is reported using a combinatorial index w composed of L bits (3GPP Group Radio Access Network, 2010). In this study case $M=6$. Θ_{WB} is also reported:

$$\Delta_{LTE\text{-}UESEL} = \left\{\Theta_{WB}, \Theta_{Dif}, w\right\}$$
$$\delta_{LTE\text{-}UESEL} = 4 + 2 + L \ \left[\text{bits}\right]$$
$$L = \log_2 \binom{N_{SB}}{M}$$

4. **MOD-TOPM:** This scheme was proposed in (Xue, Yin, Yue, & Liu, 2009) and operates similarly to LTE-UESEL just with some differences. The UE reports a 4-bit CQI representing the average quality observed within the best M subbands. Thus, instead of using differential encoding, 4-bit CQIs are employed and so wideband CQI is not required. However, the value of M is adjusted depending on the load (the number of users at each cell). The positioning of the best M must be informed to the transmitter by means of a combinatorial index w composed of L bits:

$$\Delta_{\text{LTE-UESEL}} = \left\{ \Theta_{\text{WB}}, \Theta_{\text{Dif}}, w \right\}$$

$$\delta_{\text{LTE-UESEL}} = 4 + 2 + L \left[\text{bits} \right]$$

$$L = \left\lceil \log_2 \left(\begin{array}{c} N_{\text{SB}} \\ M \end{array} \right) \right\rceil$$

5. **HI-SEL:** This scheme was proposed in (Su, Fan, Zheng, & Wang, 2007). It divides the system bandwidth into different levels, each of them with different granularities. Given that N_{PRB}=100PRBs, the implementation defines 5 levels. The number of subbands in the lth level, N_{SB}^{l} is: 1, 2, 4, 20, 100 for l = 1,2,…,5 . Correspondingly, the subband size S^l and the number of suboptimal subbands q^l in the level l is 100, 50, 25, 5 and 1, and 0, 1, 2, 3 and 4, respectively. Note that the notion of subband in the context of this strategy is not the same as in LTE and hence, the size of each of them depends on both the hierarchical level and the system bandwidth. The algorithm transmits, for each level, a CQI value for the best subband together with another CQI representing the average quality in the next best q subbands (the suboptimal subbands). In addition to the pair of CQIs, the positioning of the best and suboptimal subbands at each level must be indicated to the network by means of a combinatorial index w composed of L bits.

$$\Delta_{\text{HI-SEL}} = \left\{ \Theta_{\text{BestM}}, \Theta_q, w \right\}$$

$$\delta_{\text{HI-SEL}} = 4 + 4 + L[\text{bits}]$$

$$L = \left\lceil \log_2 \left(\sum_{l=2}^{5} \left(\left(\begin{array}{c} N_{\text{SB}}^l \\ 1 \end{array} \right) \left(\begin{array}{c} N_{\text{SB}}^l - 1 \\ q^l \end{array} \right) \right) \right) \right\rceil$$

B. Proposed Scheme: Localized ICIC

The proposed scheme relies on the fact that previous proposals and LTE mechanisms are not very efficient when static ICIC strategies are used. In such cases, UE will be measuring the quality in portions of the system bandwidth without interest by virtue of the current user classification and the bandwidth allocation pattern corresponding to the static ICIC scheme. As a result, the wideband CQI (around which subband CQIs are encoded) is shifted from the value that would be obtained if only RBs were considered.

Taking this into account, Loc-ICIC focuses on RBs when computing wideband estimates. To do this, Loc-ICIC only requires transmitting a very small amount of information (a vector $\vec{m}$ of $\left\lceil N_{\text{PRB}} / k \right\rceil$ bits) when the UE changes its current classification due to, for instance, mobility. Given the binary vector $\vec{m}$, the vector $\vec{s}$ containing the indexes of non-zero positions in $\vec{m}$ can be easily obtained. For instance, given $\vec{m}$ = [11000011], $\vec{s}$ = [0167]. The operation is as follows: the base station signals to the UE a bit stream, one bit for each SB, indicating which one is active for that UE (according to UE's classification and bandwidth allocation in the serving base station). This information does not need to be updated unless the UE changes its classification. Then, the UE estimates/transmits one differential CQI value for each SB in $\vec{s}$. With this approach, the UE focuses exclusively on the relevant part of the system bandwidth achieving more accurate descriptions of the radio channel. Figure 3a sketches the operational principle behind Loc-ICIC using FFR as example.

$$\Delta_{\text{Loc-ICIC}} = \left\{ \Theta_{\text{WB}}, \vec{\Theta} \in \mathbb{R}^{|\vec{s}|} \right\}$$

$$\delta_{\text{Loc-ICIC}} = 4 + 2 |\vec{s}| [\text{bits}]$$

V. SYSTEM MODEL

The downlink of a LTE network is considered and the interworking between different network functionalities such as CSI feedback, scheduling and so on is illustrated in the Figure 3b. This figure shows how several data structures (see Table 2) flow from one entity to another. To be precise, the scheduler allocates radio resources and shapes future transmissions to different users every Transmission Time Interval (TTI) by taking into account all these data structures.

Thus, based on the information coming from previous HARQ processes, available resources at each cell according to static ICIC, user QoS and CSI, the scheduler performs the final short term resource allocation, i.e., it defines the matrices **X**, **Y** and **T**. Having a more detailed look at this process, CQI update is done according to some CSI Feedback Scheme (CFS), say CFS_x, and hence, the central element in this study is the fact that the matrix **C** is indeed a function of the selected reporting discipline. This gives the leading role to the CSI feedback mechanism in the sense that the overall system performance depends on the accuracy of **C**.

$$C\left(t\right) = f_{\text{Reporting}}\left(CFS_x\right) \qquad (3)$$

The matrix **C** corresponds to the CQI-based channel descriptor of users in the system. Given **C**, the scheduling process also takes into account:

- Buffers status stored in the data structure **B**;
- QoS parameters for each service $s \in \emptyset$ stored in the data structure **Q**;
- Per-class/cell power/bandwidth allocation defined by the static ICIC policy by means of **P** and active/reserved bands at each cell: P_{AB}^i and $P^{i,j}$ for all $j \in \left\{\text{Ext, Int}\right\}$);
- HARQ feedback information of previous transmissions: **T**.

This framework is a convenient way to study the impact of different CSI reporting schemes on the overall system performance and user QoS (Andrews, Kumaran, Ramanan, Stolyar, Whiting, & Vijayakumar, 2001).

The user satisfaction ratio θ_s for a service s is expressed as follows:

$$\theta_s = \mu_s / \mu_s \qquad (4)$$

where $\hat{\mu}_s$ and μs are the number of connected and satisfied flows from service s respectively. In particular, a NRT service is said to be satisfied if the target bit rate RT is met. Finally, The selection of the MCS index to be used in a HARQ (re-) transmission τ, is done according to:

$$MCS^* = \underset{MCS}{\text{argmax}} \; \Gamma_\tau$$

Subject to:

$$f_{\text{eff}}\left(\vec{q}\right) \geq \gamma_{\text{eff}}^{\text{BLER} \leq 10\%}\left(\text{TBS}_\tau, \text{RV}_\tau, MCS^*\right) \qquad (5)$$

where Γ_δ represents the payload conveyed by the transmission τ and it is calculated as follows:

$$\Gamma_\tau = TBS \cdot \eta_i \cdot N_{\text{RE}} \qquad (6)$$

In the previous expression, η_i is the product of the modulation order and code rate of MCS i (3GPP Group Radio Access Network, 2010), (3GPP Group Radio Access Network, 2008). N_{RE} is the number of useful Resource Elements (RE) per PRB. In this work, $N_{RE} = (N_{SC} N_{OFDM}^{Sym}) - N_{RS}$. N_{RS} is the number of RSs within the N_{OFDM}^{Sym} symbols and its value is equal to 6. There are 8 RS per PRB, however the first two are placed in the first OFDM symbol devoted to control signaling (3GPP Group Radio Access Network, 2008) (See

Figure 3. Proposed CSI feedback scheme operation and system interworking. (a) Operational principle of Loc-ICIC (b) System interworking

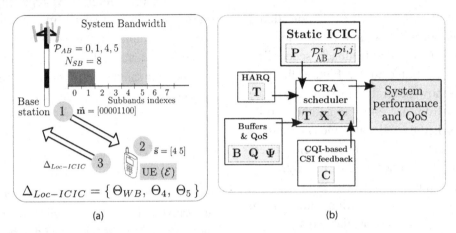

(a)   (b)

Table 2. Data structure considered in the system model

Symbol	Description
N_u	Number of users in the system.
$\hat{l}_u$	Serving cell of user u
L	Number of cells in the system.
$\hat{o}_u$	Operator containing HARQ context (MCS, TBS and RV) for user u
$T \in \mathbb{R}^{N_u}$	HARQ information. $\tau_u \in T$
$P \in \mathbb{R}^{L \times N_{PRB}}$	Power allocation matrix.
$X \in \mathbb{R}^{L \times N_{PRB}}$	Transmission map. $x_{l,n} \in \{01\}$ If $x_{l,n} = 1 \Rightarrow p_{l,n} > 0$, otherwise $p_{l,n} = 0$
$Y \in \mathbb{R}^{N_u \times N_{PRB}}$	Resource allocation matrix. $y_{u,n} \in \{01\}$. If $y_{u,n} = 1 \Rightarrow$ PRB n is assigned to user u.
$C \in \mathbb{R}^{N_u \times N_{PRB}}$	CQI map.
B	Buffer status of each flow: size, oldest packet delay, etc
ψ	Service set. $\psi = \{\text{HTTP FTP}\}$
Q	Quality of service. $Q = \{Q_{NRT}\}$

Figure 3a). The vector $\vec{q}$ contains the nominal SINR values associated to the CQIs (stored in **C**) that correspond to the PRBs where the transmission τ is going to be allocated $\gamma_{\text{eff}}^{\text{BLER} \leq 10\%}$ is the minimum effective SINR required to transmit τ with a BLER $\leq 10\%$ given TBS_τ, RV_τ and MCS*.

The mapping from a set of SINR values (vector $\vec{q}$) to the equivalent effective SINR is done as follows. Given that N_{RS}^P is the number of RSs in an arbitrary set of PRBs P and that in LTE there are 8 RS per PRB (see Figure 3a), $N_{RS}^P = 8 \mid P \mid$ always holds. The elements of the vector $\vec{\gamma}$ $(\gamma_i, i = 1, 2 ..., N_{RS}^P)$ correspond to the SINR values measured on the RSs in P and computed according to Equation 1. Then, the effective SINR for the set P is obtained from the following expression:

$$\gamma_{\text{eff}}\left(\text{P}\right) = f_{\text{eff}}\left(\vec{\gamma}\right) = \alpha_1 \cdot I^{-1}\left[\frac{1}{N_{RS}^P}\sum_{i=1}^{N_{RS}^P}I\left(\frac{\gamma_i}{\alpha_2}\right)\right] \quad (7)$$

Parameters α_1 and α_2 adapt to different Modulation and Coding Schemes (MCSs). $I(\cdot)$ is a generic function that maps each SINR value γ_1 to a performance metric that is averaged over all the samples. In this work, the Mutual Information Equivalent SINR Mapping (MIESM) or modulation constrained capacity (Brueninghaus, et al., 2005), (IEEE Broadband Wireless Access Working Group, 2008) is employed and hence:

$$I\left(\gamma_i\right) = \log_2\left(M\right)$$
$$+ \frac{1}{2\pi M}\sum_{m=1}^{M-1}g\left(\gamma_i, m\right)$$
$$\cdot g\left(\gamma_i, m\right) \quad (8)$$
$$= \int e^{-\gamma_i\left(y - x_m\right)^2} \log_2\left(\frac{e^{-\gamma_i\left(y - x_m\right)^2}}{\sum_{k=0}^{M-1}e^{-\gamma_i\left(y - x_k\right)^2}}\right)dy$$

where M is the size of the modulation alphabet, y is the channel output and x_m are the modulation symbols.

VI. RESEARCH METHODOLOGY AND NETWORK SETTING

A. Research Methodology

In order to obtain accurate and realistic performance figures associated to each of the CSI feedback schemes; this study is conducted by means of detailed LTE system level simulations. This approach allows taking into account all the elements affecting the performance of feedback schemes such as realistic ICI and fading patterns, estimation errors, processing delay and so on. In addition, more insights can be obtained about the actual impact of the CSI feedback mechanisms on final service-oriented QoS experienced by users.

The evaluation setting has been embedded in a LTE system level simulator which carefully models relevant LTE aspects such as HARQ, OFDMA structure and logical channels according to (3GPP Group Radio Access Network, 2010), (3GPP Group Radio Access Network, 2008) and (3GPP Group Radio Access Network, 2008). System level is fed by look-up tables obtained through detailed link level simulations in order to assess an accurate BLER prediction (Brueninghaus, et al., 2005), (IEEE Broadband Wireless Access Working Group, 2008). Results from link level include means to map effective SINR figures subject to different TBS, MCS and RV into transmission error probabilities. In this manner, BLER is modeled as in the actual LTE operation. Experiments were conducted by means of Monte Carlo simulations and results were obtained from 500 independent experiments with uniform randomly spread users. Each experiment simulates 60 seconds (6e4 TTIs) in order to account with traffic features and let enough time to the scheduler to converge to a stable regime.

B. Network Setting and LTE Configuration

The cellular layout corresponds to an urban and macro-cellular scenario composed of 19 sites (57 tri-sectorial cells) featuring hexagonal/regular geometry. Statistics were collected from the 3 central cells (having two interference tiers) to avoid border effects.

Channel model and users mobility deserve special attention because the choice of these parameters has an important influence on the performance of CSI feedback mechanisms, and hence, on results and conclusions. The mobility model is vehicular for urban scenarios as defined in (Correia, et al., 2001). In order to emulate low/moderate conditions, pedestrian speed of 3 km/h was assumed. The channel model is the Extended ITU Pedestrian B defined in (Sorensen, Mogensen, & Frederiksen, 2005) which features a 32.55 ns sampling grid that matches the LTE sampling rate of 30.72 MHz. Additional implementation details are shown in Table 3.

For this study, a wideband configuration of LTE has been selected (3GPP Group Radio Access Network, 2008). To be precise, the system has 1200 allocable subcarriers spaced 15 kHz (system bandwidth is 18 MHz). These subcarriers are

Table 3. Simulation and LTE parameters

Parameter	Description
Cell power and Inter-site distance	43 dBm and 1.5 km
UE noise figure	7 dB
Propagation model	3GPP's Urban macrocellular (3GPP Group Radio Access Network, 2000)
Carrier frequency (f_c)	2.14 GHz
Shadowing	Based on multiple correlated layers (Fraile, Lazaro, & Cardona, 2003) Mean and standard deviation: 0 dB and 8 dB
Channel model	Extended ITU Pedestrian B (Sorensen, Mogensen, & Frederiksen, 2005) Temporal and Frequency resolution: 1 ms and 15 kHz Maximum Doppler frequency (f_d): 5.94 Hz (f_c = 2.14 GHz and v = 3 km/h)
Mobility model	Urban vehicular (Correia, et al., 2001) User speed, Main angle and Correlation distance: 3 km/h, 90° and 20 m
Antennas	Kathrein 800 10271 Xpol TriSec Gain, Front-to-back ratio and 3 dB beam: 19.33 dBi, > 25 dB and 65°
Static ICIC configuration	SFR α =0.40, β =0.66, γ_{TH} =1.0 dB FFR α =0.40, $\hat{a}$ =0.40, γ_{TH} =1.0 dB
Target bit rate (QoS)	FTP/HTTP = {400/600} [kbps]
LTE: Transmission mode	Single-antenna port
LTE: PDCCH Capacity	$\leq$ 8 (Scheduling grants per TTI)
LTE: CSI processing delay	3 TTI
LTE: RS power boost	0 dB
LTE: Resource Allocation	Type 1 (3GPP Group Radio Access Network, 2010)

grouped in N_{PRB} PRBs each of them containing N_{SC} subcarriers. The minimum assignment the scheduler can grant to a user is one single PRB during 1 Transmission Time Interval (TTI). The total available power per cell is distributed among the PRBs according to static ICIC strategies. Note that the sum power condition is always kept. Within each TTI, 14 OFDM symbols are transmitted from which N_{OFDM}^{Sym} are devoted to data transmission. In this work, $N_{PRB} = 100$, $N_{SC} = 12$ and $N_{OFDM}^{Sym} = 11$. HARQ with Incremental Redundancy (IR) and a maximum number of 3 retransmissions is implemented (3GPP Group Radio Access Network, 2010). The minimum retransmission delay is 8 TTIs and a maximum number of 8 parallel HARQ processes per user is assumed.

Finally, Single-antenna port transmission mode (port 0) is considered in this work so one Transport Block (TB) is transmitted on the Physical Downlink Shared Channel (PDSCH) from a single physical antenna (3GPP Group Radio Access Network, 2010), (3GPP Group Radio Access Network, 2008).

C. Traffic Models

Two different traffic models are considered: Hypertext Transfer Protocol (HTTP) and File Transfer Protocol (FTP). Traffic models are defined according to the mathematical models in (3GPP Group Radio Access Network, 2004). Web browsing sessions are divided into ON/OFF periods representing web-page downloads, also referred to as packet calls, and reading times. In FTP, a session consists of a sequence of file transfers, separated by reading times.

The Medium Access Control (MAC) scheduler determines how downlink (and uplink) channels in the LTE air interface are used. The scheduler allocates radio resources in such a way as to satisfy QoS requirements and optimize system performance.

MAC scheduler design is not specified by the LTE standard. Different schedulers may result in significantly different levels of user satisfaction and system performance, and hence mobile operators implement vendor-specific solutions according to their needs. In this work, the scheduler implementation corresponds to the Capacity-driven Resource Allocation (CRA) scheduler proposed in (Marques, Wanstedt, Porto, & Freitas, 2010). The CRA scheduler dynamically controls the resource sharing among flows of different services such as delay-sensitive and rate demanding ones. The authors claim that CRA scheduler improves the joint system capacity, defined as the maximum total offered load in which all provided services fulfill the user satisfaction ratio threshold. In case of NRT services such as HTTP and FTP, it was previously indicated that a user is said to be satisfied if the target bit rate RT foreseen for its service is met. Thus, the joint system capacity concept fits perfectly to the research objectives in this work since it captures all relevant aspects of multiservice environments such as per-service QoS requirements. In addition, it is worth saying that the CRA scheduler by itself does not apply any restriction to users based on classes (Ext or Int), i.e., constraints come from the static ICIC policy which determines how much resources are assigned to each class of users.

VII. NUMERICAL RESULTS

Results are grouped into two groups:

1. High level system- and user- oriented performance metrics including: user satisfaction ratio θ per service, average user rate r and its percentile 5, $r_{5\%}$ provides a direct measure of the impact of a given CSI feedback scheme on the overall QoS. User rate r is also important from the operator point of view because it quantifies spectral efficiency, i.e.,

for a given bandwidth the higher the mean value of r, the better the system spectral efficiency is. Another interesting indicator in the ICIC context is $r_{5\%}$ which fairly represents the cell edge user rate;

2. Additional performance indicators closely related to the operation of CSI feedback schemes. The rationale behind these metrics is to better understand the performance achieved by each CSI strategy. Average energy efficiency p, BLER and MCS selection are investigated. In addition, a comparative view of the CSI reporting mechanisms in terms of required feedback overhead and computational cost at UE is also provided.

A. High Level Performance Metrics

The user satisfaction ratio θ provides a consistent way to evaluate QoS from user point of view. Figure 4 shows the resulting value of θ achieved by each CSI feedback for each static ICIC strategy, service class (HTTP, FTP) and different system loads.

As expected, IDEAL clearly outperforms the rest of its competitors no matter the scenario. However, this is at the expense of a prohibitive (indeed unfeasible) amount of feedback overhead. Thus its result is kept as an upper bound and the comparison is focused on realistic schemes. Loc-ICIC improves the QoS with respect to both LTE

Figure 4. Impact of CSI feedback schemes on UE satisfaction ratio (a) HTTP@FFR (b) FTP@FFR (c) HTTP@SFR (d) FTP@SFR

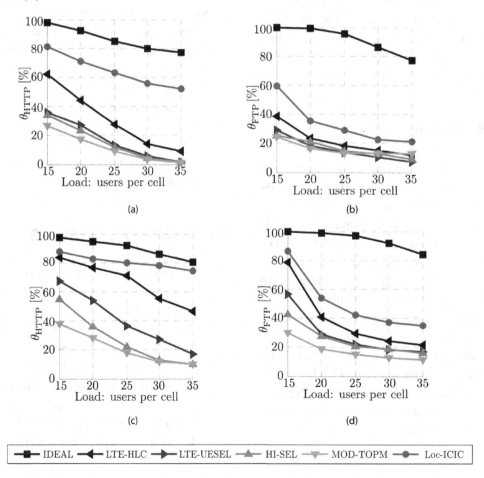

schemes and previous proposals in any case being this improvement especially significant in HTTP scenarios: Figures 4a and 4c. This is due to the more accurate wideband CQI estimation in Loc-ICIC that allows a more precise MCS selection. Of particular interest is always the case where the system load is high. In HTTP scenarios, Loc-ICIC provides gains of 40% (FFR) and 25% (SFR) with respect to the closest case, LTE-HLC. In FTP scenarios, (a service that behaves similarly to the so-called full buffer model) gains are smaller, around 9% (FFR) and 15% (SFR). Gains are smaller in FTP scenarios because web traffic is burstier and hence, there is more room for retransmissions (from which Loc-ICIC can be especially benefited from). Although a more accurate channel estimation could result in erroneous transmissions due to the time-varying nature of ICI and small scale fading, this can be, to some extent, compensated by means of retransmissions. This point will be further supported by the figures presented later on in VII-B.

Regarding the performance of 3GPP schemes, LTE-HLC and LTE-UESEL, results herein confirm some findings presented in (Donthi & Mehta, 2011). LTE-HLC clearly outperforms LTE-UESEL (now also in the context of static ICIC) despite the assumptions followed therein. However some clarifications/distinctions need to be remarked. In (Donthi & Mehta, 2011), the comparison was presented in terms of the average throughput subject to 'synthetic' scheduling policies such as greedy and proportional fair that have a clear asymptotic behavior under the full/infinite buffer assumption. The scheduler employed herein (Marques, Wanstedt, Porto, & Freitas, 2010) is multiservice and QoS oriented. This means that the scheduler, on the one hand, tries to allocate the minimum amount of resources to meet the QoS (target bit rate) of each user, and on the other hand, it tries to maximize the number of satisfied flows meaning that under heavy load conditions it focuses on users more likely to be satisfied, the rest being attended afterwards. Thus, this study

is both required and relevant as it extends previous theoretical findings to cases where analytical treatment is impossible but having great interest from a practical viewpoint.

$$R_T^{HTTP} = 600 \text{ kbps}, R_T^{FTP} = 400 \text{ kbps}$$

With respect to previous proposals, HI-SEL and MOD-TOPM, Figure 4 reveals that their performance is especially poor in the context of static ICIC, being even below of 3GPP baselines. Both HI-SEL and MOD-TOPM showed acceptable performances in (Su, Fan, Zheng, & Wang, 2007) and (Xue, Yin, Yue, & Liu, 2009) respectively. However it is worth saying that these strategies were tested under the full frequency reuse assumption for which they were explicitly designed. Moreover, no comparison with LTE reporting schemes was presented, and hence, their relative merit with respect to these important baselines was not clarified. The fact that static ICIC and its resource allocation pattern are considered sketches a completely different picture from the CSI point of view. Indeed, some of the strengths in HI-SEL and MOD-TOPM become important drawbacks in this new scenario. For instance, both HI-SEL and MOD-TOPM are reporting schemes in which only the best subbands are reported. On the one hand, MOD-TOPM is indeed a variation of LTE-UESEL without wideband CQI nor differential encoding. To some extent, wideband estimates are good in the sense that, as they favor conservative estimations, it makes possible to limit other error sources such as reporting/processing delay. On the other hand, HI-SEL always reports the quality of the best q subbands at each level (see subsection IV-A). In static ICIC the bandwidth portion reserved for exterior users receives significantly less ICI and hence, without any explicit mechanism to deal with this situation, these subbands are the most likely to be reported no matter the current UE classification.

In this study it has been found that there is an important tradeoff between reporting accurate CQI values (favoring more aggressive and efficient MCSs) and being conservative enough in order to compensate error sources inherent to practical systems. Loc-ICIC attains a good tradeoff between these two conflicting designs targets as (1) it reports channel quality at subband level in order to increase accuracy and, (2) it features differential encoding with respect to a localized bandwidth portion in order to take the average radio channel quality into account as well. This is the fundamental reason why Loc-ICIC clearly surpasses the overall QoS level offered by more generic CSI feedback schemes.

Spectral efficiency is another important performance metric from the system's viewpoint. Figure 5 shows Cumulative Distribution Functions (CDFs) of user rates (r) for two particular scenarios. Similar results, qualitatively speaking, were obtained for the rest of scenarios. Figures 5a and 5b show that Loc-ICIC improves r, showing the already commented better accuracy with respect to other strategies.

From an ICIC perspective, especial interest is placed on cell edge performance. Thus, the impact of CSI reporting on the performance of users at cell edges is shown in Figure 6. Figure 6a shows the case where HTTP users and SFR are considered. Loc-ICIC achieves gains ranging from 5% to 25% with respect the second best for low and high load conditions respectively. In case of FTP users and FFR, Figure 6b, the situation is a little bit different. In this scenario, noticeable cell edge performance gains are only feasible at low load conditions. A significant improvement of 38% was attained when 15 users per cell were allocated. However, as system load increases the gains vanish quickly. However, this is just a consequence of the scheduling policy for this particular case. The CRA scheduler aims at maximizing the number of satisfied flows which implies that, under certain circumstances; UEs that are very unlikely to be satisfied (due to their bad channel condition or resource scarcity) are jeopardized. Note that FFR is a more restrictive scheme in terms of per-cell bandwidth availability point of view. However, what it is interesting to note is the fact that Loc-ICIC always allows throughput gains to cell edge users with respect to the others CSI reporting mechanisms. As it was commented previously, this is important because ICIC aims at improving cell edge performance. Thus Loc-ICIC proves to be an excellent companion for static ICIC strategies.

Figure 5. Cumulative distribution function of users' average rate r (a) FTP@SFR (35 users per cell) (b) HTTP@SFR (20 users per cell)

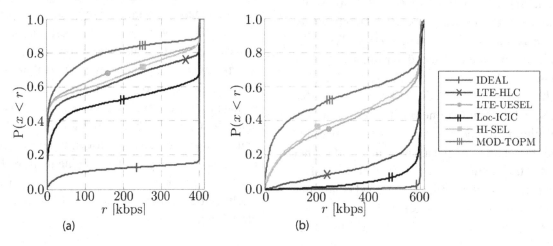

Figure 6. Cell edge performance: percentile 5 of ***r*** *(a) HTTP@SFR (b) FTP@FFR*

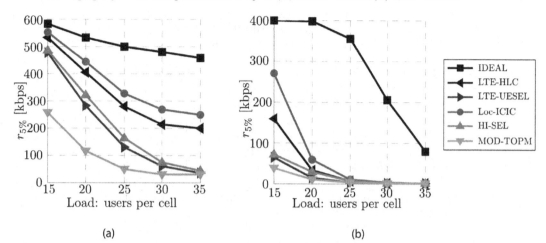

(a)   (b)

B. Additional Performance Indicators

As it was explained before, the performance of any CSI reporting strategy largely depends on its ability to achieve an adequate tradeoff between accuracy and resulting BLER. To be precise, reporting higher CQI estimations favors the selection of more spectrally efficient MCSs although the BLER can also be higher for a given SINR. However, riskier decisions are an option for certain services as errors might be compensated by the incremental redundancy in the HARQ mechanism. In fact, results show that HARQ is able to compensate BLER levels of around 15% in cases where retransmissions can be easily placed, i.e., bursty traffic scenarios. On the other hand, in situations where system load is high and users have too much data to transmit, conservative mechanisms avoiding the need for excessive retransmissions are advisable. Nevertheless, CSI feedback schemes do not operate explicitly triggered by these conditions and hence it is desirable that this balance is attained in a natural fashion.

In order to provide a deeper insight into this tradeoff, Figure 7 shows average values obtained for each CSI feedback scheme for three additional performance indicators: BLER, MCS selection and energy efficiency.

The poor performance of HI-SEL and MOD-TOPM is now explained in the light of their bad BLER performance. Indeed MOD-TOPM features the highest MCS selection figure among all realistic strategies. As a matter of fact, this is an important issue in Top-M schemes when used in conjunction with static ICIC, i.e., reporting the quality of the best subbands is only good idea if these subbands belong to the bandwidth portion over which users can be allocated, otherwise the effect is totally opposite. Focusing on Loc-ICIC and 3GPP schemes, it can be seen that Loc-ICIC features higher MCS selection due to its more accurate CQI prediction capability. Although the MCS selection difference is not so high with respect to LTE-HLC, notice the important 5% improvement in terms of BLER meaning that Loc-ICIC not only favors spectrally efficient MCSs but also reduces erroneous transmissions. On the other hand, LTE-UESEL features the issue associated to Top-M schemes in the context of static ICIC. This explains its poor performance, i.e., an unaffordable BLER > 25%. Moreover, from the energy efficiency perspective, Loc-ICIC achieves an average gain of 16% with respect to LTE-HLC, the closest case. This was expected to some extend as retransmissions imply additional energy to transmit the same information.

Figure 7. Additional performance indicators

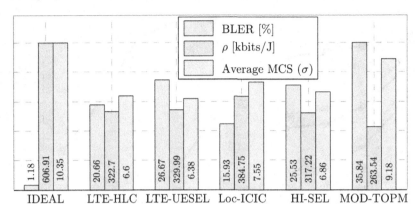

Finally, Table 4 presents a comparative analysis in terms of uplink feedback overhead and complexity. Overhead is expressed as the number of bits per aperiodic report. Complexity is measured as the number of PRBs that need to be processed in order to build the CSI report and the number of effective SINR-to-CQI mappings according to Equation 7. Note that Loc-ICIC requires different overheads depending on the selected static ICIC strategy. If FFR is employed, Loc-ICIC features the lowest overhead due to the fact that only a fraction of the whole system bandwidth is active at each cell. In case of SFR, more overhead is required but even in this case, the required overhead is 33% less than LTE-HLC, the closest mechanism from the QoS point of view. In terms of complexity at

UE, gains are also important. As Loc-ICIC only focuses on the portion of the system bandwidth of interest to each UE, the number of PRBs that need to be processed is smaller and hence the total computational cost (with its corresponding impact on battery life) is also improved.

C. Implementation Feasibility

Finally, some implementation aspects in LTE are discussed. As it was commented before, any proposal must be, as far as possible, standard-compatible, otherwise implementation would be unfeasible. This aspect has been meticulously considered in the design of Loc-ICIC. Loc-ICIC does not require any additional functionality at UE

Table 4. Overhead and complexity associated to different reporting schemes

CSI Feedback	Overhead [bits/report] $(N_{PRB} = 100)=100$	Complexity: Analized PRB // $\gamma_{eff} \rightarrow$ CQI Mappings
IDEAL	400	100//100
LTE-HLC	30	100//13
LTE-UESEL	17	100//14
HI-SEL	29	100//127
MOD-TOPM	17	100//13
Loc-ICIC	SFR: 20; FFR: 14	SFR: 64//9, FFR: 40//6

level, i.e., the mobile terminal would take the same measurements it currently does. Loc-ICIC only proposes to better localize those measurements in the frequency domain. Note that Loc-ICIC also preserves wideband CQI estimation and differential encoding, currently used in LTE. CSI feedback is user-specific and hence, existing terminals can still use LTE reporting mechanisms, i.e., coexistence between Loc-ICIC-capable terminals and legacy devices is not an issue.

The only aspect that needs to be considered is the transmission of the bit stream $\vec{m}$ (see Figure 3a) to Loc-ICIC-capable terminals. This information must be transmitted occasionally when a terminal changes its current classification. Normal wideband CQI estimations can be transmitted periodically, in a scale of tens of seconds, to account with this aspect in Loc-ICIC. The worst case scenario from the perspective of the size of $\vec{m}$ is the case studied herein (N_{PRD}=100) in which $|\vec{m}| = 13$ bits.

Assuming the hypothetical case in which a user changes its classification every 60 seconds (at speed of 3 km/h a user would walk 50 m). The additional required downlink control overhead is 0.216 bps. Even under the strong assumption that 100 users change continuously its classification every 60 s in a cell, the total aggregate at cell level would still be negligible. Therefore, having shown that the control overhead is not an issue in Loc-ICIC, the only remaining aspect is how transmit such information.

The natural choice is the 'RRC connection reconfiguration' message transmitted from the network to users (3GPP Group Radio Access Network, 2011). The purpose of this procedure is to modify a Radio Resource Control (RRC) connection, e.g. to establish/modify/release radio bearers (3GPP Group Radio Access Network, 2010). Through this control signaling, LTE provides means to send user specific information associated to their connections. As the amount of information is at most 13 bits, this info can be allocated eas-

ily in any of the several available optional fields such as the 'pdsch-ConfigDedicated' within the 'radioResourceConfigDedicated' subtree. This message is indeed transmitted to users in RRC CONNECTED state and hence it fits perfectly to the operational principle of Loc-ICIC.

In the light of the previous discussion, it is clear that Loc-ICIC can be implemented by vendors in their mobile terminals and base stations in order to offer it as an additional added value to operators.

D. Performance in Vehicular and High Mobility Scenarios

In the previous sections, performance evaluations were presented for pedestrian users. In those comparisons, CSI updating period is kept the same for all schemes under consideration. Thus, the performance gap between Loc-ICIC and the rest of schemes is due to the fact that Loc-ICIC provides more accurate information as it is focused on relevant subbands for each user and, to some extent, this information is transmitted, processed and used in time scales that make it useful (the information is still valid given the Doppler frequency for pedestrian users). However, in high speed scenarios, the coherence time is much shorter and hence, no matter how accurate the CSI is, it becomes outdated. For such scenarios, practical systems rely on either wideband channel estimations (wideband/average radio channel quality varies slower than subband counterparts) or conservative and more robust modulation and coding scheme formats.

VIII. CONCLUSION AND FUTURE WORK

QoS refers to the ability of the network to provide a desired level of service for selected traffic on the network. Typically, service levels are described in terms of throughput, latency, jitter and packet error rate and are specified for different types or streams of traffic. Designing QoS policies for evolving packet-based applications is a fundamental requirement in modern multiservice cellular systems as QoS impacts directly the Quality of Experience (QoE) of the users in the network. In this chapter, a novel aperiodic CSI feedback scheme has been proposed for LTE. The proposed solution is suitable to work in conjunction with static ICIC techniques requiring (1) minimal signaling overhead and (2) small new functionalities with respect to current LTE specifications. The proposed mechanism allows important QoS improvements when static ICIC techniques are considered. After describing the operation of this mechanism, it has been evaluated and compared with 3GPP schemes and previous proposals. This has been done in scenarios with different types of traffic. The main results can be summarized as follows:

- The proposed CSI feedback scheme is a good candidate to work in conjunction with ICIC strategies. Under such circumstances, it provides significant performance gains with respect to 3GPP feedback mechanisms and previous proposals;
- The performance of the proposed scheme is especially good with bursty traffic, where retransmissions can be easily allocated to compensate the BLER. Even though Loc-ICIC successfully keeps it lower than the rest of considered schemes;
- In addition to gains in terms of spectral/energy efficiency and overall QoS, Loc-ICIC is also able to improve the quality at cell edges improving the average rate of users. This clearly suggests that Loc-ICIC is an excellent companion of static ICIC, whose one of its main targets is improving the QoS at the cell edge and promote fairness;
- Feasibility is an important aspect. One of the most interesting features of Loc-ICIC is the fact that it can be easily implement-

ed. Modifications in LTE is minimum and maybe more important, Loc-ICIC can co-exist with native 3GPP schemes;

- Future research lines include extensions to CSI feedback schemes for vehicular and high speed scenarios. Given that channel varies too fast in such environments, predictive strategies based on previous measurements can be an interesting possibility. Finite state Markov chains could be an appropriate tool to that end. In addition, research towards periodic CSI feedback is also under study.

REFERENCES

3GPP Group Radio Access Network. (2000). *TR 25.942: RF system scenarios (v2.1.3)*. 3GPP.

3GPP Group Radio Access Network. (2004). TR 25.892: Feasibility study for orthogonal frequency division multiplexing (OFDM) for UTRAN enhancement (v6.0.0). 3GPP.

3GPP Group Radio Access Network. (2008). TS 36.201: LTE physical layer - General description (v8.2.0). 3GPP.

3GPP Group Radio Access Network. (2008). TS 36.211: Physical channels and modulation (v8.5.0). 3GPP.

3GPP Group Radio Access Network. (2010). *TS 36.213: Physical layer procedures (v9.2.0)*. 3GPP.

3GPP Group Radio Access Network. (2011). TS 36.331: Radio resource control (RRC) protocol specification (v8.14.0). 3GPP.

Agarwal, M., Guo, D., & Honig, M. (2010). Limited-rate channel state feedback for multicarrier block fading channels. *IEEE Transactions on Information Theory*, 6116–6132. doi:10.1109/TIT.2010.2080970

Agarwal, R., Majjigi, V., Han, Z., Vannithamby, R., & Cioffi, J. (2008). Low complexity resource allocation with opportunistic feedback over downlink OFDMA networks. *IEEE Journal on Selected Areas in Communications*, 1462–1472. doi:10.1109/JSAC.2008.081012

Alcatel-Lucent. (2007). *R1-072924: Incremental CQI feedback scheme and simulation results.* 3GPP.

Alcatel-Lucent. (2009). *R1-090394: CQI and CSI feedback compression.* 3GPP.

Andrews, M., Kumaran, K., Ramanan, K., Stolyar, A., Whiting, P., & Vijayakumar, R. (2001). Providing quality of service over a shared wireless link. *IEEE Communications Magazine*, 150–154. doi:10.1109/35.900644

Basukala, R., Ramli, H., Sandrasegaran, K., & Chen, L. (2010). Impact of CQI feedback rate/delay on scheduling video streaming services in LTE downlink. In *Proceedings of 12th IEEE International Conference on Communication*. Nanjing, China: IEEE.

Brueninghaus, K., Astely, D., Salzer, T., Visuri, S., Alexiou, A., Karger, S., et al. (2005). Link performance models for system level simulations of broadband radio access systems. In *Proceedings of IEEE International Symposium on Personal, Indoor and Mobile Radio Communications* (pp. 2306–2311). Berlin: IEEE.

Chen, J., Berry, R., & Honig, M. (2008). Limited feedback schemes for downlink OFDMA based on sub-channel groups. *IEEE Journal on Selected Areas in Communications*, 1451–1461. doi:10.1109/JSAC.2008.081011

Choi, Y., & Bahk, S. (2008). Partial channel feedback schemes maximizing overall efficiency in wireless networks. *IEEE Transactions on Wireless Communications*, 1306–1314. doi:10.1109/TWC.2008.060863

Correia, L. M., Fledderus, E., Meijerink, E., Perera, R., Serrador, A., Turke, U., et al. (2001). *Identification of relevant parameters for traffic modelling and interference estimation.*

Donthi, S., & Mehta, N. (2011). Joint performance analysis of channel quality indicator feedback schemes and frequency-domain scheduling for LTE. *IEEE Transactions on Vehicular Technology*, 3096–3109. doi:10.1109/TVT.2011.2159034

Ericsson. (2008). *R1-080887: CQI measurement methodology.* 3GPP.

Fraile, R., Lazaro, O., & Cardona, N. (2003). *Two dimensional shadowing model.* COST 273.

Ganapathy, H., & Caramanis, C. (2012). Queue-based sub-carrier grouping for feedback reduction in OFDMA systems. In *Proceedings of IEEE Infocom* (pp. 1098–1106). IEEE. doi:10.1109/INFCOM.2012.6195466

González, G. D., García-Lozano, M., Corvino, V., Ruiz, S., & Olmos, J. (2010). Performance evaluation of downlink interference coordination techniques in LTE networks. In *Proceedings of IEEE Vehicular Technology Conference (VTC)*. Ottawa, Canada: IEEE.

González, G. D., García-Lozano, M., Ruiz, S., & Olmos, J. (2012). An analytical view of static intercell interference coordination techniques in OFDMA networks. In *Proceedings of IEEE Wireless Communications and Networking Conference (WCNC)*. Paris: IEEE.

González, G. D., García-Lozano, M., Ruiz, S., & Olmos, J. (2012). *On the need for dynamic downlink intercell interference coordination for realistic LTE deployments.* Wireless Communications and Mobile Computing. doi:10.1002/wcm.2191

Gopalan, A., Caramanis, C., & Shakkottai, S. (2012). On wireless scheduling with partial channel-state information. *IEEE Transactions on Information Theory*, 403–420. doi:10.1109/TIT.2011.2169543

Himayat, H., Talwar, S., Rao, A., & Soni, R. (2010). Interference management for 4G cellular standards. *IEEE Communications Magazine*, 48(8), 86–92. doi:10.1109/MCOM.2010.5534591

Hitachi Ltd. (2012). *R1-122699: CQI estimation for CoMP*. 3GPP.

HTC. (2012). *R1-122323: CQI definition and feedback reduction mechanism for CoMP*. 3GPP.

Huawei. (2011). *R1-110015: Remaining issues in aperiodic CQI-only PUSCH*. 3GPP.

Huawei, HiSilicon. (2011). *R1-110021: Issues for aperiodic and periodic CSI reporting*. 3GPP.

Hur, S. H., & Rao, B. (2012). Sum rate analysis of a reduced feedback OFDMA downlink system employing joint scheduling and diversity. *IEEE Transactions on Signal Processing*, 862–876. doi:10.1109/TSP.2011.2173335

IEEE Broadband Wireless Access Working Group. (2008). *C802.16m-08/119: Link performance abstraction for ML receivers based on RBIR metrics*. IEEE.

Intel Corporation. (2012). *R1-122628: Periodic and aperiodic CSI feedback modes for DL CoMP*. 3GPP.

Irmer, R., Droste, H., Marsch, P., Grieger, M., Fettweis, G., & Brueck, S. et al. (2011). Coordinated multipoint: Concepts, performance, and field trial results. *IEEE Communications Magazine*, 102–111. doi:10.1109/MCOM.2011.5706317

ITU-R. (2008). *M.2135: Guidelines for evaluation of radio interface technologies for IMT-advanced*. ITU-R.

Kumar, S., Monghal, G., Nin, J., Ordas, I., Pedersen, K., & Mogensen, P. (2009). Autonomous inter cell interference avoidance under fractional load for downlink long term evolution. In *Proceedings of IEEE Vehicular Technology Conference (VTC)*. Barcelona: IEEE.

Marques, F. R., Wanstedt, S., Porto, F. R., & Freitas, W. C. (2010). Scheduling for improving system capacity in multiservice 3GPP LTE. *Journal of Electrical and Computer Engineering*.

Mecking, M. (2002). Resource allocation for fading multiple-access channels with partial channel state information. In *Proceedings of IEEE International Conference on Communications*. New York: IEEE.

Motorola. (2005). *R1-051334: CQI feedback scheme for EUTRA*. 3GPP.

Motorola. (2010). *R1-103187: LTE-A dynamic aperiodic SRS - Triggering, duration, timing, and carrier aggregation*. 3GPP.

NEC Group. (2009). *R1-090303: Correction to RHO definition for CQI calculation*. 3GPP.

Nokia Siemens Networks. (2007). *R1-073662: CQI per PRB versus per group of best PRBs*. 3GPP.

Olmos, J., Serra, A., Ruiz, S., García-Lozano, M., & González, G. D. (2009). Exponential effective SIR metric for LTE downlink. In *Proceedings of IEEE International Symposium on Personal, Indoor and Mobile Radio Communications (PIMRC)* (pp. 900-904). Tokyo, Japan: IEEE.

Ouyang, M., & Ying, L. (2009). On scheduling in multi-channel wireless downlink networks with limited feedback. In *Proceedings of 47th Annual Allerton Conference on Communication* (pp. 455–461). Monticello.

Panasonic, HTC. (2010b). *R1-103761: Aperiodic CQI reporting for carrier aggregation*. 3GPP.

Panasonic. (2009). *R1-090250: HARQ protocol handling of CQI-only reports.* 3GPP. Panasonic, HTC. (2010a). *R1-101262: Aperiodic CQI reporting for carrier aggregation.* 3GPP.

Qualcomm. (2012). *R1-122777: CQI definition for downlink CoMP.* 3GPP.

Qualcomm Europe. (2007). *R1-072731: Scheduling requests using CQI.* 3GPP.

Samsung. (2010). *R1-102186: Aperiodic CQI activation in CA.* 3GPP.

Samsung. (2011). *R1-110078: Simultaneous PUSCH and PUCCH transmissions in case of aperiodic CSI.* 3GPP.

Sesia, S., Toufic, I., & Baker, M. (2011). *LTE - The UMTS long term evolution: From theory to practice.* Chippenhan, UK: John Wiley & Sons. doi:10.1002/9780470978504

Sharp. (2009). *R1-092103: Control overhead analysis on aperiodic PUSCH.* 3GPP.

Sorensen, T., Mogensen, P., & Frederiksen, F. (2005). Extension of the ITU channel models for wideband (OFDM) systems. In *Proceedings of IEEE Vehicular Technology Conference* (pp. 392–396). Dallas, TX: IEEE.

Su, J., Fan, B., Zheng, K., & Wang, W. (2007). A hierarchical selective CQI feedback scheme for 3GPP long-term evolution system. In *Proceedings of International Symposium on Microwave, Antenna, Propagation and EMC Technologies for Wireless Communications* (pp. 5–8). Beijing, China: Academic Press.

Texas Instruments. (2008). *R1-080207: CQI reporting procedure for E-UTRA.* 3GPP.

Texas Instruments. (2008). *R1-080208: Differential CQI definition for E-UTRA.* 3GPP.

Tse, D., & Viswanath, P. (2005). *Fundamentals of wireless communication.* Cambridge, UK: Cambridge University Press. doi:10.1017/CBO9780511807213

Varanese, N., Vicario, J., & Spagnolini, U. (2012). On the asymptotic throughput of OFDMA systems with best-M CQI feedback. *IEEE Wireless Communications Letters*, 145–148.

Venturino, L., Prasad, N., & Wang, X. (2009). Coordinated scheduling and power allocation in downlink multicell OFDMA networks. *IEEE Transactions on Vehicular Technology*, 2835–2848. doi:10.1109/TVT.2009.2013233

Xue, Y., Yin, C., Yue, W., & Liu, D. (2009). A QoS-aware resource allocation scheme with limited feedback in downlink OFDMA systems. In *Proceedings of International Conference on Wireless Communications, Networking and Mobile Computing*. Beijing: Academic Press.

Chapter 3
Distributed Antenna Systems for Enhanced Video Transmission in LTE Public Safety Networks

Elias Yaacoub
Qatar Mobility Innovations Center (QMIC), Qatar

Nizar Zorba
Qatar Mobility Innovations Center (QMIC), Qatar

Zaher Dawy
American University of Beirut (AUB), Lebanon

ABSTRACT

In this chapter, Long Term Evolution (LTE) for public safety is investigated. Particularly, Distributed Antenna Systems (DAS) are studied, and their impact on LTE public safety networks is analyzed. Furthermore, resource allocation algorithms for the purpose of real-time video transmission, in both the Uplink (UL) and Downlink (DL) directions, are proposed, and a proportional fair scheduling algorithm, applicable in both the UL and DL directions, is presented. The proposed algorithms are compared in several scenarios with and without distributed antenna systems. In addition, Quality of Experience (QoE) metrics are used to measure the quality of the video transmissions, and joint uplink/downlink quality metrics, tailored to video transmission over public safety networks, are presented. Simulation results show large enhancements in video quality due to the application of DAS with smart resource allocation in LTE public safety networks.

INTRODUCTION

The Long Term Evolution (LTE) technology is strongly considered as a candidate for public safety networks (Motorola, 2010), either to replace or to complement the existing public safety networks.

The main advantage of LTE is to enable real-time video communication in these networks. In fact, communication in case of law enforcement, emergency, or disaster events such as terrorist attacks, floods, earthquake, hurricanes, etc., constitutes a vital component. In these critical situations, a

DOI: 10.4018/978-1-4666-4888-3.ch003

central command center would send critical information, over the wireless public safety network, to rescuing teams such as ambulances, mobile medical treatment units, and police vehicles. The critical information could include disaster related information such as electronic maps to support aid forces during their motion within a disaster area, weather conditions, nature and specifics of the disaster, safety areas, etc. (Song, 2005). Furthermore, the command center could receive information from the teams at the disaster site, process it, and then share it with other teams either on their way to, or located at, the disaster site. An example is considered in (Motorola, 2011), where videos and information from an incident location are transmitted by a helicopter to a command center, which distributes this information to the public safety teams (police, fire, etc.) heading towards, or already located at the incident location.

Distributed antenna systems (DASs), also known as distributed base stations (DBSs), are used to increase the coverage and capacity of wireless networks in a cost effective way. They consist of a central base station (BS) connected to several remote antenna heads (RAH). Although they are used in previous generations of wireless systems, DASs are receiving significant research attention for their deployment in LTE, e.g. see (Zhao, 2012). The impact of DASs on LTE uplink scheduling was studied in (Yaacoub & Dawy, 2012), and their implementation in public safety networks was investigated in (Yaacoub & Kubbar, 2012a).

In this chapter, we study the performance of LTE public safety networks in the presence of DAS. We consider video transmission, since real time video support is one of the main features that make LTE more attractive than other alternatives for next generation public safety networks. We analyze video quality of service (QoS) and quality of experience (QoE) in both the uplink (UL) and downlink (DL) directions, since effective end-to-end operation needs to be maintained in public safety networks. Hence, the objective is to perform

efficient radio resource management (RRM) in both UL and DL, and to use DAS to enhance the performance of real time video streaming.

BACKGROUND

This section presents the background information related to the contributions of the chapter. After presenting a general overview of LTE, the standardization trends for its application to public safety networks are discussed. Then, a brief overview of LTE radio resource management is presented, followed by a review of DAS implementations in wireless communication systems. Finally, the contributions of the chapter are outlined and the relation to the presented background information is described.

LTE Overview

LTE is one of the most promising technologies that have been recently specified to meet the increasing performance requirements of mobile broadband. This technology is already implemented in several countries and showing remarkable results (Bhat, 2012). LTE supports both Frequency Division Duplexing (FDD) and Time Division Duplexing (TDD) as its access techniques, where the FDD option is the most implemented one (Bhat, 2012).

Goals for this evolved system include support for improved system capacity and coverage, high peak data rates, low latency, reduced operating costs, multi-antenna support, flexible bandwidth operations, and seamless integration with existing systems. To meet these requirements, LTE is based on orthogonal frequency division multiple access (OFDMA) due to its immunity to inter-symbol interference and frequency selective fading (Ekström, 2006). However, for the LTE uplink, single carrier frequency division multiple access (SCFDMA), a modified form of OFDMA, is used. Although it has similar throughput performance and essentially the same overall complexity as OFDMA, its principal advantage is its lower peak-to-average power ratio (PAPR) (Myung, 2008).

In LTE, the available spectrum is divided into resource blocks (RBs), each consisting of 12 adjacent subcarriers. The assignment of an RB takes place every 1 ms, agreed to be the duration of one transmission time interval (TTI), or the duration of two 0.5 ms slots (Lunttila, 2007).

After the completion of the standardization of LTE Release 8, activities on further evolution of LTE, called LTE-Advanced (LTE-A), started in April 2008 with the following performance targets (3GPP TR 36.913, 2008):

- Peak DL data rates of up to 1 Gbps and peak UL data rates of up to 500 Mbps;
- Peak DL spectrum efficiency of 30 bps/Hz, with up to 8×8 multiple-input multiple-output (MIMO) antennas, and peak UL spectrum efficiency of 15 bps/Hz (with up to 4×4 MIMO);
- Average DL spectrum efficiency of up to 3.7 bps/Hz/cell (with 4×4 MIMO) and average UL spectrum efficiency of up to 2.0 bps/Hz/cell (with 2×4 MIMO);
- Cell edge DL spectrum efficiency of 0.12 bps/Hz/cell (with 4×4 MIMO) and cell edge UL spectrum efficiency 0.07 bps/Hz/cell in uplink (with 2×4 MIMO).

The work on LTE-A resulted in Release 10, finalized in March 2011. The main technology components added within the framework of LTE-A are (Astély, 2009):

- Carrier Aggregation, where multiple component carriers of 20 MHz are aggregated to lead to a total bandwidth of up to 100 MHz;
- Relays, leading to increased coverage and reduced deployment costs. It should be noted that DAS lead to the same results as re-

lays in terms of coverage expansion, while ensuring a better use of the LTE spectrum. We will refer to this point in more detail later in the chapter, in subsection "DAS vs. Relays" of the "System Model" section;

- Extended MIMO, thus increasing the data rates by allowing up to 8×8 MIMO in the DL and up to 4×4 MIMO in the UL;
- Coordinated Multipoint (CoMP) Transmission/Reception, where joint transmission/reception takes place across multiple cell sites in order to improve the cell edge performance.

Hence, LTE is well positioned to meet the requirements for the evolution of public safety systems, since it offers an all-IP system architecture, supports homogeneous and heterogeneous networks (macro, pico, and femtocells), allows single and multi-carrier transmission, tolerates flexible carrier bandwidths from below 5MHz up to 20 MHz and even 100 MHz with carrier aggregation, interworks with existing systems, provides efficient interference mitigation through intercell interference coordination (ICIC/eICIC), supports FDD and TDD transmissions, and provides broadcast services through the Multicast Broadcast Multimedia Services (MBMS/eMBMS) in addition to the unicast service (Doumi, 2013).

LTE for Public Safety

Traditionally, public safety standards such as Terrestrial Trunked Radio (TETRA) and P25 have been used to provide communications for public safety teams like police, fire and ambulance (Sharp, 2013).

These systems support medium speed data (hundreds of kilobits per second). The need for efficient real-time video transmission in UL and DL in public safety systems mandated the need for a technology enhancement in next generation public safety networks.

The National Public Safety Telecommunications Council (NPSTC) in the USA decided on LTE as their platform for this national network and spectrum in the 700MHz band was reserved for an LTE based public safety network. The TETRA and Critical Communications Association (TCCA) and the European Telecommunication Standards Institute (ETSI) also selected LTE as the technology of choice for next generation broadband public safety networks (Sharp, 2013).

The adoption of LTE for public safety has preceded the standardization efforts, and some companies started making unified devices for public safety teams, integrating TETRA for voice and traditional public safety services, while using LTE for video transmission (Motorola, 2010; Motorola, 2011). However, standardization activities are ongoing as part of LTE Release 12, where the requirements for public safety will be incorporated in the standard. The main features to be added are (Doumi, 2013; Sharp, 2013):

- Direct communications, consisting of proximity services that identify mobiles in the vicinity of each other and allow them to communicate directly, without necessarily having the communication routed through the network. This relates to the topic of device-to-device (D2D) communications that is being investigated in LTE in a broader scope than public safety and known also under the name "LTE Direct";
- Group communications, allowing efficient group communications operations, e.g. one-to-many calling, dispatching, etc., in a "push to talk" (PTT) mode.

Hence, starting from LTE Release 12, planned for freezing in mid-2014, the LTE standard will provide the necessary features enabling LTE to be used as part of a broadband public safety network. Nevertheless, the work in this chapter focuses on video transmission in public safety using intelligent UL/DL RRM with DAS. Consequently, it is compliant with the current Releases 8/10 and does not depend on the enhancements of Release 12.

Overview LTE Radio Resource Management

RRM consists of allocating the available wireless resources to the mobile users. With information about the wireless channel, the resources can be allocated to the users in an efficient way through channel-aware resource allocation. In LTE resource allocation, the input to the scheduler at the BS is the channel quality indicator (CQI). For the UL, BSs estimate the channel directly from the sounding reference signals. The sounding reference signal (SRS) is transmitted at the last symbol of the subframe (3GPP TS 36.211, 2012). For the DL, channel information is acquired through explicit feedback from the mobile devices. The DL reference signal is transmitted on the first OFDM symbol of every 0.5 ms subframe (3GPP TS 36.211, 2012). A second reference signal can be transmitted, but one is usually sufficient for FDD at low to moderate mobility, since adjacent subframes can often be used to improve channel estimation performance (Motorola, 2007). Reference signals are transmitted on selected subcarriers, and low complexity channel estimation (interpolation) is used to determine the CQI on the other subcarriers. Low complexity techniques include minimum mean squared error–finite impulse response (MMSE–FIR) and inverse fast Fourier transform (IFFT)-based channel estimators (Motorola, 2007).

It should be noted that MIMO and smart antenna technologies can be easily supported with OFDM, since with OFDMA each subcarrier becomes flat faded and the antenna weights can be optimized on a per subcarrier or per RB basis (Motorola, 2007). In the case of multiple antennas, reference signals on different subcarriers are transmitted on the different antennas. In the case of two antennas, the frequency positions of the reference signals sequence of the second antenna correspond to shifted positions of the sequence of the first antenna (3GPP TS 36.211, 2012; Motorola, 2007). In the case of 4×2 MIMO, the reference signals sequence corresponding to the four BS antennas is adjusted accordingly. Details can be found in (3GPP TS 36.211, 2012). Hence, to provide orthogonal reference signals for multi-antenna implementation, frequency division multiplexing (FDM) is used for different transmit antennas of the same cell. To provide orthogonality through different cells, code division multiplexing (CDM) is used for different cells.

The output from the scheduler consists of RB allocation in addition to the power levels and modulation and coding scheme (MCS) used. The best MCS scheme in LTE can also be selected by using Effective Exponential signal to noise ratio (SNR) Mapping (EESM), which is the interface between link level performance and system level simulations (3GPP TR 25.892, 2004; Jorguseski, 2008). EESM is used to derive throughput (usually determined via link level simulations) from signal to interference plus noise ratio (SINR) calculated on system level (Jorguseski, 2008). To simplify the simulations, the Shannon capacity formula, *log(1+SNR)*, is frequently used instead of the discrete set of MCSs. This will be the case in this chapter (Equations (3) and (7) presented later on).

Specific resource allocation algorithms are not imposed by the standards. However, the most common algorithms like round robin (RR), maximum C/I, and proportional fair (PF) scheduling are supported by LTE, with proportional fairness in time and frequency (PFTF) being the most widely implemented (Jorguseski, 2008). More details about these scheduling methods are presented in the section of this chapter entitled "LTE Radio Resource Management". The reader interested in more advanced information about resource allocation can refer to (Jorguseski, 2008; Yaacoub & Dawy, 2012) for example.

DAS Overview

This section presents a brief historical overview of DASs. It should be noted that in the existing literature, the terms distributed base station (DBS) and DAS are used interchangeably.

DASs were initially proposed to enhance indoor coverage of cellular systems where a building is treated as a single cell with several distributed antennas rather than either multiple pico cells each with a dedicated antenna or as a single cell with one central antenna (Saleh, 1987). The DAS approach allows avoiding excessive handovers in the first case and significant fading in the latter. The coverage and capacity of DASs in an indoor WCDMA system were investigated for several types of antennas in (Schuh, 2002). It was shown by Dai (2002) that maximum ratio combining (MRC) in the UL achieves a considerable capacity and coverage enhancement in a multi-cell CDMA system with DAS, but simultaneous transmission in the DL reduces performance since it increases the intercell interference (Dai, 2002). A solution for this problem was proposed in (Dai, 2005), where it was found that selecting only the RAH with best channel to the user ensures the best DAS DL performance. A similar conclusion was reached in (Hasegawa, 2003) where transmitting from the RAH with the best channel was shown to outperform the case of using the RAH as a relay while transmitting the signal directly from the BS. These results were validated in (Choi & Andrews, 2005; Choi & Andrews, 2007) from an information theoretic standpoint, where selective transmission (from only the RAH with best channel to user) was compared to maximum ratio transmission (using all the RAHs). Clark (2001) showed that selection combining (SC) in the uplink provides considerable enhancement over centralized BSs and constitutes a good tradeoff between performance and complexity when compared to MRC. A generalization of the concept of DASs was presented by Roh (2002), where each RAH consists of several antennas ensuring microdiversity, and the set of RAHs contributes to macrodiversity.

It should be noted that, in a practical scenario, installing RAHs at desired locations (e.g. equidistant along the cell boundary) might not be possible. Therefore, the performance of random placement of RAHs throughout the cell was investigated in terms of outage probability, as a lower bound on the actual performance (Zhang, 2007; Zhang, 2008). Interestingly, it was found that as the number of RAHs increases, the performance converges to that of regularly deployed RAHs. In fact, in the case of both fixed and random RAH locations, the gains achieved by a DAS system were shown to increase with the number of RAHs up to a certain limit where the gain obtained after using an additional RAH is negligible. This limit was considered to be four and seven RAHs in (Dai, 2005; Choi & Andrews, 2005), respectively, for the regular RAH positions, and seven in (Zhang, 2008) for the random RAH positions. Consequently, the investigated scenarios in this chapter will be selected within these limits.

A solution is presented for DAS cooperation via block-diagonalization and dual decomposition to maximize the weighted sum network capacity under per-antenna power constraint in (Hadisusanto, 2008). The solution is a trade-off between intercell interference mitigation, spatial multiplexing and macro diversity. Leroux (2008) proposed a protocol to manage multiuser interference in a DAS system, where users may connect to more than one RAH using the same resources, which leads to an increase in interference.

The protocol of (Leroux, 2008) was not associated to a particular multiple access scheme. However, DASs were implemented in a variety of wireless systems. For example, they were investigated for the Local Multipoint Distribution Service (LMDS) in (Highsmith, 2002). The commercial deployment of DASs was announced for WCDMA/HSPA in (Alcatel-Lucent, 2008a), and for cdma2000/EvDO in (Alcatel-Lucent,

2008b). They are currently receiving significant research attention for their deployment in LTE, e.g. (Zhao, 2012).

Conversely to (Hadisusanto, 2008; Leroux, 2008) where RAHs are considered to use the same resources without centralized control, the RAHs in this chapter are connected to a single BS, and the resources allocated to different RAHs are orthogonal subsets of the resources available at the central BS. Hence, interference is not an issue within a single cell.

Contributions of the Chapter

This chapter presents RRM algorithms applicable to LTE Release 8 and Release 10. When applied in conjunction with DAS, these algorithms are shown to lead to enhanced performance of real-time video transmission in LTE, particularly in public safety networks. In such networks, the proposed RRM techniques are applied to both UL and DL, and show significant increase in video QoE when implemented in the presence of DAS. Furthermore, a joint UL/DL QoE metric for real time video transmission over public safety networks is derived and analyzed in extreme conditions. The presence of DAS with intelligent UL and DL RRM is shown to overcome the limitations of this scenario. The presented QoE metrics can be applied to test the performance of future releases of LTE, e.g. with LTE Direct and D2D communications when applied to public safety networks. Promising preliminary results in this direction have been obtained in (Yaacoub & Kubbar, 2012b) and detailed investigations are planned in the future.

DAS IN LTE PUBLIC SAFETY NETWORKS

This section presents the details of the studied system, consisting of a DAS deployment supporting video transmission over LTE public safety networks. After describing the system model, the metrics used to assess the video quality during transmission over the LTE network are presented. Then, the LTE RRM algorithms for the UL and DL are proposed and analyzed. Finally, the simulation results are presented and assessed.

System Model

The DAS model consists of a single central BS connected to several RAHs distributed throughout the cell area. The BS centrally controls the RAHs and could be co-located with any of the RAHs or in a separate location. Although other types of media are possible, the BS is mainly connected to RAHs via fiber optic cable. Connection topologies include star, chain, tree, and ring topologies (CPRI, 2004). Each RAH consists mainly of a remote

antenna connected to the central BS. This allows centralized control to be exercised by the BS on the RAHs that in turn allow extended coverage and/or more user capacity. In addition, for fixed coverage and user capacity, the RAHs provide the users with better QoS since the distance from a user to the nearest RAH will be shorter than the distance to the central BS antenna in the conventional case, which leads to a higher SNR. Figure 1 shows examples of DAS deployment scenarios. In addition, it shows examples of six users connected to the RAHs of deployment scenarios (b) and (c).

In this chapter, a single cell scenario is considered. We compare the LTE performance in the presence and absence of DASs, for the scenarios presented in Figure 1. In the comparisons, we consider the same coverage area and the same number of users in the cell in the case of a single

Figure 1. DAS deployment scenarios

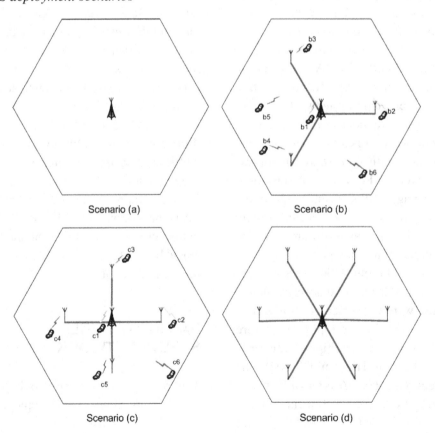

Scenario (a)   Scenario (b)

Scenario (c)   Scenario (d)

centralized BS (Scenario (a) in Figure 1) and in the case of DASs (Scenarios (b)-(d) in Figure 1). We also consider the same number of subcarriers in both cases. Hence, the RAHs are not used to ensure more frequency reuse, but rather to make a more efficient and fair use of the available subcarriers.

In the DAS scenario, the presence of the RAHs is transparent to the users who act as if there was only a single central BS in the cell. The communication between the central BS and the RAHs is via fiber optic (or microwave links having a nonoverlapping spectrum with LTE) and consequently does not consume any LTE radio resources. The presence of the RAHs contributes in enhancing the channel states of the different users by providing each user with an antenna that is closer to it than the central BS antenna. Thus, the DAS system appears as a single BS to the user. The mobility of a user heading from the area of RAH X to the area covered by RAH Y is translated in terms of decreasing channel quality on the subcarriers of RAH X and better channel quality on the subcarriers of RAH Y. Hence, the user is allocated a subset of the subcarriers of RAH Y similarly to what would happen in a single BS scenario when channel quality deteriorates on certain subcarriers and improves on others. The presence of RAHs and the actual handover occurrence are oblivious to the user. As for mobility between cells, the handover rules apply as in the case of two cells with a central BS in each.

DAS vs. Relays

As opposed to relays, the communication between the BS and RAHs does not consume any LTE radio resources, as mentioned previously. However, it should be noted that a wired connection between the central BS and the RAHs is not always feasible or easily realizable in practice. In this case, relay stations (RSs) are used instead of RAHs and the

wired connection is substituted by a wireless connection. Thus, the RS with less functionality than the BS can forward the data to remote areas of the cell and/or increase the cell capacity with reduced infrastructure cost. But in relay enhanced wireless networks, resource allocation imposes an additional challenge than scheduling with RAHs. In fact, with relays, resource allocation should be performed on the links between the BS and RS, in addition to the links between the BS/RS and the mobile users. Furthermore, the various links along each route in a communication system with RSs have generally different channel gains. Consequently, efficient scheduling decisions should be coupled with routing methods in order to ensure the best possible management and allocation of the wireless resources (Salem, 2010; Sreng, 2002).

Channel Model

This section presents the channel model adopted in this chapter. The channel gain of user k over subcarrier i on the link with RAH x can be expressed as follows (Goldsmith, 2005):

$$H_{k,i,\mathrm{dB}}^{(x)} = (-\kappa - \upsilon \log_{10} d_k^{(x)}) - \xi_k^{(x)} + 10\log_{10} F_{k,i}^{(x)} \tag{1}$$

In (1), the first factor captures propagation loss, with κ the pathloss constant, $d_k^{(x)}$ the distance in km from mobile k to RAH x, and υ the path loss exponent. The second factor, $\xi_k^{(x)}$, captures log-normal shadowing with zero-mean and a standard deviation σ_ξ, whereas the last factor, $F_{k,i}^{(x)}$, corresponds to Rayleigh fading with a Rayleigh parameter a (usually selected such that $E[a^2] = 1$).

In the traditional scenario (Scenario (a)), denoting by $x = 1$ the RAH co-located with the BS at the cell center, the channel gain between the BS and user k over subcarrier i is expressed as:

$H_{k,i} = H_{k,i}^{(1)}$. With DASs, it will transparently "appear" to user k that its channel gain with the BS over subcarrier i is:

$$H_{k,i} = \arg\max_x H_{k,i}^{(x)} \tag{2}$$

It should be noted that the above analysis applies to both the UL and DL, depending on whether i is an UL or DL subcarrier, respectively. In the rest of the chapter, whenever there is a need to distinguish between the uplink and downlink directions, we will use the superscripts (UL) and (DL) in the equations, respectively.

Data Rate Calculations in the Uplink

Letting $I_{\text{sub},k}^{(\text{UL})}$ be the set of UL subcarriers allocated to user k, $I_{\text{RB},k}^{(\text{UL})}$ the set of UL RBs allocated to user k, $N_{\text{RB}}^{(\text{UL})}$ the total number of RBs in the UL, $P_{k,\max}^{(\text{UL})}$ the total transmit power of user k, and $R_k^{(\text{UL})}$ its achievable rate in the UL. Then, the SCFDMA throughput of user k is given by:

$$R_k^{(\text{UL})}(P_{k,\max}^{(\text{UL})}, I_{\text{sub},k}^{(\text{UL})}) =$$
$$\frac{B^{(\text{UL})} \mid I_{\text{sub},k}^{(\text{UL})} \mid}{N_{\text{sub}}^{(\text{UL})}} \cdot \log_2\left(1 + \beta \cdot \Gamma_k^{(\text{UL})}(P_{k,\max}^{(\text{UL})}, I_{\text{sub},k}^{(\text{UL})})\right) \tag{3}$$

where $B^{(\text{UL})}$ is the total UL bandwidth, $\mid I_{\text{sub},k}^{(\text{UL})} \mid$ is the cardinality of $I_{\text{sub},k}^{(\text{UL})}$ and $N_{\text{sub}}^{(\text{UL})}$ is the number of UL subcarriers. β is called the SNR gap. It indicates the difference between the signal to noise ratio (SNR) needed to achieve a certain data transmission rate for a practical M-QAM system and the theoretical Shannon capacity limit (Qiu, 1999). It is given by: $\beta = \dfrac{-1.5}{\ln\left(5P_b\right)}$, where P_b denotes the bit error rate (BER). Finally, $\Gamma_k^{(\text{UL})}(P_{k,\max}^{(\text{UL})}, I_{\text{sub},k}^{(\text{UL})})$ is the SNR of user k after

Minimum Mean Squared Error (MMSE) frequency domain equalization at the receiver (Myung, 2008):

$$\Gamma_k^{(\text{UL})}(P_{k,\max}^{(\text{UL})}, I_{\text{sub},k}^{(\text{UL})}) = \left(\cfrac{1}{\cfrac{1}{\mid I_{\text{sub},k}^{(\text{UL})} \mid} \displaystyle\sum_{i \in I_{\text{sub},k}^{(\text{UL})}} \cfrac{\Gamma_{k,i}^{(\text{UL})}}{\Gamma_{k,i}^{(\text{UL})} + 1}} - 1\right)^{-1} \tag{4}$$

In (4), $\Gamma_{k,i}^{(\text{UL})}$ is the UL SNR of user k over subcarrier i. It is given by:

$$\Gamma_{k,i}^{(\text{UL})} = \frac{P_{k,i}^{(\text{UL})} H_{k,i}^{(\text{UL})}}{\sigma_{BS,i}^2} \tag{5}$$

where $\sigma_{BS,i}^2$ is the noise power at the receiver of the BS (i.e. the receiver of the RAH that is nearest to user k), and $P_{k,i}^{(\text{UL})}$ is the power transmitted by user k over subcarrier i.

The LTE standard imposes the constraint that the RBs allocated to a single user should be consecutive with equal power allocation over the RBs (3GPP TS 36.213, 2012; Lunttila, 2007; Myung, 2008). Hence, we set:

$$P_{k,i}^{(\text{UL})} = \frac{P_{k,\max}^{(\text{UL})}}{\mid I_{\text{sub},k}^{(\text{UL})} \mid} \tag{6}$$

Data Rate Calculations in the Downlink

Letting $I_{\text{sub},k}^{(\text{DL})}$ be the set of DL subcarriers allocated to user k, $I_{\text{RB},k}^{(\text{DL})}$ the set of RBs allocated to user k in the DL, $N_{\text{RB}}^{(\text{DL})}$ the total number of DL RBs, $P_{BS,i}^{(\text{DL})}$ the total power transmitted by the BS over subcarrier i, $P_{BS,\max}^{(\text{DL})}$ the maximum transmission power of the BS, and $R_k^{(\text{DL})}$ the achievable

DL rate of user k. Then, the OFDMA throughput of user k is given by:

$$R_k^{(DL)}\left(P_{BS,\max}^{(DL)}, I_{sub,k}^{(DL)}\right) = \sum_{i \in I_{sub,k}^{(DL)}} B_{sub}^{(DL)} \cdot \log_2\left(1 + \beta \cdot \Gamma_{k,i}^{(DL)}\right)$$

(7)

where $\Gamma_{k,i}^{(DL)}$ is the SNR of user k over subcarrier i, and $B_{sub}^{(DL)}$ is the subcarrier bandwidth. It is expressed as:

$$B_{sub}^{(DL)} = \frac{B^{(DL)}}{N_{sub}^{(DL)}}$$

(8)

with $B^{(DL)}$ the total usable DL bandwidth, and $N_{sub}^{(DL)}$ the total number of DL subcarriers.

In this chapter, we consider equal power transmission over the subcarriers to simplify DL resource allocation. Hence, for all i, we have:

$$P_{BS,i}^{(DL)} = \frac{P_{BS,\max}^{(DL)}}{N_{sub}^{(DL)}}$$

(9)

The DL SNR of user k over subcarrier i, $\Gamma_{k,i}^{(DL)}$ is given by:

$$\Gamma_{k,i}^{(DL)} = \frac{P_{BS,i}^{(DL)} H_{k,i}^{(DL)}}{\sigma_{k,i}^2}$$

(10)

where $\sigma_{k,i}^2$ is the noise power over subcarrier i in the receiver of user k.

QoS/QoE Metrics

This section presents the QoS and QoE metrics used to assess video quality after transmission over the cellular network. After briefly describing video encoding and simple error concealment techniques, the QoS metrics represented by loss distortion and video peak signal to noise ratio

(PSNR) are discussed. Then, relatively recent QoE metrics that better reflect the user experience are presented. Finally, a joint UL/DL video QoE metric tailored to the public safety scenario is derived.

Video Transmission and Error Concealment

We consider that video sequences are encoded into groups of pictures (GOPs) according to the H.264 standard. Each GOP consists of one I-frame and a sequence of P-frames and has a duration T_{GOP}. When a GOP is available for real-time transmission, it should be transmitted within a duration of T_{GOP}. When T_{GOP} has elapsed, all the frames that are not received are assumed lost, and the transmission of a new GOP begins. Due to the interdependencies of the video frames, the loss of a frame in a GOP leads to the loss of all subsequent frames in the GOP, until the next I-frame is received. The loss of an I-frame leads to the loss of all the frames in the GOP (Choi & Ivrlac, 2005). When video frames are lost, error concealment techniques are used. The most common approach for error concealment is known as the previous frame concealment method. It consists of repeating the last correctly received frame until the next I-frame is received (Choi & Ivrlac, 2005).

QoS Metric: Loss Distortion

To measure QoS in video transmission, one of the most widely used metrics is the mean-squared error distortion. Two types of distortion affect a video sequence: source distortion and loss distortion. Source distortion depends on the compression method at the source, whereas loss distortion corresponds to the distortion caused by lost frames during transmission over the wireless channels. The distortion for replacing a frame f, of dimensions $N_1 \times N_2$ pixels, with an estimated frame $\hat{f}$ can be computed as follows (Choi & Ivrlac, 2005):

$$D = \frac{1}{N_1 N_2} \sum_{n_1=0}^{N_1-1} \sum_{n_2=0}^{N_2-1} \left(f(n_1, n_2) - \hat{f}(n_1, n_2) \right)^2 \quad (11)$$

where $f(n_1, n_2)$ indicates the pixel value of frame f at position (n_1, n_2). The PSNR in this case can be expressed as:

$$P_{\text{SNR}}\left(f, \hat{f} \right) = \frac{\left(2^B - 1 \right)^2}{D\left(f, \hat{f} \right)} \quad (12)$$

with B the number of bits used to encode a single pixel in the picture frame (note that the video PSNR is not to be confused with signal SNR over the wireless links).

The total (or cumulative) loss distortion depends on the frame type (I-frame, P-frame) and position (in the same GOP, the loss of a P-frame f_1 leads to more distortion than the loss of a P-frame f_2 when $f_1 < f_2$). It also depends on the video coding method used and the error concealment technique adopted (duplication of last correctly received frame, etc). The total loss distortion caused by the loss of a frame f in a GOP of N_G frames with one I-frame and $(N_G - 1)$ P-frames, using the previous frame concealment method, can be obtained from (11) as follows:

$$D^{(f)} = \sum_{y=f}^{N_G} D\left(y, f - 1 \right) \quad (13)$$

The expression in (13) is obtained due to replacing all lost frames in the GOP from frame f onwards by the last correctly received frame f-1. An example is shown in Figure 2. When an I-frame is lost, it is replaced by the last correctly received frame from the previous GOP.

QoE Metric

PSNR is generally used to measure QoS in video transmission (Choi & Ivrlac, 2005), and it is calculated from the mean-squared error distortion. On the other hand, QoE is gaining significant interest as a method to quantify the multimedia experience of mobile users, e.g., see (Lee, 2012; Ou, 2011; Sohn, 2010). A survey of QoE techniques is presented in (Lee, 2012). QoE tries to measure the QoS as it is finally perceived by the end-user. For example, following (VQEG, 2003), the QoE can be related to the PSNR as follows:

$$Q = \frac{1}{1 + e^{b_1 \left(P_{SNR} - b_2 \right)}} \quad (14)$$

where b_1 and b_2 are parameters that depend on the video characteristics, and P_{SNR} is the PSNR expressed in dB. In (14), $Q = 0$ indicates the best quality and $Q = 1$ indicates the worst quality. In (Sohn, 2010), an empirical QoE metric taking into account PSNR, spatial resolution, frame rate, in addition to spatial and temporal variances was derived. A QoE metric derived in (Ou, 2011), based on the metric in (VQEG, 2003), is expressed as:

Figure 2. Error concealment example

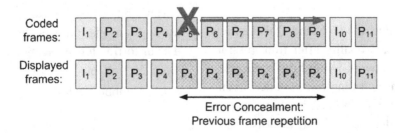

$$Q_m = Q_{\max} \left(1 - \frac{1}{1 + e^{b_1\left(P_{SNR} - b_2\right)}} \right) \cdot \frac{1 - e^{-b_3 \frac{f}{f_{\max}}}}{1 - e^{-b_3}} \quad (15)$$

where b_3 is another parameter that depends on the video characteristics, $Q_{\max}$ is a constant corresponding to maximum quality, f is the frame rate at which the video is displayed, and $f_{\max}$ is the maximum frame rate. The QoE derivations take into account user experience while playing the video and are not inherently designed to assess the transmission over wireless channels. Using the approach depicted in Figure 2, the same frame rate can be maintained after error concealment (i.e. $f = f_{\max}$), and hence (15) can be simplified to:

$$Q_m = Q_{\max} \left(1 - \frac{1}{1 + e^{b_1\left(P_{SNR} - b_2\right)}} \right) \quad (16)$$

Hence, in this chapter, we use (16) with $Q_{\max}$ = *100*, in order to display QoE on a scale from 0 to 100.

In practice, during the streaming of a stored video at the streaming server or BS, the video characteristics can be extracted offline and used to determine b_1, b_2, and b_3 in the QoE metrics. Although these parameters are difficult to extract during the streaming of a live video (e.g. live transmission during a public safety incidents), an approach for their dynamic real-time estimation is presented in (Ou, 2011). Nevertheless, the methods presented in this chapter do not need the system to be aware of these parameters. In the next section, "LTE Radio Resource Management", we present RRM techniques for LTE that are independent of these parameters. However, when these RRM techniques are applied in conjunction with DAS, they are shown to lead to enhanced video QoS/QoE. Consequently, the video dependent parameters in (16) are used to quantify the QoE in the simulation results, but the proposed methods can be implemented without knowing these parameters.

Joint UL/DL End-to-End QoE Metric

The previous QoS and QoE metrics can be applied independently to the UL and DL directions. Although a good performance in both directions generally reflects a good performance in practice, other metrics can be more representative in a public safety framework. In fact, with public safety networks, there is an interest in the end-to-end performance, where a given video transmitted from a member of the team to the command center through the BS/RAH, is routed back by this command center to other member(s) of the team in order to provide more information about the incident scene, as perceived by the first (transmitting) member. An example of joint UL/DL real-time video streaming in a public safety scenario is described in (Motorola, 2011), where a traditional approach with a single BS (without DAS) is assumed.

In the UL, users from the various public safety teams capture real-time video sequences from the disaster site. Each user transmits the video to the BS, where it will be routed to a central command center. When a GOP becomes available for transmission at a certain mobile terminal, it should be sent to the BS within a duration of T_{GOP}. When T_{GOP} has elapsed, all the frames that are not received at the BS are assumed lost, and the transmission of a new GOP begins. The command center gathers all the videos form the different users, filters, analyzes, and processes the data, and then sends back the processed information to the various public safety teams in order to take appropriate action. Hence, on the DL, when a GOP becomes available at the BS, coming from the central command center, the BS should distribute the GOP to the mobile users within a duration of T_{GOP}. When T_{GOP} has elapsed, the transmission of a new GOP begins, in order to maintain the real time streaming process. All the frames from the previous GOP that are not received at a given mobile terminal are assumed lost. Consequently, the final QoE after DL transmission depends on the QoE of the previous UL transmissions destined to the command center.

To assess this joint interdependency, we denote by $Q_{m,k}^{(UL)}$ the quality metric for the video received from user k in the UL and by $Q_{m,j}^{(DL)}$ the quality metric for the video received by user j in the DL, coming from the BS or RAH after being forwarded by the command center. Assuming there are K_j users filming the same location and sending the information to the command center to be forwarded to a specific user j, then the joint UL/DL QoE can be expressed as:

$$Q_j^{(\text{Joint UL-DL})} = \min\left(\max_{k=1,\dots,K_j} Q_{m,k}^{(UL)}, Q_{m,j}^{(DL)} \right) \quad (17)$$

In fact, there is no need to forward all the videos and risk overloading the network. The command center has to select the one with the best quality and forward it to the concerned user(s). For example, if several police vehicles are following and filming a suspect car, the movie showing the best reading of the car plate number, car brand and color, etc., can be forwarded to another police car coming from another direction and preparing to close the road in front of the suspect vehicle. This justifies the use of the "max" term inside the parentheses in (17).

If the information is to be broadcast to a group of users denoted by J, then the QoE is limited by the user having the worst DL QoE. Hence, (17) becomes:

$$Q_j^{(\text{Joint UL-DL})} = \min\left(\max_{k=1,\dots,K_J} Q_{m,k}^{(UL)}, \min_{j \in J} Q_{m,j}^{(DL)} \right) \quad (18)$$

The expression in (18) corresponds to the QoE perceived by all $j \in J$. In fact, in a broadcast scenario using LTE MBMS/eMBMS, the broadcast rate is limited by that of the user having the worst channel conditions, in order to guarantee that all users receive the video correctly, which explains the use of the second "min" expression inside the parentheses in (18). In a unicast scenario, the expression in (17) applies for each user j.

LTE Radio Resource Management

This section presents the LTE RRM algorithms used in this chapter. The subsection "Radio Resource Management in the Uplink" presents an RRM algorithm that can be applied in UL transmission. Indications on implementing it in DL unicasting are also presented. The subsection "Radio Resource Management in the Downlink" describes the RRM approach followed in the DL for broadcast/multicast using LTE MBMS/eMBMS in order to transmit a given video to a group of users using a single transmission.

Radio Resource Management in the Uplink

The resource allocation algorithm presented in this section is a utility maximization algorithm applicable to both UL and DL. Hence, we will drop the superscripts (UL) and (DL) to avoid repetition. We denote by $I_{\text{sub},k}$ the set of subcarriers allocated to user k, $I_{\text{RB},k}$ the set of RBs allocated to user k, N_{RB} the total number of RBs, K the number of users, and R_k the achievable throughput of user k. We define $U\left(R_k \mid I_{\text{RB},k} \right)$ as the utility of user k as a function of the throughput R_k given the allocation $I_{\text{RB},k}$. The resource allocation algorithm presented below consists of allocating RB n to user k in a way to maximize the difference:

$$\Lambda_{n,k} = U\left(R_k \mid I_{\text{RB},k} \cup \{n\} \right) - U\left(R_k \mid I_{\text{RB},k} \right) \quad (19)$$

where the marginal utility, $\Lambda_{n,k}$, represents the gain in the utility function U when RB n is allocated to user k, compared to the utility of user k before the allocation of n. The algorithm is described as follows:

- **Initialization:** Consider the set of available RBs $I_{avail\_RB} \subseteq \{1, 2, \cdots, N_{RB}\}$ and the set of available users $I_{avail\_users} \subseteq \{1, 2, \cdots, K\}$. At the start of the algorithm, $I_{avail\_RB} = \{1, 2, \cdots, N_{RB}\}$ and $I_{avail\_users} = \{1, 2, \cdots, K\}$.

Step 1: Find the user that has the highest marginal utility defined in (19) among all available users when the first available RB in I_{avail_RB} is allocated to it. In other words, for each RB n, find the user k^* such that:

$$k^* = \arg\max_k \Lambda_{n,k} \qquad (20)$$

Step 2: Allocate RB n to user k^*: $I_{RB,k^*} = I_{RB,k^*} \cup \{n\}$;

Step 3: Delete the RB from the set of available RBs: $I_{avail\_RB} = I_{avail\_RB} - \{n\}$;

Step 4: This step is only for the UL direction in order to guarantee the contiguity of subcarrier allocations. It is not needed for the DL. In the UL, if k^* is the same user to which RB $n-1$ was allocated, i.e. $k^* = \arg\max_k \Lambda_{n-1,k}$, keep k^* in I_{avail_users}. Otherwise, delete user k^* from the set of available users:

$$I_{avail\_users} = I_{avail\_users} - \{k^*\} \qquad (21)$$

Step5 (Iteration Step): Repeat Steps 1, 2, 3, and 4, until there are no available RBs or no available users.

The utility function depends on the data rate, and can be changed depending on the different services and QoS/QoE requirements. Letting the utility equal to the rate, the algorithm leads to a maximization of the sum-rate of the cell (also known as a max C/I approach). However, in this case, users close to the BS or RAHs will be allocated most of the resources, whereas edge users will be generally deprived from resources and will not be able to send/receive reliable video in real time. To solve this problem, utility functions providing proportional fairness are desired. It is known that the logarithmic utility function is associated with the proportional fairness for the utility-based optimization (Myung, 2008; Yaacoub & Dawy, 2012). Hence, letting $U = ln(R)$ provides proportional fairness, where ln represents the natural logarithm. Using, in the logarithm, the achievable throughput at the current scheduling instant achieves proportional fairness in frequency (PFF), whereas including the previous scheduling instants by using the cumulative throughput (since the start of the video transmission to/by the user in the DL/UL, respectively), achieves proportional fairness in time and frequency (PFTF). For more details about these methods and their relation to fairness, the reader can check (Yaacoub & Dawy, 2012). In this chapter, PFTF is selected and thus a logarithmic utility is used, since it allows a fair allocation for all users in order to transmit/receive their videos on the UL/DL.

Radio Resource Management in the Downlink

The previous algorithm applies to a unicasting scenario, where the BS/RAH is sending a different video to each user, or sending the same video to each user individually. In a public safety network, there might be a need to send the same video by the central command center to the members of the various public safety teams at the disaster site. In this case, a multicast/broadcast approach might be used in order to transmit the video once to all concerned users. This saves wireless resources by avoiding the allocation of individual RBs to each user. However, to guarantee that all users receive the data correctly, the broadcast/multicast takes place at the data rate that can be achieved by the user having the worst wireless conditions in the group. In other words, multicast transmission on a given RB is limited by the throughput achieved by the user having the worst channel conditions on that RB. Using LTE MBMS, a single RB can be dedicated in the cell to multicast the same DL video stream to the mobile users (Lu, 2009). Thus, denoting by $R_{k,n}^{(DL)}$ the DL throughput of user k over RB n, the BS selects the RB having the highest minimum throughput in order to maximize performance, i.e., according to the following:

$$n^* = \arg \max_{n} \left(\min_{k} R_{k,n}^{(DL)} \right) \qquad (22)$$

In Scenario (a) of Figure 1, all users are connected to the single BS antenna located in the cell center. Consequently, there is a high probability to have at least one user with bad channel conditions that will affect the performance in the whole network. However, in a DAS scenario, the presence of RAHs throughout the cell enhances the channel gains of all users according to (2), and the negative effects due to the user with the worst channel conditions are reduced.

Simulation Results and Analysis

This section presents the simulation results analyzing the performance of UL/DL LTE RRM in the presence of DAS on the QoS/QoE of real time video streaming. The simulation model consists of a single cell with a BS equipped with an omnidirectional antenna, or consisting of several RAHs, each having an omnidirectional antenna. The investigated RAH deployment models are shown in Figure 1. Deployment Scenario (a) consists of the

conventional centralized single BS. Deployment Scenario (b) consists of four RAHs: one located at the cell center and three located at a distance of $2R_c/3$, with R_c being the cell radius considered to be 1 km. The angular separation between these three RAHs is 120 degrees. Deployment Scenario (c) consists of five RAHs: one located at the cell center and four located at a distance of $R_c/2$, with 90 degrees angular separation between them. Finally, deployment Scenario (d) consists of seven RAHs: one located at the cell center and six located at a distance of $2R_c/3$, with 60 degrees angular separation between them. The simulation parameters are shown in Table 1. LTE parameters are obtained from (3GPP TS 36.211, 2012; 3GPP TS 36.213, 2012), and channel parameters are obtained from (3GPP TR 25.814, 2006). Users are considered to be uniformly distributed in the cell area.

QoS Results

In this section, we use the video loss distortion as a QoS metric. We simulate the video transmission in both directions, UL and DL, using the Foreman sequence, encoded in QCIF format (QCIF has a resolution of 176 × 144 pixels per frame). We consider MBMS in the DL, assuming the BS is sending the same video to all users, after aggregating, analyzing, and assessing the information it received from each user in the UL. GOPs consisting of 15 frames, one I-frame and 14 P-frames, are used, with the duration of a GOP being 0.5s. The results are averaged over 2500 iterations. In each iteration, a video sequence has to be transmitted from all mobile terminals to the BS (UL direction) under varying fading conditions, and another video sequence has to be transmitted from the BS to the mobile users using LTE MBMS (DL direction).

Figure 3 shows the average loss distortion results in dB for the UL and DL. A lower distortion indicates a better video quality. The superiority due to using DASs instead of traditional deployments is evident. In the UL, the enhancement is between 7-8 dB when Scenario (b) or (c) is used

Table 1. Simulation parameters

Parameter	Value	Parameter	Value
κ	-128.1 dB	υ	3.76
σ_ξ (dB)	8 dB	Rayleigh parameter a	$E[a^2] = 1$
$B^{(DL)}$	5 MHz	$B^{(UL)}$	5 MHz
$N_{RB}^{(DL)}$	25	$N_{RB}^{(UL)}$	25
$B_{sub}^{(DL)}$	15 kHz	$B_{sub}^{(UL)}$	15 kHz
$P_{BS,max}^{(DL)}$	5 W	$P_{k,max}^{(UL)}$	0.125 w

instead of Scenario (a), whereas the enhancement is around 10-12 dB when Scenario (d) is used. In the DL, the numbers are approximately the same in favor of DAS deployments. These results indicate that DASs could lead to significant gains in video quality, both in the UL and DL, which is highly desirable in real-time video streaming applications, especially when they relate to public safety networks.

Distortion results of Scenarios (b) and (c) are almost overlapping. Although Scenario (c) leads to slightly higher sum-rate results (not plotted here but can be found in (Yaacoub & Kubbar, 2012a)), this incremental enhancement, when subdivided among all users, is apparently not sufficient to allow the complete transmission of an additional video frame most of the time. For example, during T_{GOP}, transmitting bits corresponding to 12.1 frames with Scenario (b), or 12.9 frames with Scenario (c), is practically the same, since in both cases only 12 out of 15 frames will be correctly decoded, which leads to the same distortion, although the UL throughput is higher in the case of Scenario (c). When the number of RAHs is increased to six (Scenario (d)), this limitation is clearly overcome.

Another conclusion that can be reached from Figure 3 is that the DL distortion is higher than the UL distortion, which indicates a lower DL QoS. This is due to the use of multicasting, which limits the achievable rate to that of the worst case user. In the following subsection dedicated to QoE results, unicasting will be used in the DL using the proposed channel-aware RRM algorithm, which will allow the DL QoE to outperform that of the UL.

QoE Results

In this section, we use the video QoE metric derived in (16). A higher QoE indicates a better performance. To simulate the video transmission in both directions, UL and DL, the Football sequence is used, with GOPs consisting of 15 frames, one I-frame and 14 P-frames, having a GOP duration $T_{GOP} = 1$s. The results are averaged over 2500 iterations, where in each iteration, a video sequence has to be transmitted from the BS to each mobile user in the DL, or from each mobile terminal to the BS in the UL.

It should be noted that, although the same video sequence was used for simulation purposes, the scenario considered corresponds in practice

Figure 3. QoS (loss distortion) results for the UL and DL: Transmission of the foreman video sequence in QCIF format

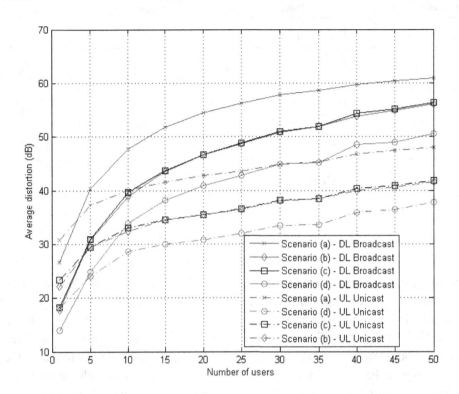

to a unicasting scenario where different videos are transmitted to (by) each user in the DL (UL).

Figure 4 show the average QoE results for the UL and DL using a video encoded in QCIF format, whereas Figure 5 shows the results of the video sequence encoded in CIF format (CIF has a resolution of 352 × 288 pixels per frame), which puts more strain on the wireless network.

It can be clearly seen from Figures 4 and 5 that the use of DASs leads to better video QoE compared to traditional deployments in both UL and DL. Furthermore, the QoE increases with the number of RAHs deployed. It can be noted that the QoE in the DL is better than in the UL, due to the higher transmission power available at the BS. The improvement is slight in the case of DAS, but large in the classic scenario of a single BS. In fact, the QoE of Scenario (a) degrades drasti-

cally as the number of users in the network increases, as shown in Figures 4 and 5, conversely to the DAS scenarios that maintain a relatively good performance. Their performance is relatively stable in Figure 4 regardless of the number of users, due to the relatively small size of the video frames that can be easily handled when the proposed RRM algorithm is used in conjunction with DAS. However, in Figure 5, it can be seen that although the QoE performance is better (compared to Figure 4) when the number of users is low (due to the better quality of CIF vs. QCIF), this performance starts degrading when the number of users becomes high. In fact, it becomes hard to allocate the resources to all users while still being able to transmit the higher number of bits required for the CIF format. However, it should be noted that in the case of Scenario (d), the QoE

Figure 4. QoE results for the UL and DL: Transmission of the football Video sequence in QCIF format

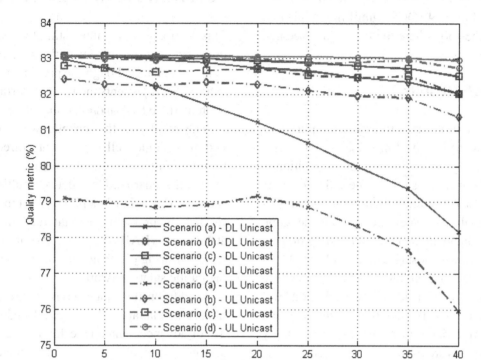

Figure 5. QoE results for the UL and DL: Transmission of the football video sequence in CIF format

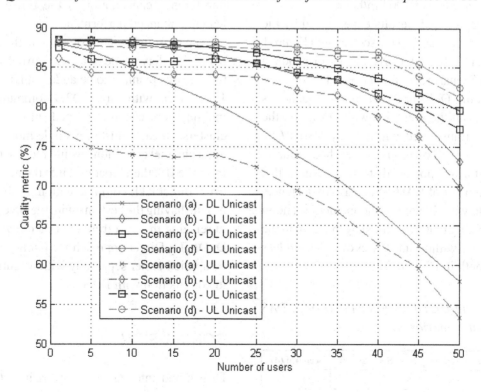

performance in Figure 5 (CIF) remains superior to that of Figure 4 (QCIF) until the number of users reaches 50, where the two values become comparable.

Joint QoE Results

In this section, in order to assess the joint UL/DL QoE metric derived in (17), we consider a team of five public safety members positioned in an incident area assumed to be at the cell edge (i.e. in a worst case scenario in terms of wireless channel qualities). They are filming the same spot in the incident area (e.g. a building on fire, an apartment with hostages held inside, etc.), and sending video to a central command center. The center selects the best video showing the best level of detail relevant to the situation at hand. This can translate to the video having the best visual quality in case all users are filming the same scene. Then the center sends the selected video to a public safety vehicle (e.g. police or ambulance) moving from the opposite cell edge towards the incident location at a speed of 100 km/hour.

The average QoE results experienced by the moving vehicle in each of the scenarios of Figure 1 are shown in Table 2. Clearly, the performance in the case of Scenario (a) is not acceptable. However, the maximum QoE for the encoded sequence is reached for all the scenarios with DAS, i.e., the video was transmitted without any losses (the reason that a QoE of 100 is not reached is due to source distortion, not loss distortion), even with a reduced number of RAHs (Scenario (b)). Hence, the vehicle was able to see the incident scene in the best quality that was filmed by the team in the incident area, without any losses over the wireless channel, both in UL and DL.

Table 2. Joint UL/DL QoE for the various DAS deployment scenarios

Scenario (a)	Scenario (b)	Scenario (c)	Scenario (d)
22.47	88.51	88.51	88.51

FUTURE RESEARCH DIRECTIONS

This section presents interesting research directions that would complement the work presented in this chapter. Although the presented list is not exhaustive, it presents the most important topics related to LTE DAS and/or public safety networks.

The results of this chapter were presented within a single cell. A possible direction for future research consists of investigating DAS in multicell scenarios. Considering multiple cells, each having a DAS deployment, represents a challenging problem where intercell interference at the various RAHs should be taken into account, while ensuring efficient and robust operation of the public safety network.

In addition, this chapter considered omnidirectional antennas at the BS and RAH locations. The use of advanced antenna techniques, e.g., smart antennas, diversity, and MIMO, is expected to lead to better results. Furthermore, allowing frequency reuse within a single cell, when implemented with advanced detection techniques like successive interference cancellation at the BS, could also lead to enhanced performance.

The most important extension in the direction of public safety would be to perform research with the features planned to be added in LTE Release 12. In fact, with direct D2D communications, mobile users can be grouped into cooperative clusters. In each cluster, a single mobile having good channel conditions would receive the video from the BS, then broadcast it to the nearby users using direct LTE communication. In the UL, the mobile having the best link with the BS could help in relaying the data from the other devices. This D2D/LTE Direct approach for public safety can be applied either separately with a central BS or in conjunction with DAS.

CONCLUSION

Distributed antenna systems were investigated in the context of LTE public safety networks. Resource allocation for the purpose of real-time video transmission, in both the uplink and downlink directions, was studied and several deployment scenarios were compared. A proportional fair scheduling algorithm, applicable in both the uplink and downlink directions, was presented. Furthermore, a quality of experience metric was used to measure the quality of the video transmissions. In addition, a joint uplink/downlink quality metric, tailored to video transmission over public safety networks, was presented and analyzed. Simulation results showed video quality can be largely enhanced due to the reduction of loss distortion in the presence of distributed antennas.

ACKNOWLEDGMENT

The authors would like to thank Dr. Osama Kubbar for his advice and feedback during the preliminary work that preceded the investigations described in this chapter.

This work was made possible by NPRP grant # 4-347-2-127 from the Qatar National Research Fund (A member of The Qatar Foundation). The statements made herein are solely the responsibility of the authors.

REFERENCES

Alcatel-Lucent. (2008a). *Alcatel-Lucent expands 3G WCDMA/HSPA portfolio with new distributed base station that offers increased deployment flexibility and lowers power requirements*. Alcatel-Lucent Press Release. Retrieved from http://www.alcatel-lucent.com/wps/portal/NewsReleases/

Alcatel-Lucent. (2008b). *Alcatel-Lucent unveils 3G CDMA/EV-DO distributed base station that offers greater deployment flexibility while lowering power requirements*. Alcatel-Lucent Press Release. Retrieved from http://www.alcatel-lucent.com/wps/portal/NewsReleases/

Astély, D., Dahlman, E., Furuskär, A., Jading, Y., Lindström, M., & Parkvall, S. (2009). LTE: The evolution of mobile broadband. *IEEE Communications Magazine, 47*(4), 44–51. doi:10.1109/MCOM.2009.4907406

Bhat, P., Nagata, S., Campoy, L., Berberana, I., Derham, T., & Guangyi, L. et al. (2012). LTE-advanced: An operator perspective. *IEEE Communications Magazine, 50*(2), 104–114. doi:10.1109/MCOM.2012.6146489

Choi, W., Andrews, J. G., & Yi, C. (2005). The capacity of multicellular distributed antenna networks. In *Proceedings of the International Conference on Wireless Networks, Communications and Mobile Computing*, (pp. 1337-1342). Maui, HI: IEEE.

Choi, W., & Andrews, J. G. (2007). Downlink performance and capacity of distributed antenna systems in a multicell environment. *IEEE Transactions on Wireless Communications, 6*(1), 69–73. doi:10.1109/TWC.2007.05207

Choi, L. U., Ivrlac, M. T., Steinbach, E., & Nossek, J. A. (2005). Analysis of distortion due to packet loss in streaming video transmission over wireless communication links. In *Proceedings of International Conference on Image Processing (IEEE ICIP 2005)*, (pp. 89-92). Genoa, Italy: IEEE.

Clark, M. V., Willis, T. M., Greenstein, L. J., Rustako, A. J., Ercegt, V., & Roman, R. S. (2001). Distributed versus centralized antenna arrays in broadband wireless networks. In *Proceedings of the IEEE Vehicular Technology Conference-Spring (VTC-Spring2001)*, (pp. 33-37). Rhodes, Greece: IEEE.

CPRI Specification V2.0. (2004). *Common public radio interface (CPRI)*. Interface Specification. CPRI.

Dai, L., Zhou, S., & Yao, Y. (2002). Capacity with MRC-based macrodiversity in CDMA distributed antenna systems. In *Proccedings of IEEE Globecom 2002* (pp. 987–991). Taipei, Taiwan: IEEE.

Dai, L., Zhou, S., & Yao, Y. (2005). Capacity analysis in CDMA distributed antenna systems. *IEEE Transactions on Wireless Communications*, 4(6), 2613–2620. doi:10.1109/TWC.2005.858011

Doumi, T., Dolan, M. F., Tatesh, S., Casati, A., Tsirtsis, G., Anchan, K., & Flore, D. (2013). LTE for public safety networks. *IEEE Communications Magazine*, 51(2), 106–112. doi:10.1109/MCOM.2013.6461193

Ekström, H., Furuskär, A., Karlsson, J., Meyer, M., Parkvall, S., Torsner, J., & Wahlqvist, M. (2006). Technical solutions for the 3G long-term evolution. *IEEE Communications Magazine*, 44(3), 38–45. doi:10.1109/MCOM.2006.1607864

Goldsmith, A. (2005). *Wireless communications*. New York, NY: Cambridge University Press. doi:10.1017/CBO9780511841224

Hadisusanto, Y., Thiele, L., & Jungnickel, V. (2008). Distributed base station cooperation via block-diagonalization and dual-decomposition. In *Proceedings of IEEE Globecom 2008*. New Orleans, LA: IEEE.

Hasegawa, R., Shirakabe, M., Esmailzadeh, R., & Nakagawa, M. (2003). Downlink performance of a CDMA system with distributed base station. In *Proceedings of the IEEE Vehicular Technology Conference-Fall (VTC-Fall 2003)*, (pp. 882-886). Orlando, FL: IEEE.

Highsmith, W. R. (2002). An investigation into distributed base station design for LMDS systems. In *Proceedings IEEE Southeastcon 2002*, (pp. 162-165). Columbia, SC: IEEE.

Jorguseski, L., Le, T. M. H., Fledderus, E. R., & Prasad, R. (2008). Downlink resource allocation for evolved UTRAN and WiMAX cellular systems. In *Proceedings of IEEE Personal, Indoor, and Mobile Radio Communications Conference (PIMRC 2008)*. Cannes, France: IEEE.

Lee, J.-S., De Simone, F., Ebrahimi, T., Ramzan, N., & Izquierdo, E. (2012). Quality assessment of multidimensional video scalability. *IEEE Communications Magazine*, 50(4), 38–46. doi:10.1109/MCOM.2012.6178832

Leroux, P., Roy, S., & Chouinard, J.-Y. (2008). A multi-agent protocol to manage interference in a distributed base station system. In *Proceedings of the International Conference on Advanced Technologies for Communications (ATC 2008)*, (pp. 421-426). Hanoi, Vietnam: ATC.

Lu, S., Cai, Y., Zhang, L., Li, J., Skov, P., Wang, C., & He, Z. (2009). Channel-aware frequency domain packet scheduling for MBMS in LTE. In *Proceedings of the IEEE Vehicular Technology Conference-Spring (VTC – Spring 2009)*. Barcelona, Spain: IEEE.

Lunttila, T., Lindholm, J., Pajukoski, K., Tiirola, E., & Toskala, A. (2007). EUTRAN uplink performance. In *Proceedings of International Symposium on Wireless Pervasive Computing (ISWPC 2007)*, (pp. 515-519). San Juan, Puerto Rico: ISWPC.

Motorola. (2007). *Long term evolution (LTE), overview of LTE air–Interface, technical white paper*. Retrieved from http://www.motorola.com/web/Business/Solutions/Industry%20Solutions/Service%20Providers/Wireless%20Operators/LTE/_Document/Static%20Files/6993_MotDoc_New.pdf

Motorola. (2010). *Real-world LTE performance for public safety*. Retrieved from http://www.motorola.com/web/Business/US-EN/NGPS/pdf/Real_World_LTE_Performance_for_Public_Safety_White_Paper.pdf

Motorola. (2011). *Barricaded suspect incident analysis: Enhancing critical incident response with public safety LTE*. Retrieved from http://www.motorola.com/web/Business/_Documents/Application%20Briefs/Static%20Files/Motorola_Barricaded_Suspect_Analysis.pdf

Myung, H. G., & Goodman, D. J. (2008). *Single carrier FDMA: A new air interface for long term evolution*. Chichester, UK: John Wiley and Sons. doi:10.1002/9780470758717

Ou, Y.-F., Ma, Z., Liu, T., & Wang, Y. (2011). Perceptual quality assessment of video considering both frame rate and quantization artifacts. *IEEE Transactions on Circuits and Systems for Video Technology, 21*(3), 286–298. doi:10.1109/TCSVT.2010.2087833

Qiu, X., & Chawla, K. (1999). On the performance of adaptive modulation in cellular systems. *IEEE Transactions on Communications, 47*(6), 884–895. doi:10.1109/26.771345

Roh, W., & Paulraj, A. (2002). Outage performance of the distributed antenna systems in a composite fading channel. In *Proceedings of the IEEE Vehicular Technology Conference-Fall (VTC-Fall 2002)*, (pp. 1520 - 1524). Vancouver, Canada: IEEE.

Saleh, A. A. M., Rustako, A. J., & Roman, R. S. (1987). Distributed antennas for indoor radio communications. *IEEE Transactions on Communications, 35*(12), 1245–1251. doi:10.1109/TCOM.1987.1096716

Salem, M., Adinoyi, A., Rahman, M., Yanikomeroglu, H., Falconer, D., & Kim, Y.-D. et al. (2010). An overview of radio resource management in relay-enhanced OFDMA-based networks. *IEEE Communications Surveys and Tutorials, 12*(3), 422–438. doi:10.1109/SURV.2010.032210.00071

Schuh, R. E., & Sommer, M. (2002). WCDMA coverage and capacity analysis for active and passive distributed antenna systems. In *Proceedings of the IEEE Vehicular Technology Conference-Spring (VTC – Spring 2002)*, (pp. 434-438). Birmingham, AL: IEEE.

Sharp, I. (2013, April). *Delivering public safety communications with LTE 3GPP*. Retrieved from http://www.3gpp.org/Public-Safety

Sohn, H., Yoo, H., De Neve, W., Kim, C. S., & Ro, Y. M. (2010). Full-reference video quality metric for fully scalable and mobile SVC content. *IEEE Transactions on Broadcasting, 56*(3), 269–280. doi:10.1109/TBC.2010.2050628

Song, J., & Trajkovic, L. (2005). Modeling and performance analysis of public safety wireless networks. In *Proceedings of 24th IEEE International Performace, Computing and Communications Conference (IPCCC 2005)*, (pp. 567-572). Phoenix, AZ: IEEE.

Sreng, V., Yanikomeroglu, H., & Falconer, D. (2002). Capacity enhancement through two-hop relaying in cellular radio systems. In *Proceedings of IEEE Wireless Communications and Networking Conference (WCNC 2002)*, (pp. 881-885). Orlando, FL: IEEE.

Third Generation Partnership Project (3GPP). (n.d.a). *3GPP TR 25.814 3GPP TSG RAN physical layer aspects for evolved UTRA, v7.1.0*. 3GPP.

Third Generation Partnership Project (3GPP). (n.d.b). 3GPP TR 25.892 feasibility study for orthogonal frequency division multiplexing (OFDM) for UTRAN enhancements, v6.0.0. 3GPP.

Third Generation Partnership Project (3GPP). (n.d.c). 3GPP TR 36.913 3GPP TSG RAN requirements for further advancements for evolved universal terrestrial radio access (E-UTRA) (LTE-advanced), version 8.0.1, release 8, 2008. 3GPP.

Third Generation Partnership Project (3GPP). (n.d.d). 3GPP TS 36.211 3GPP TSG RAN evolved universal terrestrial radio access (E-UTRA) physical channels and modulation, version 11.0.0, release 11, 2012. 3GPP.

Third Generation Partnership Project (3GPP). (n.d.e). 3GPP TS 36.213 3GPP TSG RAN evolved universal terrestrial radio access (E-UTRA) physical layer procedures, version 11.0.0, release 11, 2012. 3GPP.

Video Quality Experts Group (VQEG). (2003). *Final report on the validation of objective models of video quality assessment*. Author.

Yaacoub, E., & Dawy, Z. (2012). *Resource allocation in uplink OFDMA wireless systems: Optimal solutions and practical implementations*. Hoboken, NJ: John Wiley and Sons / IEEE Press. doi:10.1002/9781118189627

Yaacoub, E., & Kubbar, O. (2012a). On the performance of distributed base stations in LTE public safety networks. In *Proceedings of IEEE International Wireless Communications and Mobile Computing Conference (IWCMC 2012)*, (pp. 927-932). Limassol, Cyprus: IEEE.

Yaacoub, E., & Kubbar, O. (2012b). Energy-efficient device-to-device communications in LTE public safety networks. In *Proceedings of Globecom Workshops 2012 (International Workshop on Green Internet of Things)*, (pp. 391-395). Anaheim, CA: ACM.

Zhang, J., & Andrews, J. G. (2007). Cellular communication with randomly placed distributed antennas. In *Proceedings of IEEE Globecom*, (pp. 1400-1404). Washington, DC: IEEE.

Zhang, J., & Andrews, J. G. (2008). Distributed antenna systems with randomness. *IEEE Transactions on Wireless Communications*, 7(9), 3636–3646. doi:10.1109/TWC.2008.070425

Zhao, X., & Yang, X. (2012). Downlink ergodic capacity analysis for wireless networks with cooperative distributed antenna systems. In *Proceedings of IEEE International Conference on Communications (ICC 2012)*, (pp. 5911-5915). Ottawa, Canada: IEEE.

ADDITIONAL READING

Atat, R., Yaacoub, E., Alouini, M.-S., & Filali, F. (2012, January). Delay Efficient Cooperation in Public Safety Vehicular Networks Using LTE and IEEE 802.11p. *IEEE Consumer Communications and Networking Conference - Special Session Information Dissemination in Vehicular Networks (CCNC 2012 - SS IDVN)*, pp. 316-320, Las Vegas, NV, USA.

Bacchus, R., Taher, T., Zdunek, K., & Roberson, D. (2010). Spectrum Utilization Study in Support of Dynamic Spectrum Access for Public Safety. *IEEE Symposium on New Frontiers in Dynamic Spectrum*, pp. 1-11.

Bae, C., & Cho, D.-H. (2007). Fairness-Aware Adaptive Resource Allocation Scheme in Multi-Hop OFDMA Systems. *IEEE Communications Letters*, 11(2), 134–136. doi:10.1109/LCOMM.2007.061381

Blom, R., de Bruin, P., Eman, J., Folke, M., Hannu, H., Naslund, M., et al. (2008). Public Safety Communication Using Commercial Cellular Technology. *International Conference on Next Generation Mobile Applications, Services and Technologies (NGMAST 2008)*, pp. 291-296.

Bohannan, C., Zhang, L., Tang, J., Wolff, R. S., Wan, S., Gurdasani, N., & Galarus, D. (2009). QoS Enhancement and Performance Evaluation of Ad-Hoc Routing Protocols for Rural Public Safety. *IEEE International Conference on Communications (ICC 2009)*, pp. 1-5, Dresden, Germany.

Borkar, S., Roberson, D., & Zdunek, K. (2011). Priority Access for Public Safety on Shared Commercial LTE Networks. *Technical Symposium at ITU Telecom World (ITU WT)*, pp. 105-110.

Esmiol, F., Rousseau, S., Conan, V., & Bonnet, C. (2011). Distributed Multi-Level Cooperative Scheme for QoS Support in Public Safety Networks. *IEEE 8th International Conference on Mobile Adhoc and Sensor Systems (MASS 2011)*, pp. 955-961.

Gentile, C., Matolak, D. W., Remley, K. A., Holloway, C. L., Wu, Q., & Zhang, Q. (2012). Modeling Urban Peer-to-Peer Channel Characteristics for the 700 MHz and 4.9 GHz Public Safety Bands. *IEEE International Conference on Communications (ICC 2012)*, pp. 4557-4562.

Kaneko, M., & Popovski, P. (2007, June). Radio Resource Allocation Algorithm for Relay-Aided Cellular OFDMA System. *IEEE International Conference on Communications (ICC 2007)*, pp. 4831-4836, Glascow, Scotland.

Kim, M., & Lee, H. (2007, July). Radio Resource Management for a Two-Hop OFDMA Relay System in Downlink. *IEEE Symposium on Computers and Communications (ISCC 2007)*, pp. 25-31, Aveiro, Portugal.

Lee, J., Park, S., Wang, H., & Hong, D. (2007, June). QoS-Guaranteed Transmission Scheme Selection for OFDMA Multi-Hop Cellular Networks. *IEEE International Conference on Communications (ICC 2007)*, pp. 4587-4591, Glascow, Scotland.

Li, G., & Liu, H. (2006). Resource Allocation for OFDMA Relay Networks with Fairness Constraints. *IEEE Journal on Selected Areas in Communications*, *24*(11), 2061–2069. doi:10.1109/JSAC.2006.881627

Nam, W., Chang, W., Chung, S.-Y., & Lee, Y. (2007, June). Transmit Optimization for Relay-Based Cellular OFDMA Systems. *IEEE International Conference on Communications (ICC 2007)*, pp. 75-81, Glascow, Scotland.

Oyman, O. (2007, November). Opportunistic Scheduling and Spectrum Reuse in Relay-Based Cellular OFDMA Networks. [Washington DC, USA.]. *IEEE GlobeCom*, *2007*, 3699–3703.

Rangnekar, R., Feng, G., Young, A., Silvius, M. D., Fayez, A., & Bostian, C. W. (2009). A Remote Control and Service Access Scheme for a Vehicular Public Safety Cognitive Radio. IEEE Vehicular Technology Conference Fall (VTC 2009-Fall), pp. 1-5.

Rousseau, S., Benbadis, F., Lavaux, D., & Conan, V. (2011). Public Safety Situation Aware Services over Cognitive Radio Networks. *IEEE 8th International Conference on Mobile Adhoc and Sensor Systems (MASS 2011)*, pp. 962-967.

Simic, M. B. (2012). Feasibility of Long Term Evolution (LTE) as Technology for Public Safety. (2012). *20th Telecommunications Forum (TELFOR 2012)*, pp. 158-161.

Valcourt, S. A., Chamberlin, K., McMahon, B., & Kun, A. (2007). Systems Engineering of Datacasting for Public Safety Vehicles. *IEEE Conference on Technologies for Homeland Security*, pp. 45-50.

Wei, Q., He, J., & Zhang, X. (2010). Behavioral Modeling for Public Safety Communication in Wireless Mesh Networking. *International Conference on Wireless Communications Networking and Mobile Computing (WiCOM 2010)*, pp. 1-5.

Wei, Q., He, J., & Zhang, X. (2010). Key Agreement with Voting Receiver in Public Safety Mesh Networks. *International Conference on Wireless and Mobile Communications (ICWMC 2010)*, pp. 415-419.

Yaacoub, E., & Dawy, Z. (2009). A Game Theoretical Formulation for Proportional Fairness in LTE Uplink Scheduling. *IEEE Wireless Communications and Networking Conference (WCNC 2009)*, pp. 1-5, Budapest, Hungary.

Yaacoub, E., & Dawy, Z. (2010, April). A Comparison of Uplink Scheduling in OFDMA and SCFDMA. *IEEE International Conference on Telecommunications (ICT 2010)*, pp. 466-470, Doha, Qatar.

Yaacoub, E., & Dawy, Z. (2010). Uplink Scheduling in LTE Systems using Distributed Base Stations. [ETT]. *European Transactions on Telecommunications*, *21*(6), 532–543. doi:10.1002/ett.1408

Yaacoub, E., & Dawy, Z. (2011). Achieving the Nash Bargaining Solution in OFDMA Uplink Using Distributed Scheduling with Limited Feedback. *International Journal of Electronics and Communication AEU (Elsevier)*, *65*(4), 320–330. doi:10.1016/j.aeue.2010.03.007

Yaacoub, E., & Dawy, Z. (2012). A Survey on Uplink Resource Allocation in OFDMA Wireless Networks. *IEEE Communications Surveys and Tutorials*, *14*(2), 322–337. doi:10.1109/SURV.2011.051111.00121

Yang, K., Calin, D., Kaya, A. O., & Yiu, S. (2012). Coordinated Dual-Layer Beamforming for Public Safety Network: Architecture and Algorithms. *IEEE International Conference on Communications (ICC 2012)*, pp. 4095-4099.

KEY TERMS AND DEFINITIONS

Distributed Antenna Systems: A set of remote antenna heads connected to a central base station (BS) enclosure. They allow the BS to extend its coverage and provide enhanced connectivity to cell edge users.

Long Term Evolution (LTE): It is the state of the art cellular system being deployed for commercial cellular communications, and it is planned to be the next generation system for public safety broadband communications.

Orthogonal Frequency Division Multiple Access (OFDMA): It is the accessing scheme used for LTE downlink. It consists of subdividing the bandwidth into a large number of subcarriers, each having a small bandwidth where the fading can generally be considered flat.

Public Safety System: A system that allows collaboration between the various agencies concerned with public safety, like law enforcement (police), fire fighters, and medical personnel (ambulance), in order to ensure coordination and harmonious operation between these different teams in case of incidents.

Quality of Experience (QoE): QoS as perceived by the end user. It is generally a subjective measure. Objective metrics for QoE like the ones used in this chapter are generally derived taking into account subjective assessments.

Quality of Service (QoS): Measure to assess the network performance. It is an objective measure used to assess performance uniformly for all users, not taking into account the actual user experience.

Radio Resource Management: Algorithms and techniques to allocate the wireless resources and set certain parameters of the wireless system depending on the channel characteristics and interference levels, with the objective of optimizing the network performance.

Single Carrier FDMA (SCFDMA): It is the accessing scheme used for LTE uplink. It is a modified form of OFDMA that allows the subcarriers to be transmitted sequentially rather than in parallel. Its main advantage is a reduction in the signal peak to average power ratio (PAPR), which allows cheaper power amplifiers to be used in LTE handsets (UEs).

Chapter 4
On Max-SINR Receiver for Hexagonal Multicarrier Transmission System

Kui Xu
PLA University of Science and Technology, China

Youyun Xu
PLA University of Science and Technology, China

Dongmei Zhang
PLA University of Science and Technology, China

Wenfeng Ma
PLA University of Science and Technology, China

ABSTRACT

In this chapter, a novel receiver for Hexagonal Multicarrier Transmission (HMT) system based on the maximizing Signal-to-Interference-plus-Noise Ratio (Max-SINR) criterion is proposed. Theoretical analyses show that there is a timing offset between the prototype pulses of the proposed Max-SINR receiver and the traditional projection receiver. Meanwhile, the timing offset should be matched to the channel scattering factor of the Doubly Dispersive (DD) channel. The closed form timing offset expressions of the prototype pulse for Max-SINR HMT receiver over DD channel with different channel scattering functions are derived. Simulation results show that the proposed Max-SINR receiver outperforms traditional projection scheme and obtains an approximation to the theoretical upper bound SINR performance within the full range of channel spread factor. Consistent with the SINR performance improvement, the Bit Error Rate (BER) performance of the HMT system has also been further improved by using the proposed Max-SINR receiver. Meanwhile, the SINR performance of the proposed Max-SINR receiver is robust to the channel delay spread estimation errors.

DOI: 10.4018/978-1-4666-4888-3.ch004

INTRODUCTION

Orthogonal frequency division multiplexing (OFDM) systems with guard-time interval or cyclic prefix can prevent inter-symbol interference (ISI). OFDM has overlapping spectra and rectangular impulse responses. Consequently, each OFDM sub-channel exhibits a sinc-shape frequency response. Therefore, the time variations of the channel during one OFDM symbol duration destroy the orthogonality of different subcarriers, and result in power leakage among subcarriers, known as inter-carrier interference (ICI), which causes degradation in system performance. In order to overcome the above drawbacks of OFDM system, several pulse-shaping OFDM systems such as multiwavelets based OFDM system, OFDM based on offset quadrature amplitude modulation (OFDM/OQAM) system, et al., were proposed (Kumbasar V., & Kucur O., 2007, Das S., & Schniter P., 2007, Abbas H.K., Waleed A. M., & Nihad S., 2010, Gao X., Wang W., Xia X.G., Au E.K.S. & You X. H., 2011, Jung P., & Wunder G., 2007, Ma M., Jiao B., & Lee C. Y., 2008, Lin G., Lundheim L., & Holte N., 2008, Siohan P., Siclet C., & Lacaille N., 2002).

BACKGROUND

It is shown in (Strohmer T, & Beaver S., 2003, Han F. M., & Zhang X. D., 2007, Han F.M., & Zhang X.D., 2009, Han F. M., & Zhang X.D., 2010) that signal transmission through a rectangular lattice is suboptimal for doubly dispersive (DD) channel. By using results from sphere covering theory (Conway J. H. & Sloane N. J. A., 1998), the authors have demonstrated that lattice OFDM (LOFDM) system, which is OFDM system based on hexagonal-type lattice, providing better performance against ISI/ICI (Strohmer & Beaver, 2003). However, LOFDM confines the transmission pulses to a set of orthogonal ones. As pointed out in (Han & Zhang, 2007), these orthogonalized pulses destroy the time-frequency (TF) concentration of the initial pulses, hence lower the robustness to the time and frequency dispersion caused by the DD propagation channel.

In (Han & Zhang, 2007, Han & Zhang, 2009, Han & Zhang, 2010), the authors abandoned the orthogonality condition of the modulated pulses and proposed a multicarrier transmission scheme named as hexagonal multicarrier transmission (HMT) by regarding signal transmission as tiling of the TF plane. To optimally combat the impact of propagation channel, the hexagonal lattice parameters and the pulse shape of modulation waveform in HMT system are optimized jointly to adapt to the channel scattering function. It is shown that the HMT system obtains lower energy perturbation by incorporation the best T-F localized Gaussian pulses as the elementary modulation waveform, hence outperforms OFDM and LOFDM system from the robustness against channel dispersion point of view (Xu K., & Shen Y. H., 2009, Xu K., Xu Y., & Zhang D.,2011, Xu K., Lv Z., Xu Y., & Zhang D., 2013).

In HMT system, there is no cyclic prefix and data symbols of HMT signal are transmitted at the hexagonal type lattice points in TF plane. The basic mathematical operation on the received signal performed by the demodulator is a projection onto an identically structured function set generated by the prototype pulse function (Jung & Wunder, 2007, Han & Zhang,2007, Xu et al. 2013), i.e. an optimal match filter. It is shown in (Wu Jingxian, & Xiao Chengshan, 2007, Wu Jingxian, Zheng Yahong Rosa, Khaled Ben Letaief, & Xiao Chengshan, 2007, Wu Jingxian, Zheng Yahong Rosa, Khaled Ben Letaief, & Xiao Chengshan, 2005) that the optimum sampling time of wireless communication systems over DD channel is dependent on the power distribution of the channel profiles, and that zero timing offset does not always yield the best system performance. Max-SINR ISI/ICI-Shaping receiver for multicarrier modulation system is discussed in (Das & Schniter 2007), the

Max-SINR prototype pulse can be obtained by maximizing the generalized Rayleigh quotient.

In (Xu & Shen, 2009, Xu et al., 2011, Xu et al., 2013, Xu Kui, Xu Y.Y., Xia X.C, & Zhang D.M., 2012), we have presented that traditional HMT receiver proposed in (Han & Zhang, 2007, Han & Zhang, 2009, Han & Zhang, 2010) using zero timing offset prototype pulse is a suboptimal approach in the view of SINR. The receiver prototype pulse based on Max-SINR criterion for HMT system over DD channel with exponential power delay profile and U-shape Doppler spectrum was proposed. In this chapter, we will present the receiver prototype pulses based on Max-SINR criterion for HMT system over DD channel with different channel scattering functions. Theoretical analyses show that there is a timing offset between prototype pulses of the proposed Max-SINR HMT receiver and traditional HMT receiver in the SINR point of view, which is consistent with the conclusion in (Wu & Xiao, 2007, Wu et al., 2007, Wu et al., 2005). The closed form timing offset expressions of prototype pulse for Max-SINR HMT receiver over the DD channel with different channel scattering functions are derived. In general, the above mentioned timing offset of the proposed Max-SINR prototype pulses should be matched to the channel scattering function of the DD channel, including channel maximum time delay spread and the root mean square (RMS) delay spread.

Theoretical analyses and simulation results show that the proposed optimal Max-SINR receiver outperforms the traditional projection receiver in (Han & Zhang, 2007, Han & Zhang, 2009, Han & Zhang, 2010) and obtains an approximation to the theoretical upper bound SINR performance. Specifically, the SINR performance of the proposed Max-SINR HMT receiver outperforms traditional receiver using zero timing offset prototype pulse about 2dB over DD channel with uniform power delay profile and uniform Doppler spectrum. The proposed Max-SINR HMT receiver obtains an about 3dB gain over the correspond-

ing traditional HMT receiver using zero timing offset prototype pulse on the SINR performance over DD channel with exponential power delay profile and U-shape Doppler spectrum. Moreover, the proposed Max-SINR receiver obtains an about 2dB bit error rate (BER) performance gain at SNR=20dB. Meanwhile, the SINR performance of the proposed scheme is robust to the channel delay spread estimation errors.

HEXAGONAL MULTICARRIER TRANSMISSION SYSTEM

In HMT systems, the transmitted baseband signal can be expressed as (Han & Zhang, 2007, Han & Zhang, 2009, Han & Zhang, 2010):

$$
\begin{aligned}
x\left(t\right) = &\sum_m \sum_n c_{m,2n} g\left(t - mT\right) e^{j2\pi nFt} + \\
&\sum_m \sum_n c_{m,2n+1} g\left(t - mT - \frac{2}{T}\right) e^{j2\pi\left(nF+\frac{F}{2}\right)t}
\end{aligned}
\tag{1}
$$

where T and F are the lattice parameters as shown in Figure 1, which can be viewed as the symbol period and the subcarrier separation, respectively; $c_{m,2n}$ denotes the user data, which is assumed to be taken from a specific signal constellation and independent and identically distributed (i.i.d.) with zero mean and average power σ_c^2; $m \in \mathcal{M}$ and $n \in \mathcal{N}$ are the position indices in the TF plane; $\mathcal{M}$ and $\mathcal{N}$ denote the sets from which m, n can be taken, with cardinalities M and N, respectively. The prototype pulse $g\left(t\right)$ is the Gaussian window[1]:

$$
g\left(t\right) = \left(2/\sigma\right)^{1/4} e^{-\left(\pi/\sigma\right)t^2}
\tag{2}
$$

with σ being a parameter controlling the energy distribution in the time and frequency directions. The ambiguity function of Gaussian pulse is defined by:

$$A_g\left(\tau, v\right) = \int_{-\infty}^{\infty} g\left(t\right) g^*\left(t - \tau\right) e^{-j2\pi vt} dt \qquad (3)$$

$$= e^{-\frac{\pi}{2}\left(\frac{1}{\sigma}\tau^2 + v^2\right)} e^{-j\pi\tau v}$$

where $\left(\cdot\right)^*$ denotes the complex conjugate. It can also be viewed as the 2-D correlation between $g\left(t\right)$ and its shifted version by τ in time and v in frequency in the TF plane.

The original hexagonal lattice can be expressed as the disjoint union of a rectangular sublattice V_{rect1} and its coset V_{rect2}, as shown in Figure 1. The transmitted baseband signal in Equation (1) can be rewritten as:

$$x\left(t\right) = \sum_i \sum_m \sum_n c_{m,n}^i g_{m,n}^i\left(t\right) \qquad (4)$$

where $i = 1, 2$, $c_{m,n}^1$ and $c_{m,n}^2$ represent the symbols coming from V_{rect1} and V_{rect2}, respectively:

$$g_{m,n}^i\left(t\right) = g\left(t - mT - \left(i-1\right)T\big/2\right) e^{-j2\pi\left(nF + \left(i-1\right)F/2\right)t}$$

is the transmitted pulse generated by the prototype pulse $g\left(t\right)$.

The baseband DD channel can be modeled as a random linear operator H (Bello P. A., 1963):

$$\text{H}\left[x\left(t\right)\right] = \int_0^{\tau_{\max}} \int_{-f_d}^{f_d} H\left(\tau, v\right) x\left(t - \tau\right) e^{j2\pi vt} d\tau dv \quad (5)$$

where $\tau_{\max}$ and f_d are the *maximum multipath delay spread* and the *maximum Doppler frequency*, respectively. The product $\vartheta = \tau_{\max} f_d$ is referred to as the *channel spread factor* (CSF) (Bello P. A., 1963, L. Cohen, 1995). $H\left(\tau, v\right)$ is called the delay-Doppler spread function, which is the Fourier transform of the time-varying impulse response of the channel $h\left(t, \tau\right)$ with respect to t.

Figure 1. Partition of the hexagonal lattice into a rectangular sublattice V_{rect1} (denoted by ◯) and its coset V_{rect2} (denoted by ●)

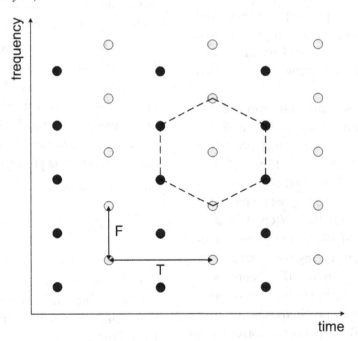

In wide-sense stationary uncorrelated scattering (WSSUS) assumption the DD channel is characterized by the second-order statistics:

$$\mathrm{E}\left[H\left(\tau,\upsilon\right)H^{*}\left(\tau_{1},\upsilon_{1}\right)\right]=S_{H}\left(\tau,\upsilon\right)\delta\left(\tau-\tau_{1}\right)\delta\left(\upsilon-\upsilon_{1}\right) \tag{6}$$

where $\mathrm{E}\left[\cdot\right]$ denotes the expectation and $S_{H}\left(\tau,\upsilon\right)$ is called the scattering function, which characterizes the statistics of the WSSUS channel. Without loss of generality, we use $\int_{0}^{\tau_{\max}}\int_{-f_{d}}^{f_{d}}S_{H}\left(\tau,\upsilon\right)d\tau d\upsilon=1$, which means that the channel has no overall path loss.

As shown in (5), the propagation channel introduces energy perturbation among the transmitted symbols. It is shown in (Han & Zhang, 2007, Han & Zhang, 2009, Han & Zhang, 2010) that the symbol energy perturbation function is dependent on the channel scattering function and the pulse shape. The properly designed HMT system with Gaussian prototype pulse achieves minimum symbol energy perturbation over DD channel. The optimality of such system in combating the ISI/ICI caused by the DD channel is guaranteed by the Heisenberg uncertainty principle and the sphere-packing theory. The choice of the system parameters (σ, T, F) to minimize such undesired energy perturbation is extensively dealt with in (Han & Zhang, 2007, Han & Zhang, 2009, Han & Zhang, 2010). In general, the pulse shape of the Gaussian window and the transmission pattern parameters T and F should be matched to the channel scattering function. The optimal system parameter for DD channels with exponential-U scattering function can be chosen as (Han & Zhang, 2007, Han & Zhang, 2009, Han & Zhang, 2010):

$$\sigma=\frac{W_{t}}{W_{f}}=\alpha\frac{\tau_{\mathrm{rms}}}{f_{d}}=\sqrt{3}\frac{T}{F} \tag{7}$$

and:

$$\sigma=\frac{W_{t}}{W_{f}}=\alpha\frac{\tau_{\mathrm{rms}}}{f_{d}}=\frac{1}{\sqrt{3}}\frac{T}{F} \tag{8}$$

The received signal is:

$$r\left(t\right)=\mathrm{H}\left[x\left(t\right)\right]+w\left(t\right) \tag{9}$$

where $w\left(t\right)$ is the AWGN having variance σ_{w}^{2}. Recently, several channel estimation schemes for multicarrier modulation system with hexagonal TF lattice have been proposed (Gao Meng, Shen Y.H., & Yuan Z.G., 2009, Gao Meng, Shen Y.H., & Xu K., 2011, Gao Meng, Shen Y.H., & Yuan Z.G., 2011) and all this schemes are suitable for HMT system.

THE MAX-SINR RECEIVER

The basic mathematical operation on the received signal performed by the demodulator is a projection onto an identically structured function set generated by the prototype pulse function, i.e. an optimal match filter (Han & Zhang, 2007, Han & Zhang, 2009, Han & Zhang, 2010).

To obtain the data symbol $\hat{c}_{m,n}^{i}$, the match filter receiver projects the received signal $r\left(t\right)$ on prototype pulse function $\psi_{m,n}^{i}\left(t\right)$, $i=1,2$, i.e.:

$$\hat{c}_{m,n}^{i}=\left\langle r\left(t\right),\psi_{m,n}^{i}\left(t\right)\right\rangle$$
$$=\sum_{j}\sum_{m',n'}c_{m',n'}^{j}\left\langle\mathrm{H}\left[\psi_{m',n'}^{j}\left(t\right)\right],\psi_{m,n}^{i}\left(t\right)\right\rangle+\left\langle w\left(t\right),\psi_{m,n}^{i}\left(t\right)\right\rangle \tag{10}$$

where:

$$\psi_{m,n}^{i}\left(t\right)=\psi\left(t-mT-\left(i-1\right)T/2\right)e^{-j2\pi\left(nF+\left(i-1\right)F/2\right)t}$$

and $\psi(t)$ is the prototype pulse at the receiver. The energy of the received symbol $c_{m,n}^i$, after projection on the filter function $\psi_{m,n}^i(t)$ over DD channel can be expressed as:

$$E_s = \mathrm{E}\left\{\left|\sum_j \sum_{m',n'} c_{m',n'}^j \left\langle \mathrm{H}\left[g_{m',n'}^j(t)\right], \psi_{m,n}^i(t-\Delta t)\right\rangle + \left\langle w(t), \psi_{m,n}^i(t-\Delta t)\right\rangle\right|^2\right\}$$

(11)

Under the assumptions of WSSUS channel and source symbols $c_{m,n}^i$ are statistically independent, (11) can be rewritten as:

$$E_s = \sigma_c^2 \int_\tau \int_v S_H(\tau,v)\left[\sum_{m,n}\left(\left|A_g(mT+\tau,nF+v)\right|^2 + \left|A_g\left((m+1/2)T+\tau,(n+1/2)F+v\right)\right|^2\right)\right]$$

$$\times d\tau dv + \sigma_w^2\left|A_g(0,0)\right|$$

(12)

We can see from Equation (12) that E_s is composed of the expectation symbol energy, ISI/ICI and additive noise. The SINR of the desired symbol $c_{m_0,n_0}^{i_0}$ can be expressed as:

$$R_{\mathrm{SIN}} = \frac{\sigma_c^2}{E_{\mathrm{IN}}}\int_\tau \int_v S_H(\tau,v)\left|A_g(\tau,v)\right|^2 d\tau dv$$

(13)

where the interference-plus-noise energy E_{IN} is the energy perturbation of the desired symbol $c_{m_0,n_0}^{i_0}$, from other symbols over time varying multipath fading channel $H(\tau,v)$. For presentation simplicity, the desired symbol $c_{m_0,n_0}^{i_0}$ is chosen as $c_{0,0}^1$. Hence, E_{IN} can be expressed as:

$$E_{\mathrm{IN}} = \sigma_c^2 \int_\tau \int_v S_H(\tau,v)$$

$$\left[\sum_{z=[m,n,i]^{\mathrm{T}}\neq[0,0,1]^{\mathrm{T}}}\left|A_{g,\psi}\left(\left(m+\frac{i}{2}\right)T+\tau,nF+v\right)\right|^2\right.$$

$$\left.+\sum_{z=[m,n,i]^{\mathrm{T}}\neq[0,0,1]^{\mathrm{T}}}\left|A_{g,\psi}\left(\left(m+\frac{i}{2}\right)T+\frac{T}{2}+\tau,nF+\frac{F}{2}+v\right)\right|^2\right]$$

$$d\tau dv + \sigma_w^2\left|A_{g,\psi}(0,0)\right|$$

(14)

Clearly, the interference-plus-noise energy function E_{IN} is dependent on the channel scattering function and the pulse shape (through its ambiguity function). According to the form of channel scattering functions, the Max-SINR receiver can be discussed in two cases (Han & Zhang, 2009, Han & Zhang, 2010). Case A: DD channel with uniform power delay profile and uniform Doppler spectrum. Case B: DD channel with exponential power delay profile and U-shape Doppler spectrum.

A: DD Channel with Uniform Power Delay Profile and Uniform Doppler Spectrum

For the DD channel with uniform power delay profile and uniform Doppler spectrum, the scattering function can be expressed as (P. Matthias, 2002):

$$S_H(\tau,v) = 1/(2\tau_{\max}f_d) \quad (15)$$

with $\tau_{\max} \geq \tau \geq 0, |v| < f_d$. We assume that[2] $\psi(t) = g(t-\Delta t)e^{j2\pi\Delta ft}$, $\Delta f < f_d$, the SINR of the received signal over the DD channel with uniform power delay profile and uniform Doppler spectrum can be expressed as:

$$R_{\mathrm{SIN}}^{\mathrm{UNI}} = \frac{\sigma_c^2}{2\tau_{\max}f_d E_{\mathrm{IN}}^{\mathrm{UNI}}}\int_0^{\tau_{\max}} e^{-\pi(\tau-\Delta t)^2/\sigma}d\tau \int_{-f_d}^{f_d} e^{-\sigma\pi(v-\Delta f)^2}dv$$

(16)

Substituting (15) into (14), the interference-plus-noise energy $E_{\text{IN}}^{\text{UNI}}$ over DD channel with uniform power delay profile and uniform Doppler spectrum in (16) can be expressed as:

$$E_{\text{IN}}^{\text{UNI}} = \frac{\sigma_c^2}{2\tau_{\max}f_d}\left\{\sum_{[m,n,i]=[0,0,1]}\frac{\int_{(m+(i-1)/2)T}^{(m+(i-1)/2)T+\tau_{\max}}e^{-\pi(\tau-\Delta t)^2/\sigma}d\tau}{\int_{-f_d}^{f_d}e^{-\sigma\pi(nF+v-\Delta f)^2}dv}\right.$$
$$\left. + \sum_{[m,n,i]\neq[0,0,1]}\frac{\int_{(m+(i-1)/2)T}^{(m+(i-1)/2)T+\tau_{\max}}e^{-\pi(\tau-\Delta t)^2/\sigma}d\tau}{\int_{-f_d}^{f_d}e^{-\sigma\pi\left(nF+\frac{F}{2}+v-\Delta f\right)^2}dv}\right\} + \sigma_w^2\left|A_{g,\psi}(0,0)\right|$$

(17)

The theoretical SINR upper bound of the received signal over the DD channel with uniform power delay profile and uniform Doppler spectrum can be expressed as:

$$R_{\text{UB}}^{\text{UNI}} = \arg\max_{\Delta t,\Delta f}R_{\text{SIN}}^{\text{UNI}}$$

(18)

Plugging (16) and (17) in (18), the Max-SINR prototype pulse can be expressed as (see Appendix 1):

$$\psi(t) = g\left(t - \frac{\tau_{\max}}{2}\right)$$

(19)

We can see from (19) that there is a timing offset between the prototype pulses of the proposed Max-SINR receiver and the traditional projection receiver.

B: DD Channel with Exponential Power Delay Profile and U-Shape Doppler Spectrum

For the DD channel with exponential power delay profile and U-shape Doppler spectrum, the scattering function can be expressed as (P. Matthias, 2002):

$$S_H(\tau,v) = \frac{e^{-\tau/\tau_{\text{rms}}}}{\pi\tau_{\text{rms}}f_d\sqrt{1-\left(v/f_d\right)^2}}$$

(20)

with $\tau \geq 0, |v| < f_d$. We assume that $\psi(t) = g(t - \Delta t)e^{j2\pi\Delta ft}$, $\Delta f < f_d$, the SINR of the received signal over the DD channel with exponential power delay profile and U-shape Doppler spectrum can be expressed as:

$$R_{\text{SIN}}^{\text{EXP}} = \frac{\sigma_c^2}{\pi\tau_{\text{rms}}f_dE_{\text{IN}}^{\text{EXP}}}\int_0^\infty e^{-\tau/\tau_{\text{rms}}}e^{-\frac{\pi}{\sigma}(\tau-\Delta t)^2}d\tau$$
$$\int_{-f_d}^{f_d}e^{-\sigma\pi(v-\Delta f)^2}\Big/\sqrt{1-\left(v/f_d\right)^2}\,dv$$

(21)

Substituting (20) into (14), the interference-plus-noise energy function $E_{\text{IN}}^{\text{EXP}}$ over DD channel with exponential power delay profile and U-shape Doppler spectrum in (21) can be expressed as:

$$E_{\text{IN}}^{\text{EXP}} = \frac{\sigma_c^2}{\pi\tau_{\text{rms}}f_d}\left\{\sum_{[m,n,i]=[0,0,1]}\int_0^\infty e^{-\tau/\tau_{\text{rms}}}e^{-\pi\left((m+(i-1)/2)T+\tau-\Delta t\right)^2/\sigma}d\tau\right.$$
$$\int_{-f_d}^{f_d}e^{-\sigma\pi(nF+v-\Delta f)^2}\Big/\sqrt{1-\left(v/f_d\right)^2}\,dv$$
$$+ \sum_{[m,n,i]\neq[0,0,1]}\int_0^\infty e^{-\tau/\tau_{\text{rms}}}e^{-\pi\left((m+(i-1)/2)T+\tau-\Delta t\right)^2/\sigma}d\tau$$
$$\left.\int_{-f_d}^{f_d}e^{-\sigma\pi\left((n+1/2)F+v-\Delta f\right)^2}\Big/\sqrt{1-\left(v/f_d\right)^2}\,dv\right\}$$
$$+\sigma_w^2\left|A_{g,\psi}(0,0)\right|$$

(22)

The theoretical SINR upper bound of the received signal over the DD channel with exponential power delay profile and U-shape Doppler spectrum can be expressed as:

$$R_{\text{UB}}^{\text{EXP}} = \arg\max_{\Delta t,\Delta f}R_{\text{SIN}}^{\text{EXP}}$$

(23)

Plugging (21) and (22) in (23), the Max-SINR prototype pulse can be expressed as $\psi(t) = g(t - \Delta t)$ and (see Appendix 2)[3]:

$$\Delta t = \frac{\sigma}{2\pi\tau_{rms}} - \frac{1}{1.76}\sqrt{\frac{\sigma}{2\pi}}$$

$$\left(\frac{3.28\sqrt{\sigma}}{\tau_{rms}} - \sqrt{\frac{3.28^2\sigma}{\tau_{rms}^2} - 3.52\left(\frac{\sigma}{\tau_{rms}^2} - 4\right)} \right) \tag{24}$$

We can see from Equations (19) and (24) that the prototype pulses of the proposed Max-SINR receiver over DD channel are functions of channel maximum delay spread and RMS delay spread, respectively. In HMT system, as shown in (Han F. M., & Zhang X. D., 2007), the prototype pulse shape of the Gaussian window and the transmission pattern parameters T and F should be matched to the channel scattering function including maximum delay spread and RMS delay spread. In other words, the RMS delay spread and the maximum delay spread are known at the HMT transceiver. Recently, several channel estimation schemes for multicarrier modulation system with hexagonal TF lattice have been proposed in (Gao et al., 2009, Gao et al., 2011, Gao et al., 2011) and all this schemes are suitable for HMT system. Hence, it is reasonable to assume that the RMS delay spread priori known in HMT system.

SIMULATION AND DISCUSSION

In this section, we test the proposed Max-SINR receiver via computer simulations based on the discrete signal model. In the following simulations, the number of subcarriers for HMT system is chosen as $N=40$, and the length of prototype pulse is set to $N_g=600$. The center carrier frequency is $f_c=5$GHz and the sampling interval is set to $T_s=10^{-6}s$. The system parameters of HMT system are $F=25$kHz, $T=1\times10^{-4}s$ and the signaling efficiency $\rho=0.8$. σ for prototype pulse g(t) is set to $\sigma = T/\sqrt{3F}$ and α in [10] is set to $\alpha =2.1$. Traditional projection receiver proposed in (Han

& Zhang, 2007, Han & Zhang, 2009, Han & Zhang, 2010) is named as Traditional Projection Receiver (TPR) in the following simulation results.

A: SINR PERFORMANCE OF THE PROPOSED MAX-SINR RECEIVER FOR HMT SYSTEM

1. **SINR Performance of HMT System over DD channel with uniform power delay profile and uniform Doppler spectrum:** The SINR performance of different receivers with the variety of σ_c^2/σ_w^2 for HMT system over DD channels with uniform power delay profile and uniform Doppler spectrum is depicted in Figure 2. The CSF is set to $\vartheta = 0.07$ and $\vartheta = 0.2$, respectively. We can see from Figure 2 that the SINR performance of the proposed Max-SINR receiver outperforms TPR scheme about 0.5~1.5dB at $\vartheta = 0.07$ and 1~3dB at $\vartheta = 0.2$, respectively. The SINR gap between the proposed Max-SINR receiver and the theoretical SINR upper bound is smaller than 0.1dB at $\vartheta = 0.07$ and 0.2, respectively.

The SINR performance with the variety of channel spread factors ϑ at $\sigma_c^2/\sigma_w^2 = 20$dB over DD channels with uniform power delay profile and uniform Doppler spectrum is depicted in Figure 3. The SINR performance of the TPR scheme is depicted for comparison. It can be seen that there is a degradation of SINR with the increasing of channel spread factor. The proposed Max-SINR receiver obtains an approximation to the theoretical upper bound SINR performance within the full range of ϑ. Meanwhile, the proposed Max-SINR receiver obtains an about 3.5dB maximum SINR gain over TPR scheme at $\vartheta =0.35$, and the SINR gain increases as the CSF ϑ increases:

Figure 2. The SINR performance of different receivers with the variety of σ_c^2/σ_w^2 for HMT system over DD channel with uniform power delay profile and uniform Doppler spectrum

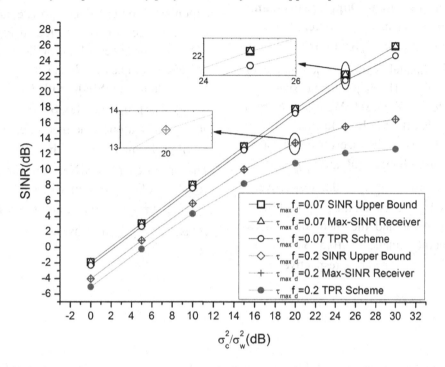

Figure 3. The SINR performance of different receivers with the variety of channel spread factors ϑ for HMT system over DD channel with uniform power delay profile and uniform doppler spectrum, $\sigma_c^2/\sigma_w^2 = 20\text{dB}$

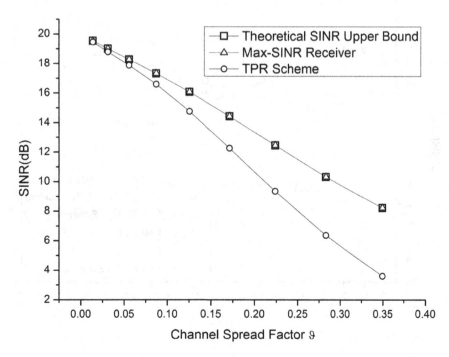

2. **Performance of HMT System over DD channel with exponential power delay profile and U-shape Doppler spectrum:** The SINR performance of different receivers with the variety of σ_c^2/σ_w^2 for HMT system over DD channels with exponential power delay profile and U-shape Doppler spectrum is depicted in Figure 4. We can see from Figure 4 that the SINR performance of the proposed Max-SINR receiver outperforms TPR scheme about 1~4dB at $\tau_{rms}f_d = 0.07$ and 1.5~3.5dB at $\tau_{rms}f_d = 0.2$, respectively. The SINR gap between the proposed Max-SINR receiver and the theoretical SINR upper bound is smaller than 0.5dB and 0.1dB at $\tau_{rms}f_d = 0.07$ and 0.2, respectively.

The SINR performance with the variety of $\tau_{rms}f_d$ at $\sigma_c^2/\sigma_w^2 = 20\text{dB}$, over DD channels with exponential power delay profile and U-shape Doppler spectrum is depicted in Figure 5. The SINR performance of the TPR scheme is depicted for comparison. It can be seen that there is a degradation of SINR with the increasing of $\tau_{rms}f_d$. The proposed Max-SINR receiver obtains an approximation to the theoretical upper bound SINR performance within the full range of $\tau_{rms}f_d$ The proposed Max-SINR receiver achieves an about 2.5dB maximum SINR gain over TPR scheme at $\tau_{rms}f_d = 0.35$, and the SINR gain increases as $\tau_{rms}f_d$ increases.

Figure 4. The SINR performance of different receivers with the variety of σ_c^2/σ_w^2 for HMT system over DD channel with exponential power delay profile and U-shape doppler spectrum

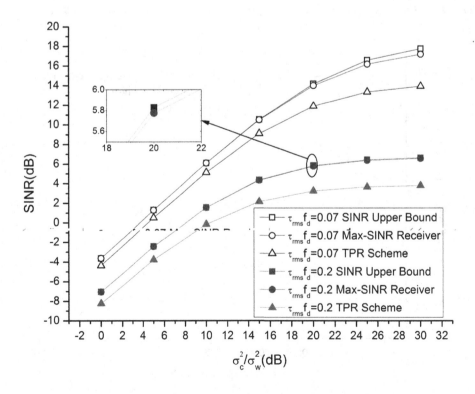

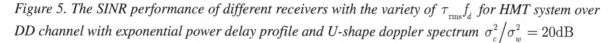

Figure 5. The SINR performance of different receivers with the variety of $\tau_{rms}f_d$ for HMT system over DD channel with exponential power delay profile and U-shape doppler spectrum $\sigma_c^2/\sigma_w^2 = 20$dB

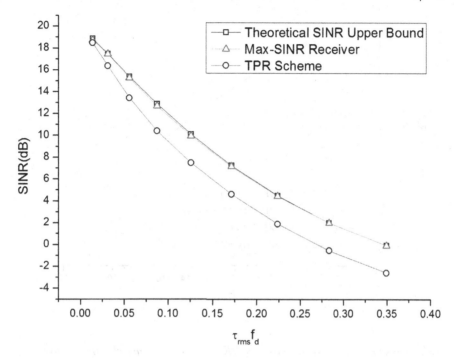

B: BER Performance of the Proposed Max-SINR Receiver for HMT System

The BER performance of the proposed Max-SINR receiver for HMT system over the DD channel with different channel scattering functions is given in Figure 6. For the DD channel with uniform power delay profile and uniform Doppler spectrum, named as DD-UNI in Figure 6, channel spread factor $\tau_{rms}f_d$ is set to 0.2, We can conclude from Figure 6 that the BER performance of the proposed Max-SINR receiver for HMT system over DD-UNI channel outperforms TPR receiver about 2dB at $E_b/N_0 = 20$dB. For the DD channel with exponential power delay profile and U-shape Doppler spectrum, named as DD-EXP in Figure 6, $\tau_{rms}f_d$ is set to 0.1. We can see from Figure 6

that the proposed Max-SINR receiver over DD-EXP channel outperforms TPR receiver on the BER performance and the performance gain is about 2.5dB at $E_b/N_0 = 20$dB.

C: Robustness of the Proposed Max-SINR Receiver against Channel Delay Spread Estimation Errors

The robustness of the proposed Max-SINR receiver against channel delay spread estimation errors is depicted in Figure 7. Estimation errors of τ_{rms} and τ_{max} for DD-EXP channel and DD-UNI channel are modeled as uniformly distributed random variables in the interval $\left[-\tau_{rms}/2, \tau_{rms}/2\right]$ and $\left[-\tau_{max}/2, \tau_{max}/2\right]$, respectively.

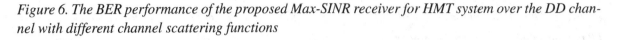

Figure 6. The BER performance of the proposed Max-SINR receiver for HMT system over the DD channel with different channel scattering functions

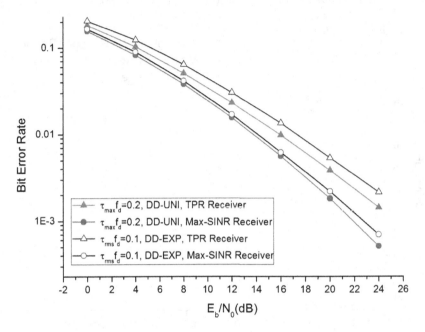

Figure 7. The robustness of the proposed Max-SINR receiver against channel delay spread estimation errors. Estimation errors of τ_{rms} and τ_{max} for DD-EXP channel and DD-UNI channel are modeled as uniformly distributed random variables in the interval $\left[-\tau_{rms}/2, \tau_{rms}/2\right]$ and $\left[-\tau_{max}/2, \tau_{max}/2\right]$, respectively

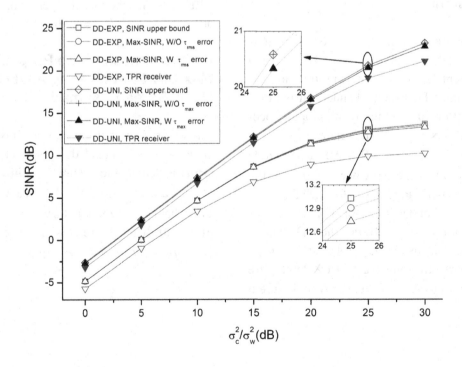

In Figure 7, the channel spread factor ϑ of DD channel with uniform power delay profile and uniform Doppler spectrum is set to 0.1. We can see from Figure 7 that the SINR gap between the SINR upper bound and the proposed Max-SINR receiver with estimation error of τ_{max} is within 0.1dB and 0.5dB at $\sigma_c^2 / \sigma_w^2 = 0$dB and 30dB, respectively.

The SINR performance of the proposed Max-SINR receiver over DD channels with exponential power delay profile and U-shape Doppler spectrum at $\tau_{rms} f_d = 0.1$ is given in Figure 7. The SINR gap between the SINR upper bound and the proposed Max-SINR receiver with estimation error of τ_{rms} is within 0.1dB and 0.7dB at $\sigma_c^2 / \sigma_w^2 = 0$dB and 30dB, respectively. SINR performance of the TPR receiver over DD-UNI and DD-EXP channel is also depicted in Figure 7 for comparison. The proposed Max-SINR receiver outperforms TPR scheme when there exists estimation errors of τ_{rms} and τ_{max}. In summary, the proposed Max-SINR receiver is robust to the estimation errors of τ_{rms} and τ_{max}.

CONCLUSION

A novel receiver based on Max-SINR criterion for HMT system over DD channel with different channel scattering functions is proposed in this chapter. Theoretical analyses show that there is a timing offset between the prototype pulses of the proposed Max-SINR receiver and the traditional projection receiver. The timing offset should be matched to the channel scattering factor of the DD channel. The closed form timing offset expressions of prototype pulse for Max-SINR HMT receiver over DD channel with different channel scattering functions are derived. Simulation results show that the proposed Max-SINR receiver outperforms traditional projection scheme and obtains an approximation to the theoretical upper bound SINR performance within the full

range of channel spread factor. Moreover, the proposed Max-SINR receiver obtains an about 2dB BER performance gain over DD channel at SNR=20dB. Meanwhile, the SINR performance of the proposed prototype pulse is robust to the channel delay spread estimation errors.

REFERENCES

Abbas, H. K., Waleed, A. M., & Nihad, S. (2010). The performance of multi-wavelets based OFDM system under different channel conditions. *Digital Signal Processing*, 20, 472–482. doi:10.1016/j.dsp.2009.06.022 doi:10.1016/j.dsp.2009.06.022

Bello, P. A. (1963). Characterization of randomly time-variant linear channels. *IEEE Transactions on Communications Systems*, 11, 360–393. doi:10.1109/TCOM.1963.1088793 doi:10.1109/TCOM.1963.1088793

Cohen, L. (1995). *Time-frequency analysis*. Englewood Cliffs, NJ: Prentice-Hall.

Conway, J. H., & Sloane, N. J. A. (1998). *Sphere packings, lattices and groups* (3rd ed.). New York: Springer-Verlag.

Das, S., & Schniter, P. (2007). Max-SINR ISI/ICI-shaping multicarrier communication over the doubly dispersive channel. *IEEE Transactions on Signal Processing*, 55, 5782–5795. doi:10.1109/TSP.2007.901660 doi:10.1109/TSP.2007.901660

Gao, X., Wang, W., Xia, X. G., Au, E. K. S., & You, X. H. (2011). Cyclic prefixed OQAM-OFDM and its application to single-carrier FDMA. *IEEE Transactions on Communications*, 59, 1467–1480. doi:10.1109/TCOMM.2011.031611.100045 doi:10.1109/TCOMM.2011.031611.100045

Han, F. M., & Zhang, X. D. (2007). Hexagonal multicarrier modulation: A robust transmission scheme for time-frequency dispersive channels. *IEEE Transactions on Signal Processing*, 55, 1955–1961. doi:10.1109/TSP.2006.890884 doi:10.1109/TSP.2006.890884

Han, F. M., & Zhang, X. D. (2009). MLSD for hexagonal multicarrier transmission with time-frequency localized pulses. IEEE Transactions on Vehicular Technology, 58, 1598–1604. doi:10.1109/TVT.2008.927032 doi:10.1109/TVT.2008.927032

Han, F. M., & Zhang, X. D. (2010). Asymptotic equivalence of two multicarrier transmission schemes in terms of robustness against time-frequency dispersive channels. IEEE Transactions on Vehicular Technology, 59, 1598–1604.

Jung, P., & Wunder, G. (2007). The WSSUS pulse design problem in multicarrier transmission. IEEE Transactions on Communications, 55, 1918–1928. doi:10.1109/TCOMM.2007.906426 doi:10.1109/TCOMM.2007.906426

Kingsbury, N. (2005). *Approximation formulae for the Gaussian error integral*. Retrieved from http://cnx.org/content/m11067/2.4/

Kumbasar, V., & Kucur, O. (2007). ICI reduction in OFDM systems by using improved sinc power pulse. Digital Signal Processing, 17, 997–1006. doi:10.1016/j.dsp.2007.03.010 doi:10.1016/j.dsp.2007.03.010

Lin, G., Lundheim, L., & Holte, N. (2008). Optimal pulses robust to carrier frequency offset for OFDM/QAM systems. IEEE Communications Letters, 12, 161–163. doi:10.1109/LCOMM.2008.071680 doi:10.1109/LCOMM.2008.071680

Ma, M., Jiao, B., & Lee, C. Y. (2008). A dual-window technique for enhancing robustness of OFDM against frequency offset. IEEE Communications Letters, 12, 17–19. doi:10.1109/LCOMM.2008.071226 doi:10.1109/LCOMM.2008.071226

Matthias, P. (2002). Mobile fading channels. West Sussex, UK: John Wiley & Sons, Ltd.

Meng, G., Shen, Y. H., & Yuan, Z. G. (2009). Maximum Doppler spread estimation by tracking the delay-subspace for LOFDM systems in doubly dispersive fading channels. In *Proc. 2009 IEEE Int. Conf. Wireless Communications and Signal Processing*. IEEE.

Meng, G., Shen, Y. H., & Yuan, Z. G. (2011). Cyclostationarity-based and super-imposed pilot-aided maximum doppler spread estimation for LOFDM systems in doubly-dispersive channels. Frequenz, 65, 93–101.

Meng, G., Shen, Y.H., & Xu, K. (2011). A low complexity frequency domain pilot time domain doubly average channel estimation for LOFDM systems. *Przeglad Elektrotechniczny*, 270-274.

Siohan, P., Siclet, C., & Lacaille, N. (2002). Analysis and design of OFDM/OQAM systems based on filterbank theory. IEEE Transactions on Signal Processing, 50, 1170–1183. doi:10.1109/78.995073 doi:10.1109/78.995073

Strohmer, T., & Beaver, S. (2003). Optimal OFDM design for time-frequency dispersive channels. IEEE Transactions on Communications, 51, 1111–1122. doi:10.1109/TCOMM.2003.814200 doi:10.1109/TCOMM.2003.814200

Wu, J., & Xiao, C. (2007). Performance analysis of wireless systems with doubly selective rayleigh fading. IEEE Transactions on Vehicular Technology, 56, 721–730. doi:10.1109/TVT.2007.891438 doi:10.1109/TVT.2007.891438

Wu, J., Zheng, Y. R., Letaief, K. B., & Xiao, C. (2005). Matched filter bound of wireless systems over frequency selective channels with receiver timing phase offset. In *Proc. IEEE Global Telecommun. Conf. (GLOBECOM05)*, (pp. 3758-3762). IEEE.

Wu, J., Zheng, Y. R., Letaief, K. B., & Xiao, C. (2007). On the error performance of wireless systems with frequency selective fading and receiver timing phase offset. IEEE Transactions on Wireless Communications, 6, 720–729. doi:10.1109/TWC.2007.05417 doi:10.1109/TWC.2007.05417

Xu, K., & Shen, Y. H. (2009). Effects of carrier frequency offset, timing offset, and channel spread factor on the performance of hexagonal multicarrier modulation systems. EURASIP Journal on Wireless Communications and Networking, 1–8.

Xu, K., Lv, Z., Xu, Y., & Zhang, D. (2013). Max-SINR based timing synchronization scheme in hexagonal multicarrier transmission. Wireless Personal Communications, 68, 1789–1805. doi:10.1007/s11277-012-0550-5 doi:10.1007/s11277-012-0550-5

Xu, K., Xu, Y., & Zhang, D. (2011). SINR analysis of hexagonal multicarrier transmission systems in the presence of insufficient synchronization for doubly dispersive channel. Frequenz, 65, 149–157. doi:10.1515/freq.2011.020 doi:10.1515/freq.2011.020

Xu, K., Xu, Y. Y., Xia, X. C., & Zhang, D. M. (2012). On Max-SINR receiver for hexagonal multicarrier transmission over doubly dispersive channel. In *Proc. 2012 IEEE Global Telecommun. Conf. (GLOBECOM12)*, (pp. 3673 - 3678). IEEE.

Xu, K., Xu, Y., Zhang, D., & Ma, W. (2013). On max-SINR receiver for HMT over doubly dispersive channel. IEEE Transactions on Vehicular Technology, 62, 2381–2387. doi:10.1109/TVT.2013.2239674 doi:10.1109/TVT.2013.2239674

ENDNOTES

[1] LOFDM system confines the transmission pulses to a set of orthogonal ones. As pointed out in (Han & Zhang, 2007), these orthogonalized pulses destroy the TF concentration of the initial pulses, hence lower the robustness to the time and frequency dispersion caused by the DD channel. On the other hand, the orthogonalized pulses are constructed from a nonorthogonal set of Gaussian pulses. As shown in (Strohmer & Beaver, 2003), the orthogonalization process needs to compute all the elements of the Gram matrix, which leads to high implementation complexity.

[2] It is shown in (Wu & Xiao, 2007, Wu et al., 2007, Wu et al., 2005) that the optimum sampling time of wireless communication systems over DD channel is dependent on the power distribution of the channel profiles, and that zero timing offset does not always yield the best system performance. In other words, there is a timing offset between the prototype pulses at the transmitter and the receiver. Meanwhile, the DD propagation channel causes transmission signal dispersion in both the time and frequency domains. Hence, we assume that there is a frequency offset between the prototype pulses at the transmitter and the receiver.

[3] In (Das & Schniter, 2007), the Max-SINR prototype pulse g of multicarrier transmission system with rectangular TF lattice over DD channel is obtained by maximizing the generalized Rayleigh quotient $\hat{g} = \arg\max \left(g^H Bg\right)/\left(g^H Ag\right)$. The solution is the generalized eigenvector of the matrix pair (B, A) corresponding to the largest generalized eigenvalue. It is shown that there is a delay between the transmitted Gaussian prototype pulse and the received Gaussian prototype pulse. In this chapter, the close form time offset expressions between the transmitted and received prototype pulse of multicarrier transmission system with hexagonal TF lattice is derived.

APPENDIX 1: PROOF OF EQUATION (19)

The SINR of the received signal over DD channel with uniform power delay profile and uniform Doppler spectrum can be expressed as:

$$R_{\text{SIN}}^{\text{UNI}} \approx \underbrace{\frac{\sigma_c^2}{2\sigma_w^2 \tau_{\max} f_d} \int_0^{\tau_{\max}} e^{-\pi(\tau - \Delta t)^2/\sigma} d\tau}_{R^{\text{UNI}}(\Delta t)} \underbrace{\int_{-f_d}^{f_d} e^{-\sigma\pi(\upsilon - \Delta f)^2} d\upsilon}_{R^{\text{UNI}}(\Delta f)} \tag{25}$$

We can see from Equation (25) that $R_{\text{SIN}}^{\text{UNI}}$ is the product of two functions $R^{\text{UNI}}\left(\Delta t\right)$ and $R^{\text{UNI}}\left(\Delta f\right)$ with respect to Δt and Δf, respectively. Hence, the optimal timing offset Δt and the optimal frequency offset Δf can be obtained independently.

The optimal timing offset Δt can be obtained by taking the partial derivative of $R_{\text{SIN}}^{\text{UNI}}$ with respect to Δt and solving the partial derivative equal to zero for Δt:

$$\frac{\partial R_{\text{SIN}}^{\text{UNI}}}{\partial \Delta t} = 0 \tag{26}$$

Plugging (25) in (26) and ignoring the constant items with respect to Δt, the partial derivative can be rewritten as:

$$\int_0^{\tau_{\max}} \frac{2\pi\left(\tau - \Delta t\right)}{\sigma} e^{\frac{-\pi(\tau - \Delta t)^2}{\sigma}} d\tau = 0 \tag{27}$$

The exponential function is a non-negative function and $2\pi\left(\tau - \Delta t\right)/\sigma$ is a monotonically increasing function. If and only if $0 < \Delta t < \tau_{\max}$, Equation (27) is solvable. Under the assumption that $0 < \Delta t < \tau_{\max}$, we can rewrite (27) as:

$$\int_{\Delta t}^{\tau_{\max}} \frac{2\pi\left(\tau - \Delta t\right)}{\sigma} e^{\frac{-\pi(\tau - \Delta t)^2}{\sigma}} d\tau +$$
$$\int_0^{\Delta t} \frac{2\pi\left(\tau - \Delta t\right)}{\sigma} e^{\frac{-\pi(\tau - \Delta t)^2}{\sigma}} d\tau = 0 \tag{28}$$

Let $\tau' = \tau - \Delta t$, we can rewrite (28) as:

$$\int_0^{\tau_{\max} - \Delta t} \frac{2\pi\tau'}{\sigma} e^{\frac{-\pi(\tau')^2}{\sigma}} d\tau' + \int_{-\Delta t}^0 \frac{2\pi\tau'}{\sigma} e^{\frac{-\pi(\tau')^2}{\sigma}} d\tau' = 0 \tag{29}$$

The exponential function is a non-negative function and $2\pi\tau'/\sigma$ is an odd function. We can rewrite (29) as:

$$\underbrace{\int_0^{\tau_{\max}-\Delta t} \frac{2\pi\tau'}{\sigma} e^{\frac{-\pi(\tau')^2}{\sigma}} d\tau'}_{\alpha(\Delta t)} = \underbrace{\int_0^{\Delta t} \frac{2\pi\tau'}{\sigma} e^{\frac{-\pi(\tau')^2}{\sigma}} d\tau'}_{\beta(\Delta t)} \tag{30}$$

Hence, $\partial R_{\text{SIN}}^{\text{UNI}}/\partial\Delta t = \alpha(\Delta t) - \beta(\Delta t)$ can be expressed as:

$$\begin{cases} \partial R_{\text{SIN}}^{\text{UNI}}/\partial\Delta t < 0, & \Delta t > \tau_{\max}/2 \\ \partial R_{\text{SIN}}^{\text{UNI}}/\partial\Delta t = 0, & \Delta t = \tau_{\max}/2 \\ \partial R_{\text{SIN}}^{\text{UNI}}/\partial\Delta t > 0, & \Delta t < \tau_{\max}/2 \end{cases} \tag{31}$$

The solution of equation $\partial R_{\text{SIN}}^{\text{UNI}}/\partial\Delta t = 0$ is $\Delta t = \tau_{\max}/2$ and the SINR of the received symbols obtains the maximum value while $\Delta t = \tau_{\max}/2$.

The optimal frequency offset Δf can be obtained by taking the partial derivative of $R_{\text{SIN}}^{\text{UNI}}$ with respect to Δf and solving the partial derivative equal to zero for Δf:

$$\frac{\partial R_{\text{SIN}}^{\text{UNI}}}{\partial\Delta f} = 0 \tag{32}$$

Plugging (25) in (32) and ignoring the constant items with respect to Δf, the partial derivative can be rewritten as:

$$\int_{-f_d}^{f_d} 2\sigma\pi\left(\upsilon - \Delta f\right) e^{-\sigma\pi\left(\upsilon - \Delta f\right)^2} d\upsilon = 0 \tag{33}$$

The exponential function is a non-negative function and $2\sigma\pi\left(\upsilon - \Delta f\right)$ is a monotonically increasing function. Under the assumption that $\left|\Delta f\right| < f_d$, we can rewrite (33) as:

$$\int_0^{f_d-\Delta f} 2\sigma\pi\upsilon' e^{-\sigma\pi(\upsilon')^2} d\upsilon' + \int_{-f_d-\Delta f}^0 2\sigma\pi\upsilon' e^{-\sigma\pi(\upsilon')^2} d\upsilon' = 0 \tag{34}$$

where $\upsilon' = \upsilon - \Delta f$. The exponential function is a non-negative function and $2\sigma\pi\upsilon'$ is an odd function. We can rewrite (34) as:

$$\underbrace{\int_0^{f_d - \Delta f} 2\sigma\pi\upsilon' e^{-\sigma\pi(\upsilon')^2} d\upsilon'}_{\kappa(\Delta f)} =$$
$$\underbrace{\int_0^{f_d + \Delta f} 2\sigma\pi\upsilon' e^{-\sigma\pi(\upsilon')^2} d\upsilon'}_{\chi(\Delta f)}$$

(35)

Hence, $\partial R_{\text{SIN}}^{\text{UNI}} / \partial\Delta f = \kappa(\Delta t) - \chi(\Delta t)$ can be expressed as:

$$\begin{cases} \partial R_{\text{SIN}}^{\text{UNI}} / \partial\Delta f < 0, & \Delta f > 0 \\ \partial R_{\text{SIN}}^{\text{UNI}} / \partial\Delta f = 0, & \Delta f = 0 \\ \partial R_{\text{SIN}}^{\text{UNI}} / \partial\Delta f > 0, & \Delta f < 0 \end{cases}$$

(36)

The solution of partial derivative $\partial R_{\text{SIN}}^{\text{UNI}} / \partial\Delta f = 0$ is $\Delta f = 0$. Meanwhile, the SINR of the received symbols obtains the maximum value while $\Delta f = 0$.

In summary, for the DD channel with uniform power delay profile and uniform Doppler spectrum, time offset and frequency offset of the Max-SINR prototype pulse at the receiver can be expressed as $\Delta t = \tau_{\max}/2$ and $\Delta f = 0$, respectively.

APPENDIX 2: PROOF OF EQUATION (24)

Under the assumption that $\psi(t) = g(t - \Delta t) e^{j2\pi\Delta ft}$, the SINR of the received signal can be expressed as:

$$R_{\text{SIN}}^{\text{EXP}} = \frac{\sigma_c^2}{\pi\tau_{\text{rms}} f_d E_{\text{IN}}^{\text{EXP}}} \int_0^\infty e^{-\tau/\tau_{\text{rms}}} e^{-\frac{\pi}{\sigma}(\tau - \Delta t)^2} d\tau$$
$$\int_{-f_d}^{f_d} e^{-\sigma\pi(\upsilon - \Delta f)^2} \bigg/ \sqrt{1 - (\upsilon/f_d)^2}\, d\upsilon \approx \frac{\sigma_c^2}{\pi\sigma_w^2 \tau_{\text{rms}} f_d}$$
$$\int_{-f_d}^{f_d} e^{-\sigma\pi(\upsilon - \Delta f)^2} \bigg/ \sqrt{1 - (\upsilon/f_d)^2}\, d\upsilon \left(\underbrace{e^{\frac{\sigma}{4\pi\tau_{\text{rms}}^2} + \frac{\Delta t}{\tau_{\text{rms}}}}}_{a(\Delta t)} \underbrace{\int_0^\infty e^{-\frac{\pi}{\sigma}\left(\tau - \Delta t + \frac{\sigma}{2\pi\tau_{\text{rms}}}\right)^2} d\tau}_{b(\Delta t)} \right)$$

(37)

where:

$$b(\Delta t) = \sqrt{\frac{\sigma}{\pi}} \int_{\sqrt{\frac{\pi}{\sigma}}\left(\frac{\sigma}{2\pi\tau_{\text{rms}}} - \Delta t\right)}^\infty e^{-x^2} dx$$
$$= \frac{\sqrt{\sigma}}{2} erfc\left(\sqrt{\frac{\pi}{\sigma}} \left(\frac{\sigma}{2\pi\tau_{\text{rms}}} - \Delta t \right) \right)$$

(38)

where $erfc(\cdot)$ is the complementary error function. If $x>0$, we may obtain an approximate solution of the complementary error function $erfc(\cdot)$ by (Kingsbury, 2005):

$$erfc\left(\frac{x}{\sqrt{2}}\right) \approx \frac{2e^{-\frac{x^2}{2}}}{1.64x + \sqrt{0.76x^2 + 4}} \tag{39}$$

We can see from Equation (37) that $R_{\text{SIN}}^{\text{EXP}}$ is also the product of two functions with respect to Δt and Δf, respectively. Hence, the optimal timing offset Δt and the optimal frequency offset Δf can be obtained independently. The optimal timing offset Δt can be obtained by solving the gradient $a(\Delta t) b(\Delta t)$ with respect to Δt to zero:

$$\frac{da(\Delta t)}{d\Delta t} b(\Delta t) + \frac{db(\Delta t)}{d\Delta t} a(\Delta t) = 0 \tag{40}$$

where $da(\Delta t)/d\Delta t = -a(\Delta t)/\tau_{\text{rms}}$ and $db(\Delta t)/d\Delta t$ can be expressed as:

$$\frac{db(\Delta t)}{d\Delta t} = e^{-\frac{\pi}{\sigma}\left(\frac{\sigma}{2\pi\tau_{\text{rms}}} - \Delta t\right)^2} \tag{41}$$

hence, Equation (40) can be rewritten as:

$$\begin{aligned}
\frac{b(\Delta t)}{\tau_{\text{rms}}} &= e^{-\frac{\pi}{\sigma}\left(\frac{\sigma}{2\pi\tau_{\text{rms}}} - \Delta t\right)^2} = \\
&\frac{\sqrt{\sigma}}{2\tau_{\text{rms}}} erfc\left(\sqrt{\frac{\pi}{\sigma}}\left(\frac{\sigma}{2\pi\tau_{\text{rms}}} - \Delta t\right)\right) \approx \\
&\frac{\sqrt{\sigma}}{\tau_{\text{rms}}} e^{-\frac{\pi}{\sigma}\left(\frac{\sigma}{2\pi\tau_{\text{rms}}} - \Delta t\right)^2} \\
&\left(1.64\sqrt{\frac{2\pi}{\sigma}}\left(\frac{\sigma}{2\pi\tau_{\text{rms}}} - \Delta t\right) + \sqrt{\frac{1.52\pi}{\sigma}\left(\frac{\sigma}{2\pi\tau_{\text{rms}}} - \Delta t\right)^2 + 4}\right)^{-1}
\end{aligned} \tag{42}$$

Equation (42) can be simplified to a quadratic equation. Under the constraint of $\Delta t > 0$, the solution of the quadratic equation can be expressed as:

$$
\Delta t = \frac{\sigma}{2\pi\tau_{\text{rms}}} - \frac{1}{1.76}\sqrt{\frac{\sigma}{2\pi}}
$$
$$
\left(\frac{3.28\sqrt{\sigma}}{\tau_{\text{rms}}} - \sqrt{\frac{3.28^2\,\sigma}{\tau_{\text{rms}}^2} - 3.52\left(\frac{\sigma}{\tau_{\text{rms}}^2} - 4\right)} \right)
$$

(43)

The optimal timing offset Δf can be obtained by solving the partial derivative $R_{\text{SIN}}^{\text{EXP}}$ with respect to Δf to zero:

$$
\frac{\partial R_{\text{SIN}}^{\text{EXP}}}{\partial \Delta f} = 0
$$

(44)

Let $\Xi(\Delta f)$ denotes the partial derivative $\partial R_{\text{SIN}}^{\text{EXP}} / \partial \Delta f$. Plugging (35) in (42) and ignoring the constant items with respect to Δf, $\Xi(\Delta f)$ can be rewritten as:

$$
\Xi(\Delta f) = \int_{-f_d}^{f_d} \frac{2\pi\sigma\left(v - \Delta f\right) e^{-\sigma\pi\left(v - \Delta f\right)^2}}{\sqrt{1 - \left(v/f_d\right)^2}}\, dv
$$

(45)

Both of the exponential function and $\sqrt{1 - \left(v/f_d\right)^2}$ are non-negative, and $2\pi\sigma\left(v - \Delta f\right)$ is a monotonically increasing function. Under the assumption that $\left|\Delta f\right| < f_d$, $\Xi(-\Delta f)$ can be expressed as:

$$
\begin{aligned}
\Xi(-\Delta f) &= \int_{-f_d}^{f_d} \frac{2\pi\sigma\left(v + \Delta f\right) e^{-\sigma\pi\left(v + \Delta f\right)^2}}{\sqrt{1 - \left(v/f_d\right)^2}}\, dv \\
&= \int_{-f_d}^{f_d} \frac{2\pi\sigma\left(-v + \Delta f\right) e^{-\sigma\pi\left(-v + \Delta f\right)^2}}{\sqrt{1 - \left(-v/f_d\right)^2}}\, dv \\
&= -\int_{-f_d}^{f_d} \frac{2\pi\sigma\left(v - \Delta f\right) e^{-\sigma\pi\left(v - \Delta f\right)^2}}{\sqrt{1 - \left(v/f_d\right)^2}}\, dv \\
&= -\Xi(\Delta f)
\end{aligned}
$$

(46)

Hence, $\Xi\left(\Delta f\right), \left|\Delta f\right| < f_d$, is a continuous odd function. Meanwhile, $\partial^2 R_{\mathrm{SIN}}^{\mathrm{EXP}} \big/ \partial \Delta f^2 = \partial \Xi\left(\Delta f\right) \big/ \partial \Delta f$ can be expressed as:

$$\frac{\partial \Xi\left(\Delta f\right)}{\partial \Delta f} = \int_{-f_d}^{f_d} \frac{2\pi\sigma \left[2\pi\sigma\left(\upsilon - \Delta f\right)^2 - 1\right] e^{-\sigma\pi\left(\upsilon - \Delta f\right)^2}}{\sqrt{1 - \left(\upsilon / f_d\right)^2}} \, d\upsilon \tag{47}$$

Practical wireless channels usually satisfy that $\vartheta = \tau_{\max} f_d \ll 1$ (Bello, 1963) and the optimal system parameter for HMT over DD channels can be chosen as $\sigma = \tau_{\max} / f_d$ (Han & Zhang, 2007). Hence, σ in (47) satisfies $\sigma \ll 1/\Delta f^2$ and $\partial \Xi\left(\Delta f\right) \big/ \partial \Delta f < 0$, $\left|\Delta f\right| < f_d$. We can conclude from Equations (46) and (47) that $\Xi\left(\Delta f\right), \left|\Delta f\right| < f_d$, is a continuous odd function and $\partial \Xi\left(\Delta f\right) \big/ \partial \Delta f < 0$, therefore, the necessary and sufficient condition of $R_{\mathrm{SIN}}^{\mathrm{EXP}}$ to obtain its maximum value is $\Delta f = 0$.

In summary, for the DD channel with exponential power delay profile and U-shape Doppler spectrum, time offset and frequency offset of the Max-SINR prototype pulse at the receiver can be expressed as Equation (43) and $\Delta f = 0$, respectively.

Chapter 5
Collaborative Mobile Clusters:
An Energy–Efficient Emerging Paradigm

Zheng Chang
University of Jyväskylä, Finland

Tapani Ristaniemi
University of Jyväskylä, Finland

ABSTRACT

Future wireless communication systems are expected to offer several gigabits data rate. It can be anticipated that the advanced communication techniques can enhance the capability of mobile terminals to support high data traffic. However, aggressive technique induces high energy consumption for the circuits of terminals, which drain the batteries fast and consequently limit user experience in future wireless networks. In order to solve such a problem, a scheme called collaborative mobile cluster is foreseen as one of the potential solutions to reduce energy consumption per node in a network by exploiting collaboration within a cluster of nearby mobile terminals. This chapter provides a detailed analysis of the energy consumption of a terminal joining the cluster and also analyzes the conditions for energy savings opportunities.

1. INTRODUCTION

By utilizing new technologies for cellular environments, such as Orthogonal Frequency Division Multiple Access (OFDMA) in the downlink, Single-carrier Frequency-Division Multiple Access (SC-FDMA) in the uplink and multiple input multiple output (MIMO) schemes, the next generation wireless network is going towards offering high data rate multimedia services to the user. As the fast growth of wireless market, multicast/broadcast services, such as IPTV will become more popular. Meanwhile, the dramatic evolution of smart phones makes changes to how we use these mobile devices. For instance, the demand for sharing content among users, watching TV and other internet activities are surprisingly arisen. In this chapter, an emerging energy efficient paradigm, namely collaborative mobile cluster (CMC) is introduced to deal with such mobile evolution. The CMC model is foreseen as a potential platform to provide broadcast services and boost up sharing capabilities for mobile users with reduced energy consumption. In this section, next generation networks as well as some other background information are briefly overviewed.

DOI: 10.4018/978-1-4666-4888-3.ch005

1.1. Background

The wireless communications industry has witnessed tremendous growth in the past decade with over four billion wireless subscribers worldwide. The first generation analog cellular systems supported voice communication with limited roaming capability. Later on, the second generation digital systems brought higher data rate and better voice quality than did their analog counterparts. The current third generation (3G) cellular network is offering high-speed data transmissions, such as VoIP, etc, to the mobile subscribers. In order to ensure the competitiveness of Universal Mobile Telecommunications System (UMTS) for the coming 10 years and beyond, concepts for UMTS Long Term Evolution (LTE) have been investigated. The focus of LTE is to provide a high-data-rate, low-latency and packet-optimized radio access technology supporting flexible bandwidth deployments (3GPP TR 25.913). In parallel, a new network architecture is designed with the goal to support packet-switched traffic with seamless mobility, quality of service and minimal latency (3GPP TR 23.882, 2009).

In the physical layer (PHY) of LTE, according to the initial requirements defined by the 3rd Generation Partnership Project (3GPP), the network should support peak data rates of more than 100 Mb/s over the downlink and 50 Mb/s over the uplink. A flexible transmission bandwidth ranging from 1.25 to 20 MHz will provide support for users with different capabilities. These requirements will be fulfilled by employing new technologies for cellular environments, such as OFDMA in the downlink, SC-FDMA in the uplink and multi antenna (or MIMO) schemes. Additionally, channel variations in the time/frequency domain are exploited through link adaptation and frequency-domain scheduling, giving a substantial increase in spectral efficiency. In order to support transmission in paired and unpaired spectrum, frequency division duplex (FDD) as well as time division duplex (TDD) modes are supported by the LTE air interface.

In the past, cellular systems (e.g. 1G) have mostly focused on transmission of data intended for a single user and not on broadcast services. Broadcast networks, exemplified by the radio and TV broadcasting networks, have on the other hand focused on covering large areas and have offered no or limited possibilities for transmission of data intended for a single user. In the next generation (e.g. 4G) networks, the support of broadcast or multicast service can be expected as an essential part and it is important for offering multimedia services to different users. For example, support of MBMS (Multimedia Broadcast Multicast Services) is a requirement for LTE and will be an integral part of LTE (3GPP TR 36.440, 2010).

1.2. Motivation

As expected, above mentioned future communication systems are going toward offering even gigabits data rate. In order to support such high data traffic, aggressive wireless technique will be utilized to the user equipments (UEs), which consequently induce high energy consumption (Chu, Chen & Fettweis, 2012). It is essential that these UEs can fully exploit the throughput gains offered by future communication systems whenever possible. Meanwhile, with the dramatic evaluations of smart phones, the way how people use cell phone is changing. Instead of simply making calls and sending short text messages, multimedia services are demonstrating the usage of cell phone. Moreover, due to the fact that the social medium and networks are becoming popular, the demand for sharing content among users is arisen as well.

On the other hand, the evaluation of wireless networks brings us facing many inherent problems. Telecommunications data volume increases approximately by an order of 10 every 5 years, which results in an increase of the associated energy consumption by approximately 16–20 percent per annum (3GPP TR 25.913, 2009). The escalation of energy consumption in wireless networks directly results in increased greenhouse gas emission, which has been recognized as a major threat to environmental protection and sustainable development. From the users' point of view, the high energy consumption restricts this due to the capacity limitation of battery and the user experience of high speed transmission would be seriously impacted. Therefore, reducing energy consumption emerges as a critical issue to prolong the battery life in the future wireless networks.

Motivated the aforementioned challenges, we introduce the CMC model, where a cluster of resource-constrained nodes that can perform receiving and decoding cooperatively and in a distributive manner. By utilizing such user-cooperation capability, the CMC is foreseen as energy efficient solutions for offering different services for users, such as broadcast services, content sharing, etc.

1.3. Related Works

For energy saving purpose, some research works have been done by improving transmitting and receiving mechanisms for a single receiver (Gür & Alagöz, 2011; Bontu & Illidge, 2009). Gür & & Alagöz (2011) introduced a resource allocation scheme which can dynamically allocate time and frequency to reduce the receiving energy consumption per single receiver. In (Bontu & Illidge, 2009), an overview of discontinuous reception (DRX) which is used in LTE to reduce receiver power consumption was presented. Meanwhile Datla, et al (2009) and Datla, et al (2012) dedicated the work on the power saving schemes for wireless distributed computing networks. However, these contributions focus more on power saving performance of computing rather than the one of communication. In (Radwan & Rodriguez,

2012), short range cooperation among MTs was proposed as a key idea to reduce the transmit energy consumption for the transmission from MTs to AP. Energy saving gains obtained by using different combination of technologies for short range communication, such as WLAN and WiMAX, WLAN and WLAN were also derived in (Radwan & Rodriguez,2012). In order to improve the throughput, Alonso-Zarate, et al (2013) introduced Multi-Radio ARQ schemes for hybrid networks combining long-range and short-range communications. However, these studies consider transmit energy consumption only.

1.4. Notations

Some key notations are summarized in Table 1.

2. DEFINING CMC: CONCEPTS, MODEL AND APPLICATIONS

2.1. CMC Concepts

As stated in the last section, the related works mainly consider the transmit energy consumption in different kinds of wireless networks. In this chapter, we consider both transmit and receive energy consumptions. Scenario under consideration includes cooperation among UEs, which has previously been studied for enhancing single transmissions. This scenario also known as Mobile Cloud is modelled as a cluster of resource-constrained nodes that can perform receiving and decoding cooperatively and in a distributive manner (Hoyhtya, Palola, Matinmikko & Katz, 2011). One CMC contains several UEs that can cooperatively receive the information data from Base Station (BS), and then exchange the received data with others. By exploiting the benefits of CMC, we are able to obtain the receiver energy consumption reduction (Chang & Ristaniemi, 2013). Such model can potentially offer several advantages over traditional AP-to-UE (or Point-

Table 1. Notations

Notations	Description
$E_{UE}^{tx/rx}$	UE total energy consumption for performing TX/RX in a CMC
$E_{BB}^{tx/rx}$	UE BB energy consumption for performing TX/RX in a CMC
$E_{RF}^{tx/rx}$	UE RF energy consumption for performing TX/RX in a CMC
P_E	UE BB power consumption for performing TX/RX in a CMC
$P_{tx/rx}$	UE RF power consumption for performing TX/RX in a CMC
$P_{tx,dist}$	UE RF power consumption for performing TX in a CMC by using unicast
$I_{tx/rx}$	Allocated number of RBUs per UE for performing TX/RX in a CMC
$T_{tx/rx}$	Time consumed performing TX/RX in a CMC
E_{UE}^{BS}	UE total energy consumption for performing RX from BS
$E_{UE}^{unicsat}$	UE total energy consumption for performing TX/RX in a CMC by using unicast
$E_{UE}^{unicsat}$	UE total energy consumption for performing TX/RX in a CMC by using multicast
E_{part}	UE energy consumption for performing RX from BS in a CMC

to-Point, P2P) networks, including reduction of energy and resource consumption per node. The links within the CMC is assumed to be device-to-device (D2D) links, where the MTs can share their received data and available resource. In this paper we provide detailed analysis of the energy consumption of a MT within the CMC and compare it with non-cooperative schemes.

2.2. CMC Model

We consider there are one Base Station (BS) and Z UEs in the system, where K UEs can form a CMC. All UEs inside CMC require the same data from BS (e.g., through a video or television channel).

Each UE can be dual-mode device, equipped with a short-range (e.g., WLAN) wireless communication technique for information exchange between devices and equipped with broadband access technique(e.g. LTE/LTE-A) for receiving from BS. The scenario is depicted in Figure 1, where K=5.

The transmission among different UEs inside a CMC can be modeled as unicast or multicast transmission. It is known that multicast transmission is an efficient method for group data transmission (Baek, Hong & Sung 2009). Through broadcast in radio channels, a multicast transmission increases transmission efficiency due to reduction of transmitted redundant data. However, wireless multicast should be adapted accord-

Figure 1. CMC model

ing to the worst channel state user in a multicast group. Hence, the system capacity of multicast transmission is affected both by the number of users and the supportable data rate of MT with worst instantaneous channel condition. On the other hand, unicast transmission utilizes wireless channel variations and obtains the multiuser diversity gain (Lee, Tcha, Seo & Lee, 2011). Meanwhile, the unicast transmission can utilize the channel variation on the expense of introducing transmission overhead for same data. Therefore, unicast transmission is costly from the radio resources point of view.

In the transmission, we invoke the Resource Block Unit (RBU) as the elementary resource

unit in our work. A RBU is defined as a certain frequency bandwidth W (e.g. 12 subcarriers in LTE) in one time slot. One example of RBU concept can be found in Figure 2, in which the colored blocks represent the RBUs. By using this concept, we can express the unicast and multicast transmission inside a CMC as shown in Figure 3. In Figure 3, we assume there are 4 UEs forming a CMC and all of them require same information data from BS. Therefore, each of them can receive 1/4 part of the data and then share it with others. If unicast is considered as the transmission strategy, more time and frequency resource will be consumed comparing with using multicast inside CMC in this case. In general, we can observe that the receive time duration is reduced, which leads to potential energy saving gain for the UEs. We will discuss the energy efficiency related issue in next section.

2.3. CMC Applications in 4G

As we stated previously, CMC model has a great potential to achieve energy saving for the next generation wireless networks. In addition to obtain energy saving performance from technique side, CMC is also foreseeable to have advantages on performing social interactions among numbers of users and improve the local services. It can be a competitive candidate for content or resource sharing purpose as well (Pederson & Fitzek, 2012). Some of examples are broadband mobile system

Figure 2. RBU concept

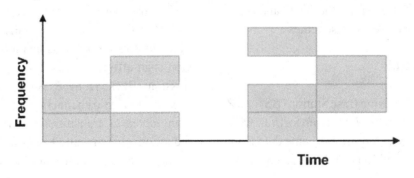

Figure 3. Receive process and transmission inside CMC

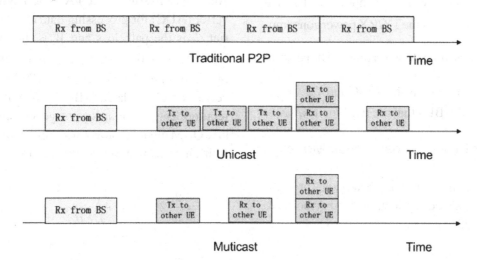

offering multimedia services, of which a typical application is for Multimedia Broadcast Multicast Service (MBMS) subscribers. Current networks, for example, have difficulties to support such kind of broadcast services for mass events, e.g. rock concerts or sport matches, especially when the receivers are spatially correlated. Furthermore, the social interaction over such content cannot be globalized, but is limited to people which are spatially or socially close to each other. Therefore, the trend tends to share the content in a more co-operative way in inter UE (or D2D) mode. Using CMC, the users closing to each other are able to watch same sport match in an energy efficient way. Also from network operator point of view, as the contents that have already been sent to UEs are not necessarily stored in the networks, resource of BS will be released. Therefore, both BS and UEs can exploit the benefits of using CMC in next generation wireless networks.

3. ENERGY EFFICIENCY OF CMC

The energy efficiency of CMC is examined in this section. As depicted in Figure 3, for the energy consumption model, we consider both transmit (TX) and receive (RX) energy consumption.

The overall TX/RX energy consumption can be categorized into baseband (BB) and RF energy consumption. The detailed models will be described in the following.

3.1. Power Consumption Model

We here model the energy consumption of the UE as the sum of BB power consumption and RF power consumption. In other words, the energy consumption of UE can be expressed as:

$$E_{UE} = E_{BB} + E_{RF} \qquad (1)$$

where E_{BB} is the BB energy consumption and E_{RF} is the RF energy consumption. Therefore, when an UE is in the TX mode, the energy consumption is:

$$E_{UE}^{tx} = E_{BB}^{tx} + E_{RF}^{tx} = (P_E + P_{tx}) \; T_{tx} I_{tx} \qquad (2)$$

and for the UE in the RX mode, we have similar definition:

$$E_{UE}^{rx} = E_{BB}^{rx} + E_{RF}^{rx} = (P_E + P_{rx}) \; T_{rx} I_{rx} \qquad (3)$$

where P_E is the power consumption for BB in a RBU and P_{tx} / P_{rx} is the TX/RX power consumption. $\dfrac{T_{tx}}{T_{rx}}$ is the time duration that an UE perform TX/RX transmission inside CMC and I_{tx} / I_{rx} is the number of RBUs that are used for TX/RX.

3.1.1. BB Power Consumption Model

The power dissipation for baseband signal processing can be modeled as (Schurgers, Aberthorne & Srivastava, 2011):

$$P_E = \left(C_E + C_R \frac{R_{s,max}}{R_s} \right) R_s \qquad (4)$$

where R_s is the symbol rate of the transmission, $R_{s,max}$ is the maximum symbol rate of the transmitter, C_E and C_R are related to system voltage level. The discussion of the BB power consumption may be out of scope of this chapter and more detailed explanations of baseband parameters are introduced in (Schurgers, et al, 2011).

3.1.2. RF Power Consumption Model

For inter-UE communication inside DMC, the transmit power dissipation of RF front-end for one single RBU can be expressed as (Datla, et al, 2009; Datla, et al, 2012):

$$P_{tx} = \beta_1 \gamma_{min} WL + \beta_2 \qquad (5)$$

where β_1 and β_2 depend on the transceiver components and channel characteristics. In particular, β_1 is related to transmitting actions on/after power amplifier (PA), such as antenna and channel gains. β_2 depends on transceiver RF circuit components, e.g., local oscillator and Digital-

Analog Converter (DAC)/Analog-Digital Converter (ADC) for processing data on one subcarrier. L is the path loss and W is the frequency bandwidth of one RBU. γ_{min} is the minimum required Signal to- Noise Ratio (SNR) at the receiver, which is related to Bit- Error-Ratio (BER) requirement. Without loss of generality we can take QAM modulation as an example, which would result in (Chang & Ristaniemi, 2012):

$$\gamma_{min} = \frac{2}{3} \left(2^b - 1 \right) ln \frac{4 \left(1 - 2^b \right)}{BER_{req}} \qquad (6)$$

where BER_{req} is the BER requirement at receiver and b is the modulation order. Also, β_1 and β_2 can be expressed as (Chang & Ristaniemi, 2012):

$$\beta_1 = \frac{\eta k_B T_o NF(\sigma_s)^{-Q^{-1}(1-P_{out})} (4\pi)^2}{G_t G_r \lambda^2 d_o^{-2}} LM \qquad (7)$$

$$\beta_2 = P_{DAC} + P_{RF} + \vartheta \qquad (8)$$

where Q^{-1} is inverse Q function. The explanation and possible values of parameters are shown in Table II (Datla, et al, 2009; Haloka, Chen, Lehtomaki, &Koskela, 2010).

3.1.3. Total Energy Consumption Model

For simplicity, we assume that each node within DMC is assigned the same resource for transmission. Thus, for each UE inside CMC, we have equal I_{tx} and T_{tx}. In addition, it is easy to observe that $I_{tx} = I_{rx} = I_{UE}$ and $T_{tx} = T_{rx} = T_{UE}$ since all UEs have same amount of data.

Using unicast scheme, the overall energy consumption an UE with considering receiving certain amount of data from BS can be expressed as:

$$E_{UE}^{unicast} = E_{UE}^{tx} + E_{UE}^{rx} + E_{part} =$$

$$(K-1)(2P_E + P_{tx} + P_{rx})T_{UE}I_{UE} + {E_{UE}^{BS}}\Big/{K} \qquad (9)$$

Similarly, using multicast scheme for transmission inside CMC, we have:

$$E_{UE}^{multicast} = E_{UE}^{tx} + E_{UE}^{rx} + E_{part} =$$

$$(KP_E + P_{tx,dist} + (K-1)P_{rx})T_{UE}I_{UE} + {E_{UE}^{BS}}\Big/{K} \qquad (10)$$

where we assume there are K UEs inside a CMC and are assigned same amount of data. Due to the features of multicast transmission, $P_{tx,dist}$ is defined as the UE with worst channel gain. E_{UE}^{BS} is the UE energy consumption when performing receiving from BS without using CMC concept. E_{UE}^{BS} can be expressed as follows:

$$E_{UE}^{BS} = MP_{UE}^{BS}T_{UE}^{BS} \qquad (11)$$

where M is the number of RBUs. T_{UE}^{BS} is the time slot duration and We assume that P_{UE}^{BS} is the circuit power of UE that is used for receiving certain amount of data in one RBU from BS.

3.2. Energy Efficiency of Different Transmission Strategies

Based on the above analysis, we can define the energy saving gain of using unicast in CMC as:

$$\xi_{unicast} = E_{UE}^{BS} - E_{UE}^{unicsat} = \frac{K-1}{K}MT_{UE}^{BS}$$

$$(P_{UE}^{BS} - \frac{P_{tx} + P_{rx}}{\rho} + \frac{\rho - 2}{\rho}P_E) \qquad (12)$$

where we have $I_{UE}T_{UE} = {MT_{UE}^{BS}}\Big/{K\rho}$, $\forall \rho > 0$.

Since the amount of data carried by subcarrier increases, the air time and frequency bandwidth

could be reduced. Here A depends on the amount of data that the subcarrier can carry, which in general, is decided by modulation and coding schemes. For example, if BPSK is invoked as modulation scheme from BS to UE and QPSK is used for inter UE communication inside DMC, we have $\acute{A} = 2$. Similarly, we have the energy saving gain when using multicast transmission as (Chang & Ristaniemi, 2013):

$$\xi_{multicast} = E_{UE}^{BS} - E_{UE}^{multicast} = \frac{M}{K}T_{UE}^{BS}$$

$$(P_{UE}^{BS} + \frac{(K-1)P_{rx} + P_{tx}}{\rho} + \frac{K}{\rho}P_E) \qquad (13)$$

Therefore, the energy efficiency performance can be denoted as:

$$EE = \frac{\hat{\imath}}{E_{UE}^{BS}} \times 100\% \qquad (14)$$

4. SIMULATION RESULTS

We present some simulation results here to illustrate the notable energy saving gain by using CMC model. EE in (13) is used as the performance metric. For baseband energy consumption, we have $R_{s,max} = 1$ MHz and $R_s = 250$ MHz. We also use the same $C_E = 8 \times 10^{-8}V^2$ and $C_R = 7 \times 10^{-7}V^2$ as in (Schurgers, et al, 2011), and $BER_{req} = 10^{-5}$. We examine the impact of size of the CMC in terms of number and distances of UEs within the cluster. Also, the effect of modulation order $\tilde{n}$ to the EE performance is studied. The D2D channel is defined according to IEEE 802.11ac (2012), where inter-UE (or D2D) distance is assumed to be around 20m unless individually mentioned.

From Figure 4, we can see that as the number of UEs increases, the energy saving gain obtained by using CMC arises as well. The energy saving percentage (or EE) reaches the 'almost' saturation level when there are 20 MTs forming a CMC. It

Table 2. TX/RX power consumption related parameters

Parameters	Description	Value
η	Power amplifier Parameter	0.2
ϑ	Power amplifier Parameter	174 mW
k_B	Boltzmann Constant	1.3806×10^{-23} J/K
T_o	Temperature	300 K
NF	Noise Figure	9 dB
σ_s	Shadow fading standard deviation	12 dB
G_t	Tx antenna gain	2 dBi
G_r	Rx antenna gain	2 dBi
λ	Signal wavelength	0.15 (2 GHz)
LM	Link margin	15 dB
W	Bandwidth of RBU	0.2 MHz
d_o	Near field distance	15m
P_{out}	Channel outage probability	1%
P_{DAC}	Power of DAC	15.4 mW
P_{RF}	Power of other RF device	131.5 MW

means that without any radio resource (e.g. RBUs) constraints, forming DMC can help nearby MTs to save energy if proper modulation and coding schemes (MCS) are used. In Figure 5, we notice that when $Á = 5$, we reach the maximal energy saving gain for all cases in this setting. Due to shorter transmit times, the increase of the energy saving as a function of modulation order can be expected. However, there's also a need for higher transmit powers with higher modulation order so a trade-off clearly exists. As we see from the

figure, when $ñ > 5$, the growth of transmit power appears to dominate the increase of E_{UE}, and thus, energy saving percentage begins to decrease from its maximum.

If we fix the number of UEs inside CMC to be 20, we could obtain the impact of value of A in Figure 6. From Figure 6, we can see that the energy efficiency can reach up to of 70% when D2D distance is shorter than break point distance d_0. In general, for same value of A, shorter D2D distance can obtain higher energy saving percent-

Figure 4. Number of UEs vs. energy efficiency gain with fixed inter UE distance of 25m

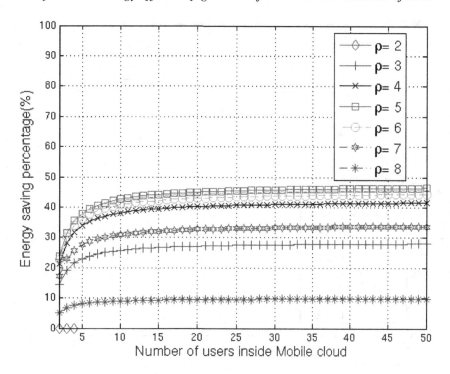

Figure 5. ρ vs. energy efficiency gain with a fixed D2D distance of 25m

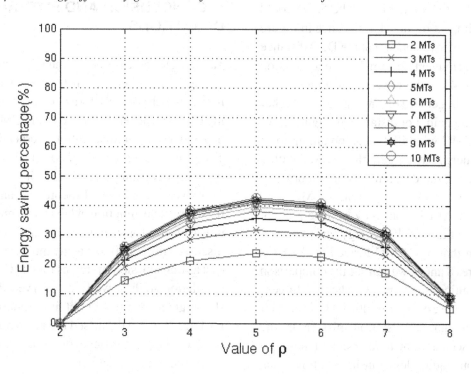

Figure 6. ρ vs. energy efficiency gain with a fixed number of UEs

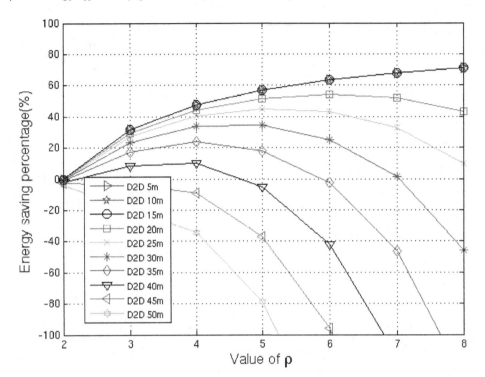

age. If we fix the value of A to be 5, we could obtain the impact of inter-UE distance in Figure 7. When A = 5, we notice that the D2D distance should not be longer that 38m. The same situation as in Figure 4 can be observed in Figure 7, in other words, larger size of CMC results in higher energy saving gain. For instance, in Figure 8, we see that a CMC with 4 UEs can obtain up to of 1.5 times energy saving gain that a CMC with 2 UEs. However, the difference is not so obvious when there are more UEs forming a CMC, e.g., a CMC with 20 UEs can only achieve a slight better (up to of around 4%) energy saving performance than that of a CMC formed by 10 UEs. From Figures 8 and 9, we can see the comparison between multicast and unicast schemes. In general, we can observe that multicast has superior performance that unicast transmission in the considered scenario due to the fact that multicast transmission requires less transmitting times than unicast.

5. CONCLUSION AND FUTURE DIRECTIONS

Targeting to decrease the total energy consumption of single UE, we studied a distributed mobile cloud model, which is formed by a number of collaborating UEs. The benefits achieved from CMC may be negated by the communication overhead inside it. Therefore, we presented a theoretical analysis on the energy consumption of UEs within the CMC. Moreover, we presented theoretical analysis on the energy consumption of UEs when multicast or unicast is used as well. Based on the analysis, we discussed the benefits of using multicast and unicast as transmission strategies for CMC. Through simulation studies, we first observed that CMC shows great potential for obtaining energy saving for UEs. We also discussed the great potential of CMC on the way to offer better broadcast services for future wireless networks.

Figure 7. D2D distance vs. energy efficiency gain with $\rho = 5$

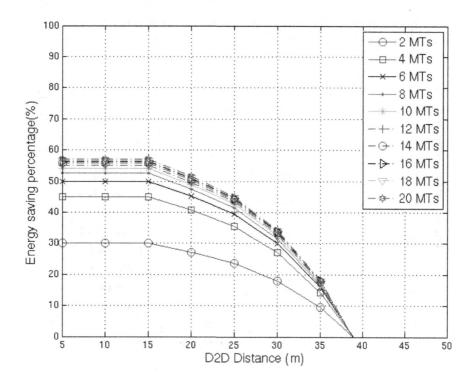

Figure 8. D2D distance vs. energy efficiency, both multicast and unicast

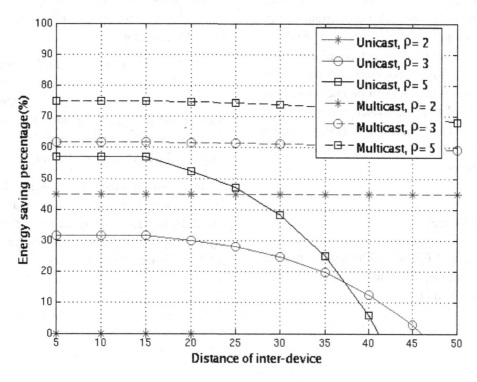

Figure 9. Number of UEs vs. energy efficiency, both multicast and unicast

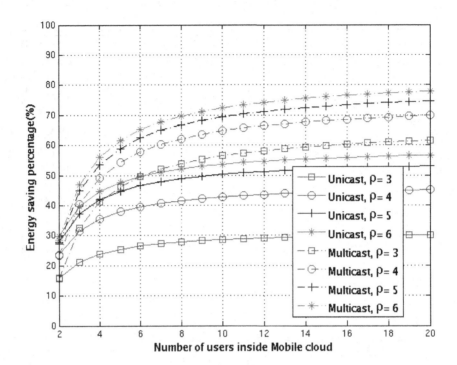

CMC maps perfectly with the social need to share with people who are close to each other. The problem is, however, that the current mobile platforms are not, or even worse not anymore, ready for this. Besides some technique issues, such as ad hoc wireless access should be featured in the cellphone. Willingness of people for selfless sharing is hard to be motivated. Going towards solving the related obstacles in both technique and social domains will be the prior objectives for future work.

REFERENCES

3GPP TR 23.882. (2009). 3GPP system architecture evolution: Report on technical options and conclusions. Author.

3GPP TR 25.913. (2009). *Requirements for evolved universal terrestrial Radio Access (UTRA) and universal terrestrial radio access network (UTRAN).* Author.

3GPP TR 36.440. (2010). Technical specification group radio access network, Evolved Universal terrestrial radio access network (E-UTRAN), general aspects and principles for interfaces supporting multimedia broadcast multicast service (MBMS) within E-UTRAN, release 9. Author.

Alonso-Zarate, J., Kartsakli, E., Katz, M., Alonso, L., & Verikoukis, C. (2013). Multi-radio cooperative ARQ in wireless cellular networks: A MAC layer perspective. *Telecommunication Systems, 52*(3), 375–385.

Baek, S. Y., Hong, Y.-J., & Sung, D. K. (2009). Adaptive transmission scheme for mixed multicast and unicast traffic in cellular systems. *IEEE Transactions on Vehicular Technology, 58*(6), 2899–2907. doi:10.1109/TVT.2008.2010515

Bontu, C., & Illidge, E. (2009). DRX mechanism for power saving in LTE. *IEEE Communications Magazine, 47*(6), 48–55. doi:10.1109/MCOM.2009.5116800

Chang, Z., & Ristaniemi, T. (2012). Reducing power consumption via collaborative OFDMA mobile clusters. In *Proceedings of IEEE Workshop on Computer-Aided Modeling Analysis and Design of Communication Links and Networks(CAMAD'12)*. Barcelona, Spain: IEEE.

Chang, Z., & Ristaniemi, T. (2013). Energy efficiency of collaborative OFDMA mobile clusters. In *Proceedings of IEEE CCNC'13*. IEEE.

Chang, Z., & Ristaniemi, T. (2013). Efficient use of multicast and unicast in collaborative OFDMA mobile clusters. In *Proc. of 77th IEEE Vehicular Technology Conference*. Dresden, Germany: IEEE.

Chu, F.-S., Chen, K.-C., & Fettweis, G. (2012). Green resource allocation tominimize receiving energy in OFDMA cellular systems. *IEEE Communications Letters, 16*(3), 372–375. doi:10.1109/LCOMM.2012.010512.2339

Datla, D., Chen, X., Newman, T. R., Reed, J. H., & Bose, T. (2009). Power efficiency in wireless network distributed computing. In *Proc. of 69th IEEE Vehicular Technology Conference*. Barcelona, Spain: IEEE.

Datla, D., Volos, H. I., Newman, T. R., Reed, J. H., & Bose, T. (2012). Wireless distributed computing in cognitive radio networks. *Ad Hoc Networks, 10*(5), 845–857. doi:10.1016/j.adhoc.2011.04.002

Gür, G., & Alagöz, F. (2011). Green wireless communications via cognitive dimension: An overview. *IEEE Network, 25*(2), 50–56. doi:10.1109/MNET.2011.5730528

Haloka, S., Chen, T., Lehtomaki, J., & Koskela, T. (2010). Device-to- device (D2D) communication in cellular network- performance analysis of optimal and practical communication mode selection. In *Proc. of 2010 IEEE Wireless Communications and Networking Conference*. Sydney, Australia: IEEE.

Hoyhtya, M., Palola, M., Matinmikko, M., & Katz, M. (2011). Cognitive engine: Design aspects for mobile clouds. In Proceedings of CogART 2011. CogART.

IEEE 802.11ac Specifications. (2012). Washington, DC: IEEE.

Lee, S. J., Tcha, Y., Seo, S.-Y., & Lee, S.-C. (2011). Efficient use of multicast and unicast channels for multicast services transmission. *IEEE Transactions on Communications, 59*(5), 1264–1267. doi:10.1109/TCOMM.2011.020811.090200

Pederson, M. V., & Fitzek, F. H. P. (2012). Mobile clouds: The new content sharing platform. *Proceedings of the IEEE, 100*, 1400–1403. doi:10.1109/JPROC.2012.2189806

Radwan, A., & Rodriguez, J. (2012). Energy saving in multi-standard mobile terminals through short-range cooperation. *EURASIP Journal on Wireless Communications and Networking, 159*. doi:10.1186/1687-1499-2012-159

Schurgers, C., Aberthorne, O., & Srivastava, M. (2011). Modulation scaling for energy aware communication systems. In *Proceedings of International Symposium on Low Power Electronics and Design*. Fukuoka, Japan: Academic Press.

Chapter 6
Energy Efficient Schemes for Base Station Management in 4G Broadband Systems

Alexandra Bousia
Technical University of Catalonia (UPC), Spain

Angelos Antonopoulos
Telecommunications Technological Center of Catalonia (CTTC), Spain

Elli Kartsakli
Technical University of Catalonia (UPC), Spain

Luis Alonso
Technical University of Catalonia (UPC), Spain

Christos Verikoukis
Telecommunications Technological Center of Catalonia (CTTC), Spain

ABSTRACT

Reducing the energy consumption in wireless networks has become a significant challenge, not only because of its great impact on the global energy crisis, but also because it represents a noteworthy cost for telecommunication operators. The Base Stations (BSs), constituting the main component of wireless infrastructure and the major contributor to the energy consumption of mobile cellular networks, are usually designed and planned to serve their customers during peak times. Therefore, they are more than sufficient when the traffic load is low. In this chapter, the authors propose a number of BSs switching off algorithms as an energy efficient solution to the problem of redundancy of network resources. They demonstrate via analysis and by means of simulations that one can achieve reduction in energy consumption when one switches off the unnecessary BSs. In particular, the authors evaluate the energy that can be saved by progressively turning off BSs during the periods when traffic decreases depending on the traffic load variations and the distance between the BS and their associated User Equipments (UEs). In addition, the authors show how to optimize the energy savings of the network by calculating the most energy-efficient combination of switched off and active BSs.

DOI: 10.4018/978-1-4666-4888-3.ch006

1. INTRODUCTION

During the last few years, the rapid and radical evolution of mobile telecommunication services along with the emerging demand for multimedia applications due to the widespread use of laptops, tablets and smart-phones have led to a growing demand for data transmission. The traffic load is experiencing a growing increase by the factor of 10 every 5 years approximately (Global Action Plan, 2007; Cisco, 2013). Overall mobile data traffic is expected to reach 11.6 exabytes per month by 2017, a 13-fold increase between 2012 and 2017 and at a Compound Annual Growth rate (GAGR) of 66% from 2012 to 2017. The mobile applications, in particular, are expected to grow in staggering rates, with mobile video showing the higher growth and getting up to 66.5%.

To meet these demands, the development of new standards and architectures is more than compulsory. Long Term Evolution (LTE), that is the natural upgrade of Universal Mobile Telecommunications System (UMTS), is an evolving wireless standard developed by the 3rd Generation Partnership Program (3GPP) as a candidate Fourth Generation (4G) system, while LTE-Advanced constitutes the most advanced version of LTE (3GPP, 2012), (Martin-Sacristan, Monserrat, Cabrejas Penuelas, Clabuig, Carrigas, & Cardona, 2009). IEEE 802.16m standard is the 4G system proposed by International Mobile Telecommunications-Advanced (IMT-Advanced). These new standards promise higher data rates for mobile phones and terminals, ubiquitous connectivity and enhanced spectral efficiency.

Along with the development of the new telecommunications standards, operators face the need to expand their wireless infrastructure in order to tackle with the challenges of future mobile networks and handle the predicted increase in mobile traffic volume. As a result, more Base Stations (BSs) are deployed and small cells alongside with the macro sites are used in high traffic areas. The telecommunications companies work towards the mass deployment of 4G systems as there are more than 4 million BSs serving mobile users, with this number expected to double by the end of 2012 (Correia et al., 2012).

The BS, called Evolved Node B (eNB) in LTE-Advanced, is the principal energy consuming entity of Information and Communications Technology (ICT) (Chen, Zhang, Zhao, & Chen, 2010), whereas mobile telephone exchange and data centers consume less energy (Motorola, 2007). The BSs consume up to 1350 Watts, while more than 50% of the total energy is consumed by the transmit antennas and the Power Amplifiers (PAs). On the other hand, data transmission is a less energy consuming contributor to wireless cellular networks. Therefore, reducing the energy consumption of BSs through a "greener" BSs operation in the cellular networks has become an important research topic. Improving the hardware and developing less consuming PAs is a way to go, but it does not promise great energy savings.

Energy efficient BSs operation can achieve significant energy consumption reduction through switching off the unused BSs by taking into account the time varying traffic conditions. Considering that access networks are usually dimensioned according to the peak hour traffic, the resources of the network are shared among the existing users, so as to meet specific Quality of Service (QoS) constraints. On the other hand, when traffic decreases due to normal load variations throughout the day, networks are over-dimensioned, resources become redundant and the existing traffic in a given area can be served by just a subset of the deployed BSs. Thus, the unnecessary BSs could be switched off in a smart way during the low traffic periods in order to save energy. After the BSs switching off, the existing traffic is served by the remaining active BSs, which, in turn, may need to increase their transmission power in order to extend their coverage area. The number of switched off BSs and the transmission power increase of the active ones leads to a tradeoff that must be configured to improve the effectiveness of the energy efficient algorithms.

Motivated by the above research challenges, this chapter is focused on energy efficient solutions for the deactivation of the unnecessary BSs during off-peak traffic conditions. Particular interest is laid on the parameters that are crucial for the determination of the most suitable BSs to be switched off. The decision of the selection of the BSs to be switched off plays a significant role in the system performance and the energy savings that can be accomplished. Most works in the literature, explained in details in Section 2, turn off the BSs according to the traffic load and give priority to the BSs that have lower traffic, while others switch off the BSs randomly. In this chapter, we present three different approaches that take into consideration (i) the distance between BSs and the associated users and (ii) the traffic load variations through time. We also show how to optimize the energy efficiency by calculating the energy consumption reduction in different combinations of network configuration where we determine the most effective combination of turned off and active BSs. To this end, a distance-aware algorithm, a dynamic distance-aware approach and a maximization scheme are presented.

The content of this chapter is organized as follows. Section 2 outlines the related work on BSs switching off schemes in the literature. In Section 3, we introduce the three proposed switching off schemes. The traffic models along with the analysis for throughput and energy efficiency are presented in Section 4. The validation of the models and the performance evaluation of the schemes are provided in Section 5. Finally, Section 6 concludes the chapter.

2. RELATED WORK

With the explosive growth of high data rate applications in wireless networks, energy efficiency has drawn rising attention from the research com-

munity. The increasing concern about the energy consumption of telecommunication networks is driving operators to manage their equipments by intelligently allocating their resources so as to optimize energy utilization and, at the same time, to provide sufficient service coverage to their users. Telecommunication operators have become very sensitive to the energy issue. They have committed themselves to reduce their energy consumption and through the energy consumption decrease, significant reduction will be achieved in terms of network cost. Therefore, from the operators' perspective, besides the energy diminution and the great ecological benefits, significant financial gains will be attained. For this reason, telecommunication companies study different approaches for energy consumption reduction in the network design, and operation planning and management. The network design refers to the proposal of energy efficient network architectures, while network planning and management include mechanisms for switching off BSs. The latter category will be the focus of our proposals. In the context of BSs planning, several works have been proposed in the literature so far. The objective of this section is to highlight the recent work on this field for UMTS and Wireless Local Access Networks (WLANs) in order to provide the reader with an up to date State-of-the-Art.

One of the major enhancements of LTE is the employment of power save mechanisms. The objective is to switch off the radio parts of the BSs when the traffic load is low. The power save operations of LTE include Discontinuous Reception (DRX) and Discontinuous Transmission (DTX). DRX and DTX policies improve significantly the network efficiency by reducing the energy consumption at the cost that the users' throughput capacity is reduced (Freescale, 2008; Vinella,& Polignano, 2009).

Apart from the power saving techniques proposed in the LTE standard, the energy efficiency of wireless networks has been examined in the literature. Some of the first attempts for BSs planning have been made in (Charaviglio, Ciullo, Meo,& Marsan, 2008; Charaviglio, Ciullo, Meo,& Marsan, 2009; Marsan, Charaviglio, Ciullo,& Meo, 2009), where different approaches for switching off a specific number of BSs in UMTS cellular networks during low traffic periods are presented. Particularly, in (Charaviglio, Ciullo, Meo,& Marsan, 2008), the authors propose an algorithm to calculate the adequate number of BSs to be switched off, as well as the duration of the switching off phase, in order to guarantee QoS constraints in terms of the blocking probability. The limitation of this work is that the switching off phase begins with the selection of a random number of BSs to be switched off and the randomness of the decision does not assure optimal energy savings. With a small number of switched off BSs, the QoS demands in terms of the number of dropped calls are fulfilled; however the energy savings are not significant. On the contrary, with very few remaining active cells, higher energy efficiency is achieved, but the active BSs suffer from a considerable transmission power increase to guarantee full coverage. In (Charaviglio, Ciullo, Meo,& Marsan, 2009), the same authors provide an extension of their former work with two main novelties. First, they use realistic data traffic patterns, with users generating voice, video and data traffic sessions and, second, they introduce the idea of network planning for switching off the BSs considering both uniform and hierarchical scenarios. The uniform scenario considers the existence of identical cells with regard to the traffic load and the transmission power, while the hierarchical scenario is represented by a network with a hierarchical cellular structure, in which one umbrella cell overlaps with six smaller cells. The umbrella cell guarantees the QoS constraints when the random switching off scheme is applied. In another work (Marsan, Charaviglio, Ciullo,& Meo, 2009), the authors propose a novel switching off scheme that optimizes the energy saving, by assuming that any fraction of cells can be switched off according to a deterministic traffic variation

pattern over time and then by accounting for the constraints resulting from the cell layout. The optimal strategy is applied in different network configurations, whose difference relies on the BSs position and they identify the best period of time that the BSs should be switched off. The restriction of this paper lies on the fact that the authors can apply their algorithms to specific network scenarios and the switching off schemes cannot be generalized. Another important aspect of the switching off strategies is examined in (Marsan, Charaviglio, Ciullo,& Meo, 2011). Since the introduction of sleep mode in the operation of BSs is considered one of the most promising approaches to reduce the energy consumption in cellular access networks, Marsan et al. point out that the time needed for a BS to change from the state of being active to being switched off and vice versa, should be examined. The goal of the authors is to clarify whether it has a marginal or a crucial impact on energy savings when the sleep mode schemes are applied. The authors study the switching off transients for one cell by measuring the amount of time that is necessary to actually switch off the BSs, while allowing terminals to handover to the corresponding active BS without overloading the signaling channels. Even though this work does not include the proposal of a novel switching off scheme, its outcome is considered fundamental for the proposition of sleeping algorithms and encourages operators to further investigate the field of network planning.

The switching off algorithms presented so far do not consider neither the daily traffic variations, nor the positions of the users, as critical parameters for the switching off decision. Towards this direction, another research group proposes several algorithms for BSs switching off. In (Zhou, Gong, Yang, Niu,& Yang, 2009), two approaches that achieve energy savings are proposed: (i) a greedy centralized algorithm where the traffic load is examined to determine whether each BS is going to be switched off or not, and (ii) a distributed algorithm where each BS locally estimates its traffic load and decides independently from the others whether it is going to be switched off. In both algorithms, the BS with the lowest traffic load concentrates the traffic of the neighboring BSs that will be then switched off. Gong et al. (Gong, Zhou, Niu, & Yang, 2010) propose an improved switching off algorithm where the BSs are switched off according to the traffic variations and so as to achieve a blocking probability constraint. The difference of this approach from previous works stands on the existence of a predefined minimum mode holding time, which refers to a time period that a BS should be active or switched off before changing from one state to another. The BSs are restricted to remain in active or switched off mode for a specific time and no noticeable performance degradation is observed. A similar idea that exploits the daily traffic load variations is considered in (Samdanis, Kutscher, & Brunner, 2010) and (Samdanis, Taleb, Kutscher, & Brunner, 2011), where the authors deal with the overlapping coverage areas of the BSs in cellular networks. Samdanis et al. (Samdanis, Kutscher, & Brunner, 2010) describe a centralized and a distributed algorithm for BSs switching off, where the BS with the maximum traffic load serves the traffic load of its neighboring BSs. Both algorithms exploit coordination mechanisms, but the switching off decision is taken in centralized and distributed way, respectively. In (Samdanis, Taleb, Kutscher, & Brunner, 2011), the same authors further analyze the energy savings of Self Organized Networks (SONs). The network is reconfigured again in both a centralized and in a distributed way, but especially in this paper the authors present the switching off algorithms that are triggered by the BS with the lowest traffic. The switching off decision guarantees certain capacity and delay constraints. Another interesting approach is presented by Fusco et al. in (Fusco, Buddhikotl, Gupta, & Venkatesan, 2011), where algorithms that minimize energy consumption by switching off BSs based on the traffic demand are proposed. Comparing to the aforementioned

works, the authors propose a mechanism where a subset of BSs is selected to remain active and power levels are assigned to each one of them, so as to achieve full coverage and adequate capacity for the network users. Then, the rest of the unneeded BSs are switched off. In these works, the traffic load appears to be an intelligent parameter to decide the suitable BSs to be switched off, even though other network characteristics, such as the BSs density and the distance between the BSs and the users, should also be taken into consideration, as well.

Another fundamental energy efficient approach has been presented by Oh et al. in (Oh, & Krishnamachari, 2007). In this paper, the daily variations of the traffic and the BSs positions are examined in order to decide the most energy efficient switching off strategy. The number of switched off BSs is fixed, calculated by an objective function that maximizes the energy efficiency of the network. The results obtained in the paper show how traffic load and BS density influence the amount of energy savings. In densely deployed areas, many BSs are switched off and the results are very promising. However, the optimal number of switched off BSs is not calculated and the network capacity is not exploited to its limits.

Apart from the previous studies, where "green" BSs planning and operation in UMTS cellular networks have been described, some analytical models are also introduced for reducing the power consumption in WLANs (Marsan, Charaviglio, Ciullo, & Meo, 2010; (Jardosh, Iannaccone, Papagiannaki, & Vinnakota, 2007). In particular, in (Marsan, Charaviglio, Ciullo, & Meo, 2010) a cluster of cells is responsible for deciding which Access Points (APs) should be switched off based on the number of associated users and the traffic load. Two policies are examined. The first algorithm is based on the number of users that are associated to each AP and the second is based on the number of active users that actually generate traffic. In the same framework, a switching off approach for dense WLANs is presented in (Jardosh, Iannaccone, Papagiannaki,& Vinnakota, 2007). In this work, the AP with the lowest traffic load is switched off first and its traffic load is served by a neighboring AP. These approaches have many similarities with the previous works for UMTS cellular networks, since the parameters used for determining the APs to be switched off are the traffic load and the number of users. An optimized network management scheme is considered in (Lorincz, Capone,& Begusic, 2011). The authors propose a centralized network approach based on the traffic load and the User Equipments (UEs) location estimations in order to decide the appropriate number of APs that should be sited in a given network configuration. The energy savings are presented in the context of different traffic patterns and a thorough survey on deployment strategies is given. Even though this work does not consider BSs switching off strategies, it identifies the density and the position of the UEs as crucial parameters that can play an important role in switching off algorithms.

Working towards a different direction, the authors of (Kolios, Friderikos,& Papadaki, 2010) provide a technique for BSs switching off by using the advantages of Store-Carry and Forward (SCF) relaying. Their algorithm proposes that cooperative relay nodes route the traffic of low utilization BSs to neighboring BSs. Thus, the routing scheme via the SCF relays allows the BSs with the lower traffic load to be switched off and their traffic to be served by the adjacent cells. The switching off decision relies only on the daily traffic load variations.

Apart from the academic groups, energy saving through BSs switching off has been thoroughly explored by the research departments of mobile operators and telecommunication companies. Telecommunication operators have an increased interest in employing sleep modes for mobile BSs and their motivation is twofold. First, energy savings through these techniques is huge, since 23% reduction in BSs energy consumption is equivalent

to 3.5 GWh of energy reduction (Sleep mode for mobile base stations cuts Jamaican operators' carbon footprint, 2013, February 26) as well as carbon emissions can be reduced significantly (Vodafone India switches off AC at towers to cut energy costs, and carbon emissions, 2013, March 20), (Telefonica – Focusing on Climate Change Pays Off For Everyone, 2010, September 8). Second, statistics verify that the mobile operators could save more than $560 millions in operational expenditure annually by turning off the unnecessary BSs (Mobile operators could save $560m+ in OPEX annually, according to new Arieso study, 2011, June 15). Alcatel in (Blume, Eckhardt, Klein, Kuehn,& Wajda, 2010) study the potentials of energy savings through network adaptation to traffic demands. The characteristics of the traffic load patterns are exploited to propose the energy efficient strategies that can be applied and turning off the BSs for long periods during the night is presented among them. In the same context, Ericsson (Ericsson, 2013) considers turning off the low power nodes as a promising solution towards a "greener" network. Another whitepaper (Huawei, 2011) presented by Huawei technologies Co. deals with the hardware technology that should be implemented in the BSs in order to allow effective switching off in the different parts of macro cells.

Even though the network operation concept has been extensively studied in the literature, there are still many challenges and open issues to be studied. The open gaps of the State-of-the-Art solutions must be investigated seeing that they provide the necessary incentives to propose new and innovative energy saving strategies. In particular, apart from the traffic load that can be used as a crucial factor to decide the appropriate BSs to be switched off, we are going to use the distance between users and BSs in switching off policies. In addition, we should ensure that the whole capacity of the network is exploited in order to find the maximum number of BSs to be switched off while still guaranteeing the QoS.

3. BASE STATION MANAGEMENT SCHEMES

As we have already mentioned, reducing energy consumption in wireless communications has recently attracted increasing attention. As indicated in the State-of-the-Art, it can generally be said that most contributions on network planning schemes focus on particular aspects of the problem and simplify the rest. Usually, they focus on proposing traffic-aware switching off algorithms and they ignore the BSs and the users position. In this section, we describe the system model where our proposed energy efficient algorithms will be applied. In addition, the three switching off algorithms are presented and the analytical models for throughput and energy efficiency calculation are given.

3.1. System Model

We consider an area covered by BSs with partially overlapping coverage areas and we focus on clusters of 7 cells, as shown in Figure 1a. Each BS is characterized by an identification number, denoted as $i \in [0, 6]$. We assume that the UEs of

each operator are uniformly distributed within each cell, noting that the terms "UE", "call" and "session" are used interchangeably. Each UE generates traffic according to a Poisson process. We adopt a typical day/night traffic profile for the traffic of each BS based on real traffic information, as shown in Figure 1b (3GPP, 2011). The peak hours are observed in the morning and during early afternoon, while during night hours the traffic is low. The dissimilarity in traffic load between busy hours and off-peak periods is also reflected on the energy consumption during high and low traffic periods. Since the network is dimensioned according to the peak traffic demand of the users, and the network capacity is adequate for serving the traffic during peak hours, during low traffic periods, the probability of having the system full is low. Thus, a number of network resources are redundant. The underutilization of these resources leads to considerable energy waste.

Three BSs switching off algorithms are presented. The main target of all schemes is to provide enhanced network energy efficiency by switching off the unnecessary BSs during low traffic conditions and our intention is to decide the subset of BSs to be switched off. The decision is very cru-

Figure 1. (a) An example of 7-cell cluster network model, (b) Daily voice traffic load variations during a 24-h weekday

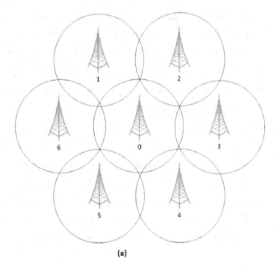

(a)

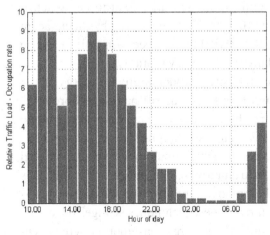

(b)

cial and we have to take into account that the QoS should not be degraded, since when we switch off some BSs and keep active only a few BSs, the coverage is restricted, and thus, some users may be in outage. Consequently, we must provide radio coverage to the parts that were served by the switched off BSs. In order to achieve increased coverage, we first must increase the transmission power of the remaining switched on BSs and before switching off a BS, we first ensure that the remaining BSs can serve the traffic of the network with the same QoS.

3.2. Distance-Aware Base Station Switching Off Scheme (DSO)

The first proposed switching off mechanism is based on the fact that the transmission power of a BS depends on its distance from the UEs. The BSs require increased transmission power to cover extended area and serve distant users. Hence, the impact of the distance on the transmission power makes it an appropriate indicator for the decision about the BSs that must be turned off. The Distance-aware Switching Off (DSO) approach proposes to switch off the BS with the maximum average distance value. Our algorithm leads to energy saving, while guaranteeing the QoS in terms of achieved throughput and outage probability of the UEs. The remaining BSs are responsible for covering the parts of the network that were covered by the switched off BSs and the proposed algorithm does not switch off any further BSs if those that remain active are not able to serve all the existing traffic at the present time in the network.

Our research work has two main contributions: (i) we consider the distance between the BSs and their associated UEs in the switching off decision in order to minimize the energy consumption of the whole network, and (ii) we apply our algorithm on the LTE-A Standard, whereas most works in this field consider older technologies.

The DSO algorithm works as follows:

Step 1: Each BS estimates the distance of its UEs and obtains the information for the distance of UEs that are associated with its neighbors through the X2 interface;

Step 2: The BSs calculate the average distance based on the results of the first step and they exchange the outcome among them;

Step 3: The BS with the maximum average distance is switched off first, if there is no QoS degradation, and the neighboring BSs deal with the possible increases in the transmission power. The algorithm is repeated from *Step 2*, until the maximum number of BSs is switched off and it is guaranteed that there is no QoS degradation.

The steps of the DSO algorithm are shown graphically in the flowchart in the Figure 2.

3.3. Dynamic Distance-Aware Base Station Switching Off Scheme (DDSO)

In the same context, we propose a second switching on/off algorithm that exploits the traffic load variations during night zone, along with the distance between the UEs and the BSs, as a parameter for the switching off decision. Comparing to the related work presented in Section 2, the main contributions of this novel dynamic distance-aware switching on/off strategy are summarized in the following: (i) This dynamic algorithm is an iterative process and its results vary according to the time changing conditions. The number of BSs that are switched off is not fixed and, in particular, the selection of the deactivated BSs depends on traffic pattern variations and the distance between the BSs and the UEs. The dynamic nature of the algorithm leads to the extension of the night zone compared to other works in the literature. More specifically, the deactivation of the BSs is progressively occurring as soon as the traffic load decreases and not during a predefined night zone. (ii) In other works in the literature, the schemes

Figure 2. Flowchart of the distance-aware switching off (DSO) algorithm

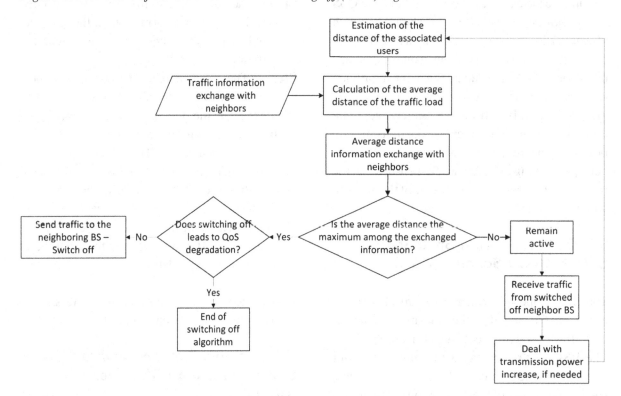

that were demonstrated were applied in a static way, with the decision taken at the beginning of the night zone. In contrast, in this work, our adaptive strategy is applied every hour in the low traffic zone, a characteristic that differentiates the Dynamic Distance-aware Switching On/Off (DDSO) scheme from our DSO algorithm, as well. (iii) Our proposal is not only to switch off the BSs, but the BSs are also switched on gradually, according to the traffic load variations, when the network resources are not sufficient for serving the existing traffic load.

Our algorithm is divided in two phases: the switching off phase that begins when the traffic load decreases and the switching on phase that begins when the traffic demand increases again, early in the morning:

- **Switching off Phase:** The switching off phase starts at 19:00 p.m. (Figure 1b) and ends at 07:00 a.m. During these hours, the

traffic load is low, and a reduced number of BSs could be used to serve the existing traffic. In a wireless network that consists of N BSs, our algorithm calculates the minimum number N_{on} of BSs that should remain active based on the traffic variations. Therefore, a maximum number of $N - N_{on} = N_{off}$ BSs will be switched off. The algorithm consists of three steps (same steps as the ones presented in the previous algorithm and shown in Figure 2) that are repeated every hour during the switch off phase. The night zone is extended and a greater amount of energy is saved. Based on the total network capacity and the desired data rate, the BSs estimate the maximum number of the UEs that can be served in the coverage area and they decide if more BSs can be switched off;

- **Switching on Phase:** In a typical traffic load scenario, since the cell load increases at 08:00 a.m., the number of active BSs is not adequate for serving the traffic load. Therefore, the BSs should be switched on gradually in order to have the appropriate number of BSs to serve the existing traffic load. At 08:00 a.m. the existing active BSs calculate the number of BSs that should be turned on in order to serve the traffic of the network based on the traffic requirements and the position of the existing UEs. The active BSs are responsible for informing the neighboring non-active BSs to be turned on. At 10:00 a.m. when the traffic load reaches its peak, all the BSs should be turned on.

3.4. Maximization Base Station Switching Off Scheme (MSO)

The two previous algorithms presented strategies for switching off different number of BSs. The objective of the third algorithm is to find the maximum number of BSs that can be switched off for a network configuration of the hexagonal grid network. In this section, we provide an extension of the previous works in order to achieve this optimization goal. We propose a novel switching off algorithm and its contribution is presented below: The key point relies on finding the optimal combination of those BSs to be switched off and those that remain active. The optimal solution maximizes the energy savings.

The algorithm is applied from 10:00 p.m. until 07:00 a.m. Our algorithm is applied at the beginning of the night zone when traffic load is low for clusters consisting of 7 cells (Figure 1a) and follows the next steps:

Step 1: Each cluster, having information about the traffic pattern given from Figure 1b, computes the average estimated traffic arrival rate for the night zone;

Step 2: For any given cluster of 7 cells, the energy consumption and the energy efficiency are computed for different combinations of switched off BSs, using the average estimated traffic rate. We assume that the traffic of a BS that is switched off is served by the neighboring BS that has the smallest identification number (the identification numbers appear in Figure 1a). The BSs that remain active increase their transmission power accordingly to keep the QoS of the overall area;

Step 3: The combination that gives the maximum energy saving is applied to our network. The BSs that remain active deal with the transmission power increases to serve the existing UEs.

The flowchart of the Maximum Switching Off (MSO) algorithm is presented in the Figure 3.

3.5. Analytical Model

In this section, an analytical model for calculating the throughput performance and the network energy efficiency achieved when applying our algorithms is developed. The same mathematical analysis is used for the three algorithms, since the network performance can be estimated in the same way and the difference relies only on the selection of the BSs to be switched off. The results are further verified by extensive simulations, presented in the following section.

In our analysis, the network traffic load is formulated as an *M/M/c* multi-server queue. The Markov chain, referring to the traffic model of one BS, represents the downlink traffic flows between the BSs and the UEs and indicates a system where: (i) the sessions in each hour and for each BS are generated according to a Poisson process and the inter-arrival times are exponential with mean value $1/\lambda$ [*s/call*], (ii) the service time is exponentially distributed with mean value equal

Figure 3. Flowchart of the maximization switching off (MSO) algorithm

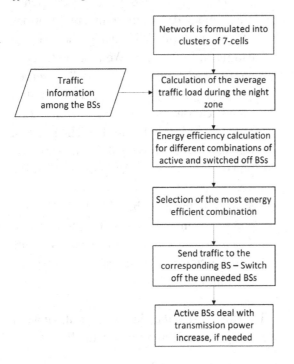

to $1/\mu$ [*s/call*], (iii) there are c servers, where c represents the maximum number of sessions that can be served simultaneously, given as $c = C/R$ with C being the total capacity of a BS and R being the constant bit rate, and (iv) the sessions are served in order of arrival. Each state of the system is characterized by the number of active sessions. The state p_n denotes the equilibrium probability of having n calls in the system. The traffic generation rate and the service rate are given by:

$$\lambda_n = \lambda, n = 0,1,2,... \tag{1}$$

and:

$$\mu_n = \begin{cases} n \cdot \mu, n = 1,2,...,c \\ c \cdot \mu, n \geq c \end{cases} \tag{2}$$

The occupation rate per server ρ is the traffic intensity, and represents the relative traffic load, shown in Figure 1b. From the traffic pattern and based on the following equations, we extract the traffic rate λ:

$$\rho = \frac{\lambda}{c \cdot \mu} \tag{3}$$

The steady state probabilities p_0 and p_n, that represent the valid transitions, are given by solving the *M/M/c* system, and are given below:

$$p_0 = \left(\sum_{n=0}^{c-1} \frac{\alpha^n}{n!} + \frac{\alpha^c}{c!} \cdot \frac{1}{1-\rho} \right)^{-1} \tag{4}$$

and:

$$p_n = \begin{cases} \dfrac{\alpha^n}{n!} \cdot p_0, n = 0,1,...,c-1 \\ \dfrac{\alpha^n}{c! \, c^{n-c}} \cdot p_0, n \geq c \end{cases} \tag{5}$$

where:

$$\alpha = \frac{\lambda}{\mu} \tag{6}$$

3.5.1. Throughput

The expected throughput $\mathrm{E}\left[T_{BS}\right]$ of a single BS is equal to the average number of served sessions in the system multiplied by the transmission rate of each session. The average throughput of a BS is calculated by the following equation:

$$\mathrm{E}\left[T_{BS}\right] = \sum_{n=1}^{c} \frac{\alpha^n}{n!} \cdot p_0 \cdot n \cdot R \tag{7}$$

3.5.2. Energy Efficiency

The ratio of the transmitted bits over the average energy consumption denotes the energy efficiency, calculated in [bits/joule] is given below:

$$\mathrm{E}\left[\eta_{BS}\right] = \frac{\mathrm{E}\left[N_{bits}\right]}{\mathrm{E}\left[E_{BS}\right]} \tag{8}$$

where $\mathrm{E}\left[N_{bits}\right]$ are the transmitted bits of one BS, calculated as the probability being in a system state multiplied by the number of session in the corresponding state and are given by the following equation:

$$\mathrm{E}\left[N_{bits}\right] = \sum_{n=1}^{c} \frac{\alpha^n}{n!} \cdot p_0 \cdot n \tag{9}$$

For any given BS, the energy consumption, $\mathrm{E}\left[E_{BS}\right]$ given in Equation (10), is modeled as a linear function, consisting of the constant part of energy required for feeding the antenna and for cooling, denoted as $\mathrm{E}\left[E_{const}\right]$, and two variable parts, which both depend on traffic load, $\mathrm{E}\left[E_{idle}\right]$ referring to the energy consumed when BS is idle without serving any UE, and $\mathrm{E}\left[E_{TX}\right]$, which corresponds to the energy for serving its traffic:

$$\mathrm{E}\left[E_{BS}\right] = \mathrm{E}\left[E_{const}\right] + \mathrm{E}\left[E_{idle}\right] + \mathrm{E}\left[E_{TX}\right] \tag{10}$$

The energy consumption is further analyzed into the power consumed by a BS during the time, t_{night} which corresponds to the total time that a BS remains active throughout the night zone and is given by the next expression:

$$\mathrm{E}\left[E_{BS}\right] = t_{night}$$
$$\cdot \left(P_{const} + P_{idle} \cdot p_0 + \sum_{n=1}^{c} P_{TX} \cdot p_n \cdot n \right) \tag{11}$$

where, P_{const} is the constant power for BS operation, P_{idle} represents the power consumed in the state p_0, where the BS is idle and no ongoing session waiting to be served and P_{TX} refers to the power consumed for serving one session.

4. PERFORMANCE EVALUATION

In order to evaluate the performance of the proposed switching off schemes and verify our analytical formulation, custom-made C/C++ simulation tools that execute the rules of the algorithms have been developed. Monte Carlo methods were employed to compare our approach to state-of-the-art algorithms. In this section, the simulation setup is described, followed by a discussion about the obtained results.

4.1. Simulation Scenario

Based on the physical layer capabilities of the LTE-Advanced standard, we assume that the overall capacity of the downlink traffic is 115 Mbps. We further assume that our traffic has an average bandwidth of 384 kbps for each session based on the G.711 codec. Each result was produced by running the simulation 1000 times, while we simulate every hour of the night zone.

To evaluate the performance of the proposed algorithms, we consider a typical urban scenario. A cellular deployment has been considered and the distance among the neighboring BSs has been set to 800 meters. Each BS has to serve the same average number of users. The UEs are uniformly distributed around the BSs and the traffic is generated according to a Poisson process. We focus on downlink traffic to measure the energy consumption in the BSs side. In LTE-Advanced, OFDMA is employed as the multiplexing scheme in the downlink. A specific number of sub-carriers and timeslots (called physical resource blocks - PRBs) are allocated to a UE for a predetermined amount of time. Spatial multiplexing allows transmitting different streams of data simultaneously on the same downlink resource block(s), while on different PRBs one single user or different users can transmit concurrently. The LTE-Advanced specification defines parameters for system bandwidth from 1.25 MHz to 20 MHz. In Evolved Universal Terrestrial Radio Access (E-UTRA), a downlink modulation scheme 16QAM is used. The adopted simulation parameters are summarized in Table 1.

To evaluate the energy efficiency of the proposed algorithms (DSO, DDSO, MSO) a research on the State-of-the-Art switching off mechanism for the LTE-Advanced standard has been conducted. Two State-of-the-Art approaches have been employed to provide a comparison for the performance of our proposed schemes: (i) a baseline scenario where all BSs are active and none of the BSs is switched off, referred as No Switching Off approach (NSO), and (ii) a network planning scheme based on the instantaneous traffic intensity, referred as Random Switching Off algorithm (RSO) (Charaviglio, Ciullo, Meo, & Marsan, 2008). The RSO algorithm considers the selection of a random number of BSs to be switched off and calculates the time that this fraction of BSs should be switched off, as already mentioned

Table 1. Simulation parameters

Parameter	Value
Bandwidth, C	115 Mbps
Transmission rate, R	384 kbps
Service time, $1/\mu$	Exponential: mean 50 s/call
Transmission power, P_{TX}	0.37 Watt
Idle power, P_{idle}	0.34 Watt
Constant Power, P_{const}	675 Watt
Inter-site distance	800 m

in Section 2. In addition, an extension of the DDSO algorithm will be used, denoted as Dynamic Traffic-aware Switching On/Off (DTSO). DTSO approach uses traffic instead of distance in order to decide which BSs will be switched off. The purpose of this comparison relies on the determination of which indicator, among distance and traffic, is better to be taken into account in a switching off policy.

4.2. Performance Results

In this section, we provide the analytical and simulation results in terms of energy efficiency and relative energy efficiency gain, as the percentage gain with respect to NSO. For the DDSO scheme, the number of active BSs and its variation through time are given, as well.

In Figure 4, the energy efficiency of the network is calculated for our proposed distance-aware scenario (DSO) and the two reference schemes, namely the baseline scheme (NSO), and the network planning switch off algorithm (RSO). From Figure 4a, comparing our proposal to the reference scenarios, we observe that energy efficiency follows the traffic load variations. When applying our scheme, a fixed number of BSs is switched off, as the switching off decision is taken in the beginning of the night zone. As a consequence, with the traffic decrease, fewer bits are transmitted and less energy is consumed. Nevertheless, since energy consumption includes a constant part that is independent of the traffic (mentioned in Section 3.5), energy decreases at a lower rate with respect to the transmitted bits, thus leading to a reduced energy efficiency. The opposite happens as traffic increases. Comparing the first switching off algorithm to traditional schemes during the night zone, we observe that the DSO approach outperforms the RSO scheme in terms of energy efficiency, without any deterioration in the overall system performance, since the existing traffic is served. The throughput of our system is not degraded in comparison to the State-of-the-Art approaches, even though it is not graphically presented. By focusing on Figure 4b, it is observed that, using our algorithm, a better system performance is achieved, as there is a significant enhancement in energy efficiency of about 40% when comparing our approach to the NSO scheme, in contrast to the 23% improvement of the State-of-the-Art RSO scheme.

The simulation results of the proposed dynamic distance-aware switching off (DDSO) algorithm comparing to the State-of-the-Art solutions are presented in Figure 5a. This algorithm improves the energy efficiency to a greater extend by employing an extended night zone and iteratively applying the switching off policy every hour. The dynamic nature of the algorithm leads to an increased number of BSs that are switched off, and thus to increasing energy savings. The energy efficiency follows the variations of the traffic, while a different number of BSs are turned off each time during the night zone.

The relative comparison of the energy efficiency is presented in Figure 5b. In this figure our dynamic algorithm is presented with respect to the NSO solution. We examine two versions of our algorithm, where in the first one the criterion for the BSs to be switched off is the distance

between the BSs and the UEs (referred as DDSO), and in the other algorithm the BSs are switched off according to the traffic (meaning that the BS with the lowest traffic is switched off, referred as DTSO). The comparison between the two different versions, the DDSO and DTSO, outlines that the algorithm that uses distance for the determination of the switching off BSs gives better performance than the scheme that uses traffic. Therefore, the selection of distance as the critical indicator in the deactivation policy is well stated as energy efficient and more effective than the traffic-aware factors. It is worth noting that for low traffic networks the energy savings of the DDSO scheme in terms of the percentage of energy efficiency can be significant, of the order of 70% compared to the baseline NSO scenario. By comparing the results of Fig.4b to the relative gain of Fig,5b, we remark that DDSO algorithm outperforms the distance aware switching off algorithm (DSO) as well as the previous works appearing in the literature (RSO).

Figure 6 depicts the number of BSs that remain active (N_{on}) during a 24-hour period. In the dynamic schemes, N_{on} decreases gradually after 19:00 p.m., as the switching off scheme is applied at the beginning of each hour and increases again

Figure 4. Distance-aware scheme: (a) Energy efficiency; (b) Relative energy efficiency with respect to NSO

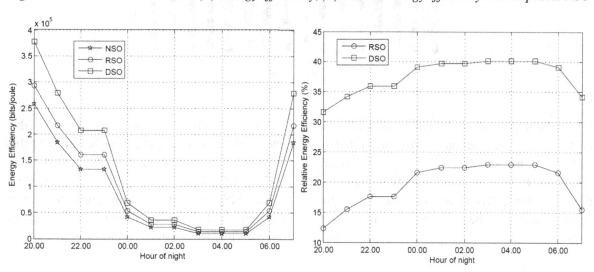

Figure 5. Dynamic distance-aware scheme: (a) Energy efficiency; (b) Relative energy efficiency with respect to NSO

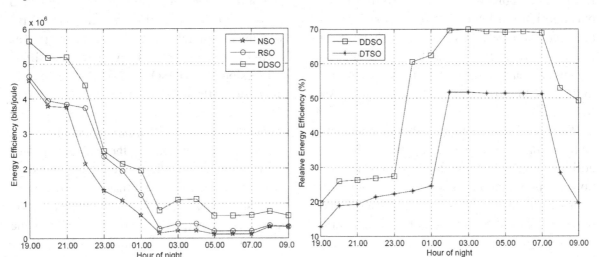

Figure 6. Comparison of energy saving schemes in terms of number of active BSs

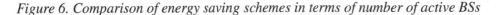

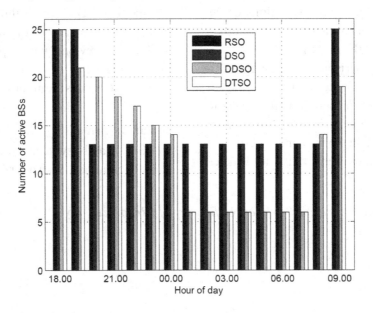

at 08:00 a.m., when the switching on strategy is employed. On the other hand, when applying the RSO algorithm and the DSO algorithm, a fixed number of the BSs are switched off. Comparing the algorithms, DDSO algorithm exploits the whole capacity of network while guaranteeing QoS.

Figure 7a shows the results with regard to the energy efficiency gains that are achieved by the maximization (MSO) and the State-of-the-Art (NSO, RSO) scenarios that we have already mentioned. MSO outperforms both approaches of the literature and the gain in energy efficiency is noteworthy. The relative comparison of the en-

Figure 7. Maximization scheme: (a) Energy efficiency; (b) Relative energy efficiency with respect to NSO

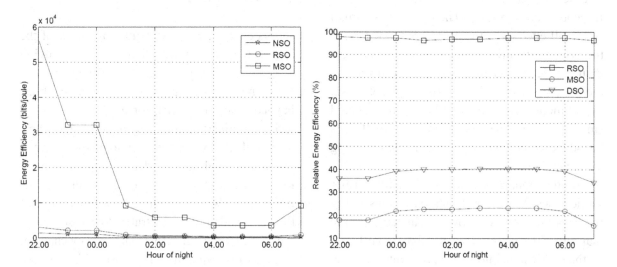

ergy efficiency with respect to NSO scheme is presented in Figure 7b. The energy saving is 96% by using our maximization technique. In addition, it is worth noting that the energy savings that we succeed in terms of the percentage of energy efficiency are of the order of 71% compared to State-of–the-Art RSO algorithm. The MSO algorithm outperforms the DSO scheme, since it exploits the capacity of network in a better way and saves the maximum energy while still guaranteeing QoS by finding the optimal combination between switched off and active BSs.

5. FUTURE RESEARCH DIRECTIONS

The energy consumption problem remains crucial and energy efficiency in cellular networks has to be significantly improved. Therefore, fundamental research for green wireless communications must be done. In our analysis, we focused on achieving energy savings through network planning by switching off BSs during periods with low activity. However, more aspects should be considered and studied towards this direction.

First of all, referring to the aforementioned works of the literature and the proposed switching

off algorithms, energy efficient solutions were presented for deactivating the redundant BSs during low traffic periods. The coverage "gap" of the switched off BSs was covered by the remaining active BSs that increased their transmission power. Still the details of the switching off schemes ought to be examined, because there might be cases where the deactivation of BSs leads to coverage holes. For example, in high traffic regions, a switching off policy may lead users to outage due to lack of network resources. The research works so far study scenarios with uniform traffic, in order to simplify the analysis. Therefore, more realistic scenario and networks configurations should be examined, because operators are willing to save energy, if and only if the service area is preserved and the QoS is not degraded. The question that remains is if it is feasible in practice for the active BSs to increase their transmission power in order to increase their coverage and what are the limitations of the coverage extension. To reduce the outage probability, relay nodes can be used to improve the network coverage and low consumption BSs can be used to maintain the QoS.

In addition, the innovative trend of heterogeneous networks can be exploited. The trend nowadays is to install low consumption nodes in order to provide service in areas where traffic load is concentrated. The existence of small cells will encourage the operators to switch off their BSs even during peak traffic hours and have their traffic served by small cells. Concerning the heterogeneous characteristic of networks, deployment strategies should be investigated since the coexistence of macro and small cells introduces additional complexity in the switching off techniques.

Another important issue that needs to be further studied consists of the traffic load variations during the days. As we have shown in this chapter, the majority of the energy efficient solutions are based on the traffic load information that unfortunately cannot be predicted. So far, we use average values of traffic load and information about real traffic data. The traffic-aware schemes provide promising results, but their behavior is degraded if the traffic load does not follow the predicted patterns. For these cases and to overcome this obstacle, either more advanced strategies must be proposed; or the energy efficient approaches must focus on real time traffic information, which implies more complicated scenarios.

Finally, the coexistence of different operators in the same metropolitan area leads to energy waste due to the increased infrastructure deployment. Therefore, significant energy can be saved if the operators cooperate and share their resources. The cooperation between operators through joint network management and roaming policies entails the proposal of advanced switching off schemes where even more BSs can be switched off. When designing cooperation algorithms, the agreements and the conditions under which the operators will be willing to cooperate formulate a problem that must be thoroughly examined.

Considering the above aspects, we conclude to the fact that there are still many open problems in the concept of energy efficient network planning, and the proposal of innovative solutions is more than compulsory.

6. CONCLUSION

In this chapter, we provided an overview of the latest research activities focused on improving energy efficiency in wireless cellular networks and three energy efficient switching off algorithms, beyond State-of-the-Art, for the LTE-Advanced architecture have been presented. These algorithms decide which BSs are more suitable to be switched off in a general cellular deployment. The main idea of the proposed schemes is that during low traffic periods, the operators switch off some of their BSs and the existing traffic load is served by the BSs that remain active. The first mechanism is based on switching off the suitable BSs according to the average distance of the associated UEs and the BSs. The second scheme proposed to dynamically switch off the BSs by considering the traffic load variations, along with the distance between the BSs and the users. The third approach was an optimization technique. The performance evaluation of the proposed switching off schemes has led to some remarkable observations that are summarized as follows:

- Compared to State-of-the-Art methods proposed for UMTS cellular networks, our solutions improve the energy efficiency to different extends, without deteriorating the total network performance, and the results are very promising.
- The decision of the best suitable BSs to be switched off is affected by the distance between BSs and users and the traffic variations.
- Finally a number of several open lines of investigation in the context of BSs dynamic operation were given. The open "gaps" give the necesary incentives for further research.

ACKNOWLEDGMENT

This work has been funded by the Research Projects GREENET (PITN-GA-2010-264759), CO2GREEN (TEC2010-20823), GREEN-T (TSI-020400-2011-16-CP8-006) and GEOCOM (TEC2011-27723-C02-01).

REFERENCES

3GPP. (2011). *3GPP TR 36.922 V10.1.0, 3rd Generation partnership project: Technical specification group radio access network: Evolved universal terrestrial radio access (E-UTRA), potential solutions for energy saving for E-UTRA, Release 10, technical report.* Author.

3GPP. (2012). *3GPP TS 36.300, V11.4.0, 3rd generation partnership project, technical specification group radio access network, evolved universal terrestrial radio access (E-UTRA) and evolved universal terrestrial radio access network (E-UTRAN), overall description, stage 2, release 11.* Author.

Blume, O., Eckhardt, H., Klein, S., Kuehn, E., & Wajda, W. M. (2010). Energy savings in mobile networks based on adaptation to traffic statistics. *Bell Labs Technical Journal, 15,* 77–94. doi:10.1002/bltj.20442

Chen, T., Zhang, H., Zhao, Z., & Chen, X. (2010). Towards green wireless access networks. In *Proceedings from CHINACOM'10: The 5th International ICST Conference on Communications and Networking in China.* Beijing, China: CHINACOM.

Chiaraviglio, L., Ciullo, D., Meo, M., & Marsan, M. A. (2008). Energy-aware UMTS access networks. In *Proceedings from WPMC'08: The 11th International Symposium on Wireless Personal Multimedia Communications.* Lapland, Finland: WPMC.

Chiaraviglio, L., Ciullo, D., Meo, M., & Marsan, M. A. (2009). Energy-efficient management of UMTS access networks. In *Proceedings from ICT'09: The 21st International Teletraffic Congress.* Paris, France: ICT.

Cisco. (2013, February 6). *Cisco visual networking index: Global mobile data, forecast update 2012-2017.* Retrieved from http://www.cisco.com/en/US/solutions/collateral/ns341/ns525/ns537/ns705/ns827/white_paper_c11-520862.html

Correia, L., Zeller, D., Blume, O., Ferling, D., Jading, Y., & Godor, I. et al. (2012). Challenges and enabling technologies for energy aware mobile radio networks. *IEEE Communications Magazine, 48,* 66–72. doi:10.1109/MCOM.2010.5621969

Ericsson. (2013, January 16). *LTE release 12 – Taking another step toward the networked society, white paper.* Retrieved from http://www.ericsson.com/news/130116-wp-lte-release-12_244129229_c

Freescale. (2008). *Long term evolution protocol overview, whitepaper.* Freescale Semiconductor.

Fusco, G., Buddhikotl, M., Gupta, H., & Venkatesan, S. (2011). Finding green spots and turning the spectrum dial: Novel techniques for green mobile wireless networks. In *Proceedings from DySPAN'11: IEEE Symposium on New Frontiers in Dynamic Spectrum Access Networks.* Aachen, Germany: IEEE.

Global Action Plan. (2007). *An inefficient truth, global action plan.* Retrieved from http://www.globalactionplan.org.uk/

Gong, J., Zhou, S., Niu, Z., & Yang, P. (2010). Traffic-aware base station sleeping in dense cellular networks. In *Proceedings from IWQoS'10: The 18th International Workshop on Quality of Service.* Beijing, China: IWQoS.

Huawei. (2011). *Improving energy efficiency, lowering CO₂ emissions and TCO*. Huawei Technologies Co., Ltd.

Jardosh, A. P., Iannaccone, G., Papagiannaki, K., & Vinnakota, B. (2007). Towards an energy-star WLAN infrastructure. In *Proceedings from HotMobile'07: The 8th IEEE Workshop on Mobile Computing Systems and Applications*. Tucson, AZ: IEEE.

Kolios, P., Friderikos, V., & Papadaki, K. (2010). A practical approach to energy efficient communications in mobile wireless networks. *Journal of Mobile Networks and Applications, 17*(2), 267–280. doi:10.1007/s11036-011-0337-z

Lorincz, J., Capone, A., & Begusic, D. (2011). Optimized network management for energy savings of wireless access networks. *Computer Networks, 55*, 514–540. doi:10.1016/j.comnet.2010.09.013

Marsan, M. A., Chiaraviglio, L., Ciullo, D., & Meo, M. (2009). Optimal energy savings in cellular access networks. In *Proceedings from ICC Workshops '09: The IEEE International Conference on Communications Workshops*. Dresden, Germany: IEEE.

Marsan, M. A., Chiaraviglio, L., Ciullo, D., & Meo, M. (2010). A simple analytical model for the energy-efficient activation of access points in dense WLANSs. In *Proceedings from e-Energy'10: The 1st International Conference on Energy-Efficient Computing and Networking*. New York, NY: e-Energy.

Marsan, M. A., Chiaraviglio, L., Ciullo, D., & Meo, M. (2011). Switch off transients in cellular access networks with sleep modes. In *Proceedings from ICC Workshops'11: The IEEE International Conference on Communications Workshops*. Kyoto, Japan: IEEE.

Martin-Sacristan, D., Monserrat, J. F., Cabrejas Penuelas, J., Calabuig, D., Garrigas, S., & Cardona, N. (2009). On the way towards fourth generation mobile: 3GPP LTE and LTE-advanced. *EURASIP Journal on Wireless Communications and Networking, 4*.

Mobile Operators Could Save $560m+ in OPEX Annually, According to New Arieso Study. (2011, June 15). Retrieved from http://www.fiercemobilecontent.com/node/18332/print

Motorola. (2007). *Node B specification sheet*. Retrieved from http://www.motorola.com

Oh, E., & Krishnamachari, B. (2007). Energy savings through dynamic base station switching in cellular wireless access networks. In *Proceedings from GLOBECOM'10: The IEEE Global Telecommunications Conference*. Miami, FL: IEEE.

Samdanis, K., Kutscher, D., & Brunner, M. (2010). Self-organized energy efficient cellular networks. In *Proceedings from PIMRC'10: The 21st IEEE International Symposium on Personal Indoor and Mobile Radio Communications*. Istanbul, Turkey: IEEE.

Samdanis, K., Taleb, T., Kutscher, D., & Brunner, M. (2011). Self organized network management functions for energy efficient cellular urban infrastructures. *Journal of Mobile Networks and Applications, 17*(1), 119–131. doi:10.1007/s11036-011-0293-7

Sleep Mode for Mobile Base Stations Cuts Jamaican Operators' Carbon Footprint. (2013, February 26). Retrieved from http://www.gsma.com/publicpolicy/sleep-mode-for-mobile-base-stations-cuts-jamaican-operators-carbon-footprint

Telefonica – Focusing on Climate Change Pays Off For Everyone. (2010, September 8). Retrieved from https://idc-insights-community.com/groups/it_agenda/sustainability/telefonica-focusing-on-climate-change-pays-off-for

Vinella, D., & Polignano, M. (2009). *Discontinuous reception and transmission (DRX/DTX) strategies in long term evolution (LTE) for voice-over-IP (VoIP) traffic under both full-dynamic and semi-persistent packet scheduling policies.* (Thesis Dissertation). Aalborg University, Aalborg, Denmark.

Vodafone India Switches off AC at Towers to Cut Energy Costs, and Carbon Emissions. (2013, March 20). Retrieved from http://articles.economictimes.indiatimes.com/2013-03-20/news/37872443_1_indus-towers-telecom-towers-vodafone-india

Zhou, S., Gong, J., Yang, Z., Niu, Z., & Yang, P. (2009). Green mobile access network with dynamic base station energy saving. In *Proceeding from MobiCom'09: The 15th Annual International Conference on Mobile Computing and Networking.* Beijing, China: ACM.

ADDITIONAL READING

3GPP. TR 25.913, v. 9.0.0 (2009), *Requirements for Evolved UTRA (EUTRA) and Evolved UTRAN (E-UTRAN).*

3GPP. (2010). *TR 36.814, v9.0.0.* Further Advancements for EUTRA Physical Layer Aspects.

3GPP. TR 25.912), v8.0.0 (2008), Feasibility Study for Evolved Universal Terrestrial Radio Access (UTRA) and Universal Terrestrial Radio Access Network (UTRAN.

3GPP. TR 25.913, v8.0.0 (2008), Requirements for Evolved UTRA (E-UTRA) and Evolved UTRAN (E-UTRAN).

3GPP. TR 36.913, v9.0.0 (2010), Requirements for Further Advancements for Evolved Universal Terrestrial Radio Access (E-UTRA) (LTE-Advanced).

Astély, D., Dahlman, E., Frenger, P., Ludwig, R., Meyer, M., & Parkvall, S. et al. (2006). A Future Radio-Access Framework. *IEEE Journal on Selected Areas in Communications, 24*(3), 693–706. doi:10.1109/JSAC.2005.862420

Badic, B., O'Farell, T., Loskot, P., & He, J. (2009). Energy efficient radio access architectures for green radio: large versus small cell size deployment. Proceedings from VTC'09 Fall: *The IEEE 70th Vehicular Technology Conference Fall.* Anchorage, AK, USA.

Bousia, A., Antonopoulos, A., Alonso, L., & Verikoukis, C. (2012). Green distance-aware base station sleeping algorithm in LTE-Advanced. Proceedings from ICC'12: *The IEEE International Conference on Communications.* Ottawa, ON, Canada.

Bousia, A., Kartsakli, E., Alonso, L., & Verikoukis, C. (2012). Dynamic energy efficient distance-aware base station switch on/off scheme for LTE-Advanced. Proceedings from GLOBECOM'12: *The IEEE Global Communications Conference.* Anaheim, CA, USA.

Bousia, A., Kartsakli, E., Alonso, L., & Verikoukis, C. (2012). Energy efficient base station maximization switch off scheme for LTE-Advanced. Proceedings from CAMAD'12: *The IEEE 17th International Workshop on Computer Aided Modeling and Design of Communication Links and Networks.* Barcelona, Spain.

Bousia, A., Katsakli, E., Antonopoulos, A., Alonso, L., & Verikoukis, C. (2013). Game Theoretic Approach for Switching Off Base Stations in Multi-Operator Environments, Proceedings from ICC'13: *The IEEE International Conference on Communications.* Budapest, Hungary.

Dahlman, E., & Parkvall, S. (2011). LTE/LTE-Advanced for Mobile Broadband, Academic Press, 2011.

Dahlman, E., Parkvall, S., Skold, J., & Beming, P. (2008). *3G Evolution: HSPA and LTE for Mobile Broadband* (2nd ed.). Academic Press.

Kawai, H., Morimoto, A., Higuchi, K., & Sawa-hashi, M. (2010). Investigations on Inter-Node B Macro Diversity for Single-Carrier Based Radio Access in Evolved UTRA Uplink. *IEICE Transactions on Communications. E (Norwalk, Conn.), 93-B*(1), 125–134.

Koudouridis, G. P., & Li, H. (2012). Distributed Power On-Off Optimisation for Heterogeneous Networks. Proceedings from CAMAD'12: *The IEEE 17th International Workshop on Computer Aided Modeling and Design of Communication Links and Networks*. Barcelona, Spain.

Larmo, A., Lindstrom, M., Meyer, M., Pelletier, G., Torsner, J., & Wiemann, H. (2009). The LTE Link Layer Design. *IEEE Communications Magazine, 47*(4), 52–59. doi:10.1109/MCOM.2009.4907407

Marsan, M. A., & Meo, M. (2009). Energy efficient management of two cellular access networks. *ACM SIGMETRICS performance. Evaluation Review, 37*(4), 69–73.

Marsan, M. A., & Meo, M. (2011). Energy efficient wireless Internet access with cooperative cellular networks. *Elsevier Journal Computer Networks, 55*(2), 386–398. doi:10.1016/j.comnet.2010.10.017

Sesia, S., Toufik, I., & Baker, M. (2011). *LTE - The UMTS Long Term Evolution: From Theory to Practice* (2nd ed.). Wiley. doi:10.1002/9780470978504

Son, K., Oh, E., & Krishnamachari, B. (2011). Energy-aware hierarchical cell configuration: from deployment to operation. Proceedings from INFOCOM WKSHPS'11: *The IEEE Conference on Computer Communications Workshops*. Shanghai, China.

Tombaz, S., Usman, M., & Zander, J. (2011). Energy efficiency improvements through heterogeneous networks in diverse traffic distribution scenarios. Proceedings from CHINACOM'11: *The 6th International ICST Conference on Communications and Networking in China*. Harbin, China.

KEY TERMS AND DEFINITIONS

Energy Efficiency: Metric that is defined as the ratio of the transmitted bits over the average energy consumption, measured in [bits/joule].

Green Communications: Field of cellular networks that deals with the proposal of energy efficient solutions.

LTE-Advanced Standard: Mobile communication standard, formally submitted as a candidate 4G system to ITU-T in late 2009.

Maximization Problem: The selection of finding the best solution among all feasible solutions.

Switching Off Schemes: Algorithms for energy saving in cellular networks where operators switch off the BSs which become redundant due to low traffic variations.

Chapter 7
Increasing Throughput of MIMO LTE–Advanced using Carrier Aggregation Feature

Aws Zuheer Yonis
University of Mosul, Iraq

Mohammad Faiz Liew Abdullah
University Tun Hussein Onn Malaysia, Malaysia

ABSTRACT

Carrier Aggregation (CA) is one of the key features in Long Term Evolution-Advanced (LTE-A) to support wider bandwidth than the bandwidth supported by LTE. In this chapter, design and implementation of LTE-A to support greater bandwidth by improving the carrier aggregation technique and deployment scenarios such as intra-band contiguous carrier aggregation, intra-band non-contiguous carrier aggregation, and inter-band non-contiguous carrier aggregation are provided. As a result, this chapter presents the first evolution case of carrier aggregation on LTE-Advanced to support bandwidth up to 120 MHz in contiguous carrier aggregation instead of 100 MHz and 100 MHz in non-contiguous carrier aggregation instead of 80 MHz, where these challenges can provide high peak data rate, low latency, and high spectral efficiency. Although LTE already in its first release provides very high performance, it can also serve as a robust structure for evolving into even higher performance, as prospectively the revolution will go on beyond LTE-A to converge future requirements emerging with increased user expectations.

INTRODUCTION

The developments of carrier aggregation in Release 10 (LTE-A) specifications are continuing to provide enhanced capacity and higher peak data rates. Some extensions are provided in Release 10, including support for User Equipment (UE) positioning and enhanced beamforming (Song & Shen, 2011). The initial version of Release 8- LTE can satisfy many of these demands in terms of the peak data rate requirements, spectral efficiency and some particular deployment scenarios which require significant new features and provide extensive support for deployment in spectrum allocations of various characteristics, with transmission bandwidths ranging from 1.4 MHz up to 20 MHz in both paired and unpaired bands. While release 10 (LTE-Advanced) transmission

DOI: 10.4018/978-1-4666-4888-3.ch007

bandwidth can be further extended with carrier aggregation (CA), where multiple component carriers are aggregated and used for transmission to/from a single mobile terminal. Carrier aggregation has two scenarios: intra-band carrier aggregation and inter-band carrier aggregation, as described in section 8, both of which can achieve higher bandwidth and throughput.

LTE standard evolution from Rel-8 to beyond Rel-11 is shown in Figure 1. Importantly, the one eminent challenge of Release 11 is carrier aggregation, whereby multiple carriers at several frequencies, and possibly of several bandwidths, are used in coupling with each other in a single cell, as explained schematically in Figure 1 (Zhang & Zhou, 2013).

In addition, this chapter also describes the two main parts of LTE-Advanced. The first part concerns the uplink (UL) and presents Single Carrier Frequency Division Multiple Access (SC-FDMA), where the data from mobiles is transmitted from user equipment (UE) to the base station (eNB). The second part covers the downlink (DL) and which presents Orthogonal Frequency Division Multiple Access (OFDMA), where data from mobiles is transmitted from the base station (eNB) to user equipment (UE).

This chapter presents LTE-A downlink designed to increase the number of component carriers which lead to reach bandwidth equal to 120 MHz in contiguous carrier aggregation, instead of 100 MHz and 100 MHz in non-contiguous carrier aggregation while it was 80 MHz only. All the

Figure 1. LTE evolution from Rel-8 to Rel-11

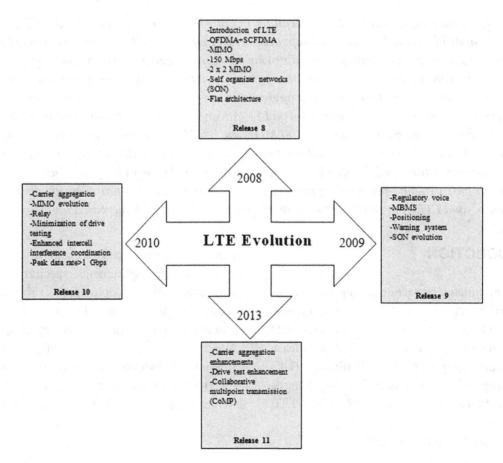

fundamentals of MIMO are included in section II, while its capacity is explained in section III. Section IV then goes on to cover the combination of MIMO with LTE-Advanced, which is followed by sections V and VI that present LTE-Advanced as peak data rate and peak spectral efficiency, respectively. The design of the downlink for LTE-Advanced is then explained in section VII, while all the scenarios of carrier aggregation are described in section VIII. Following this, all the types of intra band carrier aggregation (contiguous and non-contiguous) are included in sections IX and X. Simulation examples of these cases with all the results are included in sections XI and XIII. Finally, the main conclusions from the implementation of the proposed new design are explained in conclusion section.

BASICS OF MULTI INPUT MULTI OUTPUT (MIMO)

The use of the term MIMO is meant to differentiate it from a classical wireless system where a single antenna is used both at the transmitting and at the receiving end, called Single Input Single Output (SISO). More generally, it is common to define an antenna system related to the number of antennas at the receiver and transmitter. Figure 2 shows four antenna configurations that can characterize any wireless radio communication system: SISO, Single Input Multiple Output (SIMO) (which is characterized by a single transmit antenna and multiple receive antennas), Multiple-Input Single-Output (MISO) (which is characterized by multiple transmit antennas and a single receive antenna), and MIMO, where multiple antennas are used at both ends of the transmission. Multi antenna techniques are used in order to achieve the following parameters:

- Diversity gain;
- Array gain;
- Multiplexing gain.

The role of diversity is to increase the reliability of the radio link. Diversity gain is the gain obtained from receiving independently (or partially correlated) faded replicas of the signal. Diversity can be achieved by transmitting or receiving the signal over multiple independently fading paths (in time, frequency or space). Transmit diversity techniques attain exclusively diversity gain, while space-time-coding methods aim for a beneficial tradeoff between diversity and multiplexing.

These techniques do not require knowledge of the channel matrix that is the channel state information transmitter (CSIT). Formally, the diversity gain for a MIMO system designates the negative slope of the average error probability, P_e, versus the signal to noise ratio (SNR) and is given by:

$$d = -\lim\left(SNR \to \infty\right)\frac{\log\left(P_e\left(SNR\right)\right)}{\log\left(SNR\right)} \quad (1)$$

Array gain, also called beamforming gain, is the average increase in the receive SNR due to a coherent combining from multiple antennas at the receiver or transmitter or both. Array gain requires partial or full channel knowledge at the transmitter or receiver and depends on the number of transmit and receive antennas.

Spatial multiplexing gain is the increase of data rate at no additional power consumption obtained, for example, by transmitting multiple data streams or layers that are spatially multiplexed into the same time and frequency slot. Formally, the multiplexing gain of a MIMO transmission strategy, achieving $C(SNR)$ as the information rate at an arbitrary SNR, is defined as:

$$r = \lim\left(SNR \to \infty\right)\frac{C(SNR)}{\log(SNR)} \quad (2)$$

Figure 2. Antenna configurations

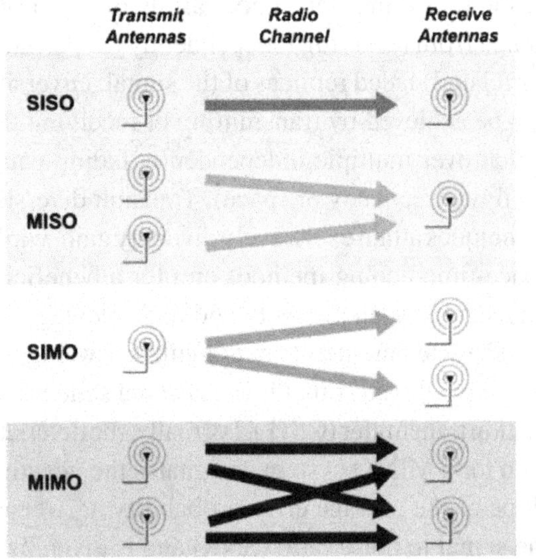

$$C_{MIMO} = E\left[log_2 \det\left(I_N + \frac{\acute{A}}{M}HH^*\right)\right] \mathrm{b/s/} Hz$$

(4)

where $\rho = \dfrac{P}{N_o}$ the received signal-to-noise ratio at each receive antenna.

If $\lambda 1 \geq \lambda 2 \geq \cdots \geq \lambda min$ are the (random) ordered singular values of the channel matrix H, then Equation (4) can be expressed as:

$$C_{MIMO} = E\left[\sum_{i=1}^{n\,min} log_2(1 + \frac{\rho}{M}\lambda_i^2)\right] =$$
$$\sum_{i=1}^{n\,min} E\left[log_2(1 + \frac{\rho}{M}\lambda_i^2)\right] b/s/Hz$$

(5)

where $n_{min} = \min (M, N)$. Let us first look at the case of low SNR where the approximation $log_2 (1 + x) \approx x$. $log_2 e$ can be used:

$$C_{MIMO} \approx \sum_{i=1}^{n_{min}} \frac{\rho}{M} E\left[(\lambda_i^2)\right] log_2 e =$$
$$\frac{\rho}{M} E\left[T_r\left[HH^*\right]\right] log_2 e =$$
$$\frac{\rho}{M} E\left[\sum_{i,j} |h_{ij}| * |h_{ij}|\right] log_2 e =$$
$$M \times \rho \times log_2 e \left[b/s/Hz\right]$$

(6)

It can be noted that at low SNR, an $M \times M$ system yields a power gain of $10 \times log_{10} (M)$ dBs relative to a single-receiver antenna. This is because the M receives antennas can coherently combine their received signals to get a power boost.

For high-SNR, where the approximation $log_2 (1 + x) \approx log_2 (x)$ can be used, the MIMO capacity formula can be expressed as:

CAPACITY OF MULTI INPUT MULTI OUTPUT

A MIMO channel consists of channel gains and phase information for links from each of the transmission antennas to each of the receive antennas as shown in Figure 3. Therefore, the channel for the M × N MIMO system consists of an N × M matrix $H_{N \times M}$ given as (Khan, 2009):

$$H = \begin{bmatrix} h_{11} & h_{12} & \cdots & h_{1M} \\ \vdots & & \ddots & \vdots \\ h_{N1} & h_{M2} & \cdots & h_{NM} \end{bmatrix}$$

(3)

where h_{ij} represents the channel gain from transmission antenna j to the receive antenna i.

In order to enable the estimations of the elements of the MIMO channel matrix, separate reference signals or pilots are transmitted from each of the transmission antennas.

The capacity of an $M \times N$ MIMO channel can be written as:

Figure 3. (M x N) MIMO system

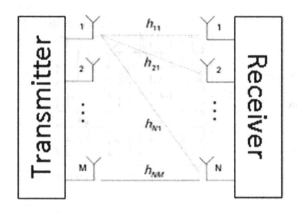

$$C_{MIMO} = \sum_{i=1}^{M} E \left[log_2 \left(\frac{\rho}{M} \lambda_i^2 \right) \right] =$$

$$\sum_{i=1}^{M} E \left[log_2 \left(\frac{\rho}{M} \right) + log_2 \left(\lambda_i^2 \right) \right] =$$

$$n_{min} \times log_2 \left(\frac{\rho}{M} \right)$$

$$+ \sum_{i=1}^{n_{min}} E \left[log_2 \left(\lambda_i^2 \right) \right] \quad b/s/Hz$$

(7)

where, $E[log_2(\lambda_i^2)] > -\infty$ for all $_i$.

The full n_{min} degree of freedom can be obtained at high SNR. It can also be noted that the maximum capacity is achieved when all the singular values are equal. Therefore, a high capacity gain would be expected when the channel matrix H is sufficiently random and statistically well-conditioned. It is important to note that the number of degrees of freedom is limited by the minimum of the number of transmission and the number of receive antennas. Therefore, a large number of transmission and receive antennas are required in order to get the full benefit from MIMO.

Observe from (6) that the capacity of a MIMO system scales linearly with the number of receive antennas at low SNR. Also note that from (7) that at high SNR, the capacity scales linearly with n_{min}. Therefore, at all SNRs, the capacity of an M × N MIMO system scales linearly with n_{min}. However, the channel matrix needs to be full rank in order to provide n_{min} degrees of freedom.

MIMO IN LTE-ADVANCED

The basic principle of MIMO is presented in Figure 4, where the different data streams are fed to the pre-coding operation and then onwards to signal mapping and OFDMA signal generation.

The reference symbols enable the receiver to separate different antennas from each other. In order to avoid transmission from another antenna corrupting the channel estimation needed for separating the MIMO streams, one needs to have each reference symbol resource used by a single transmit antenna only (Holma & Toskala, 2011).

This principle is illustrated in Figure 5, where the reference symbols and empty resource elements are mapped to alternate between antennas. This principle can also be extended to cover more

Figure 4. MIMO principles 2x2 antenna configuration (Holma and Toskala, 2011)

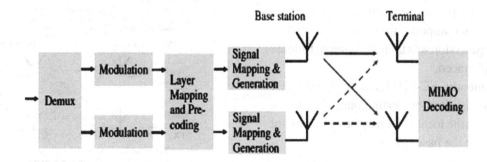

Figure 5. OFDMA reference symbols to support 2-eNodeB transmit antennas

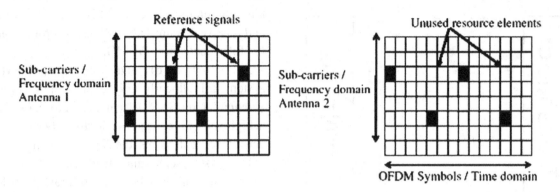

than two antennas, with the first LTE Release covering up to four antennas. As the number of antennas increases, the required SNR also increases the resulting transmitter/receiver complexity and the reference symbol overhead.

Even the LTE uplink supports MIMO technology. While the device uses only one transmit antenna, the single user data rate cannot be increased with MIMO. The cell level maximum data rate can be doubled, however, by allocating two devices with orthogonal reference signals.

Thus, the transmission at the base station is treated like a MIMO transmission, as shown in Figure 6, and the data stream is separated with MIMO receiver processing. This kind of 'virtual' or 'Multi-user' MIMO is supported in LTE Release 8 and does not represent any major implementation complexity from the device perspective as only the reference signal sequence is modified. From the network side, additional processing is required to separate the users from each other. The use of 'classical' two antenna MIMO transmission is not particularly attractive due to the resulting device impacts, thus the multi-antenna device transmission was included later in Release 10 LTE-Advanced.

Consequently, SC-FDMA is well-suited for MIMO use as users are orthogonal (inside the cell) and thus the local SNR may be very high for users close to the base station.

PEAK DATA RATE IN LTE-A

Rel-8 LTE delivers improved system capacity and coverage, improved user experience through higher data rates, reduced-latency deployment, reduced operating costs, and seamless integration with existing systems. This further advancement for LTE is known as LTE-Advanced (LTE-A). The LTE-A requirements are shown in Table 1 and focus mainly on improvements in system performance and latency reduction. From Table 1, it can be seen that the target cell and user spectral efficiencies have increased significantly. Peak data rates of 1 Gbps in the downlink and 500 Mbps in the uplink must be supported. Target latencies have been significantly reduced as well. In ad-

Figure 6. MU-MIMO principle with single transmits antenna devices (Holma and Toskala, 2011)

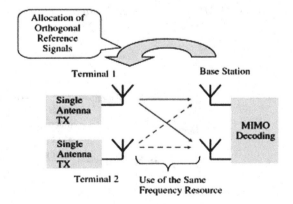

dition to advancements in system performance, deployment and operating-cost-related goals were also introduced. They include support for cost-efficient multi-vendor deployment, power efficiency, efficient backhaul, open interfaces, and minimized maintenance tasks. A comprehensive list of LTE-A requirements can be found in (Ghosh & Ratasuk, 2011).

The key features of LTE-A include, in particular, enhanced peak data rates to support advanced services and applications (100 Mbps for high mobility and 1 Gbps for low mobility (Forsberg, Horn, Moeller and Niemi, 2010).

Besides that, the cell throughput or spectral efficiency target is set at around two times higher than existing LTE systems. In order to meet the peak data rate and spectral efficiency targets set by LTE-Advanced, the air interface needs to be evolved by incorporating new radio technologies as well as improving performance of the existing techniques.

Table 1. LTE-A requirements

Feature	Requirements
Peak data rate	Downlink -1 Gbps
	Uplink - 500 Mbps
Peak spectrum efficiency	Downlink – 30 bps/ Hz (8 x 8)
	Uplink - 15 bps/Hz (4 x 4)
Average cell spectrum efficiency	Downlink - 3.7 bps/ Hz (4 x 4)
	Uplink - 2.0 bps /Hz (2 x 4)
Cell edge user spectral efficiency	Downlink - 0.12 bps /Hz (4 x 4)
	Uplink -0.07 bps/ Hz (2 x 4)
C- plane latency	50 ms from camped to active state
	10 ms from dormant to active state
U- plane latency	Reduced compared with Rel-8 (LTE)

PEAK RATES AND PEAK SPECTRAL EFFICIENCY

Many services with lower data rates such as voice services are important and still occupy a large part of a mobile network's overall capacity, but it is the higher data rate services that drive the design of the radio interface. The ever increasing demand for higher data rates for web browsing, streaming and file transfer pushes the peak data rates for mobile systems from kbps for 2G, to Mbps for 3G and close to Gbps for 4G (Hossain, Kim and Bhargav, 2011).

For marketing purposes, the first parameter by which different radio access technologies are usually compared is the peak per-user data rate which can be achieved. This peak data rate generally scales according to the amount of spectrum used, and, for MIMO systems, according to the minimum of the number of transmit and receive antennas.

The peak data rate can be defined as the maximum throughput per user assuming the entire bandwidth is being allocated to a single user with the highest modulation and coding scheme and the maximum number of antennas supported. Typical radio interface overhead (control channels, pilot signals, guard intervals, etc.) is estimated and taken into account for a given operating point. For Time Division Duplex (TDD) systems, the peak data rate is generally calculated for the downlink and uplink periods separately. This makes it possible to obtain a single value independent of the uplink/downlink ratio and a fair system comparison that is agnostic of the duplex mode.

The maximum spectral efficiency is then obtained simply by dividing the peak rate by the used spectrum allocation. The target peak data rates for downlink and uplink in LTE Release 8 were set at 100 Mbps and 50 Mbps respectively within a 20 MHz bandwidth, 7 corresponding to respective peak spectral efficiencies of 5 and 2.5 bps/Hz. The underlying assumption here is that the terminal has two receive antennas and one transmit antenna.

The number of antennas used at the base station is more easily upgradeable by the network operator, and the first version of the LTE specifications was therefore designed to support downlink MIMO operation with up to four transmit and receive antennas. When comparing the capabilities of different radio communication technologies, great emphasis is often placed on the peak data rate capabilities. While this is one indicator of how technologically advanced a system is and can be obtained by simple calculations, it may not be a key differentiator in the usage scenarios for a mobile communication system in practical deployment. Moreover, it is relatively easy to design a system that can provide very high peak data rates for users close to the base station, where interference from other cells is low and techniques such as MIMO can be used to their greatest extent. It is much more challenging to provide high data rates with good coverage and mobility, but it is exactly these latter aspects which contribute most strongly to user satisfaction. In typical deployments, individual users are located at varying distances from the base stations, the propagation conditions for radio signals to individual users are rarely ideal, and the available resources must be shared between many users. Consequently, although the claimed peak data rates of a system are genuinely achievable in the right conditions, it is rare for a single user to be able to experience the peak data rates for a sustained period, and the envisaged applications do not usually require this level of performance.

A differentiator of the LTE system design compared to some other systems has been the recognition of these 'typical deployment constraints' from the beginning. During the design process, emphasis was therefore placed not only on providing a competitive peak data rate for use when conditions allow, but also, importantly, on system level performance, which was evaluated during several performance verification steps.

System-level evaluations are based on simulations of multicell configurations where data transmission from/to a population of mobiles is considered in a typical deployment scenario. The sections below describe the main metrics used to determine system level performance. In order to make these metrics meaningful, parameters such as the deployment scenario, traffic models, channel models and system configuration need to be defined. The improvement in downlink sector spectral efficiencies on going from 2G to 4.5G systems is shown in Figure 7 (Ghosh & Ratasuk, 2011).

DOWNLINK DESIGN OF LTE-ADVANCED

The downlink LTE system is based on OFDMA an air interface transmission scheme. OFDMA is a combination of time division multiple access (TDMA) (Rumney, 2009). The basic idea of OFDMA systems is to divide the frequency spectrum into several orthogonal subcarriers using the OFDM multiplexing technique. Those frequency subcarriers are shared among users using an access technique. A scheme of a baseband OFDMA system is shown in Figure 8.

The downlink in LTE-A is represented by OFDMA. The practical implementation of an OFDMA system is based on digital technology and, more specifically, on the use of discrete fourier transform (DFT) and the inverse operation (IDFT) to move between time and frequency domain representations.

The practical implementations use the fast fourier transform (FFT). The FFT operation carries the signal from time domain to frequency domain. The Inverse-IFFT does the operation in the opposite direction. For the sinusoidal wave,

Figure 7. Improvement in downlink spectral efficiency going from 2G to 4G system (Ghosh and Ratasuk, 2011)

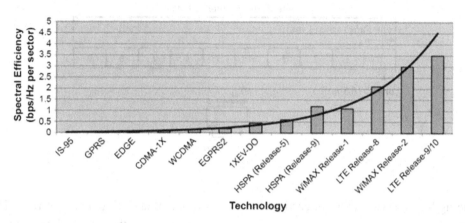

Figure 8. Downlink LTE-A system model

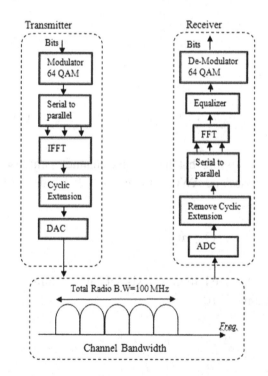

the FFT operation's output will have a peak at the corresponding frequency and zero output elsewhere. If the input is a square wave, the frequency domain output contains peaks at multiple frequencies because such waves contain several frequencies covered by the FFT operation. The FFT operation can be carried out back and forth

without losing any of the original information. Thus, for LTE, the necessary FFT lengths also tend to be powers of two, such as 512, 1024, etc.

The transmitter principle in any OFDMA system is to use narrow, mutually orthogonal subcarriers. In LTE, the sub-carrier spacing is 15 kHz, regardless of the total transmission bandwidth. Therefore, different sub-carriers are orthogonal to each other, as at the sampling instant of a single subcarrier the other sub-carriers have a zero value. The transmitter of an OFDMA system uses the IFFT block to create the signal. The data source feeds to the serial-to parallel conversion and further to the IFFT block. Each input for the IFFT block corresponds to the input representing a particular sub-carrier (or particular frequency component of the time domain signal) and can be modulated independently of the other sub-carriers. The IFFT block is followed by adding the cyclic extension, as shown in Figure 9.

Consider an OFDM system which comprises N_c carriers, occupying a bandwidth B. The OFDM symbols are transmitted in time τ_s, including a cyclic prefix of a duration denoted by τ_{cp}.

The total duration of one OFDM symbol is:

$$\tau_u = \tau_s - \tau_{cp} \tag{8}$$

Figure 9. LTE Frame structure (3rd Generation Partnership Project, 2009)

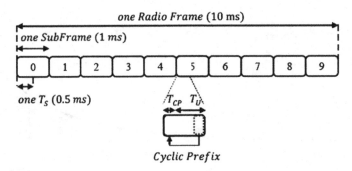

The spacing between two adjacent carriers is indicated by:

$$\beta f = 1 / \tau_u \qquad (9)$$

The purpose for adding the cyclic extension is to avert inter-symbol interference (ISI). When the transmitter adds a cyclic extension longer than the channel impulse response, the effect of the previous symbol can be averted by removing the cyclic extension at the receiver (Galih, Adiono and Kurniawan, 2010).

Figure 8 shows the baseband OFDM system model. X_k denote the complex symbols of a downlink LTE system where 16-QAM, 64-QAM and QPSK modulations can be used (Hlel, Cherif, Tlili and Siala, 2005), $U(t)$ is the filter impulse response, $h(\tau,t)$ represents the impulse response of the mobile radio transmission channel, and $n(t)$ is an additive white Gaussian noise (AWGN) with power spectral density $N_0/2$:

$$X = \begin{bmatrix} X_0 \, X_1 \ldots X_{Nc-1} \end{bmatrix}^T$$

and:

$$Y = \begin{bmatrix} Y_{0,I} & Y_{1,I} & \ldots Y_{Nc-1} \end{bmatrix}^T \qquad (10)$$

assuming that the input data of IDFT block at the transmitter and the output data of DFT block at the receiver:

$$\bar{h} = \begin{bmatrix} h_0 \, h_1 \ldots h_{Nc-1} \end{bmatrix}^T$$

and:

$$\bar{n} = \begin{bmatrix} n_0 \, n_1 \ldots n_{Nc-1} \end{bmatrix}^T \qquad (11)$$

Assuming that the sampled channel is impulse response and AWGN, the input matrix is defined as:

$$\underline{X} = \mathrm{diag}\,(X) \; and \; \underline{F}$$

The DFT-matrix (Al-Naffouri, Islam, Al-Dhahir, 2010):

$$\underline{F} = \begin{bmatrix} w_N^{0,0} & w_N^{0,1} & \cdots & w_N^{0,N_c-1} \\ w_N^{1,0} & w_N^{1,1} & \cdots & \cdot \\ \vdots & & \vdots & \ddots & \vdots \\ w_N^{N-1,0} & & \cdots & & w_N^{N-1,N_c-1} \end{bmatrix} \qquad (12)$$

where, N is the FFT size and:

$$W^{i,k}_N = (1 / \sqrt{N}) \, exp^{-j2\pi(i \, k/N)} \qquad (13)$$

Also, the channel frequency response is given by:

$$\underline{H} = DFT_N(\overline{h}) = \underline{F}\overline{h} \qquad (14)$$

and the noise in frequency domain is represented by:

$$N = \underline{F}\overline{n}. \qquad (15)$$

Assuming that the Channel Delay Spread < Cyclic Prefix Length,

The interference between the OFDM symbols can be removed. Therefore, the OFDM received signal is expressed by (Al-Naffouri, Islam, Al-Dhahir, 2010).

$$Y = DFT_N(IDFT_N(X) \ Conjunction \ \overline{h} + \overline{n}) = \underline{X}\underline{F}\overline{h} + N = \underline{X}H + N \qquad (16)$$

The relationship between the input and the output for each OFDM subcarrier can be written as:

$$Y_{k,i} = H_{K,i}X_{k,i} + N_{k,i} \qquad (17)$$

For a given symbol i, $H_{k,i}$ is the channel frequency response of the subcarrier f_k given by:

$$f_k = f_c + k/T_u \qquad (18)$$

Where, f_c is the carrier frequency and $N_{k,i}$ are obtained by applying a DFT to the vector $\overline{n}$, where $n_{k,i}$ is the result of sampling $n(t)$ at time $T_{k,i}$ given by the following equation:

$$T_{k,i} = iT_s + T_{pc} + (k \ T_u/N) \qquad (19)$$

As shown in Figure 9, each LTE radio frame duration has 10 ms (Karakaya, Arslan and Ali Cirpan, 2008), which is divided into 10 subframes.

So, each subframe is further divided into two slots, each having a 0.5 ms duration.

Figure 10 shows the physical resource block (PRB), which is a basic unit of access allocation. PRB bandwidth per slot (0.5 ms) consists of 12 subcarriers with frequency spacing of 15 kHz.

In time domain, each PRB has one slot with either 6 or 7 OFDM symbols, depending on the chosen cyclic prefix, depending on whether it is extended or normal. The transmission parameters of the LTE/OFDMA standard are shown in the following Table 2 (3rd Generation Partnership Project, 2006).

SCENARIOS OF CARRIER AGGREGATION IN LTE-ADVANCED

In Figure 11, the cases of contiguous and non-contiguous component carriers are illustrated even though, from a baseband perspective, this might not always be the case (i.e. access to large amounts of contiguous spectrum, in the order of 100 MHz, may not always be possible).

LTE-Advanced could, therefore, allow for aggregation of non-contiguous component carriers in, possibly, separate spectrum to handle situations:

Figure 10. Physical resource block

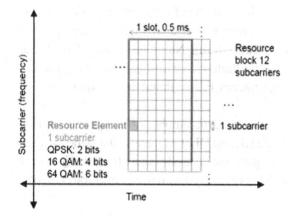

Table 2. LTE OFDMA parameters

Transmission bandwidth (MHz)	1.25	2.5	5	10	15	20
Sub-frame duration (ms)	0.5					
Sub-carrier spacing (kHz)	15					
Sampling frequency	1.92	3.84	7.68	15.36	23.04	30.72
FFT size	128	256	512	1024	1536	2048
Number of occupied sub-carriers	76	151	301	601	901	1201

Figure 11. Types of carrier aggregation for LTE-Advanced (Osseiran, Monserrat, and Mohr, 2011)

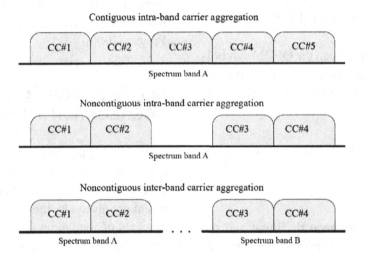

- **Intra-Band Contiguous Carrier Aggregation:** To each other within the same band. (Referring to Figure 11) (Yonis, Abdullah and Ghanim, 2012).
- **Intra-Band Non-Contiguous Carrier Aggregation:** When multiple CCs within the same band are used in a non-contiguous manner. (Referring to Figure 11).
- **Inter-Band Non-Contiguous CA:** When multiple CCs are separated along the frequency band. (Referring to Figure 11).

However, the number of component carriers in the UL and DL are typically the same for TDD deployments. Access to higher transmission bandwidths is not only useful from a peak-rate perspec-

tive, but also, and probably more important, as a tool for extending the coverage of medium data rates. Component carriers can be aggregated at different layers in the protocol stack.

LTE-ADVANCED DL INTRA BAND CONTIGUOUS CARRIER AGGREGATION

The following simulation is to generate LTE-Advanced downlink signals with carrier aggregation. The frequency band (center frequency) bandwidth of the component carrier, oversampling ratio, and the number of transmitter antennas can be changed in the parameter tab.

Figure 12. Block diagram for N x OFDMA

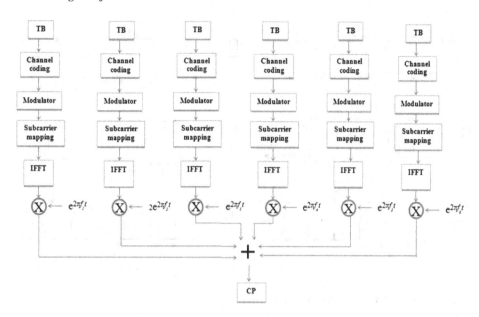

TYPES OF NON-CONTIGUOUS CA SCENARIO

Figures 13 and 14 illustrate the many possible scenarios for carrier aggregation; namely, noncontiguous component carrier. The introduction of the latter has been to support carrier aggregation in situations when sufficient contiguous component carriers are not available.

Despite the many promised advantages of carrier aggregation, the associated computational complexities are not marginal. In fact, implementing spectrum aggregation is a challenging process. It requires constant awareness of the available component carriers, the QoS requirements of the different users, the channel state information (CSI) for the requesting users over the different channels, etc. In addition, it requires additional resources to process the aggregation and de-aggregation processes at the PHY layer. For these reasons, spectrum aggregation is expected to be only applied for more capable terminals. When the bandwidth is 100 MHz, there are many scenarios supported for user 1 and user 2

as shown in Figure 13 (Akyildiz, Gutierrez-Estevez and Reyes, 2010).

This chapter presents a new method that supports more than 100 MHz, reaching to 120 MHz. The designed system is able to support more than two users and is able to send data at higher throughput and a higher peak data rate.

Figure 14 explained the examples on the possible scenarios with bandwidth of 120 MHz.

SIMULATION AND RESULTS OF CONTIGUOUS CA

The simulation of the system is used to verify the various types of intra-band carrier aggregation (two types non-contiguous and contiguous). The results showed that the CA spectrum power simulation for different bandwidths LTE-Advanced system contiguous CCs at 20 MHz, 40 MHz, 60 MHz, 80 MHz, 100 MHz, and 120 MHz; the other type of non-contiguous intra-band carrier aggregation where the bandwidth is 60 MHz, 100 MHz, and 120 MHz.

Figure 13. Scenarios of CA with bandwidth 100 MHz

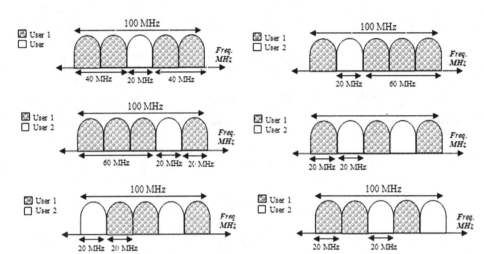

Figure 14. Scenarios of CA with bandwidth 120 MHz

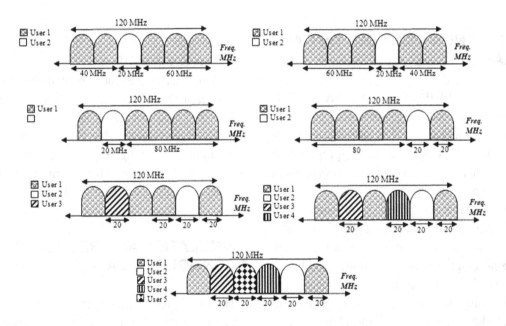

Mapping of the component carrier, from the physical layer (PHY) up to the medium access control (MAC) layer interface, is shown in Figure 15. There is one transport block (in the absence of spatial multiplexing and one Hybrid Automatic Repeat Query (HARQ) entity for each scheduled component carrier (HARQ is the control mechanism for retransmission). Each transport block is mapped to a single component carrier only. A UE may be scheduled over multiple component carriers simultaneously.

Figure 15. Data aggregation from the PHY up to MAC interface

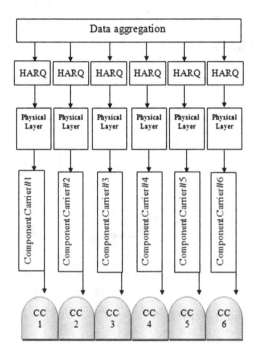

LTE-ADVANCED DOWNLINK INTRA BAND CONTIGUOUS CARRIER AGGREGATION

The following simulation generates LTE-Advanced downlink signals with carrier aggregation. The frequency band (center frequency), bandwidth of the component carrier, oversampling ratio and the number of Transmitter antennas can be changed in the parameter tab.

LTE-Advanced Downlink Component Carrier to Support 20 MHz

Generation of 20 MHz LTE-Advanced carrier aggregation (One 20 MHz component carriers) is simulated. Figure 16 shows the downloading of the 20 MHz LTE-A DL signal.

LTE-Advanced Downlink Contiguous Component Carrier to Support 40 MHz

Generation of 40 MHz LTE-Advanced contiguous carrier aggregation (Two 20 MHz component carriers) is simulated. Figure 17 shows the downloading of the 40 MHz LTE-A DL signal.

LTE-Advanced Downlink Contiguous Component Carriers to Support 60 MHz

Generation of 60 MHz LTE-Advanced contiguous carrier aggregation (Three 20 MHz component carriers) is simulated. Figure 18 shows the downloading of the 60 MHz LTE-A DL signal.

LTE-Advanced Downlink Contiguous Component Carriers to Support 80 MHz

Generation of 80 MHz LTE-Advanced contiguous carrier aggregation (Four 20 MHz component carriers) is simulated. Figure 19 shows the downloading of the 80 MHz LTE-A DL signal.

LTE-Advanced Downlink Contiguous Component Carriers to Support 100 MHz

Generation of 100 MHz LTE-Advanced contiguous carrier aggregation (five 20 MHz component carriers) is simulated. Figure 20 shows the downloading of the 100 MHz LTE-A DL signal.

Figure 16. Single CCs with aggregated channel bandwidth 20 MHz

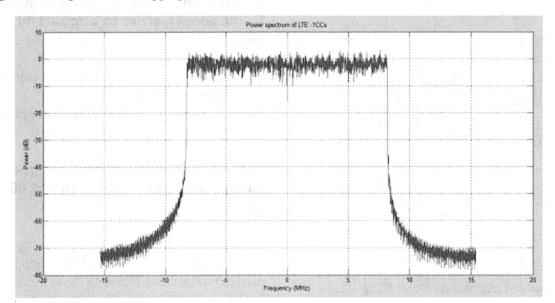

Figure 17. Contiguous CCs with aggregated channel bandwidth 40 MHz

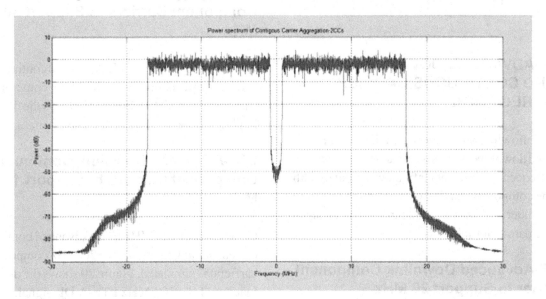

LTE-Advanced Downlink Contiguous Carrier Component to Support 120 MHz

Generation of 120 MHz LTE-Advanced contiguous carrier aggregation (Six 20 MHz component carriers) is simulated. Figure 21 shows the downloading of the 120 MHz LTE-A DL signal.

This chapter provides a proposed bandwidth for LTE-Advanced that reaches up to 120 MHz-while maintaining efficiency in the same range while increasing throughput. The aggregated throughput is the sum of the data rates that are delivered to all terminals in a network; it is usually measured in bits per second (bps).

Figure 18. Contiguous CCs with aggregated channel bandwidth 60 MHz

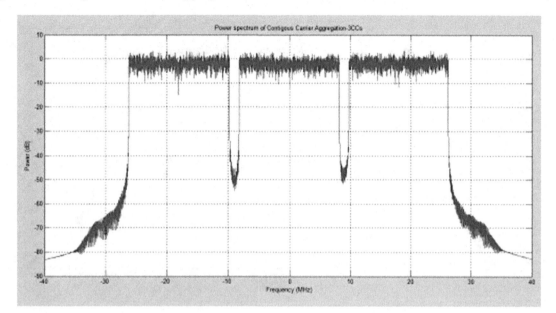

Figure 19. Contiguous CCs with aggregated channel bandwidth 80 MHz

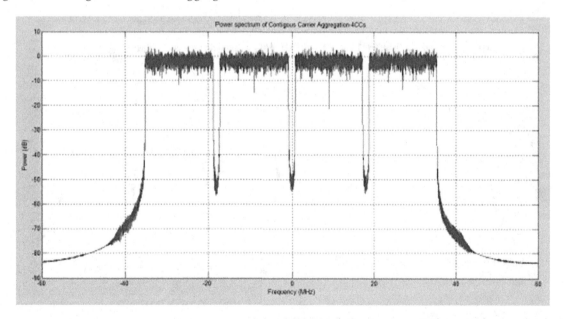

For one physical resource block (RB), the throughput equals 0.84 Mbps because the system uses 64 QAM and each block has 84 symbols for each block.

The efficiency of the system can be calculated using the following equation:

$$Efficience = \frac{Maximum Throughput}{Bandwidth} \qquad (20)$$

For LTE system with bandwidth of 20 MHz, the throughput equals to 84 Mbps, while for LTE-Advanced shown in Figure 17 with a bandwidth

Figure 20. Contiguous CCs with aggregated channel bandwidth 100 MHz

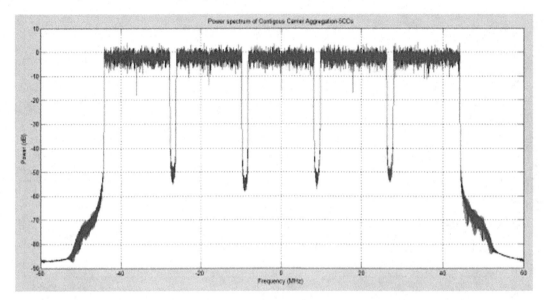

Figure 21. Contiguous CCs with aggregated channel bandwidth 120 MHz

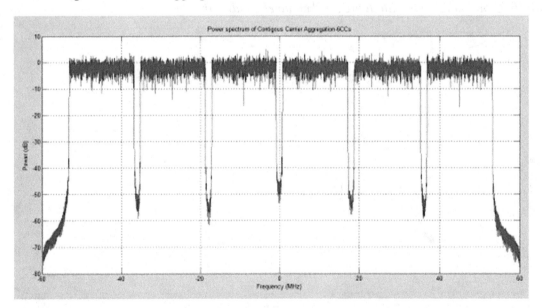

Table 3. Throughput and efficiency for 8x8 MIMO LTE-A

Bandwidth (MHz)	Throughput (Mbps)	Efficiency (bit/s/Hz)
2x20	1344	33.6
3x20	2016	33.6
4x20	2688	33.6
5x20	3360	33.6
6x20	4032	33.6

Figure 22. Relationship between throughput and bandwidth MHz

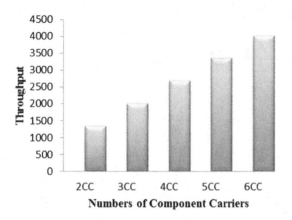

equal to 40 MHz the throughput is 1344 Mbps because the system supports 8x8 MIMO and has 2CC. The efficiency which supports bandwidth 40 MHz is 33. Table 3 shows the throughput and efficiency for different bandwidths of LTE-Advances.

Figure 22, shows the relationship between throughput and bandwidth and how throughput increases as bandwidth increases.

Figure 23 shows how the efficiency of the system which is kept on the same range while the bandwidth is increased up to 120 MHz.

Figure 23. Relationship between Efficiency and Bandwidth in MHz

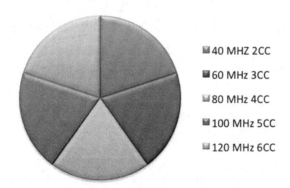

40 MHZ 2CC
60 MHz 3CC
80 MHz 4CC
100 MHz 5CC
120 MHz 6CC

SIMULATION AND RESULTS OF NON-CONTIGUOUS CA

From the different cases of the scenario of LTE-Advanced explained in section X, the following three cases are choose to show the main improvement in the performance of LTE-Advanced after increasing the bandwidth. After designing the proposed new system, it is executed using the Matlab program. The following results are obtained for non- contiguous carrier aggregation with different bandwidths (60 MHz, 80 MHz and 100 MHz).

Firstly, Downlink LTE-Advanced is designed to support 60 MHz carrier aggregation with maximum 2 component carriers as shown in Figure 24; each CCs has maximum of 20 MHz.

Secondly, to increase the throughput of the system, 3CCs are used in this step as shown in Figure 25.

The next step when the system has bandwidth carrier aggregation equal to 100 MHz with four CCs; Figure 26 shows the maximum bandwidth of LTE-Advanced.

From the above main cases of the system, increasing the bandwidth from 20 MHz to 120 MHz of 2x2 MIMO leads increased throughput from 168 to 1008 Mbps, as shown in Figure 27.

Using 4x4 MIMO with bandwidth from 20 MHz to 120 MHz leads to increased throughput from 336 to 2016 Mbps, as shown in Figure 28.

Finally, when the system haas 8X8 antennas, it is noticeable that increasing the bandwidth from 20 MHz to 120 MHz gives the advantage of increasing the throughput from 672 to 4032 Mbps as shown in Figure 29.

Figure 24. Non-contiguous CCs with aggregated channel bandwidth 60 MHz

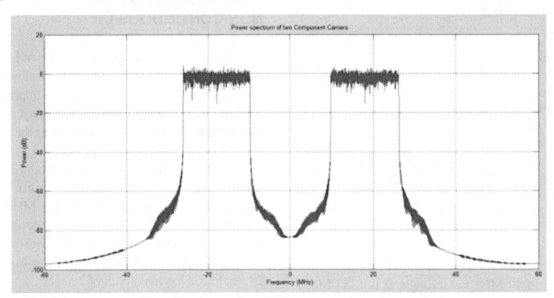

Figure 25. Non-contiguous CCs with aggregated channel bandwidth 80 MHz

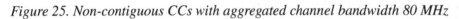

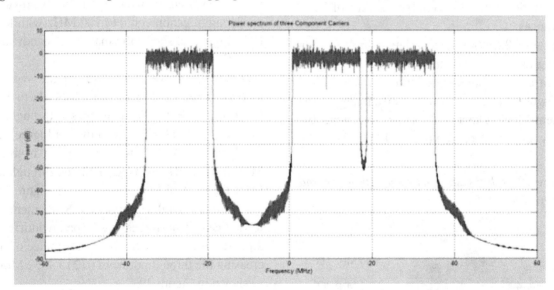

Figure 26. Non-contiguous CCs with aggregated channel bandwidth 100 MHz

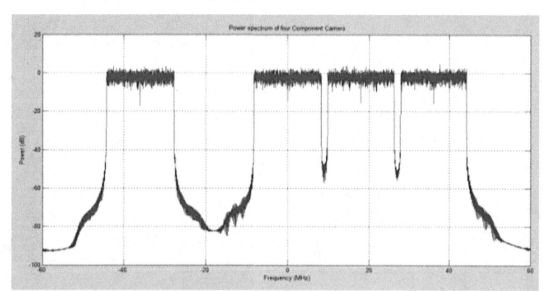

Figure 27. Relationship between throughput and bandwidth with 2x2 MIMO

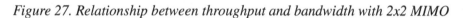

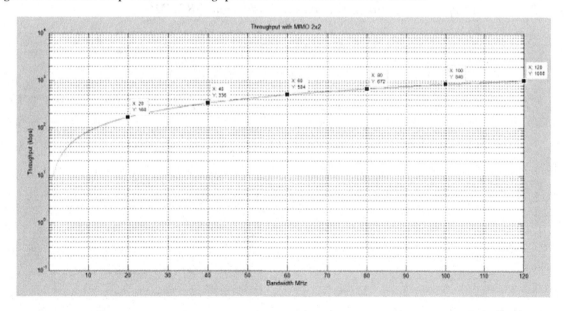

Figure 28. Relationship between throughput and bandwidth with 4x4 MIMO

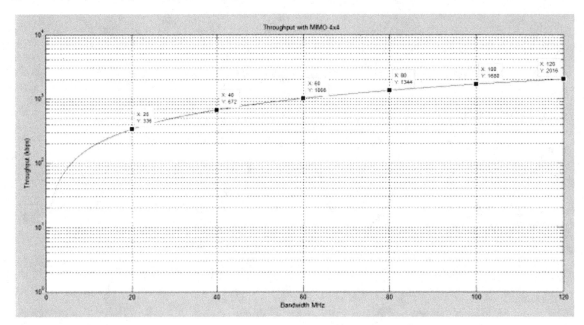

Figure 29. Relationship between throughput and bandwidth with 8x8 MIMO

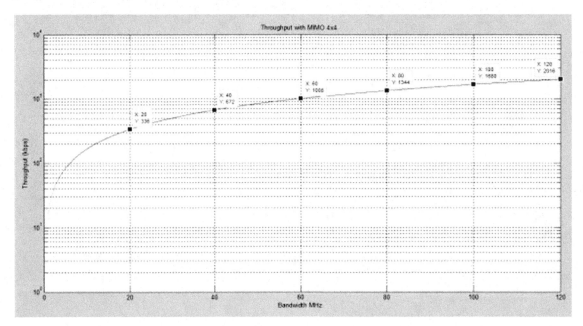

CONCLUSION

This chapter included the main technology components for LTE-Advanced. Component carrier aggregation supports Rel' 10 backward compatible bandwidth extension of up to 100 MHz, therefore the theoretical peak data rate of LTE-Advanced may be even up to 1 Gbps. CA not only helps to achieve higher peak data rates, but it also helps to achieve better coverage for medium data rates. This case allows the use of lower code rates, which would reduce the transmission power, required link budget, and interference. The design and implementation of new LTE-A that supports wider bandwidths of up to 120 MHz is done in contiguous and non-contiguous CA to improve the throughput of the system to be 4.32 Gbps within the specification, although it does present some technical challenges.

REFERENCES

3rd Generation Partnership Project. (2006). Technical specification group radio access network, physical layer aspects for evolved universal terrestrial radio access (UTRA). TR 25.814, V7.1.0.

3rd Generation Partnership Project. (2009). *Technical specification group radio access network, evolved Universal Terrestrial Radio Access (UTRA), physical channels and modulation layer.* TS 36.211, V8.8.0.

Akyildiz, I. F., Gutierrez-Estevez, D. M., & Reyes, E. C. (2010). The evolution to 4G cellular systems: LTE Advanced. *Physical Communication, 3*(4), 217–244. doi:10.1016/j.phycom.2010.08.001

Al-Naffouri, T. Y., Islam, K. M. Z., & Al-Dhahir, N. (2010). A model reduction approach for OFDM channel estimation under high mobility conditions. *IEEE Transactions on Signal Processing, 58*(4). doi:10.1109/TSP.2009.2039732

Forsberg, D., Horn, G., Moeller, W., & Niemi, V. (2010). *LTE security.* London: John Wiley & Sons. doi:10.1002/9780470973271

Galih, S., Adiono, T., & Kurniawan, A. (2010). *Low complexity MMSE channel estimation by weight matrix elements sampling for downlink OFDMA mobile WiMAX System.* Int. Jor. of Computer Science and Network Security.

Ghosh, A., & Ratasuk, R. (2011). *Essentials of LTE and LTE-A.* Cambridge, UK: Cambridge University Press. doi:10.1017/CBO9780511997082

Hlel, E. K., Cherif, S., Tlili, F., & Siala, M. (2005). *Improved estimation of time varying and frequency selective channel for OFDM systems.* Paper presented at ICECS. Tunisia.

Holma, H., & Toskala, A. (2011). *LTE for UMTS evolution to LTE-advanced* (2nd ed.). London: Academic Press. doi:10.1002/9781119992943

Hossain, E., Kim, D. I., & Bhargava, V. K. (2011). *Cooperative cellular wireless networks.* New York: Cambridge University. doi:10.1017/CBO9780511667008

Karakaya, B., Arslan, H., & Ali Cirpan, H. (2008). *Channel estimation for LTE uplink in high doppler spread.* WCNC. doi:10.1109/WCNC.2008.203

Khan, F. (2009). *LTE for 4G mobile broadband air interface technologies and performance.* New York: Cambridge University. doi:10.1017/CBO9780511810336

Rumney, M. (2009). *LTE and the evolution to 4G wireless: Design and measurement challenges.* Agilent Technologies Publication.

Song, L., & Shen, J. (2011). *Evolved cellular network planning and optimization for UMTS and LTE.* Boca Raton, FL: CRC Taylor & Francis Group.

Yonis, A. Z., Abdullah, M. F. L., & Ghanim, M. F. (2012). Effective carrier aggregation on the LTE-advanced systems. *International Journal of Advanced Science and Technology, 41,* 15–26.

Zhang, X., & Zhou, X. (2013). *LTE-advanced air interface technology.* Boca Raton, FL: CRC Press Taylor & Francis Group.

ADDITIONAL READING

3GPP. Technical Report 36.913, Requirements for further advancements for Evolved Universal Terrestial Radio Access (E-UTRA) (LTE-Advanced).

3GPP. TS 25.912, Feasibility study for evolved Universal Terrestrial Radio Access (UTRA) and Universal Terrestrial Radio Access Network (UTRAN), v7.2.0, July 2006.

Abdullah, M. F. L., & Yonis, A. Z. (2012). *Performance of LTE Release 8 and Release 10 in Wireless Communications.* IEEE International conference on cyber security, cyber warfare and digital forensic (CyberSec2012), Malaysia.

Codina, B. E. H., Rene, S., Sorensen, T. B., & Mogensen, P. (2007). *Initial performance evaluation of DFT-spread OFDM based SC-FDMA for UTRA LTE uplink.* Proceedings of IEEE 65th Vehicular Technology Conference, VTC2007-Spring, 3175–3179.

Cox, C. (2012). *An introduction to LTE/LTE-advanced, SAE and 4G mobile communications.* UK: John Wiley. doi:10.1002/9781119942825

Dahlman, E., Parkvall, S., & Sköld, J. (2011). 4G LTE/LTE-Advanced for mobile broadband. UK, Elsevier, first published.

Falconer, D., Ariyavisitakul, S. L., Benyamin-Seeyar, A., & Eidson, B. (2002). Frequency domain equalization for single-carrier broadband wireless systems. *IEEE Communications Magazine, 40*(4), 58–66. doi:10.1109/35.995852

Fazel, K., & Kaiser, S. (2008). *Multi-Carrier and spread spectrum systems from OFDM and MC-CDMA to LTE and WiMAX.* United Kingdom: John Wiley. doi:10.1002/9780470714249

Furht, B., & Ahson, S. A. (2009). *Long Term Evolution 3GPP. LTE Radio and Cellular Technology.* USA: CRC Taylor & Francis. doi:10.1201/9781420072112

Ghosh, A., Zhang, J., Andrews, J. G., & Muhamed, R. (2011). *Fundamentals of LTE: Pearson education.* USA: Prentice Hall.

Holma, H., & Toskala, A. (2012). *LTE Advanced: 3GPP. Solution for IMT-Advanced.* United Kingdom: John Wiley. doi:10.1002/9781118399439

Myung, H. G., Lim, J., & Goodman, D. J. (2006). Single Carrier FDMA for uplink wireless transmission. *IEEE Vehicular Technology Magazine, 1*(3), 30–38. doi:10.1109/MVT.2006.307304

Osseiran, A., Monserrat, J. F., & Mohr, W. (2011). *Mobile and wireless communications for IMT-Advanced and beyond.* UK: John Wiley. doi:10.1002/9781119976431

R1-051088. *Coverage comparison between UL OFDMA and SC-FDMA.* Nokia, RAN1#42, San Diego, CA, Oct. 2005.

Sacrist, D., Monserrat, F., Cabrejas, J., Calabuig, D., Garrigas, S., & Cardona, N. (2009). On the way towards Fourth-Generation mobile 3GPP. LTE and LTE Advanced. EURASIP Journal on Wireless Communications and Networking, Hindawi Publishing Corporation, 3.

Sauter, M. (2009). *Beyond 3G–bringing networks, terminals and the web together LTE, WiMAX, IMS, 4G Devices and the mobile web 2.0*. UK: John Wiley.

Sawahashi, M., Kishiyama, Y., Taoka, H., Tanno, M., & Nakamura, T. (2009). *Broadband Radio Access: LTE and LTE-Advanced*. IEEE Int. Symposium on Intelligent Signal Processing and Communication Systems (ISPACS), 224-225.

Sesia, S., Toufik, I., & Baker, M. (2011). *LTE – the UMTS Long Term Evolution from theory to practice* (2nd ed.). United Kingdom: John Wiley. doi:10.1002/9780470978504

Taha, A. M., Hassanein, H. S., & Abu Ali, N. (2012). *LTE, LTE-Advanced and WiMAX towards IMT-Advanced networks*. UK: John Wiley.

Yahiya, T. A. (2011). *Understanding LTE and its performance*. New York: Springer Science & Business Media. doi:10.1007/978-1-4419-6457-1

Yang, S. (2010). *OFDMA System analysis and design* (1st ed.). Boston, USA: Artech House.

Yi, S., Chun, S., Lee, Y., Park, S., & Jung, S. (2012). *Radio Protocols for LTE and LTE-Advanced*. Singapore: John Wiley. doi:10.1002/9781118188545

Yonis, A. Z., & Abdullah, M. F. L. (2012). *Improving Peak Data Rate in LTE toward LTE-Advanced Technology*. Int. Conference 6th SASTech2012, Organized by Khavaran Institute of Higher Education, Malaysia.

Yonis, A. Z., & Abdullah, M. F. L. (2012). Peak-Throughput of LTE-Release 10 for Up/Down link physical layer. [IJINS]. *International Journal of Information & Network Security, 1*(2), 88–96.

Yonis, A. Z., Abdullah, M. F. L., & Ghanim, M. F. (2012). Design and Implementation of Intra band Contiguous Component Carriers on LTE-A. [USA.]. *International Journal of Computers and Applications, 41*(14), 25–28. doi:10.5120/5609-7877

Chapter 8
A Massive MIMO Channel Estimation Using Circulant Jacket Matrices

Moon Ho Lee
Chonbuk National University, Korea

Md. Abdul Latif Sarker
Chonbuk National University, Korea

Kyeong Jin Kim
Mitsubishi Electronic Research Lab, USA

ABSTRACT

In this chapter, the authors investigate several fundamental issues that arise in wireless Multiple-Input and Multiple-Output (MIMO) communication over fading channels. Wireless channels are usually recognized as multipath fading channels. There are two basic aspects in wireless communication that practice the problem. Firstly, the matter of fading and secondly the disparity in the wired world. The special kinds of circulant matrices are called circulant Jacket matrices. In this chapter, the authors investigate circulant Jacket matrices in a massive MIMO channel that uses the eigenvector and the eigenvalues of this channel. In summary, they assume a perfect multipath channel with random sequences. For this system, a significant improvement in channel estimation can be seen compared to Maximum Ratio Combining (MRC), Least Squares (LS), and Minimum Mean Square Error (MMSE)-based linear channel estimations.

1. INTRODUCTION

The use of multiple antennas in the system is the principal feature of all advanced cellular wireless broadband standards in MIMO technology such as LTE in (Dahlman et al, 2008) and massive MIMO in (Toskala et al, 2012, Marzetta et al, 2010, Rusek et al, 2013 and Hoydis et al, 2013). For example, in LTE standards, up to eight anten-

nas can be employed in the BS, whereas an unlimited numbers of BS antennas are allowed in massive MIMO. Recently, the massive MIMO becomes a new research field. A variable point-to-point MIMO system is a multi-user (MU) MIMO system in (Marzetta et al, 2006 and Vishwanath et al, 2003) in which an antenna array simultaneously distributes a multiplicity of independent terminals. A MU-MIMO system is more

DOI: 10.4018/978-1-4666-4888-3.ch008

passive in the propagation environment than a point-to-point system such that under line of sight propagation states multiplexing gain vanishes for a point-to-point system, while it is retained in the MU- system. By means of a time division duplex (TDD) a channel reciprocity can be used to obtain the downlink channel from the uplink channel in (Vishwanath et al, 2003). To obtain an exact knowledge of channel state information (CSI) at the transmitter, feedback is required from the receiver in fast fading. Thus, a prohibitively large bandwidth is required for this feedback. In such a strategy, the transmitter relies on channel statistics instead of on an actual channel realization. The receiver then estimates the channel statistics and feeds them back to the transmitter or in a TDD setting the estimation may be performed at the transmitter based on uplink data. The CSI plays a key feature in the MU-MIMO system. In the forward link data transmission, the BS is required to know the forward CSI, while in the reverse link data transmission, it is required that the BS knows the reversed CSI. Multi-user MIMO operation with a large number of antennas in the BS compared with terminals was advocated in (Caire et al, 2003) which considers a single-cell TDD. The pilot symbols, through reciprocity, provide the BS with an estimate of the forward CSI, which in turn generates a linear precoder for data transmission. The time required in transmission of pilot symbols is proportional to the number of terminals served and is independent of the number of antennas in the BS as shown in (Gesbert et al, 2007). Thus, the number of terminals that can be served by the BS is limited by the channel coherence time, which itself depends on the mobility of the terminals. Even with a very noisy channel estimate, use of a more BS antennas has been always beneficial, and in the limit of an infinite number of antennas, the effects of fast fading and uncorrelated noise vanish. Thus, we can always recover the multicative matrix ambiguity from low SNR conditions by adding a sufficient number of antennas. A wireless network is considered in (Mar-

zetta et al, 2006) employing a large number of pilot symbols. The propagation medium is modeled as two-dimensional object whose wavelength spaced regular rectangular array can access a number of degrees-of-freedom and its performance becomes better proportional to the square-root of the number of antennas. If the number of BS antenna arrays grows large, the channel between the users and the BS becomes very long random vectors, which becomes pair wisely orthogonal according to fair propagation. As a result, assuming that the BS has perfect CSI, a simple MRC can remove interference from the other users without using more frequency resources. If the number of BS antennas grows large, then the channel can be estimated from the eigenvector of the covariance matrix (Werner et al, 2009) obtained from a set of received samples. In obtaining the covariance matrix, uplink pilot symbols are used in the conventional approach. However, since the channel coherence time is limited, the numbers of possible orthogonal pilot symbols being used are limited. Thus, pilot symbols have to be reused in other cells, which results in the estimates obtained in a given cell will be contaminated by pilots transmitted by the users in other cells. This is called the pilot contamination in (Jose et al, 2009 and Marzetta et al, 1999). In the proposed system, we assume that the BS comprising M antennas serves K terminals equipped with a single antenna. The terminals are located uniformly and randomly in the cell area of the BS. The propagation is assumed to be a combination of fast fading (which changes over a scale of the wavelength) and slow fading (log-normal and geometric decay). If the BS does not have perfect CSI, it estimates the channels according to the approaches proposed in (Franceschetti et al, 2009, Yin et al, 2013 and Hien et al, 2012).

In this chapter, we briefly overview the massive MIMO system in section 2. The channel estimation for massive MIMO system is described in section 3. The conclusions and future research directions are investigated in Section 4.

2. OVERVIEW OF THE MASSIVE MIMO

2.1. Why Massive MIMO?

Wireless broadband standards in MIMO technology are shown for LTE (Rel.10~11) in Figure 1 and massive MIMO in Figure 2. As shown in Figure 3, the MIMO technology is the solution in increasing capacity data rate by using detectors such as maximum ratio combining (MRC), zero forcing (ZF), MMSE, maximum likelihood detector (MLD), etc. Capacity data rate is significantly increased between release 12 and release 13.

2.2. System Model

Massive MIMO supports the dozens of user equipment (UE) and unlimited number of antennas at BS as shown in Figure 4.

2.2.1. Low SNR with Single-User

A point-to-point MIMO link is consist of a transmitter having an array of n_t antennas, a receiver having an array of n_r antennas connected by a channel such that each receive antenna is subject to the combined action of all transmit antennas. We consider the $n_t \times 1$ received vector for massive MIMO transmission (Rusek et al, 2013)

$$y = \sqrt{p}\mathrm{G}x + \mathrm{z} \qquad (1)$$

where G is the $n_r \times n_t$ propagation matrix, p is the transmission power, and z is the $n_t \times 1$ additive white Gaussian noise whose elements are independent with zero mean and variance σ^2 We assume that a signal power is normalized to one:

$$\mathrm{E}\left[\left\|x\right\|^2\right] = 1 \qquad (2)$$

The achievable rate for i.i.d. complex Gaussian inputs, under the assumption that the receiver has the perfect knowledge of the channel matrix G, measured in bit-per-symbol or equivalently bits-per-channel is:

Figure 1. 3GPP LTE (Rel.10~11)

3 GPP LTE

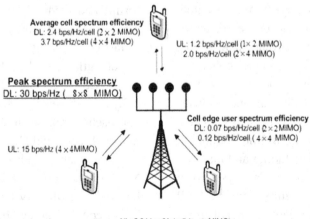

Figure 2. Massive MIMO (Rel. 11~13) system model [3]

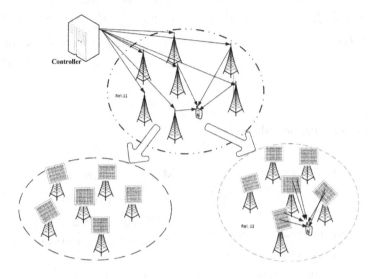

Figure 3. Massive MIMO capacity and rate demand [2]

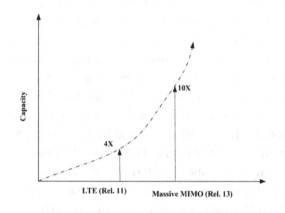

Figure 4. System model of massive MIMO

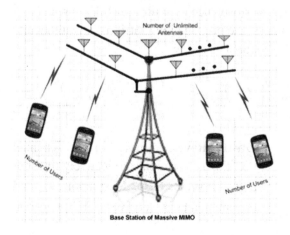

$$C = I\left(y; x\right) = \log_2 \det\left(I_{n_r} + \frac{p}{M} GG^H\right) \quad (3)$$

where $I\left(y; x\right)$ represents the mutual information, I_{n_r} denotes an $n_r \times n_r$ identity matrix and $\left\{\cdot\right\}^H$ denotes the Hermitian transpose (Foschini, 1996). In the regions of low SNRs, only beamforming gains are important and the achievable rate from Equation (3) becomes:

$$C_{p \to 0} \approx \frac{p\, Tr\left(GG^H\right)}{n_t \ln 2} \approx \frac{pn_r}{\ln 2} \quad (4)$$

Since the magnitude of a propagation coefficient is typically equal to one, we have $Tr\left(GG^H\right) \approx n_t n_r$ The expression in Equation (4), is independent of n_t, and thus, even under the most favorable propagation condition, the multiplexing gains will be lost. Moreover, from the achievable rate prospective, the use of multiple transmit antennas are of no value. If the number of transmit antennas (n_t) grows large while keeping the number of receive antennas constant, then the row-vectors of the propagation matrix are asymptotically orthogonal. As consequence of (Matthaiou et al, 2010), we can have the following if $n_t \geq n_r$:

$$\left(G^H G / n_t \right)_{n_t \gg n_r} \approx I_{n_r} \tag{5}$$

and the achievable rate from Equation (3) becomes:

$$C_{n_t \geq n_r} = \log_2 \det\left(I_{n_r} + p.I_{n_r} \right) \approx n_r \cdot \log_2\left(1 + p \right) \tag{6}$$

If the number of receive antennas (n_r) grows large while keeping the number of transmit antennas constant, then the column-vectors of the propagation matrix are asymptotically orthogonal, so that we can have the following relationship if $n_r \geq n_t$:

$$\left(G^H G / n_r \right)_{n_r \gg n_t} \approx I_{n_t} \tag{7}$$

and the achievable rate from Equation (3) becomes:

$$C_{n_r \geq n_t} = \log_2 \det\left(I_{n_t} + \frac{pGG^H}{n_t} \right) \approx n_t \cdot \log_2\left(1 + \frac{pn_r}{n_t} \right) \tag{8}$$

We can simplify a lower bound Equation (6) and an upper bound Equation (8) for a single user in the region of low signal-to-noise ratio (SNR) as follows:

$$n_r \cdot \log_2\left(1 + p \right) \leq C \leq n_t \cdot \log_2\left(1 + \frac{pn_r}{n_t} \right) \leq \min\left(n_t, n_r \right) \cdot \log_2\left(1 + \frac{p\max\left(n_t, n_r \right)}{n_t} \right) \tag{9}$$

2.2.2. High SNR with Multi-User

An $M \times K$ channel propagation matrix G in the reverse link, where M is the large antenna arrays at BS and users K, is the product of a $M \times K$ matrix H, which accounts for small scale fading and a $K \times K$ diagonal matrix $D_\beta^{1/2}$ whose diagonal elements are constitute a $K \times 1$ vector, β_k, of large scale fading coefficients:

$$G = HD_\beta^{1/2} \tag{10}$$

If $\left[G \right]_{mk} \triangleq g_{mk}$ is the coefficients for m=1,…, M and k=1,…,K, the large scale fading coefficient $\left[D_\beta^{1/2} \right]_{kk} = \sqrt{\beta_k}$ and $\left[H \right]_{mk} \triangleq h_{mk}$ describes for a small scale channel which accounts for fast fading between the K users and the BS. Then we have:

$$g_{mk} = h_{mk}\sqrt{\beta_k} \tag{11}$$

Since we assume TDD operation, the reverse link propagation matrix is merely the transpose of the forward link propagation matrix, i.e., $G \rightarrow G^T$ and the channel state information transmission (CSIT) can be obtained from uplink pilot signals. It is independent of the number of cooperating antennas at BSs and system performance can be significantly improved by increasing the number of BS antennas. Otherwise, the frequency division duplex (FDD) system requires the training overhead to collect CSIT. Thus, required complexity and bandwidth will grow linearly with the number of transmit antennas. Furthermore, training overhead will significantly limit the system performance. In multiuser MIMO with large arrays, the propagation matrix is asymptotically orthogonal as follows:

$$\left(G^H G / M \right)_{M \gg K} = D_\beta^{1/2}\left(H^H H / M \right)_{M \gg K} D_\beta^{1/2} = D_\beta \tag{12}$$

- **On the Reverse Link:** For each channel use, the K-terminals collectively transmit a $K \times 1$ vector of QAM symbols, q_r and the antenna array receives a $M \times 1$ vector.

For this uplink transmission, the received signal y_r is given by:

$$y_r = \sqrt{p_r} G q_r + z_r \tag{13}$$

where $z_r \to M \times 1$ is receiver vector noise whose components is independent and distributed as $CN(0,1)$. The reverse transmitted power is proportional to noise power as follows:

$$p_r \propto \frac{1}{\sigma^2} \tag{14}$$

The signal power is also normalized to one, $E\left\{|q_{rk}|^2\right\} = 1, \quad k = 1,...,K$. If $M = K$, the total throughput or sum rate capacity (Tse et al, 2005) is evaluated as:

$$C_{sum\_r} = \log_2 \det\left(I_k + p_r G^H G\right) \tag{15}$$

If $M \gg K$, the asymptotic sum rate is given by:

$$C_{sum\_r,M \geq K} = \log_2 \det\left(I_k + p_r M D_\beta\right)$$
$$= \sum_{k=1}^{K} \log_2\left(1 + p_r M \beta_k\right) \tag{16}$$

where the propagation matrixes are nearly orthogonal, i.e., $G^H G \approx M D_\beta$. The match filter output is given by:

$$G^H y_r = \sqrt{p_r} G^H G q_r + G^H z_r$$
$$= M \sqrt{p_r} D_\beta q_r + G^H z_r \tag{17}$$

From (2-17), we have $SNR = M p_r D_\beta$:

- **On the Forward Link:** If the base station transmits a $M \times 1$ vector and symbol x_f

through its M antennas and the terminals collectively receive a $K \times 1$ vector, then the received signal y_f is given by:

$$y_f = \sqrt{p_f} G^T x_f + z_f \tag{18}$$

where $z_f \to K \times 1$ vector of receiver noise whose components are independent and distributed as $CN(0,1)$. The forward transmitted power is proportional to noise power as follows:

$$p_f \propto \frac{1}{\sigma^2} \tag{19}$$

The total transmit power is independent of the number of antennas, o that we have:

$$E\left\{|x_f|^2\right\} = 1 \tag{20}$$

If $M = K$, the sum capacity is given by:

$$C_{sum\_f} = \max_{\{\gamma_k\}} \log_2 \det\left(I_M + p_f G D_\gamma G^H\right) \tag{21}$$

subject to $\sum_{k=1}^{K} \gamma_k = 1$. If $M \gg K$, the sum capacity has a simple asymptotic form for forward link transmission as:

$$C_{sum\_f,M \geq K} = \max_{\{\gamma_k\}} \log_2 \det\left(I_k + p_f D_\gamma^{1/2} G^H G D_r^{1/2}\right)$$
$$= \max_{\{\gamma_k\}} \sum_{k=1}^{K} \log_2\left(1 + M p_f \gamma_k \beta_k\right) \tag{22}$$

This result is correct if the propagation matrices are orthogonal which occurs asymptotically as the number of antennas grows. The transmitter uses a matched filter-based linear precoder, so that the precoder output is given by:

$$x_f = \frac{1}{\sqrt{M}} \mathbf{G}^* \mathbf{D}_\beta^{-1/2} \mathbf{D}_p^{-1/2} \mathbf{q}_f \qquad (23)$$

where q_f is the vector of QAM symbols. The receive signal will be expressed by:

$$\mathbf{y}_f = \sqrt{p_f M} \mathbf{D}_\beta^{1/2} \mathbf{D}_p^{1/2} \mathbf{q}_f + \mathbf{z}_f \qquad (24)$$

From Equation (24), the achievable rate of forward link transmission will be immediately obtained as follows:

$$C_{sum\_f,M \geq K} = \sum_{k-1}^{K} \log_2 \left(1 + M p_f p_k \beta_k \right) \qquad (25)$$

2.2.3. Uplink Transmission

2.2.3.1. For Perfect CSI

We consider the $M \times 1$ received vector at the BS for uplink transmission (Hien et al, 2011) using Equation (10) is given by:

$$\mathbf{y}_u = \sqrt{p_u} \mathbf{H} \mathbf{D}_\beta^{1/2} x_u + \mathbf{z}_u \qquad (26)$$

The received signal after zero-forcing (ZF) is given by:

$$\begin{aligned} w_{ZF\_UL} &= \mathbf{G}^\dagger \mathbf{y}_u = \mathbf{G}^\dagger \left(\sqrt{p_u} \mathbf{H} \mathbf{D}_\beta^{1/2} x_u + \mathbf{z}_u \right) \\ &= \mathbf{G}^\dagger \left(\sqrt{p_u} \mathbf{G} x_u + \mathbf{z}_u \right) \end{aligned} \qquad (27)$$

where $\mathbf{G}^\dagger \triangleq \left(\mathbf{G}^H \mathbf{G} \right)^{-1} \mathbf{G}^H$, when $M \to \infty$, from (2-10) and (2-12), $\frac{1}{M} \mathbf{G}^H \mathbf{G} \to \mathbf{D}$ and hence $\mathbf{G}^\dagger \to \frac{1}{M} \mathbf{D}^{-1} \mathbf{G}^H$ which corresponds to the

maximum ratio combining (MRC). The detection after using MRC precoding for uplink transmission we obtain:

$$\begin{aligned} w_{MRC\_UL} &= \mathbf{G}^H \mathbf{y}_u = \mathbf{G}^H \left(\sqrt{p_u} \mathbf{G} x_u + \mathbf{z}_u \right) \\ &= \left(\sqrt{p_u} \mathbf{G}^H \mathbf{G} x_u + \mathbf{G}^H \mathbf{z}_u \right) \\ &= \left(\sqrt{\frac{E_u}{M}} \frac{M \mathbf{G}^H \mathbf{G}}{M} x_u + \mathbf{G}^H \mathbf{z}_u \right) \\ &= \left(\sqrt{M E_u} \mathbf{D}_\beta x_u + \mathbf{G}^H \mathbf{z}_u \right) \end{aligned} \qquad (28)$$

where $p_u = E_u / M$ and the transmit power E_u is fixed. The signal-to-noise ratio (SNR) of the UL transmission from the kth user is given by:

$$\begin{aligned} SNR_{ku} &= \left(\sqrt{M E_u} \mathbf{D}_\beta \right)^2 / \mathbf{G}^H \mathbf{G} \\ &= M E_u \left(\mathbf{D}_\beta \right)^2 / M \mathbf{D}_\beta = E_u \mathbf{D}_\beta = M p_u \beta_k \end{aligned} \qquad (29)$$

If $M \geq K$, then the sum capacity of UL MU-MIMO for perfect CSI is given by:

$$\begin{aligned} C_{sum\_UL\_M \gg K} &= \log_2 \det \left(I_k + SNR_{ku} \right) \\ &= \sum_{k=1}^{K} \log_2 \left(1 + M p_u \beta_k \right) \end{aligned} \qquad (30)$$

2.2.3.2. For Imperfect CSI

Let s be the number of symbols used entirely for pilots p_p. The sequences of users are pairwise orthogonal. Therefore the pilot sequences used by the K users can be represented by $s \times K$ matrix $\sqrt{p_p} \psi$ which satisfies $\psi^H \psi = I_k$ where $p_p = s p_u$. The $M \times s$ received pilot matrix at the base station is given by:

$$\mathbf{Y}_p = \sqrt{p_p} \mathbf{G} \dot{\mathbf{E}}^T + \mathbf{Z} \qquad (31)$$

The minimum mean square error (MMSE) estimate of G is given by:

$$\hat{G} = \frac{1}{\sqrt{p_p}} Y_p \psi^* \tilde{D}_\beta$$

$$= \frac{1}{\sqrt{p_p}} \left(\sqrt{p_p} G \psi^T + Z \right) \psi^* \tilde{D}_\beta = \left(G + \frac{Z\psi^*}{\sqrt{p_p}} \right) \tilde{D}_\beta \tag{32}$$

where $Z\psi^* = B$ is the $M \times K$ random matrix whose elements are i.i.d. zero mean complexes Gaussian with variance σ^2 and $\tilde{D}_\beta = \left(\frac{\sigma^2}{p_p} \beta_k^{-1} + I_k \right)$ When we cut the transmission power of each user to E_u / M as in the perfect CSI case, the processed signal vector at the base station after using MRC estimation is given by:

$$\hat{w}_{MRC\_UL} = \hat{G}^H y_u$$

$$= \tilde{D}_\beta \left(G^H + \frac{\sqrt{M} B^H}{\sqrt{sE_u}} \right) \left(\sqrt{\frac{E_u}{M}} G x_u + z_u \right) \tag{33}$$

The MMSE estimation from uplink pilots and the transmit power of each user $p_u = E_u / \sqrt{M}$ where E_u is fixed and $p_p = sE_u / \sqrt{M}$. The $\overline{SNR}_{ku}$ as follows as:

$$\overline{SNR}_{ku} = sD_\beta^2 E_u^2 = sMp_u^2 \beta_k^2 \tag{34}$$

While $M \geq K$, the sum capacity of **UL MU-MIMO** for **imperfect CSI** is given by:

$$C_{sum\_UL\_M \gg K} = \sum_{k=1}^{K} \log_2(1 + sMp_u^2 \beta_k^2) \tag{35}$$

2.2.4. Downlink Transmission

2.2.4.1. For Perfect CSI

Similarly, from Equation (26), we obtain the received signal as the downlink transmission:

$$y_u = \sqrt{p_u} G x_u + z_u \tag{36}$$

where:

$$\left(GG^H / M \right)_{M \gg K} = D_\beta^{1/2} \left(HH^H / M \right) D_\beta^{1/2} = D_\beta$$

The received signal after applying the precoding based MRC is given by:

$$w_{MRC\_DL} = \left(\sqrt{p_d} H D_\beta^{1/2} \frac{H^H}{\sqrt{M}} \tilde{x}_d + z_d \right)$$

$$= \left(\sqrt{p_d} H D_\beta^{1/2} \frac{H^H}{\sqrt{M}} \tilde{x}_d + z_d \right)$$

$$= \left(\sqrt{p_d M} D_\beta^{1/2} \frac{HH^H}{M} \tilde{x}_d + z_d \right) \tag{37}$$

$$= \left(\sqrt{p_d M} D_\beta^{1/2} \tilde{x}_d + z_d \right)$$

where $x_d = \frac{H^H}{\sqrt{M}} \tilde{x}_d$ and $\frac{HH^H}{M} \rightarrow I_k$. Now the signal to noise ratio (SNR) of the DL transmission from the *kth* user:

$$SNR_{kd} = Mp_d D_\beta = Mp\beta_k. \tag{38}$$

When $M \geq K$, then the corresponding sum capacity of DL MU-MIMO for perfect CSI is given by:

$$C_{sum\_DL\_M \gg K} = \log_2 \det \left(I_k + Mp_d D_\beta \right)$$

$$= \sum_{k=1}^{K} \log_2 \left(1 + Mp_d D_\beta \right) \tag{39}$$

Similarly, from Equation (35), when, the sum rate capacity of DL MU-MIMO for imperfect CSI is as follows:

$$C_{sum\_DL\_M \gg K} = \log_2 \det(1 + sMp_d^2\beta_k^2)$$
$$= \sum_{k=1}^{K} \log_2 \left(1 + sMp_d^2\beta_k^2\right) \tag{40}$$

In Table 1, the evolution of SNR and SINR for standard precoding technique views in Appendix 1.

In Figure 5, shows the sum rates versus the number of BS antennas for $p_u = E_u / M$ and $p_u = E_u / \sqrt{M}$ with perfect and imperfect CSI using $E_u / \sigma^2 = 5\,dB$ with ZF and MRC, respectively. The ZF works well at high SNR while MRC is better at low SNR.

In Figure 6, the asymptotic distribution such as Gaussian distribution depends on the mean and the variance sum capacity function of transmit and receive antennas for uplink and downlink zero-forcing beamforming (ZF-BF) of massive MIMO scheme. If we assume ZF-BF matrix,

$$H_{K \times M} = \begin{bmatrix} -h_1- \\ \vdots \\ -h_k- \end{bmatrix} \Rightarrow W_{M \times K}$$

and

$$\|W\|_F^2 \rightarrow \frac{K}{M-K}$$

as $K, M \rightarrow \infty$, then the mean of sum capacity as follows:

$$E\left[C_{ZF}\right] = K \log_2 \left(1 + \frac{p}{\|W\|_F^2}\right) = K \log_2 \left(1 + \frac{p}{\beta}\right) \tag{41}$$

where $E\left[tr\left\{\left(HH^H\right)^{-1}\right\}\right] = \frac{K}{M-K} = \beta$ for $K \times K$ Wishart matrix with M degree of freedom. The estimated variance is given by:

$$Var\left[\|W\|_F^2\right] = E\left[\|W\|_F^4\right] - \left(E\left[\|W\|_F^2\right]\right)^2 = \beta^3 \left(\frac{\beta+1}{K^2 - \beta^2}\right) \tag{42}$$

3. CHANNEL ESTIMATION FOR MASSIVE MIMO BASED ON CIRCULANT JACKET MATRICES

3.1. Circulant Matrices

A common special kind of Toeplitz matrices-which results in a significant simplification and plays a fundamental role in developing more general results, is the circulant matrix. This circulant matrix is formed when every row of the matrix is a right cyclic shifts of the row above it so that

Table 1. Detector complexity using ZF, MF and MMSE algorithm

Detector	SNR Value for Perfect CSI	SINR Value for Imperfect CSI
ZF	$\rho_f(\alpha-1)$	$K^3(\alpha+1)$
MF	$\dfrac{\rho_f \alpha}{\rho_f + 1}$	$\dfrac{\xi^2 \rho_f (\alpha-1)}{(1-\xi^2)\rho_f + 1}$
MMSE	αK^2	$\dfrac{\xi^2 \rho_f \alpha}{\rho_f + 1}$

$\rho_f = forward\ Tx.\ power, M \rightarrow \infty, M/K = \alpha,\ \xi = Channel\ Estimation\ Reliability(0 \le \xi \le 1)$

Figure 5. Uplink sum-rate vs. the number of BS antennas where $M = 500$ *and* $K = 10$

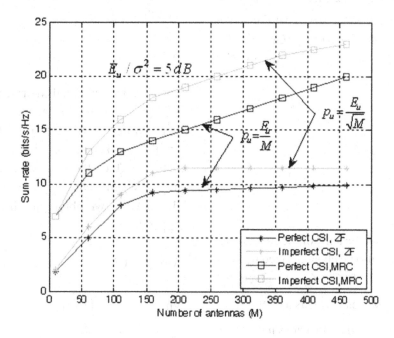

Figure 6. Sum rate capacity as function of antennas ($M = 500$ *) with users (* $k = 50$ *) when transmit* $SNR(p) = 0dB$

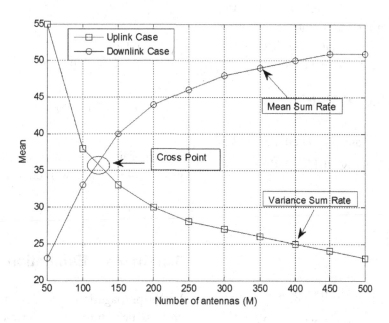

$t_i = t_{-n+i} = t_{i-n}$ for $i = 1, 2, ..., n-1$. All circulant matrices with the same size have the same eigenvectors. A circulant matrix C_n (Gray, 2006) is a Toeplitz matrix having the following form:

$$C_n = \begin{bmatrix} c_0 & c_1 & c_2 & \cdots & c_{n-1} \\ c_{n-1} & c_0 & c_1 & c_2 & \vdots \\ \vdots & c_{n-1} & c_0 & c_1 & c_2 \\ \vdots & \ddots & \ddots & \ddots & c_1 \\ c_1 & \cdots & \cdots & c_{n-1} & c_0 \end{bmatrix} \quad (43)$$

where each row is a cyclic shift of the row above it. The structure can also be characterized by noting that (i, j) entry of C, $C_{i,j}$ is given by $C_{i,j} = c_{(j-i) \bmod n}$ where each row is a cyclic shift of the row above it. Circulant matrices have been used in many applications, for example, in applications involving the discrete Fourier transform (DFT) (Lee et al, 2008) and the study of cyclic code for error correction (Lee, 2012). For the general treatment of circulant matrices we refer the reader to (Gray, 2006). Now we discuss circulant Jacket matrices in the next subsection.

3.2. Circulant Jacket Matrices

A matrix $J_N \triangleq (a_{ij})$ and is called the Jacket matrix (Lee et al, 2008 & 2012) if it's inverse satisfies:

$$J_N^{-1} = \frac{1}{N} \left\{ (a_{ij})^{-1} \right\}^T \quad (44)$$

where an operator $\{\cdot\}^T$ is the transpose of $(a_{ij})^{-1}$ The inverse matrix of the Jacket matrix can be obtained by taking the element-wise inverse. The class of Jacket matrices contains the class of real and complex-valued Hadamard matrices. The special kind of circulant matrices is the circulant Jacket matrix (Lee, 2012). Let A be a $n \times n$

circulant matrix. If there exists a Jacket matrix J such that:

$$A = J \Lambda J^{-1} \quad (45)$$

where Λ is a diagonal matrix, then we say that A is the circulant Jacket matrix similar to the diagonal matrix Λ (Lee et al, 2010). If A is the circulant Jacket matrix similar to the diagonal matrix Λ, then the main diagonal entries of Λ are all eigenvalues of A. Furthermore, since $A = J \Lambda J^{-1}$, we obtain and it is provided from Appendix 1:

$$\Lambda = J^{-1} A J \quad (46)$$

where $J_{n \times n}^{-1} = (1/n) J_{n \times n}^\dagger$. For example, let $A_2 = \begin{bmatrix} a & b \\ b & a \end{bmatrix}$ be a circulant Jacket matrix and $J_2 = \begin{bmatrix} a & a \\ a & -a \end{bmatrix}$ then we get:

$$\Lambda_2 = J_2^{-1} A_2 J_2 = \begin{bmatrix} a & a \\ a & -a \end{bmatrix}^{-1} \begin{bmatrix} a & b \\ b & a \end{bmatrix} \begin{bmatrix} a & a \\ a & -a \end{bmatrix}$$
$$= \begin{bmatrix} 2(a+b) & 0 \\ 0 & 2(a-b) \end{bmatrix} \quad (47)$$

According to (Lee et al, 2008 & 2010) In general (47) can be written as follows:

$$\Lambda_k = J_k^{-1} A_k J_k = diag\{\lambda_1, ..., \lambda_k\} \quad (48)$$

3.3. Channel Estimation

Let the propagation matrix G model independent small scale fading geometric attenuation and log-normal shadowing fading. Each element of the propagation matrix G is the channel coefficient between the *l-th* BS and the *K-th* user in the *j-th* cell. The received sample vector has a real or complex valued multivariate normal distribution, that is, $Y_i \sim N_n(0, R)$. Also, Y_i are assumed to be mutually independent. The received sample vector is modeled as:

$$Y_i = \sqrt{p} G S_{id} + Z_i \qquad (49)$$

where G is the $M \times K$ dimensional unknown deterministic propagation matrix. $Z_i \sim \left(0, R_{\hat{Z}_i}\right)$ is the M-dimensional real or complex Gaussian noise vector with the noise covariance matrix may be known or unknown. $S_{id} \sim \left(0, R_{S_{id}}\right)$ is a K-dimensional real or complex valued Gaussian signal vector with the following signal covariance matrix [13]:

$$
\begin{aligned}
R_{S_{id}} &= \mathrm{E}\left[S_{id} S_{id}^H\right] \\
&= \begin{bmatrix}
\mathrm{E}\left[s^2(1)\right] & 0 & \cdots & 0 \\
0 & \mathrm{E}\left[s^2(2)\right] & \cdots & 0 \\
\vdots & \vdots & \ddots & \vdots \\
0 & 0 & \cdots & \mathrm{E}\left[s^2(N)\right]
\end{bmatrix} \\
&= \mathrm{I}_{N \times N}
\end{aligned}
\qquad (50)
$$

where it is assumed that for each sample we get an i.i.d. Gaussian symbol with the sample covariance which can be written as $R_s = \mathrm{E}\left[s^2\right] = 1$ and S_{id} is the $m \times m$ dimensional diagonal matrix comprising of transmitted symbols $s = [s(1), \ldots s(N)]$. While the signal and noise vectors are independent of each other, the covariance matrix of Y_i can be decomposed as:

$$
\begin{aligned}
R_{Y_i} &= \mathrm{E}\left[Y_i Y_i^H\right] \\
&= \mathrm{E}\left[\left(\sqrt{p} G S_{id} + Z_i\right)\left(\sqrt{p} G S_{id} + Z_i\right)^H\right] \\
&= \mathrm{E}\left[\left(\sqrt{p} G S_{id}\right)\left(\sqrt{p} G S_{id}\right)^H\right] + \mathrm{E}\left[Z_i Z_i^H\right] \\
&= p D_\beta H R_{S_{id}} H^H + R_{Z_i} = \Phi + R_{Z_i}
\end{aligned}
\qquad (51)
$$

where, $\Phi = p D_\beta H R_{S_{id}} H^H$ and $\dfrac{H^H H}{n} = \delta_{ij} I_k$ as $n \to \infty$. Note that the columns of H are linearly independent, the covariance matrix of the signals $R_{S_{id}}$ is nonsingular with the rank k. Equivalently the $n - k$ smallest eigenvalues of Φ are equal to zero. This is a main property of a massive MIMO system which simplifies a simple eigenvalue based channel estimation (Hien et al, 2012) that does not require any particular form of the transmitted signals because circulant Jacket matrices are very fast in the computation of the eigenvalue decomposition (Lee et al, 2008). Hence multiplying (13) by H and using $\dfrac{H^H H}{n} = \delta_{ij} I_k$, we obtain:

$$
\begin{aligned}
R_{Y_i} H &= H\left(Mp D_\beta + I_k\right) = AJ\left(Mp D_\beta + I_k\right) \\
&= J\Lambda\left(Mp D_\beta + I_k\right) = \hat{R}_{Y_i}
\end{aligned}
\qquad (52)
$$

where H is a $n \times n$ channel matrix which is constructed by an $n \times n$ circulant Jacket matrix A with a $n \times n$ Jacket matrix J which decompose the eigenvalues from A and $\left(Mp D_{\beta ll} + I_k\right)$ is a diagonal matrix. Hence the estimated channel of H can be found via:

$$H = AJ = J\Lambda \quad and \quad \Lambda = J^{-1}AJ \qquad (53)$$

where J is the Jacket matrix and A is the circulant Jacket matrix that is constructed by a Jacket matrix and a diagonal Jacket matrix which is formed by the eigenvalues. Let us assume Jacket matrices are J_M and J_K are of order $M = p^m$ and $K = q^k$, respectively, i.e., $A_M = J_M \Lambda_M J_M^{-1}$ and $A_K = J_K \Lambda_K J_K^{-1}$, where A_M and A_k are two circulant Jacket matrices that can be factored as

$$J_{M = p^m} = \prod_{i=1}^{m} I_{p^{m-i}} \otimes J_p \otimes I_{p^{i-1}}$$

and

$$J_{K=q^k} = \prod_{i=1}^{k} I_{q^{k-i}} \otimes J_q \otimes I_{q^{i-1}}$$

until Jacket matrices J_p and J_q of order p and q respectively. With the aid of the properties of Kronecker products, we generate a matrix of large order $M \times K$ given by:

$$
\begin{aligned}
A_{MK} &= A_M \otimes A_K \\
&= (J_M \otimes J_K)(\Lambda_K \otimes \Lambda_K)(J_M \otimes J_K)^{-1}
\end{aligned}
\tag{54}
$$

For example, we assume that A_2 and A_3 are two matrices which can be factored as:

$$
\begin{aligned}
A_2 &= \begin{pmatrix} a_1 & b_2 \\ b_2 & a_1 \end{pmatrix} \\
&= \begin{pmatrix} a_1 & a_1 \\ a_1 & -a_1 \end{pmatrix} \begin{pmatrix} a_1+b_2 & 0 \\ 0 & a_1-b_2 \end{pmatrix} \begin{pmatrix} a_1 & a_1 \\ a_1 & -a_1 \end{pmatrix}^{-1} \\
&= J_2 \Lambda_2 J_2^{-1}
\end{aligned}
\tag{55}
$$

and

$$
\begin{aligned}
A_3 &= \begin{bmatrix} a_1 & b_2 & c_3 \\ c_3 & a_1 & b_2 \\ b_2 & c_3 & a_1 \end{bmatrix} \\
&= \begin{bmatrix} 1 & 1 & 1 \\ 1 & \omega & \omega^2 \\ 1 & \omega^2 & \omega \end{bmatrix} \\
&\cdot \begin{bmatrix} a_1+b_2+c_3 & 0 & 0 \\ 0 & a_1+b_2\omega+c_3\omega^2 & 0 \\ 0 & 0 & a_1+b_2\omega^2+c_3\omega \end{bmatrix} \\
&\cdot \begin{bmatrix} 1 & 1 & 1 \\ 1 & \omega & \omega^2 \\ 1 & \omega^2 & \omega \end{bmatrix}^{-1}
\end{aligned}
\tag{56}
$$

where $\Lambda_2 = diag(\lambda_1, \lambda_2)$ with $\lambda_1 = a_1 + b_2$, $\lambda_2 = a_1 - b_2$ and $\Lambda_3 = diag(\lambda_1, \lambda_2, \lambda_3)$ with $\lambda_1 = a_1 + b_2 + c_3$, $\lambda_2 = a_1 + b_2\omega + c_3\omega^2$, $\lambda_3 = a_1 + b_2\omega^2 + c_3\omega$, respectively. It is obvious that J_2 and J_3 in Equation (55) and Equation (56) are Jacket matrices due to the fact that:

$$
J_2^{-1} = \frac{1}{2}\begin{bmatrix} a^{-1} & a^{-1} \\ a^{-1} & -a^{-1} \end{bmatrix}, J_3^{-1} = \frac{1}{3}\begin{pmatrix} 1 & 1 & 1 \\ 1 & \omega^{-1} & \omega^{-2} \\ 1 & \omega^{-2} & \omega^{-1} \end{pmatrix}
\tag{57}
$$

Therefore, we can construct the combined matrix $A_6 = A_2 \otimes A_3$ of order 6, i.e.:

$$
\begin{aligned}
A_6 &= (J_2 \otimes J_3)(\Lambda_2 \otimes \Lambda_3)(J_2 \otimes J_3)^{-1} \\
&= (I_2 \otimes J_3)(J_2 \otimes I_3)(I_2 \otimes \Lambda_3) \\
&\cdot (\Lambda_2 \otimes I_3)(J_2^{-1} \otimes I_3)(I_2 \otimes J_3^{-1})
\end{aligned}
\tag{58}
$$

For example, a signal vector x of length 6, the data flow diagram of the fast algorithm for the signal transform $y = A_6 x$ is shown in Figure 7. It requires 16 additions and 22 multiplications for this algorithm. However, it needs 30 additions and 36 multiplications for the direct computing approach. In general, the computational complexity of this algorithm based on the Jacket matrices is shown in Table 2. It shows that the proposed algorithm of the calculation complexity is faster than that of the direct computing approach.

From Equation (53), we can observe that the k dimensional square diagonal matrix Λ_k can be solved by using short pilot sequences. Let a short pilot sequence of length τ symbols be used for uplink pilot and sequences are pair wisely orthogonal. Hence, the pilot sequences used by the K users can be denoted by $\tau \times K$ matrix $\sqrt{p_t}\psi$ which satisfies $\psi^H \psi = I_k$ where $p_t = \tau p_u$. The

$M \times \tau$ received pilot matrix at the *l-th* BS is given by:

$$Y_{t,l} = \sqrt{p_t}\Lambda_k D_\beta^{1/2} X_{t,l} + Z_{t,l} \qquad (59)$$

where $\hat{\Lambda}_k = \underset{\Lambda \in \lambda_k^k}{\arg\min} \left\| Y_{t,l} - \sqrt{p_t}\Lambda_u D_\beta^{1/2} X_{t,l} \right\|_F^2$ and λ_k is the $k \times k$ diagonal matrices. If BS equipped $M \to \infty$ antennas, H_n can be determined by using Λ_k of the covariance matrix $\hat{R}_{Y_i}$. However this covariance matrix is unavailable to use. The Gaussian distribution of the received signal indicates that the sample covariance matrix is given by:

$$\hat{R}_{Y_i} = \frac{1}{N}\sum_{i=0}^{N-1} vec\left(Y_{t,l}\right) vec^*\left(Y_{t,l}\right) \qquad (60)$$

The channel is estimated by the least-squared method of the pilot data for uplink transmission as follows:

$$\hat{G} = \frac{1}{\sqrt{P_t}} Y \hat{X}^\dagger \qquad (61)$$

The estimated received signal for maximum ratio combining can be obtained as:

$$\tilde{y}_{MRC\_ul} = \tilde{G}_{t,l}^H Y_{t,l} = \frac{1}{\sqrt{p_t}} Y_{t,l} X^{\dagger *} \qquad (62)$$

Moreover, the estimated channel covariance matrix is given by:

$$\hat{\hat{R}}_{Y_i} = \frac{1}{N}\sum_{i=0}^{N-1} vec\left(G_{t,l}\right) vec^*\left(G_{t,l}\right) \qquad (63)$$

and:

$$tr\left\{\hat{R}_{Y_i}\right\} = \frac{1}{N}\sum_{i=0}^{N-1} vec^*\left(Y_{t,l}\right) vec\left(Y_{t,l}\right) \qquad (64)$$

Similarly, we can have:

$$\begin{aligned}\hat{R}_{Y_i} &\triangleq \mathrm{E}\left[y A^H\right] \\ &= E\left[\left(\sqrt{p_u}GS_{id} + z\right) A^H\right] = \hat{R}_{Y,A}\end{aligned} \qquad (65)$$

The estimated channel covariance matrix for different signals are given by:

$$\hat{\hat{R}}_{Y,A} = \frac{1}{N}\sum_{i=0}^{N-1} vec\left(Y_{t,l}\right) vec^*\left(\hat{G}_{t,l}\right) \qquad (66)$$

Using Equation (57), Equation (63) and Equation (66), the MMSE-based channel estimation is given by:

$$\tilde{g}_{mmse} = \left(\hat{\hat{R}}_{Y,A} \hat{\hat{R}}_{Y_i}^{-1}\right) Y_{t,l} \qquad (67)$$

The relation between the require power versus the number of base station antennas using MRC

Figure 7. The data flow diagram of the signal transforms based on the eigenvalue-based decomposition

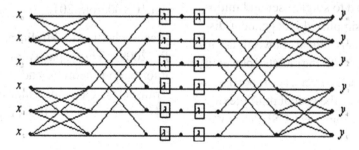

Table 2. Computation complexities of jacket based algorithms

	DCA	FA for $N = p^m$	FA for $N = p^m \cdot q^n$
AD	$N(N-1)$	$2mp^m(p-1)$	$2mp^m(p-1)+2nq^n(q-1)$
MU	N	$2m(p-1)p^m+2p^m$	$2mp^m(p-1)^2+2p^m q^n$ $+2nq^n(q-1)^2$

AD: Additions, MU= multiplications, FA= fast algorithm and DCA= direct computing approach

and MMSE detector based on imperfect CSI system has been shown in Figure 8. We set in Figure 3a, $K = 10$ and low power scaling (p_u) is proportional to $1 / \sqrt{M}$ as $M \to \infty$, then the difference performance between MRC and MMSE.

In Figure 9, shows the sum rate versus number of base station antennas M of the multicellular MMSE based detection process with $M = 90$ antennas at BS, $L = 20$ cells, users $K = 10$ in each cell, sample $N = 100$, $p_u = 20dB$ and the propagation factor $\beta_k = 0.8$ and 10 iterations.

4. CONCLUSION AND FUTURE RESEARCH DIRECTIONS

The massive MIMO is a new research field and it has appeared as an interesting and very promising approach to achieve the higher capacity demand in future such as 1000x, more stable communication links and low transmit power in wireless cellular communication system. We focus in this chapter, the propagation characteristics of massive MIMO and illustrate them using real channel measurement, a liner reception technique in uplink and downlink scenario, achievable rates for realistic channels are compared to single-user and multi-user obtained using simplified independent distribution channel models. We also investigate in this chapter with perfect CSI the radiated power of the terminals can be made inversely proportional to M, while maintaining the spatial multiplexing gains, otherwise with imperfect CSI the power can only be made proportional to the square root of M and compared three receive structures such as ZF, MRC and MMSE.

ACKNOWLEDGMENT

This work was supported by MEST-2012-002521, NRF, Republic of Korea.

REFERENCES

Caire, G., & Shamai, S. (2003). On the achievable throughput of a multiantenna Gaussian broadcast channel. IEEE Transactions on Information Theory, 49(7), 1691–1706. doi:10.1109/TIT.2003.813523

Dahlman, E., Parkvall, S., Skold, J., & Beming, P. (2007). *3G evolation HSPA and LTE for mobile broadband*. London: Academic Press. Retrieved from http://www.elsevier.com/books/3g-evolution/dahlman/978-0-12-372533-2

Foschini, G. J. (1996). Layered space-time architecture for wireless communication in a fading environment when using multi-element antennas. Bell Labs Technical Journal, 1(2), 41–59. doi:10.1002/bltj.2015

Franceschetti, M., Migliore, M. D., & Minero, P. (2009). The capacity of wireless networks: information-theoretic and physical limits. IEEE Transactions on Information Theory, 55(8), 3413–3424. doi:10.1109/TIT.2009.2023705

Figure 8. Required power vs. number of base station antennas (M) for uplink transmission

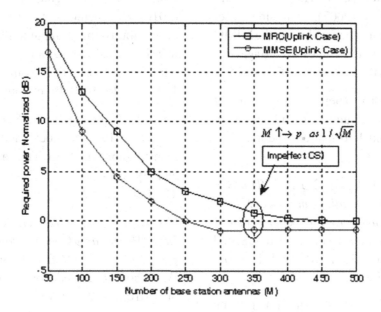

Figure 9. Sum rate vs. number of antennas (downlink transmission)

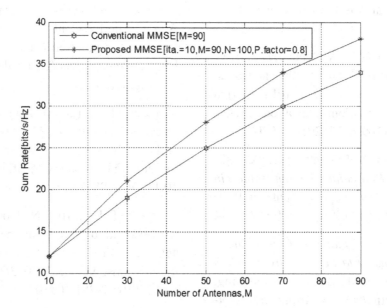

Gesbert, D., Kountouris, M., Heath, R. W., Jr., Chae, C., & Salzer, T. (2007). From single user to multiuser communications: Shifting the MIMO paradigm. IEEE Signal Processing Magazine, 24(5), 36–36. doi:10.1109/MSP.2007.904815

Gray, R. M. (2006). Toeplitz and circulant mareices: A review. Foundation and Trends in Communication and Information Theory, 2(3), 155–239.

Hien, Q. N., & Erik, L. G. (2012). *EVD-based channel estimation for multicell multiuser MIMO with very large antenna arrays.* Paper presented at the International Conference on Acoustics, Speed and Signal Processing (ICASSP). DOI: 10.1109/ICASSP.2012.6288608

Hien, Q. N., Erik, L. G., & Marzetta, T. L. (2011). *Uplink power efficiency of multiuser MIMO with very large antennas arrays.* Paper presented at Forty-Ninth Annual Allerton Conference. DOI: 10.1109/Allerton.2011.6120314

Hoydis, J., Stephan, B. T., & Debbah, D. (2013). Massive MIMO in the UL/DL of celluar networks: How many antennas do we need? IEEE Journal on Selected Areas in Communications, 31(2), 160–171. doi:10.1109/JSAC.2013.130205

Jose, J., Ashikhmin, A., Marzetta, T. L., & Vishwanath, S. (2009). *Pilot contamination problem in multi-cell TDD systems.* Paper presented at ISIT. Seoul, Korea. DOI: 10.1109/ISIT.2009.5205814

Lee, M. H. (2012). *Jacket matrices: Constructions and its applications for fast cooperative wireless signal processing.* LAP Lambert Publishing. Retrieved from http://www.amazon.com/Jacket-Matrices-Construction-Application-Cooperative/dp/3659291455

Lee, M. H., Manev, N. L., & Zhang, X. D. (2008). Jacket transforms eigenvalue decomposition. Applied Mathematics and Computation, 198(2), 858–864.

Lee, M. H., Matalgah, M. M., & Song, W. (2010). Fast method for precoding and decoding of distributive multi-input multi-output channels in relay-based decode-and-forward cooperative wireless network. IET Communications, 4(2), 144–153. doi:10.1049/iet-com.2008.0712

Lee, M. H., Zhang, X. D., Song, W., & Xia, X. G. (2012). Fast reciprocal jacket transform with many parameters. IEEE Transactions on Circuits and Systems, 59(7), 1472–1481. doi:10.1109/TCSI.2011.2177013

Marzetta, T. L., & Alexei, A. (2010). *Beyond LTE: Hundreds of base station antennas!* Paper presented at IEEE Communication Theory Workshop. Retrieved from http://www.ieee-ctw.org/2010/mon/Marzetta.pdf

Marzetta, T. L. (1999). *BLAST training: Estimating channel characteristics for high capacity space-time wireless.* Paper presented at 37th Annual Allerton Conf. Commnications, Control, and Computing. Retrieved from ftp://cm.bell-labs.com/cm/ms/who/hochwald/papers/training/training.pdf

Marzetta, T. L. (2006). *How much training is required for multiuser MIMO?* Paper presented at Fortieth Asilomar Conference on Signals, Systems, & Computers. Pacific Grove, CA. DOI: 10.1109/ACSSC.2006.354768

Marzetta, T. L. (2010). Noncooperative cellular wireless with unlimited numbers of base station antennas. IEEE Transactions on Wireless Communications, 9(11), 3590–3600. doi:10.1109/TWC.2010.092810.091092

Matthaiou, M., McKay, M. R., Smith, P. J., & Nossek, J. A. (2010). On the condition number distribution of complex Wishart matrices. IEEE Transactions on Communications, 58(6), 1705–1717. doi:10.1109/TCOMM.2010.06.090328

Rusek, F., Daniel, P., Buon, K. L., Erik, L. G., Marzetta, T. L., Edfors, O., & Tufvesson, F. (2013). Scaling up MIMO: Opportunities and challenges with very large arrays. IEEE Signal Processing Magazine, 30(1), 40–60. doi:10.1109/MSP.2011.2178495

Toskala, A. (2012). *3GPP TSG RAN workshop on Rel-12 and onwards: Samsung RWS-120002*. Retrieved from http://www.3gpp.org/Future-Radio-in-3GPP-300-attend

Tse, D., & Viswanath, P. (2005). *Fundamentals of wireless communications*. Cambridge, UK: Cambridge University Press. Retrieved from http://www.eecs.berkeley.edu/~dtse/book.html

Vishwanath, P., & Tse, D. (2003). Sum capacity of a vector Gaussian broadcast channel and uplink-downlink duality. IEEE Transactions on Information Theory, 49(8), 1912–1921. doi:10.1109/TIT.2003.814483

Vishwanath, S., Jindal, N., & Goldsmith, A. (2003). Duality, achievable rates, and sum-rate capacity of Gaussian MIMO broadcast channels. IEEE Transactions on Information Theory, 49(10), 2058–2068. doi:10.1109/TIT.2003.817421

Werner, K., & Jansson, M. (2009). Estimating MIMO channel covariances from training data under the Kronecker model. Signal Processing, 89(1), 1–13.

Yin, H., Gesbert, D., Filippou, M., & Liu, Y. (2013). A coordinated approach to channel estimation in large-scale multiple-antenna systems. IEEE Journal on Selected Areas in Communications, 31(2), 264–273. doi:10.1109/JSAC.2013.130214

ADDITIONAL READING

Chocklingam, A., & Rajan, B. S. (Soon Appear 2013). Large Scale MIMO. UK: Cambridge University Press.

Dahlman, E., & Parkvall, S. (2011). LTE/LTE-Advanced for Mobile Broadband. London: Academic Press. Retrieved from http://ytd2525.files.wordpress.com/2013/02/124879484-101565919-4g-lte-lte-advanced1.pdf.

Dahlman, E., Parkvall, S., Skold, J., & Beming, P. (2008*). 3G Evolution HSPA and LTE for Mobile Broadband*. London: Academic press. Retrieved from http://www.elsevier.com/books/3g-evolution/dahlman/978-0-12-372533-2.

Farooq, K. (2009). *LTE for 4G Mobile Broadband*. Cambridge: Cambridge University Press. Retrieved from http://www.cambridge.org/us/academic/subjects/engineering/wireless-communications/lte-4g-mobile-broadband-air-interface-technologies-and-performance.

Harri, H., & Antti, T. (2012). *LTE-Advanced 3GPP. Solution for IMT-Advanced*. UK: John Wiley and Sons, Ltd. Retrieved from http://onlinelibrary.wiley.com/book/10.1002/9781118399439.

Larmo, A., et al. (2009). The LTE Link Layer Design. IEEE Communications Magazine, 47(4), 52–59. doi:10.1109/MCOM.2009.4907407

Lee, M. H. (2012). *Jacket Matrices: Constructions and its applications for fast cooperative wireless signal processing*. Germany: LAP LAMBERT publishing. Retrieved from http://www.amazon.com/Jacket-Matrices-Construction-Application-Cooperative/dp/3659291455.

Tony, Q. S., Gulillaume, Q., DeLa, R., Ismail, G., & Marios, K. (2013). Small Cell Networks. UK: Cambridge University Press. Retrieved from http://www.cambridge.org/us/academic/subjects/engineering/wireless-communications/small-cell-networks-deployment-phy-techniques-and-resource-management.

KEY TERMS AND DEFINITIONS

2ⁿᵈ Generation Mobile Standard: System used digital communication technology with TDM, FDM, and CDMA.

3ʳᵈ Generation Partnership Project-Long Term Evolution: A project aims to improve the mobile phone standard to cope with future requirements.

4ᵗʰ Generation: Aims to provide internet protocol (IP) telephony, ultra-broadband internet access and gaming services.

Circulant Jacket Matrix: Also special types of circulant matrices is known as circulant Jacket matrix.

Circulant Matrices: Special kind of Toeplitz matrices is called circulant matrices.

Jacket Matrix: A Matrix A of order n is called Jacket.

LTE-Advanced: Mobile communication 4G standard Release 12 to Release 13.

Massive MIMO: Wireless broadband standard formally submitted as user 4G system using unlimited of BS antenna ports.

APPENDIX 1

Table 1 Proof

From Equation (23), the received forward signal for single user as follows:

$$x_f = G^T s_f + z_f \tag{68}$$

where s_f is the data vector of q_f. In *zero-forcing* (ZF) detector, the data vector of QAM symbol is given by:

$$s_f = \frac{1}{\sqrt{\gamma}} \left(G^T \right)^{\dagger} q_f = \frac{1}{\sqrt{\gamma}} G^* \left(G^T G^* \right)^{-1} q_f \tag{69}$$

where $\left(G^T \right)^{\dagger} = G^* \left(G^T G^* \right)^{-1}$. We also can express that the forward received signal for k-user using Equation (23) as below:

$$x_{fk} = \sqrt{\sum_{l=1}^{M} \left| g_{lk} \right|^2} \cdot q_{fk} + z_{fk} \tag{70}$$

since $\sum_{l=1}^{M} \left| g_{lk} \right|^2 / M \to 1$, $M \to \infty$ and $E\left[q_{fk} q_{fk}^H \right] = p_f / K$. From Equation (69) the signal to noise ratio (SNR) of the output of ZF for perfect CSI:

$$SNR = \frac{p_f}{K\gamma} = \frac{p_f}{K \cdot Tr\left(G^T G^* \right)^{-1} / K} = p_f \left(\alpha - 1 \right) \tag{71}$$

while $Tr\left(G^T G^* \right)^{-1} = 1 / \left(\alpha - 1 \right)$. For imperfect CSI the propagation matrix will be changed. Then we get the effective propagation matrix from Equation (68) as follows:

$$\hat{G}^T = \xi G^T + \sqrt{\left(1 - \xi^2 \right)} E \tag{72}$$

where ξ is reliability of estimation and $0 \leq \xi \leq 1$. The signal-to-interference-noise-ratio (SINR) of the output using Equation (72) of ZF for imperfect CSI:

$$SINR = \frac{\xi^2 p_f (\alpha - 1)}{(1 - \xi^2) p_f + 1} \tag{73}$$

Similarly, from Equation (68), we get the data vector for QAM symbol using MF as follows:

$$s_f = \frac{1}{\sqrt{\gamma}} G^* q_f \tag{74}$$

From Equation (68) and Equation (73), the signal to noise ratio (SNR) of the output of MF for perfect CSI:

$$SNR = p_f \alpha / (p_f + 1) \tag{75}$$

and:

$$SINR = \frac{\xi p_f \alpha}{p_f + 1} \tag{76}$$

The output of MMSE detector for perfect CSI, the SNR is given by:

$$SNR = MK = \frac{M}{K} \cdot K^2 = \alpha.K^2 \tag{77}$$

The signal-to-interference-noise-ratio (SINR) of the output of MMSE for imperfect CSI:

$$SINR = K^3 (\alpha + 1) \tag{78}$$

APPENDIX 2

Eigenvalue Decomposition of Circulant Jacket Matrices

Example 1: If A and B are Jacket decomposable matrices, then their Kronecker product $A \otimes B$ is also Jacket decomposable.

Let $A = T\Lambda_1 T^{-1}$ and $B = U\Lambda_2 U^{-1}$, where T and U are Jacket matrices, Λ_1 and Λ_2 are diagonal. Then we have:

$$
\begin{aligned}
A \otimes B &= \left(T\Lambda_1 T^{-1}\right) \otimes \left(U\Lambda_2 U^{-1}\right) \\
&= \left(T \otimes U\right)\left(\Lambda_1 \otimes \Lambda_2\right)\left(T^{-1} \otimes U^{-1}\right)
\end{aligned}
\tag{79}
$$

where $\left(\Lambda_1 \otimes \Lambda_2\right)$ is a diagonal matrix and $\left(T \otimes U\right)$ is a Jacket matrix. Since $T^{-1} \otimes U^{-1} = \left(T \otimes U\right)^{-1}$, we can rewrite the above equality in the following form:

$$
A \otimes B = \left(T \otimes U\right)\left(\Lambda_1 \otimes \Lambda_2\right)\left(T \otimes U\right)^{-1}
\tag{80}
$$

Hence, $A \otimes B$ is a Jacket decomposable.
Recall that a circulant matrix is said to be a matrix of the following form:

$$
C = \begin{pmatrix}
c_0 & c_1 & c_2 & \cdots & c_{n-1} \\
c_{n-1} & c_0 & c_1 & \cdots & c_{n-2} \\
c_{n-2} & c_{n-1} & c_0 & \cdots & c_{n-3} \\
\cdot & \cdot & \cdot & \cdots & \cdot \\
c_1 & c_2 & c_3 & \cdots & c_0
\end{pmatrix}
\tag{81}
$$

Since $W^{-1}CW = diag\left(f\left(x_1\right), f\left(x_2\right), ..., f\left(x_n\right)\right)$, where $f\left(x\right) = c_0 + c_1 x + \cdots + c_{n-1} x^{n-1}$ and W is the DFT matrix, it is obviously that $f\left(x_1\right), f\left(x_2\right), ..., f\left(x_n\right)$ are the eigenvalues of C:

Example 2: A matrix $A = \left(a_{ij}\right)$ is diagonalizable by the Vandermonde matrix W, if and only if A is a circulant matrix.

Let $A = W\Lambda W^{-1}$, where $\Lambda = diag\left(\lambda_1, \lambda_2, ..., \lambda_n\right)$ denote

$$
f_k\left(x\right) = a_{k1} + a_{k2} x + \cdots + a_{kn} x^{n-1}, k = 1, 2, \cdots n.
$$

Then it is easy to show that:

$$AW = \begin{vmatrix} f_1(x_1) & f_1(x_2) & \cdots & f_1(x_n) \\ f_2(x_1) & f_2(x_2) & \cdots & f_2(x_n) \\ f_3(x_1) & f_3(x_2) & \cdots & f_3(x_n) \\ . & . & . & . \\ f_n(x_1) & f_n(x_2) & \cdots & f_n(x_n) \end{vmatrix} \tag{82}$$

On the other hand, we have:

$$W\Lambda = \begin{vmatrix} \lambda_1 & \lambda_2 & \cdots & \lambda_n \\ \lambda_1 x_1 & \lambda_2 x_2 & \cdots & \lambda_n x_n \\ \lambda_1 x_1^2 & \lambda_1 x_2^2 & \cdots & \lambda_n x_n^2 \\ . & . & . & . \\ \lambda_1 x_1^{n-1} & \lambda_1 x_2^{n-1} & \cdots & \lambda_1 x_n^{n-1} \end{vmatrix} \tag{83}$$

Since $AW = W\Lambda$, we get:

$$\begin{vmatrix} f_1\left(x_j\right) = \lambda_j, \\ f_2\left(x_j\right) = \lambda_j x_j \\ . \qquad . \qquad . \\ f_2\left(x_j\right) = \lambda_j x_j^{n-1}, \quad j = 1, 2, \cdots n \\ . \qquad . \qquad . \\ f_n\left(x_j\right) = \lambda_j x_j^{n-1} \end{vmatrix} \tag{84}$$

Multiplying the first equation by x_j^{k-1} and subtracting the result from the kth equation for any $j = 1, 2, ..., n$, we obtain:

$$\begin{aligned} &\left(a_{k,1} - a_{1,n-k+2}\right) + \left(a_{k,2} - a_{1,n-k+3}\right)x_j \\ &+ \cdots + \left(a_{k,n} - a_{1,n-k+1}\right)x_j^{n-1} = 0 \end{aligned} \tag{85}$$

which means that a vector:

$$\left(\left(a_{k,1} - a_{1,n-k+2}\right), \left(a_{k,2} - a_{1,n-k+3}\right), ..., \left(a_{k,n} - a_{1,n-k+1}\right)\right) \tag{86}$$

is a solution of the following homogenous linear system:

$$
W \begin{pmatrix} z_1 \\ z_2 \\ . \\ z_n \end{pmatrix} = \begin{pmatrix} 0 \\ 0 \\ . \\ 0 \end{pmatrix} \tag{87}
$$

Since W is nonsingular matrix, this system has only the trivial (zero) solution. Thus:

$$
\begin{aligned}
\left(a_{k,1} - a_{1,n-k+2} \right) &= \left(a_{k,2} - a_{1,n-k+3} \right) \\
&= \cdots = \left(a_{k,n} - a_{1,n-k+1} \right) = 0
\end{aligned} \tag{88}
$$

Note that since, the *kth* row of A, $k = 1, 2, \ldots, n$ is a right shift by $k - 1$ positions of the first row, A is a circulant matrix:

Example 3: A matrix $A = \left(a_{ij} \right)$ is diagonalizable by a Jacket matrix which is equivalent to the DFT matrix W, if and only if $A = PBP^{-1}$, where P is a permutation matrix and B has the form:

$$
B = \begin{pmatrix}
c_1 & c_2 d_1 d_2^{-1} & c_3 d_1 d_3^{-1} & \cdots & c_n d_1 d_n^{-1} \\
c_n d_2 d_1^{-1} & c_1 & c_2 d_2 d_3^{-1} & \cdots & c_{n-1} d_2 d_n^{-1} \\
c_{n-1} d_3 d_1^{-1} & c_n d_3 d_2^{-1} & c_1 & \cdots & c_{n-2} d_3 d_n^{-1} \\
. & . & . & \cdots & . \\
c_2 d_n d_1^{-1} & c_3 d_3 d_2^{-1} & c_4 d_n d_3^{-1} & \cdots & c_1
\end{pmatrix}
$$

We first express the matrix via the of Jacket decomposition:

$$
A = T \Lambda T^{-1} \tag{89}
$$

We shall consider the case when T is equivalent to the DFT matrix W, that is, when:

$$
T = PDWEQ \tag{90}
$$

where P and Q are permutation matrices and D and E are diagonal matrices.

By Equation (91), we get:

$$
A = PDWEQ \Lambda Q^{-1} E^{-1} W^{-1} D^{-1} P^{-1} \tag{91}
$$

Since Q is a permutation matrix, the matrix $\Lambda_1 = Q\Lambda Q^{-1}$ is also diagonal and differs from Λ only in the order of diagonal elements. Since E, Λ_1, and E^{-1}, are all diagonal matrices, they can be commuted with each other. Hence, we have $E\Lambda_1 E^{-1} = \Lambda_1 EE^{-1} = \Lambda_1$. Therefore, by Equation (92), we can see that:

$$A = PDW\Lambda_1 W^{-1}D^{-1}P^{-1} = PDCD^{-1}P^{-1} = PBP^{-1} \tag{92}$$

where $B = DCD^{-1}$. According to Example 2, matrix $C = W\Lambda_1 W$ becomes circulant:

Example 4: If A and B are Jacket decomposable matrices and σ is a matrix equivalence, then the matrix $C = \begin{pmatrix} A + \sigma B\sigma^{-1} & A - \sigma B\sigma^{-1} \\ A - \sigma B\sigma^{-1} & A + \sigma B\sigma^{-1} \end{pmatrix}$ is also Jacket decomposable.

Let $A = U\Lambda_1 U^{-1}$ and $B = V\Lambda_2 V^{-1}$ are Jacket decomposable matrices, where U, V are Jacket matrices and Λ_1, Λ_2 are diagonal matrices. Then:

$$
\begin{aligned}
C &= \begin{pmatrix} A + \sigma B\sigma^{-1} & A - \sigma B\sigma^{-1} \\ A - \sigma B\sigma^{-1} & A + \sigma B\sigma^{-1} \end{pmatrix} \\
&= \begin{pmatrix} U\Lambda_1 U^{-1} + \sigma V\Lambda_2 V^{-1}\sigma^{-1} & U\Lambda_1 U^{-1} - \sigma V\Lambda_2 V^{-1}\sigma^{-1} \\ U\Lambda_1 U^{-1} - \sigma V\Lambda_2 V^{-1}\sigma^{-1} & U\Lambda_1 U^{-1} + \sigma V\Lambda_2 V^{-1}\sigma^{-1} \end{pmatrix} \\
&= \begin{pmatrix} U & \sigma V \\ U & -\sigma V \end{pmatrix} \begin{pmatrix} \Lambda_1 & 0 \\ 0 & \Lambda_2 \end{pmatrix} \begin{pmatrix} U^{-1} & U^{-1} \\ V^{-1}\sigma^{-1} & -V^{-1}\sigma^{-1} \end{pmatrix}
\end{aligned}
\tag{93}
$$

where σ is a matrix equivalence and $\begin{pmatrix} \Lambda_1 & 0 \\ 0 & \Lambda_2 \end{pmatrix}$ is the eigenvalue matrix.

Chapter 9
Exploiting Scalar Effect in Wireless Access Networks:
A Case Study and Research Directions

Rongrong Qian
Beijing University of Posts and Telecommunications (BUPT), China

Yuan Qi
Beijing University of Posts and Telecommunications (BUPT), China

ABSTRACT

"Economies of scale" (called scale effect for notational convenience in this work), as a long run concept in microeconomics, refers to reductions in unit cost as the size of a facility and the usage levels of other inputs increase (Wikipedia, 2013). This chapter applies the concept of scale effect in microeconomics to the studies of algorithmic complexity within which the scale effect can be defined as the feature that the unit complexity (i.e., complexity per instance) of the algorithm decreases as the number of instances of algorithm increases while maintaining the performance. In this chapter, the Early-Termination Fixed-Complexity Sphere Detector (ET-FSD) is developed to exploit scale effect for the multiple-antenna system, which has to detect signals of multiple users under the constraint of sum complexity (e.g., the base-station systems always encounter the run-time limit of signal detection of all the users). Based on the study of ET-FSD, future directions of scale effect research for algorithmic complexity issues appearing in wireless access networks are presented as well.

INTRODUCTION

The fundamental scenario for exploiting the scale effect (as shown in the Figure 1) is that some algorithm is instantiated for many times and all the instances are executed together under a sum complexity constraint. This algorithm shall have variable complexity, which has many parameters affecting the statistics of its complexity. It is assumed that the algorithm has instances, and the complexity of different instances (each of which is denoted by ξ_j) are random variables. Then, the sum complexity of instances is

$$S_n = \sum_{j=1}^{n} \xi_j \, .$$

DOI: 10.4018/978-1-4666-4888-3.ch009

Figure 1. Illustration of the scenario for exploiting the scale effect

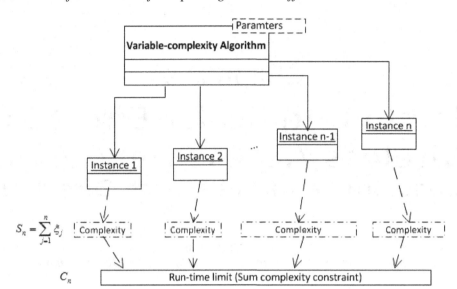

Due to the run-time limit, the sum complexity S_n cannot exceed a constraint C_n, otherwise, it leads to an outage event.

Considering the multiple-user scenario, it is proposed in this chapter to realize the full diversity multiple-input multiple-output (MIMO) detection under a polynomial constraint of unit complexity (i.e., complexity per user) by exploiting the scale effect. It is worth noting that the multiple-user scenario is a typical case of applying the scale effect, in which every algorithm is always instantiated for all the users. To be specific, the ET-FSD algorithm is developed in the multiple-user scenario, and the corresponding mathematic model primarily based on the large deviation principle is established for analyzing the scale effect. The existence of scale effect in ET-FSD can be clearly revealed by this study. Hence, one can expect that, due to the scale effect, the goal to make the MIMO detection work under a polynomial constraint of unit complexity while maintaining the full diversity performance can be accomplished.

After presenting ET-FSD as a case study, this chapter also focuses on discussing the future research directions of the scale effect study with respect to the algorithmic complexity issues in wireless access networks. Besides the MIMO detection, channel decoding algorithms (including these of Turbo codes and LDPC codes) of base-band processing in wireless access networks shall also have the scale effect. Thus this chapter will explain on the details of investigating the scale effect of channel decoding algorithms.

BACKGROUND

For the multiple-antenna system with n_T transmit and n_R receive antennas, one can use the matrix $\mathbb{C}^{n_R \times n_T}$ to represent this MIMO channel. The channel matrix considered in this study has the entries which are independent and identically distributed (i.i.d.) zero-mean complex Gaussian random variables with unit variance. If letting $\mathbb{C}^{n_T \times 1}$ be the transmit signal vector in which each entry belongs to a constellation set $\mathcal{D}$ with size m, the signal model of the MIMO channel would be written as y=Hs+v, where denotes the receive signal vector and is the zero-mean circularly symmetric complex Gaussian noise vector with covariance matrix $\mathrm{E}(vv^H)=\sigma^2 \mathrm{I}_{n_R,n_R}$.

By assuming that is perfectly known at the receiver, the maximum-likelihood (ML) detector that could minimize the average error probability, is the optimal MIMO detection scheme and can be given by

$$\tilde{s}_{ML} = \arg\min_{\tilde{s} \in \mathcal{D}^{n_T}} \left\| y\text{-}H\tilde{s} \right\|_F^2 \qquad (1)$$

The optimality of ML detector also implies that this detector is able to achieve the diversity order n_R (i.e., full diversity order) (Paulraj, Nabar, &Gore, 2003). Despite the optimal performance of average error probability, the ML detector is not a feasible scheme of MIMO detection for practical deployment because of its extremely high complexity. It can be found from (1) that the ML detector has to perform exhaustive search among all the possible candidates and thus has the exponential complexity $C_{ML} = O(m^{n_T})$.

Intensive research efforts have been spent on exploring low complexity MIMO detectors with the optimal/suboptimal performance of error probability or diversity order (Viterbo & Boutros, 1999)-(Barbero & Thompson, 2006). With some fixed performance degradation (Narasimhan, 2003), the sphere decoding (SD) has an exponential complexity (in both the worst and the average cases) of $C_{SD} = O(m^{\gamma n_T})$ with $\gamma \in (0,1)$ (Narasimhan, 2003). The fixed-complexity sphere decoder (FSD) is proved to maintain full diversity with a complexity $C_{FSD} = O(m^{\sqrt{n_T}})$ that is 'subexponential' (Jalden, Barbero, Ottersten, & Thompson, 2007). On the other hand, the linear receivers, e.g., zero-forcing (ZF) and minimum mean square error (MMSE) schemes, have low complexity but quite poor diversity order, i.e., $n_R - n_T + 1$ (Paulraj, Nabar, &Gore, 2003). Even now the topic of MIMO detection attracts many interests (Seethaler & Bolcskei, 2010)-(Seethaler, Jalden, Studer, & Bolcskei, 2011), because although a lot of prior works have been done, still

there is an imperfectness in MIMO detection, i.e., it lacks a scheme that ensures to realize the optimal performance MIMO detector under the constraint of polynomial complexity. The situation maybe more discouraging, since many MIMO detectors have their own inherent limitations (Jalden & Ottersten, 2005)(Taherzadeh & Khandani, 2010). Under these conditions, this chapter puts forth a new viewpoint:

to exploit more potential positive factors in the MIMO detectors might be one of the appropriate ideas for making the next breakthrough, for instance, to exploit scale effect in multiple-user case.

MAIN FOCUS

As an attractive scheme among the existing MIMO detectors, the FSD is highly suitable for hardware implementation owing to its fixed-complexity and parallel-computing-friendly features (Barbero & Thompson, 2006). By simply incorporating an early-termination mechanism into the FSD, one can establish the ET-FSD scheme. The main processing of ET-FSD is a constrained tree search through a tree with n_T levels where m branches originate from each node. Analogous to FSD (Jalden et al., 2007, 2009), the EF-FSD has two stages:

- The first stage is full expansion (FE) search, in which a full search is performed in levels, expanding all m branches per node. In this stage the transmit symbol judged (by FSD channel matrix reordering strategy proposed by (Jalden et al., 2009)) to have the larger noise amplification appears in the earlier level of the tree. The minimum post-processing SNR after the FE search with p levels, denoted by η_p, is defined and satisfies

$$\eta_p \triangleq \min_i \frac{\rho}{n_T} \frac{1}{[(Q_p)^{-1}]_{i,i}}$$
$$\geq \frac{\rho}{n_T} \frac{1}{\lambda_{\max}((Q_p)^{-1})} = \frac{\rho}{n_T} \lambda_1(Q_p) \qquad (2)$$

where ρ is the average receive SNR (Paulraj, Nabar, &Gore, 2003) and the inequality is obtained by following the derivations as (32)-(33) of (Narasimhan, 2003) since the largest eigenvalue shall be not less than any diagonal term of a Hermitian matrix (Lutkepohl, 1996). $\lambda_{\max}(\bullet)$ and $\lambda_k(\bullet)$ denote the maximum and the k-th smallest eigenvalue of the matrix, respectively.

- The second stage is single expansion (SE) search, in which a single search needs to be performed in the remaining n_T-p levels. The SE search expands one branch per node followed by the decision-feedback equalization (DFE) path as in previous studies (Jalden et al., 2007, 2009). Given the FSD channel matrix reordering performed in (Jalden et al., 2009), the signal model left to SE search can be written as $\bar{y} = H_{o1}s_{o1} + v$, where s_{o1} contains the symbols to be detected in the SE search and H_{o1} is the effective channel matrix left for the SE search. The Hermitian matrix $Q_p \triangleq H_{o1}^H H_{o1}$ shall be a principal sub-matrix obtained by successively removing p columns and rows from $H^H H$ according to the criterion in (Jalden et al., 2009).

The FE search has no impact on the diversity order of ET-FSD but the SE search does (Jalden et al., 2009).

While the key idea of early termination employed by ET-FSD is to adaptively set the number of levels of the FE search p_H as

$$p_H = \min \left\{ \min \left\{ p : \underbrace{\eta_{(p-1)} \geq \rho^\gamma}_{\text{early-termination criterion}} \right\}, \bar{p} \right\} \quad (3)$$

where $\gamma \in (0,1)$ is a real value and η_0 is defined by (2) with $Q_0 = H^H H$. We use p_H to denote so as to emphasize that p_H is a function of . If the FE search is assumed to have p_H levels, the overall complexity of ET-FSD would be $\xi(p_H) \triangleq O(m^{p_H})$, where $\xi(p_H)$ is defined as the overall complexity of ET-FSD when the FE search has p_H levels and it shall vary with p_H. A straight result can be derived from (Jalden et al., 2007) is that, the ET-FSD would maintain the full diversity order as the ML detector if $p_H \geq \bar{p}$, where $\bar{p}$ is

$$\bar{p} = \min\{p : (n_R - n_T)(p+1) + (p+1)^2 > n_R\} \quad (4)$$

In other words, having $p_H \geq \bar{p}$ enable ET-FSD to achieve the full diversity order (Qian, Qi, Peng, & Wang, 2013a). But the early termination as (3) surely makes the event $p_H < \bar{p}$ happen, then what the diversity order of ET-FSD exactly could be is still an open question for us, which will be answered in sketch as follows.

With the early-termination criterion of (3), one could get

$$P(p_H = j)$$
$$= \begin{cases} P(\eta_j \geq \rho^\gamma), & j = 0, \\ P\left((\eta_{(j-1)} < \rho^\gamma) \cup (\eta_j \geq \rho^\gamma)\right), & 1 \leq j < \bar{p}, \\ P(\eta_{(j-1)} < \rho^\gamma), & j = \bar{p}, \end{cases}$$

where

$$P(p_H = j) = P(\eta_{(j-1)} < \rho^\gamma)$$

for $j \geq 1$. Then, by following from (2), we can arrive at

$$P(\eta_{(j-1)} < \rho^{\gamma}) \leq \beta \left(\binom{n_T}{p-1} n_T \rho^{(\gamma-1)} \right)^{(n_R - n_T)p + p^2} \quad (5)$$

where the inequality is derived similarly as in (Jalden et al., 2007) and β is a real constant (Khoshnevis & Sabharwal, 2004). Since we use $\xi(p_H)$ to represent the complexity of ET-FSD when its FE search has p_H levels, $\xi(0)$ and $\xi(\overline{p})$ stand for two extremes of $\xi(p_H)$, which correspond to $p_H = 0$ and $p_H = \overline{p}$, respectively. Moreover, one should observe

$$P\left(\xi(p_H) = \xi(j) \right) = P\left(p_H = j \right)$$

and

$$P\left(\xi(p_H) \neq \xi(0) \right) = P\left(\eta_0 < \rho^{\gamma} \right) \quad (6)$$

Regarding the diversity order, for ET-FSD there exists the relation as:

$$d_{ET-FSD} = \min\{n_R, d_{SE}\}$$

where d_{ET-FSD} and d_{SE} denote the diversity order of ET-FSD and linear detector at the SE search, respectively. It also holds true that (Jalden et al., 2009)

$$d_{SE} \geq \lim_{\rho \to +\infty} \frac{\log P(\eta_p \leq 1)}{\log(1 / \rho)}$$

Since the early termination happens when the minimum post-processing SNR exceeds ρ^{γ}, the probability $P(\eta_p \leq 1)$ of ET-FSD never gets worse in comparison to that in FSD. In summary, the diversity order of ET-FSD is still n_R with the early-termination mechanism specified in (3). The detail

proof of the full diversity property of ET-FSD can be found in (Qian, Qi, Peng, & Wang, 2013a).

In the multiple-user scenario where the MIMO receiver has to detect the signals of n users with ET-FSD performed for each user, the existence of the scale effect will be proved in the coming part.

Solutions and Recommendations

For the considered multiple-user scenario, define

$$S_n \triangleq \sum_{j=1}^{n} \xi_j(p_H)$$

to be the sum complexity of ET-FSD of n users. And S_n/n can be named by us as the unit complexity that actually is the complexity per user.

Let us assume different users in multiple-user scenario suffer i.i.d. channel fading and have the same average receive SNR ρ for the simplification of analysis. Then, if let the random variable, $\xi_j(p_H)$, denote the complexity of the ET-FSD for the j-th user, one will get that $\xi_j(p_H)$ and $\xi_k(p_H)$ are i.i.d. random variables with $j \neq k$. This assumption should be applicable for practice because different users within a base-station might stay in different locations, thus the wireless channels they encounter could have no spatial correlation. Also current base-station systems always employ the open-loop power control such that the average receive SNR for each user at base-station side can be adjusted to an identical value.

Definition: Because of the run-time limit, there exists a constraint $C_n \left(\xi(0) < C_n / n < \xi(\overline{p}) \right)$ such that the MIMO receiver has to perform the ET-FSD for n users with the sum complexity being less than C_n, i.e., $S_n < C_n$, where C_n is called the *sum complexity constraint*.

As $\xi(0) < C_n / n < \xi(\overline{p})$, S_n shall exceed C_n with certain probability. Once $S_n \geq C_n$ occurs, due to the limit of run-time, the ET-FSD of some users shall have to unconditionally quit before completely executing the tree search, which can be seen as the detection outage and would cause performance degradation to the corresponding users. Such detection outage is undesirable; but it is inevitable. Therefore it is required to investigate the probability $P(S_n \geq C_n)$ so as to clearly recognize the impact brought by the above detection outage.

To make use of the large deviation principle, a random variable is introduced firstly as below

$$X_j(p_{\mathrm{H}}) \triangleq \begin{cases} \xi(0), & \text{if } \xi_j(p_{\mathrm{H}}) = \xi(0) \\ \xi(\bar{p}), & \text{if } \xi_j(p_{\mathrm{H}}) \neq \xi(0) \end{cases}$$

where

$$P\Big(X_j(p_{\mathrm{H}}) = \xi(0)\Big) = P\Big(\eta_0 \geq \rho^\gamma\Big)$$

and

$$P\Big(X_j(p_{\mathrm{H}}) = \xi(\bar{p})\Big) = P\Big(\eta_0 < \rho^\gamma\Big)$$

Observe that $X_j(p_{\mathrm{H}}) \geq \xi_j(p_{\mathrm{H}})$, one can further define and get

$$\bar{S}_n \triangleq \sum_{j=1}^{n} X_j(p_{\mathrm{H}}) \geq S_n \tag{7}$$

Several theoretic results of $\bar{S}_n$ could be derived as follows.

Theorem (The Cramer's theorem for empirical average [Hollander, 2008]): Since $X_j(p_{\mathrm{H}})$ satisfies

$$\varphi(t) = \mathrm{E}\Big(e^{tX_j(p_{\mathrm{H}})}\Big) < +\infty, \quad \forall t \in \mathbb{R}$$

for all $\delta > 0$, it is true that

$$\lim_{n \to +\infty} \frac{1}{n} \log P\left(\frac{1}{n}\bar{S}_n \geq \mathrm{E}\Big(X_j(p_{\mathrm{H}})\Big) + \delta\right) \\ = -I\Big(\mathrm{E}\Big(X_j(p_{\mathrm{H}})\Big) + \delta\Big) \tag{8}$$

where $I(\bullet)$ is a rate function defined as

$$I(z) = \sup_{t \in \mathbb{R}} \Big(zt - \log \varphi(t)\Big)$$

Theorem (Detail proof provided in (Qian et al., 2013a)): The closed-form expression of $I\Big(\mathrm{E}\Big(X_j(p_{\mathrm{H}})\Big) + \delta\Big)$ in (8) can be obtained as Equation 9 in Box 1 where

$$\Delta_\zeta \triangleq \zeta(\bar{p}) - \zeta(0)$$

and

$$P_* = 1 - P\Big(X_j(p_{\mathrm{H}}) = \xi(0)\Big) = 1 - P\Big(\xi_j(p_{\mathrm{H}}) = \xi(0)\Big)$$

Box 1. Equation 9

$$I\Big(\mathrm{E}\big(X_j(p(\mathbf{H}))\big)\Big) + \delta = \log \frac{\delta[1 - P_*] + \Delta_\zeta P_*[1 - P_*]}{\Delta_\zeta P_*[1 - P_*] - \delta P_*} \left[P_* + \frac{\delta}{\Delta_\zeta}\right] - \log \frac{\Delta_\zeta[1 - P_*]}{\Delta_\zeta[1 - P_*] - \delta}$$

One can observe from (9) that $I\left(\mathrm{E}(X_j(p(\mathbf{H}))) + \delta\right)$ is independent of n. By combining (5), (6) and (9).

$$\lim_{\rho \to +\infty} \frac{I\left(\mathrm{E}\left(X_j(p(\mathbf{H}))\right) + \delta\right)}{\log \rho} \geq \frac{\delta(1 - \gamma)(n_R - n_T + 1)}{\Delta_\zeta} \tag{10}$$

Furthermore, (8) can also be interpreted as, $\forall \varepsilon > 0$, there exists a number N, for any $n \geq N$, it satisfies the equation in Box 2.

The relationship above allows us to calculate

$$\lim_{\rho \to +\infty} \frac{nI\left(\mathrm{E}\left(X_j(p(\mathbf{H}))\right) + \delta\right) - n\varepsilon}{\log \rho}$$

$$\leq -\lim_{\rho \to +\infty} \frac{\log P\left(\frac{1}{n}\bar{S}_n \geq \mathrm{E}(X_j(p(\mathbf{H}))) + \delta\right)}{\log \rho}$$

$$\leq \lim_{\rho \to +\infty} \frac{nI\left(\mathrm{E}\left(X_j(p(\mathbf{H}))\right) + \delta\right) + n\varepsilon}{\log \rho}$$

which further yields, by recalling from (10),

$$-\lim_{\rho \to +\infty} \frac{\log P\left(\frac{1}{n}\bar{S}_n \geq \mathrm{E}(X_j(p(\mathbf{H}))) + \delta\right)}{\log \rho}$$

$$= \lim_{\rho \to +\infty} \frac{nI\left(\mathrm{E}\left(X_j(p(\mathbf{H}))\right) + \delta\right)}{\log \rho}$$

$$\geq \frac{n\delta(1 - \gamma)(n_R - n_T + 1)}{\Delta_\zeta}$$

This finally implies

$$P\left(\frac{1}{n}\bar{S}_n \geq \mathrm{E}(X_j(p(\mathbf{H}))) + \delta\right) \dot{\leq} \rho^{-n\delta(1-\gamma)(n_R - n_T + 1)/\Delta_\zeta} \tag{11}$$

Given both the relations in (7) and (11), it can be obtained that

$$P\left(\frac{1}{n}S_n \geq \mathrm{E}(X_j(p(\mathbf{H}))) + \delta\right) \dot{\leq} \rho^{-n\delta(1-\gamma)(n_R - n_T + 1)/\Delta_\zeta} \tag{12}$$

From (12), it is known that, if

$$C(n)/n = \mathrm{E}\left(X_j(p(\mathbf{H}))\right) + \delta$$

the detection outage probability

$$P\left(S(n)/n \geq \mathrm{E}\left(X_j(p(\mathbf{H}))\right) + \delta\right)$$

has an asymptotic upper bound that is directly determined by n. As long as n is large sufficiently such that

$$n > \frac{n_R \Delta_\zeta}{\delta(1 - \gamma)(n_R - n_T + 1)}$$

the detection outage would give rise to a vanishing performance gap (with increasing ρ) between ET-FSD in multiple user scenario and ML performance, by applying the approach of analyzing

Box 2.

$$e^{-n\left(I\left(\mathrm{E}\left(X_j(p(\mathbf{H}))\right) + \delta\right) + \varepsilon\right)} < P\left(\frac{1}{n}\bar{S}_n \geq \mathrm{E}(X_j(p(\mathbf{H}))) + \delta\right) < e^{-n\left(I\left(\mathrm{E}\left(X_j(p(\mathbf{H}))\right) + \delta\right) - \varepsilon\right)}$$

vanishing gap to the ML performance developed in (Jalden & Elia, 2011). Herein the vanishing performance gap actually implies no loss of diversity order (Jalden & Elia, 2011). And also this performance gap should in principle become smaller as n increases, with respect to (12). Meanwhile, $C(n)/n = \mathrm{E}\left(X_j(p(\mathbf{H}))\right) + \delta$ can be seemed as the constraint of the unit complexity, for which $\mathrm{E}\left(X_j(p(\mathbf{H}))\right)$ is a decreasing function of ρ that tends to ξ(0) as ρ increases, according to (5). Therefore, (12) clearly show that scale effect exists in ET-FSD.

FUTURE RESEARCH DIRECTIONS

The so-called scale effect is newly introduced to the studies of algorithmic complexity including MIMO detection, while it shall be found that similar effect named multiuser diversity has already been recognized and attracts intensive interests in network and information-theoretic researches (see the references (Zhang, Lv, & Wang, 2008) (Tajer & Wang, 2010) and therein). The similarity between scale effect and multiuser diversity is that both of them stand for the benefits arising in multiple-user scenario. On the other hand, scale effect differs from multiuser diversity because the former quantifies the reduction of complexity while multiuser diversity always represents the increase of network throughput and channel capacity.

The scale effect in fact ubiquitously exists in current base-station systems, and in future it might play more important role in baseband signal processing owing to the trends of the green radio and centralized base-station processing systems (Qian, Qi, Peng, & Wang, 2012). The development of ET-FSD and the corresponding analysis of scale effect for ET-FSD in preceding part of this chapter show a case study of exploiting scale effect of algorithmic complexity, from which we can find many directions for future research, which are related to wireless access network.

1. **Extending results of ET-FSD:** For the scale effect of ET-FSD, the assumption given above requires that all the users encounter the same system configurations (including the number of antennas, average receive SNR) such that the complexity of ET-FSD of all the users are i.i.d. random variables. While in practical wireless access network, the system configurations for all the users are not necessarily the same, in which case we shall have to analyze the scale effect of ET-FSD with non-i.i.d. complexity of different users. Then the results obtained and the analytical method used therein would not be sufficient for exploiting scale effect of ET-FSD in real wireless access network, and thus further extensions are needed.

2. **Extending results of general MIMO detection:** In fact ET-FSD is not the only feasible scheme of MIMO detection being capable of exploiting the scale effect. For instance, the scale effects oriented MIMO detector (SEOD) is developed by (Qian, Qi, Peng, & Wang, 2011) under the multiple-user assumption, which is proved to have the scale effect as well via theoretic analysis in (Qian, Qi, Peng, & Wang, 2013). The similarity between ET-FSD and SEOD lies in that, both of them are variable-complexity, and the statistics of their complexity distribution can be identified. From this observation, we feel that it is also interesting to analyze the scale effect of general MIMO detectors, for which the study is not restricted to a certain scheme. In general, any MIMO detection algorithm with variable complexity shall have the scale effect. The challenge left for us is how to derive the closed-form expression of rate function as obtained in (9).

3. **Extending results of channel decoding algorithms:** Besides MIMO detection, the concept of scale effect could be generalized to a large range of algorithmic complexity studies in which variable-complexity algorithm is instantiated for many times and all

the instances of the algorithm are performed under a certain sum complexity constraint. At least, one can find that, for the channel decoding in current wireless access network, it is worth exploiting the scale effect so as to improve the utility of computation resources. The reasons can be listed as below:

a. Channel decoding algorithms including these of Turbo codes and LDPC codes always work in iterative fashion combining with some early termination mechanism, and thus they have the variable complexity.

b. In wireless access networks whatever in 2G, 3G or 4G systems, the channel decoding is always involved. Especially, in 4G systems, the iterative decoding algorithms of Turbo codes and LDPC codes shall be employed.

c. Within the base-station systems of wireless access network, the channel decoding generally dominates the overall computational complexity of baseband processing. For example, in LTE system, the channel decoding of Turbo codes could cost more than 80% of the computational power spent on the baseband processing considering the peak rate service. Thus, the complexity behavior of channel decoding shall be a key factor for the real-time processing in baseband of base-station systems.

d. It is also well known that, the base-station systems of wireless access network are multiple-user systems. The channel decoding shall be performed for each accessed user.

Since for the algorithms of channel decoding in wireless access network it is meaningful to exploit the scale effect, one can then directly follow the methodology developed for ET-FSD, e.g., by making use of the analytical methods of large deviation.

4. **More useful analytical tools for scale effect:** For analyzing the scale effect, the large deviation theory is a proper theoretic tool. We shall also point out that the weak law of large numbers (derived by Chebyshev inequality) and Chernoff bound theory (Proakis, 1995) are useful as well to the theoretic derivation for the scale effect.

5. **Extensions in centralized base-station systems (Qian et al., 2012):** Traditional base-station systems are multiple-user systems, in which the variable-complexity algorithms shall have the scale effect, especially when there are a large number of users accessing to the systems. However, a base-station just serves the access of users within one cell; then the number of simultaneously accessing users is always limited by the capacity of the base-station and thus cannot be quite large (e.g., hundreds of users at most). Actually, in both industries and academics, a new innovative technology for wireless access network, called centralized base-station systems, attracts much attention. The key point of centralized base-station system technology lie in that, rather than separate base-stations but a centralized and virtual pool of computational resources bears the computational workloads of physical (PHY) and media access control (MAC) processing of wireless access network. The capacity of such computational resources can be capable of handling the workloads of quite many base-stations. Therefore, in centralized base-station systems, the scale effect would be more notable. Or one can say that, the factor that the scale effect becomes more notable is one of advantages of centralized base-station

systems in comparison with traditional base-station systems (Qian et al., 2012). In order to let readers clearly understand the key difference between traditional base-station and centralized base-station system, we note that the PHY/MAC processing of traditional base-station system is performed for UEs accessed in one cell while that of centralized base-station system could be for UEs accessed in a large number of cells. We also note that the concept of Wireless Network Cloud proposed by IBM (Lin & Shao, 2010) and the concept of C-RAN proposed by China Mobile Institution (China Mobile Research Institute, 2010) are two typical scenarios of the centralized base-station, which have attracted special attentions from industries and academics.

SCALE EFFECT IN 4G: FROM THEORETICAL STUDY TO PRACTICE

The study of scale effect in the preceding is mainly on the theoretical aspect. Now it is interesting for us to be aware of how to exploit the scale effect of MIMO detection and other algorithms in 4G systems. We firstly take the LTE/LTE-A systems for example. In LTE/LTE-A system, both e-NodeB and UE could equip with multiple antennas. 3GPP technical specifications have already explicitly defined the space-time codes for LTE/LTE-A downlink (3GPP, 2013), while for uplink the e-NodeB receiver can detect the spatial multiplexing signals from multiple UEs with SC-FDMA-based multiple-access technology (Ghosh, Ratasuk, Mondal, & Mangalvedhe, 2010) in which case the MIMO detection would be used by e-NodeB and the scale effect can be exploited. Moreover, the coordinated multi-point processing (CoMP) is one of the key technologies in LTE-A system (Daewon, Hanbyul, Clerckx, & Hardouin, 2012), which could enable multiple e-

NodeB systems of neighborhood jointly detect the uplink signal from UE that might have multiple transmit antennas and send uplink signal with spatial multiplexing technology. If more than one UE exist in CoMP e-NodeB systems, it is able to exploit the scale effect.

If to implement the MIMO detection in 4G systems without exploiting the scale effect, it is preferred to adopt the fixed-complexity algorithms, e.g., ZF, MMSE and FSD, which shall be friendly to hardware realization (Paulraj, Nabar, &Gore, 2003). While for the fixed-complexity algorithms, it is always unable to achieve the optimal (near optimal) performance of error probability with low cost of complexity. Then through exploiting the scale effect, to achieve the optimal (near optimal) performance at the cost of quite low complexity could be hopefully possible in 4G systems.

On the other hand, the iterative decoding algorithm of Turbo codes and/or LDPC codes should be the indispensable part of baseband processing in 4G broadband wireless access systems such as LTE and LTE-A (3GPP, 2013a), which always consumes the most of the computational power in baseband. Since each e-NodeB of 4G is a typical multiple-access system, we can exploit the scale effect of iterative decoding algorithm in 4G by following the analytic approach developed in this study for ET-FSD.

CONCLUSION

This chapter firstly presents a case study of exploiting scale effect in wireless access network. ET-FSD scheme is developed to exploit the scale effect of MIMO detection in the multiple-user scenario. It should be clear now that, although for a single-user MIMO detection there has been no scheme that can rigorously achieve the full diversity while spending the polynomial worst-case complexity, it is still possible for ET-FSD in multiple-user scenario to get the full diversity under the polynomial constraint of unit complexity. On the basis of the case study, future research directions of exploiting the scale effect in wireless access network are provided as well.

REFERENCES

3GPP Website, (2013a). *3GPP TS 36.211: Evolved universal terrestrial radio access (E-UTRA), physical channels and modulation, V11.2.0*. Author.

3GPP Website, (2013b). *3GPP TS 36.212: Evolved universal terrestrial radio access (E-UTRA), multiplexing and channel coding, V11.2.0*. Author.

Abediseid, W., & Damen, M. (2011). Lattice sequential decoder for coded MIMO channel: Performance and complexity analysis. *IEEE Transactions on Information Theory*. PMID:22287795

Agrell, E., Eriksson, T., Vardy, A., & Zeger, K. (2002). Closest point search in lattice. *IEEE Transactions on Information Theory*, *48*(8), 2201–2214. doi:10.1109/TIT.2002.800499

Barbero, L. G., & Thompson, J. S. (2006). Performance analysis of a fixed-complexity sphere decoder in high-dimensional MIMO systems. In *Proc. IEEE ICASSP 06*. IEEE.

China Mobile Research Institute. (2010). *C-RAN: The road towards green RAN*. C-RAN.

Daewon, L., Hanbyul, S., Clerckx, B., & Hardouin, E. (2012). Coordinated multipoint transmission and reception in LTE-advanced: deployment scenarios and operational challenges. *IEEE Communications Magazine*, *50*(2), 148–155. doi:10.1109/MCOM.2012.6146494

Damen, M. O., Gamal, H. E., & Caire, G. (2003). On maximum likelihood detection and the search for the closest lattice point. *IEEE Transactions on Information Theory*, *49*(10), 2389–2402. doi:10.1109/TIT.2003.817444

Ghosh, A., Ratasuk, R., Mondal, B., & Mangalvedhe, N. (2010). LTE-advanced: Next-generation wireless broadband technology. *IEEE Wireless Communications*, *17*(3), 10–22. doi:10.1109/MWC.2010.5490974

Goldberger, J., & Leshem, A. (2011). MIMO detection for high-order QAM based on a Gaussian tree approximation. *IEEE Transactions on Information Theory*, *57*(8), 4973–4982. doi:10.1109/TIT.2011.2159037

Hollander, F. (2008). *Large deviations*. Washington, DC: American Mathematical Soc.

Jalden, J., Barbero, L. G., Ottersten, B., & Thompson, J. S. (2007). Full diversity detection in MIMO systems with a fixed-complexity sphere decoder. In *Proc. IEEE ICASSP 2007*. IEEE.

Jalden, J., Barbero, L. G., Ottersten, B., & Thompson, J. S. (2009). The error probability of the fixed-complexity sphere decoder. *IEEE Transactions on Signal Processing*, *57*(7), 2711–2720. doi:10.1109/TSP.2009.2017574

Jalden, J., & Elia, P. (2011). Sphere decoding complexity exponent for decoding full rate codes over the quasi-static MIMO channel. *IEEE Transactions on Information Theory*. PMID:22287795

Jalden, J., & Ottersten, B. (2005). On the limits of sphere decoding. In *Proc. ISIT 2005*. ISIT.

Khoshnevis, A., & Sabharwal, A. (2004). On diversity and multiplexing gain of multiple antenna systems with transmitter channel information. In Proc. *Allerton Conference on Communication, Control and Computing*. Academic Press.

Lin, Y., & Shao, L. (2010). Wireless network cloud: Architecture and system requirements. *IBM Journal of Research and Development*, *54*(1), 4:1-4:12.

Lutkepohl, H. (1996). *Handbook of matrices.* Chichester, UK: Wiley.

Narasimhan, R. (2003). Spatial multiplexing with transmit antenna and constellation selection for correlated MIMO fading channels. *IEEE Transactions on Signal Processing, 51*(11), 2829–2838. doi:10.1109/TSP.2003.818205

Paulraj, A., Nabar, R., & Gore, D. (2003). *Introduction to space-time wireless communications.* Cambridge, UK: Cambridge University Press.

Proakis, J. G. (1995). *Digital communications* (4th ed.). New York: McGraw-Hill International.

Qian, R., Qi, Y., Peng, T., & Wang, W. (2011). Scale effects oriented MIMO detector. In *Proc. IEEE PIMRC 2011.* IEEE.

Qian, R., Qi, Y., Peng, T., & Wang, W. (2012). Exploiting scalar effects of MIMO detection in cloud base-station: Feasible scheme and universal significance. In *Proc. IEEE Globecom Workshops (GC Wkshps) 2012.* IEEE.

Qian, R., Qi, Y., Peng, T., & Wang, W. (2013). On the scale effects oriented MIMO detector: Diversity order, worst-case unit complexity and scale effects. *Signal Processing, 93*(1), 277–287. doi:10.1016/j.sigpro.2012.08.006

Qian, R., Qi, Y., Peng, T., & Wang, W. (2013a). Scale effect analysis of early- termination fixed-complexity. *EURASIP Journal on Advances in Signal Processing.* doi:10.1186/1687-6180-2013-125

Seethaler, D., & Bolcskei, H. (2010). Performance and complexity analysis of infinity-norm sphere-decoding. *IEEE Transactions on Information Theory, 56*(3), 1085–1105. doi:10.1109/TIT.2009.2039034

Seethaler, D., Jalden, J., Studer, C., & Bolcskei, H. (2011). On the complexity distribution of sphere decoding. *IEEE Transactions on Information Theory, 57*(9), 5754–5768. doi:10.1109/TIT.2011.2162177

Taherzadeh, M., & Khandani, A. K. (2010). On the limitations of the naïve lattice decoding. *IEEE Transactions on Information Theory, 56*(10), 4820–4826. doi:10.1109/TIT.2010.2059630

Tajer, A., & Wang, X. (2010). Multiuser diversity gain in cognitive networks. *IEEE/ACM Transactions on Networking, 18*(6), 1766–1779. doi:10.1109/TNET.2010.2048038

Viterbo, E., & Boutros, J. (1999). A universal lattice code decoder for fading channels. *IEEE Transactions on Information Theory, 45*(5), 1639–1642. doi:10.1109/18.771234

Wikipedia. (2013). Retrieved from http://en.wikipedia.org/wiki/Economies of scale

Zhang, X., Lv, Z., & Wang, W. (2008). Performance analysis of multiuser diversity in MIMO systems with antenna selection. *IEEE Transactions on Wireless Communications, 7*(1), 5297–5311.

ADDITIONAL READING

Part of the chapter was presented in IEEE PIMRC 2012, Sydney. Please refer to: Qian, R., Qi, Y., et al. (2012a). ET-FSD: A feasible scheme of MIMO detection to exploit scalar effects. Paper presented at Proc. IEEE Personal Indoor and Mobile Radio Communications (PIMRC), 2226 - 2230.

Chapter 10
MEMS–Enabled Smart Beam–Steering Antennas

Hadi Mirzajani
Sahand University of Technology, Iran

Habib Badri Ghavifekr
Sahand University of Technology, Iran

Esmaeil Najafi Aghdam
Sahand University of Technology, Iran

ABSTRACT

In recent years, Microelectromechanical Systems (MEMS) technology has seen a rapid rate of evolution because of its great potential for advancing new products in a broad range of applications. The RF and microwave devices and components fabricated by this technology offer unsurpassed performance such as near-zero power consumption, high linearity, and cost effectiveness by batch fabrication in respect to their conventional counterparts. This chapter aims to give an in-depth overview of the most recently published methods of designing MEMS-based smart antennas. Before embarking into the different techniques of beam steering, the concept of smart antennas is introduced. Then, some fundamental concepts of MEMS technology such as micromachining technologies (bulk and surface micromachining) are briefly discussed. After that, a number of RF MEMS devices such as switches and phase shifters that have applications in beam steering antennas are introduced and their operating principals are completely explained. Finally, various configurations of MEMS-enabled beam steering antennas are discussed in detail.

1. INTRODUCTION

Wireless communication systems, like their wired counterparts, have some fundamental challenges (Vanderveen, 1997):

1. Limited allocated spectrum which results some limitation on capacity.

2. Because of uncertainty in radio propagation environment and the mobility of users signal fading and spreading in time, space and frequency increases.

3. Power limitation which is the main constraint in any mobile and hand held device and system.

DOI: 10.4018/978-1-4666-4888-3.ch010

Figure 1. Disorder in the received signal in wireless communication systems

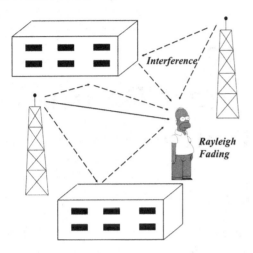

Moreover, interference due to frequency reuse in cellular wireless communication systems is another challenge. Many efforts have been done to investigate potential technologies in order to alleviate such undesired effects. Some of these potential methods that researchers find are multiple access schemes, channel coding and equalization and smart antenna employment.

Figure 1 shows the main problem with wireless communication systems that smart antennas are used to alleviate that effect (Winters, 1998).

The main idea which smart antennas are working on, is sometimes referred to as human listening system by an intuitive example (Bellofiore, 2002). A person can determine the Direction-of-Arrival (DOA) of an acoustic signal by a three stage process as flow;

Firstly, the listener hears the acoustic wave by his/her acoustic sensors (ears), and then because the ears are separated with each other, the acoustic wave arrives at different times to each ear. Finally, the human brain, which is a sophisticated processor, does a lot of computations and determines the location of the source of the acoustic wave. In order to intuitively understand the above mentioned information, consider three persons in a room, which both of them are carrying on a conversation

with the listener which is located between them, as shown in Figure 2.

As the listener moves around the room, he/she receives the acoustic signals from two persons. His/her brain computes the difference of the acoustic signal received from each person and predicts their location. Then the brain can add the strength of acoustic signal from each ear in order to focus on the intended user in specific location. Moreover, if the number of speakers increases, the human brain can enhance the received signal from the intended user and tune out unwanted interferences. Therefore, the listener has the ability to distinguish the desired speaker from many speakers and only focus on it. Conversely he/she can respond the intended speaker by orientating his/her transmitter (mouth).

Transmitting the same idea into wireless communication systems, the antenna plays the role of ear and mouth and the signal processing unit immediately after the antenna works as human brain. A schematic diagram of a smart antenna system is shown in Figure 3 (Baltersee, 1998; Balanis, & Ioannides, 2007).

Figure 2. An example for understanding the concept of smart antennas

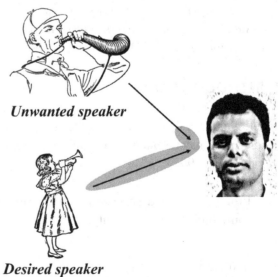

Unwanted speaker

Desired speaker

Figure 3. A conceptional view of a smart antenna

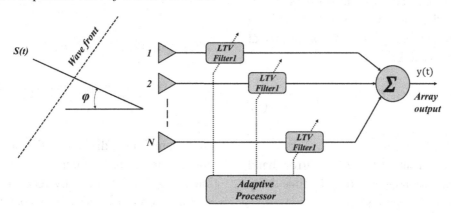

The smart antenna is consists of three segments which are; antenna array, patternforming network, and adaptive processor.

The antenna array consists of N antennas to receive and transmit signals. The physical arrangement of the antenna array can put fundamental limitations on the capability of the smart antenna and can be chose arbitrarily depending on required specifications. The output of each antenna element is an input for patternforming network. In petternforming network, the outputs of the antennas are processed by Linear Time Variant (LTV) filters. In fact, these filters determine the directional pattern of the smart antenna. Finally, in order to produce the overall output $y(t)$, the output of the LTV filters is summed to each other. Adaptive processor determines the complex weights of the LTV filters. The signals and known system properties used for determining the weights are:

- The received signals by the antenna array which are $x_n(t)$, $n=1,2,...,N$.
- The output of the smart antenna ($y(t)$).
- The spatial structure of the antenna array.
- The temporal structure of the received signal.
- Feedback signals from the mobiles.
- Network topology.

The functioning principle of a smart antenna can be easily explained using a simple example (Baltersee, 1998; Balanis, & Ioannides, 2007). In this example, two identical omnidirectional antennas are assumed in a uniform linear array (ULA) which is shown in Figure 4.

It is assumed that the signal-of-interest $S(t)$ is generated by a source in the far-field of smart antenna. As shown in Figure 4, the incident signal on the antenna array is a uniform plane wave. Considering the distance d between two antennas, antenna 2 experiences a time delay of $\Delta\tau$ respect to antenna 1. The time delay can be calculated as:

$$\Delta\tau = \frac{d\sin\varphi}{\nu_0} \qquad (1)$$

Figure 4. A uniform linear array with two antenna elements

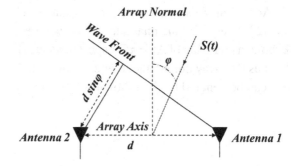

Where d is distance between two antenna elements and ν_0 is the wave speed. Now by knowing d and measuring $\Delta\tau$ the angle φ direction-of-arrival can be found by using:

$$\varphi = \sin^{-1}\left[\frac{\nu_0 \Delta\tau}{d}\right] \qquad (2)$$

If the signal of interest $S(t)$ is a narrow band signal with carrier frequency of f_c the time delay $\Delta\tau$ corresponds to a phase shift of:

$$\Delta\psi = 2\pi \frac{d \sin \varphi}{\lambda_c} \qquad (3)$$

where λ_c is wavelength of the carrier frequency (f_c). It is clear that for an incoming signal in the direction of perpendicular to the array normal with $\varphi = 0$, both time delay and phase shift between two antennas are zero.

Now we consider that an interfering signal $n(t)$ with the same carrier frequency comes on the array. For example, the direction of $S(t)$ and $n(t)$ are set to $0°$ and $30°$, respectively. The complex antenna weights can be denoted as $\omega_1 = \omega_{1,1} + j\omega_{1,2}$ and $\omega_2 = \omega_{2,1} + j\omega_{2,2}$, respectively.

Hence, array output due to $S(t)$ can be calculated by:

$$\begin{aligned} S(t) &= s(t)\left[(\omega_{1,1} + j\omega_{1,2}) + (\omega_{2,1} + j\omega_{2,2})\right] \\ &= s(t)\left[(\omega_{1,1} + \omega_{2,1}) + j(\omega_{1,2} + \omega_{2,2})\right] \end{aligned} \qquad (4)$$

According to Equation 3, for a distance of $d=\lambda/2$ between two antennas and $\varphi=30°$, antenna 2 shows a phase lag of $\Delta\psi=\pi/2$ respect to antenna 1. Thus the array output due to interfering signal $n(t)$ can be denoted by the following:

$$\begin{aligned} N(t) &= n(t)\left[(\omega_{1,1} + j\omega_{1,2}) + e^{-j\frac{\pi}{2}}(\omega_{2,1} + j\omega_{2,2})\right] \\ &= n(t)\left[(\omega_{1,1} + \omega_{2,2}) + j(\omega_{1,2} - \omega_{2,1})\right] \end{aligned} \qquad (5)$$

As previously discussed, the main goal of a smart antenna is to completely cancel out the interfering signal and fully recover the desired signal. In order to achieve this goal using Equations 4 and 5 it is necessary that:

$$\omega_{1,1} + \omega_{2,1} = 1 \qquad (6)$$

$$\omega_{1,2} + \omega_{2,2} = 0 \qquad (7)$$

$$\omega_{1,1} + \omega_{2,2} = 0 \qquad (8)$$

$$\omega_{1,2} - \omega_{2,1} = 0 \qquad (9)$$

Solving Equation 6 to 9 yield the followings:

$$\omega_{1,1} = \omega_{1,2} = \omega_{2,1} = 1/2$$

and

$$\omega_{2,2} = -1/2 \qquad (10)$$

or

$$\omega_1 = 1/2(1 + j)$$

and

$$\omega_2 = 1/2(1 - j) \qquad (11)$$

Hence, for the smart antenna shown in Figure 4, in order to completely cancel out the interfering signal and completely recover the desired signal the weight of ω_1 and ω_2 must be as above.

In a general case, smart antennas can be divided into two main categories as;

1. Switched beam antennas
2. Adaptive arrays

In switched beam antennas a limited number of predefined patterns exist while in adaptive arrays the beam of the antenna can theoretically directed to any desired location in a real time manner.

Figure 5 compares their operation in the presence of one desired signal and two interferences.

From the figure, both of the antennas direct the maximum beam of the antenna radiation pattern in the direction of the signal-of-interest. However, the adaptive array chose a more accurate placement of the maximum beam of the antenna. From the interference rejection point of view, both antennas place the signal-not-of-interest outside of the main lob of the antenna, but again the adaptive array places these signals in the minimum gain points of the antenna pattern.

The chapter is organized as follows, Section 1 deal with the need for smart antennas and gives an introduction about these antennas by the aid of an intuitive example. In section 2, micromachining techniques which are used for fabrication of RF

MEMS devices are presented. After that, different RF MEMS devices which have applications in antenna reconfigurations are presented and their operating principles are completely discussed. Section 3 introduces various ways of radiation pattern reconfiguration by RF MEMS technology and gives an in depth overview for such antennas.

2. MICROMACHINING AND RF MEMS TECHNOLOGY

Micromachining

The ability in making physically small objects received much attention with the introduction of integrated circuit (IC) fabrication technology in the 1960s. In that technology, different photographic and etching techniques have been used in order to print circuits on a wafer. Since the circuits could be scaled, and still perform the same function, a race has been arose to develop various ways of transferring more circuits on a single semiconductor wafer. It is very beneficial to increase the number of the circuits which can be printed on a wafer, because by this way the functionality is increased and costs are decreased.

The successful progress which was displayed in IC industry, motivated the electronic engineers to apply the same concept of integrated electronic manufacturing technique into different fields such

Figure 5. Operation of the switched beam antenna and adaptive arrays in presence of one desired signal and two interferences

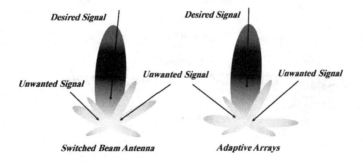

as; mechanics, optics, and fluidics with the hope of the same performance enhancement and cost effectiveness which was previously experienced by the semiconductor industry (Senturia, 2001). One fundamental difference between microelectronic ICs and Microelectromechanical structures is that, the firs is two dimensional and is fixed, whereas the latter is three dimensional and have moving parts. Generally there is two different ways of creating such moveable Microelectromechanical systems, namely; surface micromachining and bulk micromachining.

Surface Micromachining

In surface micromachining different layers of thin-films are deposited and patterned in order to create the three-dimensional structure. Different layers which are deposited, can be categorized as structural and sacrificial layers. Sacrificial layer is a layer which is used for creation of free standing layer (structural layer) and will be etch out in release process. Structural layer is a layer that acts as mechanical moving part. In order to

create a surface micromachined micromechanical device a regular pre-defined steps of thin-film deposition, lithography, dry and wet etching must be taken. Different materials can be used as structural layer and sacrificial layers. Each of them has respective etchants which can selectively etch the sacrificial layer and leave the structural material intact (Senturia, 2001; Bustillo et al., 1998; Williams, and Muller, 1996). In order to intuitively understand the process of the surface micromachining, the fabrication process flow of a free standing structure is schematically outlined in Figure 6. Firstly, in order to electrically isolating between substrate and structural layer, a silicon nitride layer is deposited (a). A silicon oxide layer is deposited as sacrificial layer and also is patterned in order to open a window for creation of anchor of the structural layer (b). The structural layer is deposited and patterned (c). And finally the structural layer is released by etching out the sacrificial layer (d) (Varadan et al., 2003).

Figure 6. Process flow for a typical surface micromachining technology

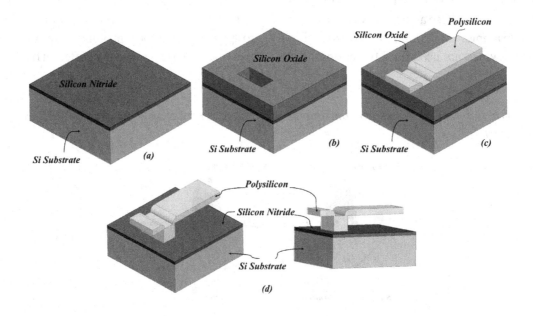

Bulk Micromachining

As opposed to surface micromachining, bulk micromachining is creation of micromechanical structures in the bulk of the wafer. This process is extensively used for fabrication of suspended membranes which have applications in pressure sensors and accelerometers. A structure which is formed by bulk micromachining is shown in Figure 7.

As it is apparent from the figure, in fact bulk micromachining is creating trenches in the bulk of the wafer by etching. By wisdom combination of highly-directional etchants, non-directional etchants, and the wafer's crystallographical orientation, the etching rates are manipulated in order to create various mechanical structures within the bulk of the wafer (Bryzek et al., 1994). Usually in bulk micromachining processes, two or more wafers are bounded in order to form the final device structure. For example, Figure 8 shows a frequency reconfigurable microstrip patch antenna which is composed of two segments, namely, upper and lower (Nasiri et al., 2013, Mirzajani et al., 2012). The upper layer is fabricated by a process combination of surface and bulk micromachining and then is mounted over a RF module (lower segment).

Figure 7. A bulk micromachined structure

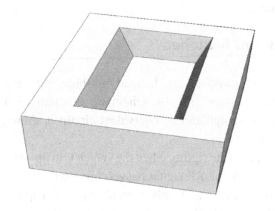

RF MEMS Technology

Today, because of increasing demand for compact, low cost, high performance and intelligent wireless communication systems, there is a growing tendency for the devices and components which can meet the above mentioned requirements. Such devices and components must be designed in such a way that they can perform different tasks and also be fabricated monotonically onto a single chip.

Microelectromechanical systems (MEMS) technology is an emerging technology which have revolutionized the RF systems by realization of devices and components which have unique characteristics such as low power consumption, high linearity and low loss. Moreover, tunable characteristics of the RF MEMS devices make them so attractive in reconfigurable structures such as filters and antennas (Rebeiz, 2003). Incorporating RF MEMS in antenna structures provide different advantages such as configurability in polarization, frequency and radiation pattern. Among many RF MEMS devices and components, switches and phase shifters are extensively used in antenna structures in order to achieve radiation pattern reconfiguration. In the rest of this section different configurations and operating principles of MEMS-based switches and phase shifters will be discussed.

RF MEMS Switches

Switches are one of the most well-known RF MEMS devices. Many institutes and universities worldwide have done extensive research in design, simulation, fabrication, and characterization of these devices and made a lot of progress. RF MEMS switches are generally fabricated by surface micromachining process and have a mechanically suspended structure (a cantilever or a clamped-clamped beam). Actuating this

Figure 8. Frequency reconfigurable microstrip patch antenna fabricated by surface and bulk microma-chining processes (Mirzajani et al., 2012)

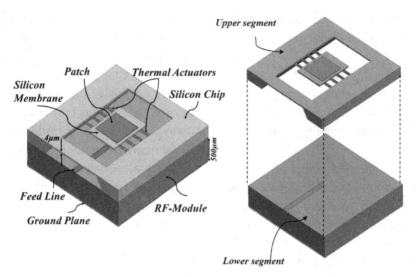

suspended structure opens or closes the transmission line of the RF signal. These switches can be categorized into series or shunt switches (Rebeiz, 2003; Varadan et al., 2003; Liu, 2010).

Series Switches

Series switches are placed in series with transmission line. In fact in series switches there is a discontinuity in the transmission line, with actuating the switch, the mechanical suspended part of the switch collapse on the discontinuity and connect the two transmission lines to each other and makes a short circuit. A schematic view of a series switch and its equivalent circuit is shown in Figure 9.

In figure above, C_s and R_s denote capacitance and resistance between transmission line and switch. Series switches can be divided into ohmic contact and capacitive contact switches. In ohmic contact switches the connection between transmission line and suspended part of the switch is a metal to metal contact. Ohmic contact switches can operate in lower frequencies respect to capacitive contact switches however because of ohmic resistance between transmission line

and switch the insertion loss increases and also these kind of switches encounter some reliability problems like as micro-welding (Rebeiz, 2003). In capacitor contact switches there is an isolator layer on the transmission line which prevents the direct connection between T-line and switch. These switches have not the problem of resistive contact switches but in turn, work in upper frequencies respect to resistive switches and also charge trapping in dielectric layer between T-line and switch may cause some uncertainty in switch operation (Rebeiz, 2003). Figure 10 shows a close up view of contact region of a RF MEMS capacitive switch.

Shunt Switches

Shunt switches are located in shunt with the transmission line. A schematic diagram of a shunt switch and its equivalent circuit is shown in Figure 11.

From the figure, when the switch is in up-state position, the RF signal passes through the transmission line and only a small value is capacitively coupled to suspended part of the switch and hence to ground. This value of RF signal leakage

Figure 9. (a) A schematic view of a series switch and (b) its equivalent circuit

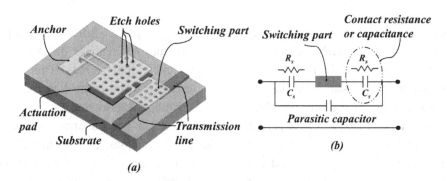

Figure 10. A closed up view of contact region of a RF MEMS capacitive switch

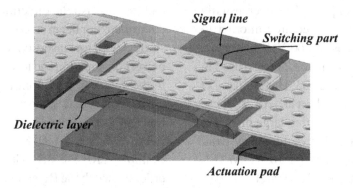

Figure 11. (a) Schematic diagram of a shunt switch and (b) its equivalent circuit

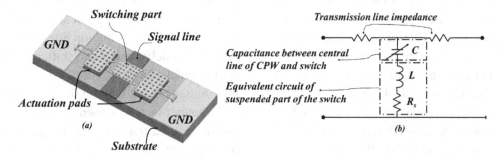

directly increases the insertion loss of the switch. In order to decrease this leakage the initial gap between transmission line and suspended structure can be increased. In down-state position, the switch is collapsed on the central line of the CPW line and connects it to the ground plane, in this state the RF signal is completely directed to the ground and the switch is off. Shunt switches, like their series counterparts, can have ohmic and capacitive contacts.

Actuation Mechanism

Different actuation methods such as electrostatic, electro-thermal, piezoelectric and their combinations can be used as the derive mechanism of these switches. The most dominant actuation mechanism of RF MEMS switches (series and shunt) is electrostatic actuation method. In that way, by applying an actuation voltage between actuation pad and suspended part of the switch (Figures 9 and 11) an electrostatic force deflects the suspended part downward toward the transmission line. The most interesting property of electrostatic actuation is its near zero power consumption. However, usually a large actuation voltage is required in order to reach desired deflections (50-60 Volts) (Rebeiz, 2003). Electro-thermal actuators are also used in switch structures (Rebeiz, 2003; Daneshmand et al., 2009; Qui et al., 2003; He et al., 2012). These actuators are capable of creating large displacements with considerable forces, also they work with low actuation voltages (< 10 Volts) (El-buken et al., 2009; Yan, 2002; Varona, et al, 2008). The main disadvantage of switches fabricated by this actuation method is their power consumption problem. However a kind of latching mechanism can be used in switch structure which can considerably decrease the power consumption of the switch. In fact, the switch consumes power while transition between on and off states (Daneshmand et al., 2009; Agrawal, 2004; Qui, et al, 2003; Oberhammer, & Stemme, 2006; Khazaai, & Qu, 2012; Moseley et al, 2006; Nordquist et al, 2009). Both electrostatic and electro-thermal actuators fabrication process is compatible with CMOS fabrication process (Elbuken et al., 2009). Piezoelectric actuators have zero power consumption and use low voltage levels. However, fabrication of piezoelectric materials with the capability of creating required forces and deflections is challenging (Xiang, & Shi, 2009).

RF MEMS Phase Shifters

Generally a phase shifter is a two port network which imposes a phase difference between its input and output signals. This value of phase difference can be controlled by an external dc bias voltage. Phase shifters have extensive applications in phased array antennas. In these kinds of antennas, the antenna is composed of an n×m array and each of these elements is feed by a phase shifter and they experience a phase difference among their exited signals respect to each other. By this way, the shape of the antenna pattern and also the direction of its beam can be controlled. For beam steering applications, phase shifters with low insertion loss, light weight, low power consumption and low cost of fabrication are in the center of attention. Because of their near ideal characteristics, recently considerable attention has been received for fabrication of the beam steering antenna by RF MEMS components. For example, a RF MEMS switch can be designed in order to switch the RF signal into different signal paths or can be distributed on a transmission line as capacitive shunt switches in order to change the effective capacitive load of the transmission line.

Different RF MEMS phase shifters are; 1. Distributed MEMS transmission line phase shifters, 2. Switches delay line phase shifters, 3. Distributed parallel plate capacitors phase shifters, 4. Interdigitad capacitor phase shifters and etcetera.

Among the above mentioned phase shifters, distributed transmission line phase shifters (DMTL) are dominant in MEMS-based beam steering antenna design.

These kinds of phase shifters are composed of a number of periodically distributed MEMS capacitive shunt switches. As previously discussed, capacitive shunt switches consist of a metal bridge which is suspended over central line of a coplanar wave guide (CPW) transmission line. The bridge is anchored in its two ends on the CPW ground planes (Figure 11). By applying an actuation voltage between suspended bridge and central line of CPW transmission line, the bridge deflects down toward the central line. This deflection changes the total capacitance load of the transmission line which causes a change in transmission line phase and velocity which in turn causes a phase shift (Muldavin, & Rebeiz, 2000a; Muldavin, & Rebeiz, 2000b; Palei et al, 2005; Wang et al, 2008; Du, Bao, & Jiang, 2013). A schematic diagram of such a phase shifter and its circuit model is shown in Figure 12.

The phase shifter can be modeled as a lumped capacitance C_t and inductance L_t with a parallel variable capacitor, inductor and resistor where (Barker, Rebeiz, 1998a):

$$C_t = \frac{\sqrt{\varepsilon_{r,eff}}}{cZ_0} \qquad (12)$$

$$L_t = C_t Z_0^2 \qquad (13)$$

In above equations $\varepsilon_{r,eff}$ is effective dielectric constant of the unloaded CPW transmission line and c is free space velocity. In a case of CPW transmission line, Z_0 and $\varepsilon_{r,eff}$ are related to its physical parameters.

The characteristic impedance Z and phase velocity v of a DMTL phase shifter can be approximated by the following equations (Barker, Rebeiz, 1998b):

$$Z = L_t (C_t + \frac{C}{s})^{-1} \qquad (14)$$

$$\nu = \left[L_t \left(C_t + \frac{C}{s} \right) \right]^{-1/2} \qquad (15)$$

which C/s is the distributed MEMS capacitance on the loaded line.

The phase shift per unit length of the DMTL is calculated by:

$$\Delta\phi = \frac{\omega Z_0 \sqrt{\varepsilon_{r,eff}}}{c} \left[\frac{1}{Z_{lu}} - \frac{1}{Z_{ld}} \right] \qquad (16)$$

where Z_{lu} and Z_{ld} corresponds to DMTL characteristic impedance when the MEMS bridge is in up and down state positions, respectively.

Figure 12. (a) A schematic view and (b) circuit model of a DMTL phase shifter

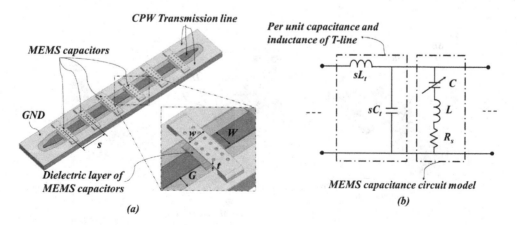

3. MEMS-ENABLED SMART BEAM-STEERING ANTENNA CONFIGURATIONS

Beam steering antennas are widely used in military and commercial applications such as radar systems and wireless communications. RF MEMS devices and circuits have attracted interest in applications such as electronic beam-steering systems, particularly in the millimeter-wave frequency band, due to their near-ideal signal performance and compatibility with semiconductor fabrication technology. The following section introduces the state-of-the-art antenna architectures and on-chip antennas in beam-steering front-ends.

Radiation pattern reconfigurable antennas using RF MEMS technology usually fall into three categories. The first design uses RF MEMS switches in antenna structures in order to connect different directional patches to each other or reconfigure the geometry of a multimode antenna. The second design uses RF MEMS phase shifters in antenna feed network in order to impose a phase difference among different antenna elements. And the third design uses different MEMS actuation methods in order to mechanically actuate the antenna and change its mechanical orientation. In the rest of this section these methods will be discussed.

BEAM-STEERING BY RF MEMS SWITCHES

RF MEMS switches can be incorporated in antenna structures in a number of ways in order to achieve radiation pattern reconfiguration. First method is using RF MEMS switches in order to connect the feed network to a specific patch which is pointed to a specific direction. A conceptional operating principle of these kinds of antennas is shown in Figure 13.

As it is apparent from the figure, by activating each of the RF MEMS switches, the respective antenna will be exited and radiate in the predefined direction. A practical design of this idea is proposed in (Cetiner et al., 2003). As shown in Figure 14 (Cetiner et al., 2003), two switches are used in the feed line of the two coplanar waveguide (CPW) slot antennas in order to activate them. Each of these antennas has a specific radiation pattern with specific directivity. Switch S1 is used for activation of antenna A1 and switch S2 is used for activation of antenna A2. The main problem with this design is that, the antenna which is not activated can disturb the radiation pattern of the activated antenna and can make side lobs and change the radiation pattern of the antenna from the desired one.

Figure 13. Conceptional operating principle of activating different feeding paths using MEMS switches in order to achieve different radiation patterns

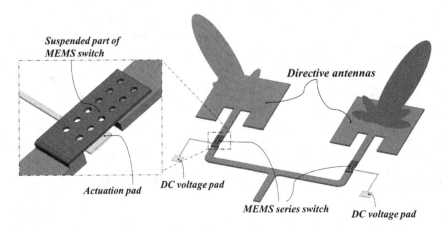

Figure 14. A schematic view of monolithic RF-MEMS switched diversity antenna

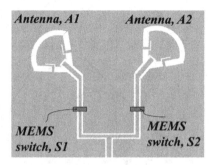

The second method is using MEMS switches in order to reconfigure the geometry of a multimode antenna in order to operate at different modes. A spiral antenna can be used as a multimode radiator (Huff & Bernhard, 2006). A schematic view of the antenna is shown in Figure 15. The antenna is a single-turn microstrip spiral antenna. The antenna is feed by a SMA connector which is connected to the interior end of the spiral. Commercially available packaged RF MEMS switches are used in this design. The on/off configuration of the switches in order to change the antenna radiation pattern, are as follow; for end-fire radiation, switch 1 is closed and switch 2 is open and for broadside radiation switch 1 is open and switch 2 is closed.

As discussed above, switches can be incorporated in geometry of a multimode antenna in order to operate at different modes. In that way, the antenna structure consists of several segments of metallic geometries which are connected to each other through RF MEMS switches (Cetiner et al., 2003; Pringle et al., 2004). In some applications which require a large number of reconfiguration modes, the switching circuitry becomes very complex and can severely degrade the performance of the reconfigurable antenna. A new technique is proposed in (Li et al., 2012; Rodrigo et al., 2011) in order to alleviate that problem. A schematic view of the antenna proposed in (Li et al., 2012; Rodrigo et al., 2011) is shown in Figure 16. In that design, the switching network is separated from the drive antenna. In fact, the switching network is located on top side of the parasitic layer and the parasitic layer is located over the drive antenna in such a way that there is not any physical connection between them. Configurability in antenna properties comes by coupling the electromagnetic energy from the drive antenna to the parasitic layer by mutual coupling. The RF MEMS switches are located between the reconfigurable parasitic pixels. By judicious activation of RF MEMS switches the upper layer geometry of the parasitic layer changes which in turn changes the mode of the operation. This method

Figure 15. A schematic view of the antenna proposed in (Huff & Bernhard, 2006)

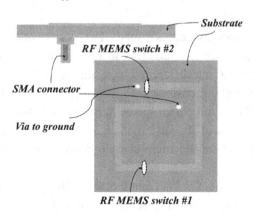

Figure 16. A schematic view of the reconfigurable antenna proposed in (Li et al., 2012; Rodrigo et al., 2011)

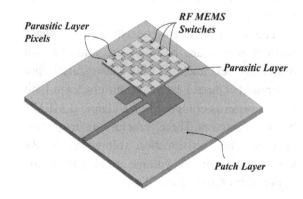

of reconfiguration provides a lot of advantages over previous methods in terms of design and fabrication.

BEAM-STEERING BY USING MEMS PHASE SHIFTERS IN ANTENNA FEED NETWORKS

In phased array antennas, each radiating element is connected to a feed line which provides specific phase shift. In order to point the radiation beam of the antenna into a specific direction, the provided phase shift must be changed according to that direction. One solution for that application is using RF MEMS phase shifters in antenna feed networks which can provide several phase states or a continuous tuning of the phase delay which is controlled by a DC voltage (Fernández-Bolaños et al., 2010).

As previously discussed, phase shifters with low insertion loss, low power consumption and low cost of fabrication are very attractive for phased array antennas. A conceptional operating principle of the phased array antennas is shown in Figure 17 (Varadan et al., 1995).

From the figure, the direction of the beam can be tuned by controlling the phase difference among different antenna elements. A practical implementation of this idea is presented in (Sundaram et al., 2008). In this design, 3-bit distributed transmission line phase shifters are monolithically integrated in a two element slot antenna in order to achieve a MEMS-based electronically steerable antenna array. The configuration of the antenna is shown in Figure 18.

The antenna system consists of 3-bit phase shifters which are between the antenna and power divider. Each of 3-bit phase shifters are composed of three 1-bit phase shifters. Each 1-bit phase shifter is composed of 2 identical MEMS bistable varactors. These varactors are in up-state position when no actuation voltage exists. By applying an actuation voltage around 200 V, the upper plate of the varactor deflects downward and

Figure 17. Operating principle of phased array antennas (Varadan et al., 1995)

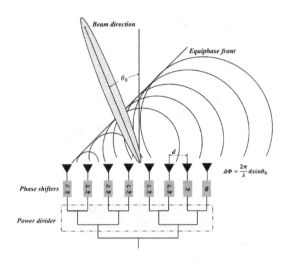

Figure 18. A schematic diagram of proposed antenna in (Sundaram et al., 2008)

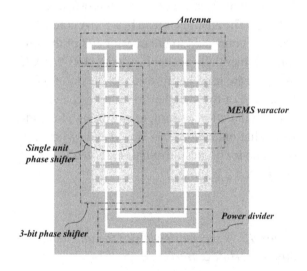

increases the capacitance. The corresponding capacitance for varactors in up and down state positions for different phase shifter units with different dimensions are summarized in Table 1.

The main performance of the antenna for the actuation of the different phase shifter units in right side of the antenna is summarized in Table 2.

Topalli et al in (Topalli et al., 2008) proposed a new electronically scanning phased-array an-

Table 1. different capacitances and corresponding phase shifts for different phases shifter units (Sundaram et al., 2008)

Phase Shifter Unit	Up-State Capacitance (fF)	Down-State Capacitance (fF)	Phase Shift at 9.1 GHz
1	66	141	10°
2	83	251	15°
3	110	427	18°

tenna which was monotonically integrated with RF MEMS phase shifters. The antenna was designed to operate at 15 GHz and was composed of 4 linearly placed microstrip patch antennas. Four 3-bit low loss Distributed MEMS Transmission Line (DMTL) phase shifters were incorporated in antenna structure. DMTL phase shifters are composed of RF MEMS switches and Metal-air-Metal capacitors. The overall dimension of the antenna system is 6cm × 5cm and is fabricated by surface micromachining on 500-μm-thick Pyrex 7740 glass substrate. Experimental results show that the phase shifter can provide a phase shift of 20°/50°/95° and their combinations by an insertion loss of 1.5 dB at 15 GHz. It was observed that the beam of the antenna can be tilted by 4° and 14° when the phase shifts are 20° and 50°, respectively.

BEAM-STEERING BY MECHANICALLY ACTUATED ANTENNAS

Although electronic scanning antennas offer fast scan speeds, capability to track multiple targets,

low probability of interception and etcetera, they suffer from some limitations such as requiring many phase shifter units which make the final design expensive and decreases radiation efficiency of the antenna when the beam of the antenna is far away from the broadside of the antenna. Moreover, the phase shifters have usually high insertion loss which decreases the signal-to-noise (SNR) ratio of the system (Kang et al., 2002).

The idea in mechanically beam steering antennas is to mechanically rotate the antenna orientation in order to point the antenna beam into the desired direction (Hutchings et al., n.d.; Woten et al., 2009). A conceptional view of such a design is shown in Figure 19.

A micromachined 1-Dimensional beam steering antenna was proposed in (Chauvel et al., 1997). A schematic view of the antenna is shown in Figure 20.

The antenna is composed of two segments; upper and lower segments. A 1.5-μm-thick gold layer is electroplated over 100-μm-thick quartz substrate as a microstrip patch antenna. The upper layer is suspended over the actuation pads by two torsional hinges. By applying an actuation voltage

Table 2. Performance of the antenna respect to different phase shifts of phase shifter units in right side of the antenna (Sundaram et al., 2008)

Phase Shifter States	Return Loss at 9.1 GHz (dB)	Beam Steering Angle at 9.1 GHz
All units up	35	0°
Unit 1 actuated	25	5°
Unit 2 actuated	40	15°
Unit 3 actuated	47	18°
All units down	25	20°

Figure 19. A Conceptional illustration of mechanically beam steering antennas

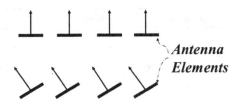

between electrostatic actuators and ground of the antenna which is on the back side of the quartz substrate, the antenna can rotate about the torsional hinges. The dimensions of the actuation pads are optimized by the use of FEM (Finite Element Method) simulations. The actuation pads are created in an inclined shape in order to decrease the required actuation voltage. For creation of lower layer a (110) oriented silicon wafer is formed by the use of adequate KOH etchant solution. Evaporation is used in order to deposit gold layer as actuation pad. In order to electrically isolating between actuation pads, silicon substrate and upper layer electrodes SiO_2 is used.

Another design example is a V-band micromachined 2-dimendional beam steering antenna which is driven by magnetic force (Baek et al., 2003). A schematic diagram of this design is shown in Figure 21.

From the figure, the antenna system is composed of an array of 2×2 patch antennas. The

Figure 20. Schematic diagram of the antenna proposed in (Chauvel et al., 1997)

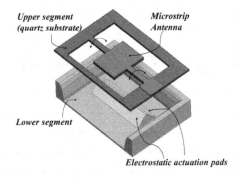

platform which antenna array is located on can be rotated about the X and Y axes. Hence, the antenna can have a 2-D beam steering. In this design, Benzocyclobutene (BCB) which is a kind of silicon-containing polymer is used as substrate material of the antenna for the purpose of flexibility. Also it has a good microwave property such as low dielectric material and low tangential loss. Magnetic actuation is used as the drive mechanism of the antenna. Compared to their previous work, (Baek et al., 2001) this actuation method both increased the rotation angle and also decreased the required actuation voltage.

CONCLUSION

Today, there is a rapid growth in the number and functionality of components and devices in communications and wireless systems. This drastic advancement is mainly because of the tremendous achievement of the semiconductor and electronics industries that enable large amounts of information and data to be processed in a quick and inexpensive way. The need for tinier and more versatile devices in, e.g., mobile phones, automotive radar transceivers, GPS receivers, and remote sensors, is enabling intensive integration and the development of novel technologies to achieve the technological requirements. RF MEMS technologies including tunable capacitors, micromachined inductors, resonators, switches, and tunable filters are emerging as enabling technologies that can fulfill the requirements for the next generation of components and devices. Although the technology is still maturing, MEMS is attractive for RF and wireless systems.

Because of having good performance in high frequencies, low cost of fabrication and tunable characteristics of RF MEMS devices and components, these devices are good candidates respect to their semiconductor counterparts for integration in antenna structures. Employing these devices in antenna structures provides different recon-

Figure 21. A schematic diagram of the 2-D beam steering antenna proposed in (Baek et al., 2003)

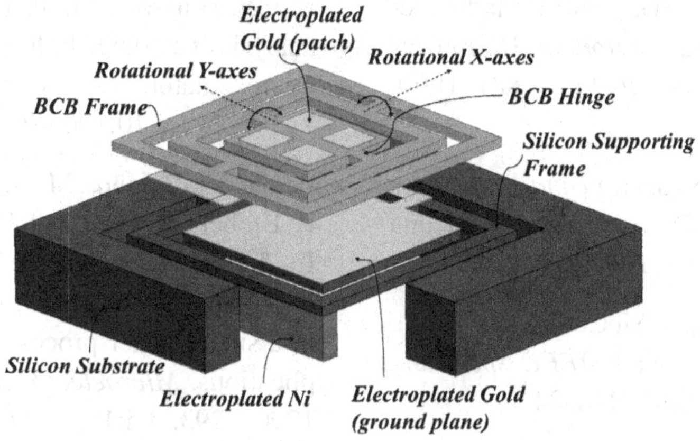

figuration mechanisms such as reconfiguration in frequency, polarization and radiation pattern. Also these devices allow for monolithic fabrication of antenna systems which considerably decreases the losses due to the connectors and system complexity. In this chapter, firstly a brief introduction about smart antennas was presented and their operating mechanism was explained by an example. Then, different micromachining techniques which can be used for fabrication of RF MEMS devices were introduced. After that, different RF MEMS devices which could be incorporated in antenna structures were discussed and then various methods of beam steering techniques by RF MEMS technology were completely studied. The antennas studied in this chapter can be a promising choice for next generation wireless communication systems.

REFERENCES

Agrawal, V. (2004, September). A latching MEMS relay for DC and RF applications. In *Proceedings of the 50th IEEE Holm Conference on Electrical Contacts and the 22nd International Conference on Electrical Contacts* (pp. 222-225). IEEE.

Baek, C. W., Song, S., Cheon, C., Kim, Y. K., & Kwon, Y. (2001). 2-D mechanical beam steering antenna fabricated using MEMS technology. In *Microwave symposium digest* (Vol. 1, pp. 211–214). IEEE.

Baek, C. W., Song, S., Park, J. H., Lee, S., Kim, J. M., Choi, W., & Kwon, Y. (2003). A V-band micromachined 2-D beam-steering antenna driven by magnetic force with polymer based hinges. *IEEE Transactions on Microwave Theory and Techniques, 51*(1), 325–331. doi:10.1109/TMTT.2002.806516

Balanis, C. A., & Ioannides, P. I. (2007). Introduction to smart antennas. *Synthesis Lectures on Antennas, 2*(1), 1–175. doi:10.2200/S00079ED-1V01Y200612ANT005

Baltersee, J. (1998). *Smart antennas and space-time processing*. Aachen University of Technology, Institute for Integrated Signal Processing Systems.

Barker, N. S., & Rebeiz, G. M. (1998a). Distributed MEMS true-time delay phase shifter and wideband switches. *IEEE Microwave Guided Wave Letters,* 1881–1890.

Barker, S., & Rebeiz, G. M. (1998b). Distributed MEMS true-time delay phase shifters and wideband switches. *IEEE Transactions on Microwave Theory and Techniques*, *46*(11), 1881–1890. doi:10.1109/22.734503

Bellofiore, S. (2002). *Smart antenna systems for mobile platforms*. (Ph.D. dissertation). Arizona State University, Phoenix, AZ.

Bryzek, J., Peterson, K., & McCulley, W. (1994). Micromachines on the march. *IEEE Spectrum*, *31*(5), 20–31. doi:10.1109/6.278394

Bustillo, J. M., Howe, R. T., & Muller, R. S. (1998). Surface micromachining for microelectromechanical systems. *Proceedings of the IEEE*, *86*(8), 1552–1574. doi:10.1109/5.704260

Cetiner, B. A., Qian, J. Y., Chang, H. P., Bachman, M., Li, G. P., & De Flaviis, F. (2003). Monolithic integration of RF MEMS switches with a diversity antenna on PCB substrate. *IEEE Transactions on Microwave Theory and Techniques*, *51*(1), 332–335. doi:10.1109/TMTT.2002.806521

Chauvel, D., Haese, N., Rolland, P. A., Collard, D., & Fujita, H. (1997). A micro-machined microwave antenna integrated with its electrostatic spatial scanning. In *Proceedings Tenth Annual International Workshop* (pp. 84-89). IEEE.

Daneshmand, M., Fouladi, S., Mansour, R. R., Lisi, M., & Stajcer, T. (2009). Thermally actuated latching RF MEMS switch and its characteristics. *IEEE Transactions on Microwave Theory and Techniques*, *57*(12), 3229–3238. doi:10.1109/TMTT.2009.2033866

Du, Y. J., Bao, J. F., & Jiang, J. W. (2013). A new design of multi-bit RF MEMS distributed phase shifters for phase error reduction. *Microsystem Technologies*, *19*(2), 237–244. doi:10.1007/s00542-012-1649-z

Elbuken, C., Topaloglu, N., Nieva, P. M., Yavuz, M., & Huissoon, J. P. (2009). Modeling and analysis of a 2-DOF bidirectional electro-thermal microactuator. *Microsystem Technologies*, *15*(5), 713–722. doi:10.1007/s00542-009-0789-2

Fernández-Bolaños, M., Vasylchenko, A., Dainesi, P., Brebels, S., De Raedt, W., Vandenbosch, G. A. E., & Ionescu, A. M. (2010). Dipole antenna and distributed MEMS phase shifter fully integrated in a single wafer process for beam steering applications. *Microelectronic Engineering*, *87*(5), 1290–1293. doi:10.1016/j.mee.2009.10.009

He, X. J., Lv, Z. Q., Liu, B., & Li, Z. H. (2012). High-isolation lateral RF MEMS capacitive switch based on HfO_2 dielectric for high frequency applications. *Sensors and Actuators. A, Physical*. doi:10.1016/j.sna.2012.03.013

Huff, G. H., & Bernhard, J. T. (2006). Integration of packaged RF MEMS switches with radiation pattern reconfigurable square spiral microstrip antennas. *IEEE Transactions on Antennas and Propagation*, *54*(2), 464–469. doi:10.1109/TAP.2005.863409

Hutchings, D. A., El-Shenawee, M., & Tung, S. (n.d.). *Electromagnetic characterization of broadband MEMS antenna*. Academic Press.

Kang, N. W., Cheon, C., & Jung, H. K. (2002). Feasibility study on beam-forming technique with 1-D mechanical beam steering antenna using niching genetic algorithm. *IEEE Microwave and Wireless Components Letters*, *12*(12), 494–496. doi:10.1109/LMWC.2002.805954

Khazaai, J. J., & Qu, H. (2012). Electro-thermal MEMS switch with latching mechanism: Design and characterization. *IEEE Sensors Journal*, *12*(9), 2830–2838. doi:10.1109/JSEN.2012.2194736

Lakshminarayanan, B., & Weller, T. M. (2006). Design and modeling of 4-bit slow-wave MEMS phase shifters. *IEEE Transactions on Microwave Theory and Techniques, 54*(1), 120–127. doi:10.1109/TMTT.2005.860332

Li, Z., Mopidevi, H., Kaynar, O., & Cetiner, B. A. (2012). Beam-steering antenna based on parasitic layer. *Electronics Letters, 48*(2), 59–60. doi:10.1049/el.2011.2787

Liu, A. Q. (2010). *RF MEMS switches and integrated switching circuits* (Vol. 5). Berlin: Springer. doi:10.1007/978-0-387-46262-2

Mirzajani, H., Nasiri, M., & Ghavifekr, H. B. (2012). A new design of MEMS-based wideband frequency reconfigurable microstrip patch antenna. In *Proceedings of Mechatronics and its Applications (ISMA), 2012 8th International Symposium on* (pp. 1-6). IEEE.

Moseley, R. W., Yeatman, E. M., Holmes, A. S., Syms, R. R. A., Finlay, A. P., & Boniface, P. (2006). Laterally actuated, low voltage, 3-port RF MEMS switch. [IEEE.]. *Proceedings of Micro Electro Mechanical Systems, 2006*, 878–881.

Muldavin, J. B., & Rebeiz, G. M. (2000a). High-isolation CPW MEMS shunt switches: 1: Modeling. *IEEE Transactions on Microwave Theory and Techniques, 48*(6), 1045–1052. doi:10.1109/22.904743

Muldavin, J. B., & Rebeiz, G. M. (2000b). High-isolation CPW MEMS shunt switches: 2: Design. *IEEE Transactions on Microwave Theory and Techniques, 48*(6), 1053–1056. doi:10.1109/22.904744

Nasiri, M., Mirzajani, H., Atashzaban, E., & Ghavifekr, H. B. (2013). Design and simulation of a novel micromachined frequency reconfigurable microstrip patch antenna. *Wireless Personal Communications*, 1–24.

Nordquist, C. D., Baker, M. S., Kraus, G. M., Czaplewski, D. A., & Patrizi, G. A. (2009). Polysilicon based latching RF MEMS switch. *IEEE Microwave and Wireless Components Letters, 19*(6), 380–382. doi:10.1109/LMWC.2009.2020025

Oberhammer, J., & Stemme, G. (2006). Active opening force and passive contact force electrostatic switches for soft metal contact materials. *Journal of Microelectromechanical Systems, 15*(5), 1235–1242. doi:10.1109/JMEMS.2006.882810

Palei, W., Liu, A. Q., Yu, A. B., Alphones, A., & Lee, Y. H. (2005). Optimization of design and fabrication for micromachined true time delay (TTD) phase shifters. *Sensors and Actuators. A, Physical, 119*(2), 446–454. doi:10.1016/j.sna.2004.10.006

Pringle, L. N., Harms, P. H., Blalock, S. P., Kiesel, G. N., Kuster, E. J., Friederich, P. G., & Smith, G. S. (2004). A reconfigurable aperture antenna based on switched links between electrically small metallic patches. *IEEE Transactions on Antennas and Propagation, 52*(6), 1434–1445. doi:10.1109/TAP.2004.825648

Qui, J., Lang, J. H., Slocum, A. H., & Strumpler, R. (2003). A high-current electrothermal bistable MEMS relay. [IEEE.]. *Proceedings of Micro Electro Mechanical Systems, 2003*, 64–67.

Rebeiz, G. M. (2003). *RF MEMS theory, design and technology*. Hoboken, NJ: Wiley.

Rodrigo, D., Damgaci, Y., Unlu, M., Cetiner, B. A., Romeu, J., & Jofre, L. (2011). Antenna reconfigurability based on a novel parasitic pixel layer. In *Proceedings of the 5th European Conference on Antennas and Propagation* (EUCAP) (pp. 3497-3500). IEEE.

Senturia, S. D. (2001). *Microsystem design* (Vol. 3). Boston: Kluwer Academic Publishers.

Sundaram, A., Maddela, M., Ramadoss, R., & Feldner, L. M. (2008). MEMS-based electronically steerable antenna array fabricated using PCB technology. *Journal of Microelectromechanical Systems*, *17*(2), 356–362. doi:10.1109/JMEMS.2008.916291

Topalli, K., Civi, O. A., Demir, S., Koc, S., & Akin, T. (2008). A monolithic phased array using 3-bit distributed RF MEMS phase shifters. *IEEE Transactions on Microwave Theory and Techniques*, *56*(2), 270–277. doi:10.1109/TMTT.2007.914377

Vanderveen, M. C. (1997). *Estimation of parametric channel models in wireless communications networks*. (Ph.D. dissertation). Stanford University, Department of Scientific Computing and Computational Mathematics, Palo Alto, CA.

Varadan, V. K., Jose, K. A., Varadan, V. V., Hughes, R., & Kelly, J. F. (1995). A novel microwave planar phase shifter. *Microwave Journal*, *38*(4), 244–255.

Varadan, V. K., Vinoy, K. J., & Jose, K. A. (2003). *RF MEMS and their applications*. Hoboken, NJ: Wiley.

Varona, J., Tecpoyotl-Torres, M., Escobedo-Alatorre, J., & Hamoui, A. A. (2008). Design and fabrication of a MEMS thermal actuator for 3D optical switching applications. In *Proceedings of IEEE/LEOS Summer Topical Meetings*, (pp. 31-32). IEEE.

Wang, J., Ativanichayaphong, T., Huang, W. D., Cai, Y., Davis, A., Chiao, M., & Chiao, J. C. (2008). A distributed MEMS phase shifter on a low-resistivity silicon substrate. *Sensors and Actuators. A, Physical*, *144*(1), 207–212. doi:10.1016/j.sna.2007.12.027

Williams, K. R., & Muller, R. S. (1996). Etch rates for micromachining processing. *Journal of Microelectromechanical Systems*, *5*(4), 256–269. doi:10.1109/84.546406

Winters, J. H. (1998). Smart antennas for wireless systems. *IEEE Personal Communications*, *5*(1), 23–27. doi:10.1109/98.656155

Woten, D. A., El-Shenawee, M., & Tung, S. (2009). Planar broadband dual-linearly polarized MEMS steerable antenna. In *Proceedings of Antennas and Propagation Society International Symposium, 2009* (pp. 1-4). IEEE.

Xiang, H. J., & Shi, Z. F. (2009). Static analysis for functionally graded piezoelectric actuators or sensors under a combined electro-thermal load. *European Journal of Mechanics. A, Solids*, *28*(2), 338–346. doi:10.1016/j.euromechsol.2008.06.007

Yan, D. (2002). *Mechanical design and modeling of MEMS thermal actuators for RF applications*. (Doctoral dissertation). University of Waterloo.

KEY TERMS AND DEFINITIONS

Actuation: The act of making mechanical deflection or deformation in a mechanically suspended micro-scale device by applying an actuation voltage.

Buck Micromachining: The process of making micro-scale devices by etching the bulk of the silicon.

Coplanar Wave Guide (CPW): A kind of transmission line which its ground plane is located inplainly with the signal line.

Micromachining: The process of making micro-scale devices and components by the aid of conventional IC fabrication techniques.

Phase Shifter: Is a two port network which is used to impose a defined phase difference between its input and output signals without the loss of signal power.

Sacrificial Layer: A layer which is used for creation of free standing structures and is etched out in release process.

Signal-of-Interest: A signal which is intended for receiving of transmitting.

Smart Antenna: An antenna which can dynamically change its radiation pattern in order to receive the desired signal and reject the interferences.

Structural Layer: A layer that acts as mechanical moveable part.

Surface Micromachining: The process of making micro-scale devices in the surface of the silicon by deposition and etching of different layers of structural and sacrificial layers.

Section 2
MAC Layer Issues

Chapter 11
Hierarchical QoS Admission Control Mechanism for IEEE 802.16j Mobile Multi-Hop Relay WiMAX Network

Rohaiza Yusoff
Universiti Teknologi MARA, Malaysia

Mohd Dani Baba
Universiti Teknologi MARA, Malaysia

Muhammad Ibrahim
Universiti Teknologi MARA, Malaysia

ABSTRACT

This chapter presents some performance issues in Worldwide Interoperability for Microwave Access (WiMAX) network and focus on the capability of non-transparent relay in Mobile Multi-Hop Relay (MMR) WiMAX Network. In this work, an admission control mechanism with hierarchy Quality of Service (QoS) is developed for the relay architecture. An open source-based simulator is used to evaluate the three types of QoS classes, which are Unsolicited Grant Access (UGS), Real Time Polling Service (rtPS), and Non-Real Time Polling Service (nrtPS). Two scenarios of non-transparent relay topologies are set up for different numbers of subscribers with different types of QoS application classes. Three performance metrics, which are bandwidth utilization, number of slots used, and number of admitted service flow, are observed and plotted in graph. The results show the hierarchy-based QoS admission control mechanism can enhance the throughput of provided services by 35% compared to the conventional method without the admission control approach.

DOI: 10.4018/978-1-4666-4888-3.ch011

INTRODUCTION

The field of wireless communications have experience tremendous changes recently in response to user demand for ubiquitous communication from anywhere, anytime and anyone. The role of government in supporting the vendors to deliver the most efficient services will convince the users of their continuous support. Therefore, many approaches were developed and deployed in order to satisfy the user demands.

WiMAX enables the delivery of last mile wireless broadband access as an alternative to wired broadband like cable and Digital Subscriber Line (DSL). WiMAX provides fixed, nomadic, portable and mobile wireless broadband connectivity. The two driving forces of modern internet are broadband and wireless. The WiMAX standard combines the two, delivering high-speed broadband internet access over a wireless connection.

With the rapid advancement in telecommunication technology today, Mobile Multi-hop Relay (MMR) Worldwide Interoperability for Microwave Access (WiMAX) network standard was introduced in early 2009 through IEEE Standard for Local and metropolitan area networks Part 16: Air Interface for Broadband Wireless Access Systems Amendment 1: Multiple Relay Specification to enable mobile communication with low cost base station offered.

Role of Relay Station

A Relay Station (RS) is a radio system that helps to amplify and retransmit the signal to the uncovered Base Station (BS) area. The implementation of RS in certain topology is to enhance the network capacity especially for shadowed places. RS is also effective in extending the network coverage region at the edge of cell boundary. There are few types of RS which is categorized according to their functionality. Fixed RS is usually for permanent deployment and long term purpose. It is used to eliminate the coverage holes at val-

ley area, penetration into large building and to enhance coverage for shadowed area. Fixed RS is also used for multi-hop relay in order to penetrate targeted area. Sometimes fixed RS can be found in underground facilities to provide signals for users. Another position for fixed RS is near the edge of the cell to support weak signal from BS and to helps handoff process efficiently.

Figure 1 shows several usages of fixed RS in WiMAX architecture. Another type is Mobile RS which is placed on moving object such as an RS on underground train to ensure the passengers in the train able to continuously communicate while travelling. This RS has to connect and handoff from immediate BS to another in the fastest way while serving its subscribers.

Ad-hoc RS is a temporary RS which can be deployed for a certain time period such as to provide coverage in a big event or peak usage season. The main purpose of ad-hoc RS is to increase the network capacity being served by existing BS so that user did not get any difficulties to get connected in crowded area. This kind of portable RS give benefits not only to user but also to vendor in order to broadcast any live events.

As for this work, the focus is on fixed type RS with non-transparent mode and distributed scheduling. Several enhancement and features of the fixed RS have also been done.

The biggest difference between conventional WiMAX and MMR WiMAX is that in MMR network, the system enables mobile stations to communicate with a base station through intermediate relay stations. In conventional WiMAX network architecture, signals are transferred between base station and mobile terminals. In MMR network architecture, the whole cell is divided into two regions: BS region and RS region. The users near the base station which belong to BS region are connected directly to BS while users in the relay region, out of BS region are connected to RS. Hence, RS pretends to be a Mobile Station (MS) for BS and to be a BS for MS.

Figure 1. Usages of relay stations in WiMAX architecture

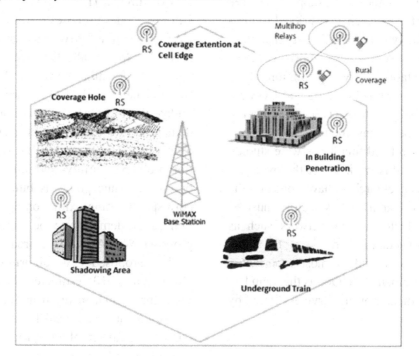

Two different relay modes are defined in the IEEE 802.16j which are transparent and non-transparent relay. Transparent relay usually used to enhance the network capacity while non-transparent relay is to enhance the network coverage. Transparent relay does not forward framing information to BS and this mode has lower complexity which only operates in two-hop network topology in centralized scheduling. Scheduling is one of the most crucial factors which influence the quality of service (QoS) in WiMAX network.

Admission Control

Admission control is a process of regulating traffic volume particularly for wireless mobile networks. In this context, it is more to QoS procedure which controls and determines how the resources of the system are allocated by the available connections with various requirements. The slots for the relay link are the main resource for the admission control algorithm. Slot is the minimum time frequency

resource allocated by WiMAX system standard. A series of slots are assigned to a given user which is called the user's data region. The scheduling algorithm implemented in WiMAX system allocates data regions for different users, according to their demand, QoS requirements and channel conditions.

Basically, an admission control mechanism works together with scheduling technique in order to deliver an efficient traffic in the network. This research is focused on the admission control coupled with Round Robin scheduler to avoid overwhelming the limited radio resources due to many user connections.

Objective of Research Work

The objective of this work is to develop the admission control mechanism by assigning hierarchy priority to three QoS classes; UGS, rtPS and nrtPS. After that, the performance analysis on the admission control mechanism is carried out to determine whether it can support the three QoS classes. This research is restricted to non-transparent relay type for distributed scheduling within one cell network which comprises of Base Station, Relay Station and Mobile Station. Three types of QoS classes; rtPS, nrtPS and UGS are employed and assigned to one type of application for each subscriber at any one time.

Some of the related literatures were studied and discussed in this work to get the overview of what the other researchers have done and the focus of their research. A few factors must be considered in deploying any network such as the capacity of users, time processing for single and multiple requests and the most important is their QoS requirement. The QoS is the main key performance indicator of the services offered by the vendors.

RELATED WORKS

Recently, there is much technology advancement in the broadband wireless access networks. In WiMAX family, the architecture affects the chronology of working network system. For example, the mesh WiMAX topology does not use relay station in order to transmit the data packet. Since the technology is growing, more techniques are required to fulfil the role. Admission control works together with scheduling technique in order to deliver an efficient traffic in network. In this literature review, some scheduling techniques are discussed.

Call Admission Control (CAC) scheme for IEEE 802.16e that satisfies both bandwidth and delay guarantee to the admitted connections has been proposed in (Kalikivayi, Misra, & Saha, 2008). Numerical results show that the proposed CAC scheme is the better choice for admission control in terms of blocking and dropping probabilities of the connections and bandwidth utilization of the system.

Bo Rong in (Bo, Yi, Kejie, Hsiao-Hwa, & Guizani, 2008) proposes a framework of a 2-D CAC to accommodate various features of WiMAX networks. Specifically, they decomposed the 2-D uplink and downlink WiMAX CAC problem into two independent 1-D CAC problems and formulate the 1-D CAC optimization, in which the demands of service providers and subscribers are jointly taken into account. To solve the optimization problem, a utility- and fairness-constrained optimal revenue policy is built, as well as its corresponding approximation algorithm. Simulation results demonstrate the effectiveness of the proposed WiMAX CAC approach.

The proposed CAC algorithm by (Wan & Hwangjun, 2010) estimates the expected network throughput in the near future by using a measurement-based local linear model and the control parameter of the proposed scheduling algorithm, and performs its own functions based on information. Then the algorithm periodically updates the control parameter to pursue an effective trade-off between the QoS of video streaming and the network utilization. Simulation results present a strong performance in the proposed video streaming system.

In (Ben-Jye, Yan-Ling, & Chien-Ming, 2007) they proposed an adaptive polling approach with cost-based CAC for increasing utilization of access channel and network reward, and reducing polling delay. Two mechanisms are proposed in their study, including a two-level adaptive scheduling mechanism for scheduling a dynamic polling list for QoS-based SSs and a cost-based call admission control mechanism for determining whether to accept a new incoming service flow or not. Numerical results indicate that the proposed approach outperforms IEEE 802.16 standard in fractional reward loss and average delay significantly.

State-dependent admission control scheme by (Tarhini & Chahed, 2008) where the degree of acceptance of flows depends on the density of the users in a given location. The latter refers to different areas in a single OFDMA-based WiMAX cell wherein users are allowed to move internally between those areas as well as externally to other cells. The developed analytical model which allows deriving some performance measures such as blocking and dropping probabilities. The results quantify how these metrics vary with the load as well as the admission strategies. The density-based AC algorithm is shown to lower the dropping probability of on-going calls without increasing too much the blocking probability of new ones.

As a conclusion, the performance of basic rtPS, UGS and nrtPS indicates that although they can guarantee in fulfilling their respective tasks, an enhancement into the services would give a more significant throughput to the network. Most of the CAC proposed are for Mobile WiMAX network and adding a RS in the system would give some behavioural effect.

METHODOLOGY

The main focus of this chapter is to address two major problems of call admission control and scheduling in MMR WiMAX network. The current IEEE standard does not specify the specific scheduler and admission control strategy for MMR WiMAX. A hierarchical admission control mechanism would give a better results and this approach is enhanced to support QoS requirement as one of the better solutions.

Furthermore, without admission control, the system transmission faces high collision which causes significant drop in throughput. Besides that, mobile user handover is also being investigated to observe the effect of RS in the network topology

Hierarchical QoS Admission Control Mechanism

The hierarchical QoS admission control mechanism for MMR WiMAX network is developed by using the Network Simulator version 2 (NS2) that supports National Chiao Tung University network

simulator (NCTUns) module package with hierarchical QoS priority mechanism. NCTUns platform uses native Linux TCP/IP stack and interacts with real devices in virtual networks. It allows experiments with real applications without the need to change the real applications. Users may use remote simulations and concurrent simulations so that it is easier to create simulation servers by taking the advantage of multiple cores or processors.

The admission control is performed during the initial ranging request process of RS-MS. The IEEE 802.16j has specified the initial ranging process. Ranging is a process of acquiring the correct timing offset, and physical parameters, such as transmit power level, frequency offset and others, so that the MS can communicate with the BS correctly. BS performs measurements and feedback while MS performs the necessary adjustments. The sequences of ranging process can be seen in Figure 3.

The word hierarchy represents the priority or arrangement of certain group so as in this approach, each of QoS classes is assigned a hierarchy. Their hierarchy is numbered from one to three as we only consider three types of QoS classes; UGS, rtPS and nrtPS. The mechanism is applied when slots left are not enough or the available bandwidth cannot satisfy minimum sustained rate. All three QoS classes require different minimum sustained rate and for each applications will be tabulated in the table. If the available slot is greater or equal to minimum required slots, the request is accepted.

In this study, the slots reserved by the RS have no limitation. This means an RS has the opportunity to use all the slots reserved for all RSs in BS. Therefore, it can be said that the limit of an RS can be less or equal to the reserved relay slots in BS and the limits of each RSs are adjusted automatically by applying this mechanism. Both UGS and rtPS classes are used for real time applications which need more bandwidth resources compared to nrtPS so that they need to be prioritized. The hierarchy number of UGS class is one, rtPS class is two and nrtPS class is three. The lower number has higher priority and more chance to be served if they happen in the same time. The mechanism is then applied into the simulator to observe the behavioural.

Simulation

Mobile Relay WiMAX topology was configured as in Figure 2 using non-transparent relay types consisting of one host, one BS, two RSs and ten MSs. The MSs will send the data at different time and observe the throughput and number of served subscribers in uplink mode. This simulation study also includes the variety of MS density, by varying MS from five to fifteen.

BS height is set to 30m; RS is 20m and all the MSs are set to 1.5 m. The MSs are position carefully to ensure the connection existed through the RS and the BS coverage is adequate to serve two RSs only. In order to match the OFDMA standard (Tao, Weidong, Hsiao-Hwa, & Qiang, 2007), the WiMAX system model is configured according to OFDMA parameters as tabulated in Table 1. The system employed QPSK ½ modulation with 6 bytes of slot size for 623 available slots for the downlink transmission with frame duration of 5ms (Wang, Chen, & Chuang, 2010).

In order to maintain link connectivity, 30% of the available slot is reserved for nrtPS connection so that the system is not craving while the higher class of QoS are being served at certain time. Implementation of admission control will take place during ranging process as ranging respond procedure which can be seen in Figure 3 in bold arrow.

In our implementation, other than we improve the use of radio resources we also manage the subscribers based on requested applications by assigning hierarchy priority for each of them. The UGS class will be assigned as the highest priority followed by rtPS and nrtPS which will utilize the radio resources accordingly. Basic algorithm is represented by the flow chart shown in Figure 4. The available connection of rtPS and nrtPS will degrade slightly about 10% if the UGS application does not have enough slots. If there are unused slot at the neighbour RS, it will pass the slot to the required RS to cover the task.

Generally UGS class will have the highest priority followed by rtPS class and lastly nrtPS. The mechanism is applied if and only if the available unused slots are more than 30%. This mechanism will benefit both real time traffic and non-real time application. Besides that, the unused slot in the neighbouring RS will also be optimized.

Figure 2. Topology drawn for simulation

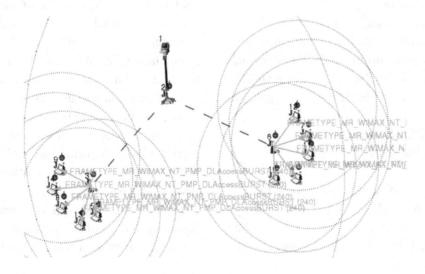

Table 1. OFDMA parameter used

OFDMA Parameters	Value
FFT-Size	1024
DL Sub-Carriers Allocation	30
UL Sub-Carriers Allocation	35
Bandwidth	10MHz
Sampling Factor	28/25
Sampling Frequency	11.2MHz
CP Ratio	1/8
CP Time	11.425us
Symbol Time	102.825us
Frame Duration	5ms
Physical Slot	0.357143us
TTG/RTG	90PS

Performance Analysis

The simulation is performed on the original network configuration to observe the performance and the effect of new admission control for non-transparent RS on certain topology. Besides that, the average throughput received, and number of subscribers being served for the uplink transmission is also studied. The proposed admission control mechanism is then tested with variety of QoS classes in order to compare their performance with the conventional mechanism by using the NCTUns simulation tools.

For case one, simulation is performed using rtPS class to observe the throughput and number of MSs being served for the uplink transmission. The proposed mechanism and the conventional

Figure 3. Ranging process with admission control used slot

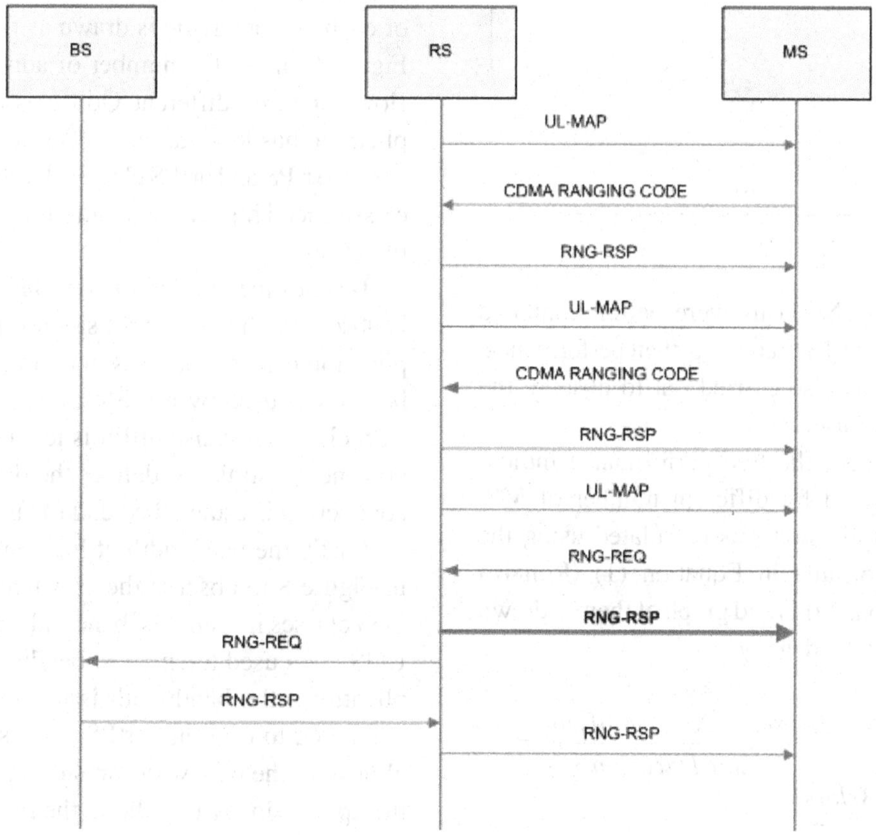

Figure 4. Flow of admission control used

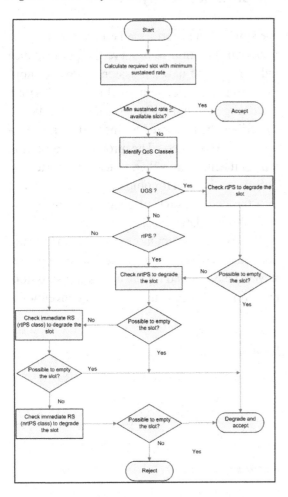

mechanism by NCTUns were being simulated respectively in order to compare their performance. Simulation was also carried out to observe the number of slot used.

For case one, the tree performance indicators are analysed for different number of MS. Bandwidth utilization was calculated using the throughput formula in Equation (1) (Rohaiza Yusoff & Baba, 2011) and graph of them is drawn for different MSs density.

$$Throughput = \frac{Slot\,size * Number\,of\,slot}{Frame\,Duration} = \frac{\left(6\,bytes * 623\,slots\right)}{5\,ms}$$

Figure 5 shows the graph of the number of admitted request served by MSs for rtPS class in different density of MSs. The request is initiated at different time and while the time increases, more MSs is successfully served. When it is analysed per RS basis, the allocated slots per each RS change according to its population. In the low population, the degradation of the calls starts later than the higher population. It was because at the beginning more bandwidth was requested. The overall performance for different number of MSs is then summarized in one single graph. As the number of MS is increases, the percentage of bandwidth utilization is also increases (R. Yusoff, Baba, & Ibrahim, 2011). The higher density of MSs leads to faster bandwidth being utilized.

In case two, three types of applications are used in order to observe the effect of QoS classes to the proposed admission control mechanism. The three types of QoS namely the UGS, rtPS and nrtPS were used in the simulation and result of each characteristic is drawn as figures below. Figure 6 shows the number of admitted service flow for three different QoS classes. UGS application has less number of service flows compared to rtPS and nrtPS classes. It is because UGS classes need higher bandwidth for each of its application.

Besides the number of admitted service flow is observed, the number of slot used for each application is also plotted as in Figure 7. The number of slot used by nrtPS classes is higher than rtPS classes because nrtPS is less complex with no time constraint to deliver the data as long as connection is established end to end.

Lastly the bandwidth utilization is plotted as in Figure 8 to observe the effectiveness of each QoS classes in using the bandwidth provided. As UGS class used the highest bandwidth in its applications, the bandwidth is utilized earliest as compared to rtPS and nrtPS classes. At the end, almost all the bandwidth was utilized by each of the application which shows the result of 0.96 or 96%.

Figure 5. Graph of performance for different number of MSs

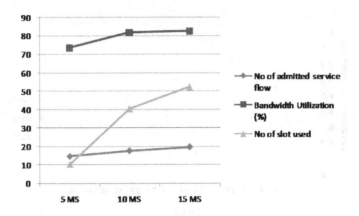

Figure 6. Number of admitted request for different QoS classes

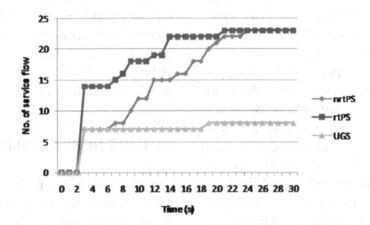

Figure 7. Number of slot used for different QoS classes

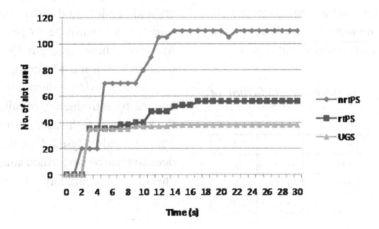

Figure 8. Bandwidth utilization for different QoS classes

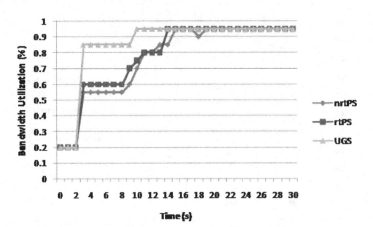

From the results, it shows that when the radio resources are being used wisely, it gives some enhancement and increase the bandwidth utilization. This benefit is important to system since there are varieties of application used by users and they are still able to serve each of them and satisfy the desired QoS requirement. Summary of three performance indicator for each QoS class is tabulated in Table 2. High class QoS such as UGS has lower number of service flow and number of slot but it utilizes the most bandwidth.

The simulation for rtPS QoS class with admission control process in non-transparent relay mode shows that by employing useful scheduling technique it is possible to increase the overall performance of Mobile Relay WiMAX network. In general, there are few factors that affect the efficiency of certain network and we have to plan well to avoid interference and signal losses.

Table 2. Summary of performance indicator of each QoS classes

Performance Indicator	nrtPS	rtPS	UGS
No. of Service Flow	14.81	18.16	6.71
No. of Slot Used	85.65	44.58	33.58
Bandwidth Utilization (%)	76.29	78.06	85.48

Figure 9 shows the comparison between the proposed hierarchical admissions controls mechanism with the existing module which does not employ any admission control procedure. Indicates another 35% of bandwidth provided is being successfully utilized.

FUTURE RESEARCH DIRECTIONS

Nowadays, the access to data is one of the basic needs in communication system. The tremendous growth of free applications has attracted people to use and gets benefits from them. The flexibility and cost effective offered by relay WiMAX architecture gives huge opportunity to researchers and vendors to discover new techniques and innovation towards better performance. In order to discover new paradigm, QoS parameter as the main indicator must be complied.

The admission control algorithm can be enhanced by introducing cognitive module where the behaviour of the users in a cell can be sensed, observed and analysed. Then the admission control decision can be performed automatically without checking the degradation level of each RS.

Figure 9. Comparison of bandwidth utilization between proposed hierarchical admission control and existing module

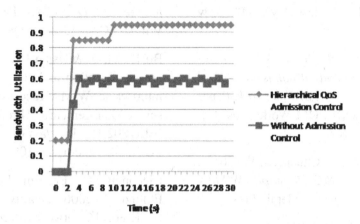

CONCLUSION

The hierarchical QoS based admission control mechanism has been successfully implemented to minimize the wastage of radio resources and also to increase the system capability in general. As in this work, the suffering of low QoS class has been mitigated based on priority admission control mechanism. The result shows 35% performance enhancement has been achieved with the proposed method and also increases the number of MS being served.

In general the performance of the proposed hierarchical QoS admission control mechanism for non-transparent RS in Mobile Relay WiMAX network is capable to increase the bandwidth utilization. Besides that, various applications instead of one QoS classes can be run in enhanced module.

To achieve the desired optimum performance, further research should be carried out on the proposed platform before deploying the network. The selection of relay types and modes is important to manage the fairly connected network with maximum throughput. Future research can also explore other factors such as fading variance, path selection or frequency reuse for various network topologies.

REFERENCES

Ben-Jye, C., Yan-Ling, C., & Chien-Ming, C. (2007). *Adaptive hierarchical polling and cost-based call admission control in IEEE 802.16 WiMAX networks.* Paper presented at the Wireless Communications and Networking Conference. New York, NY.

Bo, R., Yi, Q., Kejie, L., Hsiao-Hwa, C., & Guizani, M. (2008). Call admission control optimization in WiMAX networks. *IEEE Transactions on Vehicular Technology, 57*(4), 2509–2522. doi:10.1109/TVT.2007.912595

Kalikivayi, S., Misra, I. S., & Saha, K. (2008). *Bandwidth and delay guaranteed call admission control scheme for QOS provisioning in IEEE 802.16e mobile WiMAX.* Paper presented at the Global Telecommunications Conference. New York, NY.

Tao, J., Weidong, X., Hsiao-Hwa, C., & Qiang, N. (2007). Multicast broadcast services support in OFDMA-based WiMAX systems. *IEEE Communications Magazine, 45*(8), 78–86. doi:10.1109/MCOM.2007.4290318

Tarhini, C., & Chahed, T. (2008). *Density-based admission control in IEEE802.16e mobile WiMAX.* Paper presented at the Wireless Days, 2008. New York, NY.

Wan, K., & Hwangjun, S. (2010). *A novel combined packet scheduling and call admission control for video streaming over WiMAX network.* Paper presented at the GLOBECOM Workshops (GC Wkshps). New York, NY.

Wang, S.-Y., Chen, H.-Y., & Chuang, S.-W. (2010). *NCTUns tool for IEEE 802.16j mobile WiMAX relay network simulations.* Academic Press.

Yusoff, R., & Baba, M. D. (2011). *Performance analysis of transparent and non-transparent relays in MMR WiMAX networks.* Paper presented at the 2011 IEEE Symposium on Industrial Electronics & Applications. Malaysia.

Yusoff, R., Baba, M. D., & Ibrahim, M. (2011). *Weighted QoS admission control for IEEE 802.16j WiMAX networks.* Paper presented at the Computer Applications and Industrial Electronics (ICCAIE). New York, NY.

ADDITIONAL READING

Abichar, Z., Yanlin, P., & Chang, J. M. (2006). WiMax: The Emergence of Wireless Broadband. *IT Professional, 8*(4), 44–48. doi:10.1109/MITP.2006.99

Ahmad, I., & Habibi, D. (2010, 6-10 Dec. 2010). *Call Admission Control Scheme for Improved Quality of Service in WiMAX Communication at Vehicular Speeds.* Paper presented at the Global Telecommunications Conference (GLOBECOM 2010), 2010 IEEE.

Belghith, A., & Nuaymi, L. (2008). *Comparison of WiMAX Scheduling Algorithms and Proposals for the rtPS QoS Class.* Paper presented at the Wireless Conference, 2008.

Bo, R., Yi, Q., & Hsiao-Hwa, C. (2007). Adaptive power allocation and call admission control in multiservice WiMAX access networks [Radio Resource Management and Protocol Engineering for IEEE 802.16]. *Wireless Communications, IEEE, 14*(1), 14–19. doi:10.1109/MWC.2007.314546

Cicconetti, C., Lenzini, L., Mingozzi, E., & Eklund, C. (2006). Quality of service support in IEEE 802.16 networks. *Network, IEEE, 20*(2), 50–55. doi:10.1109/MNET.2006.1607896

Conniq.com. (2012). Introduction to FDM, OFDM, OFDMA, SOFDMA Retrieved Jan, 2012, from http://www.conniq.com/WiMAX/fdm-ofdm-ofdma-sofdma-02.htm

Erwu, L., Dongyao, W., Jimin, L., Gang, S., & Shan, J. (2007). *Performance Evaluation of Bandwidth Allocation in 802.16j Mobile Multi-Hop Relay Networks.* Paper presented at the Vehicular Technology Conference, 2007.

Freitag, J., & Fonseca, N. L. S. d. (2007). *WiMAX Module for NS2 Simulator.* Paper presented at the International Symposium on Personal, Indoor and Mobile Radio Communication.

Ghazal, S., Mokdad, L., & Ben-Othman, J. (2008). *Performance Analysis of UGS, rtPS, nrtPS Admission Control in WiMAX Networks.* Paper presented at the ICC 2008.

Ghosh, D., Gupta, A., & Mohapatra, P. (2007). *Admission Control and Interference-Aware Scheduling in Multi-hop WiMAX Networks.* Paper presented at the Mobile Adhoc and Sensor Systems, 2007.

Ghosh, D., Gupta, A., & Mohapatra, P. (2009). *Adaptive Scheduling of Prioritized Traffic in IEEE 802.16j Wireless Network*. Paper presented at the Wireless and Mobile Computing, Networking and Communications, 2009.

Gupta, A., Ghosh, D., & Mohapatra, P. (2010). Scheduling Prioritized Services in Multihop OFDMA Networks. *Networking, IEEE/ACM Transactions on, 18*(6), 1780-1792.

IEEE. (2007). *Part 16: Air interface for fixed and mobile broadband wireless access systems: Multi-hop relay specification*. IEEE Baseline Document for Draft Standard for Local and Metropolitan Area Networks.

IEEE Standard for Local and metropolitan area networks Part 16: Air Interface for Broadband Wireless Access Systems Amendment 1: Multiple Relay Specification. (2009). *IEEE Std 802.16j-2009 (Amendment to IEEE Std 802.16-2009)*, c1-290.

Jo, O., & Cho, D.-H. (2007). *Traffic Adaptive Uplink Scheduling Scheme for Relay Station in IEEE 802.16 Based Multi-hop System*. Paper presented at the Vehicular Technology Conference, 2007.

Kilic, E. (2010). Quality Of Service Aware Dynamic Admission Control. In *IEEE 802.16j Non-Transparent Relay Networks*. Middle East Technical University.

Le, Y., Wu, Y., & Zhang, D. (2009). *An Improved Scheduling Algorithm for rtPS Services in IEEE 802.16*. Paper presented at the Vehicular Technology Conference, 2009.

Lee, H., Kwon, T., & Cho, D.-H. (2006). *Extended-rtPS Algorithm for VoIP Services in IEEE 802.16 System*. Paper presented at the IEEE ICC 2006.

Lee, H., Kwon, T., Cho, D.-H., Lim, G., & Chang, Y. (2006). *Performance Analysis of Scheduling Algorithms for VoIP Services in IEEE 802.16e Systems*. Paper presented at the Vehicular Technology Conference, 2006.

Nie, C., Korakis, T., & Panwar, S. (2008). *A Multi-hop Polling Service with Bandwidth Request Aggregation in IEEE 802.16j Networks*. Paper presented at the Vehicular Technology Conference, 2008.

Okuda, M., Zhu, C., & Viorel, D. (2008). Multihop Relay Extension for WiMAX Network - Overview and Benefits of IEEE 802.16j Standard. *Fujitsu Sci Tech, 44*, 292–302.

Peters, S. W., & Heath, R. W. (2009). The future of WiMAX: Multihop relaying with IEEE 802.16j. *Communications Magazine, IEEE, 47*(1), 104–111. doi:10.1109/MCOM.2009.4752686

Peters, S. W., Robert, W., & Heath, J. (2009). The Future of WiMAX: Multihop Relaying with IEEE 802.16j. *IEEE Communications Magazine*, 104–111. doi:10.1109/MCOM.2009.4752686

Valencia, C. (2009). *Scheduling Alternatives for Mobile WiMAX End-to-End Simulations and Analysis*. Carleton University.

KEY TERMS AND DEFINITIONS

Bandwidth: A range of frequencies within a given band, in particular that used for transmitting a signal.

Communication: The imparting or exchanging of information by speaking, writing, or using some other medium.

Network: A group or system of interconnected people or things. A complete system that connecting sender and receiver to deliver the data.

Quality of Service (QoS): QoS is the key factor in delivering communication system.

Relay: A device to receive, reinforce, and re-transmit a radio or television signal. Relay is like a simple base station that able to extend coverage and enhance network capacity.

Throughput: The amount of material or items passing through a system or process. One of parameter to measure the successful of data sent and received.

Worldwide Interoperability for Microwave Access (WiMAX): Wireless communication system that enable mobility with large coverage area.

Chapter 12
Scheduling Algorithms and Radio Resource Management in WiMAX

Yasser Sadri
Department of Computer Engineering, Osku Branch, Islamic Azad University, Osku, Iran

Mohammdhossein Norouzibeirami
Department of Computer Engineering, Osku Branch, Islamic Azad University, Osku, Iran

ABSTRACT

The IEEE 802.16 has defined wireless access systems called WiMAX. These systems provide high-speed communications over long distances. To support multimedia applications, some service classes with Quality of Service (QoS) requirements are defined in IEEE 802.16, but the QoS scheduler is not standardized. The scheduling mechanism has a significant effect on the performance of WiMAX systems for use of bandwidth and radio resources. Some scheduling algorithms have been introduced by researchers. This study focuses on scheduling techniques proposed for WiMAX. The authors analyze a number of WiMAX scheduling algorithms in the Point-to-Multi-Point (PMP) mode and highlight their main points.

INTRODUCTION

The Worldwide interoperability for Microwave Access (WiMAX), based on IEEE 802.16 (IEEE 802.16 Working Group, 2004) is the main technology for the last mile fixed and mobile Broadband Wireless Access (BWA) systems to provide high speed data-rate and QoS guarantees for deferent types of multimedia traffic.

The IEEE 802.16 standard defines a connection-oriented BWA system with a central controller named the Base Station (BS). Other devices in this standard are Subscriber Stations (SSs) that

are the sources and destinations of connections. The BS controls the income and outcome of SSs to the network and is responsible for sharing the radio resources among all the SSs because of QoS requirements.

In order to support QoS for different traffic types, the IEEE 802.16 Media Access Control (MAC) defines several bandwidth (BW) request-allocation mechanisms and five QoS classes of service that support diverse service flows: Unsolicited Grant Service (UGS), real-time Polling Service (rtPS), extended real-time Polling Service (ertPS), non-real-time Polling Service (nrtPS), and Best Effort (BE). However the QoS scheduler is

DOI: 10.4018/978-1-4666-4888-3.ch012

not standardized in IEEE 802.16. The scheduling mechanism has a significant effect on the performance of WiMAX systems for use of bandwidth and radio resources. The choice of which scheduling algorithm to use for IEEE 802.16 is an open question. Some scheduling algorithms have been introduced by researchers.

This study focuses on scheduling algorithms proposed for BS in WiMAX. We evaluate a number of WiMAX scheduling methods in the PMP mode.

The rest of the chapter is organized as follows: The *Background* section presents a description of the IEEE 802.16 standard. The main focus of the chapter is titled *Scheduling Mechanism in WiMAX*, which provides an overview of problems and related works related to scheduling algorithms. Then, the *future research directions* section is presented, followed by concluding remarks.

BACKGROUND

WiMAX stands for Wireless Metropolitan Area Networks (Wireless MAN). This system supports PMP architecture with an optional mesh topology. In PMP mode, a BS centrally allocates Downlink (DL, from the BS to the SSs) and Uplink (UL, from the SSs to the BS) resources to SSs. All SSs are only allowed to communicate with a BS. In mesh mode, multi-hop communication is possible between SSs. In this section, we provide a description of the Physical (PHY) and MAC layers of the IEEE 802.16 standard.

WiMAX PHY Layer

Under the PMP mode, the standard supports a range of frequencies from 2 to 66 GHz, which includes the licensed and license-exempt bands. Depending on the range of frequencies, a Line-Of-Sight (LOS) or Non-Line-Of-Sight (NLOS) propagation mode may be used. Three types of modulation can be used: QPSK, 16-QAM, and

64-QAM. QPSK is the only mandatory modulation defined by the standard.

IEEE 802.16 defines five different PHY techniques:

1. Wireless MAN-SC (Single Carrier): In this technique, PHY layer single carriers are used to transmit information for frequencies beyond 11GHz in a LOS condition.
2. Wireless MAN-SCa: This technique also relies on a single carrier transmission scheme, but for frequencies between 2 GHz and 11GHz.
3. Wireless MAN-OFDM (Orthogonal Frequency Division Multiplexing): This technique is based on a Fast Fourier Transform (FFT) with a size of 256 points. It is used for PMP links in a NLOS condition for frequencies between 2 GHz and 11GHz.
4. Wireless MAN-OFDMA (OFDM Access): This technique, also referred to as mobile WiMAX, is also based on a FFT and possesses a size of 2048 points. It is used in a NLOS conditions for frequencies between 2 GHz and 11GHz.
5. Wireless MAN-SOFDMA (Scalable OFDMA): This technique employs an OFDMA PHY layer that has been extended in IEEE 802.16e, where the size is variable and can take different values: 128, 512, 1024, and 2048.

Both communications, DL and UL, are time multiplexed by means of Time Division Multiple Access (TDMA). Both sub-frames may use Time-Division Duplexing (TDD), where the DL and UL sub-frames share the same frequency but are separated in time or Frequency-Division Duplexing (FDD), in which both channels operate on separate frequencies.

WiMAX MAC Layer

In the MAC layer, three sub-layers have been defined in the IEEE 802.16 standard: the Service-Specific Convergence Sub-layer (CS), the Common Part Sub-layer (CPS) and the security sub-layer. Figure 1 shows WiMAX protocol stack.

The MAC CPS provides the core MAC functionality of system access, bandwidth allocation, connection establishment, and connection maintenance. On the other hand, the MAC CS resides on top of the MAC CPS. The CS performs the following functions, utilizing the services of the MAC:

- Receiving packet Protocol Data Units (PDUs) from the higher layer and classifying them into the appropriate connection.
- Delivering the resulting CS PDUs to the MAC Service Access Point (SAP) associated with the service flow for transport to the peer MAC SAP.
- Receiving the CS PDUs from the peer MAC SAP.

The sending CS is responsible for delivering the MAC Service Data Unit (SDU) to the MAC SAP. The MAC SDU is responsible for delivering the MAC to peer MAC SAP in accordance with the QoS, fragmentation, concatenation, and other transport functions associated with a particular connection's service flow characteristics. The receiving CS is responsible for accepting the MAC SDU from the peer MAC SAP and delivering it to a higher-layer entity. ATM CS is used for ATM protocols. The packet CS is used to transport all packet-based protocols such as Internet Protocol (IP) and IEEE 802.3 (Ethernet).

The security sub-layer provides subscribers with privacy, authentication or confidentiality across the broadband wireless network. It does this by applying cryptographic transforms to MAC PDUs carried across connections between SS and BS. In addition, the security sub-layer provides operators with strong protection from theft of service. The BS protects against unauthorized access to these data transport services by securing the associated service flows across the network. The security sub-layer employs an authenticated

Figure 1 WiMAX protocol stack (IEEE 802.16 Working Group, 2004)

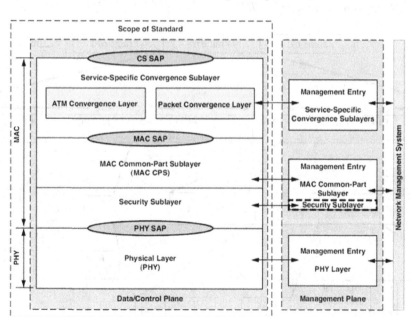

client/server key management protocol, in which the server at the BS controls distribution of keying material to client SS (IEEE 802.16 Working Group, 2004).

In PMP mode, the access to the medium is frame based. The MAC frame is divided in two sub-frames: DL and UL. Figure 2 shows the WiMAX MAC frame in TDD mode.

In both cases, TDD and FDD modes, the DL sub-frame starts with a *frame preamble* used by the PHY layer for synchronization and equalization. The Frame Control Header (FCH) comes next, which is composed of management messages and is used to convey control information directed to every SS. DL-Burst 1 contains the broadcast messages; Two of such management messages are the DL-MAP and UL-MAP, which indicate the assigned bandwidth to the connections or SSs and their corresponding burst profiles, in both directions, the DL and UL, respectively. By this means, each SS knows when and for how long the data should be received from the BS or transmitted to the BS. Other management messages, periodically transmitted, are the DCD and UCD

messages, where indicate the PHY characteristics of the PHY channel in both directions.

The BS allocates the time slots of the frame, using QoS-criteria, according to the needs defined by SSs. In the TDD mode, the sizes of the DL and UL sub-frames are dynamically determined by the BS and are broadcast to the SSs through the DL-MAP and UL-MAP messages at the beginning of each frame. The Tx/Rx Transition Gap (TTG) is used between the DL burst and the next UL burst. This gap allows time for the BS to switch from transmit to the receive mode and for SSs to switch from receive to the transmit mode. The Rx/Tx Transition Gap (RTG) is inserted between the UL burst and the subsequent DL burst. Its meaning is similar to TTG, but in an inverse sense (Delicado et al., 2012).

Bandwidth Requests

Bandwidth requests refer to the mechanism that SSs use to indicate to the BS that they need UL bandwidth allocation. The IEEE 802.16 standard defines a random access mechanism or broadcast polling, in which the BS assigns part of the UL

Figure 2 WiMAX MAC frame structure in TDD

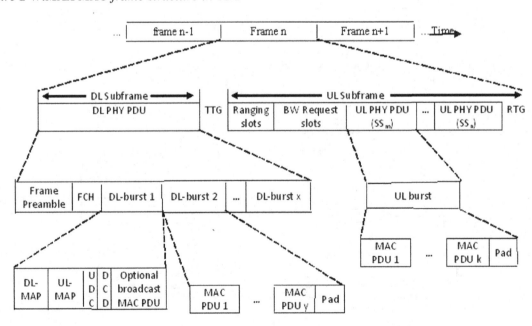

sub-frame to be used by the SSs to place their BW-requests. This period is composed of mini-slots, which can be used by the contending SSs to place their BW-request messages. The BS is responsible for establishing the contention period size in each frame. Obviously, in the case that two or more SSs, if they select the same time slot to send their respective BW-request messages, a collision will result. In order to solve potential conflicts during the contention period in the UL sub-frame, the standard defines a collision resolution method based on a truncated binary exponential back-off algorithm, with the initial and maximum back-off window values established by the BS through the UCD message (Chuck, Chen, & Chang, 2010). Since the UL sub-frame is used to transmit data packets and the contention period is defined in it, limiting the contention period size is one of the main issues to be addressed. In other words, the longer the contention period is, the lower the capacity available for data transmission will be. However, there is a clear trade-off between the contention period size and the actual collision probability. Therefore, reducing the number of signaling messages can leads to reducing the probability of collisions (Delicado et al., 2012).

Grant

In IEEE 802.16, grants can be allocated based on two modes:

1. **Grant Per Connection (GPC):** The BS entity decides the specific connection to grant the bandwidth to. As this mode is more controlled and saves scheduling decisions at the SS, it introduces additional overhead as now the UL-MAP must have grant information for each connection.
2. **Grant Per SS (GPSS):** BS grants bandwidth based on the aggregate of requests. Grant is communicated to the SS via its primary CID (Connection Identifier). It is then up to the SS to decide how to distribute the bandwidth.

The SS itself has to apply a certain level of scheduling logic to decide which connection to allocate the grant to.

For a SS, bandwidth requests reference individual connections while each bandwidth grant is addressed to the SS's basic CID, not to individual CIDs. Since the request honored is non-deterministic, when the SS receives a shorter transmission opportunity than expected (scheduler decision, request message lost, etc.), no explicit reason is given. In all cases, based on the latest information received from the BS and the status of the request, the SS may decide to perform back-off and request again or discard the SDU.

A SS may use Request Information Elements (IEs, that are broadcast) directed at a multicast polling group if is a member of or directed at its Basic CID. In all cases, the Request IE burst profile is used, even if the BS is capable of receiving the SS with a more efficient burst profile. To take advantage of a more efficient burst profile, the SS should transmit in an interval defined by a Data Grant IE directed at its Basic CID. Because of this, unicast polling of a SS would normally be done by allocating a Data Grant IE directed at its Basic CID. Also note that in a Data Grant IE directed at its Basic CID, the SS may make bandwidth requests for any of its connections.

Poling

Polling is the process by which the BS allocates bandwidth to the SSs specifically for the purpose of making bandwidth requests. These allocations may be to individual SSs or to groups of SSs. Allocations to groups of connections and/or SSs actually define bandwidth request contention IEs. The allocations are not in the form of an explicit message, but are contained as a series of IEs within the UL-MAP (IEEE 802.16 Working Group, 2004).

SCHEDULING MECHANISM IN WIMAX

WiMAX Scheduling: Issues and Problems

The key components of the WiMAX QoS guarantees are the admission control and the bandwidth allocation in BS. IEEE 802.16 defines adequate signaling schemes to support admission control and bandwidth allocation, but does not define the algorithms for them. This absence of definition allows more flexibility in the implementation of admission control and bandwidth allocation.

The research problem being investigated here is, after connections are admitted into the WiMAX network, how to allocate bandwidth resources and perform scheduling services so that the QoS requirements of the connections can be satisfied. As studied in (Fattah & Leung, 2002), efficient link utilization, delay bound, throughput, fairness, low implementation complexity, and scalability are the most required features for a resource scheduler in wireless multimedia networks.

Scalability means that an algorithm should efficiently operate as the number of connections increases. On the other hand, since the BS has to handle many simultaneous connections and decisions have to be made during the short WiMAX frame duration, the scheduling algorithms have to be simple, fast, and use minimum resources such as memory; consequently, an algorithm should has low implementation complexity. The same applies to the scheduler at the SS (So-in et al., 2010).

Moreover, the IEEE 802.16 protocol covers MAC and PHY layers, and there are several challenges for scheduling.

WiMAX Scheduling and MAC Layer

The greatest challenge of the MAC layer is handling the diverse service types, which requires its scheduling scheme to perform effectively with respect to QoS criteria and to achieve fairness among different types of traffic.

QoS

Generally, time-dependent and other non-functional requirements are expressed as QoS requirements. These requirements describe what is needed from the underlying network to ensure that, for example, the temporal relationship in a stream can be preserved (Tanenbaum & Steen, 2007). In WiMAX networks, the principal mechanism for providing QoS is to associate packets traversing the MAC interface into a service flow as identified by the CID. A service flow is a unidirectional flow of packets that is provided a particular QoS. The SS and BS provide this QoS according to the QoS Parameter Set defined for the service flow. Service flows exist in both the UL and DL directions and may exist without actually being activated to carry traffic. The requirements for QoS include the following (IEEE 802.16 Working Group, 2004):

- A configuration and registration function for pre-configuring SS-based QoS service flows and traffic parameters.
- A signaling function for dynamically establishing QoS-enabled service flows and traffic parameters.
- MAC scheduling and QoS traffic parameters for UL service flows
- QoS traffic parameters for DL service flows.
- Service Classes that grouping service flow properties so that upper-layer entities and external applications (at both the SS and BS) may request service flows with desired QoS parameters in a globally consistent way.

Service Classes, also known as scheduling services, are the data handling mechanisms supported by the MAC scheduler for data transport on a connection. Each connection is associated with a single data service. Each data service is associated with a set of QoS parameters that quantify aspects of its behavior. Four services are supported by IEEE 802.16d (IEEE 802.16 Working Group, 2004):

The Unsolicited Grant Service (UGS) provides Constant Bit Rate (CBR) data flows, such as T1/E1 and Voice over IP (VoIP) without silence suppression. The QoS parameters of UGS service are the maximum sustained traffic rate, minimum reserved traffic rate, tolerated jitter, maximum latency, and request/transmission policy.

The real-time Polling Service (rtPS) is designed for applications with real-time requirements which generate variable size data packets on a periodic basis, such as MPEG video streams. QoS guarantees are given as maximum latency, maximum sustained traffic rate, assurance of minimum traffic rate, and request/transmission policy.

The non-real-time Polling Service (nrtPS) is designed to support non-real-time services that require variable size bursts on a regular basis such as FTP services. The maximum sustained traffic rate, minimum traffic rate guarantees, and request/transmission policy are provided to nrtPS connections.

The Best Effort (BE) service, such as HTTP services, is designed to support data streams for which no minimum service level is required and, therefore, may be handled on a space-available basis. The mandatory QoS service flow parameters for this scheduling service are Traffic Priority, and Request/Transmission Policy.

The IEEE 802.16e (IEEE 802.16 Working Group, 2004), adds a new service class called extended real-time Polling Service (ertPS). This service is designed for real-time traffic with variable data-rates, such as VoIP service with silence suppression. The ertPS is built on the efficiency of both UGS and rtPS. This service uses a grant mechanism similar to that of UGS connections. Moreover, grants allocated periodically can be used to send bandwidth requests to inform the BS of the grant size. The BS does not change the size of UL allocations until it has received another bandwidth request from the SS. The QoS parameters of ertPS are minimum reserved traffic rate, maximum latency, request/transmission policy, and tolerated jitter.

WiMAX Forum (2008) classifies applications into five categories as shown in Table 1. Each application has its own characteristics such as throughput, latency, and jitter constraints to assure a good quality of user experience.

The Figure 3 shows the scheduling mechanism in both the BS and SS. Generally, two types of scheduling mechanisms are defined in IEEE 802.16: Data transmission scheduling and UL request/grant scheduling.

Data transmission scheduling selects the data for transmission in a particular frame/bandwidth allocation and is performed by the BS for DL and by the SS for UL. In addition to whatever other factors the scheduler may deem pertinent, the

Table 1. WiMAX application and service classes (WiMAX Forum, 2008)

Applications	Throughput Guideline		Latency Guideline		Jitter Guideline		QoS Classes
Multiplayer Interactive Gaming	Low	50 kbps	Low	< 25 ms	N/A		rtPS and UGS
VoIP and Video Conference	Low	32-64 kbps	Low	<160	Low	< 50 ms	UGS and ertPS
Streaming Media	Low to High	5 kbps to 2 Mbps	N/A		Low	< 100 ms	rtPS
Web Browsing and Instant Messaging	Moderate	10 kbps to 2 Mbps	N/A		N/A		nrtPS and BE
Media Content Downloads High	High	> 2 Mbps	N/A		N/A		nrtPS and BE

following items are taken into account for each active service flow (IEEE 802.16 Working Group, 2004):

- The scheduling service specified for the service flow.
- The values assigned to the service flow's QoS parameters.
- The availability of data for transmission.
- The capacity of the granted bandwidth.

Uplink request/grant scheduling is performed by the BS with the intent of providing each associated SS with bandwidth for UL transmissions or opportunities to request bandwidth. By specifying a scheduling service and its associated QoS parameters, the BS scheduler can anticipate the throughput and latency needs of the UL traffic and provide polls and/or grants at the appropriate times. Table 2 summarizes the scheduling services and the poll/grant options available for each.

Fairness

Aside from assuring the QoS requirements, left over resources should also be allocated fairly. However, the fairness definition is complex in wireless networks. As described in (Wengerter et al., 2005), a fair resource allocation usually does not produce equal connection data-rates because the diverse connections also suffer from diverse channel conditions, network states, and dynamics. Moreover, WiMAX needs to provide QoS guarantees for different scheduling services. Therefore, for fairness, it is necessary to consider QoS guarantees for different class connections. Two types of fairness have been defined in (Chen et al., 2009):

1. Intra-class fairness: the connections within the same class achieve an equal degree of QoS.
2. Inter-class fairness: the connections with QoS requirements achieve exactly what they

Figure 3. Scheduling in the BS and in the SS (Sadri & Khanmohammadi, 2013)

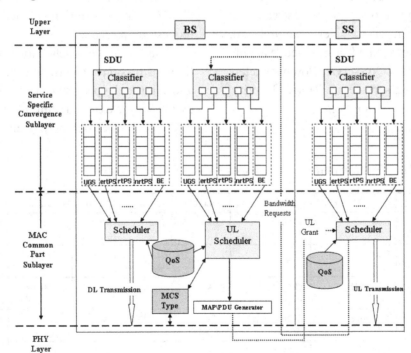

Table 2 Scheduling services and corresponding poll/grant options

Scheduling Type	Piggy Back Request	Bandwidth Stealing	Polling
UGS	Not Allowed	Not Allowed	Poll Me (PM) bit is used to request a unicast poll for bandwidth needs of non-UGS connections.
ertPS	Allowed	Not Allowed	Unicast, Multicast, Broadcast, and Polling.
rtPS	Allowed	Allowed	Unicast and Group Polling.
nrtPS	Allowed	Allowed	Unicast, Multicast, Broadcast, and Polling.
BE	Allowed	Allowed	Unicast, Multicast, Broadcast, and Polling.

require, and those without QoS requirements equally share the remaining resources.

WiMAX Scheduling and PHY Layer

The total data-rate in a WiMAX network is adaptive since Adaptive Modulation and Coding (AMC) are deployed in the PHY layer and the number of bytes each time slot can carry depends on the Modulation and Coding Scheme (MCS). The system takes one of three different modulation schemes. On the UL, QPSK is mandatory, while 16-QAM and 64-QAM are optional. The DL supports QPSK and 16-QAM, while 64-QAM is optional.

Furthermore, the system can use various Forward Error Correction (FEC) schemes on the UL as well as the DL. The combinations of PHY modulation and FEC schemes used between the BS and the SSs are termed as DL or UL burst profiles. The Signal-to-Noise Ratio (SNR) threshold of receivers is used by AMC to select different burst profiles in order to maximize the network throughput and maintain the Bit Error Rate (BER) under a preset level. To fully utilize the flexible and robust PHY layer, the WiMAX system equips a flexible Radio Link Control (RLC) scheme, which is responsible for transition from one PHY scheme to another. The RLC is capable of switching between different PHY bursts (Ma & Lu, 2009).

WiMAX transceivers support various transmission modes with different MCSs correspond-ing to different data transmission rates. In order to guarantee a certain BER, receivers have their own SNR thresholds and minimum receiver sensitivity requirements corresponding to different MCSs. Table 3 shows the MCSs based on the SNR thresholds on a targeted predefined bit error rate ($BER \leq 1 \times 10^{-6}$) in WiMAX PMP systems. These thresholds are taken from the SNR assumptions values that are proposed in Table 266 of the IEEE 802.16 standard for OFDM and in Table 338 for OFDMA (IEEE 802.16 Working Group, 2004).

Each data transmission rate corresponds to a SNR requirement. High data-rates require high SNR in order to keep BER under the pre-set level. Higher SNR require higher transmission power under the same channel condition (Lu & Ma, 2011). Therefore, the scheduler needs to use the channel state condition information and the resulting BER in deciding the MCS for each user. Moreover, for mobile users, the power is very

Table 3. AMC receiver SNR requirement

Modulation	Coding Rate	Receiver SNR (db)
BPSK	1/2	6.4 – 9.3
QPSK	1/2	9.4 – 11.1
	3/4	11.2 - 16.3
16-QAM	1/2	16.4 – 18.1
	3/4	18.2 – 22.6
64-QAM	2/3	22.7 -24.3
	3/4	>= 24.4

limited; therefore, the SS scheduler also needs to optimize the transmission power.

WiMAX Scheduling: Solutions and Techniques

Because the various service classes that are defined in IEEE 802.16, the scheduling mechanisms are classified into two groups:

1. Intra-class mechanisms that are used to management of connections within a same service class.
2. Inter-class mechanisms that attempt to manage the connections with deferent service classes.

On the other hand, the scheduling algorithms are divided into two types; priority and non-priority algorithms. In priority algorithms, some of connections have a priority based on one or more characteristics (e.g. delay or throughput).

Moreover, some scheduling algorithms consider the channel characteristics for decision making processes. These techniques are known as cross-layer and/or opportunistic schemes. Figure 4 shows the mechanism of cross-layer scheduling. Other algorithms do not rely on channel states in making their decisions.

In (Naja et al., 2012) the scheduling algorithms fall into three categories:

*   Simple Scheduling Algorithms
*   Cross-Layer Scheduling Algorithms
*   Hierarchical Scheduling Algorithms

Simple algorithms are considered for all classes in order to provide QoS, flow isolation and fairness. This is the case for First-In First-Out (FIFO), Weighted Fair Queuing (WFQ), and Earliest Deadline First (EDF) algorithms, among others.

Channel conditions are the main factors in the design of cross-layer scheduling algorithms. Temporary Removal Scheduler (TRS) and maxi-

Figure 4. Cross layer diagram as proposed in (Song et al., 2009)

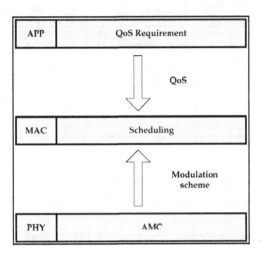

mum Signal-to-Interference Ratio (mSIR) are two examples of cross-layer methods.

The hierarchical category combines several queuing disciplines in more than one layer. Once bandwidth is assigned to each class using the first layer scheduling algorithms, a legacy algorithm is executed within each class in the second layer. An important aspect of algorithms in this category is the overall allocation of bandwidth among the scheduling services.

In (Ali et al., 2009), the scheduling mechanisms are classified into Homogeneous, Hybrid and Opportunistic algorithms.

The homogeneous category uses scheduling algorithms which were originally proposed for wired networks, but are also used in WiMAX. Generally, these algorithms don't consider the link channel quality. Some examples of these algorithms are: Round Robin (RR), Weighted Round Robin (WRR), Deficit Round Robin (DRR), Earliest Deadline First (EDF), Weighted Fair Queuing (WFQ), etc.

The hybrid category employs multiple legacy schemes in an attempt to satisfy the QoS requirements of the multi-class traffic in WiMAX networks. Some of the algorithms in this category also address the issue of variable channel conditions in WiMAX. Two examples of this type of algorithms are EDF+WFQ+FIFO (Karim et al., 2010) and EDF+WFQ (Ali et al., 2009).

This chapter studies some common scheduling schemes and divides them into three categories:

- Classic Algorithms
- Cross-Layer Algorithms
- Knowledge base Algorithms

An algorithm may fall into more than one group, but we classify algorithms based on the more specific characteristics of them.

Classic Algorithms

These algorithms are the simple and/or hybrid schemes that were studied in wired networks. The extended versions of these algorithms also fall into this category. The disadvantage of these algorithms is that they do not consider the SNR of connections. As a consequence, system throughput decreases when these algorithms are used.

RR

One classic algorithm is The Round Robin (RR). This algorithm allocates resources in a fixed and equal manner and provides no priority. Basically, the algorithm services the backlogged queues in a round robin fashion. Each time the scheduler pointer stops at a particular queue, one packet is dequeued from that queue and the scheduler pointer goes to the next queue.

The RR algorithm is studied in (Ball et al., 2006) for WiMAX systems. The RR scheduler is simple and easy to implement, and can be implemented in both inter- and intra-class mechanisms. This technique is not suitable for systems with different levels of priority and systems with strongly varying sizes of traffic because it does not consider user QoS requirements. However, RR can be suitable for BE connections as an intra-class scheduler because the BE service class has

no throughput or delay guarantees. Therefore, the RR scheduler can provide fairness for this type of connection.

WRR

A RR scheduler is based on static weights called Weighted Round Robin (WRR). This algorithm is proposed in (Chen et al., 2005; Ali et al., 2009) for BS in WiMAX. The WRR algorithm determines the allocation of bandwidth among the SSs based on their weights. In (Ali et al., 2009), WRR assigns a weight to each SS with respect to its minimum reserved traffic rate (T^{min}) as follows:

$$w_i = \frac{T_i^{\min}}{\sum_{j=1}^{n} T_j^{\min}} \tag{1}$$

where W_i is the weight of SS_i, and n is the number of SSs.

While the formulation is almost simple, there are no considerations for the BE service class, which does not have a specific minimum reserved traffic rate. Also, the delay parameter, very important for real-time applications, is not considered in WRR. Furthermore, as evaluated in (Ali et al., 2008), the WRR algorithm does not perform well when the traffic contains variable-sized packets. Finally, these types of algorithms disregard the SNR at the user location.

DRR

In (Cicconetti et al., 2006) a Deficit Round Robin (DRR) scheduler is used for the SS scheduler. The DRR or Deficit Weighted Round Robin (DWRR) scheduler associates a fixed quantum (Q i) and a deficit counter (DC i) with each flow i. At the start of each round and for each flow i, DC i is incremented by Q i. The head of the queue i is acceptable in queuing if DC i is greater than the length of the packet waiting to be sent (L i). In this case, DC i is decremented by L i. At each round, at most one packet can be sent (and then queued) for each flow. DRR operates with packet sizes and relies on knowledge of the head-of-line packet per connection, which is not known from the BS perspective on the UL. However, it can suitable for DL in BS and UL in SS.

WFQ

The Weighted Fair Queuing algorithm is a packet-based approximation of the Generalized Processor Sharing (GPS) algorithm. GPS is an idealized algorithm that assumes a packet can be divided into bits and each bit can be scheduled separately (Parekh & Gallager, 1993). WFQ is employed for UL traffic in WiMAX with different size packets. The WFQ scheduler assigns finish times to the packets. So, the packets are selected in increasing order according to their finish times. The finish times of the SS packets are calculated based on the size of the packets and the weight assigned to the SS. This algorithm has been evaluated in (Ali et al., 2008) for OFDM. The WFQ algorithm results in superior performance as compared to the WRR algorithm in the presence of variable size packets. The WFQ can be also used to guarantee the data-rate due to dynamic change of weights. The main disadvantage of WFQ is its complexity. Moreover, it does not consider the start time of a packet, therefore the system performance may decrease when many packets occur in the priority region.

EDF

The Earliest Deadline First (EDF) was originally proposed for real-time applications in wide area networks (Khan et al., 2010). The EDF algorithm is proposed for WiMAX in (Chen et al., 2005). This algorithm assigns a deadline to each packet and allocates bandwidth to the SS that has the packet with the earliest deadline (Hussain et al., 2009). The deadlines can be assigned to the packets of the SSs based on the SSs maximum delay requirement. Since each SS specifies a value for the maximum

latency parameter, the arrival time of a packet is added to the latency to form the tag of the packet. The EDF algorithm is suitable for real-time connections. However, EDF is a greedy algorithm. It schedules all the arriving packets according to ascending order of deadlines, which may leads to starve the packets that have no critical deadline.

Other Algorithms

A Dynamic Allocating Priority Queue (DAPQ) scheduling scheme is defined in (Esmailpour & Nasser, 2009), where each traffic type gets a portion of the resource. If an assigned bandwidth is unused, it will be allocated to another traffic type. Importantly, this solution needs an efficient tuning of the bandwidth reservation percentages.

The authors in (Wongthavarawat & Ganz, 2003) adopted a two layer scheduling scheme where bandwidth between different service classes is allocated with strict priority in the first layer, and each service class has its own scheduling algorithm in the second layer.

Borin and da Fonseca (2007) consider three types of queues with various level priorities for UL scheduling. The first type is used to schedule UGS, ertPS, and rtPS with critical delay. The second queue is used for rtPS and nrtPS connections, which sorts them by minimum reserved bandwidth. In last queue the remained bandwidth is allocated for BE connections. This method does not consider radio conditions and SNR of connections. One problem of this method is that users with high minimum reserved traffic rates and BE connections may never be served.

In (Tsai, Jiang, & Wang, 2006) a UL scheduler with a Call Admission Control (CAC) mechanism is developed by using a token bucket algorithm to characterize traffic flows. Their proposed CAC is based on the estimation of bandwidth usage of each traffic class, while the delay requirement of rtPS flows is met. Each connection is controlled by token rate r_i and bucket size b_i. Then, they find an appropriate token rate by analyzing Markov

Chain state and according to delay requirements of connections. In their Uplink Packet Scheduling Algorithm, the EDF algorithm is adopted. There is a database that records the number of packets that need to be sent during each frame of every rtPS connection. The disadvantage of this mechanism is that depends on the estimation model that is used.

An Adaptive Bandwidth Allocation (ABA) model for multiple traffic classes was proposed in (Sheu & Huang, 2011). In order to promise the quality of real-time traffic and allow more transmission opportunity for other traffic types, the ABA algorithm first serves the UGS connections. Then, polling bandwidth is allocated for rtPS service to meet their delay constraints and for the nrtPS to meet their minimum throughput requirements. For the BE service, the ABA algorithm will prevent it from starvation. The ABA algorithm assigns initial bandwidth, UGS, rtPS, nrtPS and BE, based on the requested bandwidth of UGS, the required minimum bandwidth of rtPS and nrtPS and the queue length of BE service respectively. If remaining bandwidth exists, the ABA then assigns extra bandwidth for the rtPS, nrtPS and BE services (Teixeira & Guardieiro, 2012).

Cross-Layer Algorithms

mSIR

The maximum Signal-to-Interference Ratio (mSIR) Scheduler is proposed in (Ball et al., 2005; Belghith & Nuaymi, 2008) for IEEE 802.16 networks. It allocates radio resources to users which have the highest Signal-to-Interference Ratio (SIR). This method allows highly efficient utilization of radio resources; but it may starve the users with a small SNR.

TRS

The Temporary Removal Scheduler (TRS) is proposed in (Ball et al., 2005) where a scheduling list is defined for TRS. The scheduling list contains all the SSs that can be served at the next frame. TRS includes identifying the packet call power (depending on radio conditions) and then temporarily removing them from scheduling list for a certain adjustable time period TR. When TR expires, the temporarily removed packet is checked again. If an improvement is observed in the radio channel, the packet can be added to the scheduling list again; otherwise the process is repeated for another TR duration. In poor radio conditions, the whole process can be repeated up to L times then the removed packed is added to the scheduling list, independently of the current radio channel condition.

The TRS can be combined with other schedulers. The combined scheduler with RR is called TRS+RR. For example, if there are k packet calls and only one of them is temporary removed, each packet call has a portion equal to $1/(k-1)$ of the whole channel resources. TRS can be associated with the mSIR scheduler that called TRS+mSIR. This scheduler assigns the whole channel resources to the packet call that has the maximum value of the SNR. The station to be served has to belong to the scheduling list (Belghith & Nuaymi, 2008).

ODRR

The Opportunistic Deficit Round Robin (O-DRR) scheduler (Rath et al., 2006) is used for UL. The BS polls subscribers periodically. After each period, the BS determines the set of subscribers that are acceptable for transmitting and the required bandwidth. A number of conditions such as queue should not be empty and the received SNR should be above a minimum threshold verified by an SS. Once these conditions are satisfied, the subscriber can be accepted to transmit during a given frame of the current scheduling epoch. The scheduled set changes dynamically depending on the wireless link state of subscribers. At the beginning of each scheduling epoch, the BS resets the acceptable and scheduled sets and repeats the above mentioned process.

Other Algorithms

The authors in (Lera et al., 2007) addressed a channel-aware scheduling algorithm with a per-flow channel error compensation technique based on the typical features of the WiMAX system: class-based QoS guarantees and per-flow resource assignment. The Worst-Case Fair Weighted Fair Queuing+ (WF2Q+) algorithm was suggested to manage the flow-level and class-level granularity per-class queues to provide the targeted QoS to each WiMAX service class while achieving fairness among traffic flows belonging to the same class. Paper (Kwon et al., 2005) gave out a cross-layer adaptive architecture for the IEEE 802.16e OFDMA system.

The strategy proposed in (Lihua et al., 2007) enhanced the architecture in (Kwon et al., 2005) by proposing a joint packet scheduling and a sub-channel allocation scheme.

In (Liu et al., 2006) a priority-based scheduler has been proposed at the MAC layer where each connection employs the AMC scheme at the PHY layer. The authors defined a priority function (PRF) for each connection admitted in the system and updated it dynamically depending on the wireless channel quality, QoS satisfaction and service priority through a MAC-PHY cross-layer procedure.

The method in (Lu & Ma, 2011) further enhanced the proposals in (Liu et al., 2006) and (Lihua et al., 2007), that proposed a cross-layer MAC protocol and QoS support framework associated with a two-stage opportunistic scheduling scheme with adaptive power control scheme to provide QoS support traffic in single carrier WiMAX PMP networks.

Knowledge Base Algorithms

Generally, classical scheduling algorithms only provide some limited aspects of QoS; because, it is difficult or even impossible to design mathematical models. The difficulty may result from time-dependent system behaviors, dynamics, and uncertainty in wireless communication environment. Knowledge base and expert systems perform well under these conditions.

FQFC

A fairness and QoS guaranteed scheduling approach with fuzzy controls (FQFCs) is proposed in (Chen et al., 2009) for WiMAX OFDMA systems. The controllers, respectively, adjust priority and transmission opportunity (TXOP) for each connection according to QoS requirements and service classes. The FQFC scheduler assigns two variables with fuzzy inference values for each connection with CID i, which is, the priority p_i and the maximum number of packets $TXOP_i$ that connection i can transmit in a frame duration. The FQFC scheduler first initializes the two variables based on the characteristics of connections and adjusts them, respectively, by two fuzzy controllers to adapt to the dynamics of system. As shown in Figure 5, the priority controller adjusts p_i according to channel quality, QoS requirements, and service classes (Chen et al., 2009).

With the priority, the FQFC decides the transmission order of connections. The TXOP controller adapts $TXOP_i$ according to transmission rate and the queue length difference between two contiguous transmissions of the MAC layer.

However, the throughput is not guaranteed for real-time connections whereas the throughput is one of the QoS requirements for this type of service classes.

FIS

In (Sadri & Khanmohamadi, 2013) a fuzzy based scheduling system is proposed for compounds of rtPS and nrtPS services in WiMAX networks. The Fuzzy Inter-class Scheduler (FIS) addresses the problem of latency control for rtPS applications and throughput control for nrtPS to provide QoS requirements for these types of service.

This scheme defines a model of bandwidth requests scheduling for IEEE 802.16d WiMAX

Figure 5. The FQFC scheduling mechanism (Chen et al., 2009)

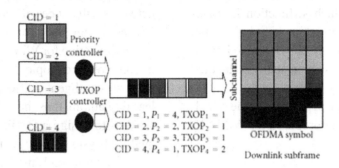

systems. There exist 4 classes of traffic, where each traffic class has its own queue q_i; i = 1: 4. The bandwidth request of subscribers SS_j with same class is integrated in same queues q_i. q_1 denotes the queue for UGS traffic that has the highest priority because of specifications of this class. q_N denotes the queue for best effort traffic, which has no predefined delay and throughput requirements. Then this work focus on remainder of queues q_i; i=2,3. The role of the FIS is to decide which queue should be serviced at this time of scheduling. Figure 6 represents the schematic of scheduling system.

Other Algorithms

A scheduling algorithm based on learning automata is proposed for WiMAX UL real-time traffic in PMP architecture in (Misra, Banerjee, & Wolfinger, 2012). The main objective of this

work is providing QoS to real-time traffic. This algorithm provides dynamic channel allocation to a number of SSs with different service flows, based on environment requirements, namely, requested bandwidth, number of packets dropped, and service flow class. This method does not consider SNR.

In (Taghipoor, Tavassoli, & Hosseini, 2010) The Reinforcement Learning (RL) scheduler is based on the model of packet scheduling described by Hall and Mars (1998). The aim is to use different scheduling policies depending on which queues are not meeting their delay requirements. The state of the system represented by a set of N -1 binary variables $\{s_1: s_{n-1}\}$, where each variable si indicates whether traffic in the corresponding queue qi .

At each timeslot, the scheduler must select an action a ∈ $\{a_1: a_N\}$, where ai is the action of choosing to service the packet at the head of queue

Figure 6. FIS scheduling mechanism (Sadri & Khanmohamadi, 2013)

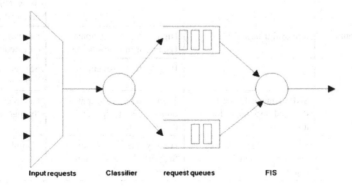

qi. The scheduler makes this selection by using a scheduling policy Π, which is a function that maps the current state of the system son to an action a. If the set of possible actions is denoted by A, and the set of possible system states is denoted by S, then Π: S→A.

Table 4 represents main points of some scheduling algorithms that are proposed for WiMAX.

FUTURE RESEARCH DIRECTIONS

The appearance of multimedia applications with high data-rate and QoS requirements has made an epoch in telecommunications technology and distributed systems. Due to development of multimedia networks, the particularly case assessments and preparations for improving performance of networks will not be sufficient; Special protocols and serious attempts are needed to guarantee QoS.

Optimization for WiMAX scheduler is still an ongoing research topic. For future work, we will propose intelligent and expert systems such as learning automatons, neural networks and fuzzy systems to design a flexible, punctual and fully qualified system based on the QoS requirement, radio conditions and fairness for increasing system performance in WiMAX networks.

Furthermore, as studied in (So-in et al., 2010), WiMAX systems have several holes to fill in, for example, polling mechanism, back-off and overhead optimization, and so on. WiMAX can support reliable transmission with Automatic Retransmission Request (ARQ) and Hybrid ARQ (HARQ)

Table 4. Scheduling mechanisms

Scheduler	Channel Aware	DL/ UL	Decision Parameter	Pros	Cons
RR	No	Both	None	Very simple	Unfair (variable packet size), cannot meet QoS requirements
WRR		Both	Static weights	Simple; meets the throughput guarantee	Unfair (variable packet size)
DRR		DL	Fixed quantum	Simple, supports variable packet sizes	Not fair on a short time
WFQ		Both	Dynamic weights	Supports throughput and delay, Fairness	Complex
EDF		Both	Deadline	Meets the relative delay guarantee	Greedy in decision, starves the connections with high deadline. Needs to know the arrival time of the packets.
mSIR	Yes	Both	SNR	Highest system throughput	SSs having a poor SIR may be scheduled after an excessive delay. Not useable for real-time connections.
TRS		Both	Removal time and SNR	High system throughput. Useful for mobile stations.	not useable for real-time connections.
ODRR		UL	SNR	High system throughput.	SSs having a poor SIR may not be serves.
FQFS		DL	SNR, delay and jitter for rtPS and throughput for nrtPS connections	High system throughput. Supports throughput and delay, Fairness.	Complex. Don't supports throughput for rtPS connections
FIS		Both	SNR, delay for rtPS and throughput for nrtPS connections	High system throughput. Supports throughput and delay.	Complex

(Sayenko, Alanen, & Hamalainen, 2008). Future research on scheduling should consider the use of these characteristics. The use of Multiple-Input Multiple-Output (MIMO) with multiple antennas to increase the bandwidth makes the scheduling problem even more sophisticated. Also, the multihops scenario also needs to be investigated for end-to-end service guarantees. With user mobility, future schedulers need to handle base station selection and hand-off. All these issues are still open for research and new discoveries.

CONCLUSION

In this chapter, we present the state of the art of WiMAX scheduling mechanisms. Firstly, we present the features of the WiMAX PHY and MAC layers and of the WiMAX scheduling classes. The main components of MAC layer are also presented. After that, we explained the key issues and challenges existing in the development of scheduling mechanisms. A classification of the scheduling mechanisms was also made. So, we present a synthesis table of the scheduling mechanisms performance where we highlight the main points of each of them.

All the proposed WiMAX algorithms could not be studied in this chapter, but we have shown some relevant proposals. The goals of the scheduling mechanisms are basically to meet QoS guarantees for all service class, to maximize the system throughput, to maintain fairness, to have less complexity, and so on. Each algorithm has its own characteristics.

Classic algorithms generally are simple in complexity. However, they do not explicitly consider all the required QoS parameters of the traffic classes in WiMAX. Moreover, these algorithms do not consider SNR of connections; therefore system throughput is decreased using these methods. The cross-layer algorithms consider some QoS

requirements of deferent traffic such as the average delay, average throughput in WiMAX. Main advantage of these algorithms is the consideration the channel quality of connections. Generally, current scheduling algorithms only provide some limited aspects of QoS; because, it is difficult or even impossible to design mathematical models. The difficulty may result from time-dependent system behaviors, dynamics, and uncertainty in wireless communication environment. Knowledge base and expert systems perform well under these conditions. However, the proposed intelligent systems do not consider all QoS parameters in decisions.

REFERENCES

Ali, N. A., Dhrona, P., & Hassanein, H. S. (2008). A performance study of scheduling algorithms in point-to-multipoint WiMAX networks. In *Proceedings of IEEE Conference on Local Computer Networks (LCN 2008)*. Montreal, Canada: IEEE.

Ali, N. A., Dhrona, P., & Hassanein, H. S. (2009). A performance study of scheduling algorithms in point-to-multipoint WiMAX networks. *Computer Communications*, *32*, 511–521. doi:10.1016/j.comcom.2008.09.015

Ball, C. F., Treml, F., Gaube, X., & Klein, A. (2005). Performance analysis of temporary removal scheduling applied to mobile WiMAX scenarios in tight frequency reuse. In *Proceedings of the 16th Annual IEEE International Symposium on Personal Indoor and Mobile Radio Communications*. IEEE.

Ball, C. F., Treml, F., Ivanov, K., & Humburg, E. (2006). Performance evaluation of IEEE802.16 WiMAX scenarios with fixed and mobile subscribers in tight reuse. *Eur Trans Telecommun*, *17*(1), 203–218. doi:10.1002/ett.1102

Belghith, A., & Nuaymi, L. (2008). *Design and implementation of a QoS-included WiMAX module for NS-2 simulator*. Paper presented at the First International Conference on Simulation Tools and Techniques for Communications Networks and Systems, SIMUTools 2008. Marseille, France.

Borin, J. F., & da Fonseca, N. L. S. (2007). Uplink scheduling with quality of service in IEEE 802.16 networks. In *Proceedings of the 50th Annual IEEE Global Telecommunications Conference (GLOBECOM '07)*, (pp. 2503–2508). Washington, DC: IEEE.

Chen, C., Lee, J., Wu, C., & Kuo, C. (2009). Fairness and QoS guarantees of WiMAX OFDMA scheduling with fuzzy controls. *EURASIP Journal on Wireless Communications and Networking*. doi:10.1155/2009/512507

Chen, J., Jiao, W., & Guo, Q. (2005). An integrated QoS control architecture for IEEE 802.16 broadband wireless access systems. In *Proceedings of Global Telecommunications Conference*, GLOBECOM'05. ACM.

Chuck, D., Chen, K. Y., & Chang, J. M. (2010). A comprehensive analysis of bandwidth request mechanisms in IEEE 802.16 networks. *IEEE Transactions on Vehicular Technology*, *59*(4), 2046–2056. doi:10.1109/TVT.2010.2040642

Cicconetti, C. et al. (2006). Quality of service support in IEEE 802.16 networks. *IEEE Network*, *20*(2), 50–55. doi:10.1109/MNET.2006.1607896

Delicado, J., Delicado, F. M., & Orozco-Barbosa, L. (2012). *RPSF: A new QoS bandwidth request mechanism for the IEEE 802.16*. J Telecommun Syst. doi:10.1007/s11235-010-9392-1

Esmailpour, A., & Nasser, N. (2009). Packet scheduling scheme with quality of service support for mobile WiMAX networks. In *Proceedings of IEEE WLN* (pp. 1040–1045). IEEE.

Fattah, H., & Leung, C. (2002). An overview of scheduling algorithms in wireless multimedia networks. *IEEE Wireless Communications*, *9*(5), 76–83. doi:10.1109/MWC.2002.1043857

Hall, J., & Mars, P. (1998). *Satisfying QoS with a learning based scheduling algorithm*. Durham, NC: School of Engineering, University of Durham. doi:10.1109/IWQOS.1998.675236

Hussain, M. A. R., et al. (2009). Comparative study of scheduling algorithms in WiMAX. In *Proceedings of National Conference on Recent Developments in Computing and its Applications (NCRDCA '09)*. New Delhi, India: NCRDCA.

IEEE 802.16 Working Group. (2004). *IEEE standard for local and metropolitan area networks – Part 16: Air interface for fixed broadband wireless access systems*. Author.

Karim, A. et al. (2010). Modeling and resource allocation for mobile video over WiMAX broadband wireless networks. *IEEE Journal on Selected Areas in Communications*, *28*(3), 354–365. doi:10.1109/JSAC.2010.100407

Khalil, A., & Ksentini, A. (2007). Classification of the uplink scheduling algorithms in IEEE 802.16. In *Proceedings of International Workshop on Dynamic Networking (IWDYN' 07)*. IWDYN.

Khan, M. A. S. et al. (2010). Performance evaluation and enhancement of uplink scheduling algorithms in point to multipoint WiMAX networks. *European Journal of Scientific Research*, *42*(3), 491–506.

Kwon, T., Lee, H., Choi, S., Kim, J., Cho, D.-H., & Cho, S. et al. (2005). Design and implementation of a simulator based on a cross-layer protocol between MAC and PHY layers in a WiBro compatible IEEE 802.16e OFDMA system. *IEEE Communications Magazine*, *43*(12), 136–146. doi:10.1109/MCOM.2005.1561931

Lera, A., Molinaro, A., & Pizzi, S. (2007). Channel-aware scheduling for QoS and fairness provisioning in IEEE 802.16/WiMAX broadband wireless access systems. *IEEE Network, 21*(5), 34–41. doi:10.1109/MNET.2007.4305171

Lihua, W., Wenchao, M., & Zihua, G. (2007). A cross-layer packet scheduling and sub channel allocation scheme in 802.16e OFDMA system. In *Proceedings of Wireless Communications and Networking Conference*, (pp. 1865–1870). IEEE.

Liu, Q. et al. (2006). A cross-layer scheduling algorithm with QoS support in wireless networks. *IEEE Transactions on Vehicular Technology, 55*(3), 839–847. doi:10.1109/TVT.2006.873832

Lu, J., & Ma, M. (2011). Cross-layer MAC protocol and holistic opportunistic scheduling with adaptive power control for QoS in WiMAX. *J Wireless Pers Commun., 61*, 19–40. doi:10.1007/s11277-010-9996-5

Ma, M., & Lu, J. (2009). QoS provisioning mechanism in WiMAX. In M. Ma (Ed.), *Current technology developments of WiMAX systems*. Berlin: Springer. doi:10.1007/978-1-4020-9300-5_5

Misra, S., Banerjee, B., & Wolfinger, B. E. (2012). *A learning automata-based uplink scheduler for supporting real-time multimedia interactive traffic in IEEE 802.16 WiMAX networks*. ComCom. doi:10.1016/j.comcom.2012.06.016

Naja, R., Helou, M. E., & Tohmé, S. (2012). *WiMAX double movable boundary scheme in the vehicle to infrastructure communication scenario*. J Wireless Pers Commun. doi:10.1007/s11277-011-0389-1

Parekh, A., & Gallager, R. (1993). A generalized processor sharing approach to flow control in integrated services networks: The single node case. *IEEE/ACM Transactions on Networking, 1*, 344–357. doi:10.1109/90.234856

Rath, H. K., Bhorkar, A., & Sharma, V. (2006). *An opportunistic DRR (O-DRR) uplink scheduling scheme for IEEE 802.16-based broadband wireless networks*. Paper presented at the IETE International Conference on Next Generation Networks (ICNGN). Mumbai, India.

Sadri, Y., & Khanmohamadi, S. (2013). An intelligent scheduling system using fuzzy logic controller for management of services in WiMAX networks. *The Journal of Supercomputing*. doi: doi:10.1007/s11227-010-0523-y

Sadri, Y., & Khanmohammadi, S. (2013). A QoS aware dynamic scheduling scheme using fuzzy inference system for IEEE 802.16 networks. *Wireless Personal Communications*. doi:10.1007/s11277-013-1138-4

Sayenko, A., Alanen, O., & Hamalainen, T. (2008). ARQ aware scheduling for the IEEE 802.16 base station. In *Proc. IEEE Int. Conf. Communications*. Beijing, China: IEEE.

Sheu, T.L., & Huang, K.C. (2011). Adaptive bandwidth allocation model for multiple traffic classes in IEEE 802.16 worldwide interoperability for microwave access networks. *IET Communications, 5*(1), 90–98. doi:10.1049/iet-com.2010.0005

So-in, C., Jain, R., & Tamimi, A. (2010). Scheduling in IEEE 802.16e mobile WiMAX networks: Key issues and a survey. *IEEE Journal on Selected Areas in Communications, 27*(2), 156–151. doi:10.1109/JSAC.2009.090207

Song, J., Li, J., & Li, C. (2009). A cross-layer scheduling algorithm based on genetic algorithm. In *Proceeding of the Seventh Annual Communication Networks and Services Research Conference*. Moncton.

Taghipoor, M., Tavassoli, G., & Hosseini, V. (2010). *Guarantee QoS in WiMAX networks with learning automata*. Paper presented at ITNG 2010. Las Vegas, NV.

Tanenbaum, A. S., & Steen, M. V. (2007). *Distributed systems: Principles paradigms* (2nd ed.). Academic Press.

Teixeira, M. A., & Guardieiro, P. R. (2012). Scheduling mechanisms. In R. C. Hincapie, & J. E. Sierra (Eds.), *Quality of service and resource allocation in WiMAX*. InTech.

Tsai, T., Jiang, C., & Wang, C. (2006). CAC and packet scheduling using token bucket for IEEE 802.16networks. *The Journal of Communication*, *1*(2), 30–37.

Wengerter, C., Ohlhorst, J., & vonElbwart, A. G. E. (2005). Fairness and throughput analysis for generalized proportional fair frequency scheduling in OFDMA. In *Proceedings of the 61st IEEE Vehicular Technology Conference (VTC '05)*, (vol. 3, pp. 1903–1907). Stockholm, Sweden: IEEE.

WiMAX Forum. (2008). *WiMAX system evaluation methodology V2.1*. Retrieved from http://www.wimaxforum.org/technology/documents/

Wongthavarawat, K., & Ganz, A. (2003). Packet scheduling for QoS support in IEEE 802.16 broadband wireless access systems. *International Journal of Communication Systems*, *16*(1), 81–96. doi:10.1002/dac.581

Chapter 13
Analysis of VoIP Traffic over the IEEE 802.16 Protocol

Luis Ortiz
National Autonomous University of Mexico, Mexico

Victor Rangel
National Autonomous University of Mexico, Mexico

Javier Gomez
National Autonomous University of Mexico, Mexico

Miguel Lopez-Guerrero
Metropolitan Autonomous University – Iztapalapa, Mexico

ABSTRACT

Voice over Internet Protocol (VoIP) is one of the fastest growing applications for the Internet today and is a very important service because mobile users can utilize voice services more cheaply compared with most mobile systems. A crucial application over these networks is VoIP over the Worldwide Interoperability for Microwave Access (WiMAX), which is one of the technologies in Broadband Access Networks based on IEEE 802.16 standards. It provides high throughput broadband connections over long distances, which supports Point to Multi-Point (PMP) wireless access. A hurdle, however, is the number of voice connections that can be supported. Since VoIP requires short end-to-end delays, supporting as many VoIP users as possible in a mobile broadband wireless access network, considering limited radio resources, becomes a very important issue. In this chapter, the authors use a theoretical model and an algorithm to evaluate the performance of some of the most important VoIP codecs.

INTRODUCTION

Broadband Wireless Access (BWA) networks will revolutionize the way wireless communication is used today for the transmission of mobile, nomadic and fixed digital applications and services for the next generation of cellular systems. Global trends

indicate that Long Term Evolution (LTE) release 8 (LTE Standard, 2009), LTE-Advanced (LTE release 10, 2011) and IEEE 802.16m-2011 (IEEE 802.16m, 2011) will emerge as new technologies to provide data rates above 300 Mbps, or even higher than 1 Gbps with advanced PHY (physical) layer characteristics. These new systems are

DOI: 10.4018/978-1-4666-4888-3.ch013

the best BWA technologies that will support the increased demand of fourth generation (4G) traffic, which will include a larger number of subscribers and active simultaneous requested services per a mobile user such as video conferencing and video streaming applications using a very large radio bandwidth.

BWA has become the best option to meet residential and small business demand for high speed Internet access and multimedia services. However, the wide-scale adoption of BWA systems will be determined by its ability to overcome cost and performance barriers. If BWA can meet these challenges, it could easily be the next revolution in wireless systems after WLAN.

The great demand for high speed Internet access, voice and video applications, combined with the global tendency to use wireless devices, have given sprouting for BWA networks. A solution for BWA networks are the IEEE 802.16m-2011 and the IEEE 802.16e-2005 (IEEE 802.16e, 2005) standards which supports mobility speeds up to 120 km/h with an asymmetrical link structure and allows Subscriber Stations (SSs) to have a handheld form factor, well suited for mobile devices, like PDAs (Personal Digital Assistants), cell phones, laptops, tablets, among others.

The diverse options offered by the BWA standards have increased the interest of the research community, manufactures, and operators about what type of performance can be expected from IEEE 802.16-2004 (IEEE 802.16, 2004), IEEE 802.16e-2005 and recently IEEE 802.16m-2011 protocols in the near future. In the rest of this chapter we refer to these three versions of the standard only as IEEE 802.16.

As the BWA has had one of the most notable growing up in recent years on the telecommunications industry's history, the growing up has driven the demand of high speed Internet data services. Broadband users around the world hope these services can support speed web browsing, high data rates on file downloads, interactive games

and real time multimedia applications as such as conferences and VoIP (Voice over IP) services.

With the constant development of mobile devices a great deal of attention has been attracted by VoIP services, because it is expected to be widely supported by mobile wireless networks, such as the IEEE 802.16 protocol. These multimedia applications are very important because mobile users can utilize VoIP services cheaper than mostly actual mobile systems. Therefore, supporting as many VoIP users as possible in a mobile wireless network using limited radio resources is a very important issue.

However, performance of VoIP services is affected by several issues defined in the IEEE 802.16 standard, as such as signaling overhead of MAP messages, ranging regions and wasted symbols due to "rectangulation and quantization", among others.

Here we defined "rectangulation" as the process of allocating bandwidth resources in the downlink (DL) channel on a square or rectangle region of the frame structure. Also we defined "quantization" as the process of allocating these resources using the minimum allocation unit, denominated "quantum map". Considering Partial Usage of Sub-Channels (PUSC), a quantum map or a slot in the DL channel is one subchannel per two OFDMA (Orthogonal Frequency Division Multiple Access) symbols. A quantum map in the uplink (UL) channel is one subchannel per three OFDMA symbols, as we depicted in Figure 1.

These settings seriously affect VoIP service performance because a VoIP packet allocation generally does not fit well in the DL and UL reservation space and usually multiple quantum maps are required. Signaling overhead of MAP messages also affects VoIP services, because such overhead increases when the Base Station (BS) schedules small-sized VoIP packets.

Some studies have evaluated VoIP performance taking into consideration mapping overhead (So, 2007) and (So 2009). However, in these studies neither wasted resources in the DL channel due to

Figure 1. Quantum map dimensions for DL and UL channels

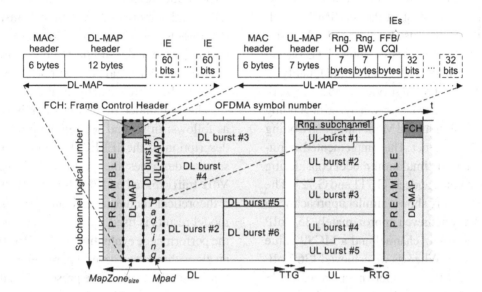

quantization and rectangulation were considered nor ranging and contention signaling on the UL channel were taken into account. A previous work presented an analytical model to evaluate VoIP performance (So, 2008). This study takes into account the quantization and ranging regions in the DL and UL channels, respectively. However, wasted symbols due to rectangulation were not considered. The performance of some speech codecs has been evaluated in (Kaarthick, Yeshwenth, Nagarajan & Rajeev, 2009) and (Lee, Kim & Cho, 2008). In (Lee, Kim & Cho, 2008) wasted symbols were considered, however they were considered as a result of variations of VoIP inter-arrival times and packet sizes. Moreover, in (Kaarthick, Yeshwenth, Nagarajan & Rajeev, 2009) and (Lee, Kim & Cho, 2008), the mapping overhead was not considered and the performance optimization of speech codecs based on OFDMA symbols for UL and DL channels was not approached.

Other study has evaluated the performance of VoIP services (Yu, Wang, & Zhang, 2009). In this study a novel uplink performance analysis model focusing on the VoIP services in TDD-OFDMA (Time Division Duplex-Orthogonal Frequency Division Multiple Access) based WiMAX net-

work is proposed. Here a two-state MMPP was used to model the aggregated VoIP traffic. They also implemented a Point-To-Multipoint (PMP) network model. However, they assume that the channel SNR in each SS is as good enough as achieve the best Modulation and Coding Scheme, this mean they suppose the channel capacity is stable. Although they also consider a fixed VoIP packet length with the same stack protocols (RTP, UDP and IP), the system network model was not overloaded and ranging and contention signaling on the UL channel weren't taken into account.

Persistent scheduling has been used to avoid signaling MAP overhead in (Shrivastava & Vannithamby, 2009), however more signaling overhead could be created to avoid resource wastage due to "resource holes" created when VoIP are de-allocated/reallocated. Moreover loss of MAP containing persistent allocation/de-allocation information could have serious consequences if the error control mechanism doesn't respond quickly. Also, this error control mechanism creates more signaling MAP overhead.

Recently, a similar study has analyzed the performance of VoIP services on a LTE (Long Term Evolution) network in (Asheralieva, Khan

& Mahata, 2011). In this study a Fully Dynamic (FD) and a Semi-Persistent Packet (SMP) scheduling technique was used. This work identifies and analyzes the features of above LTE packet scheduling techniques to enhance the Quality of Service's (QoS) of VoIP services. Here, the VoIP capacity of a LTE network was analyzed depending on channel bandwidth and Modulation and Coding Schemes (MCS) values. They implemented a similar OPNET based simulation model considering two different voice codecs: G.711 and G.723. The results of this study show a similar approach with our study. They achieved approximately 35 VoIP users using a 5MHz channel and a MCS9 value for G.711 codec. Whereas we achieved 136 VoIP users with a 20MHz channel and a similar MCS (16-QAM3/4). This mean we almost achieved four times the number of VoIP users using a channel bandwidth four times greater than the channel bandwidth they used. However, considering G.723 codec they achieved 150 VoIP users using the 5MHz channel and the MCS9 value while we achieved 720 VoIP users considering 16-QAM3/4 MCS and the 20MHz channel. This is more than four times the number of VoIP users they achieved. In few words our proposal can compete with new technologies and even could be better.

In this chapter, we present a performance optimization of a mobile WiMAX network in order to support the maximum number of VoIP streams, using most common codecs: G.711, G.729, G.728 and G.723.1. A theoretical model was used which considers several issues that affects the performance of VoIP codecs, as such as wasted symbols due to rectangulation and quantization, signaling overhead of MAP messages, ranging regions from the UL channel, and a balanced amount of OFDMA symbols for each channel (UL and DL), to compensate the signaling overhead of MAP messages in the DL channel. Several modulations and codifications were taken into account in order to evaluate the performance of different VoIP codecs using three packet encapsulations types: without Header Suppression (-HS), with

Header Suppression (+HS) (Rangel, 2002; ETSI, 2001) and compressed Real-time Transport Protocol (+cRTP) (Casner & Jacobson, 1999). We also implemented a simulation model to analyze end-to-end delays and other important issues that could not be approached by the theoretical model.

The remainder of this chapter is organized as follows: In second section we present a brief description of the IEEE 802.16 protocol. Third section describes the performance analysis of VoIP traffic based on IEEE 802.16 systems; here a theoretical model to validate the simulations model results is used. In section four we present the performance evaluation for VoIP traffic using an algorithm to test several parameter configurations. Finally, section five presents and discusses the conclusions of this chapter.

IEEE 802.16 PROTOCOL DESCRIPTION

The Medium Access Control (MAC) protocol of the IEEE 802.16 standard defines both Frequency Division Duplex (FDD) and Time Division Duplex (TDD) transmission technics. A DL channel conducts transmissions from a BS to SSs, with Point Multi Point (PMP) wireless access using a frequency channel for FDD or a time signaling frame for TDD. Here, multiple SSs share one slotted UL channel via TDD on a demand basis for voice, data and multimedia traffic. Upon receiving the demand for bandwidth, the BS handles bandwidth allocation by assigning UL grants based on requests from SSs. A typical signaling frame for TDD includes a DL subframe and a UL subframe. In turn, the DL subframe includes a Preamble, Frame Control Header (FCH), and a number of data bursts for SSs as is depicted in Figure 2.

The Preamble is used for synchronization and equalizations, and contains a predefined sequence of well-known symbols at the receiver. The FCH specifies the burst profile and length of at least one DL burst immediately following the FCH.

Figure 2. Frame structure for IEEE 802.16 MAC protocol

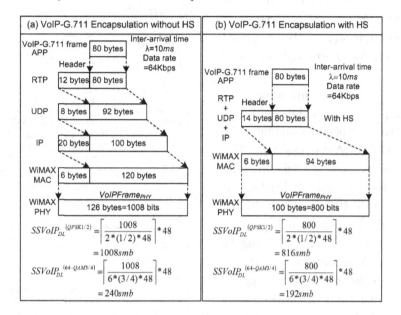

The DL-MAP and UL-MAP are MAC management messages that include Information Elements (IEs) in order to define the access and the burst start time in the DL and UL direction, respectively. These messages are broadcasted by the BS following the transmission of the FCH.

Upon entering the BWA network, each SS has to go through the Initialization and Registration process setup as define the IEEE 802.16 standard. After this setup is completed, a SS can create one or more connections over which their data are transmitted to and from the BS. SSs request transmission opportunities using the UL subframe. The BS collects these requests and determines the number of ODFMA symbols (grant size) that each SS will be allowed to transmit in the UL subframe. This information is broadcasted in the DL channel by the BS in each UL-MAP. The UL-MAP message contains the IE which describes the use of the UL subframe, such as maintenance, contention and reservation access. After receiving the UL-MAP, a SS will transmit data in the predefined reserved ODFMA symbols indicated in their corresponding IEs. These ODFMA symbols are transmission opportunities assigned by the BS

using a QoS class, such as UGS (Unsolicited Grant Service) for CBR (Constant Bit Rate) traffic, rtPS (real-time Polling Service) and ertPS (extended real-time Polling Service) for VBR (Variable Bit Rate), nrtPS (non real-time Polling Service) for non real-time bursty traffic, and BE (Best Effort) for traffic such as Internet, email and all other non real-time traffic.

PERFORMANCE ANALISYS OF VOIP TRAFFIC

In this section, we present the performance analysis of the IEEE 802.16 MAC protocol when VoIP traffic is transmitted using a 20 MHz channel. The theoretical model we have derived for the performance analysis can also be used to study other applications. However, in this study we evaluate CBR traffic to stress the network with short VoIP packets, when the service class UGS is used. From Figure 2, we can see that the DL subframe comprises of a Preamble, a FCH (Frame Control Header), a DL-MAP message, a UL-MAP message and DL bursts. According to the standard

(IEEE Std. 802.16e, 2005) Preamble and FCH are constant sizes, but DL-MAP and UL-MAP are of variable size. Here DL bursts are also constants since they are used to transport fixed-size VoIP frames.

Therefore in order to know the number of VoIP streams supported in the DL subframe ($VoIPstreams_{DL}$), we just need to compute the available number of OFDMA symbols at the PHY layer in the DL subframe (Avl_{smbDL}), take away the overhead (FCH, DL-MAP and UL-MAP), and compute how many DL VoIP bursts fits in the last symbols, (considering the total wasted symbols, if so). Similarly, we follow the same procedure to compute the number of VoIP streams supported in the UL subframe ($VoIPstreams_{UL}$). We just need to compute the available number or OFDMA symbols at the PHY layer in the UL subframe (Avl_{smbUL}), take away the ranging regions and computing how many UL VoIP bursts fits in the last symbols (in this case there are no wasted symbols). Finally, the maximum number of VoIP streams supported ($MaxVoIPstreams$) in a 20 MHz channel for the transmission of voice traffic will be the minimum of $VoIPstreams_{DL}$ and $VoIPstreams_{UL}$:

Theoretical Model

For the modeling of the IEEE 802.16 protocol, we used the parameters given in Table 1. These parameters include the default values given by the standard (IEEE Std. 802.16e, 2005). As the grants (used to transmit data traffic) have to be reserved in quantum map units, the available number of OFDMA symbols has to be rounded to multiples of quantum maps. Hence, the available number of OFDMA symbols in the DL subframe is given by Equation (1):

$$Avl_{smbDL} = \left| \frac{OFDMA_{smbDL} - 1}{Qsmb_{DL}} \right| * Qsmb_{DL} * Data_{sbcrDL}$$

(1)

Table 1. MAC and PHY layer parameters for a 20 MHz channel

Parameter	Definition	Default Value	
$Frame_d$	Frame duration	5ms	
FCH_{sbch}	FCH subchannels	1	
FCH_{smb}	FCH symbols	2	
FFB_{smb}	Symbols for Fast Feed Back Channel Quality Information (FFB/CQI)	6	
FFB_{sbch}	Subchannels for FFB/CQI.	1	
$IErng_{bytes}$	Ranging information element size (bytes)	7	
$MACHdr_{bytes}$	MAC header (bytes)	6	
N	Number of VoIP streams	-	
$OFDMA_{smb}$	OFDMA symbols (see Table 2)	θ[0-5]	
Rng_{smbBW}	Symbols for ranging and Band Width (BW) request	1	
Rng_{smbHO}	Symbols for ranging HandOff (HO)	2	
Rng_{sbchBW}	Subchannels for ranging and BW request	6	
Rng_{sbchHO}	Subchannels for ranging HO	6	
		Subframe	
		UL	DL
$Data_{sbcr}$	Data Subcarriers	1120	1440
$IEsize_{bits}$	Information element size (bits)	32	60
$MapHdr_{bytes}$	Map header (bytes)	7	12
$Qsmb$	Quantum symbol size	3	2
$RepCnt$	Repetition count	1	4
$SbCh$	Subchannels	70	60
$SbCr_{sbch}$	Subcarriers per Subchannel	16	24

here we have taken out one OFDMA symbol for the Preamble, where: $OFDMA_{smbDL}$ - number of OFDMA symbols used in the DL subframe, $Qsmb_{DL}$ - quantum symbol size for the DL subframe (in OFDMA symbols), $Data_{sbcr}$ - data subcarriers in the DL subframe.

According to the standard (IEEE Std., 2005), $OFDMA_{smbDL}$ can be set to different values (denoted by "θ" in Table 2). Thus, DL and UL subframes

Table 2. UL and DL subframe configuration

Configuration	$OFDMA_{smb}$	
	UL	DL
θ0	9	38
θ1	12	35
θ2	15	32
θ3	18	29
θ4	21	26
θ5	24	23

can have a different number of OFDMA symbols as shown in Figure 3. For each VoIP codec, modulation and codification, we derived an algorithm that chooses the best configuration from Table 2 in order to achieve the maximum number of VoIP streams on each channel.

One of the performance problems is the *"signaling overhead of control messages"* (SOCM) consumed in the DL subframe. This is the space consumed in the DL subframe by the FCH, DL-MAP and UL-MAP. The map zone size ($MapZone_{size}$) computes the number of OFDMA symbols consumed by SOCM as the number of VoIP streams increases. Thus, $MapZone_{size}$ is given by:

$$MapZone_{size} = FCH_{size} + Map_{sizeDL} + Map_{sizeUL} \qquad (2)$$

where Map_{sizeDL} is the length of the DL-MAP subframe; Map_{sizeUL} is the length of the UL-MAP subframe as shown in Figure 2; and FCH_{size} is the length of the frame control header given by:

$$FCH_{size} = \left\lceil \frac{FCH_{smb} * FCH_{sbch} * SbCr_{sbchDL}}{Qmap_{DL}} \right\rceil * Qmap_{DL} * RepCnt_{DL} \qquad (3)$$

where FCH_{smb}, FCH_{sbch} and $SbCr_{sbchDL}$ are the number of OFDMA symbols, the number of subchannels and the number of subcarriers per subchannel assigned to the FCH region, respectively; $RepCnt_{DL}$ is the DL repetition count; and $Qmap_{DL}$ is the DL quantum map given by:

$$Qmap_{DL} = Qsmb_{DL} * SbCr_{sbchDL} \qquad (4)$$

where $Qsmb_{DL}$ is the length of the quantum symbol in the DL subframe. In (3) we rounded the FCH size to multiples of the minimum reservation unit in the DL channel, the DL Quantum MAP ($Qmap_{DL}$).

The DL-MAP subframe contains Information Elements (IEs) used by the SSs to decode their grants in the DL subframe. The DL-MAP size (Map_{sizeDL}) depends on the number of VoIP streams (N) allocated in the DL subframe. Therefore the DL-MAP size is defined as Equation 5 in Box 1

Box 1. Equation 5

$$Map_{sizeDL} = \left\lceil \frac{\left(MACHdr_{bytes} + MapHdr_{bytesDL}\right) * 8 + N * IEsize_{bitsDL}}{Qmap_{DL}} \right\rceil \left(\frac{Qmap_{DL}}{RepCnt_{DL}^{-1}} \right);$$

for $N = 0, 1, 2, 3, \ldots$

Figure 3. Variable number of OFDMA symbols for DL and UL subframes

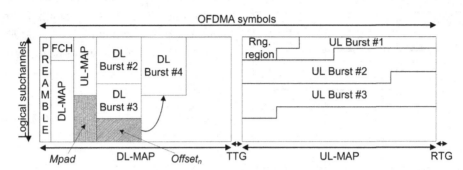

where $MACHdr_{bytes}$ is the generic MAC header; $MapHdr_{bytesDL}$ is the DL-MAP header; and $IEsize_{bitsDL}$ is the DL IE size as is shown at the top of Figure 2.

In (3) and (5), $RepCnt_{DL}$ is used because the BS must ensure that SOCM for SSs operation are correctly received. Similarly, we computed the UL-MAP size as Equation 6 in Box 2 where $MapHdr_{bytesUL}$ is the UL-MAP header; $IErng_{bytes}$ is the Ranging IE size; $IEsize_{bitsUL}$ is the UL IE size; and $RepCnt_{UL}$ is the UL repetition count.

In (6), $IErng_{bytes}$ is used by the HO region, the BW Requests region and the FFB/CQI region. Then, the number of VoIP streams supported in the DL subframe is defined by Equation 7 in Box 3 where $CIntArv_{time}$ is the codec inter-arrival time

(see Table 3); $Frame_d$ is the Frame duration; $SS\text{-}VoIP_{DL}$ is the DL VoIP stream size; $Mpad$ is the padding of map zone wasted by $MapZone_{size}$; and $Wstsmb_{(N)}$ is the total wasted symbols in the DL subframe.

Both $Mpad$ and $Wstsmb_{(N)}$ are wasted symbols due to rectangulation and quantization. $max(N)$ means the maximum N such that $Avl_{smbDL}-MapZone_{size}-N*SSVoIP_{DL}-Mpad-Wstsmb_{(N)} \geq 0$. In order to compute $SSVoIP_{DL}$ we need to obtain the VoIP frame size at the PHY layer ($VoIPFrame_{PHY}$) and then apply the modulation and codification overhead factor. Thus, the DL VoIP stream size is defined by:

Box 2. Equation 6

$$Map_{sizeUL} = \left\lceil \frac{\left(MACHdr_{bytes} + MapHdr_{bytesUL} + 3*IErng_{bytes}\right)*8 + N*IEsize_{bitsUL}}{Qmap_{DL}} \right\rceil \left(\frac{Qmap_{DL}}{RepCnt_{UL}^{-1}}\right);$$

for $N = 0,1,2,3,\ldots$

Box 3. Equation 7

$$VoIPstreams_{DL} = \frac{CIntArv_{time}*max(N)}{Frame_d} \left| Avl_{smbDL} - MapZone_{size} - N*SSVoIP_{DL} - Mpad - Wstsmb_{(N)} \geq 0;\right.$$

for $N = 0,1,2,3,\ldots$

Table 3. Codecs characteristics

Codec	Bit Rate	Codec Inter-Arrival Time (ms) $CIntArv_{time}$	VoIP Frame Size (Application Layer)
G.711	64 Kbps	10	80 bytes
G.723	5.3 Kbps	30	20 bytes
G.726	32 Kbps	10	40 bytes
G.728	16 Kbps	2.5	40 bits (5 bytes)
G.729	8 Kbps	10	10 bytes

$$SSVoIP_{DL} = \left\lceil \frac{VoIPFrame_{PHY}}{M * cc * Qmap_{DL}} \right\rceil * Qmap_{DL} \quad (8)$$

where *M* is the number of bits per symbol (2 for QPSK, 4 for 16-QAM and 6 for 64-QAM); and *cc* is the convolutional coding rate (1/2, 2/3, 3/4 or 5/6).

For the performance analysis, the most common VoIP codecs were considered, such as G.711, G.723, G.726, G.728 and G.729). These are described as follows:

1. Codec G.711 (ITU-T, 1988) was considered in order to stress the IEEE 802.16 network and because this codec will be used for quality voice calls. G.711 is the mandatory codec according to the ITU-T H.323 conferencing standard (ITU-T, 2009), which uses Pulse Code Modulation to produce a data rate of 64 kbps at the application layer. This codec creates and encapsulates an 80-byte VoIP frame every 10 ms.

2. According to the ITU, IETF and the VoIP Forum, G.723.1 (G.723 from now on); (ITU-T, 2006) is the preferred speech codec

for Internet telephony applications. This codec generates a data rate of 5.3 kbps at the application layer, where a 20-byte VoIP frame is generated every 30 ms.

3. Codec G.726 uses Adaptive Differential Pulse Code Modulation (ADPCM) scheme according to the ITU G.726 recommendation (ITU-T, 1990). This codec generates a data rate of 32 kbps at the application layer, where a 40-byte VoIP frame is generated every 10 ms.

4. According ITU 6.728 recommendation (ITU-T, 1992), codec G.728 uses Low-Delay Code Exited Linear Prediction (LD-CELP) and generates a data rate of 16 kbps at the application layer and a 40-bit VoIP frame is generated every 2.5 ms.

5. Codec G.729 uses Conjugate-Structure Algebraic-Code-Excited Linear Prediction (CS-ACELP) speech compression algorithm, approved by ITU (ITU-T, 2007). It is mostly used in VoIP applications where bandwidth must be conserved. It generates a 10-byte VoIP frame every 10 ms, producing a data rate of 8 kbps.

As an example to obtain the $SSVoIP_{DL}$, Figure 4 illustrates the encapsulation process for G.711 and G.723 codecs using two different modulations QPSK1/2 (*M*=2, *cc*=1/2) and 64-QAM3/4 (*M*=6, *cc*=3/4).

According to (Ortiz et al, 2011) and (Rangel, 2002), header suppression (HS) is possible, so we can disregard fixed fields of the RTP, UDP and IP headers. This results in a reduction from 40-bytes to 14-bytes of header as shown in Figure 4. This reduction of RTP+UDP+IP headers (VoIP frame overhead), will increase system performance as indicated in the following sections.

Figure 4. VoIP encapsulation for G.711 and G.723 codecs, with and without header suppression

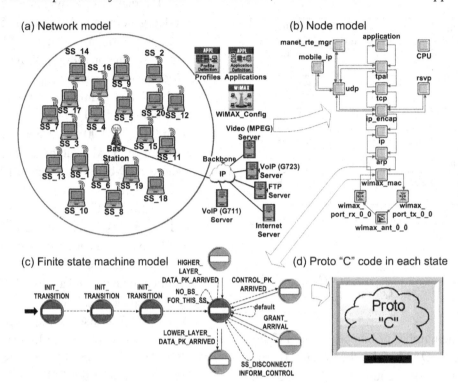

As we mentioned, padding symbols are wasted by the $MapZone_{size}$, this is because the map zone has to fill the symbols from the last subchannels to form a rectangle region, as it is shown in Figure 2. Thus wasted padding symbols by the $MapZone_{size}$ are defined by Equation 9 in Box 4.

With each grant being allocated at the last subchannels of the DL subframe, it could be possible that data allocation does not fit well into these subchannels. So, data allocation has to be moved to start at the next OFDMA symbol of the first subchannel. This generates an offset as is shown in Figure 5.

Thus, the offset generated by the *n*th data allocation is defined as Equation 10 in Box 5 where $SbCh_{DL}$ are subchannels on the DL subframe. This expression considers the previous VoIP streams already allocated in the DL subframe ((n-1)*$SSVoIP_{DL}$) and the total wasted symbols due to all previous data allocations in the DL subframe ($Wstsmb_{(n-1)}$).

Therefore, the total wasted symbols in the DL subframe due to N VoIP streams allocations is obtained as:

Box 4. Equation 9

$$Mpad = \left(\left\lceil \frac{MapZone_{size}}{Qsmb_{DL} * Data_{sbcrDL}} \right\rceil * Qsmb_{DL} * Data_{sbcrDL} \right) - MapZone_{size}$$

Figure 5. Offset generated by data allocation

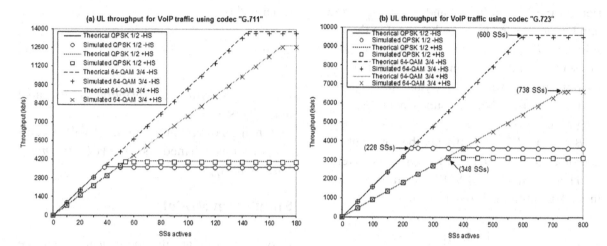

Box 5. Equation 10

$$Offset_n = \left| SbCh_{DL} - Mod \left(\frac{\dfrac{(n-1) * SSVoIP_{DL} + Wstsmb_{(n-1)}}{Qmap_{DL}}}{SbCh_{DL}} \right) \right| * Qmap_{DL}; \qquad \text{for n} \geq 1$$

$$Wstsmb_{(N)} = \sum_{n=1}^{N} Goffset_n \qquad (11)$$

where $Goffset_n$ is the grant offset wasted.

We need to guarantee that $Offset_n$ corresponds to a grant that was tried to be allocated at the last subchannels of the DL subframe. Hence, the grant offset wasted by the *n*th $SSVoIP_{DL}$ allocation in the DL subframe is defined by:

$$Goffset_n = \begin{cases} Offset_n; & if\ Offset_n < SSVoIP_{DL} \\ 0 & otherwise \end{cases}$$

$$(12)$$

We also need to know the number of VoIP streams supported in the UL subframe. Thus, the available number of OFDMA symbols in the UL subframe (Avl_{smbDL}) is computed as:

$$Avl_{smbUL} = \begin{matrix} \left(\left\lfloor \dfrac{OFDMA_{smbUL}}{Qsmb_{UL}} \right\rfloor * Qsmb_{UL} * Data_{sbcrUL} \right) \\ -Rng_{smbHO} * Rng_{sbchHO} * SbCr_{sbchUL} \\ -Rng_{smbBW} * Rng_{sbchBW} * SbCr_{sbchUL} \\ -FFB_{smb} * FFB_{sbch} * SbCr_{sbchUL} \end{matrix}$$

$$(13)$$

where $OFDMA_{smbUL}$ is the number of OFDMA symbols used in the UL subframe; $Qsmb_{UL}$ is the quantum symbol size for the UL subframe (in

OFDMA symbols); $Data_{sbcrUL}$ is the data subcarriers in the UL subframe; and $SbCr_{sbchUL}$ is the number of subcarriers per subchannel in the UL subframe. Rng_{smbHO} and Rng_{sbchHO} are the number of symbols and subchannels used for ranging handoff, respectively. Rng_{smbBW} and Rng_{sbchBW} are the number of symbols and subchannels used for ranging and bandwidth (BW) request, respectively. FFB_{smb} and FFB_{sbch} are the number of symbols and subchannels used for FFB/CQI, respectively.

Then, the number of VoIP streams supported in the UL subframe is obtained as:

$$VoIPstreams_{UL} = \left(\frac{CIntArv_{time}}{Frame_d} \right) \left\lfloor \frac{Avl_{smbUL}}{SSVoIP_{UL}} \right\rfloor \quad (14)$$

where $SSVoIP_{UL}$ is the UL VoIP stream size given by:

$$SSVoIP_{UL} = \left\lceil \frac{VoIPFrame_{PHY}}{M * cc * Qmap_{UL}} \right\rceil * Qmap_{UL} \quad (15)$$

where $Qmap_{UL}$ is the UL quantum map, which is defined by:

$$Qmap_{UL} = Qsmb_{UL} * SbCr_{sbchUL} \quad (16)$$

where $Qsmb_{UL}$ is the length of the quantum symbol in the UL subframe.

Finally, the maximum number of VoIP streams supported is defined as $min(VoIPstreams_{DL}, VoIPstreams_{UL})$.

Simulation Model

In order to validate the theoretical model, we implemented a WiMAX mobile simulation model based on the OPNET MODELER package v.16. At the top level of the IEEE 802.16 network model are the network components, for example the BS, SSs and servers, as is shown in Figure 6 (a).

The next hierarchical level, Figure 6 (b), defines the functionality of a SS in terms of components such as traffic sources, TCP/UDP, IP, MAC and PHY interfaces. The operation of each component is defined by a Finite State Machine (an example of which is shown in Figure 6 (c).)

Figure 6. IEEE 802.16 simulation model

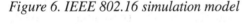

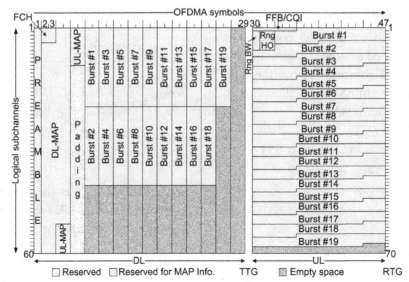

Finally the actions of a component at a particular state are defined in Proto-C code (see Figure 6 (d).) This approach allows modifications to be applied to the operation of the IEEE 802.16 MAC protocol and different optimizations and enhances to be tested. The parameters used for the simulation model were the same as the theoretical model defined in Table 1.

Results

The performance analysis of VoIP traffic in a WiMAX Mobile network is of great importance for the 4G Telecommunications' community. This study determine the maximum number of SS that can support a VoIP phone call so that a WiMAX Mobile network when being implemented in a real scenario is not overloaded. Having an over-dimensioned network would result in a lower system performance.

For the performance analysis we modeled a 20 MHz TDD channel, using the configuration parameters as indicated in Table 1. For the first performance scenario, we evaluated two different codecs, G.711 and G.723. G.711 was chosen because is used for quality voice calls and thus it consumes more allocation resources than the other ones. In contrast, G.723 was chosen because is the preferred speech codec for Internet telephony applications and thus it consumes low allocation resources. For each codec we also employed two modulations: QPSK with convolutional coding = 1/2 (QPSK1/2) and 64-QAM with convolutional coding = 3/4 (64-QAM3/4). This was done with

the target to find out the extremely point for which both codecs can support the maximum number of SS making a VoIP phone call.

Figure 7 shows the network performance in terms of system throughput and Figure 8 shows the mean access delay, for codecs G.711 and G.723, using the theoretical and simulation model.

We considered different frame configurations (see Table 2) in order to evaluate the system throughput and find out the maximum number of VoIP streams supported. In Figure 7 we can see the throughput for the UL direction, both models (theoretical and simulation) were used, and results are in good agreement. We also found the same throughput for the DL direction, thus Figure 7 also applies for the DL channel. In Figure 7a, the maximum number of quality phone calls (*VoIP-streams*) supported was of 38 using G.711 codec with QPSK1/2, without HS (-HS) and θ3. This is the result of having 38 outgoing VoIP streams in the UL subframe and 38 ingoing VoIP streams in the DL subframe.

When HS and θ4 frame configuration is considered this number is increased by 42.1%, so the maximum number of quality phone calls grows to 54. This is because considering HS, the VoIP frame overhead is reduced considerably and more VoIP streams can be allocated. By changing the modulation to 64-QAM3/4 and using a θ3 frame configuration without considering HS, the maximum number of quality phone calls becomes of 144. However, when HS is employed, this number increases to 170 when a θ2 frame configuration is used, resulting in an 18% increase.

Figure 7. Maximum throughput of VoIP traffic in a 20 MHz channel

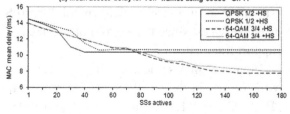

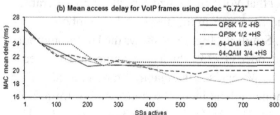

Figure 8. VoIP traffic mean access delay in a 20 MHz channel

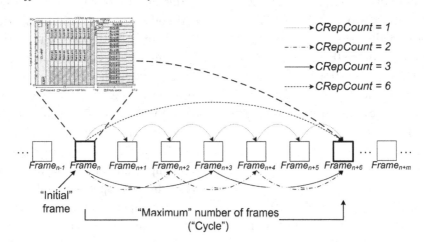

Although more VoIP streams are supported, we can see a throughput reduction (8.13%); this is because considering HS, the resources consumed by the new VoIP streams allocated, are less than the resources consumed by the previous VoIP frame overhead. Thus reducing the throughput from 13.8 Mbps (= 144 SSs * 96 Kbps, where DL-MAP + UL-MAP = 4.1 Msmb/s) to 12.8 Mbps (= 170 SSs * 75.2 Kbps, where DL-MAP + UL-MAP = 4.9 Msmb/s). Moreover in this case, more OFDMA symbols were configured to DL subframe (θ2), to compensate for resources consumed by signaling overheads of MAP messages.

Figure 9 shows the allocations of VoIP streams (bursts) in both directions, DL and UL, where the empty space could not be allocated for the transmission of VoIP traffic, since it is not possible to have fragmented VoIP frames when UGS is used and due to the rectangulation and quantization process. However most of this empty space is allocated for the transmission of more VoIP bursts when 64-QAM3/4 and HS are considered, due the fact that VoIP bursts size is reduced considerable and fits better in the unscheduled symbols.

Similarly, Figure 7b shows the UL throughput for codec G.723, which also applies to DL direction. We can see the maximum number of VoIP phone calls is increased considerably from 228 (with -HS, θ4, QPSK1/2) to 348 (with +HS, θ3, QPSK1/2). Here, there was an increase of 52.6% on VoIP phone calls.

However, these VoIP phone calls are performed with a medium quality, since MOS (Mean Opinion Score) = 3.6 for codec G.723, compared to MOS = 4.4 for codec G.711. Once again we can see a throughput reduction (15.6%) due VoIP frame overhead reduction. By using 64-QAM3/4, the number of VoIP phone calls can be increased from 600, (with -HS, θ2) to 738 (with HS, θ1). Here the increase was of 23% on VoIP phone calls, but the throughput reduction was so important (43.5%). When a big amount of VoIP phone calls is considered for HS, the VoIP frame overhead reduction is significant. Moreover, when small sized VoIP frames are considered (for instance G.723, with 64-QAM3/4) VoIP bursts fit better into the last subchannels of DL subframe and thus fewer symbols are wasted. This analysis can be directly applied to fixed nodes, where the modulation type can be negotiated with the BS at connection setup, however for mobiles nodes, it is recommended to use QPSK1/2 for bandwidth estimation and use unscheduled symbols for nrtPS or BE services, since these types of service can support fragmentation.

Figure 8 shows the mean access delay of VoIP frames in the UL direction. According to "PacketCable™ 1.5 Specifications, Audio/Video

Figure 9. MAP and VoIP burts allocation for codec G.711-QPSK1/2

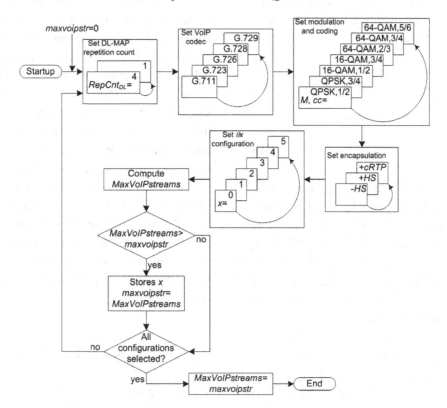

Codecs" (Cable Television Laboratories, Inc., 2009), in order two estimate the one-way delay we need to know: 1) Coding delay (comprised of Encoding and Decoding delays), 2) Access delay (comprised of MAC access delay+ transmission delay + propagation delay), and 3) Look-ahead delay. The coding + look-ahead delays are constants and accounts for 20 ms and 67 ms for codec G.711 and G.723, respectively. In Figure 8a, for codec G.711 we see the simulated mean access delays is under 15 ms, plus coding + look-ahead delays the point to point (PtP) delay becomes under 45ms, which is under the maximum PtP delay allowed for VoIP calls, 150ms. For codec G.723, as shown in Figure 8b, the simulated mean access delay was under 27ms, this delay becomes less than 94ms when coding + look-ahead delays are considered which is still below the maximum PtP delay.

PERFORMANCE OPTIMIZATION FOR VOIP TRAFFIC

In order to carry out the performance optimization for VoIP traffic, we designed an algorithm which chooses the best θ frame configuration from Table 2 in order to achieve the maximum number of VoIP phone calls. We evaluated the performance of codecs, G.711, G.723, G.726, G.728 and G.729 using different modulations and codings (QPSK1/2, QPSK3/4, 16-QAM1/2, 16-QAM3/4, 64-QAM2/3, 64-QAM3/4 and 64-QAM5/6). We also evaluated the performance of VoIP traffic considering two repetition counts for FCH and DL-MAP (*RepCnt*=4 and *RepCnt*=1, respectively); moreover HS and cRTP were also considered.

The operating principle of the algorithm is based on the coding repetition count (*CRepCount*), which is defined by:

$$CRepCount = \begin{cases} 1; & if \quad \dfrac{CIntArv_{time}}{Frame_d} < 1 \\ \dfrac{CIntArv_{time}}{Frame_d} & otherwise \end{cases}$$

$$(18)$$

The coding repetition count means the number of frames that a VoIP stream has to wait in order to be allocated, as is shown in Figure 10. Here, we can see a VoIP stream that is allocated every frame (*CRepCount*=1), one that is allocated every two frames (*CRepCount*=2), another one that is allocated every three frames (*CRepCount*=3) and finally one more that is allocated every six frames (*CRepCount*=6). As we can see, in this terms *Frame$_n$*=*Frame$_{n+6}$*. We called this as a "cycle", because based on the fact that VoIP streams are CBR traffic, every six frames have to be allocated the same VoIP streams.

Therefore, if *Frame$_n$* is filled with data allocations (for UGS traffic), *Frame$_{n+6}$* will be filled too. This means that only *Frame$_{n+1}$* to *Frame$_{n+5}$* have available symbols for more data allocations. Although this algorithm can model, different VoIP codecs simultaneously, we modeled one VoIP codec at a time in order to evaluate the performance of each VoIP codec individually.

In Figure 11 we show the algorithm used to optimize VoIP traffic performance. This algorithm begins by initializing a temporary variable, *maxvoipstr*. This variable stores the maximum number of VoIP streams reached at any iteration. Then in a Round Robin (RR) mode, each of the configuration parameters is selected. First, the DL-MAP repetition count is selected (1 or 4). Then, a VoIP codec, a modulation and codification are selected. Next, a packet encapsulation (-HS, +HS or +cRTP) is selected.

Finally, θ frame configuration is selected. Once all parameters were selected, the algorithm computes the maximum number of VoIP streams supported (*MaxVoIPstreams*), using the theoretical model described in section II. This value is compared with the maximum number of VoIP streams reached (*maxvoipstr*), and the higher value of these two variables is stored into the *maxvoipstr* temporary variable. This guarantees that at the end of all iterations, the maximum number of VoIP streams reached will be stored into *maxvoipstr*. Therefore, Table 4 shows the maximum number of VoIP streams reached with the best θ frame configuration for the different VoIP codecs modeled, using different packet encapsulation types. Here, the FCH and DL-MAP repetition count (DLr) is also indicated.

DISCUSSION AND CONCLUSION

The performance optimization presented in this chapter indicates that VoIP streams under different configurations can be supported by the WiMAX mobile protocol. There are however performance issues that need to be considered. The general trend from the results was that the system would comfortably support a number of active SSs making a VoIP phone call, where the maximum system throughput is obtained at the point when all available OFDMA symbol are scheduled. After that point, even a slight increase in the number of VoIP phone calls results in system instability. Performance deterioration is not gradual and the packet access delay increases rapidly after the threshold point if there is no control on the traffic accepted. Results shown in Figure 7 and 8 were obtained using a call admission control (CAC) scheme at call setup (using the simulation model), that computes the available number of OFDMA symbols in each direction (DL and UL). A new call is accepted if there are enough available symbols to allocate SSVoIP [smb/s] in each direction. In general, it was demonstrated

Table 4. Maximum number or VoIP streams

Codec	Mod & cc	DLr	-HS	+HS	+cRTP
G.711	QPSK1/2	4	38/θ3	54/θ4	64/θ4
G.711	QPSK3/4	4	64/θ4	76/θ4	84/θ4
G.711	16-QAM1/2	4	76/θ4	90/θ3	102/θ3
G.711	16-QAM3/4	4	116/θ3	136/θ3	144/θ3
G.711	64-QAM3/4	4	144/θ3	170/θ2	170/θ2
G.711	64-QAM5/6	4	144/θ3	170/θ2	200/θ2
G.723	QPSK1/2	4	228/θ4	348/θ3	432/θ3
G.723	QPSK3/4	4	306/θ3	432/θ3	510/θ2
G.723	16-QAM1/2	4	408/θ3	510/θ2	600/θ2
G.723	16-QAM3/4	4	510/θ2	600/θ2	738/θ1
G.723	64-QAM3/4	4	600/θ2	738/θ1	738/θ1
G.723	64-QAM5/6	4	600/θ2	738/θ1	924/θ0
G.726	QPSK1/2	4	64/θ4	84/θ4	90/θ3
G.726	QPSK3/4	4	84/θ4	116/θ3	136/θ3
G.726	16-QAM1/2	4	102/θ3	144/θ3	144/θ3
G.726	16-QAM3/4	4	144/θ3	170/θ2	200/θ2
G.726	64-QAM3/4	4	170/θ2	200/θ2	246/θ1
G.726	64-QAM5/6	4	200/θ2	246/θ1	246/θ1
G.728	QPSK1/2	4	22/θ3	36/θ3	50/θ2
G.728	QPSK3/4	4	34/θ3	50/θ2	61/θ1
G.728	16-QAM1/2	4	36/θ3	50/θ2	61/θ1
G.728	16-QAM3/4	4	50/θ2	61/θ1	77/θ0
G.728	64-QAM3/4	4	61/θ1	77/θ0	77/θ0
G.728	64-QAM5/6	4	61/θ1	77/θ0	77/θ0
G.729	QPSK1/2	4	84/θ4	144/θ3	170/θ2
G.729	QPSK3/4	4	116/θ3	170/θ2	200/θ2
G.729	16-QAM1/2	4	144/θ3	200/θ2	246/θ1
G.729	16-QAM3/4	4	170/θ2	246/θ1	246/θ1
G.729	64-QAM3/4	4	200/θ2	246/θ1	308/θ0
G.729	64-QAM5/6	4	246/θ1	308/θ0	308/θ0
G.711	QPSK1/2	1	44/θ4	56/θ4	72/θ5
G.711	QPSK3/4	1	72/θ5	90/θ5	108/θ5
G.711	16-QAM1/2	1	90/θ5	108/θ5	120/θ4
G.711	16-QAM3/4	1	136/θ4	160/θ4	192/θ4
G.711	64-QAM3/4	1	192/θ4	240/θ4	240/θ4
G.711	64-QAM5/6	1	192/θ4	240/θ4	280/θ4
G.723	QPSK1/2	1	270/θ5	408/θ4	576/θ4
G.723	QPSK3/4	1	360/θ4	576/θ4	720/θ4
G.723	16-QAM1/2	1	480/θ4	720/θ4	840/θ4

continued on following page

Table 4. Continued

Codec	Mod & cc	DLr	-HS	+HS	+cRTP
G.723	16-QAM3/4	1	720/θ4	840/θ4	1236/θ3
G.723	64-QAM3/4	1	840/θ4	1236/θ3	1236/θ3
G.723	64-QAM5/6	1	840/θ4	1236/θ3	1800/θ2
G.726	QPSK1/2	1	72/θ5	108/θ5	108/θ5
G.726	QPSK3/4	1	108/θ5	136/θ4	160/θ4
G.726	16-QAM1/2	1	120/θ4	192/θ4	192/θ4
G.726	16-QAM3/4	1	192/θ4	240/θ4	280/θ4
G.726	64-QAM3/4	1	240/θ4	280/θ4	412/θ3
G.726	64-QAM5/6	1	280/θ4	412/θ3	412/θ3
G.728	QPSK1/2	1	27/θ5	48/θ4	70/θ4
G.728	QPSK3/4	1	40/θ4	70/θ4	103/θ3
G.728	16-QAM1/2	1	48/θ4	70/θ4	103/θ3
G.728	16-QAM3/4	1	70/θ4	103/θ3	150/θ2
G.728	64-QAM3/4	1	103/θ3	150/θ2	150/θ2
G.728	64-QAM5/6	1	103/θ3	150/θ2	150/θ2
G.729	QPSK1/2	1	108/θ5	192/θ4	240/θ4
G.729	QPSK3/4	1	136/θ4	240/θ4	280/θ4
G.729	16-QAM1/2	1	192/θ4	280/θ4	412/θ3
G.729	16-QAM3/4	1	240/θ4	412/θ3	412/θ3
G.729	64-QAM3/4	1	280/θ4	412/θ3	600/θ2
G.729	64-QAM5/6	1	412/θ3	600/θ2	600/θ2

that with the use of header suppression, bandwidth efficiency is considerably increased to a large extent, achieving a much higher figure regarding the maximum number of VoIP streams sustainable. We observed that considering HS and cRTP, VoIP streams fits better into DL subframe and fewer symbols are wasted. Therefore more VoIP burst can be allocated instead of VoIP frame overhead. In addition by considering cRTP, the RTP, UDP and IP headers can be reduced to only two bytes where no UDP checksums are sent. Moreover, system performance highly depends of the DL-MAP repetition count.

For the performance optimization, we used the default value RepCnt=4, however, having RepCnt=1, and combined with cRTP, the number of VoIP-G.723 phone calls that the WiMAX mobile system could support, increases up to 1800 for 64-QAM5/6. Further research will focus on performance analysis of VoIP with mobile SSs considering also silence suppression that reduces VoIP bandwidth by a 60%.

ACKNOWLEDGMENT

This research was funded by grants PAPIIT IN114713 and PAPIIT IN114813 from DGAPA, National Autonomous University of Mexico. By research funds from CONACyT MEXICO 105279 and 105117.

REFERENCES

Asheralieva, A., Khan, J. Y., & Mahata, K. (2011). Performance analysis of VoIP services on the LTE network. In *Proceedings of Australasian Telecommunication Networks and Applications Conference,* (pp. 1-6). doi:10.1109/ATNAC.2011.6096638

Cable Television Laboratories, Inc. (2009). *PacketCable™ 1.5 specifications, audio/video codecs.* Retrieved from http://www.cablelabs.com/specifications/PKT-SP-CODEC1.5-I02-070412.pdf

Casner, S., & Jacobson, V. (1999). *Compressing IP/UDP/RTP headers for low-speed serial links.* Cisco Systems, RFC 2508. Retrieved from http://www.ietf.org/rfc/rfc2508.txt

ETSI. ES 200 800 v.1.3.1. (2001). *Digital video broadcasting: Interaction channel for cable TV distribution systems (CATV).* Retrieved from http://www.etsi.org/deliver/etsi_es/200800_200899/200800/01.03.01_60/es_200800v010301p.pdf

ITU-T. Rec. G.711. (1988). *Pulse code modulation (PCM) of voice frequencies.* Retrieved from http://www.itu.int/rec/T-REC-G.711-198811-I/en

ITU-T. Rec. G.726, 40, 32, 24, 16 kbit/s. (1990). *Adaptive differential pulse code modulation (ADPCM).* Retrieved from http://www.itu.int/rec/T-REC-G.726-199012-I/en

ITU-T. Rec. G.728. (1992). *Coding of spech at 16 kbit/s using low-delay code excited linear prediction.* Retrieved from http://www.itu.int/rec/T-REC-G.728-201206-I/en

ITU-T. Rec. G.723.1. (2006). *Dual rate speech coder for multimedia communications transmitting at 5.3 and 6.3 kbit/s.* Retrieved from http://www.itu.int/rec/T-REC-G.723.1-200605-I/en

ITU-T. Rec. G.729. (2007). *Coding of speech at 8 kbit/s using conjugate-structure algebraic-code-excited linear prediction (CS-ACELP).* Retrieved from http://www.itu.int/rec/T-REC-G.729-201206-I/en

ITU-T. Rec. H.323. (2009). *Packet-based multimedia communications systems.* Retrieved from http://www.itu.int/rec/T-REC-H.323-200912-I/en

Kaarthick, B., Yeshwenth, V. J., Nagarajan, N., & Rajeev. (2009). Investigating the performance of various vocoders for a fair scheduling algorithm in WiMAX. In *Proceedings of the First Asian Himalayas International Conference on Internet,* (pp. 1-5). doi:10.1109/AHICI.2009.5340356

Lee, H., Kim, H.-D., & Cho, D.-H. (2008). Extended-rtPS+ considering characteristics of VoIP codecs in mobile WiMAX. In *Proceedings of the IEEE 19th International Symposium on Personal, Indoor and Mobile Radio Communications,* (pp. 1-5). IEEE. doi:10.1109/PIMRC.2008.4699724

LTE-Advanced. (2011). *LTE, evolved universal terrestrial radio access (E-UTRA), physical channels and modulation (3GPP. TS 36.211 version 10.3.0 Release 10),* ETSI, TS 36.211 version 10.3.0. Retrieved from http://www.etsi.org/deliver/etsi_ts/136200_136299/136211/10.03.00_60/ts_136211v100300p.pdf

Ortiz, L., Rangel, V., Gomez, J., Aquino, R., & Lopez-Guerrero, M. (2011). Performance optimization of mobile WiMAX netwoks for VoIP stream. In *Proceedings of the 11th International Conference on Knowledge in Telecommunication Technologies and Optics,* (pp. 165-169). Szczyrk, Poland: KTTO.

Rangel, V. (2002). *Performance evaluation and optimisation of the DVB/DAVIC cable modem protocol.* Retrieved from http://ethos.bl.uk/OrderDetails.do?uin=uk.bl.ethos.251309

Shrivastava, S., & Vannithamby, R. (2009). Performance analysis of persistent scheduling for VoIP in WiMAX networks. In *Proceedings of the IEEE 10th Annual Wireless and Microwave Technology Conference*, (pp. 1-5). IEEE. doi:10.1109/WAMICON.2009.5207296

So, J. (2007). A downlink performance analysis of VoIP services over an IEEE 802.16e OFDMA system. *IEEE Communications Letters, 11*, 155–157. doi:10.1109/LCOMM.2007.061565

So, J. (2008). Performance analysis of VoIP services in the IEEE 802.16e OFDMA system with inband signaling. *IEEE Transactions on Vehicular Technology, 57*(3), 1876–1886. doi:10.1109/TVT.2007.909261

So, J. (2009). Performance analysis of a semi-fixed mapping scheme for VoIP services in wireless OFDMA systems. In *Proceedings of the Fifth International Conference on Wireless and Mobile Communications,* (pp. 13-17). doi:10.1109/ICWMC.2009.10

Standard, L. T. E. (2009). *Evolved universal terrestrial radio access (EUTRA), physical channels and modulation (release 8).* Retrieved from http://www.etsi.org/deliver/etsi_ts/136200_136299/136211/08.08.00_60/ts_136211v080800p.pdf

IEEE Std. 802.16-2004. (2004). *IEEE standard for local and metropolitan area networks part 16: Air interface for fixed broadband wireless access systems.* doi:10.1109/IEEESTD.2004.226664

IEEE Std. 802.16e. (2005). *IEEE standard for local and metropolitan area networks part 16: Air interface for fixed and mobile broadband wireless access systems: Amendment 2: Physical and medium access control layers for combined fixed and mobile operation in licensed bands.* doi:10.1109/IEEESTD.2006.99107

IEEE Std. 802.16m. (2011). *IEEE standard for local and metropolitan area networks part 16: Air interface for broadband wireless access systems, amendment 3: Advanced air interface.* doi:10.1109/IEEESTD.2011.5765736

Yu, K., Wang, X., & Zhang, L. (2009). Uplink performance analysis of VoIP services in TDD-OFDMA WiMAX networks. In *Proceedings of the Fourth International Conference on Communications and Networking in China* (pp. 1-5). doi:10.1109/CHINACOM.2009.5339799

KEY TERMS AND DEFINITIONS

Header Suppression: Is the process to remove redundant information in packet headers using known rules. These suppression rules help in reconstructing the header correctly at the receiving end. The rules are agreed in advance between the source and the destiny. In general, these rules are designed in such a way that fields of the header that do not change for the entire duration of the service flow are suppressed.

Orthogonal Frequency Division Multiple Access (OFDMA): It's a telecommunications technique that enables the multiplexing of data streams from multiple users onto the downlink and the uplink channel. Here different users can be allocated different subsets of the OFDM (Orthogonal Frequency Division Multiplexing) tones. It's facilitates the exploitation of frequency diversity and multiuser diversity to significantly improve the system capacity.

OPNET Modeler: It's an event driven network simulation platform that was created to help on the design and test of communication protocols and simulate the data networks performance.

Performance Analysis: Is the most significant outcome that a system must produce in order to meet the objectives for what the system was created.

Quality of Service: It´s a guarantee by a data network to satisfy a set of predetermined service performance constraints for the user in terms of the end-to-end delay, available bandwidth, probability of packet loss, etc., where enough resources must be available during the service invocation to keep the guarantee.

Quantum Map: Is the minimum allocation unit.

Rectangulation: Is the process of allocating bandwidth resources in the downlink channel on a square or rectangle region of the frame structure.

VoIP Codecs: There are algorithms that are used to convert voice signals into digital data to be transmitted over the Internet Protocol.

Worldwide Interoperability for Microwave Access (WiMAX): It's a last mile wireless broadband technology that uses the IEEE 802.16 set of protocols to provide connectivity to terminals in the order of tens of Mbps within coverage areas in the order of tens of kilometers.

Chapter 14
An Intelligent Scheduling Architecture for Mixed Traffic in LTE–Advanced Networks

Rehana Kausar
Queen Mary University of London, UK

Yue Chen
Queen Mary University of London, UK

Michael Chai
Queen Mary University of London, UK

ABSTRACT

In this chapter, an intelligent scheduling architecture is presented for the downlink transmission of LTE-Advanced networks to enhance the Quality of Service (QoS) provision to different traffic types while maintaining system level performance such as system throughput and fairness. Hebbian learning process and K-mean clustering algorithm are integrated in the time domain of the proposed scheduling architecture to intelligently allocate the available radio resource to Real Time (RT) and Non-Real Time (NRT) traffic types. The integration of these algorithms allows just enough resource allocation to RT traffic and diverts the remaining resource to NRT traffic to fulfil its minimum throughput requirements. System level simulation is set up for the performance evaluation, and simulation results show that the proposed scheduling architecture reduces average delay, delay violation probability, and average Packet Drop Rate (PDR) of RT traffic while guaranteeing the support of minimum throughput to NRT traffic and maintaining system throughput at good level.

INTRODUCTION

The rapid development in all IP based next generation mobile communication networks, such as Long Term Evolution-Advanced (LTE-A), is expected to support the outburst of high-speed packet based applications. These applications have a large variety of QoS requirements such as reduced latency and packet loss rate and high throughput. Radio Resource Management (RRM) faces challenges when come across such a large variety of conflicting QoS requirements (Zhen,

DOI: 10.4018/978-1-4666-4888-3.ch014

Yu-Kwong, Jianzhou, 2009). This is due to, limited radio resource, rapidly changing wireless channel conditions and ever increasing number of mobile users. Packet scheduling being one of the cores of RRM is very crucial to make an effective utilization of available radio resource (Rehana, 2010). In a scheduling algorithm, variable QoS requirements of different traffic types must be analysed and weighted appropriately to reach at a balanced solution (Zhen, Yu-Kwong, & Jianzhou, 2009).

The classic packet scheduling algorithms are Round Robin (RR), MAX C/I and Proportional Fairness (PF) algorithms. RR algorithm allocates resources cyclically thus achieving the maximum fairness. MAX C/I and PF algorithm exploit multiuser diversity to enhance system throughput. MAX C/I algorithm allocates a Physical Resource Block (PRB) to a user with the highest channel gain on that PRB, and can maximize the system throughput (Harri & Antti, 2009). PF algorithm takes both system throughput and fairness among users into consideration and allocates resources to users based on the ratio of their instantaneous throughput and acquired time averaged throughput (Stefania, Issam, & Matthew, 2009). However, RR, MAX C/I and PF algorithms aim only at improving fairness, system throughput or the trade-off between fairness and system throughput, respectively. QoS requirements, for example delay requirements of RT traffic or minimum throughput requirements of Non NRT traffic, are not considered at all. In the next generation of mobile communication networks, apart from system throughput and user fairness, the crucial point is to fulfill users' QoS requirements in a multi-service and multi-user mixed traffic environment. This is because of resource contention among users of different traffic types. To allocate radio resources efficiently and intelligently in such complex environments is very challenging.

QoS Aware Scheduling

Several scheduling algorithms are presented to achieve higher performance to fulfil QoS requirements of different traffic types, in the next generation of mobile communication.

A low complexity QoS aware PF multicarrier algorithm is presented for OFDM system in (Zhen, Yu-Kwong, & Jianzhou, 2009). The objective is to achieve PF in the system while improving QoS performance. A greedy method based multi carrier PF criterion is proposed with the consideration that traditional single carrier PF is not suitable for OFDM systems. A sub-carrier reassignment procedure is used to further improve QoS performance. This paper proposes Packet Scheduling (PS) algorithm specifically for the multimedia traffic and improves QoS, throughput and fairness in the system. However, there is a need to analyze the behaviour of the proposed algorithm when the system has to deal with different traffic types such as interactive, background traffic, etc. In (Jani, Niko, Martti, & Mika, 2008), a service classification scheme is used which classifies mixed traffic into different service specific queues and grants different scheduling priorities to them. QoS of RT traffic is improved at the cost of system spectral efficiency, when the RT queue is granted the highest priority and fairness is significantly improved when fair scheduling is used in the Time Domain (TD) to pick users from the queues instead of strictly prioritizing RT traffic queue. Fair scheduling picks users one-by-one from each queue and strict priority empties queues one after the other, giving the highest priority to RT queue. Conventional PF and MAX C/I are used to sort the priority of users in the queues, which improves system throughput and fairness among users. However, the QoS of RT and NRT traffic can be improved by using service specific queue sorting algorithms to prioritize users. In (Gutierrez, Bader, & Pijoan, 2008), an urgency factor is used to boost the priority of a particular traffic type. When any packet from a queue is about to exceed its upper bound of delay requirement, its priority is increased by adding an urgency factor. Although most of the packets are sent when they are nearly ready to expire, achieving a lower PDR thus guaranteeing the required QoS to RT traffic but at the cost QoS to NRT traffic and system performance.

In mix traffic scenarios, Queue State Information (QSI) becomes very important in addition to Channel State Information (CSI). It can make scheduling decision even more efficient; especially in QoS aware scheduling algorithms, it is very crucial. Typically this implies to minimize the amount of resources needed per user and thus allows for as many users as possible in the system, while still satisfying whatever QoS requirements there may exist (Toskala & Tiirola, 2006). A time domain multiplexing (TDM) system based Modified Largest Waited Delay First (M-LWDF) is presented in (Andrews et al., 2001) which takes into account of both QSI and CSI. This algorithm serves a user with the maximum product of Head of Line (HOL) packet delay, channel condition and an arbitrary positive constant. This constant is used to control packet delay distribution for different RT users. It updates the queue state after each TTI rather than updating after each sub-carrier allocation. M-LWDF significantly improves the support of QoS guarantees to the RT and NRT traffic for TDM systems. In (Sanjay & Alexander, 2000), an exponential (EXP) rule is proposed for scheduling multiple flows that share a time-varying channel. The EXP rule is applied in M-LWDF as one of the parameters that equalizes the delays of different RT packets to reduce the PDR of RT traffic due to time-out. M-LWDF algorithm is applied in a Frequency Domain Multiplexing (FDM) system in (Parimal, Srikrshna, & Aravind, 2005) to optimize sub-carrier allocation in Orthogonal Frequency Division Multiple Access (OFDMA) based networks. It shows improved performance

in terms of QoS but like M-LWDF updates the queues state after each TTI rather than after each sub-carrier allocation. In Sum Waiting time Based Scheduling (SWBS) algorithm (Jun, Na, An, & Haige, 2009), M-LWDF for OFDMA-based systems is modified by updating the queue status after every sub-carrier allocation. It takes into account RT and NRT traffic types and provides better QoS for both services. The results show that the support of provision of QoS guarantees in terms of delay and PDR for RT and minimum throughput for NRT traffic is improved. However the system level performance in terms of system throughput and user fairness, which is not the focus SWBS, is reduced In (Haipeng et al., 2008) an adaptive algorithm with Connection Admission Control (CAC) design is proposed. Due to large number of users and limited number of PRBs, CAC restricts the on-going connections to provide required QoS and makes decisions whether to reject or accept new connections. It improves the QoS of RT traffic by prioritizing RT users and delaying users of other traffic types. In (Kian, Simon, & Angela, 2008), a prioritizing function is used for packet data scheduling in OFDMA systems to satisfy QoS requirements of RT and NRT traffics. Priority is associated to different traffic types by setting different values of the prioritizing function. This algorithm allocates resources in a static way by setting the value of priority function for different traffic types and cannot cope with the highly dynamic variation of wireless channel conditions. In (Leandros & Anthony, 1993), a server allocation scheme to parallel queues with randomly varying connectivity is presented. The allocation decision is based on the connectivity and on the lengths of the connected queues only. The main aim of the work, in (Leandros & Anthony, 1993), is to stabilize different queues. However this allocation policy minimizes the delay and maximizes throughput for the special case of symmetric queues, i.e. queues with equal arrival, service, and connectivity.

As described in the above and the references therein, the PS algorithms improve scheduling performance in different domains separately such as system throughput, user fairness, and QoS of RT and NRT traffic types. The Combined consideration of service level (QoS) and system level performance (system throughput and user fairness) improvement has got very little or no attention despite the fact that it is very crucial. Scheduling performance in different domains needs to be united in an efficient PS architecture so that the system can be made cost effective and radio resources may be utilized at the best. PS performance in different areas can be improved jointly by an intelligent Packet Scheduling Architecture (PSA) which is capable to make scheduling decisions adaptive to the environment and to the achieved performance in terms of QoS of different traffic types. The detailed traffic types can be considered in PSA to make the PS algorithms more realistic. To understand the use of the use of Artificial Intelligence (AI) in scheduling, an overview of machine learning based scheduling is given in the following paragraphs.

Machine Learning Based Scheduling

To enhance the scheduling performance in different domains, AI is integrated in communication networks. The AI technologies offer many new and exciting possibilities for the next generation of communication networks (Jinning & Nicholson, 1987). Learning rules in AI, for a connectionist system, are algorithms or equations which govern changes in the weights of the connections in the network. One example of such learning procedure for two-layer network is Hebbian Learning Rule, which is based on a rule initially proposed by Hebb in 1949. It states how much the weight of the connection between two units should be increased or decreased in proportion to the product of their activation (Hebb, 1949). Hebbian learning rule was used in (Khozeimeh, Haykin, 2010) for dynamic spectrum management in Cognitive Radio (CR)

to estimate the presence of primary users (PUs) in the environment; PUs is the licensed users and allowed to operate in the spectrum band bought by the wireless service provider. It helps in preventing collisions of CR units with PUs.

To deal with the variable QoS requirements of different users demanding a service, clustering is fairly good technique to integrate in scheduling algorithms to rearrange users' priority according to their QoS requirements. It is a technique to group together a set of items having similar characteristics (Srivastava, Cooley, Deshpande, & Tan, 2000). In scheduling domain, where there is always a need to change priorities of different users according to their QoS requirements, clustering is a good technique to make groups of users with similar QoS requirements. It helps in setting priorities of users by sorting these groups in a proper way. Clustering gives variable priorities to different users belonging to same traffic type. Clustering based scheduling gives variable priorities to different users belonging to the same service type. For example in [PSPP07], a clustering based scheduling algorithm is used to organise users of a network into groups based on the number of their requests per channel. The transmission priority then starts from the group with the highest requests. It improves network performance in terms of higher network throughput while keeping mean packet delay at lower levels as compared to the conventional scheduling algorithms (Petridou, Sarigiannidis, Papadimitriou, Pomportsis, 2007).

As the aim of the proposed work is to consider the joint scheduling performance in different domains and to design an intelligent scheduling architecture, which works adaptive to the changing network conditions, system load and the archived QoS of different traffic types.

This chapter focuses on scheduling performance in different domains such as, service level, user level and system level. It integrates AI techniques in the scheduling architecture to improve QoS support at service level and user level along with maintaining good system level performance in terms of system throughput and user fairness. It integrates Hebbian learning process and K-mean clustering algorithm in the scheduling architecture. Hebbian learning process is used to adaptively distribute available resource in different traffic types based on average PDR of RT traffic. K-mean clustering is used to group RT users based on PDR of individual RT users. Creating such groups and prioritising them properly could lead to higher network performance without aggravating the scheduling algorithm.

CROSS-LAYER SCHEDULING IN LTE-ADVANCE NETWORKS

Dynamic resource scheduler is a Medium Access Control (MAC) layer entity in eNB and it allocates physical layer resources for the downlink and the uplink transmission. Scheduler should take into account of the traffic volume and QoS requirements of each User Equipment (UE) when sharing resources between UEs. QoS is defined as the ability of a network to provide a service to the end user at a given service level. A service level corresponds to a set of objective parameters called QoS parameters that relate directly to the end user experience, for example packet delay or bit rate (David, Man, & Renaud, 2006). Scheduler may assign resources by taking into account the radio channel conditions of UEs, measured at eNB or reported by the UEs and QoS requirements.

Layer 2 is split into MAC, Radio Link Control (RLC), and Packet Data Convergence Protocol (PDCP) sub-layers. The interface between RLC and MAC is called logical channels. The type of logical channels is defined by the data it carries, which may be either control data or user data. MAC sub-layer offers services to RLC sub-layer via logical channels. The interface between MAC and physical layer is called transport channel. Transport channels are services offered by layer 1 to the MAC layer over the air interface by defining how and with which characteristics data

is transferred. For each UE scheduled in a TTI, a Transport Block (TB) is generated carrying user data, which is delivered on the transport channel. Physical channels are used to finally transmit the data over the air interface by defining the exact physical characteristics of the radio channel (INA-CON GmBh 2009). The overview of channels is shown in Figure 1.

The main services and functions of MAC layer of the main general systems (LTE/LTE-Advanced) include (3GPP TS 36.300 v8 2012):

- Mapping between logical channels and transport channels;
- Multiplexing/de-multiplexing of RLC Packet Data Units (PDUs) into/from TBs delivered from/to the physical layer or transport channels;
- Traffic volume measurement reporting;
- Error correction through Hybrid Automatic Repeat Request (HARQ);
- Priority handling between logical channels of one UE;
- Priority handling between UEs by dynamic scheduling;
- Transport format selection;
- Padding.

Figure 1. Radio channel types

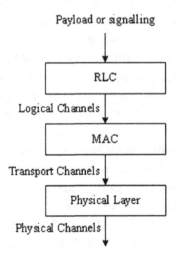

There is one MAC entity in one cell. MAC generally consists of several functional blocks such as transmission scheduling function, per UE functions, Multimedia Broadcast Multicast Service (MBMS) functions, MAC control functions, Transport block generation (3GPP TS 36.300 v8 2012).

Figure 2 shows a TD view of frames and packet timelines of LTE/LTE-Advanced downlink transmission. The radio access technology for the downlink transmission in LTE/LTE-Advanced networks is OFDMA. In OFDMA-based networks, the minimum allocation unit is one PRB having a resolution of 180 kHz in the FD and 1 ms in the time domain. In the frequency domain, 1 PRB consists of 12 sub-carriers and in the time domain it comprises 14 OFDM symbols. Radio resource allocation may be valid for one or more Transmission Time Intervals (TTIs) where each TTI is equivalent to 1ms. For more information on OFDMA readers should read (Erik, Stefan, Johan, & Per, 2007; Hui & Guoqing, 2005). A full frame is 10 ms but in LTE/LTE-Advanced networks normally consider in terms of 1 ms sub-frame, which is the entity that contains TBs. A TB carries a MAC Protocol Data Units (PDUs), which are formed from MAC Service Data Units

(SDUs). Mac SDUs contain RLC PDUs, which are formed from RLC SDUs. Then within the RLC header there can be a number of PDCP PDUs. PDCP PDUs are formed from PDCP SUDUs and there is an arbitrary relationship between the IP packets coming in, which form SDUs and how the RLC PDUs are formed. Therefore the maximum effective use of the radio resource in a fixed TTI can be made (FreeScale White Paper, 2008).

CROSS-LAYER PACKET SCHEDULING ARCHITECTURE

A schematic diagram of the scheduling architecture is shown in Figure 3. It consists of Traffic Differentiator, TD Scheduler and FD Scheduler stage.

The input to this architecture is mixed traffic, which consists of service requests of users with variable QoS requirements. It is differentiated into four queues based on traffic types: Control Traffic (i.e. control information), RT Traffic (i.e. real time voice), NRT Traffic (i.e. streaming video) and Background Traffic (i.e. email, SMS). Users in these queues are sorted according to QoS requirements of these traffic types, QSI and CQI reports. For example, control information of all

Figure 2. Time domain view of the LTE downlink

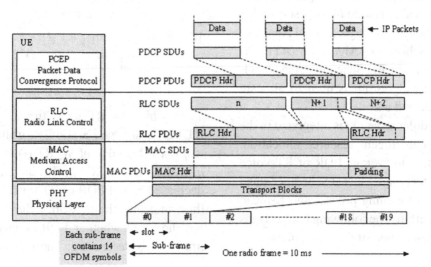

Figure 3. The cross layer packet scheduling architecture

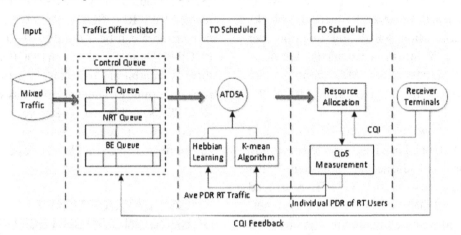

Resource Allocation to Real Time and Non Real Time Traffics

users is equally important so control data is scheduled in First Come First Serve (FCFS) manner. In addition control queue is prioritised over the remaining queues and is scheduled first. This is because control traffic contains scheduling information of all scheduled users e.g. which PRBs are scheduled to which users. That is why it is very important to send this information to the users before the actual data transmission. Two service specific queue sorting algorithms for both RT and NRT traffics are used, to prioritise users. The detailed explanation of these algorithms can be found in (Rehana, 2010). Background traffic has no QoS requirement, however to make a good trade-off between system throughput and user fairness, PF algorithm is used to sort users in this queue. At TD Scheduler stage, a novel Adaptive Time Domain Scheduling Algorithm (ATDSA) is proposed and at the FD Scheduler stage Modified PF (M-PF) algorithm is used to allocate PRBs to the selected users.

At TD Scheduler stage, AI is integrated in the ATDSA for an intelligent resource allocation, which is adaptive to average PDR of RT voice traffic. The AI techniques at TD Scheduler stage include Hebbian Learning process and K-mean clustering algorithm. The following two sections give detailed description of these techniques.

Hebbian Learning process is used to make an intelligent distribution of the available radio resource between RT and NRT traffic types. By definition, Hebbian Learning rule learns the environment in terms of the activity rate of a parameter and takes decisions based on comparison of current and previous occurrence of that activity. It is integrated in ATDSA to compare average PDR of RT traffic in the current TTI with the average PDR values in previous TTIs and changes the weight of RT traffic based on (1).

$$W\_RT(t) = \begin{cases} W\_RT(t-1) + \varsigma \\ PDR\_RT(t) > PDR\_RT(t-1) \\ W\_RT(t-1) - \varsigma \quad Otherwise \end{cases}$$

(1)

In which W_RT (t) is the weight given to RT traffic at time t and η is learning rate and $0 < \eta < 1$. The value of W_RT (t) is increased by η, if the PDR of RT traffic increases and it is decreased by η if PDR of RT traffic decreases. It thus, indicates the network behaviour by showing the trend whether PDR is increasing with time or it is decreasing. The value of η is set in such a way that after 10 consecutive increments in W_RT, PDR of RT traffic becomes equal to PDR threshold Γ, which is an appropriate time for analysing network behaviour. At this point, a change in resource allocation to RT traffic is triggered, which is calculated by (2). This adaptive change in resource allocation allows just enough radio resource to the RT traffic, to keep average PDR of RT traffic under the PDR threshold. The remaining radio resource is allocated to the NRT traffic to support minimum throughput guarantee. In addition to minimum throughput support to NRT traffic, resources are also allocated to background traffic to prevent any starvation and enhance fairness among users of different traffic types. To understand how the resource allocation is triggered consider the following.

Let C be the total capacity and λ C is the proportion of C allocated to RT traffic then (1-λ) C is the proportion of capacity allocated to NRT traffic. The initial value of λ is set according to traffic pattern and network load. Traffic patterns considered in this algorithm include, RT traffic dominant, NRT streaming video traffic dominant, background traffic dominant and equal distribution of RT and NRT traffic types. The network load in all simulations varies from 50 active users to 100 active users. Thus the initial value of λ depends on these two factors. Afterwards by using Hebbian Learning process the value of λ is changed adaptively based on (2).

$$\lambda(t+1) = \lambda(t) + W\_RT(t) * 1PRB \qquad (2)$$

In which λ (t) is the proportion of radio resource allocated to RT traffic at time t and 1 PRB is the minimum resource allocation unit in LTE/LTE-Advanced networks. The proportion of radio resource allocated to NRT traffic is further divided in NRT streaming video traffic and background traffic in such a way that when throughput requirements of streaming video traffic are fulfilled, the remaining radio resource is allocated to background traffic.

Hebbian learning process is shown in Figure 4. The input to this process is Average PDR values of RT traffic, which are saved in a vector during each TTI. It compares current PDR value with previous values and changes the weight of RT traffic accordingly. When the PDR of RT traffic becomes equal to the PDR threshold that is equivalent to 10 consecutive increments in the weight of RT traffic, an action is triggered as shown in the Figure 4.

Scheduling Order of Real Time Users

To reduce delay violation probability of RT traffic and to improve PDR fairness among RT users, clustering is used to group RT users based on their individual PDR values. Users with higher PDR values are clustered in one group and the ones with comparatively low PDR values, which are

Figure 4. Hebbian learning process

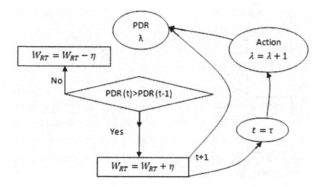

not near to the delay/PDR threshold, are clustered in another group. By sorting these groups and prioritizing them appropriately, delay violation probability can be reduced significantly. It also improves PDR fairness among RT users. For the clustering process, K-mean clustering algorithm is used, which is widely used clustering algorithm. The schematic diagram of K-mean clustering algorithm is shown in Figure 5 and the process is described in the following.

Let the clustering process is represented by *Clus* where *num* represents the number of clusters to be created having one central point known as Centroid, *X* represents the set of RT users to be clustered i.e. *X={x1, x2,...xn}* and *μ1, μ2,...* represent each of the *num* clusters consisting of |*Clus_1*|, |*Clus_2*|,...|*Clus_num*| members that is RT users. The Clustering process *Clus* is defined as an assignment of RT users to the group of users that is clusters.

$$Clus: \{1, 2,...n\} \rightarrow \{1, 2,...num\} \qquad (3)$$

Users belonging to the same cluster have similar requirements in terms of their PDR and dissimilar requirements to the users belonging to other clusters. Similarity in clustering is fundamental to make appropriate groups of users. The dissimilarity between the requirements of two users is evaluated by distance measure. For this, each user of set *X* is assigned to its nearest Centroid based on Euclidean distance as given in (4).

$$C_i = \min_{i=1,2...x} || x\_i - \mu\_k ||^2 \qquad (4)$$

In which C_i is the Centroid to which x_i is assigned and μ_k is the *kth* Centroid. The squared Euclidean distance uses the same equation as the Euclidean distance but does not take the square root while evaluating dissimilarity. The mean of PDR values of all users assigned to a Centroid is calculated and the position of each Centroid is updated by the mean of PDR values assigned to it. This process is repeated until no Centroid is shifted in the next iteration, resulting in *num* clusters. Considering all clusters, the clustering process is guided by the cost function *J*, which is the sum of distances between each user and the Centroid to which it is assigned, as given in (4). The optimization objective is to minimize *J* so that the dissimilarity between the users of same cluster becomes minimum or null.

$$J = \sum_{i=1}^{num} \sum_{x\_j \in c\_j} dist\left(x_i, c\_j\right) \qquad (5)$$

Figure 5. K-mean clustering algorithm

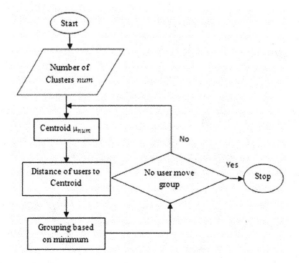

K-mean clustering algorithm, used in the proposed work is summarized in Figure 6. The input is a set of users i.e. X with their PDR values in a given TTI and the number of clusters *num* with a central point called Centroid. With this information K-mean clustering algorithm is applied to make clusters of RT users based on their individual PDR values. These clusters are then sorted (sortedClusters) in an order that a cluster with the highest value of Centroid becomes at the top of the list and the one with the lowest value of Centroid become at the end (bottom) of the list. The clusters of users are then fitted in the time domain scheduler according to the capacity proportion of RT traffic as described in previous section. The order of users (userClustered) in the scheduled cluster is kept same as in the Traffic Differentiator stage. Only the users with lower/no PDR values are skipped to give priority to users with higher PDR values. Finally these users are scheduled, S, in the FD by allocating PRBs to the users. Frequency domain multiuser diversity is exploited by allocating a PRB to each user at which this user has good channel conditions.

Figure 6. K-mean clustering algorithm

```
Algorithm: K-mean Clustering

Input: A set K of k users having a k × 1 matrix of PDR
on a given TTI, the upper bound on the PDR is τ and
the number of clusters is num.
Output: The scheduling order S of users.
    1:  /*Function Clustering*/
    2:  (Clus, num = K − mean (X, num)
    3:  SortedClusters=Sort(Centroids)
    4:  userClustered=Rearrange users
    5:  /*Function Scheduling*/
    6:  S=Schedule(userClustered)
```

SYSTEM MODEL AND PERFORMANCE METRICS

An OFDMA-based system is considered to evaluate the performance of the proposed scheduling architecture. The minimum allocation unit is one PRB, which consists of 12 sub-carriers in each Transmission Time Interval (TTI) of 1 ms duration. There are k=1, 2, ...K mobile users and m=1, 2, ...M number of PRBs. The downlink channel is a fading channel within each scheduling drop. The received symbol at the mobile user is the some of the additive white Gaussian noise (AWGN) and the product of actual data and the channel gain, as given in (6).

$$Y(t) = X(t)*H(t) + G(t) \qquad (6)$$

In which $Y(t)$ is the received symbol from eNodeB to the user, $X(t)$ is the input data symbol, $H(t)$ is the channel gain and G(t) is the complex Guassian noise. In an OFDMA system, eNodeB sends data to the users on the sub-channels that are allocated to them. It is assumed, as in (Jani, Niko, Martti, & Mika, 2008; Jun, Na, An, & Haige, 2009), that the power allocation is uniform, p = P/M on all sub-channels, where P is the total transmit power of eNodeB and p is the power allocated at a sub-channel. At the start of each scheduling drop, it is assumed as in (Jani, Niko, Martti, & Mika, 2008; Jun, Na, An, & Haige, 2009) that the CQI is perfect and is known by eNodeB.

The achieved throughput of a user k at sub-channel m is calculated by (7) as in most of the literature on LTE/LTE-Advanced.

$$C_{(k,m)}(t) = B \times \log_2 \left[1 + \frac{|H_{k,m}(t)|^2}{\sigma^2 \tau} P_m(t) \right] \qquad (7)$$

In which, B is the total available bandwidth of each PRB (sub-channel), σ is the noise power density and τ is a constant signal-to-noise gap and has a simple relationship with the required Bit Error Rate (BER) as given as τ = -ln(5BER/1.5).

The performance of the scheduling architecture is evaluated by average delay, delay violation probability average PDR and PDR fairness of RT traffic, minimum throughput guarantee to NRT streaming video traffic, system throughput and throughput fairness among all users. The delay violation probability is measured by users' packet loss ratio. The packet loss ratio (equivalent PDR) of the *kth* user is defined as the ratio of number of packets dropped to the number of total packets arrived and is given by (8).

$$\text{PDR}_k^{RT} = \frac{n_k^{dropped}}{n_k^{arrived}} \qquad (9)$$

And the delay violation probability is given by (10) (Jun, Na, An, & Haige, 2009).

$$\text{Delay Violation Probability} = \max_{k \in RT}(\text{PDR}_k^{RT}) \qquad (10)$$

The performance of long-term throughput guarantee for NRT streaming video traffic is evaluated by the minimal throughput among all NRT streaming video users, which is given by (10) (Jun, Na, An, & Haige, 2009).

$$r_{min} = \min_{k \in NRT}\left(r_k\right) \qquad (11)$$

In which r_k is the throughput achieved by *kth* NRT users. The system throughput is the sum of throughput achieved by all users including RT and NRT users. Fairness among users is calculated by using Raj Jain's fairness index (Chisung, 2007).

$$Fairness = \frac{\left[\sum_{i=1}^{K} R_k\right]^2}{K \sum_{i=1}^{K}(R_k)^2} \qquad (12)$$

In which R_k is the time average throughput of user *k*. In addition to throughput fairness among all users, PDR fairness is also evaluated for RT users, which is calculated by taking the standard deviation of PDR of all RT users.

SIMULATION MODEL AND SIMULATION RESULTS

Simulation Model

A single cell with one eNodeB and a system bandwidth of 10 MHz is considered. The wireless environment is typical Urban Non Line of Sight (NLOS) and the LTE/LTE-Advanced system works with a carrier frequency of 2GHz. The most suitable path loss model in this case is COST 231 Walfisch Ikegami (WI) (Harri & Antti, 2009) as used in most of the literature on LTE/LTE-Advanced. Users are assumed to have a uniform distribution and the total number of RT users is assumed to be equal to the total number of NRT users as in (Jun, Na, An, & Haige, 2009). The delay budget for RT traffic is 40 ms in the OFDMA-based LTE-Advanced networks (Jun, Na, An, & Haige, 2009; Ekstrom et al., 2006). Total eNodeB transmission power is 46dBm (40w) and the maximum BER requirement is 10^{-4} for all users. The simulation parameters used for system level simulation are based on (3GPP TSG-RAN TR25.814, 2006) and these are typical values used in most of literature on LTE/LTE-Advanced. These parameters are listed in Table 1.

Table 1 Simulation parameters

Parameter	Value/ Comment
Cell topology	Single cell
Cell Radius	1 km
UE distribution	Random
Smallest distance from UE to eNodeB/m	35 m
Path Loss model	COST 231 Walfisch-Ikegami (WI) model
Shadow fading standard deviation/dB	8 dB
System bandwidth/MHz	10 MHz
PRB bandwidth/kHz	180 kHz
Carrier frequency/GHz	2 GHz
BS transmission power	46dBm(40w)
Traffic model	Full buffer

SIMULATION RESULTS

The performance of the proposed packet scheduling scheme ATDSA is evaluated and compared against QoS aware mixed traffic packet scheduling algorithm (abbreviated as MIX in all results) (Jani, Niko, Martti, & Mika, 2008) and SWBS (Jun, Na, An, & Haige, 2009). The packet arrival process is Poisson distribution with 0.35 ON time.

Figure 7 shows average delay of RT traffic verses total number of active users. Average delay increases with the number of users for all algorithms as shown. However ATSA shows the least delay as compared to MIX and SWBS. It shows 33% and 48% lower delay as compared to MIX and SWBS, respectively. This is because ATDSA takes into account of the individual users' delay and PDR demands.

Figure 8 shows delay violation probability of RT users' verses total number of active users. It increases with the number of users for all algorithms as expected. The delay violation probability shown by the proposed ATDSA is reduced significantly because of the integration of K-mean clustering algorithm in the time domain of scheduling architecture, more specifically when system is under higher network load. The reason is that queues build up when the number of users increase and results in PDR at higher system loads. And the ultimate goal of integrating K-mean clustering is to improve the performance of individual RT users with respect to their PDR, which is achieved without violating scheduling performance in other domains such as, throughput of NRT traffic and overall system performance. MIX shows the highest delay violation probability because of lack

Figure 7. Average packet delay of RT traffic

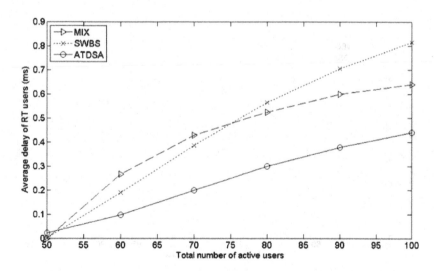

Figure 8. Delay violation probability of RT traffic

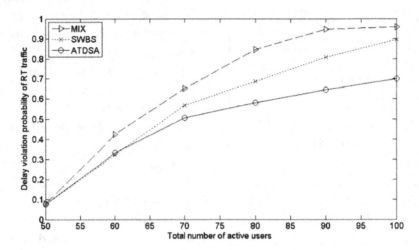

of service specific queue sorting algorithms. SWBS however shows lower delay violation probability than MIX because it considers delay requirements of RT traffic.

The average PDR of RT traffic is shown in Figure 9. It increases with the number of users for all algorithms. The proposed ATDSA shows lower PDR than MIX and SWBS at higher system loads. However at lower system loads (50 and 60 active users), PDR for all algorithms is almost same, which is because at lower system loads, the available radio resource is enough to satisfy QoS of all RT users. The improved performance of ATDSA is because it adaptively changes resource allocation to RT traffic based on its average PDR by integrating Hebbian Learning process.

To evaluate PDR fairness among RT users, the standard deviation of PDR of all RT users' verses total number of active users is shown in Figure 10. The proposed ATDSA shows significantly lower STD as compared to MIX and SWBS, indicating the highest PDR fairness among RT

Figure 9. Average PDR of RT traffic

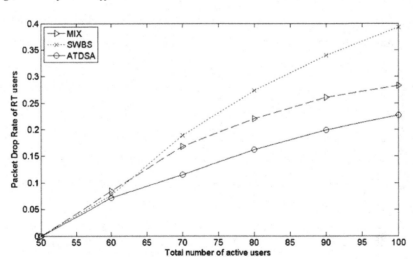

Figure 10. Minimum throughput of NRT traffic

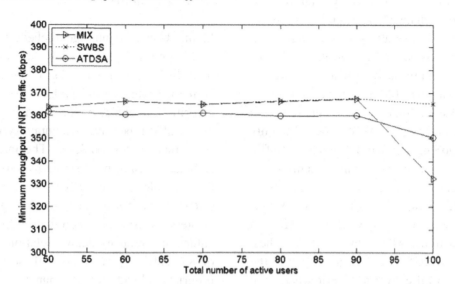

users. This is because of the integration of K-mean clustering algorithm which aims to prioritise users with higher PDR values. Mix due to lack of service specific queue sorting shows the highest STD of PDR hence the least PDR fairness. SWBS uses QoS aware strategies and shows lower STD as compared to MIX.

Figure 11 shows the overall system throughput verses total number of active users. It increases with the number of users for all algorithms. MIX achieves the highest system throughput at all system loads because of its channel dependent queue sorting algorithms. The proposed ATDSA achieves almost same throughput as MIX at lower system loads, however there is slight decrease at higher system loads. This is because at higher system loads, due to probability of higher PDR, RT traffic is prioritised. And RT users

Figure 11. System throughput

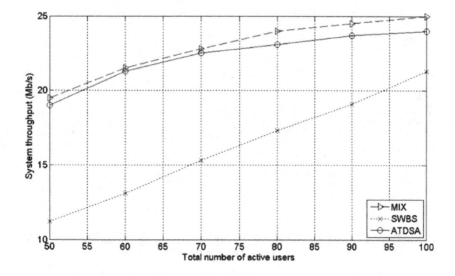

reaching their PDR threshold may not have comparatively good channel conditions thus cause a slight decrease in overall system throughput at higher system loads. SWBS algorithm achieves the lowest system throughput which is lower by a significant value of 10Mbps at lower and 5Mbps at higher system load, when compared with ATDSA. This is because SWBS is designed only to improve QoS provision to RT and NRT traffic types and is less concerned with system overall performance.

Figure 12 shows the fairness index verses total active users, achieved by ATDSA, MIX and SWBS algorithms. MIX achieves the highest fairness due to its fair scheduling policy in the time domain specifically in s scenario where total number of RT and NRT users is equal. However the proposed ATDSA shows slightly lower fairness than MIX and achieves a high fairness index value above 9 at all system loads. This is because of the integration of Hebbian Learning process, which allocates just enough resource to RT traffic and diverts the remaining resource to NRT traffic types to prevent any starvation. SWBS shows the lowest fairness index at all system loads because its main focus is on QoS provision to RT and NRT traffic types.

CONCLUSION

In this chapter, an intelligent scheduling architecture is presented for the downlink transmission of LTE-Advanced networks. It integrates Hebbian Learning process and K-mean clustering algorithm, to enhance QoS provision to RT and NRT traffic types and to maintain system overall performance at good level. The integration of Hebbian Learning process intelligently distributes the available radio resource between RT and NRT traffic types. The K-mean clustering algorithm clusters RT users based on their individual PDR values and reduces delay violation probability of RT traffic by prioritizing these clusters appropriately. In addition it enhances PDR fairness among RT users. System level performance in terms of system throughput and user fairness is maintained at good level by exploiting multiuser diversity in the Td and FD, and by allocating just enough resources to RT traffic and distributing the remaining to NRT traffic types.

Figure 12. Fairness among users

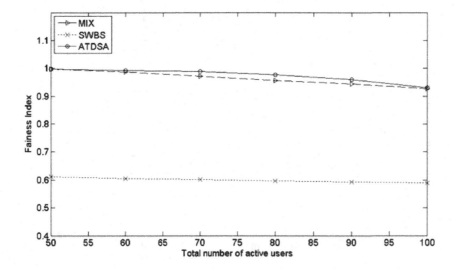

REFERENCES

Andrews, P., Kumaran, K., Ramanan, K., Stolyar, A., Whiting, P., & Vijayakumar, R. (2001). Providing quality of service over a shared wireless link. *Communication Magazine, 39,* 150–154. doi:10.1109/35.900644

David, S. I., Man, L., & Renaud, C. (2006). *QoS and QoE management in UMTS cellular networks.* West Sussex, UK: John Willey & Sons Ltd.

Ekstrom, H., Furuskar, A., Karlsson, J., Meyer, M., Parkvall, S., Torsner, J., & Wahlqvist, M. (2006). Technical solution for 3G LTE. *IEEE Communications Magazine, 44,* 38–45. doi:10.1109/MCOM.2006.1607864

Erik, D., Stefan, P. L., Johan, S., & Per, B. (2007). *3G evolution, HSPA and LTE mobile broadband.* Burlington, UK: Academic Press Elsevier.

FreeScale White Paper. (2008). *Long term evolution protocol overview* (Document No. LTEPTCLOVWWP). Retrieved on June 1, 2013 from http://www.freescale.com/files/wireless_comm/doc/white_paper/LTEPTCLOVWWP.pdf

3GPP TS 36.300 v8. (2007). *Evolved universal terristarial radio acess (E-UTRA) and evolved universal terristerial radio access networks (E-UTRAN), release 8 (2007-2012).* Author.

3GPP TSG-RAN TR25. 814. Version 7.0.0. (2006). Physical layer aspects for evolved UTRA. Author.

Gutierrez, I., Bader, F., & Pijoan, J. L. (2008). *Prioritization function for packet scheduling in OFDMA systems.* Paper presented at the Wireless Internet Conference. Brussels, Belgium.

Haipeng, L. E. I., Mingliang, A. Z., Yongyu, C., & Dacheng, Y. (2008). Adaptive connection admission control algorithm for LTE systems. In *Proceedings of IEEE Vehicular Technology Coference VTC* (pp. 2336-2340). IEEE.

Harri, H., & Antti, T. (2009). *LTE for UMTS OFDMA and SC-FDMA based radio access.* West Sussex, UK: John Wiley and Sons Ltd.

Hebb, D. O. (1949). *The organization of behaviour.* New York: John Wiley & Sons.

Hui, L., & Guoqing, L. (2005). *OFDMA-based broadband wireless networks: Design and optimization.* Hoboken, NJ: John Willey & Sons.

Jani, P., Niko, K. H., Martti, M., & Mika, R. (2008). *Mixed traffic packet scheduling in UTRAN long term evaluation downlink.* Paper presented at Indoor nas Radio Mobile Communication IEEE 19th International Symposium. New York, NY.

Jinning, A. J. I., & Nicholson, P. L. S. (1987). *Artificial intelligence in communication networks.* Paper presented at the Conference on Computing Systems and Information Technology. New York, NY.

Jun, S., Na, Y., An, L., & Haige, X. (2009). Opportunistic scheduling for heterogeneous services in downlink OFDMA system. In *Proceedings of IEEE Computer Society* (pp. 260-264). IEEE.

Khozeimeh, F., & Haykin, S. (2010). Self-organizing dynamic spectrum management for cognitive networks. In *Proceedings of Communication Networks and Services Research Conference* (pp. 1-7). Montreal, Canada: CNSR.

Kian, C. B., Simon, A., & Angela, D. (2008). Joint time-frequency domain proportional fair scheduler with HARQ for 3GPP LTE systems. In *Proceedings of IEEE Vehicular Technology Coference VTC* (pp.1-5). Calgary, Canada: IEEE.

Leandros, T., & Anthony, E. (1993). Dynamic server allocation to parallel queues with randomly varying connectivity. *IEEE Transactions on Information Theory, 39,* 466–478. doi:10.1109/18.212277

Parimal, P., Srikrshna, B., & Aravind, R. (2005). A sub-carrier allocation algorithm for OFDMA using buffer and channel state information. In *Proceedings of Vehicular Technology Conference*. IEEE.

Petridou, S. G., Sarigiannidis, P. G., Papadimitriou, G. I., & Pomportsis, A. S. (2007). Clustering based scheduling: A new approach to the design of scheduling algorithms for WDM star networks. In *Proceedings of Communication and Vehicular Technology in the Benilux* (pp. 1–5). Delft, The Netherlands: Academic Press. doi:10.1109/SCVT.2007.4436255

Sanjay, S., & Alexander, L. S. (2000). *Scheduling for multiple flows sharing a time-varying channel: The exponential rule*. Bell Labs, Lucent Technologies.

Srivastava, J., Cooley, R., Deshpande, M., & Tan, P. N. (2000). Web usage mining: Discovery and application of usage patterns from web data. *ACM SIGKDD Explorations*, *1*, 12–23. doi:10.1145/846183.846188

Stefania, S., Issam, T., & Matthew, B. (2009). *The UMTS long term evolution forum theory to practice*. Hoboken, NJ: John Willey & Sons Ltd.

Toskala, A., & Tiirola, E. (2006). UTRAN long term evaluation in 3GPP. In *Proceedings of IEEE Personal Indoor and Mobile Radio Communications Conference* (pp. 1-5). Helsinki, Finland: IEEE.

Zhen, K., Yu-Kwong, & Jianzhou, W. (2009). A low complexity QoS aware proportinal fair multi-carrier scheduling algorithm for OFDM systems. *Vehiculer Transaction on IEEE Technology, 58,* 2225-2235.

Chapter 15
Best-M Feedback Technique in 4G-LTE Systems

Hani H. Alyazidi
Florida Institute of Technology, USA

ABSTRACT

The feedback load is an important parameter with a large impact in Orthogonal Frequency Division Multiple Access (OFDMA) techniques, as a feedback over each one of the subcarriers will induce a non-acceptable signaling load in the system, so that some optimization and feedback reduction strategies are required to meet practical systems demands. The decision over the best strategy for feedback optimization highly depends on the number of available users in the system. The authors obtain the users' effect on the system through a feedback strategy over a subset of the subcarriers showing the best channel conditions, where a closed form expression of the obtained data rate is formulated to exactly indicate the effect of the number of users, the operating SNR, and/or the available number of feedback bits in the system. Quality of Service (QoS) is also obtained using the Symbol Error Rate (SER). The performance of the presented scheme is compared to the one-bit feedback strategy, where interesting conclusions are obtained.

1. INTRODUCTION

One of the most interesting techniques for modern broadband communications is the Orthogonal Frequency Division Multiple Access (OFDMA); Hoshyar et al. (2010) mentioned that efficiently converts a broadband frequency selective channel into a set of flat fading sub channels (subC) that are easily equalized. Its low complexity and high performance has pushed it into commercial standards as 3GPP LTE 4th generation for cellular communication systems (European Telecommunications Standards Institute, 2011). A further advantage of OFDMA in comparison

to its predecessor OFDM is its suitability for Multiuser scenarios, as it can provide service to several users at the same time, where each user will be allocated a bundle of subCs, while in OFDM all the subCs are awarded to a single user. Commercial systems require resources distribution among the customers, so that the OFDMA option was the implemented option in the standards. For any multiuser wireless scheme to be efficient, adaptation to the channel conditions must be accomplished, where Chen et al. (2012) stated the opportunistic scheduling is an efficient approach to select the best user for each one of the subCs. The Adaptive Coding and Modulation (ACM)

DOI: 10.4018/978-1-4666-4888-3.ch015

strategy is another helpful tool to adapt the transmitted signal to the channel conditions (Simon & Alouini, 2004). The challenge of employing any adaption to the channel characteristics is that the transmitter must know information about the channel before the transmission starts, and this is done through feedback from the receiver to the transmitter.

Modern wireless communication standards are characterized by being dynamic, where several options are available within the same standard. The most typical example is related to the Multiple Input Multiple Output (MIMO) techniques within the LTE technology (Hoshyar et al., 2010),where up to 13 different options are allowed in the standard, and each operator can choose the most suitable option for its implementation. This is a very interesting and challenging paradigm in modern wireless systems, as each operator must have an internal R&D department, where the engineers must be in charge of doing applied research for their scenario conditions, user's profiles and service characteristics, among others. This also opens the door for the research groups across the Globe to propose new techniques and strategies to improve the current wireless systems, by adapting the proposals to each operator demands. This is a very important characteristic in comparison to the rigid standardization process of GSM for example, where a single option is envisaged and the possibility to have some impact on the standard changes is minor for their search community.

In OFDMA this is a major handicap as each subC has a different performance, so that the transmitter must be aware about the channel quality from all users and over all the subCs, representing a feedback load that is prohibitive in practical systems. Based on the large amount of required feedback (Changhee & Shroff, 2009), some proposals targeted random users and subCs selection (Zorba et al.,2009), while others developed a single bit feedback to indicate an ON-OFF state over all the subCs (Sanayei & Nosratinia, 2007). But in order to extract the gain from OFDMA systems,

channel information is required and thus, the solution seems to be through feedback reduction techniques. Trivellato et al. (2009) mentioned each user is allowed to feedback over one subC, the one showing the highest Signal-to-Noise-Ratio (SNR), thus largely decreasing the feedback load, but then the achieved data rate is far from the maximum achievable one. In recent standardization activities of the 3GPP for the LTE technology (European Telecommunications Standards Institute, 2011), (Sesia et al., 2009), the option of Best-M scheme is recommended (Pedersen et al., 2007), where each user is asked to feedback the M subCs showing largest SNR values.

The heterogeneity of applications in the current and future telecommunication system necessitates characterization of the QoS, in terms of several metrics based on the required design (Jindal & Ramprashad, 2011).These metrics can be interpreted by minimum required rate and maximum tolerable SER for the reception quality, among others. This chapter tackles the aforementioned QoS for the Best-M scheme, where the serviced user has strict QoS demands in terms of its reception SER.

In order to optimize the Best-M feedback strategy and to characterize all the involved parameters, this chapter obtains the closed form expressions for its data rate and SER performance. Furthermore, with both the SER and data rate expressions, the system throughput is also obtained (Kim & Lee, 2012). Therefore, the Best-M scheme can be easily optimized by any commercial operator and/or manufacturer to account for each operating scenario conditions. In order to compare it to other feedback strategies, the resultant amount of feedback bits for the Best-M scheme is obtained. Thanks to the mathematical formulated expressions, interesting results are obtained about the impact of the number of available users, the average SNR and the allowed feedback load.

The remainder of this chapter is organized as follows: while section 2 deals with the Background, then system model in section 3, in section

4 the user opportunistic scheduling is presented together with its statistical distributions, followed by section 5 with the ACM technique. The data rate and feedback load in 3GPP LTE systems are presented in closed form expressions for the Best-M feedback strategy in section 6, while section 9 tackles the SER and throughput also in closed form expressions. Section 8 shows the numerical results and simulations to check for the mathematically formulated results, then Debate the future research direction in section IX, Finally the chapter draws the conclusions in section 10.

2. BACKGROUND

A. Wireless System Development

Mobile communication has seen a realized variance through the passing centuries, starting with the first generation (1G) systems in the 1980s. The 1G system was relied on analog technologies and applied analogue Frequency Modulation (FM) techniques. There were a lot of vital examples of 1G systems such as the Advanced Mobile Phone System (AMPS) relied on FM technology for voice transmission and digital signaling for control information, the Total Access Cellular System (TACS), the Narrowband AMPS (NAMPS) and the Nordic Mobile Telephone System (NMT-900), where it depends on Frequency Division Multiple Access (FDMA) having each channel allocate to a solitary frequency within a cluster of cells (Kim & Lee, 2012).

In the 1990s with the appearance of a lot of conflicts in the 1G and as a result to the persistent raise in the number of subscribers, a recent second generation (2G) relied on digital modulation techniques have showed. The 2G system submitted more capacity and higher data rate, and it also used multiple access techniques like Time Division Multiple Access (TDMA) and Code Division Multiple Access (CDMA) and FDMA.

Examples of 2G contain the Global System for Mobile communications (GSM), the United States Digital Cellular (USDC) standards IS-54 and IS-136, the Pacific Digital Cellular (PDC) and the cdmaOne. For a lot the terms "2G" and "3G" are formally explained, where in between came two undefined generations invented for marketing aims, the 2.5G and 2.75G, where they were used to represent 2G-systems that have a packet switched field along with the circuit switched field (Kim & Lee, 2012).

B. Multiuser Scenario

LTE systems are based on multiuser scenario. In multiuser system the Base Station (BS) communicates with several geographically different users at the same time. A fundamental characteristic of the wireless channel is the fading of the channel strength due to multipath. The multipath propagation results in deep fades which are principle reasons for symbol error. Diversity provides a good solution for fading in single user scenario where all streams are transmitted to one user (Molisch, 2010). The concept of multiuser diversity states that if one subcarrier is in fading for one user, there is a high probability that subcarrier is not in fading for another user (Floren et al., 2003). Therefore, the multiuser diversity benefits from a large number of users in that, many users in a system lead to a high probability that one of the users has a good channel at any given time where multiuser diversity results from the independent channel variation across users. The basic principle to maximize multiuser diversity is to transmit to the users with the largest SNR at each channel. This results in maximum system throughput (Bingham et al., 1989) (Peebles, 2002). Maximizing the throughput is an important goal of the LTE and other modern wireless systems. However, achieving this goal leads to an unfair resource allocation between the individual users (Sanayei & Nosratinia, 2005). The users close to the base station occupy most of the subcarriers whereas users at the cell edge are dropped at the scheduling. Thus, a practical goal of scheduler design is to maximize multiuser diversity subject to fairness and QoS constraints (Viswanath et al., 2002).

C. Channel Quality Indication (CQI)

The benefit from multiuser diversity comes at the cost of feedback overhead that is used to convey the CQI to the transmitter. CQI plays an important role in modern wireless systems such as LTE systems. CQI can be defined as a message that is sent by the user to the BS to describe the current DL channel quality of that user. Feedback overhead is a considerable drawback especially in multicarrier systems where many subcarriers are used. Such a drawback would also be increase in the multiuser scenario, because feedback is required from each user.

Based on the uplink rate allowed for CQI feedback we can have different schemes such as full CQI feedback (Leke & Cioffi, 1997) threshold (Alouini & Gesbert, 2004), and Best–M feedback schemes (Kang & Kim, 2012).

Full feedback approach means knowledge of all subcarriers gain across all user, which is not realistic especially when channel condition change quickly in time. Moreover, full feedback consumes a lot of uplink bandwidth. This approach has usually been justified for a time division duplex (TDD) technique which is based on channel reciprocal at the uplink and downlink (Keller & Hanzol, 2000). However, in FDD based communication and also in practical TDD systems full information is difficult to obtain.

The channel is complex so both its phase and amplitude must be fed back to the transmitter side (Caire & Shamai, 2003). However, this leads to a large signaling load which makes its implementation is not practical. On the other hand, with no CQI at all implementation of Adaptive Coding Modulation (ACM) could not be implemented which would have negative implication on the system performance. Therefore, it seems that some sort of partial CQI is the most tractable option to obtain the benefits from the channel adaptation techniques, without significant increase in signaling load.

The system cannot provide service to all the users at the same time, so scheduling is required. CQI from all the users is required in order to accomplish the user's selection and transmitter processing techniques. The feedback from all the users and over all the OFDMA subcarriers is impractical. The feedback overhead becomes a more serious in multichannel system like OFDMA, where we have tens of shared channels. Consequently, different approach is needed to reduce feedback overhead.

D. Scheduling

Scheduling algorithms has a significant impact on network performance. In fact, it is an important tool to achieve the multiuser diversity gain. Therefore, a lot of research is dedicated to improvement of scheduling. The most basic strategy for scheduling is called Round Robin Technique (Changhee & Shroff, 2009). In this technique the channel conditions of different users are not taken into consideration, and the selection of the scheduled user is done either through a random selection or through an ordering of the users. This strategy provides the lowest scheduling delay results, but at the cost of the lowest data rate performance.

Another popular system called Lazy Scheduling is covered in (Uysal et al., 2002). The scheduling objective in this case is to save in the amount of transmitted power. The transmitter will consider the channel situation (e.g., through the feedback SNR value) to decide whether to transmit or not. The decision is typically based on the Shannon theorem. If the SNR is low and a predefined data rate is required, a large amount of transmitted power is required to increase the SNR value and meet the data rate target. Therefore, if the feedback SNR value is small, the transmitter decides to stop the transmission (in order to save in the power).

It waist till the channel conditions are improved to resume the transmission process. This scheme achieves a considerable power saving, but at the cost of larger delay in the service and the overall throughput reduction (Andrews et al., 2004).

A large number of proposals tackle the users scheduling from the Data Link Control (DLC) layer .At this layer the emphasis is on the users scheduling from the packets arrival and queue point of view (Neely et al., 2003) Such proposals do not take into consideration the channel characteristics. This proposal is focused users scheduling over OFDMA where the channel metrics (mainly it's SNR) are very important, without taking the queue states into consideration, so that all DLC based scheduling strategies are out of the scope of this thesis.

Esmailpour and Nasser (2011) presented a Fair scheduler to support quality of service requirements by exploiting the fluctuations in the channel quality. The illustrated algorithms are analyzing the accumulative channel feedback knowledge to propose fair scheduling. This scheduler does not consider only current situation of the channel state to schedule the transmission to users. Instead, it tackles a predefined relation between the current state condition (instantaneous value of SNR) and the average value of the channel conditions within a period of time. This value will increase the channel capacity, taking into account that the time delay to be minimized. The time varying channel and location dependent error problems in wireless scheduling are discussed by Sezgin et al. (2008), where Li et al. (2009) stated the paper focus is on exploiting the multiuser channel diversity in a real-time situation. The proposed technique uses the opportunistic null of the inter-cell interference in different fading schemes with little scattering or slow fading.

Some authors propose techniques such as opportunistic beam forming to increase the multiuser diversity (Viswanath et al., 2002). With these techniques the same signal is transmitted over multiple antennas with different transmissions power. This increases the channel diversity of users, which leads to improved opportunistic gain. Max Weight is another opportunistic scheduler that selects the user with the highest product of queue length and transmission rate (Wong et al., 1999).

In fact, opportunistic scheduling has been proposed not only to improve capacity or QoS, but also to minimize the overall transmission power (Elliott, 2002).

E. Feedback Reduction

In order to employ scheduling, CQI of all users at the scheduling time is required .Thus, when consider multicarrier systems such as OFDMA, the total required feedback information is quite large. Therefore, many reduction feedback schemes are introduced.

Codded feedback strategy is developed with a large number of randomly generated matrices. As the codebook length is increased, the accuracy of the channel approximation is increased, and in the asymptotic case with infinite codebook entries, this scheme compares to the full CSI performance. But memory limitations and processor search within the codebook entries make this transmission strategy to offer an imperfect CSI at the transmitter side. Even though, it remains as an attractive tradeoff performance-feedback load (Chang et al., 2011).

Covariance Feedback is proposed for the LTE standard, where the LTE Base Station is equipped with more than one antenna, for what is known as the Multiple Input Multiple Output (MIMO) systems. A possible approach to reduce the quantity of the overhead information is to feed back the channel covariance instead of the full channel information (Jafar & Goldsmith, 2004), This seems to be appropriate in the case of a highly scattered channel, offering a zero mean complex Gaussian random vectors but with a known non-white covariance matrix. It is also reasonable to find this scenario in a too fast channel that offers problems to track its mean (Ting et al., 2007).

Ramalingam and Wang (2008) studied previous work when both mean and covariance information are available at the transmitter. The covariance matrix is optimized to maximize the throughput of the channel. The contributions were extended for wideband OFDM (Barriac & Madhow, 2006).

Using a single receiving antenna with perfect channel state in the receiver, Visotsky and Madhow (2000) shown that, although beam forming is not optimal for the non-channel state information (CSI), partial information can be enough to improve the system capacity. The author considers two cases (Visotsky & Madhow, 2000): mean (SNR) feedback, where no correlation is present in the channel; and covariance feedback with a zero mean and with any given correlation matrix. It is shown that beam forming is close to optimal strategy if there are strong paths present which can be exploited by the approach.

By feeding back just the instantaneous channels quality (Molisch et al., 2003), Antenna selection is an alternative technique to reduce the overhead feedback. Here user feeds back its channel quality relative to each one of the transmitting antennas. The BS scheduler selects the best user for each one of the transmitting antennas and forwards its information.

Blum et al. (2002) mentioned the capacity of MIMO with antenna selection has been studied for cases with limited feedback. It was shown that the antenna selection system increases the capacity using only a minimal amount of feedback, where the paper ignores any error and delay that may present in the feedback signal.

By exploiting diversity for MISO at the transmit side with the help of a feedback channel, Winters (1983) establishes a very simple antenna selection algorithm. The transmit antenna must be switched when the received SNR is below a predefined threshold.

The work presented a principle for choosing antenna subsets which have the ability to enhance the capacity of the channels (Gore et al., 2000). Antenna selection methods are used in low rank

channels to enhance the capacity in an effective way. Alkhansari and Gershman (2004) stated the technique explored two different iterative methods depending on both incremental and decremented analysis, to latter study the outage probability of the transmit antenna system employing space time coding (Gore & Paulraj, 2002). It has been shown that when CSIT is perfect, antenna selection preserves the diversity gains. Different approaches were proposed to reduce feedback overhead. Focusing on single input single output (SISO) various methods to reduce the amount of feedback have been suggested. The problem in employing an opportunistic scheme in OFDM network is the large amount of required feedback to pass from the mobile to the base station (BS). To deal with this problem, Floren et al. (2003) proposes an opportunistic scheme in which the sub channels are clustered into groups and then only the maximum value of each cluster is feedback to the BS. The cluster size can be chosen so that the feedback can be reduced without much degradation in throughput performance. Since the sub bands with higher channel gain can be assigned to the user, the performance loss is relatively small. However, the paper does not consider fairness or other quality of service QoS parameters.

The idea of reducing the feedback through thresholding was proposed by (Alouini & Gesbert, 2004). The users send feedback if their SNR values are greater than a predefined threshold without quantization. Although, the feedback overhead is reduced while multiuser diversity gain is preserved, this approach can suffer from the case where all users are below the threshold, so the multiuser gain is wasted at that instant (Sanayei & Nosratinia, 2007), (Pedersen et al., 2007).

In multiuser scenario some quantity of CSIT is required; otherwise multiuser gains within this scenario are wasted in (Sharif & Hassibi, 2005). Using flat fading model the author in (Sharif & Hassibi, 2005), extend the work done for the case of MIMO (Viswanath et al., 2002). Instead of using a single beam, multiple random beams were used. The base station BS randomly constructs M beams and transmits data to the users with maximum SINR for each beam. Therefore, by searching just for the best user in the network the amount of feedback reduced.

3. SYSTEM MODEL

A wireless broadband downlink communication system is considered in this chapter, where the total bandwidth is equally partitioned into S subcarriers or sub channels (subC) through the OFDMA technology. A total of N single antenna users are available in the system and asking for service from the transmitter at the Base Station (BS). Each subC is showing a different performance from all the other subCs (i.e., frequency uncorrelated scenario), but all of them are modeled following the same statistical distribution, so that this chapter will now present the mathematical formulation for a single subC.

The subC response h(t) between each user and the BS is modeled as a quasi-static block fading model, that independently changes between consecutive time intervals (i.e., time uncor-related channel) with independent and identically distributed (i.i.d.) complex Gaussian entries $\sim CN (0, 1)$. The received signal yn(t) for the nth user is expressed as:

$$y_n(t) = h_n(t)x_n(t) + z_n(t) \qquad (1)$$

where xn(t) is the transmitted symbol, and zn(t) is an additive zero mean white Gaussian noise with variance σ2. The received SNR γn(t) is obtained as:

$$^3{}_n(t) = \frac{|h_n(t)|^2}{\tilde{A}2} \qquad (2)$$

and for easiness in the notation from now on, the time index is dropped whenever possible.

4. USERS SCHEDULING

The optimality of the scheduling is achieved with the SNR feedback from all the users (Chen et al., 2012), and enabling the BS to select the user showing the largest SNR value at each scheduling time, for what is known as Opportunistic Scheduling (Chen et al., 2012), so that the system benefits from the multiuser availability and achieves the data rate optimality. In the practice, there are a lot of obstacles that should be taken into account before this mechanism is used, for the reason to give fairness and to guarantee that the user's requirements are satisfied, in real, the channel conditions are various and varied over the users as the wireless channel is random. Any technique that would be suggested for its implementation in practical systems, cannot only be targeted to increase the data rate, but also to consider the various users and operator demands. Relied on this, a tradeoff will be noticed between the increase of the data rate, the users fairness and the satisfaction of the users/operator QoS demands (Esmailpour & Nasser, 2011).

The elementary strategy for scheduling named the Round Robin technique (Simon & Alouini, 2004), where the channel terms over the different users are not taken into account, and the selection of the scheduled user is done even through a random selection or through an ordering of the users. This strategy provides the lowest scheduling delay results, but at the cost of the lowest data rate performance.

One of the proposals called Lazy Scheduling (Sezgin et al., 2008), where the scheduling objective is to save in the amount of transmitted power. The transmitter will consider the channel situation (e.g., through the feedback SNR value) to decide even to transmit or not. The decision is based on the Shannon theorem, where if the SNR is low and predefined data rate is required, a larger amount of transmitted power is required to increase the SNR value and meet the data rate demand. Therefore, if the feedback SNR value is small, the transmitter decides to stop the transmission (in order to save in the amount of power), and wait till the channel conditions change (larger SNR is obtained), from where the word Lazy stems. The scheme achieves a considerable power saving, but at the cost of larger delay in the service.

A huge number of proposals treatment the users scheduling from the Data Link Control (DLC) layer, that focus on the users scheduling from the packets arrival and queue point of view (Li et al., 2009), without taking into account the channel features. This proposal is focused on a user's scheduling through OFDMA where the channel metrics (fundamentally its SNR) are significant, without taking the queue states into account, so that all DLC based scheduling strategies are out of the domain of this thesis.

Therefore, the BS will accomplish a hybrid approach so that if the SNR information is not available, Changhee and Shroff (2009) stated the random Scheduling will be performed. Moreover, if no feedback information will be available, then the BS cannot apply ACM as asked in the 3GPP LTE standard; and a fixed modulation and coding strategy will be applied, pushing down the achieved data rate. In order to be employed in the data rate formulation of the Best-M scheme, we now present the mathematical characterization of the opportunistic scheduling. Notice that the measured SNR values at the receiver side for i.i.d. complex Gaussian channels has a probability distribution function (PDF) (Chen et al., 2012), given as

$$f(x) = \sigma^2 e^{-(x\sigma^2)} \tag{3}$$

where the SNR cumulative distribution function (CDF) is then formulated as

$$F(x) = 1 - e^{-(x\sigma^2)} \tag{4}$$

As the BS will select the user with the largest SNR value (i.e., $\max 1 \leq n \leq N \gamma n$), then the serving SNR value for the selected user through opportunistic scheduling will have a CDF as

$$C(x) = (F(x))^N = [1 - e^{-(x\sigma^2)}]^N \tag{5}$$

and its corresponding PDF given by

$$c(x) = N\left[1 - e^{-(x\sigma^2)}\right]^{N-1}\left[\sigma^2 e^{-(x\sigma^2)}\right] \tag{6}$$

For the case of Random Scheduling, where the BS will arbitrary select a user for transmission, the PDF and CDF are given in Equations (3) and (4), respectively.

5. ADAPTIVE CODING AND MODULATION

One of the main tools available at the transmitter side to combat the continuous changes in the wireless channel is the use of the Adaptive Coding and Modulation (ACM) strategy.

Where the BS constantly changes both the employed Code and Modulation to send the data to the selected user, where the change is performed each channel characteristics update, assumed to be each coherence time. Based on each application quality requirements, usually set as the required Symbol Error Rate (SER), each SNR range will be mapped to a given Code and Modulation that can guarantee the required SER value. ACM has been employed in the 3GPP LTE standard, (European Telecommunications Standards Institute, 2011) mentioned where 16 different levels (code and modulation) are considered (Sesia et al., 2009), each user will measure its received SNR value and it will compare it to a predefined mapping table SNR-ACM, where for each SNR value, it will select the most appropriate ACM level. Table

1 shows an example of the SNR mapping that is performed over realistic measurements in practical LTE scenarios, where the different levels of ACM are stated. K = 16 different levels are defined in the standard, so that the user can indicate which one matches its SNR value. Therefore, the Channel Quality Indicator (CQI) in this case is not the SNR value, but its mapping to the ACM table; so that if the SNR value is within the kth level (i.e., $\alpha_k \leq SNR < \alpha_{k+1}$), then the CQI for the kth interval is sent back to the BS, where α_k is the lower edge for the kth ACM level.

The scheduling strategy has a major impact on the ACM performance, as the serving SNR value (i.e., the SNR value of the selected user) will have a different range for its operation, and therefore, the probability to select each ACM level. Notice that with random scheduling, the SNR values for the serving user will have a lower average in comparison to opportunistic scheduling, so that the probability to employ the high modulations (i.e., high data rate) will be

lower with the consequent decrease in the system data rate.

With 16 different ACM levels, 4 different bits are required in the feedback process for each CQI value, but as in OFDMA, the user has to report its CQI over each subC, then the feedback load will be very large, and therefore, next section will discuss how to reduce it.

6. BEST-M FEEDBACK SCHEME

There are different proposal for reduction of CQI feedback load. The document focuses on the one "bit_and_best-M_" schemes. These two interesting schemes are very popular, mainly because of their data rate and feedback performance.

One bit strategy was presented in (Sanayei & Nosratinia, 2007), and it is based the work given in (Alouini & Gesbert, 2004). This strategy relies on the ON-OFF keying concept applied to OFDMA communication. The receiver compares

Table 1. SNR mapping in 3GPP - LTE systems

SNR (dB)	CQI	Modulation	M	df	Code rate	Data Rate (R)
out of range	0	out of range	out of range	out of range	out of range	out of range
-7.27	1	QPSK	4	10	0.076	0.157
-4.76	2	QPSK	4	8	0.118	0.231
-2.06	3	QPSK	4	6	0.188	0.371
0.61	4	QPSK	4	5	0.301	0.608
2.81	5	QPSK	4	4	0.421	0.873
4.69	6	16QAM	16	10	0.571	1.171
6.29	7	16QAM	16	8	0.367	1.476
8.69	8	16QAM	16	6	0.473	1.917
11.37	9	16QAM	16	5	0.608	2.401
13.11	10	16QAM	16	4	0.451	2.692
16.44	11	64QAM	64	10	0.550	3.338
19.62	12	64QAM	64	8	0.657	3.813
23.01	13	64QAM	64	6	0.751	4.341
26.19	14	64QAM	64	5	0.854	5.215
28.66	15	64QAM	64	4	0.929	5.348

its measured SNR for every one of the OFDMA sub-channels, and compares it to a predefined threshold (γth). If the measured SNR is larger than the threshold, the bit "1" is sent back to the BS; otherwise the receiver feeds back a bit "0". With this minimal amount of feedback, the BS can accomplish scheduling over all the receivers that send a "1" by randomly choosing one of them. The calculation of the resultant data rate largely depends on the predefined threshold. There is a disadvantage of this strategy. If the SNR of all users are below the predefined threshold, the BS will randomly select a user between all the available ones. This ultimately reduces resultant data rate.

In modern wireless systems, there is a true need for feedback, not only for scheduling, but also for the ACM operation as in LTE system. Therefore, 1-bit is insufficient for the modern wireless system to operate, so an improved and modified feedback strategy must be implemented. The Best-M technique stands out as a very attractive option (Pedersen et al., 2007).

The idea behind the Best-M is that, each user is allowed to feedback the SNR values only over a small subset (M) of OFDMA subCs. The M subCs are the ones showing the largest SNR values for that user. The feedback obviously includes the indexes of the M subCs. Allocating each subC to the user with the largest SNR value for that subC, results in an increase of the system data rate. For the subCs where no user made a feedback on them, the BS will randomly select a user.

The author in (Sanayei & Nosratinia, 2007) establishes a system that gets the required CQI information based on compressing SNR using a discreet cosine transform DCT. Moreover, Alouini and Gesbert, (2004), the idea was to report only the measurements M with the highest SNR. The feedback overhead and performance rely on the M parameters. Increasing M leads to improve performance but also the feedback overhead increase. Additionally, it might be difficult to set appropriate value for M in this system.

To deal with such a problem the idea of threshold-based scheme was proposed by (Pedersen et al., 2007). The basic idea of this paper is to report the highest SNR sub-channel and all the other measurements within a threshold which is a good solution to limit CSI feedback. The results from this study conclude that allowing each user to report CQI for the M best parts of the entire subcarriers is sufficient for the system to achieve the multiuser diversity gain using frequency domain packet scheduling. However the performance of the system is sensitive to the choice of the feedback subcarriers M.

To cover this problem, it has shown that the Best-M CQI feedback reduces the multi user diversity gain as M is increased. Therefore, optimal system is required to choose small values of M to fully benefit from multiuser diversity but with reduction in the overhead feedback. Previously, studies the Best-M performance in terms of bit error rate and the probability of outage using round-robin scheduling. In the same paper the work extend to multi antenna transmission schemes such as antenna selection. The throughput of the system achieved by the use of Best-M feedback with opportunistic user scheduling was evaluated numerically in (Pedersen et al., 2007).

The only way to achieve channel knowledge at the transmitter side in Frequency Division Duplexing (FDD) systems like the 3GPP LTE FDD systems (adapted version in almost all countries Worldwide) is through the feedback link. And as previously commented, the feedback over all the subCs in OFDMA systems is impractical, so that feedback reduction is required in commercial systems.

One of the interesting proposals in literature, Akbari et al. (2010) suggested allowing each user to feedback the SNR values only over a small subset (M) of OFDMA subCs, where these M subCs are the ones showing the largest SNR values for that user. The feedback obviously includes the indexes of the M subCs. Now with this strategy, the BS can extract the multiuser gain from the scenario as it will allocate each subC to the user with the largest SNR value in that subC, boosting the system data rate. For the subCs where no user made a feedback on them, the BS will randomly select a user for those subCs.

European Telecommunications Standards Institute (2011) declared that the Best-M scheme is proposed by the 3GPP LTE standard for the manufacturers to include it through the OFDMA subCs allocation process, so that the contribution of this chapter is in studying this scheme and providing closed form expressions for its data rate, SER and feedback load, characterizing all the system parameters that affect the Best-M scheme, as well as their impact on the system performance.

Therefore to accomplish these tasks, it is very important to provide the probability to operate each one of the different ACM levels that we obtain thanks to the formulated CDFs in section (III).

For the case with opportunistic scheduling, where the user reporting the largest CQI is selected, the CDF for this CQI feedback is a modified version of the SNR-CDF in Equation (5), as now only 16 different ACM levels can be selected, while Equation (5) is for the SNR feedback (i.e., infinite number of ACM levels.).

Also, two (or more) users can have different SNR values, but both are within the same ACM level, so that both feed the same value.

To account for this phenomena, the modified CDF for the opportunistic scheduling under the above CQI feedback in 3GPP LTE systems, and for each one of the ACM levels (αk, αk+1), we formulate it as

$$CC(x) = \sum^N (N)(F(\alpha k))^{N-n}(F(\alpha k+1) - F(\alpha k))^{n-1} F(x) \quad n=1 \quad n \quad (7)$$

with F (x) from Equation (4). With further mathematical manipulations, the previous expression we rewrite it as

$$CC(x) = \frac{(F(\alpha k + 1))^N - (F(\alpha k))^N}{F(\alpha k) - F(\alpha k)} F(x) \quad (8)$$

and its PDF cc(x) evaluates by derivation the CDF expression to state as

$$cc(x) = \frac{(F(\alpha k + 1))^N - (F(\alpha k))^N}{F(\alpha k + 1) - F(\alpha k)} f(x) \quad (9)$$

The number M in the commercial LTE system will not be large (i.e., $M \in (10-20)$), while the most typical number of subCs in commercial systems will be within the options $S = \{512, 1024\}$, and it is expected that $N \in (8 - 15)$ users are accessing the system at the same time. Therefore, not all the subCs will be requested, and therefore, some of them will be empty and the BS couldn't apply opportunistic scheduling over them, leaving the BS with the only option of random subC allocation to the users. It is important to obtain the probability for each situation in order to formulate the data rate, and to know how to optimize the system based on the amount of allowed feedback values M. For a given subC, the scheduling outage probability Pr is defined as the probability that no user selects this subC as one of its best M ones (Peebles, 2002), so that no feedback is sent back to the BS over this subC. We define it as

$$P^r = [1 - \tfrac{M}{S}]^N \quad (10)$$

Then the probability Ps that at least one user feeds back on a given subC, and opportunistic scheduling is performed by the BS, is the complementary probability given by

$$P_s = 1 - P_r = 1 - [1 - \tfrac{M}{S}]^N \quad (11)$$

where it is highly expected that only 1 user feedback over each subC due to the practical relation between M and S in commercial systems. We consider that one single feedback user is available per subC whenever that subC is in the non-outage case (i.e., this subC is one of the best M subCs for this user). On the other hand for the outage case, the scheduling is random thus making the PDF of the serving SNR as in Equation (3).

Based on the obtained probabilities in Equations (10) and (11), we can mathematically represent the resultant average data rate (in bps/Hz) as

$$R_{BestM} = P_s R_s + P_r R_r \qquad (12)$$

where R_r is the achieved data rate when the subC is in the outage case and random selection is performed over it; while R_s corresponds to the data rate in the subCs where opportunistic scheduling is accomplished. As previously commented, the BS that has not received any value over a specific subC, it will randomly allocate a user to that subC, and employing the lowest ACM level, to increase the probability P_c of correctly decoding at the receiver side. P_c corresponds to the probability that the measured SNR at the randomly selected user is larger than the detection threshold for the lowest ACM level, and we calculate it from Table 1, as

$$P_c = 1 - F(-7.27dB) \qquad (13)$$

where $F(x)$ is shown in Equation (4), as the user in this case is randomly selected. With this probability obtained, now the achievable data rate, measured in (bps/Hz), in the subCs with random selection is obtained, also from Table 1, as

$$Rr = 0.157 \, Pc \qquad (14)$$

Now the last parameter that must be obtained is the expression for R_s, that we formulate as

$$R_s = \sum_{k=1}^{K-1} P_k R_k \qquad (15)$$

where Rk is the resultant data rate for the correspondent kth ACM level, as shown in the last column of Table 1, on the other hand, Pk denotes the probability to operate each one of the ACM levels that we obtain as

$$P_k = CC(\alpha_{k+1}) - CC(\alpha_k) \qquad (16)$$

that is presented in closed form expression thanks to the formulated CDF in Equation (8).

The last topic that we will tackle in this section is the calculation of the feedback load in LTE by employing the Best-M scheme. The LTE system supports 16 ACM levels, and then 4 bits are required for each CQI value. As the Best-M scheme allows M feedback values, then the feedback load for this scheme, we obtain it as

$$FL = N(4M + M[\log_2(S)] \qquad (17)$$

where $[\log_2(S)]$ indicates the ceil function, while N is the number of available users in the scenario, as discussed in the system model. The second part of the FL expression is related to the indication of which are the selected subCs, as the user not only sends the CQI value, but also on which subC.

7. SER PERFORMANCE

The resource allocation and users scheduling one of main subjects in wireless communications, the basic which is a sensitive function because of resource reduction and the exorbitant price of available resources. From a networking view, the resource allocation is executed in the MAC layer, where the channel is favoured to the user with the most suitable network parameters (queue length, delay threshold, VIP user, ...) as it is supposed that all users channels shows the same transmitting terms. otherwise, researchers in the information theory domain concentrate on another resource allocation policy, which based on PHY layer parameters about users' channel terms, allocates the resources to the user with the best channel, so that to raise the system performance. This alternative policy chooses the users assuming the existence of equal system parameters to all the users.

The scheduling policy is clearly various whenever thresholds or trade-offs are considered, because in a threshold relied on scheduling scheme, channel terms can be used for all the users satisfying the QoS thresholds, which provides higher system performance as the Multiuser diversity previously debated is partially used. Broadly, more efficient employment of the system resources is potential when threshold approaches are followed, which added to the practical approach that thresholds supplied in real systems, make the study of this influence OFDMA and QoS scheduling to be very likely.

The resource allocation is one of the major tools that the system can use to meet the QoS limitation that are existing in wireless scenarios. The scheduler can manage the resources to vitally allocate them in such a manner that QoS needs are fulfilled, simultaneously, high system performance is provided with related to sum rate. The employment of OFDMA provides additional levels of freedom that the scheduler can used in meeting the system needs, but at the same time, an efficient resource allocation is needed to optimize the system performance. Remind the higher system sum rate that OFDMA systems define to the system, where several users can simultaneously be serviced by the central transmitting unit. Consequently from a system point of view, these higher capabilities have to be dynamically managed to strike the system needs.

One of the main QoS indicators in practical systems is the Symbol Error Rate (SER), which shows the amount of correctly received bits at the receiver side.

Within LTE, the objectives are to increase the data rate but also the offered quality, where the SER indicator outstands as a basic metric for engineers. For Best-M scheme, the total SER (SER_t) has to account for the achievable SER during the opportunistic allocation SER_s as well as during the random SubCs allocation SER_r. We obtain SER_t as

$$SER_t = P_s\,SER_s + P_r\,SER_r. \tag{18}$$

As the BS does not know the channel characteristics during the random allocation, then the symbols are transmitted through the least available ACM interval where QPSK modulation is employed. The expression of SER when the subCs are randomly selected SER_r can be written as

$$SER_r = Q\left(\sqrt{\tfrac{2}{\sigma^2}}\right) \tag{19}$$

where Q represents the Q-function (Simon & Alouini, 2004).

On the other hand when the opportunistic scheduling is accomplished, SER_s depends on the SER value in each ACM level SER_k and the probability P_k to employ that interval. We formulate it as

$$SER_s = \sum_{K=1}^{K-1} SER_K P_k \tag{20}$$

and the SERk for the kth ACM interval we obtain Equation 21 (Box 1) where df_k is the free distance in the modulation employed within the kth ACM level, R_k is the correspondent data rate while M_k is an indicator of the ACM level. All parameters are presented in Table 1. To derive the complete relation of the probability of error from the comparison of the trellis path with all zero path at the first event, especially when there are many pos-

Box 1. Equation 21

$$SER_k = \sum_{d=dfree_k}^{\infty} 2B_k \Omega_k N \sum_{n=1}^{N-1} \binom{N-1}{n}(-1)^{n-1}\left(\tfrac{1}{n}\right)\left[1 - \sqrt{\frac{3r_k R_k d}{2n(M_k-1)3r_k R_k d}}\right]$$

sible paths in different d with larger value than the previous. Convolution encoder transfer function in (Jindal & Ranprashad, 2011) provides a complete description of all possible paths that integrate with zero paths by summing the error probability for all possible path distances as upper bounded error probability in the following equation. Cleary when using ACM, we include some coding that helps to correct the error at the receiver side. The basic and widely used convolution coding is used, so that the receiver side uses trellis paths to recover the transmitted symbols.

Newly defined parameters are

$$B_k = \begin{cases} 2^{\frac{d-d_{free_k}}{2}} & (d \text{ even}) \\ 0 & (d \text{ odd}) \end{cases} \tag{22}$$

and variable Ω_k as

$$\Omega_k = \left(\frac{\sqrt{M_k} - 1}{\sqrt{M_k}} \right). \tag{23}$$

enabling to put all parameters back to Equation (18) and in a closed form expression.

A. Throughput

Throughput is a considered as an important measure for the superiority of a wireless data link. Attaining highest throughput is the goal of resource allocation technique. Throughput is described as the quantity of data bits obtained devoid of error per second and this amount is always required being as high as probable. Maximal throughput has been considered as the objective of resource allocation method. In fact, the achievable throughput is an important parameter in realistic systems where the operator is not only interested in obtaining the largest data rate, but also at the minimum errors (i.e successfully transmitted symbols).

A lot of variables influence the throughput of a wireless information scheme containing the package dimension, the transmission rate, the amount of overhead bits in every package, the obtained signal power, the obtained noise power spectral density.

The throughput Th is one of the most important metrics for operators as it reflects the amount of delivered error-free data rate, as it constitutes the useful data rate for the customers (Kim & Lee, 2012). It is based on both the data rate and SER formulations, so that its equation is obtained as

$$Th = (1 - SER_t) R_t \tag{24}$$

Also presented in a closed form expression thanks to the already formulated results in Equations (12) and (18)

8. SIMULATION RESULTS

In order to check for the Best-M scheme and to validate the mathematically obtained closed form expressions, Monte Carlo simulations are carried out on a wireless downlink single-cell scenario running OFDMA, where the total bandwidth is divided in 512 subCs, which is one of the most typical options for LTE development. 64 subCs are employed for Guard Band to the right and 64 to the left. Another 20 subCs are employed for DC synchronization, resulting in S = 376 subCs user for data transmission; where each subC shows a bandwidth of 15 KHz (European Telecommunications Standards Institute, 2011). The users are uniformly distributed in the cell with i.i.d. complex gaussian channel and showing average SNR values in the interval (-10, 30) dB reflecting their position in the cell, where they are fixed along the coherence time (T_c=20ms), and allowed to move at the end of each T_c. A transmission power of 1 Watt is employed.

Figure 1 shows the Best-M scheme performance in a scenario with a variable number of available users and a fixed M = 4, where a larger number of users translates into a greater Multiuser gain, that is exploited by the Best-M strategy to achieve higher performance. The simulations are compared to the mathematical results obtained in Equation (12), where a very close behaviour is obtained that slightly drifts from the simulation result for an increasing number is users. The reason behind this drift is that as the number of users increases, more than one user may ask for the same subC, while in the CDF formulations in section V we assumed a single user per subC.

For a better understanding of the presented results, a comparison is accomplished to the performance of the 1-bit feedback strategy (Sanayei & Nosratinia, 2007), that is employed as a benchmark scheme, where each user feedbacks a single bit to indicate if its measured SNR is above or below a predefined threshold. Obviously, sending 1 bit over all the S subCs translates into a larger feedback load than the Best-M scheme, then for a fair comparison, for each number of users, the feedback load for the Best-M scheme is calculated with Equation (17), and then the 1

bit feedback scheme is allowed to use the same amount of feedback, it is a "Partial" 1 bit feedback strategy that we employ to guarantee fairness among the compared schemes. Two different thresholds are selected for the 1 bit feedback, allowing employing 16QAM or 64QAM. The results show that by increasing the number of users, both schemes also benefit from the Multiuser gain, but at a slower pace than the Best-M strategy.

In an alternative scenario, the number of users is fixed to N = 15, and the system runs under a variable number of allowed feedback load, indicated through the value of M. The behavior of the 3 considered schemes is shown in Figure 2, where again, the Best-M strategy is the one showing the largest system data rate performance. The Mathematically obtained results show a slight drift of the simulations for the same reason, previously discussed.

Now related to the QoS performance, Figure 3 shows the Best-M scheme SER performance in a scenario with a variable average SNR value. The values of M = 4 and N = 10 are considered, where a larger average SNR value translates into a better scenario for communications with the consequent decrease in the error rate. The simula-

Figure 1. The scheme statistics rate for a changeable amount of clients in the cell

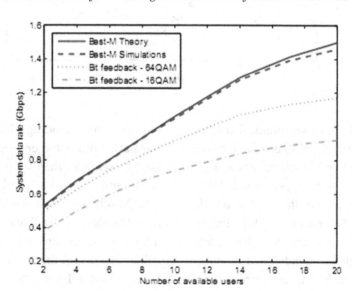

Figure 2. The system data rate for a variable amount of feedback represented through the number of M feedback values

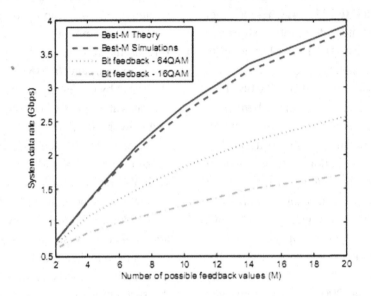

Figure 3. The resultant SER for A variable average SNR value in the scenario

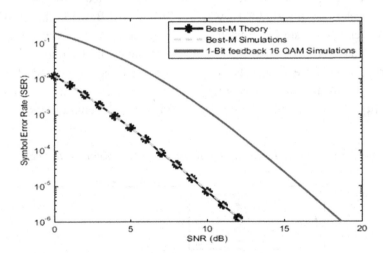

tions are compared to the mathematical results obtained in Equation (18), where a very close behavior is obtained. For a better understanding of the presented results, a comparison is accomplished to the performance of the 1-bit feedback strategy (Sanayei & Nosratinia, 2007), that is employed as a benchmark scheme, where each user feedbacks a single bit to indicate if its measured SNR is above or below a predefined threshold.

old. Obviously, sending 1 bit over all the S subCs translates into a larger feedback load than the Best-M scheme, then for a fair comparison, for each number of users, the feedback load for the Best-M scheme is calculated with Equation (17), and then the 1 bit feedback scheme is allowed to use the same amount of feedback. The threshold value selected for this truncated 1 bit feedback is obtained from Table 1 to employ 16QAM. The results show that by increasing the average SNR, both schemes behavior are enhanced, but always showing better performance for the Best-M strategy.

In an alternative scenario, the SER threshold is fixed to 10−3 and M = 4 and the effect of the number of users is checked for the throughput QoS metric. The behavior of the 2 considered schemes is shown, where again, the Best-M strategy is the one showing the largest performance. The Mathematical obtained results show a slight drift of the simulations for an increasing number is users. The reason behind this drift is that as the number of users increases, more than one user may ask for the same subC, while in the CDF formulations in section V we assumed a single user per subC as it is appeared in Figure 4.

9. FUTURE RESEARCH DIRECTIONS

The LTE system is required to offer a large data rate. The LTE system receives a lot of attention from operators and manufacturers to provide customers with good service. Here are some additional work that related to what have done in this thesis.

1. Extend the Best-M feedback scheme whenever perfect CSI is not available. The purpose of this research would be determining a robust Best-M feedback scheme.

2. In this research the SER and error probability in the system have been used as principle of QoS. The way of correcting an error in the system has not been considered. The Acknowledgement (ACK) could be a feasible way to re-transmit the failed symbols. How the ACK would affect the transmission and feedback on the Best-M system is an interesting point for future research.

3. Latest specification documents for LTE standard (Rel 12, March 2013) have included the carrier aggregation. This will increase the amount of sub channels and the whole performance of the Best-M scheme will be affected. The impact of the subcarrier aggregation on Best-M is a very interesting topic for the future.

4. The latest LTE specification documents (Rel 12, March 2013) have also enabled the option of network sharing, so that the total subcarriers are shared among two networks. This will restrict the available subcarriers

Figure 4. The resultant throughput for a variable number of users in the scenario

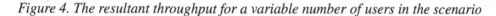
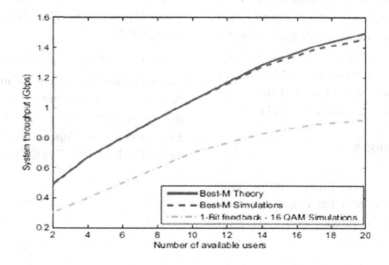

for allocation across different users, and definitely impact the Best-M behavior. The characterization of this feature is interesting topic for a future work.

10. CONCLUSION

The Study has presented the performance of the Best-M feedback scheme in 4G-LTE systems. The data rate expression is obtained in closed form expression, where all the involved parameters are characterized. Extensive simulations are carried out to check for the validity of the obtained results, where a very close performance is shown. A further comparison of the One-Bit feedback strategy is accomplished to present the benefits of the Best-M strategy, also the presented the QoS performance of the Best-M feedback scheme in 4G-LTE systems, and the SER with the throughput expressions that are obtained in closed form formulations, where all the involved parameters are characterized. The mathematical results were possible thanks to the formulated CDF expression for the developed scenario with the CQI feedback option where a very close performance is shown. The chapter has presented the energy performance of the Best-M feedback Sachem in 4G LTE systems. In addition the study of the feedback effect and how it induces additional energy consumption in the system, the simulation result shows how the amount of wasted energy decreases for an increasing number of users, moreover, it shown that the amount of the energy that the system consumed it different if we have feedback from all subCs.

Recommendations

1. Pay more attention and seek improvements on the LTE system from operators and manufacturers to provide customers with good service.

2. Search for the best technique for the feedback process in OFDMA systems, and it will fully develop its performance through closed form expressions.

3. To propose new techniques and strategies to improve the current wireless system.

4. Increasing the average SNR, both schemes Behavior is enhanced, but always showing better performance for the Best-M strategy.

5. Always seek for more feedback regarding Best-M strategy in 4G-LTE systems, through the presented QoS.

REFERENCES

Akbari, A., Hoshyar, R., & Tafazolli, R. (2010). *Energy-efficient resource allocation in wireless OFDMA systems*. Istanbul, Turkey: Institute of Electrical and Electronics Engineers PIMRC. doi:10.1109/PIMRC.2010.5671913

Alkhansari, M. G., & Gershman, A. B. (2004). Fast antenna subset selection in MIMO systems. *Institute of Electrical and Electronics Engineers Transformation on Signal Processing, 52*, 339–347.

Alouini, M. S., & Gesbert, D. (2004). *How much feedback is multi-user diversity really worth?* Paris: Institute of Electrical and Electronics Engineers ICC.

Andrews, M., Kumaran, K., Ramanan, K., Stolyar, A., Vijayakaumar, R., & Whiting, P. (2004). Scheduling in a queuing system with asynchronously varying service rates. *Probability in the Engineering and Informational Sciences, 18*, 191–217. doi:10.1017/S0269964804182041

Barriac, G., & Madhow, U. (2006). Space-time precoding for mean and covariance feedback: Application to wideband OFDM. *Institute of Electrical and Electronics Engineers Trans Communication, 54,* 96–10.

Bingham, N. H., Goldie, C. M., & Teugels, J. L. (1989). Regular variation. In *Encyclopedia of mathematics and its applications.* Cambridge, UK: Cambridge University Press.

Blum, R. S., Winters, J. H., & Sollenberger, N. R. (2002). On the capacity of cellular systems with MIMO. *Institute of Electrical and Electronics Engineers Communications Letters, 6*(6), 242–244.

Caire, G., & Shamai, S. (2003). On the achievable throughput of multi-antenna Gaussian broadcast channel. *Institute of Electrical and Electronics Engineers Transaction on Information Theory, 49,* 1691–1706. doi:10.1109/TIT.2003.813523

Chang, J., Lu, I. T., & Li, Y. (2011). *Efficient adaptive double codebook based CSI prediction for SU/MU MIMO OFDM systems.* Houston, TX: Institute of Electrical and Electronics Engineers Globecom.

Changhee, J., & Shroff, N. B. (2009). Performance of random access scheduling schemes in multi-hop wireless networks. Institute of Electrical and Electronics Engineers / Association for Computing Machinery Transactions on Networking, 17.

Chen, Y., Alouini, M. S., Tang, L., & Khan, F. (2012). Analytical evaluation of adaptive-modulation-based opportunistic cognitive radio in nakagami-m fading channels. *IEEE Transactions on Vehicular Technology,* 61.

Elliott, R. (2002). A measure of fairness of service for scheduling algorithms in multiuser systems. In *Proceedings of Institute of Electrical and Electronics Engineers Canadian Conference Electrical Comparison. Engineer. (CCECE02).* CCECE.

Esmailpour, A., & Nasser, N. (2011). Dynamic QoS-based bandwidth allocation framework for broadband wireless networks. Institute of Electrical and Electronics Engineers Transactions on Vehicular Technology, 60.

European Telecommunications Standards Institute. (2011). *3GPP TS 36.213: Technical specification group radio access network (E-UTRA), physical layer procedures, V10.1.0.* Author.

Floren, F., Edfors, O., & Molin, B. A. (2003). *The effect of feedback quantization on the through-put of a multiuser diversity scheme.* Paper presented at the Institute of Electrical and Electronics Engineers Global Telecommunication Conference (GIOBE-COM, 2003). San Francisco, CA.

Gore, D., Nabar, R., & Paulraj, A. (2000). *Selecting an optimal set of transmit antennas in wireless systems.* Istanbul, Turkey: Institute of Electrical and Electronics Engineers ICASSP.

Gore, D. A., & Paulraj, A. J. (2002). *MIMO antenna subset selection with space-time coding.* Istanbul, Turkey: Institute of Electrical and Electronics Engineers Transformation on Signal Processing. doi:10.1109/TSP.2002.803337

Hoshyar, R., Shariat, M., & Tafazolli, R. (2010). Subcarrier and power allocation with multiple power constraints in orthogonal frequency-division multiple access systems. Institute of Electrical and Electronics Engineers Communications Letters, 14.

Jafar, S. A., & Goldsmith, A. J. (2004). Transmitter optimization and optimality of beamforming for multiple antenna systems with imperfect feedback. *Institute of Electrical and Electronics Engineers Transformation Wireless Communication, 3*(4), 1165–1175.

Jindal, N., & Ramprashad, S. (2011). *Optimizing CSI feedback for MU-MIMO: Tradeoffs in channel correlation, user diversity and MU-MIMO efficiency*. Budapest: IEEE. doi:10.1109/VETECS.2011.5956557

Jindal, N., & Ranprashad, S. (2011). *Optimizing CSI feedback for MU-MIMO: Tradeoffs in channel correlation, user diversity and MU-MIMO efficiency*. Budapest: Institute of Electrical and Electronics Engineers VTC Spring. doi:10.1109/VETECS.2011.5956557

Kang, M., & Kim, K. S. (2012). Performance analysis and optimization of best-m feedback for OFDMA systems. Institute of Electrical and Electronics Engineers Communications Letters, 16.

Keller, T., & Hanzol, L. (2000). Adaptive modulation techniques for duplez OFDM transmission. *Institute of Electrical and Electronics Engineers Transaction on Vehicular Technology, 49*(5), 1893–1906.

Kim, S., & Lee, J. (2012). To cooperate or not to cooperate: System throughput and fairness perspective. *Institute of Electrical and Electronics Engineers Journal on Selected Areas in Communications, 30*.

Leke, A., & Cioffi, J. M. (1997). A maximum rate loading algorithm for discrete multi-tone 8 modulation systems. proce. *Institute of Electrical and Electronics Engineers Global Telecommunication Conference, 3*(1), 514-158.

Li, I., Xin, W., Hanqi, Z., & Morgera, S. D. (2009). *Integrating retransmission diversity with real-time scheduling over wireless links*. Baltimore, MD: CISS. doi:10.1109/CISS.2009.5054752

Molisch, A. (2010). *Wireless communication* (2nd ed.). New York: Wiley and Sons.

Molisch, A. F., Win, M. Z., & Winters, J. H. (2003). Reduced–complexity transmits/receives diversity system. *Institute of Electrical and Electronics Engineers Transformation on Signal Processing, 51*(11), 2729–2738.

Neely, M. J., Modiano, E., & Rohrs, C. E. (2003). Power allocation and routing in multi-beam satellites with time varying channels. *Institute of Electrical and Electronics Engineers Trans. Networking, 11*(1), 138–152. doi:10.1109/TNET.2002.808401

Pedersen, K. I., Monghal, G. I., & Kovács, Z. (2007). *Frequency domain scheduling for OFDMA with limited and noisy channel feedback*. Baltimore, MD: IEEE VTC. doi:10.1109/VETECF.2007.378

Peebles, P. (2002). *Probability, random variables, and random signal principles*. New York: McGraw Hill.

Ramalingam, N., & Wang, Z. (2008). *MIMO transmitter optimization with mean and covariance feedback for low SNR*. New Orleans, LA: Institute of Electrical and Electronics Engineers GLOBECOM. doi:10.1109/GLOCOM.2008.ECP.840

Sanayei, S., & Nosratinia, A. (2005). *Exploiting multiuser diversity with only 1- bit feedback*. Paper presented at the Institute of Electrical and Electronics Engineers Wireless Communication Networking Conference. New Orleans, LA.

Sanayei, S., & Nosratinia, A. (2007). Opportunistic downlink transmission with limited feedback. Institute of Electrical and Electronics Engineers Transactions on Information Theory, 53.

Sesia, S., Toufik, I., & Baker, M. (2009). *LTE the UMTS long term evolution: From theory to practice*. New York: John Wiley and Sons. doi:10.1002/9780470742891

Sezgin, A. Jorswieck, E., & Charafeddine, M. (2008). Interaction between scheduling and user locations in an OSTBC coded downlink system. Siegel, Germany: ITG-SCC.

Sharif, M., & Hassibi, B. (2005). On the capacity of MIMO broadcast channel with partial side information. Institute of Electrical and Electronics Engineers Transaction on Inform Theory, 51(2).

Simon, M. K., & Alouini, M. S. (2004). *Digital communication over fading channels.* New York: Wiley and Sons. doi:10.1002/0471715220

Ting, P., Wen, C., & Chen, J. (2007). An efficient CSI feedback scheme for MIMO-OFDM wireless systems. Institute of Electrical and Electronics Engineers Transformations on Wireless Communications, 6.

Trivellato, M., Tomasin, S., & Benvenuto, N. (2009). On channel quantization and feedback strategies for multiuser MIMO-OFDM downlink systems. Institute of Electrical and Electronics Engineers Transactions on Communications, 57.

Uysal, E., Prabhakar, B., & ElGamal, A. (2002). Energy efficient packet transmission over a wireless link. *Association for Computing Machinery/ Institute of Electrical and Electronics Engineers* Transactions on Networking, (10).

Visotsky, E., & Madhow, U. (2000). *Space-time transmit precoding with imperfect feedback.* Istanbul, Turkey: ISIT.

Viswanath, P., Tse, D.N.C., & Iaroia, R. (2002). Opportunistic beam forming using dumb antenna. *Institute of Electrical and Electronics Engineers transactions on information theory, 48*(6), 1277-1294.

Winters, J. H. (1983). Switched diversity with feedback for dpsk mobile radio systems. *Institute of Electrical and Electronics Engineers Transformations on Vehicular Technology, 32*(1), 134–150.

Wong, C., Cheng, R., Lataief, K., & Murch, R. (1999). Multiuser OFDM with adaptive subcarrier, bit, and power allocation. *Institute of Electrical and Electronics Engineers Journal on Selected Areas in Communications, 17*(10), 1747–1758. doi:10.1109/49.793310

Zorba, N., Perez-Neira, A.I., Foglar A., & Verikoukis, C. (2009). Cross layer QoS guarantees in multiuser WLAN systems. *Springer Wireless Personal Communications, 51.*

KEY TERMS AND DEFINITIONS

Base Station (BS): Is a radio signal receiver/ transmitter that works as the hub of wireless network and it can work as a gateway between wired networks and wireless networks.

Channel State Information (CSI): Is an information that describes the properties of the communication link which known as "channel properties" and describes how a signal transmits between the transmitter and the receiver.

Dynamic Resource Allocation (DRA): Is a technique of finding addresser for users automatically and it is used to increase the efficiency of using the bandwidth and therefore getting closer to the theoretical upper bound on channel capacity.

Long Term Evolution (LTE): Is wireless networking standard that is used in high speed networks for mobile phones as well as it depends on the GSM/EDGE and UMTS/HSPA network techniques.

Orthogonal Frequency Division Multiple Accesses (OFDMA): Dividing the available bandwidth into several frequency bands and therefore each band is reserved for specific station and it belongs to the station along the time.

Quality of Service (QoS): This term addresses all the related aspects of the telephony and computer networks, such as service response time, loss, signal-noise ratio SNR, interrupts and so on.

Symbol Error Rate (SER): Is a ratio that is used to determine error rate as well as it is suited to multi-node amplify-and-forward cooperative communication M-PSK constellation systems with the mean channel gains is derived.

Chapter 16
QoS and Mobility Management Issues on Next Generation Mobile WiMAX Networks

Sajal Saha
Narula Institute of Technology, India

Asish K. Mukhopadhyay
Bengal Institute of Technology and Management, India

Anup Kumar Bhattacharjee
National Institute of Technology, India

ABSTRACT

Selection of a MIMO (Multiple Input Multiple Output) antenna to achieve high throughput, minimize errors, and optimize data speed is an important design issue. Radio resource management to provide Quality of Service (QoS) in WiMAX involves dynamic scheduling of resources according to the user's priority, based classes Platinum, Gold, Silver, and Bronze. Mobility and handoff management in WiMAX is another important issue involving location update, signaling traffic and service delay, and call blocking and dropping. This chapter focuses on some issues concerning MIMO configuration to improve transmit diversity, developing an appropriate scheduling algorithm to improve QoS, and presenting a novel mobility management protocol THMIP (Three Level Hierarchical Mobile IP) in IEEE 802.16e environment to reduce signaling cost with respect to QoS parameters like throughput, end-to-end delay, interference, path loss, bit error rate, and Signal-to-Noise Ratio (SNR). For the simulation, the authors use OPNET Modeler and MATLAB.

INTRODUCTION

Ever increasing demand for higher bandwidth cannot be met with existing Digital Subscriber Line (DSL) cable Internet and other non-optical wired solutions requiring the installation of transmission cables. Wireless technologies eliminate the need for such installations. WiMAX is a solution for wireless broadband communication. WiMAX is flexible, robust, affordable and economically feasible and, therefore, assures high bandwidth communication and networking solutions of up to 48 Mbps (fixed downlink) and 7 Mbps (fixed uplink), even in the remote areas with a coverage area of 8 Km (Andrews, Ghosh, & Muhamed, 2007).

DOI: 10.4018/978-1-4666-4888-3.ch016

Mobile WiMAX provides 9.4 Mbps for downlink and 3.3 Mbps for uplink across a coverage area of 3 km. Its high speed data enables various multimedia applications, along with the conventional telephony service.

The original WiMAX standard, IEEE 802.16(2001), specifies a 10 to 66GHz range for fixed and nomadic services. This, however, has gradually (Yarali, Rahman, 2008) evolved to IEEE 802.16m (2011) through various stages as shown in Table 1. WiMAX operates in both licensed and unlicensed bands. Unlicensed band operates on the 2.4 Ghz and 5.8 Ghz frequencies. Licensed band operates on 700 Mhz, 2.5 Ghz.

BACKGROUND STUDY

A group formed by the industry and standardization forums and agencies in telecommunication such as Internet Engineering Task Force (IETF), 3rd Generation Partnership Project (3GPP2), DSL forum, Open Mobile Alliance (OMA) and Intel joined hands to form WiMAX forum (with more than 470 members to date) in 2003 to conceptualize WiMAX towards its deployment.

Etemad (2008) describes the brief overview, technology, architecture, interface, network specification of WiMAX and its evolution through the WiMAX forum. The new WiMAX standard IEEE 802.16m, proposed in 2011 (as Advance WiMAX), illustrates the extended features need to meet the requirements of ITU-R/IMT advanced 4G and support the mobility of 500km/hr. This standard is scheduled to be on the market by 2013.

The main promises of WiMAX are high throughput and expanded coverage. (Nuaymi, 2007), (Belghith & Nuaymi, 2008) for all QoS classes of WiMAX use, unsolicited grant service (UGS), real time polling service (rtPS), non-real time polling service (nrtPS) and best effort (BS). A different type of data uses a different type of QoS class to obtain maximum throughput while using the minimum bandwidth. This paper also provides a thorough analysis of mobile WiMAX architecture using the NS-2 module.

Table 1. Comperative study of different QoS service classes

	UGS	rtPS	nrtPS	ertPS	BE
Maximum sustained traffic rate	Yes	Yes	Yes	Yes	Yes
Minimum reserved traffic rate	(Can be present)	Yes	Yes	Yes	--
Request/transmission policy	Yes	Yes	Yes		Yes
Tolerated jitter	Yes	--	--	Yes	--
Maximum latency	Yes	Yes		Yes	
Traffic priority	--	Yes	Yes	Yes	Yes
Piggyback grant request	Allowed	Not allowed	Not allowed	Extended piggyback	Not allowed
Bandwidth stealing	Allowed	Not allowed	Not allowed	Allowed	Not allowed
Unicast polling	PM (Poll-Me) bit can be used	Allowed	Allowed	Allowed	Allowed
Contention -based polling	Not allowed	Not allowed	Allowed	Allowed	Allowed
Differentiated Services	EF*	AF2,AF3**	AF1	AF4	Default
Application	T1/E1 transport,fixed size packet on periodic basis	MPEG video	FTP with guaranteed minimum throughput	VoIP	HTTP,web browsing

*EF(expedidate forwarding)

**AF(Assured forwarding)

Besides the IEEE 802.16 architecture, there are several options for the wireless network vendors to implement WiMAX, along with Bluetooth, Wifi or 3G. These technologies (Dhawan, 2007) provide a number of affordable wireless solutions for more sophisticated mobile applications. Although they differ in data rates, distance covered effective bandwidth usage and minimum interference.

The MAC layer of IEEE 802.16m defines four different QoS classes with their scheduling, according to the applications. Khalil and Ksentini (2007) made an attempt to compare different scheduling services like Proportional Fair Scheduling algorithm, Cross-layer Scheduling Algorithm, and TCP aware uplink Scheduling algorithm. Liu, Wang, and Giannakis (2006) tried to optimize the resources in cross layer scheduling algorithm by providing k fixed slots to ugs out of the n slots (n>k) of radio resources. (n – k) slots were allocated to rtPS, nrtPS. Slots were dynamically assigned based on an algorithm defined by Liu, Wang, and Giannakis (2006).

WiMAX is expected to arise as the main Broadband Wireless Access (BWA) technology providing voice, data and video services with different types of QoS (Ahmed). Designing an efficient vendor-specific scheduling algorithm with high throughput and minimum delay is challenging for system developers. In this work, a detailed simulation study has been carried out for appropriate scheduling algorithms such as WFQ, Round Robin, WRR and Strict-Priority. The performance of each scheduler has been analyzed and evaluated for different QoS classes.

The demand for high speed broadband wireless system is increasing rapidly (Khalil & Ksentini, 2007). In this context, the IEEE 802.16 standard introduces several interesting advantages including variable and high data rate, last mile wireless access, point to multipoint communication, large frequency range and QoS for various types of applications. The scheduling architecture must ensure good bandwidth utilization. In this work, a

classification based on the scheduling mechanism has been used in the different propositions. Some studies are based on traditional algorithms but also adopted new methods and mechanisms that are proposed for the new standard in order to provide QoS. Mobility management during handoff creates a huge burden over the system as shown by Aguado, Jacob, Berbineau, & Samper, (2010). It proposes several enhancement techniques to reduce handoff latency and improve QoS, and end to end performance. However, this paper does not consider the increased handoff latency due to multiple inter domain movement of the mobile node (MN). In this work, the proposed solution addresses the issue by introducing a three-level hierarchical mobility management architecture (Saha & Mukhopadhyay, 2011) using a fluid flow model.

MIMO

Multiple Input Multipul Output (MIMO) antennas are now being used to operate at higher data rates with potential diversity. The array of antennas at each end of the communications circuit has the combined effect of minimizing errors and optimizing data speed.

MIMO helps improve wireless access in WiMax by:

- Connecting 802.11n Wi-Fi hotspots with each other and to the Internet.
- Offering a wireless alternative to cable and DSL for last mile broadband access.
- Providing high speed mobile data and telecommunication services for 4G and Long Term Evolution (LTE).

According to Shannon-Wiener legacy (Sibille, Oestges, & Zanella, 2010) one can theoretically control the output (which is determined by a specific target) using feedback as an error correction

Figure1. Wiener's approach

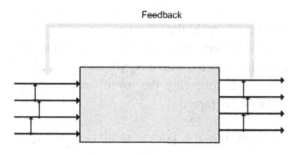

mechanism. The framework and the introduction of feedback mechanisms has already been studied and investigated with only partial knowledge of the wireless medium.

Wiener's Approach

According to Wiener's Approach (Figure 1), the transmitters obtain the information of the signal at the receiver end, and measure the degree of error if present. In this case, the input and output lines are not necessarily connected sequentially i.e. input 1 can be connected to input 4. When the receiver gets the signal, it sends the feedback to the input side so that the transmitters may have the information about the percentage of signal finally carried to the receiver and the error can be easily measured. Here, the concept of multiple input multiple output is used and the feedback generated from the MIMO antenna is used to control and tune the receiver.

MIMO Channel Capacity

Compared to a conventional single antenna system, the channel capacity of a multiple antenna system with N_T transmit and N_R receive antennas can be increased by the factor of min (N_T, N_R), without using additional transmit power or spectral bandwidth. Due to the increasing demand for faster data transmission in telecommunication systems, MIMO antenna systems are (Hughes & Sweldens,

2000; Foschini, 2002; Paulraj, Nabar, & Gore, 2008) implemented in broadband wireless access networks such as Mobile WiMAX

MIMO has three functionalitieslike Beam forming, Spatial Multiplexing and Spatial or Antenna Diversity.

Beam forming deals with the numbers of transmitter and receiver antennas. Multiple replicas of the radio signal from different directions in space give rise to spatial diversity which can increase the transmission reliability of the fading radio link. A basic idea of diversity techniques is to convert Rayleigh fading wireless channel into a more stable Additive White Gaussian Noise (AWGN) like channel without any catastrophic signal fading.

In spatial Multiplexing techniques, multiple independent data streams are simultaneously transmitted by multiple transmit antennas, thereby achieving a higher transmission speed. When spatial-multiplexing techniques are used, the maximum achievable transmission speed equals the capacity of the MIMO channel; however, when diversity techniques are used, the achievable transmission speed can be much lower than the capacity of the MIMO channel [5].

The MIMO channel capacity must be analyzed in detail to determine the optimum number of transmit and receive antennas which will lead to a situation where the transmission speed is optimum for the channel capacity.

The matrix $M \in C^{N_R \times N_T}$ has a singular value decomposition (SVD), represented as $M = U\Sigma V^*$ where U is a (m x m) unitary matrix. V^* (conjugate transpose of V) is (p x p) real unitary matrix. Σ is (m x p) rectangular diagonal matrix. The diagonal elements of Σ are singular values of matrix M, denoting them by $\alpha_1, \alpha_2 \ldots \alpha_{Nmin}$ where $N_{min} = $ min (N_T, N_R). Assuming that the diagonal elements of Σ are ordered singular value of matrix M, the rank of M corresponds to number of non-zero singular values i.e. rank$(M) \leq N_{min}$. Now if $N_{min} = N_T$, then

$$M = U \Sigma V^*$$

$$= \underbrace{\left[U N_{\min} \ U_{NR-N\min} \right]}_{0NR-N\min} \underbrace{\left(\Sigma N_{\min} V^* \right)}_{U\Sigma} = U N_{\min} \Sigma N_{\min} V^*$$

Here $U_{N\min} \in C_R^{N} {}^{xN\min}$ and $\sum N_{\min} \in C^{N\min xN\min}$ becomes square matrix. Similarly if $N\min = N_R$ then,

$$M = U \underbrace{\left[\Sigma N_{\min} \ 0_{NT-N\min} \right]}_{V_{NT-N\min}^*} \underbrace{\left(V^* N_{\min} = U \right)}_{\Sigma V^*} \Sigma N_{\min} V^* N_{\min}$$

Here $V_{N\min} \in C_T^{N} {}^{xN\min}$ becomes $N_{\min}$ right singular values. With Eigen Decomposition, $MM^* = U\Sigma\Sigma^*U^* = P\Lambda P^*$. Now if $P=U$, $P^*P = I_{NR}$ and $\Lambda \in C_R^{N} {}^{xN}{}_R$ diagonal matrix, then

$$\lambda_i = \begin{cases} \alpha_i^2, & \text{if } i = 1, 2 \dots N_{\min} \\ 0, & \text{if } i = N_{\min} + 1 \dots N_R \end{cases}$$

Channel Capacity in MIMO

The capacity of n_m sub channels with SNR equal to $(S/N)/n_m$ is much greater than that of a single channel with SNR S/N.

Using useful matrix theory Capacity of MIMO channel

$$C_{MIMO} = W \sum_{i=1}^{n_m} \log_2(1 + S / N.\lambda_i / N_T)$$

W is the channel bandwidth. At high SNR, SNR becomes infinity,

$$\begin{aligned} C_{MIMO} / W &= \sum_{i=1}^{n_m} \log_2(S / N.\lambda_i / N_T) \\ &= \sum_{i=1}^{n_m} \left(\log_2(S / N) + \log_2(\lambda_i) - \log_2(N_T) \right) \\ &= n_m \log_2(S / N) - n_m \log_2(N_T) + \log_2\left(\prod_{i=1}^{n_m} \lambda_i \right) \\ &= n_m \log_2(S / N) - n_m \log_2(N_T) + \log_2 \det(MM^*) \end{aligned}$$

$n_m \log_2(10)/10 = .332 \ n_m$ bits/s/HZ/dB,

where n_m is multiplexing gain.

It is the general form of the MIMO channel capacity equation where $N_R \leq N_T$ is, the following also holds following the useful matrix theory discussed before,

$$\log_2 \det(MM^*) \leq n_m \log 2(N_T N_R / n_m) \leq n_m \log_2(N_T).$$

Channel Capacity of Random MIMO Channels

The MIMO channel (Yong Soo Cho, 2010) changes randomly. Therefore, M is a random matrix, which means that channel capacity is also randomly time varying. In practice, we assume that random channel is an ergodic process. We consider the outage channel capacity of MIMO. The outage probability is defined as

$$P_{out}(R) = \Pr(C(M) < R) \tag{1}$$

Here if the MIMO channel capacity is $C = E\{C(\bar{M})\}$, the system is said to be in outage if the decoding error probability cannot be made arbitrarily small with a transmission speed of R bps/HZ. Then, the ε-outage channel capacity is the largest possible data rate such that the outage probability in Equation (1) is less than ε. In other words, it is corresponding to $C\varepsilon$ such that $P(C(M) \leq C\varepsilon) = \varepsilon$.

Figure 2 shows the variation of the Ergodic capacity with the cumulative distribution function (CDF). We survey on for the random MIMO channel when channel state information (CSI) is not available at the transmitter side. Figure 2 shows the CDFs of the random 2x2 and 4x4 MIMO channel capacities when SNR is 10dB, in which $\varepsilon = 0.01$-outage capacity is indicated. Here, increasing the number of transmit and receive antennas increases the channel capacity of MIMO, thus increasing reliability.

Figure 2. Ergodic capacity vs. CDF

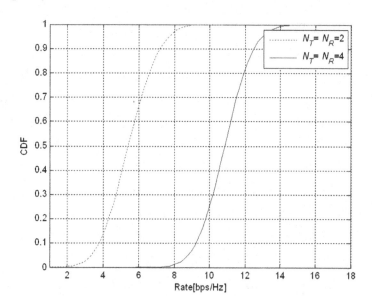

- A random process is Ergodic if its time average converges to the same limit for almost all realizations of the process; for example, for a discrete random process X[n], $1N\sum n = 1NX[n] \rightarrow EX[n]$ as N-> infinity.

We compute the Ergodic channel capacity of MIMO channel when SNR is varied, when CSI is not known on the transmitter side. Figure 3 shows the Ergodic channel capacity as a varying numbers of antennas under the same condition for Figure 1.

The above result shows that increasing the transmit and receive antennas channel capacity also increases the complexity. So, for optimization, a combination of 4x4 transmit and receive antennas is the best choice.

Antenna Diversity and Space Time Coding

Antenna diversity, or Spatial diversity, is used to mitigate multipath fading. Multiple antennas may undergo different degrees of interference. One antenna may experience selective fading, while another antenna may experience flat fading. Multiple array antennas combine the signal at the receiver side to obtain the maximum signal strength. The goal of antenna diversity is to convert an unstable time varying wireless fading channel into a stable AGWN-like channel without significant instantaneous fading.

Antenna diversity can be realized in several ways (see also Figure 4) such as:

1. **Space Diversity:** Sufficiently separated (more than 10l) multiple antennas are used to implement independent wireless channels.

2. **Polarization Diversity:** Independent channels are implemented using the fact that vertically and horizontally polarized paths are independent.

3. **Time Diversity:** The same information is repeatedly transmitted at sufficiently separated (more than coherence time) time instances.

4. **Frequency Diversity:** The same information is repeatedly transmitted at sufficiently separated (more than coherence bandwidth) frequency bands.

Figure 3. Ergodic capacity vs. SNR

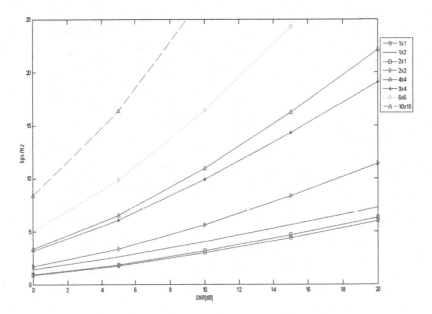

Figure 4. Various antenna configurations

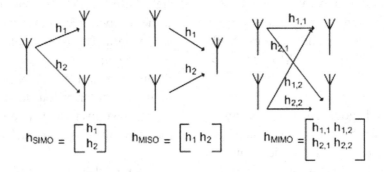

5. **Angle Diversity:** Multiple receive antennas with different directivity are used to receive the same information-bearing signal at different angles.

6. **Receive Diversity:** Receive diversity requires the use of a multiple number of receiver antennas, and all computational burdens are on receiver side. However, it may cause high power consumption for mobile units in the case of the downlink.

7. **Transmit Diversity:** Diversity gain can also be achieved by space-time coding (STC) on the transmit side, which requires only simple linear processing on the receiver side for decoding. In order to further reduce the computational complexity in mobile units, differential space-time codes can be used, which do not require CSI estimation at the receiver side (Tarokh, Seshadri, & Calderbank, 1998; Hochwald & Sweldens, 2000; Hughes & Sweldens, 2000).

Alamouti's Space Time Code

Well known Space Time Bloc Code (STBC) is Alamouti's code, a complex orthogonal space-time code specialized for the case of two transmit antennas.

In the Alamouti encoder, two consecutive symbols x1 and x2 are encoded with the following space-time codeword matrix:

$$X = \begin{pmatrix} X1 & -X2^* \\ X2 & X1^* \end{pmatrix}$$

The Alamouti is an encoded signal that is transmitted from the two transmit antennas over two symbol periods. During the first symbol period, two symbols x1 and x2 are simultaneously transmitted from the two transmit antennas. During the second symbol period, these symbols are transmitted again, where $-x2^*$ is transmitted from the first transmit antenna and $x1^*$ is transmitted from the second transmit antenna. Here, we assume the channels are independent of Rayleigh fading channels and perfect channel estimation is done at the receiver. Alamouti coding achieves the same diversity order as 1x2MRCtechnique (Paulraj, Nabar, & Gore, 2008) (implied by the same slope of the BER curves). The 2 x2 Alamouti technique achieves the same diversity order as 1x4 MRC techniques. So, from Alamouti's coding scheme we can conclude that it is better to increase the number of antennas on the transmitter side and balance them the number of antennas on the receiver side. Only increasing the number of antennas on the receiver side is not beneficial because the 2x2 has been shown to give better results than both 1x2 and 1x4 transmit receive antenna combinations. Since diversity gain is the measurement of the signal to interference ratio, the 2x2 scheme also improves the signal power.

It is important to add that an increase in diversity gain also increases channel capacity.

Antenna Selection Technique and Diversity Gain

We know channel capacity is the determinant of transmission reliability. So we have to find the optimum number of transmit and receive antennas to increase channel capacity of MIMO.

Since P antennas are now used among N_T transmit antennas, the effective channel now can be represented by P columns of $M \in N_T^N \times N_R$. If p_i denotes the index of ith selected column, i=1,2,3,..P, then the effective channel model will be modeled by N_R x P matrix which is denoted by $M_{\{a1,a2,a3....aP\}} \in C_R^N \times P$. Let $x \in C^{P \times 1}$ denote the space time coded stream mapped into P selected antennas, then the received signal y is represented as:

$$Y = \sqrt{(Ex/P)}. M_{\{a1,a2,a3....aP\}} x + z$$

where $z \in C_R^N \times 1$ is additive noise vector. The channel capacity of this system under this equation depends on the number of transmit and receive antennas (see also Figure 5).

A set of P transmit antennas must be selected out of N_T transmit antennas so as to maximize the channel capacity. When the total transmitted power is limited by P, the channel capacity of the system using P selected transmit antennas is given by:

$$C = \max \log_2 \det(I_{NR} + (Ex/PN_0)M_{(a1,a2...aP)}$$
$$R_{xx}M^*_{(a1,a2...aP)})bps/HZ...R_{xx,(a1,a2...aP)} \qquad (2)$$

Here R_{xx} is the PxP covariance matrix. We assume equal power is allocated to all transmit antennas, i.e. $R_{xx} = I_P$. So, the channel capacity for $\{a_i\}_{i=1}^P$ is:

$$C_{\{a1,a2...aP\}} \triangleq \log_2 \det(I_{NR} + (Ex/N_0)$$
$$M_{\{a1,a2...aP\}} M^*_{\{a1,a2...aP\}})bps/HZ \qquad (3)$$

Figure 5. Antenna selection with P RF modules and N_T transmit antennas ($P < N_T$)

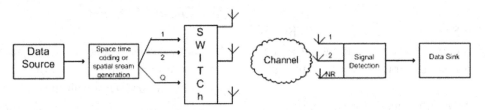

We can find the optimal selection of P antennas from the Equation (3). In order to maximize channel capacity, one should choose maximum capacity antennas, i.e.

$$\{a_1^{opt}, \ a_2^{opt}, \ a_3^{opt}\} = \arg \max C_{\{a1,a2,...aP\}} \\ \{a1, \ a2, \ aP\} \in A_p \qquad (4)$$

Here, A_p represents the set of all possible antennas with P selected antennas. $| A_P | = \begin{pmatrix} N_T \\ P \end{pmatrix}$ that is considering all possible antenna combination in Equation (4).

Figure 6 shows the variation of channel capacity with respect to SNR using Equation 2 for different antenna configurations.

QoS Service Classes in WiMAX

The IEEE 802.16 standard provides powerful tools that achieve different QoS constraints. The 802.16 standard MAC Layer provides QoS differentiation for the different types of applications that might operate over 802.16 networks, through five defined scheduling service types, also called QoS classes.

This classification into these scheduling service classes facilitates bandwidth sharing between different users. Every user has a quality of scheduling service class, also known as QoS class. According to this parameter, the BS scheduler allocates the necessary amount of bandwidth required for each application. This mechanism allows an efficient and adapted distribution of the existing resources.

Therefore, a real-time application, such as a video application, will have the priority in bandwidth allocation in comparison with FTP or email applications. This is not the case; for example, with the presently used Wi-Fi system, where all services have exactly the same level of QoS.

Scheduling services represent the data handling mechanisms supported by the MAC scheduler for data transport on a given connection. Uplink request (grant) scheduling is performed by the BS based on the scheduling service type, with the intent of providing each subordinate SS with a bandwidth for uplink transmissions and opportunities to request this bandwidth, when needed. As already mentioned in this chapter, that each connection is associated with a single data service flow and each service flow is associated with a set of QoS parameters. These parameters are managed using the DSA and DSC MAC management messages dialogues. Four scheduling services were defined in 802.16e:

1. Unsolicited Grant Service (UGS)
2. Real-time Polling Service (rtPS)
3. Non-real -time Polling Service (nrtPS)
4. Best effort (BE)

A fifth scheduling service type for 802.16e was later added:

1. Extended Real-time Polling Service (ertPS)

Each of these scheduling services has a mandatory set of QoS parameters that must be included in the service flow definition when the scheduling

Figure 6. Channel capacity vs. SNR

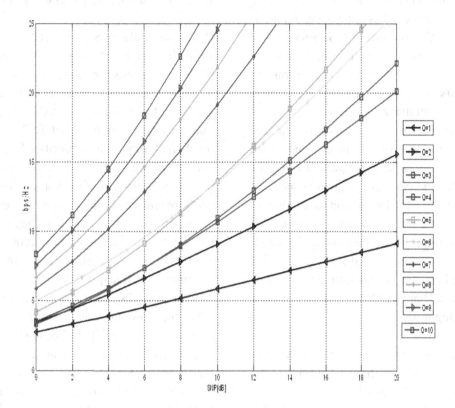

service is enabled for a service flow. Table 1 gives the mandatory service flow QoS parameters for each of the four scheduling services defined in 802.16m. At present, the minimum reserved traffic rate parameter of UGS must have the same value as the maximum sustained traffic rate parameter. Concerning ertPS, 802.16e indicates that the key service IEs are the maximum sustained traffic rate, the minimum reserved traffic rate, the maximum latency and the request/transmission policy.

Uplink request/grant scheduling is performed by the BS in order to provide each Subscriber station (SS) with a bandwidth for uplink transmissions and opportunities to request a bandwidth, when needed. By specifying a scheduling service and its associated QoS parameters, the BS scheduler can anticipate the throughput and latency needs of the uplink traffic and provide polls and/or grants at the appropriate times.

Unsolicited Grant Service (UGS)

Unsolicited grant service is a service flow in which the transmission system automatically and periodically provides a defined number of timeslots and fixed packet size that is used by a particular receiver. UGS is commonly used to provide services that require a constant bit rate (CBR) such as audio streaming or leased line (e.g. T1 or E1) circuit emulation.

UGS provides a constant bit rate for a single connection. A subscriber device may need additional bandwidth for an additional service that is added to a connection or to temporarily provide more bandwidth on the UGS connection. To request more bandwidth on a UGS connection, a poll me bit or slip indicator bit may be used.

A poll me bit is a signaling message in a data field within the header of a data packet that indicates that the device would like to be polled.

The poll me bit indicates to the base station that the subscriber device needs to be polled for a service other than for the current UGS service. For transmission to synchronous connections, timing inaccuracies may result in the need to transfer additional bits if the clock of one connection is slightly faster than the other connection.

When the buffer of the faster connection indicates the number of bits to be transmitted may soon run out, a slip indicator bit may be used. The slip indicator is a signaling message within the header of a data packet that indicates that the data transmission queue of that device is changing (slipping) and that the device needs more bandwidth to keep up with the transmission queue. This allows the base station to temporarily assign additional bandwidth until the transmission buffer has caught up.

- UGS flows are buffered separately from each other and from flows in service classes such as nrtPS and BE.
- UGS service flows are given strictly higher priority versus nrtPS and BE service flows, which implies that the system serves nrtPS and BE packets only after it has finished transmitting all outstanding UGS packets (Figure 7).

Real-Time Polling Service (rtPS)

Real-Time Polling Service (rtPS), on the other hand, is designed to support real-time service flows that generate variable size data packets on a periodic basis, such as video (Figure 8). The service offers real-time, periodic, unicast request opportunities, which meet the flow's real-time needs and allow the Subscriber Station (SS) to specify the size of the desired grant. A major drawback to using this QoS approach is the impact on the overall sector throughput. Polling overhead can reach up to 60% when using the 3.5MHz channel. This service requires more request overhead than UGS, but supports variable grant sizes for optimum data transport efficiency.

Unlike UGS, polling overhead exists even when the flows are idle, and for as long as they are active. Non-Real-Time Polling Service (nrtPS) is a service class that is intended to support non-real-time service flows that require variable size data packets and a minimum data rate, such as FTP. This is accomplished by offering unicast polls on a regular basis, which ensures that the service flow receives requests even, during network congestion

Figure 7. UGS

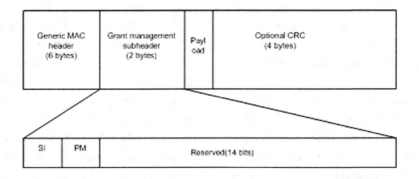

Figure 8. rtPS

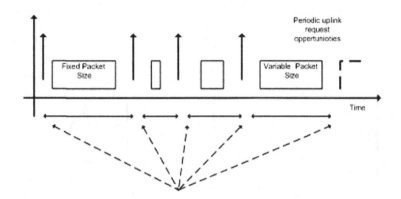

Non-Real Time Polling Service (nrtPS)

The nrtPS is designed to support delay-tolerant data streams consisting of variable-size data packets for which a minimum data rate is required. The standard considers that this would be the case, for example, for an FTP transmission. In the nrtPS scheduling service, the BS provides unicast uplink request polls on a 'regular' basis, which guarantees that the service flow receives request opportunities, even during network congestion. The standard states that the BS typically polls nrtPS CIDs on an interval on the order of one second or less. In addition, the SS is allowed to use contention request opportunities, i.e. the SS may use contention request opportunities as well as unicast request opportunities. Figure 9 shows the nrtPS mechanism.

Best Effort (BE)

The BE service is designed to support data streams for which no minimum service guarantees are required and, therefore, may be handled on a best available basis. The SS may use contention request opportunities as well as unicast request opportunities when the BS sends any. The BS does not have any unicast uplink request polling obligation for BE SSs. Therefore, a long period can run without transmitting any BE packets,

typically when the network is in the congestion state. Figure 10 shows the BE mechanism.

THMIP: A NOVEL MOBILITY MANAGEMENT SCHEME INWIMAX

Roaming in WiMAX is termed as missing piece of WiMAX puzzle. Chammakhi Msadaa, Camara, and Filali (2010) and Aguado, Jacob, Berbineau, and Samper (2010) highlighted the mobility management issues as amendment of IEEE 802.16d. Aguado, Jacob, Berbineau, and Samper (2010) describes some enhancement techniques to reduce the handoff latency limited to intra domain mobility. This paper does not consider the increased handoff latency due to multiple inter domain movement of the MN.

If a MN is moving from home Access Service Network (ASN) to visit an ASN randomly, a new Binding Update (BU) is required for each registration to the ASN and that is to be notified to HA co-locate in Connectivity Service network (CSN) to complete the handoff process. The total process increases air link resource utilization, handoff latency and subsequently increases call dropping probability. We propose (Saha & Mukhopadhyay, 2011; 2012) a new mobility management scheme – an amendment of the IEEE 802.16e standard which provides enhancements related to mobility management. In our proposed Three Level

Figure 9. nrtPS

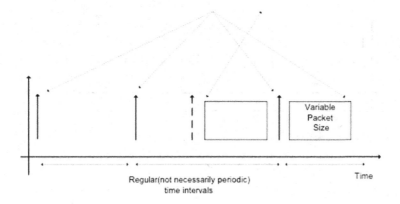

Figure 10. BE

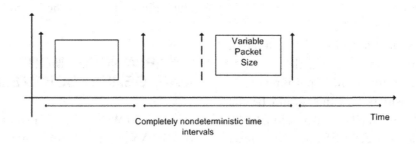

Hierarchical Mobile IP (THMIP) architecture, we consider a cluster of ASN placed in a three level hierarchy as shown in Figure 11. The root node of the hierarchy is called the Pilot ASN (PASN) which may change periodically based on the topology. As MN changes its point of attachment from home ASN to the visited ASN, the MN updates the home agent (HA) with an address called the regional care of address (RCoA) as its current location. All packets destined for the MN are intercepted by Pilot Mobility Agent (PMA), which encapsulates it and sends it to the MN's current address. If the MN changes its current point of attachment within the same domain, it gets a new address after registration, called the local care of address (LCoA) from the foreign agent serving it. The Timing diagram of THMIP is shown in Figure 12.

The MN needs to register the LCoA to the PMA and its mobility is transparent to the HA. HA is updated with new RCoA whenever the MN moves from one ASN to another. For frequent inter-ASN domain movement, multiple locations update to previous ASN increase the service delay. To get out of this problem, location update to previous AR is permitted up to two times. In third attempt, movement of the MN updates CoA to HA again with RCoA (Regional Care of Address). A tunnel is to be established previous ASN and current ASN to reduce packet loss. Hence the signaling burden is evenly distributed among the network and signaling overhead is reduced drastically. The timing diagram (Figure 12) shows the two scenarios of single inter ASN domain movement and 3m times inter ASN domain movement where m is any positive integer. Certain assumptions are taken in carrying out the simulation. Among these, two important assumptions are: (1) Three level hierarchy of ASN. And (2) Multiple inter ASN domain movement of MN.

Figure 11. THMIP architecture

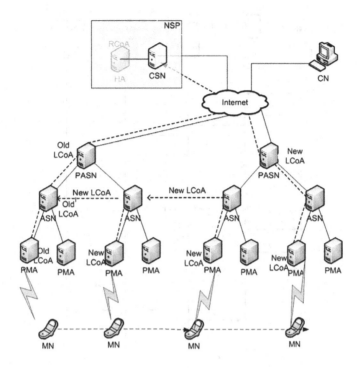

Results and Discussion

Figure 13 shows an example of a WiMAX architecture.

Here a two MN, Mobile_1_1 and Mobile_2_1 are located under Base stations BS_1 and BS_2 QoS service class using 5Mbps as maximum available bandwidth and 1.5 Mbps as minimum available bandwidth.

Static Scenario

Figure 14 shows the throughput of mobile_1_1. The call takes 20s to establish and the data transfer rate is constant at 3.04 mbps.

Figure 15 shows the discrete packets sending from Mobile_1_1 to Mobile_2_1 at certain instant of time.

Mobility Scenario with Node Movement Path

Now Mobile_1_1 is going to the cell under BS_2 from BS_1 and Mobile_2_1 is going to the cell under BS_1 from BS_2. Handoff will occur.

The mobility of the Mobile_1_1 varies from 10 KMPH to 100 KMPH and each of the cases we try to figure out the fluctuation in throughput and packet drop to define the complete agility of the system. For each of the cases, scheduling algorithm rtPS (real time polling service) is used just like in a real-life situation (see Figures 16, 17, 18, and 19).

Test Case 1: Speed: 60 KMPH-As the speed increases, throughput drops to 2.5 mbps. Therefore, the drop in throughput is $(((3.04 - 2.5)/3.04)*100) = 17.7\%$, which is less than a 20% drop.

Figure 12. Timing diagram of THMIP

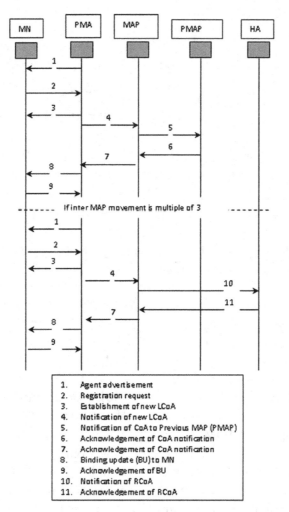

1. Agent advertisement
2. Registration request
3. Establishment of new LCoA
4. Notification of new LCoA
5. Notification of CoA to Previous MAP (PMAP)
6. Acknowledgement of CoA notification
7. Acknowledgement of CoA notification
8. Binding update (BU) to MN
9. Acknowledgement of BU
10. Notification of RCoA
11. Acknowledgement of RCoA

Figure 13. WiMAX architechture

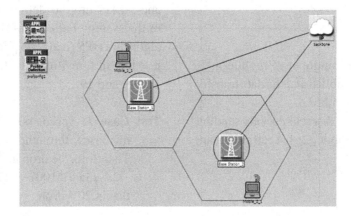

Figure 14. Throughput at static condition

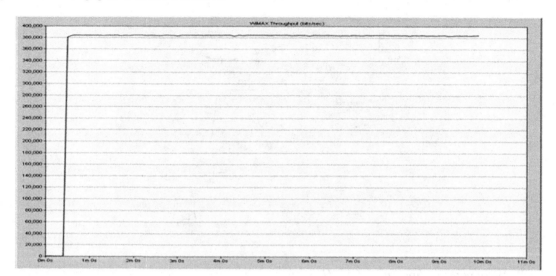

Figure 15. Packets sending from Mobile_1_1 to Mobile_2_1

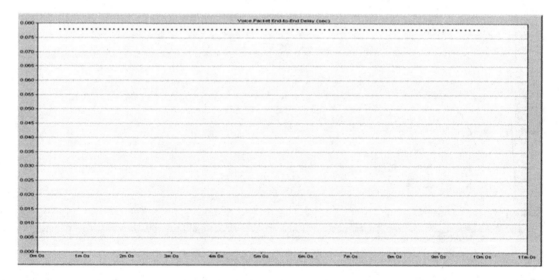

Test Case 2: Speed 90 KMPH-At 90 KMPH throughput is 2.5 mbps, so the system in these conditions is also agile.

Test Case 3: Speed 100 KMPH

As Mobile_1_1 increases speed to 100 KMPH and moves towards BS 2 changing its point of attachment, handoff occurs at 150 ms. Because of the handoff and the NLOS environment, there is a dip in throughput and throughput remains unaltered subsequently. The average throughput at 100 KMPH is 1.6mbps. The drop in throughput is $(((3.04 - 1.6)/3.04)*100) = 47.4\%$.

From the above 3 test cases it is apparent that the throughput drop for mobile_1_1 is marginal at up to 90 KMPH. At 100 KMPH, however, throughput to the system drops abruptly. Initially, rtPS was taken as the QoS service class for real-time service. Later, a comparative analysis was made with other QoS service classes (BE, UGS,

Figure 16. Trajectery path on MN

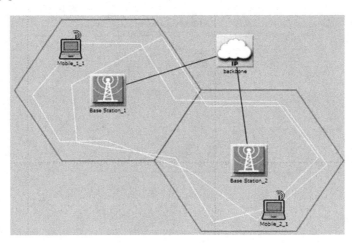

Figure 17. Average throughput at 90 KMPH

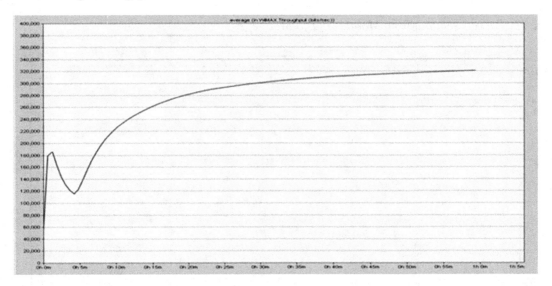

rtPS, ertPS). Figure 20 compares the throughput for different QoS service classes. It is evident from Figure 20 that throughput for the BE service class is maximum and ertPS is minimum. Figure 21 shows the comparative uplink packet drop analysis of different service classes. Figure 21 depicts that packet drop for rtPS is maximum and BE is minimum. We can conclude from Figures 20 and 21 that the BE service class can be used with the exception of some specific conditions.

Important parameters taken into account for the simulations are shown in Table2. The speed

of mobile_1_1 is set at 60 KMPH for the simulation. Figure 22 shows the change in throughput for different OFDM modulation techniques. The QPSK ½ was used as the constant modulation scheme throughout the simulation. Figure 23 shows the downlink packet drop with respect to the change in speed of mobile_1_1. There is an avalanche of packet drop at 60 KMPH due to the handoff condition which arises. Figure 24 shows the variation of path loss in dbvs speed of both the MN.

Figure 18. Average throughput at 100 KMPH

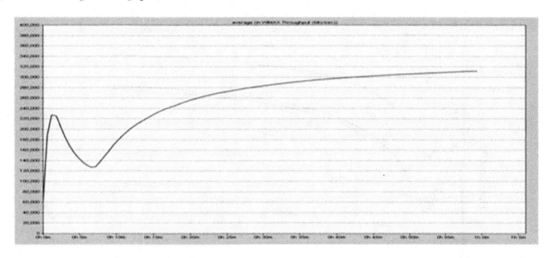

Figure 19. Actual throughput at 100 KMPH

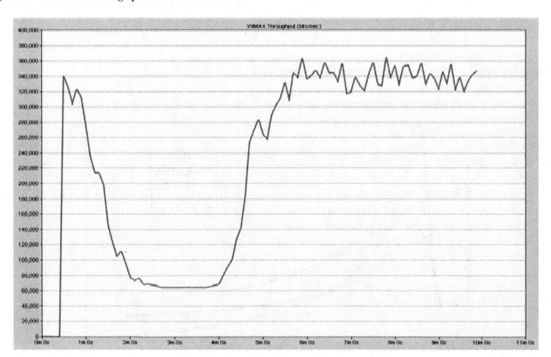

Figure 20. Throughput variation of different QoS service classes

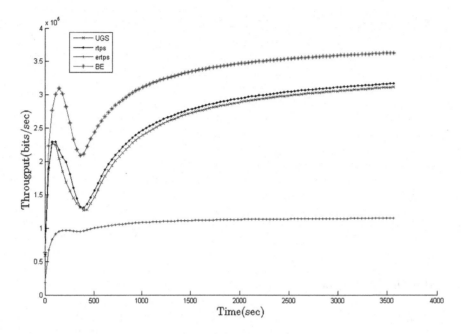

Figure 21. Uplink packet drop of different QoS service classes

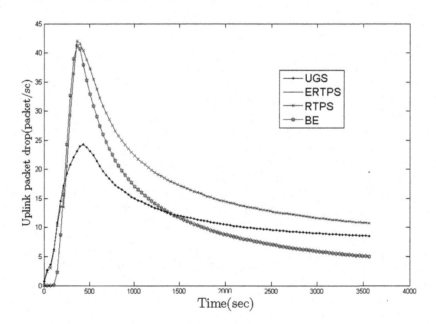

Table 2. Some important parameters taken in simulation

Min. MN velocity	40 km/hr
Max. MN velocity	100 km/hr
User density	200MN/cell
Frequency Bandwidth used	2.3-2.4 Ghz
Channel Bandwidth	8.75/10 Ghz
FFT size	1024
Modulation Technique	QPSK 1/2
RF multiple access mode	OFDMA
MIMO antenna selection	4x4
No. of Carriers	2
Transmission power	Max. 20watt
Cyclic Prefixes	1/8
RCV Buffer size	64kbytes

Figure 22. Variation of speed for different modulation technique of OFDM

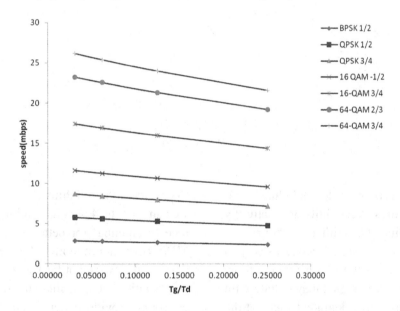

CONCLUSION

It is very important to provide QoS to guarantee diversifying requirements of different applications in WiMAX. The system requirement of the next generation of mobile WiMAX is supposed to be based on IEEE 802.16m, which is still in the letter ballot stage. It is obvious that it requires a better MIMO solution to achieve higher spectral efficiency which lack in interim release 1.5 by WiMAX forum and lower handoff latency with faster mobility (500 km/hr) through efficient mobility management.

The greatest challenge of MIMO antennas is multipath fading in non-line-of-sight (NLOS) environments where a transmitted signal may

Figure 23. Downlink packet drop vs. variation of speed

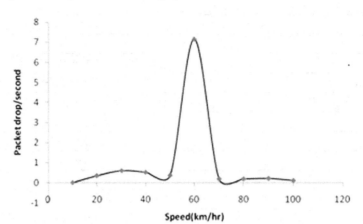

Figure 24. Path loss vs. variation of speed

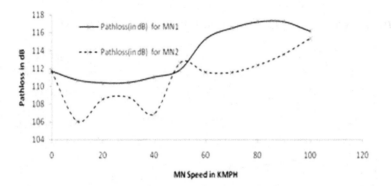

bounce off a myriad of obstacles including building, roads, structures, trees, hills and naturally occurring impediments. With each bounce, a separate instance of the signal makes its way to the destination receiver with a variation in time. These multiple bounced signal may collide with one another resulting in a degraded signal at the receiver. So there is a trade off in proper selection of antenna ratio to achieve high throughput with minimized error. We find the best feasible selection of antennas are $N_T=4$ and $N_R=4$. These provide the best MIMO channel capacity using optimal antenna selection technique. Because channel capacity is the main determinant of reliability[1] in signal transmitting and receiving and our main goal is to find the optimum number of antennas

to provide good reliability in the case of MIMO, we can take the 4x4 combination of transmit and receive antennas for better channel capacity of MIMO or better reliability. It is important to note that reliability cannot be 100% achieved. A 4x4 combination of transmit and receive antennas can only provide better channel capacity than any other antenna. It is also important to note that MIMO antenna selection should have a QPSK1/2 modulation scheme to optimize performance. The BE QoS service classes can be used in general conditions to obtain maximum throughput, low latency and low BER.

The WiMAX forum estimates that approximately 133 million people will use WiMAX by the end of 2012. Mobility management is the key

Table 3. Assured forwarding (AF) behavior group

	Class 1 (lowest)	Class 2	Class 3	Class 4 (highest)
Low Drop	AF11 (DSCP 10)	AF21 (DSCP 18)	AF31 (DSCP 26)	AF41 (DSCP 34)
Med Drop	AF12 (DSCP 12)	AF22 (DSCP 20)	AF32 (DSCP 28)	AF42 (DSCP 36)
High Drop	AF13 (DSCP 14)	AF23 (DSCP 22)	AF33 (DSCP 30)	AF43 (DSCP 38)

challenges to meet the requirements of 133 million users. Mobility management is also closely related with the handoff management. When a MN changes its point of attachment from one WiMAX coverage area to another, an IP layer assisted hand off is required. Handoff latency time requires location update, excessive signaling traffic and service delay which may lead to call blocking and call dropping to the MN. THMIP seems to support frequent user movement and performs the binding update to the HA with a minimum cost and minimum handoff latency to provide seam mobility to user.

ACKNOWLEDGMENT

Authors are thankful to AICTE for the financial support of this research work under AICTE, RPS scheme (file no: 8023/BOR/RID/RPS-72/2009-10), India.

REFERENCES

Aguado, M., Jacob, E., Berbineau, M. I., & Samper, L. (2010). QoS challenges in handover process. In Tang, Seok-Yee, Muller, Peter, Sharif, Hamid (Eds.). WiMAX Security and Quality of Service: An End-to-End Perspective. John Wiley & Sons. 213-238.

Ahmadi, S. (2009). An overview of next-generation mobile WiMAX technology. *IEEE Communications Magazine, 47*(6), 84–98. doi:10.1109/MCOM.2009.5116805

Al-Howaide, A. Z., Doulat, A. S., & Khamayseh, Y. M. (2011). Performance evaluation of different scheduling algorithms. In Wimax. International Journal of Computer Science, Engineering and Applications (IJCSEA). 1(5).81-94.

Alcatel (2006). WiMAX, making ubiquitous high-speed data services a reality.

Andrews, J. G., Ghosh, A., & Muhamed, R. (2007). *Fundamentals of WiMAX: Understanding broadband wireless networking*. Prentice Hall.

Belghith, A., & Nuaymi, L. (2008). Design and implementation of a qo-included WiMAX module for NS-2 simulator. *1st international conference on Simulation tools and techniques for communications, networks and systems & workshops (Simutools '08).*

Chammakhi Msadaa, I., Camara, D., Filali, F., (2010). Mobility management in WiMAX networks. In Tang, Seok-Yee, Muller, Peter, Sharif, Hamid (Eds.). WiMAX Security and Quality of Service: An End-to-End Perspective. John Wiley & Sons. 221-250.

Cho, Y. S. Kim Jaekwon, Yang W. Y., Kang C. G. (2010). MIMO-OFDM wireless communications with MATLAB. John Wiley & Sons

Dhawan, S. (2007). Analogy of promising wireless technology on different frequencies: Bluetooth, WiFi and WiMAX. *2nd International Conference on Wireless Broadband and Ultra Wideband Communications(AusWireless 2007).*

EDX (2007). WiMAX uplink and downlink design considerations.

Etemad, K. (2008). Overview of mobile WiMAX technology and evolution. *IEEE Communications Magazine, 46*(10), 31–40. doi:10.1109/MCOM.2008.4644117

Foschini, G. J. (2002). Layered space-time architecture for wireless communication in a fading environment when using multi-element antennas. *Bell Labs Technical Journal., 1*(2), 41–59. doi:10.1002/bltj.2015

Hochwald, B. M., Sweldens, W. (2000). Differential unitary space–time modulation. *IEEE Transactions on Communications. 48*(12).2041-2052.

Hughes, B. L., & Sweldens, W. (2000). Differential space–time modulation. *IEEE Transactions on Information Theory, 46*(7), 2567–2578. doi:10.1109/18.887864

INTEL (2007). Mobile broadband brought to you by WiMAX.

Jain, A., Verma, A. K. (n.d.) Comparative study of scheduling algorithm for WiMAX.

Khalil, A., & Ksentini, A. (2007). *Classification of the uplink scheduling algorithms in IEEE 802.16.* IRISIA.

Liu, Q., Wang, X., & Giannakis, G. B. (2006). A cross-layer scheduling algorithm with QoS support in wireless networks. *IEEE Transactions on Vehicular Technology, 55*(3), 839–847. doi:10.1109/TVT.2006.873832

Nuaymi, L. (2007). *WiMAX: Technology for broadband wireless access.* John Wiley & Sons. doi:10.1002/9780470319055

Paulraj, A., Nabar, R., & Gore, D. (2008). *Introduction to space-time wireless communication.* Cambridge University Press.

Rashwan, A. H., Hesham, B. M. E., & Ali, H. H. (2009). Comparative assessments for different WiMAX scheduling algorithms. *World Congress on Engineering and Computer Science- WCECS 2009. 1.*

Saha, S., & Mukhopadhyay, A. K. (2011). THMIP-A novel mobility management scheme using fluid flow model. *2nd International Conference on Emerging Trends and Applications in Computer Science, (NCETACS - 2011).*

Saha, S., & Mukhopadhyay, A. K. (2012). Mobility management issues for next generation wireless networks. In Abawajy, Pathan, J. M., Rahman, Pathan, M. A., Deris, M. (Eds.). Network and Traffic Engineering in Emerging Distributed Computing Applications. Information Science Reference. 247-274.

Sibille, A., Oestges, C., & Zanella, A. (2010). *MIMO: From theory to implementation.* Academic Press.

IEEE Standard (2004b). 802.16-2004.Part 16: Air interface for fixed broadband wireless access system.

IEEE Standards (2004a). IEEE Standard for local and metropolitan area networks, air interface for fixed broadband wireless access systems.

IEEE Standards (2005). IEEE Standard for local and metropolitan area networks. Air interface for fixed broadband wireless access systems. Amendment 1: Management information base.

IEEE Standards (2006). 802.16e-2005 and IEEE Std 802.16-2004/Cor1-2005-IEEE Standard for local and metropolitan area networks. Part 16: Air interface for fixed and mobile broadband wireless access systems. Amendment 2: Physical and medium access control layers for combined fixed and mobile operation in licensed bands and corrigendum 1.

Tarokh, V., Seshadri, N., Calderbank, A. R. (1998). Space-time codes for high data rate wireless communication: performance criterion and code construction. *IEEE Transactions on Information Theory. 44*(2).744 – 765.

WiMAX Forum. (2006a). Mobile WiMAX – Part 1: A technical overview and performance evaluation.

WiMaX Forum. (2006b). WiMaX end-to-end network systems architecture; Stage 2, Release 1: architecture tenets, network reference architecture, reference points.

WiMAX Forum. (2006c). WiMAX end-to-end network systems architecture; Stage 3, Release 1: detailed protocols and procedures.

WiMAX Forum. (2007). Deployment of mobile WiMAX™ networks by operators with existing 2G & 3G networks.

WiMAX Forum. (2009). Network architecture (Stage 2: Architecture tenets, reference model and reference points).*1*(Release 1.0 Version 4).

WiMAX Forum. (2010). Proxy mobile IPv4. 3gpp2 RFC 5563

Yarali, A., & Rahman, S. (2008). WiMAX broadband wireless access technology: Services, architecture and deployment models. *Canadian Conference on Electrical and Computer Engineering, CCECE 2008.* 77-82.

ADDITIONAL READING

Ahson, S. A., & Ilyas, M. (2008). *WiMAX Handbook*. CRC Press.

Chen, J.-C., & Zhang, T. (2003). *IP-based next-generation wireless networks: Systems, architectures, and protocols*. John Wiley & Sons.

Chen, K. C., & de Marca, J. R. B. (2008). *Mobile WiMAX*. John Wiley & Sons. doi:10.1002/9780470723937

Deb, S., Mhatre, V., & Ramaiyan, V. (2008). WiMAX relay networks: Opportunistic scheduling to exploit multiuser diversity and frequency selectivity. *Proceedings of the 14th ACM international conference on Mobile computing and networking- MobiCom '08.* 163-174.

Esmailpour, A., & Nasser, N. (2010). Quantifying quality of service differentiation for WiMAX networks. *International Conference on Multimedia Computing and Information Technology (MCIT).* 121-124.

Esseling, N., Walke, B. H., & Pabst, R. (2005). Fixed relays for next generation wireless systems. In A. R. K. Pahlavan (Ed.), *Ganesh, R., Kota, S. L* (pp. 72–93). Springer, US: Emerging Location Aware Broadband Wireless Ad Hoc Networks. doi:10.1007/0-387-23072-6_5

Ghosh, D., Gupta, A., & Mohapatra, P. (2008). Scheduling in multihop WiMAX networks. *Mobile Computing and Communications Review., 12*(2), 1–11. doi:10.1145/1394555.1394557

Kasch, W. T., Ward, J. R., & Andrusenko, J. (2009). Wireless network modeling and simulation tools for designers and developers. *IEEE Communications Magazine, 47*(3), 120–127. doi:10.1109/MCOM.2009.4804397

Li, Q., Lin, X., Zhang, J., & Roh, W. (2009). Advancement of MIMO technology in WiMAX: from IEEE 802.16d/e/j to 802.16m. *IEEE Communications Magazine, 47*(6), 100–107. doi:10.1109/MCOM.2009.5116806

Molisch, A. F. (2010). *Wireless communications* (2nd ed.). John Wiley & Sons.

Omar, S.-M., Slock, D. T. M., & Bazzi, O. (2010). Receiver diversity with blind and semi-blind FIR SIMO channel estimates. *Proceedings of the 4th International Symposium on Communications, Control and Signal Processing(ISCCSP 2010).*

Rahman, M. A., Pakštas, A., Wang, F. Z. (2009). Review: Network modelling and simulation tools, simulation modeling practices and theory. *Science direct. 17*(6). 1011-1031.

Rao, G.S.V.R.K., Radhamani, G. (2007). WiMAX: Λ wireless technology revolution. A*uerbach Publications.*

Sim, S., Han, S.-J., Park, J.-S., & Lee, S.-C. (2009). Seamless IP mobility support for flat architecture mobile WiMAX networks. *IEEE Communications Magazine, 47*(6), 142–148. doi:10.1109/ MCOM.2009.5116811

Zhang, Y. (Ed.). (2009). *WiMAX network planning and optimization.* CRC Press. doi:10.1201/9781420066630

KEY TERMS AND DEFINITIONS

Additive White Gaussian Noise (AWGN): Additive white Gaussian noise (AWGN) is a channel model in which the only impairment to communication is a linear addition of wideband or white noise with a constant spectral density (expressed as watts per hertz of bandwidth) and a Gaussian distribution of amplitude. The model does not account for fading, frequency selectivity, interference, nonlinearity or dispersion. However, it produces simple and tractable mathematical models which are useful for gaining insight into the underlying behavior of a system before these other phenomena are considered.

Assured Forwarding (AF): The IETF defines the Assured Forwarding behavior in RFC 2597 and RFC 3260. Assured forwarding allows the operator to provide assurance of delivery as long as the traffic does not exceed some subscribed rate. Traffic that exceeds the subscription rate faces a higher probability of being dropped if congestion occurs. The AF behavior group defines four separate AF classes with Class 4 having the highest priority. Within each class, packets are given a drop precedence (high, medium or low). The combination of classes and drop precedence yields twelve separate DSCP encodings from AF11 through AF43 (see Table 3). Some measure of priority and proportional fairness is defined between traffic in different classes. Should congestion occur between classes, the traffic in the higher class is given priority. Rather than using strict priority queuing, more balanced queue servicing algorithms such as fair queuing or weighted fair queuing (WFQ) are likely to be used. If congestion occurs within a class, the packets with the higher drop precedence are discarded first. To prevent issues associated with tail drop, more sophisticated drop selection algorithms such as random early detection (RED) are often used.

Beam Forming: Beam forming or spatial filtering is a signal processing technique used in sensor arrays for directional signal transmission or reception. This is achieved by combining elements in a phased array in such a way that signals at particular angles experience constructive interference while others experience destructive interference. Beam forming can be used at both the transmitting and receiving ends in order to achieve spatial selectivity. The improvement compared with omni directional reception/transmission is known as the receive/transmit gain (or loss).

Cumulative Distribution Function: In probability theory and statistics, the cumulative distribution function (CDF), or just distribution function, describes the probability that a real-valued random variable X with a given probability distribution will be found at a value less than or equal to x. Cumulative distribution functions are also used to specify the distribution of multivariaterandom variables.

Ergodicprocess: Insignal processing, a stochastic process is said to be ergodic if its statistical properties (such as its mean and variance) can be deduced from a single, sufficiently long sample (realization) of the process.

Expatiate Forwarding (EF): The IETF defines Expedited Forwarding behavior in RFC 3246. The EF Per hop behavior(PHB) has the characteristics of low delay, low loss and low jitter. These characteristics are suitable for voice, video and other real-time services. EF traffic is often given strict priority queuing above all other traffic classes. Because an overload of EF traffic will cause queuing delays and affect the jitter and delay tolerances within the class, EF traffic is often strictly controlled through admission control, policing and other mechanisms. Typical networks will limit EF traffic to no more than 30%—and often much less—of the capacity of a link.

Spatial Diversity/Antenna Diversity: Antenna diversity uses multiple antennas to improve the quality and reliability of wireless link and reduce multipath fading. Multiple antennas both at the sender and receiver side offer to receive the same signal of different quality due to fading. All the signals are processed through switching, combining and dynamic control to protect against fading.

Rayleigh Fading: Rayleigh fading is a statistical model for the effect of a propagation environment on a radio signal, such as that used by wireless devices.Rayleigh fading models assume that the magnitude of a signal that has passed through such a transmission medium (also called a communications channel) will vary randomly, or fade, according to a Rayleigh distribution—the radial component of the sum of two uncorrelated Gaussianrandom variables.

Singular Value Decomposition: In linear algebra, the singular value decomposition (SVD) is a factorization of a real or complexmatrix, with many useful applications in signal processing and statistics.Formally, the singular value decomposition of an m×n real or complex matrix M is a factorization of the form $M = U\Sigma V^*$ where U is an m×m real or complex unitary matrix, Σ is an m×nrectangular diagonal matrix with nonnegative real numbers on the diagonal, and V* (the conjugate transpose of V) is an n×n real or complex unitary matrix.

Section 3
Network Access Issues

Chapter 17
Access Network Selection in a 4G Environment

Vasuky Mohanan
School of Computer Science, Universiti Sains Malaysia, Malaysia

Rahmat Budiarto
Networked Computing Center, Surya University, Indonesia

Sivakumar Ramakrishnan
School of Materials and Mineral Resources Engineering, Universiti Sains Malaysia, Malaysia

ABSTRACT

4G networks provide bandwidth of up to 1Gbps for a Mobile Node (MN) that is moving at pedestrian speed. On the other hand, it also supports mobile nodes that can move at a speed of 250 km/hr with bandwidths value of 100 Mbps. This sets the premise of a network that supports diverse needs. This goal will be harder to achieve if Network Selection Problems (NSP) are not addressed comprehensively. NSP refers to the selection of target access network selection from a collection of Candidate Networks (CNs) when MNs are moving from one access network into another. The most logical way of achieving this is to select the "best" network. This translates to identifying performance values of the CNs. The analysis in this chapter shows clearly that access network selection done based on limited criteria is detrimental in achieving optimum communication. Instead, this chapter suggests a framework that would be complementary to a 4G network.

INTRODUCTION

According to International Telecommunications Union Radio Standardization Sector (ITU-R), a 4G network must be able to provide bandwidth of up to 1Gbps for mobile nodes that are moving at pedestrian speed. Additionally, a 4G network must also enable a MN that's moving at the speed of 250 km/hr to achieve a bandwidth of 100 Mbps. As per these requirements, a 4G network is expected to satisfy diverse needs spreading over two extreme ends. On one hand, mobile nodes (MN) moving at pedestrian speeds achieve very high throughput and conversely, high speed MNs are also capable of achieving high throughput. In order to satisfy these seemingly opposing needs, an efficient and intelligent access network selection mechanism is needed. Current access network selection mecha-

DOI: 10.4018/978-1-4666-4888-3.ch017

nism chooses the next target network to handover to by using limited set of criteria. Access network selection mechanism that uses single or limited criteria to decide candidate network (CN) ranking increases the chance of handing over to unsuitable target network. This is because limited criteria may not define a context wholly. This in turn will be detrimental to the level of quality of service (QoS) achieved. So far, ITU-R has recognized 2 candidate technologies to support 4G network namely LTE-Advanced and IEEE 802.16m. Both these standardizations are capable of meeting ITU-R's 4G requirements. Unfortunately, the technical benefits these technologies espouses will not trickle down to the communicating MNs unless the access network selection method makes the right decision and selects the best target network. An access network selection method in a 4G environment must take into account various criteria from all the main stakeholders (user, MNs, and CNs) in order to provide a holistic solution. This scenario is made even more challenging by the fact that MNs are now capable of connecting to different types of access networks using multiple interfaces. A typical scenario facing an access network selection method is a large pool of CNs of different access types to choose from, for MNs of varying speeds, each running multiple applications that have its own set of QoS requirements that must be satisfied. Another reality facing access network selection is to enable Always Best Connected (ABC) to MNs by choosing the best target network. ABC can mean different things for all the three main stakeholders hence the need to collect necessary criteria values from all three. It is very challenging to support ABC in a 4G environment as MNs in this environment can go up to 250 km/hr speed thereby the changing of access network connection will occur often and rapidly. Researchers have shown that two of the most popular mechanism used to collect criteria values is through mean value of past sessions (MVP) and most recent value (MRV). Both these mechanisms are mirror opposites of

each other and both have been criticized, MVP for not taking into account recent changes and MRV for not considering historical data. Mobility scenarios in a 4G network are highly dynamic therefore a hybrid of both these methods would be more suitable in identifying the respective criteria values. The access network selection mechanism must also be flexible in adapting to fast changing environment i.e. a MN that suddenly moves at high speed, a CN that is increasingly choked with large amount of traffic and a user who's running two different applications with diverse needs. Current access network selection mechanism use single or limited criteria to identify the context on which the selection occurs and this will not scale up to the more challenging 4G environment. Current access network selection methods tend to allot static weights to the criteria. Predetermined weights that are fixed will not correctly represent a scenario that has changed. The next section in this chapter proceeds by discussing and analyzing current and popular network selection problem (NSP) solutions. Next, a thorough discussion on the chosen 4G candidate technologies is done. Based on the literature review of existing approaches on NSP as well as the technicalities of 4G candidate technologies, a new framework that we believe will be more suited to the dynamic 4G environment that would also be complementary to the 4G candidate technologies is presented. The next section presents results that emphasize the efficacy of this new framework. Thereafter, a section on how this proposed framework can be implemented is presented. Next, recommendations and suggestions for future improvements are discussed followed by conclusion.

RELATED WORK

This section focuses on literature in the area of network selection. Essentially, a method that solves NSP consists of two main components: 1) a weight specification component and 2) a ranking component. Firstly, methods that allocate weights of importance to attributes are discussed followed by methods that solve the issue of ranking of CNs. Hybrid methods that implements both these components is also discussed. Also, current and popular approaches in solving NSP are also presented. This in turn will help determine the emerging trends in the area of NSP. Constraints and /or disadvantages of these methods are also highlighted.

Weight Allocation Models

Analytical Hierarchy Process (AHP)

AHP is primarily a weighting mechanism. Attributes that are pivotal in making the right decisions must be given weight indicating its importance. AHP was created in 1977 to assist in decision making for unstructured problems. AHP can easily consider a multitude of attributes simultaneously prior to making its decision. Moreover, AHP can handle both quantitative and qualitative data (Charilas, Markaki, Psarras & Constantinou, 2009). The attributes under consideration must be arranged in a hierarchical structure first, descending from an overall goal to criteria, to sub criteria and alternatives in successive level (Saaty, 1990). The decision maker has to indicate his/her preferences by comparing the criteria and sub criteria and alternatives with respect to the overall goal. AHP uses pair-wise comparison to derive the weights for each attribute. Pair wise comparison means the importance of an attribute is derived by comparing it with another attribute. The fundamental AHP scale of 1 to 9 is used to indicate importance whereby 1: Equally important, 3: Moderately more important, 5: Strongly more important, 7: Very strongly more important, 9: Extremely more important. Assume AHP is considering 3 attributes: A_1, A_2, and A_3 with W_1, W_2 and W_3 as its weight respectively. Firstly, a matrix of pair wise ratios is built.

$$
\begin{pmatrix}
 & A1 & A2 & A3 \\
A1 & W_1/W_1 & W_1/W_2 & W_1/W_3 \\
A2 & W_2/W_1 & W_2/W_2 & W_2/W_3 \\
A3 & W_3/W_1 & W_3/W_2 & W_3/W_3
\end{pmatrix}
\begin{pmatrix}
W_1 \\
W_2 \\
W_3
\end{pmatrix}
$$

The matrix A has the following properties: A(i, j) whereby i refers to the row and j refers to the column, $a_{ij} = w_i/w_j$, i, j = 1, 2, ...n, and satisfies the reciprocal property $a_{ji} = 1/a_{ij}$. The matrix is multiplied by a vector of weights giving the results *nw*. If *n* is the eigenvalue of the matrix then *w* is the eigenvector associated with it. (Saaty, 1990). The eigenvector *w* is calculated through the following steps (Charilas, Markaki, Nikitopoulos & Theologou, 2008).:

1. The elements of each line of the matrix are added up: $S_i = \Sigma_i a_{ij}$ for each i
2. For each line of the matrix, the weight of each element is estimated by calculating the quotient of the value S_i via the sum of all the elements of the matrix: $wi = si/\Sigma_i\Sigma_i a_{ij}$. The elements of vector *w* are normalized, so that their sum is equal to 1.
3. The square of the matrix is calculated and all the procedure steps are repeated until two successive approaches do not differ appreciably in the frame of desirable precision.

The AHP scale used to indicate weight is detailed in Table1 (Saaty, 1990).

As opposed to other network selecting methods, AHP has been used primarily as means to determine the weights of the attributes in question. And these weights are subsequently fed into scoring mechanisms to determine the rank of the candidate networks (Charilas & Panagopoulos, 2010; Wu, Yang & Hwang, 2009; Song & Jamalipour, 2005; Zequn et al, 2009). Therefore, AHP on its own does not present itself as a suitable holistic network selection solution as it focuses on assigning weights to the attributes. The rank-

Table 1. AHP scale

Intensity of Importance on an Absolute Scale	Definition	Explanation
1	Equal importance	Two activities contribute equally to the objective
3	Moderate importance of one over another	Experience and judgement strongly favour one activity over another
5	Essential or strong importance	Experience and judgement strongly favour one activity over another
7	Very strong importance	An activity is strongly favoured and its dominance demonstrated in practice
9	Extreme Importance	The evidence favouring one activity over another is of the highest possible order of affirmation
2,4,6,8	Intermediate values between the two adjacent judgements	When compromise is needed
Reciprocals	If activity i has one of the above numbers assigned to it when compared to activity j, then j has the reciprocal value when compared with i	
Rationals	Ratios arising from the scale	If consistency were to be forced by obtaining n numerical values to span the matrix.

ing aspect of NSP is not addressed by AHP. Nevertheless, AHP is a simple efficient method that can decompose a complex network selection problem into a hierarchical structure thus making it easier to tackle. Also, a serious lacking of AHP is that it only handles attribute values that are crisp and precise. The next section discusses ways to overcome this issue.

Fuzzy AHP

Fuzzy AHP in an extension of AHP whereby the comparison ratios are expressed as fuzzy numbers that are provided through linguistic terms (Charilas et al.,, 2009. Not all attribute values can be expressed objectively in discrete numbers. Therefore, fuzzy numbers are used to express subjective criteria values. Examples of objective criteria are delay, jitter packet loss and examples of subjective criteria are reliability, seamlessness, security etc (Charilas & Panagopoulos, 2010). Conversion scales are then used to convert these linguistic variables into crisp values. Fuzzy Inference System (FIS) is another fuzzy logic based system that uses the weight determined by the

inference system by applying a series of rules (Charilas & Panagopoulos, 2010). FIS has been criticized for not being scalable and adaptive (Charilas & Panagopoulos, 2010) as it contains a high number of rules, therefore adaptive network based FIS (ANFIS) was developed. ANFIS uses a back propagation learning algorithm in order to define rules. As ANFIS generates its own rules by using a learning algorithm, it needs to be trained often so that it performs at an optimal standard. Generally, the methods discussed in this section were designed to handle imprecise or vague criteria values. But, essentially, as its predecessor AHP, these techniques are also not holistic as it only handles the weight allocation portion of NSP.

RANKING TECHNIQUES

Electre

Elimination Et Choix Traduisant la Realite (ELECTRE) or Elimination and Choice Expressing Reality was created to handle multiple criteria real world problems regarding making decisions about choosing the best actions from a given set of actions (Figueira, Mousseau & Roy, 2005). ELECTRE methods comprise of two main procedures: construction of one or several outranking relation(s) and exploitation (Figueira et al.,, 2005). ELECTRE uses binary outranking relation S that is defined as "at least as good as". By using S to describe the relations between two actions namely *a* and *b*, the following result occurs:

- *a* S *b* – a is strictly preferred to b.
- *b* S *a* – b is strictly preferred to a.
- *a* S *b* and *b* S *a* – a is indifferent to b and vice versa.
- Not *a* S *b* and not *b* S *a* – a is incomparable to b and vice versa.

Exploitation is performed on the outranking relationship(s) to derive recommendations regarding which action to undertake. Network selection problem using ELECTRE can be modelled as P = (A, C, w) (Charilas et al., 2009) where,

A={ 1, ..., n} denotes the candidate networks being considered.
C={1, ..., m} denoting the number of attributes impacting the decision.
W={1, ..., m} denotes the weights assigned to the attributes.

Let's say the attributes involved are Delay, Jitter, Cost and Throughput and there are n candidate networks in the running, the following matrix is built:

$$
\begin{bmatrix}
D1 & J1 & C1 & T1 \\
D2 & J2 & C2 & T2 \\
\cdots & \cdots & \cdots & \cdots \\
DN & JN & CN & TN
\end{bmatrix}
$$

Next, a reference network matrix is built indicating the desired values for the corresponding attributes. As the attributes in question have different units of measurements, normalization procedure is executed on both matrices. The relative importance of each attribute is indicated by weights and these weights are incorporated on the candidate networks matrix as shown:

$$
\begin{bmatrix}
WDD1 & WJJ1 & WCC1 & WTT1 \\
WDD2 & WJJ2 & WCC2 & WTT2 \\
\cdots & \cdots & \cdots & \cdots \\
WDDN & WJJN & WCCN & WTTN
\end{bmatrix}
$$

How the weights were derived is not a focus of this method. Electre just makes use of the weight. Electre uses these matrices to derive ranking of CNs. This is done by identifying the degree of satisfaction or dissatisfaction of one candidate network compared to another and is expressed using concordance and discordance matrices (Charilas et al., 2009). These matrices are created using concordance and discordance sets respectively. Given two candidate networks x and y, concordance set reveals which of the attributes in x is superior compared to y and the discordance set identifies which attributes are lacking. Next, the net concordance and net discordance indices are calculated for all candidate networks. The net concordance (Ci) and discordance (Di) indexes are calculated using the following formula (Charilas et al., 2009). The net concordance indices reflect the relative measure of dominance of candidate network *i* over all the other alternatives compared to the relative measure of dominance of all the other alternatives over *i*. Conversely, the net discordance indices reflect the measure of weakness of candidate network i over all the other alternatives compared to the relative measure of weakness of the other alternatives as opposed to i.

$$
\mathrm{Ci} = \sum_{\substack{j=1 \\ j \neq i}}^{j=n} Cij - \sum_{\substack{j=1 \\ j \neq i}}^{j=n} Cji \quad \mathrm{Di} = \sum_{\substack{j=1 \\ j \neq i}}^{j=n} Dij - \sum_{\substack{j=1 \\ j \neq i}}^{j=n} Dji
$$

Finally, the ranking of candidate networks is executed using these net concordance and discordance indexes as well as taking the average of these two rankings. Based on (Charilas et al., 2009; Figueira et al., 2005; Kuo, Yang, Huang, 2008), ELECTRE assumes that the importance of each criteria increases or decreases monotonically. Because of this characteristic, Electre is not suitable when faced with conflicting objectives. For example, let's say the user indicates that cost as well as seamlessness is of equal importance. The network selected must provide high throughput but at a low cost. This is not possible as the cost increases as higher throughput is provided. Therefore, a monotonically increasing function for throughput will yield an expensive network. Therefore, a balance has to be achieved, whereby a network that satisfies the minimum throughput requirement of the executing application that also provides the service at a low cost can be possibly identified. This cannot be achieved using ELECTRE.

Simple Additive Weighting (SAW)

In a network selection method, SAW is usually use to rank the candidate networks based on their scores. Once all the attributes from all the candidate networks are assigned weights, SAW will determine the overall score of a candidate network by summing up the weights (Kassar, Kervella & Pujolle, 2008; Stevens-Navarro & Wong 2006). The following formula is used to identify the score of candidate network *i* where n is the number of attributes, r is the normalized attribute value and w refer to the weight (Wu et al.,, 2009):

$$Score\left(i\right) = \sum_{j=1}^{n} wjrij$$

Hence, SAW is hardly a holistic solution to the network selection problem due to its limited application.

Multiplicative Exponential Weighting (MEW)

MEW is similar to SAW in that MEW is also a scoring mechanism (Stevens-Navarro & Wong 2006). The score of a candidate network i where n is the number of attributes is the weighted product of the attributes (Wu et al.,, 2009, Márquez-Barja, et al., 2011) as shown in the following formula:

$$Score\left(i\right) = \prod_{j=1}^{n} xij^{wj}$$

Whereby x_{ij} denotes attribute j of network i and w_j refer to the weight. This score does not have an upper bound (Stevens-Navarro & Wong 2006), therefore, the score is compared against an ideal solution (Wu et al.,, 2009, Márquez-Barja, et al, 2011). As MEW is similar to SAW, the weakness of SAW is present in MEW as well whereby, it provides solution to one aspect of a network selection problem and ignores the other aspects ergo presenting itself as a non holistic solution. Furthermore, both SAW and MEW makes the implicit assumption that the utility of an attribute increases or decreases monotonically when there is an increase or decrease with the attribute value. This makes optimization such as minimum values for attributes instead of the best, unattainable.

Technique for Order Preference by Similarity to Ideal Solution (TOPSIS)

TOPSIS is essentially a ranking mechanism whereby the best network is the one that is closest in distance towards the ideal solution and also has the furthest distance from the negative solution (Olson, 2004). The key to TOPSIS is accurate weights (Zhang, 2004). Basically, TOPSIS is a ranking mechanism that performs differently when assigned weights using different techniques (Zhang, 2004). According to (Zhang, 2004), TOPSIS method consists of the following steps:

1. Obtain performance data for n alternatives for k criteria.
2. Convert raw measures xij into standardized measures sij.
3. Assign importance weights wk to each criterion.
4. Identify ideal solution, which refers to the best performance/values of each criterion.
5. Identify the negative solution, which are the worst performance/values of each criterion.
6. Develop distance measure for each criteria both from ideal (D+) and negative solution (D).
7. Use the following formula to determine ration R for each alternative.

$$R = \frac{D^-}{D^- + D^+}$$

8. The alternatives are ranked based on R values.

Based on step 4 and 5 above, it is quite clear that utilities towards the attributes increases/ decreases monotonically as only the best or worst performance values are taken into consideration. Also, solves only a subset of NSP.

Grey Relational Analysis (GRA)

According to (Charilas et al, 2008) GRA is based on building grey relationships between elements of two series in order to compare them quantitatively. One of the series refers to the ideal values for all attributes (called reference sequence) in consideration whereas the second series are attribute values from the candidate networks in consideration (called comparability sequence) Based on (Charilas et al, 2008; Kuo et al, 2008), GRA is implemented using the following steps:

1. **Grey Relational Gathering:** This involves the process of classifying the elements of series into 3 groups namely: larger-the-better, smaller-the better, nominal-the best. Lower, upper and moderate bounds of series elements are defined and finally normalization of the attribute values is done.
2. **Reference Sequence Definition:** Ideal target sequence is determined.
3. **Grey Relational Coefficient (GRC) is Calculated:** GRC is used to describe how the reference sequence and all comparability sequences are similar as well as vary.
4. **Grey Relational Grade Calculation:** Ranks the candidate networks based on their GRC values whereby the network with the highest GRC value is the best candidate network among the alternatives.

Assuming that there are n candidate networks $(S_1, S_2, S_3 ... S_n)$ having k attributes each. Upper bound u_j is defined as $\max\{s_1(j), s_2(j) ... s_n(j)\}$ and similarly lower bound l_j is equivalent to $\min\{s_1(j), s_2(j) ... s_n(j)\}$ whereby j = 1, 2, 3 ... k. A moderate bound m_j lies between u_j and l_j Normalization $(S^*_i(j))$ is achieved using the following equations:

$$s_0^*(j) = 1 - \frac{|s_i(j) - m_j|}{\max\{u_j - m_j, m_j - l_j\}} \qquad (1)$$

$$s_0^*(j) = 1 - \frac{|s_i(j) - u_j|}{u_j - l_j\}} \qquad (2)$$

$$s_0^*(j) = 1 - \frac{|s_i(j) - l_j|}{u_j - l_j} \qquad (3)$$

Equation 1 is used for the nominal-the-best attributes. Equation 2 is used for the larger-the-better attributes; Equation 3 is used for the smaller-the-better attributes. Next, the reference series is defined using u_j, l_j and m_j. GRC is calculated using the following formula:

$$\Gamma(s_0, s_i) = \frac{1}{k} \sum_{i=1}^{k} \frac{\Delta_{min} + \Delta_{max}}{\Delta_i + \Delta_{max}},$$

where

$$\Delta_i = |\, s_0^*(j) - s_i(j)\,|,$$
$$\Delta_{max} = \max_{(i,j)}(\Delta i),$$
and
$$\Delta_{min} = \min_{(i,j)}(\Delta i).$$

The network with the highest GRC value is ranked first. Authors in (Ng, 1994), uses a distinguishing coefficient to weaken the effect of a large ▲ max thereby enlarging the significance difference of the relational coefficient using the following formula:

$$\Gamma(s_0, s_i) = \frac{1}{k} \sum_{i=1}^{k} \frac{\Delta_{min} + \zeta \cdot \Delta_{max}}{\Delta_i + \zeta \cdot \Delta_{max}}$$

where $\zeta \in [0,1]$.

Based on the formulas above, we can derive that when attributes values are increasing or decreasing, the utility or suitability of those attributes does not necessarily increase or decrease monotonically as in the case of nominal-the-best. This aspect of GRA renders it suitable to satisfy conflicting objectives. For example, when cost needs to be balanced against other criteria, then the candidate network that provides the nominal-the-best values at a fraction of the cost may be ranked first. This can only be achieved when using GRA as oppose to all the other methods discussed. Other methods tends to always look for the "best" network in all aspects, which may be unlikely, and even if it finds a network that has the highest (i.e. bandwidth) or lowest (i.e. delay), chances are all the other MNs are also eyeing the same said network. This will increase the network's load rendering very unattractive and though it has the best of everything,

may not be able to serve the MN as it suppose to. Similar to previously discussed methods, GRA is not a holistic solution for NSP.

Hybrid Methods

Hybrid methods are network selection methods that combine two or more of the above discussed strategies to identify target network. Most techniques that attempts to overcome NSP emphasizes on weightage and ranking mechanism. Therefore, the hybrid methods that are discussed below do just that.

SAW and MEW

A combination of SAW and MEW was used in (Savitha, & Chandrasekar, 2011) to solve network selection problem for a vertical handover scenario. This proposed work uses only four attributes to base its decision which is not sufficiently enough to gauge the context. Moreover, the speed of the MN is not included as one of the deciding attribute. As previously discussed, MN's mobility speed will vary vastly in a 4G environment and this has to be factored in. Moreover, no discussion was done on how to resolve conflicting objectives. Additionally, user preference was not considered either. ABC has different meaning to each and every user. When this is not captured, then ABC can never be fully provided.

AHP and GRA

A hybrid method using AHP and GRA is used in (Charilas et al, 2008; Song & Jamalipour, 2005) as a network selection mechanism. The proposed method in (Song & Jamalipour, 2005) uses only user preference and network parameters to make its decision. Again, this method is not holistic as it does not consider MN parameters. It also uses fixed allocation of weights. The technique used to derive the network parameter values is not discussed. The solution designed in (Charilas et al, 2008), presented two different methods used to calculate AHP weight. The first method derives the weight by calculating the contribution of each parameter to the total QoS. The second method calculates each parameter's weight according to network performance. This research focuses on identifying the best method between these two in deriving the weights. Both methods when applied give results of different usefulness. Therefore, the discussion in this work does not address network selection per se but instead looks at different ways to define QoS in terms of AHP weights.

Fuzzy AHP and Electre

This combination was proposed in (Charilas et al, 2009). Fuzzy AHP was used to allocate weights to the attributes whereas Electre was used to rank CNs. User preference was indicated by using cost as a factor. It is not sufficient to assume that a single criterion is able to represent user preference. Furthermore, attributes were not collected from the MN. Therefore, an essential stakeholder's viewpoint has been neglected. Also, the proposed mechanism was evaluated using a numerical example. No simulation studies were done to prove the efficacy of this solution.

Fuzzy Logic and ANFIS

This combination was proposed in (Çalhan & Çeken, 2010). Unfortunately, this proposed mechanism uses attributes collected only from CNs. User preference as well MN's attribute values were not taken into account. The simulation scenario used to evaluate this method is limited as it uses a MN that moved at same speed on a straight line generating only voice traffic. A modification of this method was suggested in (Çalhan & Çeken, 2012) whereby Genetic Algorithms were used instead of ANFIS. Genetic Algorithms were used to obtain optimized membership functions off line

and this was fed to the fuzzy logic engine. Due to the volatile nature of wireless networks this technique may not produce optimal results at all times as uncertainties are not captured.

Fuzzy Logic, AHP and Genetic Algorithm

These combined methods were proposed in (Alkhawlani & Ayesh, 2008). It uses three parallel fuzzy logic subsystems to reduce complexities that are normally inherent in AI based network selection solutions. This scheme was tested using only four criteria which would hardly constitute a well realized context. The authors further modified their solution by using an enhanced version of AHP (Alkhawlani & Alsalem, 2010). This version also did not collect any attributes from the MN.

4G CANDIDATE TECHNOLOGIES

This section introduces the two candidates chosen as technologies that can support 4G network. Technical characteristics of these technologies are presented here.

IEEE 802.16m

IEEE 802.16m is an enhancement of IEEE 802.16e that was designed to meet ITU-R's 4G requirements. According to (WiMax Forum, 2010) IEEE 802.16m provides improved performance in the following areas:

1. Coverage and spectral efficiency.
2. Data and VoIP capacity.
3. Latency and QOS.
4. Seamless Internetworking.
5. Energy efficiency.
6. Support for Advanced Features and Services.

These enhancements are supported by changes incorporated into IEEE 802.16m's Physical and Medium Access Control (MAC) Layer (Figure 1). According to (Maeder, 2009), the Physical layer allows advanced multi-antenna techniques. Single and multi-user MIMO techniques are designed to provide spectral efficiency. Backward compatibility is supported using Time Division Duplexing (Srinivasan & Hamiti, 2009). Both TDD and Frequency Division Duplexing (FDD) is supported in this version. The Physical layer is designed to support adaptive burst profiling of subscriber stations. IEEE 802.16m MAC layer is divided into 3 sublayers namely: Convergence Sublayer (CS), Common Part Sublayer (CPS) and Privacy Sublayer (PS). CS task is to map data from upper layers into matching MAC Service Data Units (SDU). It also performs payload suppression to increase link efficiency though this operation is optional. CPS provides the core functionality of the MAC layer such as bandwidth allocation, establishing connection, maintaining QOS, packet fragmentation and packing. Multiple MAC PDUs and SDUs can be concatenated to increase throughput (Eklund, Marks, Stanwood & Wang, 2002).

Figure 1. IEEE 802.16m MAC and PHY layer

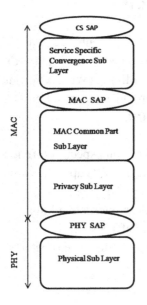

PS supports secure communication by providing mechanism for encryption, authentication and privacy key management.

MAC layer uses Hybrid Automatic Request (HARQ) to ensure successful packet transmission and receipt. IEEE 802.16m allows up to 16 parallel HARQ communication channels to mitigate communication latency.

Long Term Evolution Advanced (LTE-A)

LTE-A by 3rd Generation Partnership Project (3GPP) is another candidate technology for 4G networks. Based on (Pelcat et al, 2013) LTE is capable of providing the same advantages as IEEE 802.16m and more such as:

1. Flexible spectrum that adaptable towards constraints in different countries.
2. Simple network architecture.
3. Spatial flexibility in terms of small cell for densely populated areas and larger cell for sparsely populated areas.
4. Can support variable bandwidth.

The physical layer of LTE-A supports Orthogonal Frequency Division Multiple Access (OFDMA) for downlink communication. OFDMA allows flexibility in the number of users and data rate supported simultaneously. The uplink uses single carrier –FDMA(SC-FDMA) as uplink channel does not require as much bandwidth. SC-FDMA supports better peak to power ratio. (Tran, Shin, Y., & Shin, O. S. 2012) but in order to support carrier aggregation LTE-A also implements clustered SC-FDMA. Similar to IEEE 802.16m, LTE-A also supports MIMO antenna technology. According to (Akyildiz, Gutierrez-Estevez & Reyes, 2010; ETSI TS, 2013), LTE-A's MAC layer performs the following tasks:

1. Multiplexing and demultiplexing of packet data units.
2. Scheduling information reporting that decides both uplink and downlink radio parameters.
3. Error correction using HARQ.
4. Logical Channel Prioritizing.
5. Transport format Selection.
6. Mapping between logical and transport channels.
7. Priority handling with dynamic scheduling.

MAC layer receives data from radio link control (RLC) layer as logical channels. The logical channels data are mapped to transport channels by the MAC layer and passed to the physical layer. Transport channels are Service Access Points (SAP) between MAC and physical layer whereas logical channels are SAP between MAC and RLC layer. Figure 2 presents the LTE protocol stack. RRC refers to radio resource control layer, PDCP is packet data convergence protocol and NAS is non-access stratum.

PROPOSED FRAMEWORK

This section introduces a new framework in solving NSP. This method is more suited for the 4G network as it is holistic and incorporates dynamic weights. This technique will be able to gauge

Figure 2. LTE-A Protocol Stack

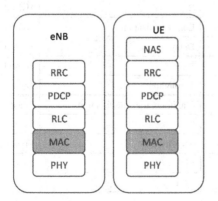

the context on which network selection occurs thereby ensuring the benefit of a 4G network is duly shared with the MNs. Dynamic weightage mechanism ensures an adaptable network selection mechanism that would be more suited to the volatile 4G network. A holistic network selection must encompass all the 3 vital steps in a network selection problem namely (Mohanan, Budiarto & Zainon, 2012):

1. Identifying the attributes values to be collected, how to collect them and the value collecting techniques used.
2. Allotment of weights to the attributes.
3. Ranking of CNs.

A holistic network selection as defined in (Mohanan, Budiarto & Zainon, 2012) can be further enhanced by adding that a holistic network solution must address the needs of all the 3 main stakeholders of this issue namely, users, MNs and CNs. Any network selection solution that does not address all the aforementioned subtasks holistically only provides sub solutions that may work excellently in solving a sub problem. An overall mechanism is needed so that a comprehensive solution is devised. Ergo, a holistic network selection model using H-AHP-GRA. This model addresses each of the subtasks as following:

The attributes collected must be comprehensive enough to correctly reflect the environment where the network selection is to occur. These attributes are collected from 3 sources: the user, MN and the corresponding CNs. How the values are collected is not addressed by this framework. IEEE 802.21 can facilitate the process of collecting the necessary information from the CNs, even if the CN is of a different access type. H-AHP-GRA uses a hybrid of the two most popular value collecting techniques namely mean value of past sessions (MVPS) and most recent values (MRV). As opposed to previous approaches that either does not focus on this aspect at all (Bari & Leung, 2009) or uses a singular technique without regards to its suitability in collecting different kinds of information. Table 2 lists the attributes value that H-AHP-GRA must collect as well as the techniques used.

As shown in Table 2, attribute value that are fixed are those that do not change. Others used a hybrid of MRV and MVPS as MRV indicates current scenario and MVPS is needed to predict future scenario. This is vital as the mapping of a prospective CN does not just depend on current values but also for future values. A CN that is suitable for the current scenario may not be compatible in the near future and vice versa.

As indicated by Table 2, user preferences is collected offline and can be changed manually by the user whenever their preferences changes.

The success of a network selection solution is not just based on selecting the best network; it should be the network that best serves the user's needs. Each individual user may exhibit different needs and preferences; therefore it is vital to identify user preferences comprehensively. Users are required to indicate how much more one aspect is more important than another, essentially filling up a matrix of importance similar to an AHP matrix. This may be a tedious affair, but is of utmost importance to ensure the highest level of user satisfaction is attained. Based on applications, the weights assigned to different attributes reflects

the importance of one attribute over another. For example, for streaming applications, the weight assigned to throughput is higher compared to delay and jitter. Each attributes involved in making the network selection decision is assigned weights indicating relative importance. Table 3 shows there are four traffic classes each in IEEE 802.11e, 802.16e and 3GPP and each of this traffic classes have different QoS needs. Authors in (Saaty & Alexander, 1989; Charilas & Panagopoulos, 2010; Ze-qun, et al. 2009) have shown how to match and correlate the QOS indicators of these standards as reflected in Table 4. This way, selecting a target network that is of different access type will not pose a challenge as their performance values can be compared objectively.

IEEE 802.21 Media Independent Handover's Information service can be used to collect this information from neighbouring networks. The proposed scheme uses AHP to calculate the weights of various traffic parameters. Authors in (Charilas & Panagopoulos, 2010) indicate that AHP is an easy to use method with low complexity and scalable. A simple algorithm with low complexity such as AHP is more suitable for high-speed MNs because an algorithm with high complexity will not be scalable for high-speed MNs (Márquez-Barja et al, 2011). High-speed MNs will be a staple feature of a 4G network.

Table 2. Attribute collection techniques

User	Method	MN	Method	CN	Method
Preferences	Once-Offline	QOS requirement of applications	Once	Bandwidth	Hybrid
		Speed	Hybrid	Load / Utilization	Hybrid
		Travel trajectory	Hybrid	Delay	Hybrid
				Jitter	Hybrid
				Throughput	Hybrid
				Maximum transmission unit	Fixed Value
				Coverage area	Fixed
				Security level	Fixed
				Link quality	Hybrid
				Cost	Fixed

Table 3. IEEE 802.16e, 802.11e and 3GPP Traffic Class

		802.11e	802.16e	3GPP
C1	AC_VO (voice)	UGS, eRT-VR	Conversational
C2	AC_VI (video)	Rt-VR	Streaming
C3	AC_BK (background)	Nrt-VR	Background
C4	AC_BE (best-effort)	BE	Interactive

Table 4. QOS Parameter Mapping Table

802.21	802.11	802.16	3GPP
Max bit rate	Peak data rate	Max. sustained traffic rate	Max bit rate
Min bit rate	Min data rate	Min reserved traffic rate	Guaranteed bit rate
Packet error rate	Packet error rate	Packet error rate	SDU error ratio
Delay	Delay bound	Max latency	Transfer delay
Jitter	Jitter	Tolerated jitter	Delay variation
Priority	User priority	Traffic priority	Traffic handling priority

There have been many researches (Wu et al,..,
2009; Yang, Wu & Huang, 2008; Ze-qun et al.
2009) that use AHP to select the best CN. Although
the authors in (Wu et al.,, et al., 2009; Yang et al.,
2008; Ze-qun et al. 2009) uses IEEE 802.21 to
facilitate collecting of relevant information, none
of them factored in the speed, travelling trajectory of the MNs into their solution and therefore
deemed not suitable for high-speed MNs. Therefore the proposed scheme as described below aims
to overcome these shortcomings.

AHP uses pair-wise comparison to derive the
weights for each attribute. The fundamental AHP
scale of 1 to 9 is used whereby 1: Equally important, 3: Moderately more important, 5: Strongly
more important, 7: Very strongly more important,
9: Extremely more important. Equation 4 shows
pair-wise comparison of an AHP matrix.

$$\begin{pmatrix} 1 & RS_{12} & RS_{13} \\ 1/RS_{12} & 1 & RS_{23} \\ 1/RS_{13} & 1/RS_{13} & 1 \end{pmatrix} \quad (4)$$

RS_{ij} are relative scores that indicate how much
more important objective i is compared to j (Kassar, Kervella & Pujolle, 2008). Generally, C1 class
traffic requires stringent priority, delay and jitter
requirements. Therefore, by applying Equation
(4), the following AHP matrix for C1 traffic is
derived and depicted in Table 5. Also, added to
Table 5 is the user preference consideration with
regards to cost whereby the AHP score of 1 indicates that cost is of utmost importance for the
user. Also, assume that the user has indicated that
quality of experience is of medium importance.
This is translated to AHP score of 5 for bit rate
and packet error rate (PER). Related work (Wu et
al.,, 2009) has shown that by taking into account
only the QoS requirements of class C1, the weight
usually accorded to PER and bit rate is 7. The
weights of the decision criteria can be identified
by calculating the eigenvector of the AHP matrix
and the eigenvalue that approximately equals the
number of accessed elements (Pesola, Pönkänen
& Markopoulos, 2004)

Table 5. AHP matrix for C1

C1	Priority	Bit Rate	Delay	PER	Jitter	Cost
Priority	1	3	1	3	1	1
Bit Rate	1/3	1	1/3	1	1/3	1/3
Delay	1	3	1	3	1	1
PER	1/3	1	1/3	1	1/3	1/3
Jitter	1	3	1	3	1	1
Cost	1	3	1	3	1	1

Unlike other related works (Ali-Yahiya, Sethom & Pujolle, 2007, Jung, Choi, Youn & Song, 2010; Yang et al.,, et al. 2008), attributes that are impacted by the MN's speed are changed accordingly at the point of network selection. Authors in (Márquez-Barja, et al. 2011) have indicated that MNs moving at high speeds experience a higher number of dropped packets, lower throughput and higher delay than expected. This would translate to higher weights for the relevant attributes based on MN's speed. This means the relevant weights are assigned dynamically as opposed to static allocation (Ali-Yahiya et al., 2007, Jung et al.,2010; Yang et al.,, et al. 2008). Assuming the MN is moving at high speed, this would be reflected in the changing of the AHP score for PER and bit rate to 3. The AHP score for the delay attribute remains the same as C1 traffic is very sensitive towards delay and this weight is already reflected in Table 5. The final AHP score of the attributes is presented in Table 5. In actuality, the weights assigned should be fluid, indicating the dynamic nature of the MN.

Also, collected values for throughput and coverage area are refined to reflect throughput and coverage experienced. This is done by factoring in speed (Throughput Experienced -TE) and travel trajectory (Maximum Coverage Experienced-MCE). TE for the same CN is different based on MN's speed. If the MN is slow moving, TE is higher for that CN. Similarly, if the MN is moving at high speed, TE for the same CN would identified as lower. This is because a MN that is moving at high speed will cut across the CN's coverage area faster, resulting in a lower TE. Most network selection algorithms will choose the CN with the biggest coverage area. Unfortunately, this value is not indicative of the maximum coverage experienced (MCE). Figure 3 highlights how travel trajectory changes MCE even for CNs or access points (AP) with the same coverage areas.

AP1 and AP2 both have the same coverage area. The MCE is higher for AP2 due to the travel trajectory. If travelling trajectory is included as one of the attributes collected then MCE can be defined reflecting Quality of Experience rather than theoretical Quality of Service. When MN's moves from x_1y_1 to x_2y_2 (Figure 1), the MCE value for AP2 (access point) is larger than AP1. This is because d^2, the distance travelled in AP2 is larger than d^1, the distance travelled in AP1 (from $x'_1y'_1$ to x'_2y_2'). Whatever the QoS value offered by AP1, it is experienced for a shorter

Figure 3. Impact of travelling trajectory

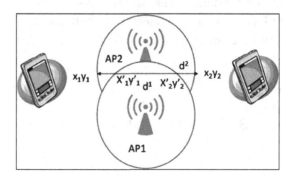

duration compared to the QoS offered by AP2. Therefore, a CN's score should reflect its MCE.

Also, as shown in (Ali-Yahiya et al, 2007), GRA is suitable for situations where both non monotonic and monotonic utilities are used for the attributes. Due to this inherent nature of the GRA technique, it sometimes opts to select a CN that gives a closest match to the reference set values and not necessarily the best. Due to this ability, GRA is well suited to handle conflicting objectives. Other works using GRA (Ali-Yahiya et al, 2007; Kumbuza & Ventura, 2006; Yang et al., et al, 2008) uses a single reference network using maximum or minimum value for the attributes. This is done on the assumption that attributes have monotonic utilities. Unlike the previous approaches, H-AHP-GRA uses multiple reference networks based on applications requirements similar to (Ali-Yahiya et al, 2007). Before network selection occurs, multiple reference networks and its associated attribute weights are built. Additionally, some of these weights may change dynamically based on MN's mobility pattern. Due to the availability of multiple reference networks, the selection of different CNs for different applications can be done. This in turn will improve load balancing. Unlike (Ali-Yahiya et al, 2007), H-AHP-GRA uses a holistic approach towards the problem of network selection by factoring in user preference, uses dynamic weights and addresses the issue of balancing conflicting objectives.

RESULTS

Simulation was implemented in NS version 3.12 to check the efficacy of the proposed framework in terms of the impact of the MN's mobility towards the number of dropped packet and throughput achieved. This simulation involves 2 MNs, one of which is static and the other is moving at different speeds. A UDP traffic flow is sent from the static MN towards the moving MN. The MNs implement IEEE 802.11b standard. Figure 4 shows how when

the MN moves an increasing speed, the number of packets dropped are higher. The simulation is set up so that the receiver is inundated with packets and has to drop the packets. But, as shown in Figure 4 when the receiver MN is immobile, the number of dropped packet is 0. This changes drastically when the same MN starts to move. The graph in Figure 5 shows throughput is reduced as the MN move at increasing speed. Even though the reduction in the value of throughput achieved is small, the trend shows when MN's speed increases the throughput is lower. Even though this simulation is executed using IEEE 802.11b and the speed is reflected in m/s the end result is an MN's speed impacts both the number of dropped packet as well as throughput achieved. The repercussion should be more severe for a 4G network as the MN can go up to speed of 250 km/hr.

H-AHP-GRA IMPLEMENTATION MECHANISM

This section discusses the method in which the proposed method can be implemented (Mohanan et al, 2012). The MN must be a Media Independent Handover (MIH) capable device. The current serving access point (AP) is a network side Media Independent Handover Function (MIHF) instance and is capable of exchanging MIH messages with a MIH-enabled MN. Similarly, the CN's AP is also MIH enabled. The old and new access rout-

Figure 4. Dropped packet vs. Speed

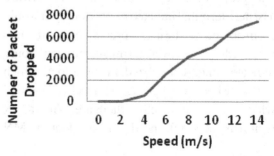

Figure 5. Throughput vs. Speed

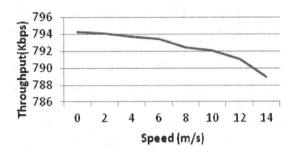

crs are also MIHF enabled. First, user preference information is collected offline. This information can be modified anytime the user wants to change his/her preferences. For example, the user says that cost is extremely more important (AHP scale 9) than fulfilling QoS. This can be translated to having the smaller the better equation applied to the cost attribute and nominal the best to the QOS requirements. Conflicting objectives can also be satisfied by our proposed method. If the user is running streaming application but extreme importance is given to cost (essentially this will renders conflicting objectives as streaming applications require massive bandwidth which in turn will incur more cost), nominal the best can be applied to the attribute bandwidth. Weights based on traffic class or application can be allotted once using AHP matrix. IEEE 802.21 then can be used to collect the necessary attribute values from all candidate networks using the hybrid method. Based on MN's speed, some of the assigned weights might be changed. Based on MN's travelling trajectory and speed, MCE and TE are identified respectively. Next, GRA is applied to rank the alternatives. Our proposed scheme falls under the network assisted-terminal initiated methodology. It would seem obvious as the user's preference is indicated in the MN. Moreover, terminal initiated would indicate a non-centralized methodology which will scale better as oppose to a centralized method which network-initiated methods are. When a MN is moving at a high speed, it means that the MN

is in a vehicle. Otherwise it should be moving at pedestrian speed. MN's speed can be identified using Global Positioning System (GPS). Prediction of MN's traveling trajectory can also be facilitated by using GPS. Using GPS to identify speed and travelling trajectory is feasible as shown in (IEEE Standard, 2009; Kassar, Kervella & Pujolle,2007; Pal Singh, Bambos, Srinivasan & Clawin, 2002).

FUTURE RESEARCH DIRECTIONS

Recent researches (Kaleem, Mehbodniya, Yen & Adachi, 2013) have shown that collection of multiple attributes is often necessary to properly define the context on which the network selection is going to occur. Assigning of priority weights to those attributes is also a 'must-have' in a network selection solution. Also, the availability of MNs with multiple interface is a common scenario therefore accessing heterogeneous networks in order to achieve ABC is very much feasible. (Kaleem et al., 2013; de Miranda Rios, de Lira Gondim & de Castro Monteiro, 2012). Also, the trend shows that not all attributes values can be expressed as crisp numbers. Therefore, many researchers(Kaleem et al.,, 2013; de Miranda Rios et al., 2012). have shown that converting imprecise umbers using fuzzy logic might be a necessity. Additionally, related works have shown that acquiring user preference values are vital to provide ABC (Kaleem et al., 2013; Mohanan et al., 2012). Also, ABC can be construed differently for different users (Mohanan, et al 2012) therefore it is a vital parameter to determine ABC. As shown in (Mohanan, et al 2012), GRA is the only ranking mechanism that caters to ranking based on minimum the best values. This capability is vital in resolving conflicting objectives in trying to attain ABC. As opposed to H-AHP-GRA that collects user's preference values offline manually, emerging trends show that self learning algorithms are preferred (Wang et al., 2012). How far this will be adapted into network selection solutions is yet to be seen. However, a self learning algorithm needs time and training data to learn and when a user changes his/her preference regularly then this impedes the success of the learning algorithm.

CONCLUSION

This chapter has shown how access network selection mechanism can affect the QoS achieved by MNs. Even though 4G networks are capable of providing high bandwidth for MNs that moves at high speeds, this chapter has shown that the benefit of 4G network may not trickle down towards the MNs because the access network selection is not efficient. The importance of a holistic access network selection methodology and the impact it has on QoE is highlighted in this chapter. The method proposed in this chapter is more suited for a 4G network as the volatile and dynamic 4G environment context is better defined using this method. This method is comprehensive by taking into accounts the view of all the three main stakeholders in a NSP scenario: user, MN and CN. The three main phases of network selection is included in this proposed method. It is dynamic in reflecting the current mobility scenario of the MN. It is applicable in situation whereby the utilities of the attributes can be both monotonic as well as non-monotonic. This in turn makes it attractive in achieving conflicting objectives. In some cases, the CN that is chosen may not be the one providing the best QoS far exceeding the application requirements but instead selects the network that matches the closest. In essence, this may be against the ABC concept but by using this method, MN is always best connected in a way that serves all optimization objectives that may be conflicting. This solution has the ability to select different CNs for different applications that are executing at the same time, therefore providing

load balancing and ABC. It also uses a hybrid method in collecting the attribute values in order to correctly identify the context in which the network selection occurs. Additionally, the all important factor of user preference is incorporated into the proposed scheme. This will provide individualized ABC for every user.

REFERENCES

3GPP TS 23.107. (2007). *UMTS—Quality of service (QoS) concept and architecture, version 7.1.0, release 7*. Retrieved from http://www.3gpp. org/ftp/Specs/html-info/23107.htm

Akyildiz, I. F., Gutierrez-Estevez, D. M., & Reyes, E. C. (2010). The evolution to 4G cellular systems: LTE-advanced. *Physical Communication*, *3*(4), 217–244. doi:10.1016/j.phycom.2010.08.001

Ali-Yahiya, T., Sethom, K., & Pujolle, G. (2007). Seamless continuity of service across WLAN and WMAN networks: Challenges and performance evaluation. [IEEE.]. *Proceedings of Broadband Convergence Networks*, *2007*, 1–12.

Alkhawlani, M., & Ayesh, A. (2008). Access network selection based on fuzzy logic and genetic algorithms. *Advances in Artificial Intelligence*, *8*(1), 1. doi:10.1155/2008/793058

Alkhawlani, M. M., & Alsalem, K. A. (2010). Radio network selection for tight-coupled wireless networks. In *Proceedings of Informatics and Systems (INFOS), 2010 the 7th International Conference on Informatics and Systems* (pp. 1-8). IEEE.

Bari, F., & Leung, V. C. M. (2009). Use of non-monotonic utility in multi-attribute network selection. In *Wireless technology* (pp. 21–39). New York: Springer. doi:10.1007/978-0-387-71787-6_2

Çalhan, A., & Çeken, C. (2010). An adaptive neuro-fuzzy based vertical handoff decision algorithm for wireless heterogeneous networks. In Proceedings of Personal Indoor and Mobile Radio Communications (PIMRC), (pp. 2271-2276). IEEE.

Çalhan, A., & Çeken, C. (2012). An optimum vertical handoff decision algorithm based on adaptive fuzzy logic and genetic algorithm. *Wireless Personal Communications*, 64(4), 647–664. doi:10.1007/s11277-010-0210-6

Charilas, D., Markaki, O., Nikitopoulos, D., & Theologou, M. (2008). Packet-switched network selection with the highest QoS in 4G networks. *Computer Networks*, 52(1), 248–258. doi:10.1016/j.comnet.2007.09.005

Charilas, D. E., Markaki, O. I., Psarras, J., & Constantinou, P. (2009). Application of fuzzy AHP and ELECTRE to network selection. In *Mobile lightweight wireless systems* (pp. 63–73). Berlin: Springer. doi:10.1007/978-3-642-03819-8_7

Charilas, D. E., & Panagopoulos, A. D. (2010). Multi-access radio network environment. *IEEE Vehicular Technology Magazine*, 5(4), 40–49. doi:10.1109/MVT.2010.939107

de Miranda Rios, V., de Lira Gondim, P. R., & de Castro Monteiro, C. (2012). Use of fuzzy logic for networks selection in heterogeneous wireless environment. In *Proceedings of Advanced Communication Technology (ICACT), 2012 14th International Conference on* (pp. 798-803). IEEE.

Eklund, C., Marks, R. B., Stanwood, K. L., & Wang, S. (2002). IEEE standard 802.16: A technical overview of the WirelessMAN/sup TM/air interface for broadband wireless access. *IEEE Communications Magazine*, 40(6), 98–107. doi:10.1109/MCOM.2002.1007415

ETSI TS 136 321 V10.7.0. (2013). *LTE, evolved universal terrestrial radio access (E-UTRA), medium access control (MAC) protocol specification (3GPP. TS 36.321 version 10.7.0 release 10)*. Retrieved from http://www.etsi.org/deliver/etsi_ts/136300_136399/136321/10.07.00_60/ts_136321v100700p.pdf

Figueira, J., Mousseau, V., & Roy, B. (2005). ELECTRE methods. In *Multiple criteria decision analysis: State of the art surveys* (pp. 133–153). New York: Springer.

Gakhar, K., Gravey, A., & Leroy, A. (2205). IROISE: A new QoS architecture for IEEE 802.16 and IEEE 802.11e interworking. In *Proceedings of the 2nd International Conference on Broadband Networks (BROADNETS'05)* (pp. 607-612). Berlin: Springer.

IEEE Standard. (2009) Standard for Local and Metropolitan Area Networks- Part 21: Media Independent Handover. *IEEE Std 802.21-2008*. doi: 10.1109/IEEESTD.2009.4769367

Jung, B. Y., Choi, M. S., Youn, H. Y., & Song, O. (2010). Vertical handover based on the prediction of mobility of mobile node. In *Proceedings of Pervasive Computing and Communications Workshops (PERCOM Workshops), 2010 8th IEEE International Conference on* (pp. 534-539). IEEE.

Kaleem, F., Mehbodniya, A., Yen, K. K., & Adachi, F. (2013). A fuzzy pre-processing module for optimizing the access network selection in wireless networks. In *Proceedings of Advances in Fuzzy Systems*. Academic Press.

Kassar, M., Kervella, B., & Pujolle, G. (2007). Architecture of an intelligent inter-system handover management scheme In *Proceedings of Future Generation Communication and Networking (FGCN 2007)* (Vol. 1, pp. 332-337). IEEE.

Kassar, M., Kervella, B., & Pujolle, G. (2008). An overview of vertical handover decision strategies in heterogeneous wireless networks. *Computer Communications, 31*(10), 2607–2620. doi:10.1016/j.comcom.2008.01.044

Kumbuza, X., & Ventura, N. (2006). Using the global positioning system (GPS) to add intelligence to wireless handover in WLAN. In *Proceedings of Electro/Information Technology, 2006 IEEE International Conference on* (pp. 23-26). IEEE.

Kuo, Y., Yang, T., & Huang, G. W. (2008). The use of grey relational analysis in solving multiple attribute decision-making problems. *Computers & Industrial Engineering, 55*(1), 80–93. doi:10.1016/j.cie.2007.12.002

Maeder, A. (2009). *IEEE 802.16m for IMT-advanced: The next step in WirelessMAN evolution.* Retrieved from http://www3.informatik.uniwuerzburg.de/euroview/2009/data/slides/Session1-Maeder-slides-handout.pdf

Márquez-Barja, J., Calafate, C. T., Cano, J. C., & Manzoni, P. (2011). An overview of vertical handover techniques: Algorithms, protocols and tools. *Computer Communications, 34*(8), 985–997. doi:10.1016/j.comcom.2010.11.010

Mohanan, V., Budiarto, R., & Zainon, W. M. N. W. (2012). Holistic network selection for wireless mobile nodes in a 4G environment. In *Proceedings of Communications (APCC), 2012 18th Asia-Pacific Conference on* (pp. 53-58). IEEE.

Ng, D. K. (1994). Grey system and grey relational model. *ACM SIGICE Bulletin, 20*(2), 2–9. doi:10.1145/190690.190691

Olson, D. L. (2004). Comparison of weights in TOPSIS models. *Mathematical and Computer Modelling, 40*(7), 721–727. doi:10.1016/j.mcm.2004.10.003

Pal Singh, J., Bambos, N., Srinivasan, B., & Clawin, D. (2002). Wireless LAN performance under varied stress conditions in vehicular traffic scenarios. In *Proceedings of Vehicular Technology Conference, 2002* (Vol. 2, pp. 743-747). IEEE.

Pelcat, M. et al. (2013). Physical layer multi-core prototyping. *Lecture Notes in Electrical Engineering, 171.* doi:10.1007/978-1-4471-4210-2_4

Pesola, J., Pönkänen, S., & Markopoulos, A. (2004). Location-aided handover in heterogeneous wireless networks. *Wireless Personal Communications, 30*(2-4), 195–205. doi:10.1023/B:WIRE.0000049399.43650.9f

Saaty, T. L. (1990). How to make a decision: The analytic hierarchy process. *European Journal of Operational Research, 48*(1), 9–26. doi:10.1016/0377-2217(90)90057-I

Saaty, T. L., & Alexander, J. M. (1989). *Conflict resolution: The analytic hierarchy approach.* New York: Praeger.

Savitha, K., & Chandrasekar, C. (2011). Vertical handover decision schemes using SAW and WPM for network selection in heterogeneous wireless networks. *arXiv preprint arXiv:1109.4490.*

Song, Q., & Jamalipour, A. (2005). A network selection mechanism for next generation networks. In *Proceedings of Communications, 2005* (Vol. 2, pp. 1418–1422). IEEE.

Srinivasan, R., & Hamiti, S. (Eds.). (2009). *IEEE 802.16m system description document (SDD): IEEE 802.16 task group m.* Retrieved from http://www.ieee802.org/16/tgm/docs/80216m-09_0034r2.zip

Stevens-Navarro, E., & Wong, V. W. S. (2006). Comparison between vertical handoff decision algorithms for heterogeneous wireless networks. In *Proceedings of Vehicular Technology Conference, 2006* (Vol. 2, pp. 947-951). IEEE.

Tran, T. T., Shin, Y., & Shin, O. S. (2012). Overview of enabling technologies for 3GPP LTE-advanced. *EURASIP Journal on Wireless Communications and Networking*, (1): 1–12.

Wang, H., Wang, Z., & Feng, G., L.V. H., Chen, X., & Zhu, Q. (2012). Intelligent access selection in cognitive networks: A fuzzy neural network approach. *Journal of Computer Information Systems*, 8(21), 8877–8884.

WiMax Forum. (2010). *WiMax and the IEEE 802.16m air interface standard*. Author.

Wu, J. S., Yang, S. F., & Hwang, B. J. (2009). A terminal-controlled vertical handover decision scheme in IEEE 802.21-enabled heterogeneous wireless networks. *International Journal of Communication Systems*, 22(7), 819–834. doi:10.1002/dac.996

Yang, S. F., Wu, J. S., & Huang, H. H. (2008). A vertical media-independent handover decision algorithm across Wi-Fi™ and WiMAX™ networks. [IEEE.]. *Proceedings of Wireless and Optical Communications Networks*, 2008, 1–5.

Ze-qun, H., Song-Nan, B., & Jung, J. (2009). A MIH services based application-driven vertical handoff scheme for wireless networks. In *Proceedings of INC, IMS and IDC, 2009* (pp. 1428-1431). IEEE.

Zhang, W. (2004). Handover decision using fuzzy MADM in heterogeneous networks. In *Proceedings of Wireless Communications and Networking Conference, 2004* (Vol. 2, pp. 653-658). IEEE.

Chapter 18
An Optimum Routing Technique for MANET over LTE Cellular Networks

Farukh M. Rahman
RMIT University, Australia

Mark A. Gregory
RMIT University, Australia

ABSTRACT

Mobile Ad Hoc Networks (MANET) is a peer-to-peer communication technique that can transmit voice or data from one mobile device to another without the support of fixed infrastructures. Multi-hop routing has improved in the last few decades and MANET is considered one of the latest trends in modern cellular communications. Studies have been carried out to find optimum routing techniques for MANET, but the majority of the works are within IEEE 802.11 environments. Long Term Evolution (LTE) series 8, which is an IP-based architecture, can offer the added benefit of co-operative communication and reduced transfer latency. Earlier research articulated a new MANET algorithm called IP Address Associated 4-N Intelligent Routing Algorithm (IPAA4NIR), which provided fast, reliable, and energy-efficient communications. This book chapter incorporates IPAA4NIR with co-operative communications to obtain an optimum routing technique for MANET using LTE cellular networks. The chapter also includes the statistical analysis of the proposed algorithm and simulations using OPNET modeller. A comparison with other prominent algorithm shows the proposed algorithm can use the added features of LTE and provides an optimum communication technique for MANET devices.

INTRODUCTION

Mobile Ad Hoc Network (MANET) is a communication technique which allows mobile devices to communicate with each other without every mobile within the network being connected to the fixed infrastructure. Whenever a call is established between two mobile devices in a conventional cellular network, traffic is sent from the initiator mobile device to the base station and then transmitted through the access and transmission medium to the destination mobile device. In a MANET environment, traffics is sent from source to destination using intermediate nodes as routers. MANET can

DOI: 10.4018/978-1-4666-4888-3.ch018

have at least one node connected with the fixed network which can allow other devices to communicate with the external world using the node as a gateway. A MANET node communicates directly with another node if both of them are within the transmission radius. Otherwise the sender finds intermediate nodes which can act as routers and transmit data to the destination node. In MANET every mobile device functions as a router and forwards the packet towards the destination node using a multi-hop technique.

Figure 1 represents a MANET model using LTE cellular network where all the mobile nodes can communicate with each other using intermediate nodes as routers. MANET also allows at least one nominated device to be connected to the IP backbone via eNodeB or Gateway so the other devices can communicate with external world using the nominated device as a router. Accordingly MANET is a self-configuring, autonomous and easily deployable network. It can be utilized to provide rapid communications at disaster affected areas, military operations, multi-hop large networks and at social or sporting events where the fixed infrastructure is unable to support traffic demands. In spite of MANET concepts being introduced several decades ago, recent technology advances have provided the opportunity to enhance MANET through the introduction of mesh and advanced node-to-node relay capabilities. This technology

not only eliminates the requirement for fixed infrastructures but provides convenience as well. Therefore customers are planning to embrace ad-hoc technology for convenience whereas service providers are planning to utilize the technology for minimizing infrastructure costs.

Current cellular networks that are a combination of circuit and packet switching cannot utilize the multi-hop characteristic of MANET efficiently. With the introduction of LTE (moving towards IMT-Advanced), MANET benefits from the use of IP and fast packet switching concepts. LTE supports a peak download limit of 300Mbps and upload limit of 75Mbps on a 20 MHz bandwidth which is considerably faster than it's predecessor. LTE also uses the Evolved Packet Core (EPC) architecture and operates in a separate wireless spectrum from 2G and 3G. LTE has a packet switched radio interface to align with it's all IP based network. Every LTE cell includes mobile nodes and an eNodeB which communicates with the outside network or IP backbone. Being an IP based architecture LTE provides the option of co-operative communication where an intermediate node will not only relay the packet but amplify as well. This is done by size matching of sent and received messages. Therefore LTE cellular networks are promising as an emerging technology for providing low cost but better quality voice services as well as ubiquitous and fast

Figure 1. An LTE MANET Model

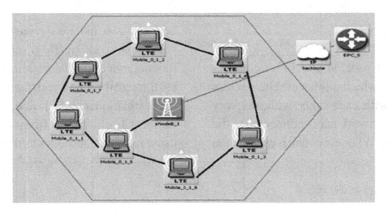

data services. Currently more than 20 telecommunication operators are using LTE for 30 million subscribers across the globe. With these added benefits and continuous growth, LTE is deemed to expand multi-hop routing in the next decade.

With the advancement of LTE, MANET is deemed to be using the IP based architecture to provide optimum ad hoc benefits. As MANET is an autonomous data transfer technology, finding the optimum routing technique has been identified as a research challenge. An ideal MANET routing algorithm should provide reliable, energy efficient and fast data transmission between nodes without any reliance on fixed infrastructures. Earlier research proposed IP Address Associated 4-N Intelligent routing algorithm for MANET where the sender used to select a subset of 4 neighbouring nodes towards the direction of the destination. Based on an intelligent matrix including distance, residual battery level and reputational value, sender used to determine the next hop among the subset. The loop was being followed for each consequent intermediate node until the communication was established between sender and receiver. LTE can provide the added benefit of co-operative communications where an intermediate node will not only relay the information but will amplify also. This is a feature of LTE and was not available through IEEE 802.11. This book chapter incorporates 4-N Intelligent routing algorithm with cooperative communication. An LTE series 8 MANET network model is developed using OPNET simulator and the proposed algorithm is implemented to determine the optimum output. The algorithm is also compared with three other prominent algorithms identified in the literature. Results highlight the proposed algorithm provides fast and reliable MANET communications utilizing LTE technologies.

Literature Review

Most of the innovative researches require significant literature reviews. The algorithm discussed in this book chapter incorporates 4-N Intelligent Routing with co-operative communications and simulation in LTE environment to have the optimum MANET Routing. This research is inspired by surveys mainly into two trends: MANET Routings and Implementation within LTE cellular networks. Key researches within these two trends are discussed below:

MANET Routing

Identifying the enormous prospect of MANET, researchers are trying to develop an optimum routing technique which will be fast, reliable and energy efficient. However developing one algorithm covering all the three aspects are still a challenge.

Path Duration is a key element which outlines the overall reliability of Mobile Ad Hoc Networks. Namuduri (2012) proposed an analytical model to estimate the path duration. The proposed model prescribes the relationship between path duration and design parameters such as node density, transmission range, number of hopes and node mobility. Whenever an intermediate node in a live MANET network loses it's capacity to act as a router, the link discontinues. The mobile node has to find alternate route which is an added overhead. Therefore it is really important to predict the path duration.

Broadcast is the simplest, oldest and most widely used approach for communications. Here the sender transmits the data to all the nodes within its transmission radius. However this can cause Broadcast storm which results wasting bandwidth and energy. Khabbazian and Bhargava

(2009) segmented the approach and proposed two broadcast routing algorithm called "Sender based" and "Receiver based". Sender based Algorithm selected a subset of neighbouring nodes and sent the broadcast message within the subset. Receiver based algorithm ensured each node will disregard any message it received earlier so that one node can broadcast the message at a time.

The advancement of Global Position System (GPS) has made MANET routing convenient. Researchers have proposed opportunistic routing where sender node can identify the next hop towards the destination based on their GPS location and Multicast or Unicast the message towards destination. Yang, Yin, and Yuan (2009) proposed a position based opportunistic routing (POR) where several forwarding candidates cache the packet that has been received using MAC interception. Latiff and Fisal (2007) proposed a quadrant based directional routing protocol (Q-DIR) where sender select a quadrant towards the destination based on the GPS location and limited the multicasting towards the quadrant. Another approach to improve route stability is to use the acknowledgement notification. Vetrivelan and Reddy (2010) proposed a novel restricted scenario model for MANET routing. The algorithm included mobility mapping and investigated the effect of mobility on MANET transmission efficiency.

Mobile nodes can often be non static and high mobility can cause link breakage. Once a link is interrupted or broken the sender has to discover another route which will cause significant route discovery overhead. Zhang, Wang, Xia, and Sung (2013) proposed a neighbour coverage based probabilistic rebroadcast protocol for reducing routing overhead. This is obtained by proposing a novel rebroadcast delay to find the rebroadcast order and accurate coverage ratio by sensing neighbour coverage knowledge.

Most of the MANET devices are battery operated. Low battery level of a MANET device will cause packet dropping which results poor communication. This can also lead towards link

failure and every link failure requires route discovery overhead to re-establish the communication. Therefore it is very prominent for every MANET device to be power efficient and to use energy efficient routing. An energy-efficient MANET algorithm is proposed by Lu and Zhu (2013) to resolve QoS multicast routing problem. Authors proposed a solution to the problem by finding the delay constrained multicast tree and reduce the total energy consumption. Naruephiphat et al. (2009) proposed a MANET routing algorithm which can provide extended network lifetime by evenly distributing the load across the network instead of one node relaying the message for the entire communication.

Like any cellular network, MANET operates in a dynamic topology where nodes constantly joins and leaves the network. To identify all the nodes correctly, every MANET device joins the network is assigned with an IP Address. Al-Shurman and Al-Mistarihi (2010) proposed a dynamic address allocation protocol to identify each node appropriately. Simulation results establish the algorithm obtains minimum end-to-end delay and has less overhead. Authors included the idea of a "Tree based address allocation scheme" and proposed an IP Address allocation technique for a new network, for nodes joining the network and for the nodes leaving the network. Due to the shortage of IP version 4 (IPv4) using only 32-bit addressing, IP version 6 (IPv6) is getting momentum. IPv6 is the latest version of Internet Protocol (IP) and uses 128-bit addressing scheme.

Fridman, Weber, Graff, Breen, Dandekar, and Kam (2012) presents a software library which helps MANET designing. OMAN design engine works on the principle of considering the network requirements and allocating resources which satisfy the input constraints and delivers performance objectives. Cooperative communications is proposed by Guan, Yu, Shengming, Leung, and Mehrvar (2012) which allows to share their antennas to form a virtual antenna array and offers enhanced performances. This has been considered in IEEE802.16j standard and integrated into 3GPP LTE networks. According to Cooperative communications, users share their resources to enhance the transmission quality. Here the multiple sources serve as a relay for one another. In a cooperative network, there are usually a source, destination and few intermediate relay nodes. Here the intermediate nodes relay the information instead of treating it as interface. Relaying can be done in two ways: Amplify and forward; Decode and forward. In Amplify and forward, the relay node increases the energy of the signal. In Decode and forward, the relay nodes will perform physical layer decoding and forward to the destination.

Djahel, Zhang, Nait-Abdesselam, and Murphy (2012) deals with back off cheating technique in MANETs operating in IEEE 802.11 mobility network and proposed a novel scheme. Authors proposed HsF-MAC which allows MANET nodes to re-calculate the back off value used by their 1-hop neighbours and immediately detect the misbehaving ones. Advantage of HsF-MAC over the existing solutions is its ability to reveal the identity of the MANET node that doesn't choose its back off properly after one successful transmission of an RTS frame. Consecutively the impact of the cheater node on the bandwidth fair-share is counteracted efficiently and treated effectively (Djahel et al., 2012).

LTE

Long Term Evolution (LTE) series 8 is the next generation cellular network supporting a peak download rate of 300Mbit/s and upload rate of 75Mbit/s. The advancement of LTE has improved voice, video and data communication among users. LTE is the advanced technology from third generation mobile network and it's mobility management is considerably different.

Long term Evolution (LTE) is an emerging technology providing quality voice communication and fast internet access. Piro et al. (2011) presented an open-source framework known as LTE_Sim to provide end-to-end performance verification. The model simulates uplink and downlink scheduling strategies in multi-user environment including user mobility, radio resource, frequency reuse etc. the model is tested using software scalability test and performance was evaluated against LTE network.

Zhang, Hong, and Xue (2012) presents a new architecture to reduce inter-cell interference for uplink and improve uplink capacity for Long Term Evolution. Authors analyse the probability of selecting a relay station within inner circle of the cell. Then developed an analytic mode to compute uplink capacity. Simulation results showed the uplink capacity can be improved when the key parameters are appropriately selected.

LTE uses a logical combination of several techniques to reduce the channel-state feedback. Donthi and Mehta (2011) proposed a closed-form expression for the throughput achieved by the feedback schemes of LTE. Analysis provided the combined effects of three most critical components of the entire system: throughput—scheduler, multiple-antenna mode and the feedback scheme. The effect brings out its dependence on system parameters such as the number of resource blocks per sub-band and the rate adaptation thresholds. Analysis provides an independent theoretical reference and a prompt system parameter optimization tool to an LTE system designer and theoretically helps to understand the characteristic of OFDMA feedback reduction techniques.

In LTE, the Mobility Management Entity (MME) is responsible for the mobility management function. MME is connected to various evolved Node Bs (eNodeB) cells and few cells are grouped to develop Tracking Areas (TAs). Few TAs form TA Lists (TALs). In an LTE network whenever a mobile node moves out of a Tracking area, it reports the new location to the MME. If any mobile device wants to connect to the LTE network, MME requests the cell in TAL to page the device. Liou, 2013 investigates the performance of LTE paging and proposes the best paging sequence for cells.

Gupta, Jha, Koc, and Vannithamby (2013) explores the traffic characteristics of emerging mobile internet applications and how they differ from more traditional applications. Authors investigate their impact on LTE device power and air interface and analyse their merits and demerits. Authors also discusses the solutions adopted by 3GPP including the latest developments in LTE release 11 to handle these issues. Gupta et al. (2013) present potential future research directions in this field. After simulation authors find that the user assistance mechanism adopted in 3GPP is an effective technique to assist the network in setting a favourable RRC configuration to save UE power. Potential solutions that can be explored to address the power issues in future 3GPP Releases.

While LTE release 8 which was finalised in 2008 and currently ongoing on a broad scale, Parkvall, Furuskar, and Dahlman (2011) proposed the Evolution of LTE towards IMT Advanced. Currently LTE is constantly evolving to meet growing requirements. LTE series 9 was finalized in 2009. However 3rd Generation Partnership Project (3GPP) finished LTE release 10 in 2010 which supersedes the capabilities of LTE release 8 and 9.

OPERATIONAL PRINCIPLE

The book chapter discusses a MANET Algorithm which can be implemented in an LTE cellular network to provide optimum ad hoc routing. So the overall network model has two aspects: MANET routing and LTE architecture. These two aspects are discussed in the next sections.

MANET

Unlike conventional mobile networks, MANET does not require all the nodes to be connected with the centralized control constantly. Here only one or two MANET nodes are connected to the external network which acts as the gateway for all the remaining nodes within the network. When a device initiates a call, the initiator searches for the destination mobile within it's transmission radius. If the destination resides within the sender's transmission radius, communication is established directly. Else the initiator refers to the routing table located within the core network for the GPS location of the destination. Based on the location information of the destination, initiator determines the intermediate nodes towards the destination and call is established using intermediate nodes as router. Accordingly MANET permits node to communicate with each other without the support of the fixed infrastructure. However for data calls or for call towards distant geographical area, sender can use the gateway MANET node to access the core network and establish communication. While MANET is easily deployable, convenient and cost efficient, it is important to establish and maintain an optimum communication is various scenarios. MANET operating principles are discussed over the next sections.

If two mobile nodes are located at location (x1,y1) and (x2,y2), d is the distance between the two nodes and θ is the angle, then:

$$d = \sqrt{(x2 - x1)^2 + (y2 - y1)^2}$$

$$\theta = \tan^{-1}\left\{(x2 - x1)/(y2 - y1)\right\}$$

Path Duration is one of the key elements which outline the overall reliability of Mobile Ad Hoc Networks. Whenever an intermediate node in an operating MANET network loses its capacity to act as a router, the link discontinues. The mobile node has to find alternate route which is an added overhead. Therefore it is really important to predict the location of the nodes and determine path duration. The main protocols for MANET routing are Dynamic Source Routing (DSR) and Ad hoc On-demand Distance Vector (AODV) protocol.

Figure 2. Model for anticipating MANET paths

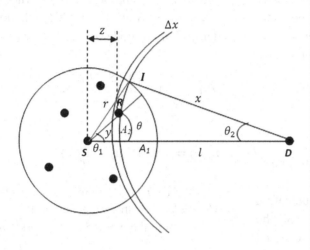

I	Point of intersection between the circles drawn at S and D
y	Distance between Sender and Relay.
r	Transmission radius of the sender node.
θ	Angle between SR and SD.
$a_{int}(x)$	Area of intersection between the circles drawn at S with radius r and at D with radius x.
Δx	Width of the strip formed by two arcs drawn from D.
X	Distance between Destination and Relay.
Ł	Parameter of position distribution representing node density

DSR selects a path based on the minimum number of hops towards the destination and AODV selects the first available route.

Figure 2 which is inspired by Namuduri (2012) represents an analytical model for anticipating MANET paths where *S = Source, D = Destination, R=Relay node*. If a MANET node selects another node located at distance x from the destination considering no other node is present within $a_{int}(x)$ but another node within the stripe $a_{arc(x,\Delta x)}$, then probability of random variable *X* can be given by:

$(x \leq X \leq x + \Delta x) =$ Pr(number of nodes in $a_{int}(x)$) $\times$ Pr(at least one node in $a_{arc(x,\Delta x)}$)

where $a_{int}(x)$ and $a_{arc(x,\Delta x)}$ are the areas where source node looks for a relay node. If the PDF of X can be represented as a function of x, then,

$$fX(x) = \begin{cases} e^{-Aa_{int}(x)(1-e^{-Aa_{arc(x,\Delta x)}};} & (l-r) \leq x \leq l \\ 0 \end{cases}$$

If $A_1 + A_2 =$ area of intersection between circles drawn at *S* and *D*, then $a_{int}(x)$ and $a_{arc(x,\Delta x)}$ can be calculated as:

$$a_{int}(x) = A_1 + A_2$$
$$= r^2 \left[\theta_1 - \frac{\sin(2\theta_1)}{2} \right] + x^2 \left[\theta_2 - \frac{\sin(2\theta_2)}{2} \right]$$

where

$$\theta_1 = \cos^{(-1)}\left[\left(\frac{r^2 + l^2 - x^2}{2rl} \right) \right]$$

and

$$\theta_2 = \cos^{(-1)}\left[\frac{(x^2 + l^2 - r^2)}{2xl} \right]$$

$$x = \sqrt{l^2 + r^2 - 2lz} \quad \text{and} \quad z = \sqrt{\frac{l^2 + r^2 - x^2}{2l}}$$

If z is the distance covered by the relay hop, then

$$a_{int}(z) = r^2 \left[\theta_1(z) - \frac{\sin 2\theta_1(z)}{2} \right]$$
$$+ \left(l^2 + r^2 - 2lz \right) \left[\theta_2(z) - \frac{\sin 2\theta_2(z)}{2} \right]$$

In MANET, nodes can be mobile or static based on the traffic condition. Relative velocity plays an import role as one node can be static in compared with another. If the sender is static then the relative velocity between sender and the intermediate node can be expressed as:

$$v_r = \sqrt{v_1^2 + v_2^2 - 2v_1 v_2 \cos \alpha}$$

where α is the angle between v_1 (sender) and v_2 (node).

A link become active once a communication path is established between two nodes and the duration the link is active is called Link Residual Life. This can be expressed as:

$$t = \frac{d}{v_r}$$

where t = Link Residual Life and d = distance between v_1 (sender) and v_2 (node).

Paths between MANET nodes are dependent on the number of hops. If a path has h hops betweensource and the destination then the path duration will be:

$$t_{path} = \min(t_1, t_2, t_3 ..... t_h)$$

The average number of hops can be calculated by dividing end-to-end distance divided by average relay node distance:

$$E[H] = \frac{l}{E[Z]}$$

Mobile nodes can often be non-static and high mobility can cause link breakage. Once a link is interrupted or broken the sender has to re-broadcast the message to re-establish the link. Therefore rebroadcasting plays a vital role in MANET communications.

If N(S) is the neighbour set of sender node and n_1 is a neighbouring node where $i=1,2.....$ any number, from Zhang (2013) the rebroadcast delay $T_d(n_i)$ of node (n_i) can be represented as:

$$T_p(n_i) = 1 - \frac{\left| N(S) \cap N(n_i) \right|}{\left| N(S) \right|}$$

$$T_d(n_i) = \text{Max Delay} \times T_p(n_i)$$

where $T_d(n_i)$ is the delay ratio of node n_i and *MaxDelay* is a small constant delay.

Additional coverage ratio of node n_i

$$R_a(n_i) = \frac{\left| U(n_i) \right|}{\left| N(n_i) \right|}$$

Therefore the connectivity factor

$$F_c(n_i) = \frac{N_c}{\left| N(n_i) \right|}$$

where $N_c = 5.1774 logn$ where n is the number of nodes in the network.

Lastly the rebroadcast probability

$$P_{re}(n_i) = F_c(n_i).R_a(n_i)$$

Energy consumption has always been considered as one of the biggest challenges in wireless networks due to a majority of mobile nodes being battery operated. Higher energy loss will result in packets being dropped and unreliable transmission across the network. As highlighted in earlier researches, a normalized link capacity cost is:

$$C_{i,j} = E_{i,j}(B_{init}/B_i)$$

where $E_{i,j}$ is the energy consumption for link (i,j), B_{init} is the initial battery level and B_i is the residual battery level.

The total energy consumed by a node is:

$$E_{TOT} = E_{TX} + E_{RX}$$

where E_{TX} is energy consumed for packet transmission and E_{RX} is energy consumed when receiving packets.

Energy consumed to transmit data b for a distance of d:

$$E_{TX}(b,d) = (E_{ELEC} \times b) + (\in_{fs} \times b \times d^2)$$

where $\in_{fs}$ =10pJ/bit/m^2 is the energy consumed in free space at the output transmitter for a transmitting range of one meter. For N-node location aided routing, if a node i has neighbours x,y,z, the energy consumption can be calculated as:

$$E_{TX}(i) = \max \left\{ E_{TX}(b, d_{ix}), E_{TX}(b, d_{i,y}), E_{TX}(b, d_{iz}) \right\}$$

The energy consumed by the receiving node $E_{RX}(b) = E_{elc}xb$ where E_{elec} is the energy expended in the radio electronics which is equal to 5-nJ/bit [8].

On the other hand minimum energy required for a link between nodes

$$P_{i,j} = k_1(r_{i,j})^\beta + k_2$$

where $r_{i,j}$ is the Euclidean distance and k_1 is a constant dependent on the properties of the antenna, k_2 is a constant responsible for the electronics overhead and digital processing. β is the path loss exponent and k_2 is a constant that accounts for the overheads of electronics and digital processing.

There can be three types of transmission in MANET. Direct transmissions, Multiple-hop transmission and Cooperative transmission. Cooperative transmission or communications is an added feature for modern day communications where the users share their resources to enhance the transmission quality (Guan et al., 2012). Recently the interest towards cooperative communications has increased due the benefits of Multiple Antenna systems. Inspite MIMO(Multiple input multiple output) can provide similar benefits, it is difficult for some mobile devices to support multiple antennas due to risk factor of added size and increased cost. In a cooperative network, there are usually a source, destination and few intermediate relay nodes. Here the intermediate nodes relay the information instead of acting as interference only. Relaying can be done by Amplify and forward. In this process the relay node increases the energy of the signal and decode and forward, the relay nodes will perform physical layer decoding and forward to the destination. Therefore in cooperative communications an intermediate node not only acts as a router but as an Amplifier also (Guan 2012.) This is done by size matching and the transmission latency is eliminated by amplification. This characteristic is predominantly available with LTE. Figure 3 provides the operational principle of Cooperative Communications along with direct transmission and Ad Hoc routing.

LTE

LTE which stands for Long Term Evolution is a standard for mobile and high speed data terminals. The goal of LTE is to increase the capacity and speed for wireless data transmission. LTE provides a peak data rate of 300Mbps downlink and 75Mbps uplink on a 20MHz bandwidth It uses IP based architecture (Evolved packet core – EPC) and operates in a separate wireless spectrum from 2G and 3G. LTE provides a peak download rate of 300Mbit/s and upload rate of 75Mbit/s. LTE can maintain connectivity with fast moving objects and provides smooth transition or handover while an object is moving from one cell to another. It supports both of broadcast and multicast. LTE supports carrier bandwidth from 1.4 MHz to 20 MHz and supports both Frequency Division Multiplexing and Time Division Multiplexing. LTE cell sizes can range from tens of metres radius up to 100 km. Lower frequency bands are generally

Figure 3. Cooperative communications

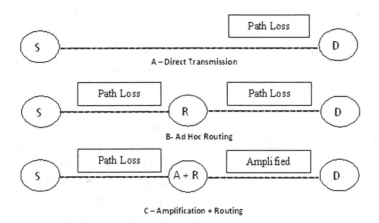

used in rural areas whereas high frequency bands are used in Metros to accommodate high density traffic. According to LTE architecture, 5 km is the optimal cell size, 30 km provides moderate traffic and macro cells with up to 100 km cell sizes support the minimum acceptable performance. LTE supports at least 200 active data clients in every 5Mhz cell. The LTE network consists of a set of cells, network nodes within the cells and a gateway to communication with external networks. Every LTE cell is identified by a unique identifying number.

LTE provides the access part of Evolved Packet System (EPS) which is a purely IP based architecture. LTE was developed to meet the requirement of high data speed and seamless cellular handshaking. LTE is an access network where User Equipments (UE) are connected with evolved Node B (eNodeB) to form a Cell. Each eNodeB is then connected to EPC. LTE does not have any centralized intelligent controller and eNodeBs are connected with each other by X2 interface whereas uses S1 interface to connect with the core network. As shown in Figure 4 this architecture speeds up the call connection and provides seamless handover between cells.

LTE has a packet switched radio interface and to align with it's all IP based network, the voice switch techniques had to be redesigned. Currently there are three different types of voice call

Figure 4. LTE Interface architecture

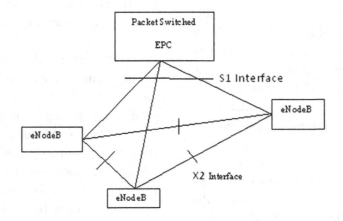

approach: Voice over LTE, Circuit Switched Fall-back and Simultaneous voice and LTE. Voice over LTE approach includes voice service being delivered as usual data packets within the LTE bearer which is not dependent on existing circuit switching techniques. According to Circuit Switched Fall-back approach, data are provided as per packet switching techniques but whenever a voice call is initiated, it falls back into Circuit switching techniques. LTE provides seamless data services whereas Circuit Switching provides the voice calls. However this approach is not available across every type of mobile devices or handset. High price and additional power consumption is another drawback of LTE.

Within any cellular network, each User Equipment (UE) or mobile device's location are tracked so that incoming calls can be established within a shorted possible timeframe. This is done by efficient mobility management and paging. Due to the mobile nature of user equipment, whenever an UE moves out of one call and connects with another cell, it reports the new location to the cell via paging. In LTE, Mobility Management Entity (MME) manages the entire function of keeping the location table updated. Whenever a call is indented for any mobile device connected with an LTE network, MME asks the last interacted cell to page the location of UE. If the last interacted cell fails to provide the information, all cells within the in Tracking Area (TA) are asked to page the location of user equipment. If the TA fails to provide the location information, then all the cells in the Tracking Area List (TAL) are asked to page the UE. LTE MME Architecture is shown in Figure 5 which is inspired by Liou (2013.)

LTE release 8 uses Orthogonal Frequency division Multiplexing (OFDM) for downlink radio access technology and Discrete Fourier Transform Spread OFDM (DFTS-OFDM) on uplink. DFTS-OFDM allows more efficient power amplification which provides the opportunity for reduced terminal power consumption. Alongside, equalization of the received signal is direct with conventional OFDM. Thus OFDM on downlink and DFTS-OFDM on uplink minimizes terminal complexity as well as overall reduction of power consumption.

OVERVIEW OF PROPOSED ALGORITHM

4-N Intelligent MANET Routing Algorithm utilizes neighbour node location information to select a four node subset in the direction of the

Figure 5. LTE Mobility Management Entity (MME) Architecture

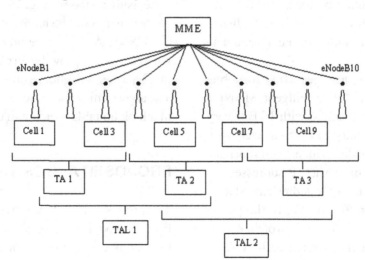

destination node. The sender node with a packet to transmit initiates a location and energy status enquiry signal. The recipient neighbour nodes reply with the required information. The transmission of location and energy status enquiry messages and the response messages are network traffic overhead and for this reason the proposed algorithm aims to limit the selection of neighbour nodes to receive packets. If there are insufficient nodes in the direct path to the destination node, intermediate nodes utilize the same algorithm steps and the process continues until traffic successfully reaches the destination node. Where possible, nodes in the destination node quadrant are utilized as intermediate nodes, however quadrant based routing may result in an inefficient transmission path or delays due to node locations.

The proposed algorithm utilises GPS based location aided routing in conjunction with a limited broadcast approach where the sender selects a subset of four neighbouring nodes in the direction of the destination node. In a conventional quadrant based location aided algorithm the selected subset of nodes are limited towards one quadrant only and can cause a longer routing path. The proposed algorithm is independent of quadrant limitations and can utilize the shortest distance or most efficient path for the next hop. The Ad Hoc On-Demand Distance Vector (AODV) routing protocol is used for this purpose. AODV is a distance vector routing protocol that operates when required. Routes will only be established when a node wants to communicate or send data to another node.

This paper proposes to allocate IPv6 to mobile devices to make the 4-N Intelligent MANET routing algorithm compatible with LTE. Every node requires an identity to be connected with the network and provided with a 128-bit private IP address. The use of private IP addresses necessitates the use of network address translation at the gateway for traffic moving to the public Internet. IPv6 is a significant revision of the earlier IPv4 which was used in earlier research. As IPv4

was running out of addresses an improved IPv6 was developed to deal with the long-anticipated problem, improve security and other features and is being used in LTE networks. IPv6 uses 128 bit addressing which allows 2^{128} addresses. In this paper when a new MANET network is initialized all of the hosts are assigned with individual IP addresses and the addresses are allocated for each node until they are within the network. However for new nodes having a valid MAC address will also be provided with an IP address which will be reused once the node leaves the network.

The source node is provided with the location information of neighbouring nodes and the associated IP addresses which are periodically updated in the routing table. This information permits the source node to use less overhead to find out the next hop or destination which results in higher throughput, less End-to-End delay and more efficient bandwidth utilization.

The key values for measuring the battery operated MANET nodes energy status are: reputation value; residual battery level; and energy efficiency. Reputation value is a decimal value between 1 to 10 representing the node data packet success rate. Residual battery level is the node residual battery power level using an index range from 1 to 10. If a node has 80% battery level then the node's residual battery level will be index value 8. Energy efficiency is the overall energy rating of a node using an index range from 1 to 10. This key value depends on the hardware and other factors.

If Node A has an overall energy rating of 23 whereas node B provides an overall energy rating of 22, sender will choose node A as the next hop. The algorithm proposes to store the energy status in a look up table which will change over time.

PROPOSED ALGORITHM

The proposed IP Address Associated 4-N Intelligent MANET Routing Algorithm incorporating Cooperative Communications is

1. A Mobile Ad Hoc Network is established.
2. All the eligible nodes are assigned with valid IP Addresses.
3. Information (M) need to be transmitted is put into a message format.
4. Sender loads the location and IP Addresses of neighbouring nodes using Location Aided Protocol.
5. Sender selects a subset of maximum 4 closest nodes towards the direction of the destination.
6. Send the location and energy status request to the 4 neighbour nodes.
7. Nodes within the subset reply with location information and energy status.
8. IF, No reply received from subset of nodes, Identify nodes and Re-send information request. Go to 5.
9. ELSE, Sender updates the look-up table including location information, IP Addresses and energy status of adjacent nodes.
10. Sender determines the next hop based on shortest distance and overall energy rating.
11. Sender transmits M to the next hop.
12. Receiving node sends acknowledgement signal and compares the size of the sent signal.
13. IF, No Acknowledgement signal received
    a.   RESEND M, Go to 11.
14. Compare the Sent packet size with Received packet size
15. IF the difference is higher than Tolerance level.
    a.   Amplify the packet.
    b.   Else Go to 16.
16. IF M has reached destination
    a. Deliver the packet
17. Continue loop until M reaches Destination. Go to 4

NETWORK SIMULATION

A real-time LTE MANET environment was created using OPNET Modeller and the proposed algorithm was simulated using the network as shown in Figure 6. The proposed algorithm is first analysed and then compared with the results found for three prominent algorithms.

According to the model in Figure 6, device Mobile_0_3_5 has to communicate with Mobile_0_6_2 which is located in another cell. At the start of MANET communications, every device in the network is assigned with a valid IPv6 address. Then device Mobile_0_3_5 selects a subset of four nodes towards the destination and sends a location IP address and energy status request to the subset. Each node that receives the location and energy status request responds with the requested information. Based on the information provided, the device Mobile_0_3_5 selects the device Mobile_0_1_2 as the next hop. If the next hop was not found, the source device would continue to search for a suitable next hop device. Upon receiving the packet, Mobile_0_1_2 sends an acknowledgement notification to the sender. Then Mobile_0_1_2 matches the received message with the sent message. According to cooperative communications Mobile_0_1_2 amplifies the message to minimize transmission latency. Mobile_0_1_2 follows the same steps and selects Mobile_0_1_5 as the next hop. Subsequently Mobile_0_1_5 amplifies the signal and follows the same loop to find next hop or destination. As the destination Mobile_0_6_2 was within the transmission radius of Mobile_0_1_5, the loop discontinues after the packet is delivered to the destination node. The simulation call volume was 1000 Erlang and the voice encoder scheme used was G.711 with the type of service set to 'Best Effort (0)'.

Figure 6. Simulation of proposed model within LTE architecture

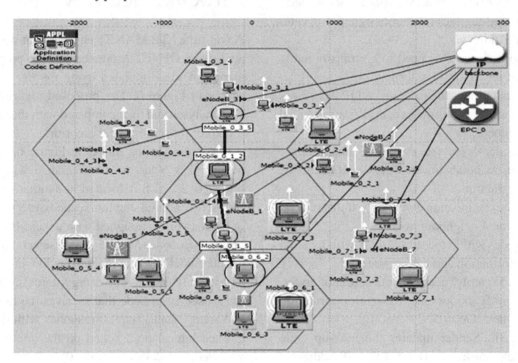

Model: Mobile Ad Hoc Networks (MANET)
Operational Mode: Long Term Evolution (LTE) Rel. 8
Simulation Tool: OPNET Modeler V 16 ad 17.5
Node Transmission Power: .005W
PHY Profile: LTE 20MHz FDD
Mobility Parameter: 5 m/s
Number of eNoeB: 7
Number of UE: 35

RESULTS

The proposed IP Address Associated 4-N Intelligent MANET Routing Algorithm (IPAA4NIR) incorporated with Cooperative Communication is simulated using Opnet Modeller. Initially the uplink and downlink performances are analysed to identify the algorithm's suitability within LTE architecture. Then the proposed algorithm is compared with 3 other prominent algorithms to analyse overall routing performance.

Figure 7 includes LTE MAC traffics sent for Uplink and Downlink. Here Uplink includes the total MAC traffics sent by all UEs within the network. This includes MAC overhead. Whereas Downlink provides total downlink LTE MAC traffic sent by all eNodeBs in the network. This also includes MAC overhead.

Figure 8 includes LTE Uplink and Downlink delays in seconds. Here the Uplink Delay is measured by the time between traffic arriving at the LTE layer from UEs and when it is delivered to the higher layer of corresponding eNodeBs. LTE Downlink delay is measured by the time traffic arrives at the LTE layer of the eNodeBs until it is delivered to the higher layer of UEs.

Figure 9 includes the LTE uplink and Downlink throughputs in Packet / Secs. Here Uplink is the total uplink LTE traffic delivered from LTE layer to higher layer. It is collected by all the eNodeBs in the network. Whereas Downlink is the total download traffic delivered from LTE layer to the higher layer in packets/sec. It is collected by all the UEs in the network.

Figure 7. LTE MAC traffics sent (packets/sec)

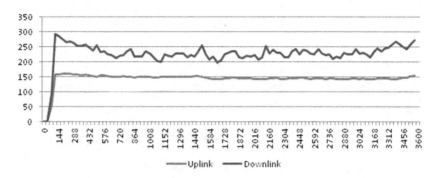

Figure 8. LTE uplink and downlink delay (secs)

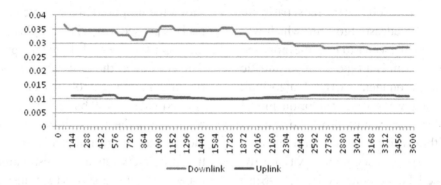

Figure 9. LTE uplink and downlink throughputs (packets/secs)

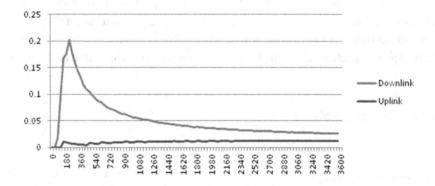

Figure 10 provides LTE MAC Traffic Received. Here Uplink provides total number of uplink LTE MAC traffics sent by all UEs in the network. Whereas Downlink provides the total number of downlink LTE MAC traffics sent by all eNodeBs in the network.

Analysis of the above high level results establishes the algorithm's compatibly and optimum performance using LTE architecture. Three other algorithms were also implemented at three other scenarios of the same network model and their performances are compared.

Figure 10. LTE MAC traffic received (packets/secs)

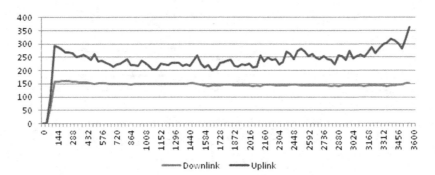

Sender based algorithm proposed by Khabbazian and Bhargava (2009) is the most basic but commonly used broadcast algorithm which was simulated in the model scenario 1. As the proposed IPAA4NIR algorithm is a type of opportunistic routing, another prominent MANET algorithm proposed by Yang, was considered for the model scenario 2. Here the authors proposed a novel NPOR algorithm which provided an interesting alternate algorithm with added complexity. Lastly, an open source LTE Cellular model (LTE-Sim) proposed in (Piro, Grieco, Boggia, Capozzi, & Camarda 2011) was simulated in the model scenario 3. The results have been collected, analysed and presented in this section.

Simulation results in Figure 11 show the proposed IPAA4NIR algorithm achieved the highest

transmission rate, close to 2200 bps. Figure12 shows the proposed algorithm can send up to 17 packets per sec which is the highest rate found for the algorithms tested. Figure13 provides traffic delivery rate at the destination node. For a traffic sending rate of 2300 bps and delivery rate of approximately 1900 bps, the proposed algorithm achieved a higher transmission reliability rate than the compared algorithms. Figure 14 includes the traffic delivery rate at the destination in terms of packets. Figure 15 shows the transmission rate at LTE layer. Achieving a reduced packet loss rate was a focus of the research and Figure 16 shows that the proposed algorithm drops fewer packets than the compared algorithms.

MANET is an Ad-Hoc routing network. A common phenomenon is observed that packets

Figure 11. Transmission rate (bit/secs)

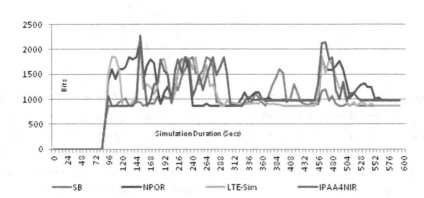

Figure 12. Transmission rate (packets/secs)

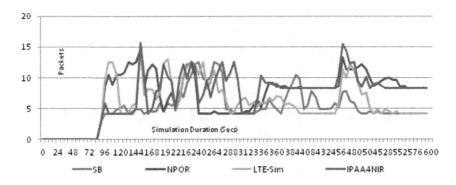

Figure 13. Traffic delivered at destination (bps)

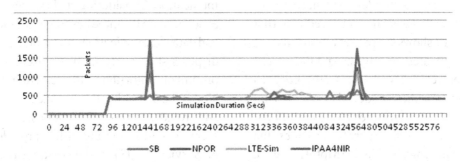

Figure 14. Traffic delivered at destination (packets/sec)

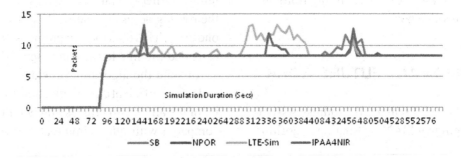

Figure 15. Load at the LTE layer

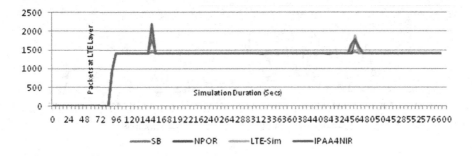

Figure 16. Packets dropped by various algorithms

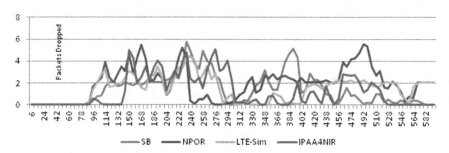

are not sent to the destination or next hop on the first instance. To provide reliable communication it was found that the sender may need to re-transmit packets that were not delivered with first effort. Figure 17 shows the packet retransmission rate for the compared algorithms and the overall result was more reliability when using the proposed algorithm. Intermediate nodes also play a vital role in MANET communication along with source and destination nodes. Figure18 provides the throughput of intermediate device Mobile_0_1_5. The proposed algorithm distributes the traffic equally among intermediate nodes to maintain energy efficiency which is proven by high through-put of intermediate nodes.

CONCLUSION AND FUTURE WORK

This book chapter discusses IP Address Associ-ated 4-N Intelligent MANET Routing Algorithm

and how the algorithm can provide optimum performance by incorporating Cooperative Com-munication. Considering quality, speed and power efficiency are the three key trends for mobile voice and data communications, the proposed algorithm displays superiority in all the trends over other prominent algorithms. By selecting subset of 4 Nodes the algorithm limits unnecessary flooding and provides fast communications. By cooperative communication the algorithm provides Quality of Service (QOS) to the packets. Transmission latency is supplemented by this technique which can provide clear communication. Lastly the In-telligent Energy Matrix aids the sender to spread the routing across the network rather than using one node. This distribution provides uniform and extended lifetime to the entire network.

In spite the algorithm provides fast, reliable and power efficient communication, the complex-ity of the algorithm utilizes higher CPU cycles in compared with other simple algorithms. Future

Figure 17. Packets re-transmission by intermediate nodes

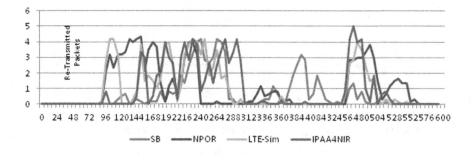

Figure 18. Throughput by intermediate node

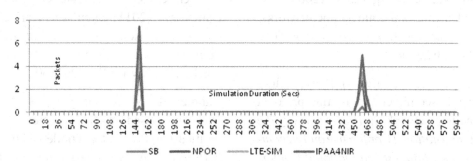

work might include simplifying the algorithm to find alternatives to minimize CPU cycles. Moreover, the algorithm is simulated with the mobility speed of 5 m/s. Performance analysis is required for nodes with high mobile speed above 40 m/s.

Apart from few scopes of improvement, Simulation results prove the proposed algorithm can be considered as an optimum routing technique for MANET communications.

REFERENCES

Al-Shurman, M., & Al-Mistarihi, A. Q. (2010). Network address assignment in mobile ad hoc networks. In *Proceedings of 2010 International Congress on Ultra Modern Telecommunications and Control Systems and workshops (ICUMT)*. ICUMT.

Djahel, S., Zhang, Z., Nait-Abdesselam, F., & Murphy, J. (2012). Fast and efficient countermeasure for MAC layer misbehaviour in MANETs. *IEEE Wireless Communications Letters, 1*(5), 540–543. doi:10.1109/WCL.2012.080112.120367

Donthi, S. N., & Mehta, N. B. (2011). Joint performance analysis of channel quality indicator feedback schemes and frequency-domain scheduling for LTE. *IEEE Transactions on Vehicular Technology, 60*(7). doi:10.1109/TVT.2011.2159034

Fridman, A., Weber, S., Graff, C., Breen, D. E., Dandekar, K. R., & Kam, M. (2012). OMAN: A mobile ad hoc network design system. *IEEE Transactions on Mobile Computing*, 1179–1191. doi:10.1109/TMC.2011.176

Ghosh, A., Ratasuk, B., Mangalvedehe, N., & Thomas, T. (2010). LTE-advanced: Next generation wireless broadband technology. *IEEE Wireless Communication, 17*(3), 10–22. doi:10.1109/MWC.2010.5490974

Guan, Q., Yu, F.R., Shengming, J., Leung, V.C.M., & Mehrvar, H. (2012). Topology control in mobile ad hoc networks with cooperative communications. *IEEE Wireless Communications*, 74-79. doi: 10.1109/MWC.2012.6189416

Gupta, M., Jha, S., Koc, A., & Vannithamby, R. (2013, February). Energy impact of emerging mobile internet applications on LTE networks: Issues and solutions. *IEEE Communications Magazine*. doi:10.1109/MCOM.2013.6461191

Indrasinghe, S., Pereira, R., & Haggerty, J. (2010). Efficient address management for mobile ad hoc networks. In *Proceedings of International Conference on Broadband, Wireless Computing, Communication and Applications*. Academic Press.

Khabbazian, M., & Bhargava, V. (2009). Efficient broadcasting in mobile ad hoc networks. *IEEE Transactions on Mobile Computing, 8*(2). doi:10.1109/TMC.2008.94

Latiff, A. A., & Fisal, N. (2007). Power reduction quadrant based directional routing protocol in mobile ad hoc network. In *Proceedings of the 2007 IEEE International Conference on Telecommunication and Malaysia International Conference on Communications*. IEEE.

Lim, S., Yu, C., & Das, C. (2009). RandomCast: An energy-efficient communication scheme for mobile ad hoc networks. *IEEE Transactions on Mobile Computing, 8*(8).

Liou, R.-H., & Lin, Y.-B. (2013). An investigation on LTE mobility management. *IEEE Transactions on Mobile Computing, 12*(1). doi:10.1109/TMC.2011.255

Lu, T., & Zhu, J. (2013). Genetic algorithm for energy-efficient QoS multicast routing. *IEEE Communications Letters, 17*(1). doi:10.1109/LCOMM.2012.112012.121467

Namuduri, K., & Rendse, R. (2012). Analytical estimation of path duration in mobile ad hoc networks. *IEEE Sensors Journal*, 1828–1835. doi:10.1109/JSEN.2011.2176927

Naruephiphat, W., & Charnsripinyo, C. (2009). Routing algorithm for balancing network lifetime and reliable packet delivery in mobile ad hoc networks. In *Proceedings of Ubiquitous, Automatic and Trusted Computing, UIC-ATC 2009, Symposium and Workshop*. UIC-ATC.

Parkvall, S., Furuskar, A., & Dahlman, E. (2011, February). Evolution of LTE toward IMT-advanced. *IEEE Communications Magazine*. doi:10.1109/MCOM.2011.5706315

Piro, G., Grieco, L., Boggia, G., Capozzi, F., & Camarda, P. (2011). Simulating LTE cellular system: An open-source framework. *IEEE Transactions on Vehicular Technology, 60*(2), 498–513. doi:10.1109/TVT.2010.2091660

Rahman, F. M., & Gregory, M. A. (2011a). Quadrant based intelligent energy controlled multicast algorithm for mobile ad hoc networks. In *Proceedings of 13th International Conference on Advanced Communication Technology (ICACT)*, (pp. 1298 – 1303). Phoenix Park, Korea: ICACT.

Rahman, F. M., & Gregory, M. A. (2011b). 4-N intelligent MANET routing algorithm. In *Proceedings of Telecommunication Networks and Applications Conference (ATNAC)*. Melbourne, Australia: ATNAC. doi: 10.1109/ATNAC.2011.6096664

Rahman, F. M., & Gregory, M. A. (2012). IP address associate 4-N intelligent MANET routing algorithm utilizing LTE cellular technology. In *Proceedings of Telecommunication Networks and Applications Conference (ATNAC)*. Brisbane, Australia: ATNAC. doi: 10.1109/ATNAC.2012.6398077

Vetrivelan, N., & Reddy, A. V. (2010). Modelling and analysing a novel restricted angle scenario model in MANET. In *Proceedings of IEEE Regional Conference 10 (TENCON 2010)*. IEEE.

Vijaykumar, H., & Ravichandran, M. (2011). Efficient location management of mobile node in wireless mobile ad hoc network. In *Proceedings of the National Conference on Innovations in Emerging Technology*, (pp. 77-84). Academic Press.

Yang, S., Yeo, C. K., & Lee, B. S. (2012). Toward reliable data delivery for highly dynamic mobile ad hoc networks. *IEEE Transactions on Mobile Computing, 11*(1).

Yang, X., Yin, J., & Yuan, S. (2009). Location-aided opportunistic routing for mobile ad hoc networks. In *Proceedings of 5th International Conference on* Wireless Communications, Networking and Mobile Computing. Academic Press.

Zhang, H., Hong, P., & Xue, K. (2012). Uplink performance of LTE-based multi-hop cellular network with out-of-band relaying. In *Proceedings of IEEE Consumer Communications and Networking Conference (CCNC),* (pp. 817 – 821). IEEE.

Zhang, X. M., Wang, E. B., Xia, J. J., & Sung, D. K. (2013). A neighbour coverage-based probabilistic rebroadcast for reduced routing overhead in mobile ad hoc networks. *IEEE Transactions on Mobile Computing, 12*(3).

Chapter 19
Physical Cell Identifier Assignment in Dense Femtocell Deployment

Jan Oppolzer
Czech Technical University in Prague, Czech Republic

Robert Bestak
Czech Technical University in Prague, Czech Republic

ABSTRACT

In this chapter, the authors deal with a mechanism of Physical Cell Identifier (PCI) assignment for dense femtocell scenarios within LTE/LTE-Advanced networks. After describing the need for femtocells in future Self-Organizing Networks (SONs), the problem is presented. The chapter discusses background information such as related works in this research field and current assignment methods. Subsequently, challenges are defined, and two mechanisms to assign PCIs are proposed. Both the mechanisms are capable of assigning collision-free PCIs and solving any future confusion events that may occur as the network grows in terms of the number of femtocells. To evaluate the algorithms, a model is described and simulation results for two different scenarios are presented.

INTRODUCTION

As the numbers of various mobile devices such as laptops, or recently very popular smart phones and mostly tablets, is increasing, the demand for reliable high speed mobile data by customers is growing as well. Zhang and De la Roche (2010) estimate that up to 2/3 of calls and overwhelming 90% of data transfers in cellular networks take place indoors and, at the same time, poor signal coverage affects up to 30% of businesses and 45% of households. Therefore, a solution for improving

such an unacceptable situation has to be developed otherwise operators and third party service providers will suffer from high opportunity costs.

Customers expect the same service quality anytime and anywhere, but that is very challenging for operators mainly when taking into account the higher operating frequencies and capacity requirements. With higher frequency, higher penetration signal loss and worse signal propagation make signal quality indoor massively reduced. Such a problem could be solved easily by various approaches. The easiest one is building

DOI: 10.4018/978-1-4666-4888-3.ch019

more macrocells; however, such a naive approach is very time-consuming, technically and legally complicated, too costly, and brings new issues, e.g. higher interference among adjacent macrocells, higher total energy consumption of the network, etc. This is why employing small cells, primarily femtocells, into mobile networks is shown as the most promising solution.

Small cells, such as picocells, metrocells and femtocells, are a family of Base Stations (BSs) with smaller covered area compared to conventional outdoor microcells or macrocells. In fact, this kind of BSs is usually deployed indoors, e.g. at homes, in offices, residential towers, shopping malls, city centres, etc. Macrocells, microcells and picocells are installed, owned and operated by operators and usually have greater capacity. Metrocells and primarily femtocells are, in general, installed, owned and operated by customers. They can place and switch on-off their BS anywhere and anytime without any operator's intervention. Customers only have to plug it into electricity and a decent Internet Protocol (IP) backhaul, such as Digital Subscriber Line (DSL), Wireless Fidelity (Wi-Fi), cable, etc., to connect the BS to the operator's core network.

Small cells are an essential constituent of a Self-Organizing Network (SON), which is a concept representing future mechanism of operating a mobile network (Hämäläinen, Sanneck, & Sartori, 2012). This concept allows automatic configuration, continuous optimization and autonomous healing of all kinds of problems. The SON approach will decrease capital expenditure using resource optimization and reduce operating costs by minimizing human work. It is basically the only way how to properly and primarily efficiently operate a mobile network with growing number of cells of various types.

Nowadays, the SON concept still poses certain challenges that have to be satisfactorily solved in order for this concept to be reliable, efficient and finally adopted by operators. These challenges among others include frequencies reuse, interfer-

ence mitigation, power consumption optimization, backhaul security, or cell identification.

One very important part of the whole small cell family represents femtocells. Femtocell Access Points (FAPs) are small, low-power and low-cost personal or enterprise BSs intended for improving (mainly indoor) signal coverage, enhancing capacity and Quality of Service (QoS), offering new services to customers and also for increasing customer retention (Chambers, 2008; Zhang & De la Roche, 2010). FAPs also might help new mobile operators to enter the market. When new operators reach roaming agreements with existing operators to use their outdoor Macrocell Base Stations (MBSs), they can build a new network without huge financial investments at the beginning.

There are three different operational FAP modes – open, closed and hybrid mode. Open mode is very similar to classical macro/micro BS – any user in the area covered by the FAP can connect and make calls or data transmissions. The closed mode is the very opposite, only users being part of a given Closed Subscriber Group (CSG) can connect to and use the FAP. The hybrid mode is a mix between the previous two modes, so defined users can connect and utilize the FAP; however, undefined users might connect and use the FAP with low priority when the FAP is in idle mode. Open mode is preferred by operators because they achieve expansion of their network with almost no expenses. Contrary to that fact, customers prefer closed mode as none except allowed users can use the FAP.

Metrocells, basically femtocells with greater transmitting power and larger covered area, are deployed in trial runs in the streets of Newcastle and Bristol in the United Kingdom (Curtis, 2012a) to offload data traffic from mobile devices to Virgin Media's fibre optic network. In the trials, data transmission was three times faster within 200m radius of the metrocell compared to existing 3G networks. In addition to faster data rates, signal strength is sufficient to penetrate most buildings while achieving high user experience.

Curtis (2012b) also estimates that by 2016 small cells collectively with Wi-Fi will carry up to 60% of mobile traffic. The report states that small cells are nowadays more and more used to offload mobile data traffic, although small cells were primarily thought to improve (mainly indoor) coverage.

The aim of this chapter is one particular aspect of a SON concept, i.e. cell identification which is performed by assigning a Physical Cell Identifier (PCI). We discuss the PCI assignment in case of femtocell environment but the presented proposal is applicable to other small cells and even any combination of them, too.

BACKGROUND

Since femtocells are still not deployed in great numbers, operators usually choose their PCIs by network planning tools manually. However, it is definitely not the best way, although it works in networks with a few FAPs. A problem will emerge as the number of femtocells will largely increase. Moreover, customers are obliged not to move their devices, because every FAP has its identifier fixed to its location and moving it to a different part of a city or country could cause conflicts, i.e. collision and/or confusion events. It means that every customer buying a FAP has to report the address where the FAP will be used. Therefore, if FAPs are to be mass deployed in the future and fulfil their purpose, PCIs have to be assigned automatically without any operator's manual planning or any other human intervention which is costly and may be the source of unintended misconfiguration.

The other method used nowadays is random PCI assignment. Customers do not have to report their address where their FAP will be operating, but there is a problem with PCI confusions as only PCI collisions are avoided with scanning radio spectrum for adjacent PCIs.

Most works in the field of PCI assignment are aimed at macrocell level (Amirijoo et al., 2008) and that is completely different situation compared

to femtocell level. There is an effort for correct and automatic PCI selection to macrocells using centralized assignment and graph theory approach by Liu, Li, Zhang, & Lu (2010a); however, we see an issue in the assumption that geographic position is known to a central entity. This is true for outdoor macro BSs but not for indoor FAPs where obtaining geographic location is nearly impossible. Therefore, we consider this assumption as highly questionable for FAPs. Moreover, as stated in (3GPP R3-091018, 2008), centralized PCI assignment is not capable of eliminating all collision events in a heterogeneous network. This claim is supported by simulation results where 500 FAPs were deployed under a macrocell, which could not be considered as a mass deployment.

A partially distributed PCI assignment mechanism is proposed by Liu, Li, Zhang, & Yu (2010b). In our opinion, the presented solution is usable only for a relatively small number of static and permanent macro BSs. In dense FAP scenarios, the probability of a confusion event is too high and this work is not concerned with solving such events.

Dividing the PCI range (3GPP R1-083424, 2008), which is rather small, among FAPs, e.g. based on the type of access (open, closed and hybrid) etc. is unsuitable. There may be hundreds of FAPs under one macro BS and we could easily run out of identifiers very quickly in one type of FAPs while having unused PCIs in the other type of FAPs. Using different PCI division in particular macro cell to better distribute PCIs does not solve the mentioned problem because of macrocell boarders. A User Equipment (UE) could be very easily confused in a situation where a particular PCI belongs to a FAP with closed access in one macrocell, while belonging to a FAP with open access in the adjacent macrocell.

Another method for automated PCI allocation that divides the PCI range between macrocells and femtocells is proposed in an article by Wu, Rui, Xiong, & Guo (2010). However, the presented simulation considers only 10 macrocells and 8 femtocells which is very few and does not represent expected future dense FAP deployment.

Dynamic reservation schemes (Lee, Jeong, Saxena, & Shin, 2009) have been also proposed yet. Despite the fact we find dividing PCI range as ineffective as stated above, the main issue in the article is that they are considering only 500 FAPs per macrocell at the maximum and that we find as an insufficient number not corresponding with future large-scale FAP deployment in areas such as city centres, office buildings etc.

IDENTIFIER ASSIGNMENT

Every working BS has various parameters defined. One of them is a PCI (3GPP 36.211, 2011) which is broadcasted by each BS as the identifying signature used in, for example, handover procedures, etc. The PCI is composed of 168 unique groups each containing three identities. In summary, there are 504 PCIs for the whole network in LTE standard. This limited range of PCIs, common for macrocells and small cells as well, is insufficient and therefore PCIs are unavoidably reused within the network. In order to avoid complications in the network, PCIs have to be selected correctly with two major requirements (i.e. collision-free and confusion-free assignment) and one minor requirement in mind (i.e. none small cell should be assigned a PCI belonging to a macrocell).

Challenges

While selecting a PCI, there may arrive two problems – a collision event and a confusion event (3GPP R3-080812, 2008). In fact, there is another issue resulting from a situation that also MBSs need an identifier as described below, but its severity is lower.

A collision event occurs when neighbouring cells use the same PCI as shown in Figure 1. Mutual interference on the physical layer leads to

Figure 1. A collision event

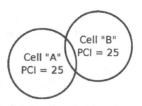

such called coverage hole, because a UE cannot distinguish cells from each other. This is very severe problem and must be avoided.

A confusion event has no such severe impact when emerged contrary to a collision event. It is caused when more cells with common neighbour have identical PCI as illustrated in Figure 2. Those cells confuse the common neighbour and in such a situation radio measurements are impossible to complete properly as well as making a handover, because it is unfeasible to distinguish cells from each other by just using PCIs. In this situation, a Global Cell Identifier (GCI) of a cell could be utilized; however, decoding a GCI takes too much time compared to decoding a PCI and therefore it is not the right way.

Additional issue occurs in a network with lots of small cells under a macrocell or in a network with PCI range limited to a few identities. In such networks, when a small cell has the same PCI as a macrocell, the small cell operations might interfere with macrocell operations which might lead to handover failure. This is the reason why PCIs assigned to macrocells should not be reused by any small cell.

Figure 2. A confusion event

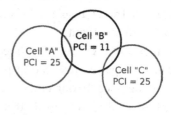

Proposed Mechanism

We suggest a fully distributed algorithm based on the shortest paths in graph theory. Firstly, it assists FAPs to avoid causing any collision events employing integrated UE capabilities to scan surrounding radio spectrum. Secondly, it also helps FAPs to solve all confusion events making use of mutual communication without any cooperation with any central intelligence in the network. Since 3GPP LTE Release 10, also known as LTE-Advanced, direct X2 interface between neighbouring FAPs is supported (3GPP TS 36.300, 2011) so adjacent cells are able to communicate mutually.

However, before any X2 interface can be established, a FAP needs to select its PCI. The PCI range from which the FAP may choose its identifier can be standardized or obtained from the Operation and Maintenance Centre (O&M). The selected identifier must not produce a collision event. This is achieved by listening the radio spectrum using incorporated UE when the FAP is powered on in order to acquire neighbouring PCIs which must be avoided. From the remaining pool, a collision-free PCI is randomly selected. Afterwards, X2 interfaces with neighbouring cells are established and maintained (3GPP R3-082228, 2008), so potential confusion events can be resolved by changing the PCI.

FAPs connected via X2 interface build mutual Neighbour Relations (NRs) and interchange their Neighbour Relation Tables (NRTs) (3GPP R3-081414, 2008) composed of a list of neighbouring PCIs. This process can be repeated with further neighbours to be aware of a larger area. In this way, FAPs know distant cells that are out of their radio range hence can avoid choosing improper or suboptimal PCI when reselection is requested to resolve a confusion event.

In case that any FAP discovers a confusion event, it can manage the reselection process in order to solve the issue. In our study, we propose two approaches called 'random method' and 'smart method'. While the random method is simpler and faster, the smart method produces lesser overhead in the network. As such it is more effective due to rebuilding fewer NRs when an identifier has been changed.

In the random method, the FAP perceiving a confusion event just randomly selects a cell causing the confusion and requests it to change its PCI.

On the other hand, the smart method determines what cell will change its PCI based on the number of its neighbouring cells. This is done in order to minimize network overhead because after a FAP reselects its PCI new NRs have to be built with neighbouring FAPs.

In both approaches, a FAP that is asked to change its PCI scans radio spectrum to avoid selecting a PCI that would produce a collision or new confusion event.

From Figure 3 can be seen the principle of the proposed smart method. As cell "B" encounters a confusion event produced by cells "A" and "C" having identical PCI, "B" will ask both neighbours how many adjacent cells they have. Since cell "A" has fewer neighbours then cell "C", it is requested to change its identifier.

As long as a FAP is not in radio range of any other FAP (we call it as a "standalone FAP"), its selected PCI can produce neither collision nor confusion event. Thus, our algorithm is not interested in such a cell until a neighbour is discovered and a problem detected.

Model Description

In the initial phase of our simulation model, a network topology is created. It represents a graph. First, a macrocell with a specific radius is established. Second, a defined number of FAPs is generated using uniformly distributed pseudo-random numbers. All the FAPs have the same radius and are allowed to overlap each other no more than the defined percentage of their mutual area. The PCI range a FAP can select from is also defined.

Every single FAP represents a vertex and all the links between FAPs (i.e. X2 interfaces) represent

Figure 3. Proposed mechanism: "Smart method." Cell "A" is requested to change its PCI because it has fewer neighbours.

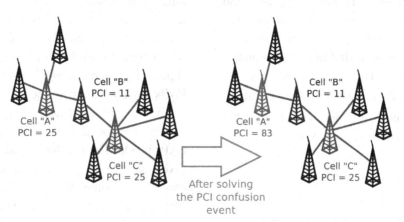

edges between them. For all the vertices their mutual distances are calculated and according to following formula, where x and y, $(x,y) \in V$ their adjacency is decided $\|x,y\| \leq 2r_F$.

In the formula, $\|x,y\|$ represents Euclidean distance between neighbouring FAPs x and y. r_F is a femtocell radius which is identical for all FAPs. The edges are weighted either with Euclidean distance or with the number of hops, *hs*, between corresponding vertices.

Next step is to compute the shortest paths between all the vertices allowing the algorithm to assign collision-free and confusion-free PCIs as described subsequently in the following paragraphs.

To select a collision-free PCI for a FAP, a collision domain $M_i^{hs=1} \in V$ for FAP$_i$ has to be identified at first. Let u be a newly introduced vertex, i.e. FAP$_u$, in the graph G. Then $M_u^1 = \left\{ v \mid (u,v) \in E \right\}$, i.e. M_u^1 consists of a list of neighbouring cells in range of the FAP$_u$ including their PCIs that may produce a collision. Then, all the PCIs (if there are any) are excluded from the predefined range of available PCIs for assignment and from the remaining pool a PCI is randomly chosen. This is the way how collisions are effectively avoided because the number of PCIs

is always high enough for such a selection. Figure 4 shows FAP domains $M_u^1, M_u^2, M_u^3, M_p^1$ and M_q^1.

After a collision-free PCI is chosen, the algorithm is checking confusions. Initially, a confusion domain for a particular FAP is identified. Let us assume that vertices $\{p,q\} \in M_u^1$ are causing a confusion event to vertex *u* (we call them as "confusion producers"). The identifier on some of the cells causing confusion has to be changed. In our simulation, there are two ways for reselecting the problematic PCI to solve confusion events. It is either random method or smart method.

Figure 4. FAP domains $M_u^1, M_u^2, M_u^3, M_p^1$ and M_q^1. for vertices u, p and q

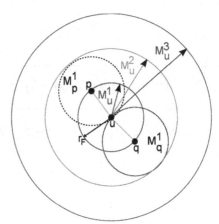

In the first approach, random method, u detecting confusion randomly chooses between p and q and asks one of them to reselect its PCI. Whereas in the second approach, smart method, u detecting confusion at first asks neighbours p and q to report their first FAP domains where , i.e. M_p^1 and M_p^1. Then, based on the FAP domain sizes, u selects the cell which will change PCI according to the following equations:

$$| M_p^1 | < | M_q^1 | \mapsto p, \quad | M_p^1 | \geq | M_q^1 | \mapsto q.$$

In random method as well as in smart method, if there are more than just two "confusion producers", the algorithm continues until there is a confusion event present.

Naturally, in both the methods, the FAP changing PCI scans its radio spectrum to avoid choosing a PCI that is used by one of its neighbours in order to evade a collision event. Moreover, such FAP also asks its neighbours what PCIs they hear in order to avoid making a new confusion event to another cell.

Our algorithms are further improved by taking into account larger neighbourhood. In a situation when u asks p and q to report their FAP domains, it can also asks about more distant neighbours, i.e. , denoted as M_p^2 and M_p^2 as the first formula in Box 1. And similarly for M_p^2. This formula can be generalized for $hs > 2$ is the second formula in Box 1.

The second approach, smart method, may take longer time to solve a confusion event due to asking for the number of neighbours, however, lower overhead, created by establishing new NRs with neighbouring FAPs after a new PCI is assigned, is generated in the network. Thus, the FAPs' backhauls are not needlessly utilized.

Figure 5 demonstrates a very simple simulation in a macrocell with a radius of 100 m and 80 FAPs inside. The red dots represent vertices, i.e. FAPs, and the integers next to red dots are PCIs assigned. The blue lines symbolize edges between vertices, i.e. those FAPs are adjacent and thus can communicate mutually using X2 interface. The real numbers next to blue lines represent weights, i.e. distances between FAPs in metres.

Scenario 1: Results and Discussion

In our first simulation we created a topology containing 2500 FAPs inside a macrocell with a radius of 564 m, i.e. covered area is 1 km^2. All the FAPs have a radius of 10 m and they are allowed to overlap each other no more than 30%. The same topology is used for random method and smart method as well. The range of PCIs available for assignment is set step by step from 20 to 480 identifiers with a step of 20, thus there is always a sufficient number of PCIs available for macrocells and/or operator's testing purposes. All the simulation parameters are summarized in Table 1.

Box 1.

$$M_p^2 = \left\{ w \in V \mid \exists v, v \in M_p^1 \ \& \ w! \in M_p^1 \ \& \ w \neq u : (v, w) \in E \right\}$$

$$M_n^{hs} = \left\{ z \in V \mid \exists w, w \in M_n^{hs} \ \& \ z! \in M_n^{hs} \ \& \ z \neq w : (w, z) \in E \right\}$$

Table 1. Simulation #1 parameters

Parameter	Value
Macrocell radius	564 m
Macrocell area	1 km²
Number of FAPs	2500
FAP radius	10 m
FAP overlapping	≤ 30%
PCI range	20-480
PCI step	20

As can be seen from Figure 6, random method causes higher overhead in the network than smart method. When a FAP changes PCI, it has to build a new NRs with neighbours, i.e. let the neighbouring cells know that it has changed its identifier. Building a new NR means two messages are exchanged between the adjacent FAPs. The first one is a message where the FAP announces its new PCI and the second is an acknowledgement from the neighbour reflecting the change.

Figure 7 shows absolute difference in the number of messages sent through the network according to method used – random or smart. As the number of PCIs available for assignment is increasing, the number of messages is decreasing. It is caused by lower probability of a FAP to select confusing PCI that has to be changed later in order to solve a confusion event.

In Figure 8, there is depicted the percentage improvement in the number of messages required to be sent when using smart method instead of random method. The improvement is computed for every PCI range available for assignment which

Figure 5. A simulation demonstration

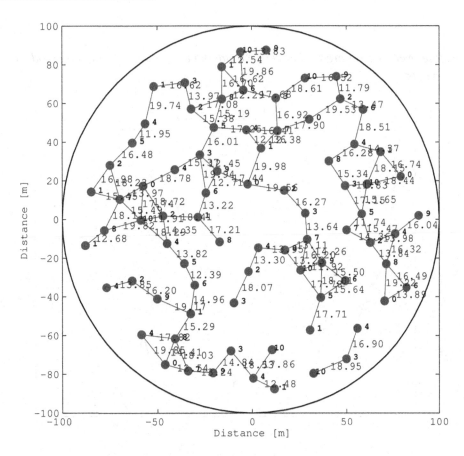

Figure 6. Overhead in the network produced by solving PCI confusion events using "random method" and "smart method"

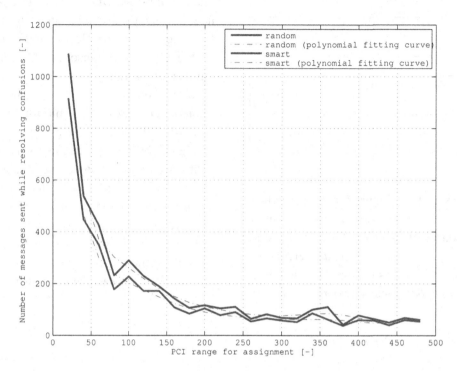

Figure 7. Absolute overhead difference between "random method" and "smart method" while solving PCI confusion events

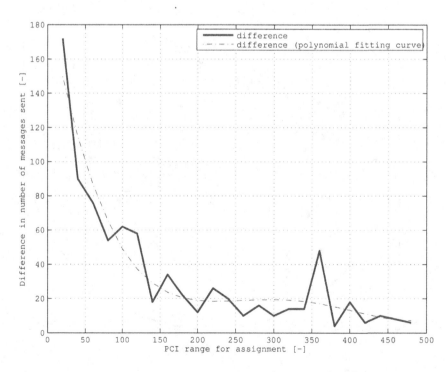

Figure 8. Percentage overhead difference between "random method" and "smart method" while solving PCI confusion events

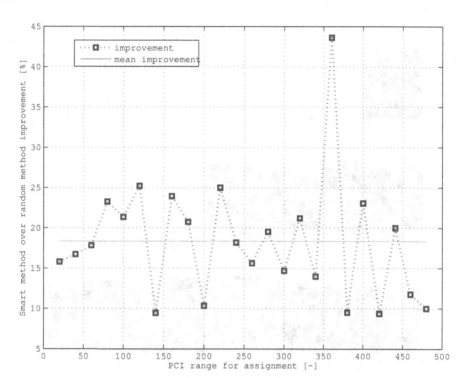

has been set from 20 to 480 with a step of 20 PCI as mentioned earlier. It can be seen from the graph that mean improvement of smart method over random method is about 18%.

Histograms shown in Figure 9 illustrate the distribution of identifiers in the network when 80, 280 and 480 PCIs are available for assignment. It denotes that assigned PCIs are uniformly distributed no matter how large the PCI range is. This means that no PCI is preferred by the algorithm and thus all the PCI are evenly selected by femtocells. Although the histograms are only for smart method, histograms for random methods are almost the same.

Scenario 2: Results and Discussion

Another simulation was developed to obtain the overhead produced by different number of hops, *hs*, in order to minimize the probability of a confusion event after PCI reselection has been run. Since the greater *hs*, the greater PCI range is required; minimal PCI range has been increased from 20 to 80 PCIs. Otherwise the algorithm is unable to converge, i.e. select correct collision-free and confusion-free PCIs. To simulate various FAP densities, the number of FAPs under a macrocell has been set from 500 to 2500. All the parameters are summarized in Table 2.

There is a certain number of "standalone FAPs" which do not have any neighbour. Figure 10 illustrates their number as a function of femtocell density. In a simulation with 1000 FAPs, almost half the femtocells composing the topology are standalone FAPs; however, as they are not connected components of the graph they do not represent any problem so we are not dealing with them in any special way.

In Figure 11, network overhead in the meaning of establishing new NRs during confusion events solving is shown. In this particular result with hs=1, new confusion events might be produced.

Figure 9. Histograms of PCI usage for various PCI ranges (80, 280 and 480 identifiers) for the smart method

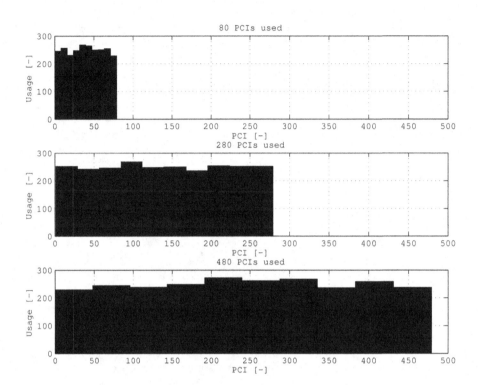

Such a behaviour is caused by FAPs requested to change PCIs. When, for example, FAP_u has to change PCI while hs=1, it only scans radio environment to find out immediate neighbours, i.e. FAP domain M_u^1. Therefore, only collision-free assignment is achieved and new potential confusion event might be created. We call those confusions as "residual confusions". Although the

Table 2. Simulation #2 parameters

Parameter	Value
Macrocell radius	564 m
Macrocell area	1 km²
Number of FAPs	500; 1000; 1500; 2000; 2500
FAP radius	10 m
FAP overlapping	≤ 20%
PCI range	80-480
PCI step	10
Number of hops, *hs*	1; 2; 3

number of residual confusions is lower than the number of confusions before the reselection process, still there might be customers with misconfigured FAPs. In our simulation, residual confusions represented less than 2% of the whole topology. In absolute numbers, up to 46 FAPs were still misconfigured. In order to evade this issue parameter *hs* has to be increased to *hs*≥2.

Figures 12 and 13 show the same function; however, greater FAP domains are scanned during reselection process. The number of hops, *hs*, is increased to , respectively . In these results no residual confusions are thus present. Higher *hs* parameter is a solution to residual confusions, but produces higher overhead. Another advantage is more spread PCIs across the network, because average distance between the same identifiers is increasing. In this manner, when the network grows, the probability of a confusion event is therefore reduced.

Figure 10. The amount of standalone FAPs as a function of femtocell density

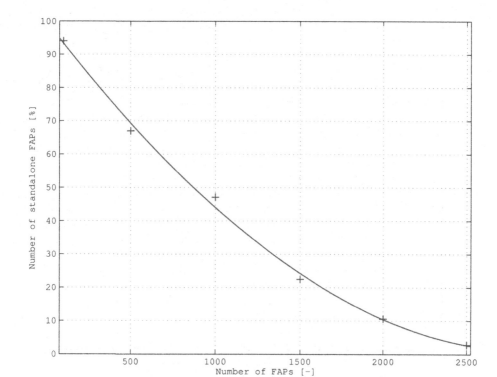

Figure 11. Network overhead caused by establishing new NRs, hs=1

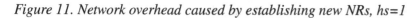
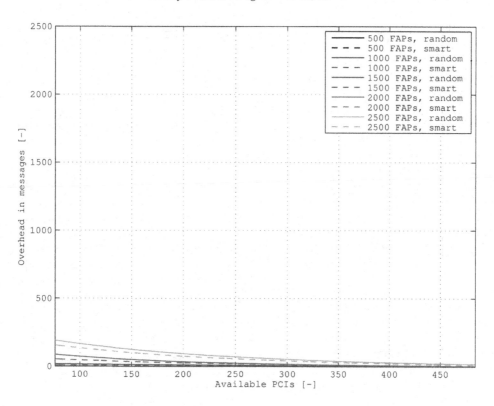

Figure 12. Network overhead caused by establishing new NRs, hs=2

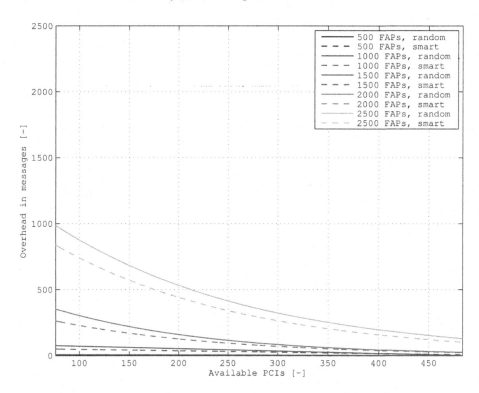

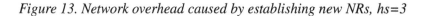

Figure 13. Network overhead caused by establishing new NRs, hs=3

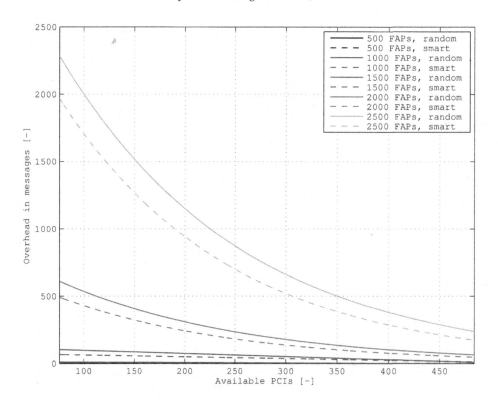

Overhead is counted as in previous simulation which means for *n* neighbours of a FAP reselecting PCI *2n* signalling messages are exchanged in the network.

FUTURE RESEARCH DIRECTIONS

From the point of view of a macrocell, confusion events will be always present if there are more FAPs than the number of PCIs available for assignment. Thus, future research should focus on a technique that will ensure intelligent PCI reuse within a macrocell. Additionally, femtocells should not reuse PCIs that are assigned to adjacent macrocells in order to evade issues where a femtocell interferes with macrocell operations.

In future research, more simulation models should be developed and compared. Model represented by a single macrocell only is very far from reality, where there are always more macrocells in range of UEs or FAPs. Further enhancement to any future model is a grid road topology, multi-floor buildings with apartments, etc. To achieve even more realistic simulation results, individual femtocells should have slightly varying covered area to model attenuation caused by walls and other propagation issues.

CONCLUSION

The mechanism we propose for PCI (Physical Cell Identifier) selection, i.e. collision-free and confusion-free assignment, in dense FAP (Femtocell Access Point) deployments is a fully distributed algorithm that does not depend on any central entity in the network. It is based on graph theory and the shortest paths. Collision events are avoided using integrated UE (User Equipment) and confusion events are solved automatically without any external intervention. A FAP that encounters a confusion event can manage it itself by means of mutual communication with the FAPs producing the confusion via X2 interface. Then, the FAP producing confusion event is requested to change its PCI. There are two approaches. The first is called random method and the second is called smart method. Both the methods solve the confusion events; however, smart method minimizes useless network overhead compared to random method. The overhead is caused by recreating NRs with adjacent cells. And since smart method selects a FAP to change its PCI which has the least number of neighbours, the overhead is lowered as can be observed from our simulation results. Smart algorithm performs better than random algorithm even when various PCI ranges, FAP densities or the amount of neighbourhood information is taken into account.

REFERENCES

3rd Generation Partnership Project. (2008a, April 3). *Solution(s) to the 36.902s automated conguration of physical cell identity use case (R3-080812)*. Retrieved from http://www.3gpp.org/ftp/tsg_ran/WG3_Iu/TSGR3_59bis/docs/

3rd Generation Partnership Project. (2008b, August 18-22). *Framework for distributed PCI selection (R3-082228)*. Retrieved from http://www.3gpp.org/ftp/Specs/html-info/TDocExMtg--R3-61--26795.htm

3rd Generation Partnership Project. (2008c, August 18-22). *LS on CSG identification (R1-083424)*. Retrieved from http://www.3gpp.org/ftp/Specs/html-info/TDocExMtg--R1-54--26793.htm

3rd Generation Partnership Project. (2008d, May 4-8). *PCI collision may be unavoidable in the presence of HeNBs (R3-091018)*. Retrieved from http://www.3gpp.org/ftp/Specs/html-info/TDocExMtg--R3-64--27300.htm

3rd Generation Partnership Project. (2008e, May 5-9). *Exchange of eUTRAN neighbour information (R3-081414)*. Retrieved from http://www.3gpp.org/ftp/Specs/html-info/TDocExMtg--R3-60--26790.htm

3rd Generation Partnership Project. (2011a). *LTE, evolved universal terrestrial radio access (E-UTRA), physical channels and modulation (V10.3.0)*. Retrieved from http://www.etsi.org/deliver/etsi_ts/136200_136299/136211/10.03.00_60/ts_136211v100300p.pdf

3rd Generation Partnership Project. (2011b, December 22). TS 36.300 V10.6.0 evolved universal terrestrial radio access (E-UTRA) and evolved universal terrestrial radio access network (E-UTRAN). Retrieved from http://www.3gpp.org/ftp/Specs/archive/36_series/36.300/36300-a60.zip

Amirijoo, M., Frenger, P., Gunnarsson, F., Kallin, H., Moe, J., & Zetterberg, K. (2008). Neighbor cell relation list and physical cell identity self-organization in LTE. [IEEE.]. *Proceedings of Communications Workshops*, *2008*, 37–41.

Chambers, D. (2008). *Femtocell primer*. Retrieved from www.lulu.com

Curtis, S. (2012a, June 6). Small cells and WiFi to carry 60% of mobile traffic by 2016. *Techworld*. Retrieved from http://news.techworld.com/networking/3362145/small-cells-and-wifi-to-carry-60-of-mobile-traffic-by-2016/

Curtis, S. (2012b, September 26). Virgin media business to offer small cells as a service. *Techworld*. Retrieved from http://news.techworld.com/networking/3400674/virgin-media-business-to-offer-small-cells-as-a-service/

Hämäläinen, S., Sanneck, H., & Sartori, C. (Eds.). (2012). *LTE Self-Organising Networks (SON), Network Management Automation for Operational Efficiency*. Wiley.

Lee, P., Jeong, J., Saxena, N., & Shin, J. (2009). Dynamic reservation scheme of physical cell identity for 3GPP LTE femtocell systems. *Journal of Information Processing Systems*, *5*(4), 219. doi:10.3745/JIPS.2009.5.4.207

Liu, Y., Li, W., Zhang, H., & Lu, W. (2010a). Graph based automatic centralized PCI assignment in LTE. In *Proceedings of Computers and Communications (ISCC), 2010 IEEE Symposium on* (pp. 919-921). IEEE.

Liu, Y., Li, W., Zhang, H., & Yu, L. (2010b). Distributed PCI assignment in LTE based on consultation mechanism. In *Proceedings of Wireless Communications Networking and Mobile Computing (WiCOM), 2010 6th International Conference on* (pp. 1-4). IEEE.

Wu, T., Rui, L., Xiong, A., & Guo, S. (2010). An automation PCI allocation method for eNodeB and home eNodeB cell. In *Proceedings of Wireless Communications Networking and Mobile Computing (WiCOM), 2010 6th International Conference on* (pp. 1-4). IEEE.

Zhang, J., & De la Roche, G. (2010). *Femtocells: Technologies and deployment*. New York: Wiley. doi:10.1002/9780470686812

ADDITIONAL READING

Ali, N. A., Taha, A. E. M., & Hassanein, H. S. (2011). *LTE, LTE-advanced and WiMAX: Towards IMT-advanced Networks*. Wiley.

Boccuzzi, J., & Ruggiero, M. (2010). *Femtocells: design & application*. McGraw-Hill Professional.

Chandrasekhar, V., & Andrews, J. (2009). Uplink capacity and interference avoidance for two-tier femtocell networks. *Wireless Communications. IEEE Transactions on*, *8*(7), 3498–3509.

Chandrasekhar, V., Andrews, J., & Gatherer, A. (2008). Femtocell networks: a survey. *Communications Magazine, IEEE, 46*(9), 59–67. doi:10.1109/MCOM.2008.4623708

Choi, B. G., Cho, E. S., Chung, M. Y., Cheon, K. Y., & Park, A. S. (2011, January). A femtocell power control scheme to mitigate interference using listening TDD frame. In *Information Networking (ICOIN), 2011 International Conference on* (pp. 241-244). IEEE.

Chowdhury, M. Z., Bui, M. T., & Jang, Y. M. (2011, June). Neighbor cell list optimization for femtocell-to-femtocell handover in dense femtocellular networks. In *Ubiquitous and Future Networks (ICUFN), 2011 Third International Conference on* (pp. 241-245). IEEE.

De La Roche, G., Glazunov, A. A., & Allen, B. (2013). *LTE-Advanced and Next Generation Wireless Networks Channel Modelling and Propagation*. Wiley.

De La Roche, G., Valcarce, A., López-Pérez, D., & Zhang, J. (2010). Access control mechanisms for femtocells. *Communications Magazine, IEEE, 48*(1), 33–39. doi:10.1109/MCOM.2010.5394027

Holma, H., & Toskala, A. (2011). *LTE for UMTS: evolution to LTE-advanced*. Wiley. doi:10.1002/9781119992943

Korowajczuk, L. (Ed.). (2011). *LTE, WiMAX and WLAN network design, optimization and performance analysis*. Wiley. doi:10.1002/9781119970460

Lee, K., Kim, S., Lee, S., & Ma, J. (2011, February). Load balancing with transmission power control in femtocell networks. In *Advanced Communication Technology (ICACT), 2011 13th International Conference on* (pp. 519-522). IEEE.

Li, Y., & Feng, Z. (2011, January). Enterprise femtocell network optimization based on neural network modeling. In *Consumer Communications and Networking Conference (CCNC), 2011 IEEE* (pp. 1130-1131). IEEE.

Liang, Y. S., Chung, W. H., Ni, G. K., Chen, Y., Zhang, H., & Kuo, S. Y. (2012). Resource Allocation with Interference Avoidance in OFDMA Femtocell Networks. *Vehicular Technology. IEEE Transactions on, 61*(5), 2243–2255.

Lin, X., Guo, C., Zeng, Z., & Li, D. (2012, September). A novel interference avoidance scheme based on blind polarization signal processing for cognitive Femtocell network. In *Wireless Personal Multimedia Communications (WPMC), 2012 15th International Symposium on* (pp. 40-44). IEEE.

Lu, Z., Sun, Y., Wen, X., Su, T., & Ling, D. (2012, July). An energy-efficient power control algorithm in femtocell networks. In *Computer Science & Education (ICCSE), 2012 7th International Conference on* (pp. 395-400). IEEE.

Pathan, A. S. K. (2010). *Security of self-organizing networks: MANET, WSN, WMN, VANET*. Auerbach Pub. doi:10.1201/EBK1439819197

Ramiro, J., & Hamied, K. (Eds.). (2011). *Self-Organizing Networks (SON), Self-Planning, Self-Optimization and Self-Healing for GSM, UMTS and LTE*. Wiley. doi:10.1002/9781119954224

Saeed, R. A., Chaudhari, B. S., & Mokhtar, R. A. (2012). *Femtocell Communications and Technologies: Business Opportunities and Deployment Challenges*. IGI Publishing.

Saunders, S., Carlaw, S., Giustina, A., Bhat, R. R., Rao, V. S., & Siegberg, R. (2009). *Femtocells: opportunities and challenges for business and technology*. Wiley. doi:10.1002/9780470748183

Sauter, M. (2010). *From GSM to LTE: An introduction to mobile networks and mobile broadband.* Wiley. doi:10.1002/9780470978238

Sesia, S., Toufik, I., & Baker, M. (2009). *LTE: the UMTS long term evolution.* New York: John Wiley & Sons. doi:10.1002/9780470742891

Wolf, S. (2010). *Optimization Problems in Self-Organizing Networks.* Logos Verlag Berlin GmbH.

Xia, P., Chandrasekhar, V., & Andrews, J. G. (2010). Open vs. closed access femtocells in the uplink. *Wireless Communications. IEEE Transactions on, 9*(12), 3798–3809.

Xia, P., Chandrasekhar, V., & Andrews, J. G. (2010, December). CDMA uplink capacity in both open and closed access two-tier femtocell networks. In GLOBECOM Workshops (GC Wkshps), 2010 IEEE (pp. 648-652). IEEE.

Yi, S., Chun, S., Lee, Y., Park, S., & Jung, S. (2012). *Radio Protocols for LTE and LTE-advanced.* Wiley. doi:10.1002/9781118188545

Zhang, X., & Zhou, X. (2012). *LTE-advanced air interface technology.* CRC PressI Llc.

KEY TERMS AND DEFINITIONS

Closed Subscriber Group (CSG): A group of defined users allowed utilizing a femtocell which is set to closed mode.

Femtocell Access Point (FAP): A personal (or enterprise) base station installed, owned and operated by a customer. It is intended to improve (indoor) signal coverage, increasing Quality of Service, offering new services to customers, etc.

PCI Collision: An event where two neighbouring femtocells have identical identifier assigned resulting in so-called coverage hole. UEs are not able to communicate with any femtocell due to interference.

PCI Confusion: An event where more femtocells use identical identifier and have a common neighbour which is not able to distinguish those cells. Such a problem results in, for example, handover failure due to ambiguous destination.

Physical Cell Identifier (PCI): An identifier composed of 168 unique groups each containing three identities used as an identifying signature during, for example, handover procedures, etc.

Self-Organizing Network (SON): A future concept of operating a mobile network that allows automatic configuration, continuous optimization and autonomous healing of all kinds of problems.

Small Cells: Base stations operated by customers or any other third parties that are connected via a backhaul to operator's core network.

Compilation of References

3rd Generation Partnership Project (3GPP). (n.d.a). 3GPP TR 25.814 3GPP TSG RAN physical layer aspects for evolved UTRA, v7.1.0. 3GPP.

3rd Generation Partnership Project (3GPP). (n.d.d). 3GPP TS 36.211 3GPP TSG RAN evolved universal terrestrial radio access (E-UTRA) physical channels and modulation, version 11.0.0, release 11, 2012. 3GPP.

3GPP Group Radio Access Network. (2000). TR 25.942: RF system scenarios (v2.1.3). 3GPP.

3GPP Group Radio Access Network. (2004). TR 25.892: Feasibility study for orthogonal frequency division multiplexing (OFDM) for UTRAN enhancement (v6.0.0). 3GPP.

3GPP Group Radio Access Network. (2008). TS 36.201: LTE physical layer - General description (v8.2.0). 3GPP.

3GPP Group Radio Access Network. (2008). TS 36.211: Physical channels and modulation (v8.5.0). 3GPP.

3GPP Group Radio Access Network. (2010). TS 36.213: Physical layer procedures (v9.2.0). 3GPP.

3GPP Group Radio Access Network. (2011). TS 36.331: Radio resource control (RRC) protocol specification (v8.14.0). 3GPP.

3GPP TR 23.882. (2009). 3GPP system architecture evolution: Report on technical options and conclusions. Author.

3GPP TR 25.913. (2009). Requirements for evolved universal terrestrial RadioAccess (UTRA) and universal terrestrial radio access network (UTRAN). Author.

3GPP TR 36.440. (2010). Technical specification group radio access network, EvolvedUniversal terrestrial radio access network (E-UTRAN), general aspects and principles for interfaces supporting multimedia broadcast multicast service (MBMS) within E-UTRAN, release 9. Author.

3GPP TS 23.107. (2007). UMTS—Quality of service (QoS) concept and architecture, version 7.1.0, release 7. Retrieved from http://www.3gpp.org/ftp/Specs/html-info/23107.htm

3GPP TS 36.300 v8. (2007). Evolved universal terristarial radio acess (E-UTRA) and evolved universal terristerial radio access networks (E-UTRAN), release 8 (2007-2012). Author.

3GPP. (2011). 3GPP TR 36.922 V10.1.0, 3rd Generation partnership project: Technical specification group radio access network: Evolved universal terrestrial radio access (E-UTRA), potential solutions for energy saving for E-UTRA, Release 10, technical report. Author.

3GPP. (2012). 3GPP TS 36.300, V11.4.0, 3rd generation partnership project, technical specification group radio access network, evolved universal terrestrial radio access (E-UTRA) and evolved universal terrestrial radio access network (E-UTRAN), overall description, stage 2, release 11. Author.

3rd Generation Partnership Project (3GPP). (n.d.b). 3GPP TR 25.892 feasibility study for orthogonal frequency division multiplexing (OFDM) for UTRAN enhancements, v6.0.0. 3GPP.

3rd Generation Partnership Project (3GPP). (n.d.c). 3GPP TR 36.913 3GPP TSG RAN requirements for further advancements for evolved universal terrestrial radio access (E-UTRA) (LTE-advanced), version 8.0.1, release 8, 2008. 3GPP.

3rd Generation Partnership Project. (2006). Technical specification group radio access network, physical layer aspects for evolved universal terrestrial radio access (UTRA). TR 25.814, V7.1.0.

3rd Generation Partnership Project. (2008a, April 3). Solution(s) to the 36.902s automated conguration of physical cell identity use case (R3-080812). Retrieved from http://www.3gpp.org/ftp/tsg_ran/WG3_Iu/TSGR3_59bis/docs/

3rd Generation Partnership Project. (2008b, August 18-22). Framework for distributed PCI selection (R3-082228). Retrieved from http://www.3gpp.org/ftp/Specs/html-info/TDocExMtg--R3-61--26795.htm

3rd Generation Partnership Project. (2008c, August 18-22). LS on CSG identification (R1-083424). Retrieved from http://www.3gpp.org/ftp/Specs/html-info/TDocExMtg--R1-54--26793.htm

3rd Generation Partnership Project. (2008d, May 4-8). PCI collision may be unavoidable in the presence of HeNBs (R3-091018). Retrieved from http://www.3gpp.org/ftp/Specs/html-info/TDocExMtg--R3-64--27300.htm

3rd Generation Partnership Project. (2008e, May 5-9). Exchange of eUTRAN neighbour information (R3-081414). Retrieved from http://www.3gpp.org/ftp/Specs/html-info/TDocExMtg--R3-60--26790.htm

3rd Generation Partnership Project. (2009). Technical specification group radio access network, evolved Universal Terrestrial Radio Access (UTRA), physical channels and modulation layer. TS 36.211, V8.8.0.

3rd Generation Partnership Project. (2011a). LTE, evolved universal terrestrial radio access (E-UTRA), physical channels and modulation (V10.3.0). Retrieved from http://www.etsi.org/deliver/etsi_ts/136200_136299/136211/10.03.00_60/ts_136211v100300p.pdf

3rd Generation Partnership Project. (2011b, December 22). TS 36.300 V10.6.0 evolved universal terrestrial radio access (E-UTRA) and evolved universal terrestrial radio access network (E-UTRAN). Retrieved from http://www.3gpp.org/ftp/Specs/archive/36_series/36.300/36300-a60.zip

Abbas, H. K., Waleed, A. M., & Nihad, S. (2010). The performance of multi-wavelets based OFDM system under different channel conditions. Digital Signal Processing, 20, 472–482. doi:10.1016/j.dsp.2009.06.022 doi:10.1016/j.dsp.2009.06.022

Abediseid, W., & Damen, M. (2011). Lattice sequential decoder for coded MIMO channel: Performance and complexity analysis. IEEE Transactions on Information Theory. PMID:22287795

Agarwal, M., Guo, D., & Honig, M. (2010). Limited-rate channel state feedback for multicarrier block fading channels. IEEE Transactions on Information Theory, 6116–6132. doi:10.1109/TIT.2010.2080970

Agarwal, R., Majjigi, V., Han, Z., Vannithamby, R., & Cioffi, J. (2008). Low complexity resource allocation with opportunistic feedback over downlink OFDMA networks. IEEE Journal on Selected Areas in Communications, 1462–1472. doi:10.1109/JSAC.2008.081012

Agrawal, V. (2004, September). A latching MEMS relay for DC and RF applications. In Proceedings of the 50th IEEE Holm Conference on Electrical Contacts and the 22nd International Conference on Electrical Contacts (pp. 222-225). IEEE.

Agrell, E., Eriksson, T., Vardy, A., & Zeger, K. (2002). Closest point search in lattice. IEEE Transactions on Information Theory, 48(8), 2201–2214. doi:10.1109/TIT.2002.800499

Aguado, M., Jacob, E., Berbineau, M. I., & Samper, L. (2010). QoS challenges in handover process. In Tang, Seok-Yee, Muller, Peter, Sharif, Hamid (Eds.). WiMAX Security and Quality of Service: An End-to-End Perspective. John Wiley & Sons. 213-238.

Ahmad, I., & Habibi, D. (2008). A novel mobile WiMAX solution for higher throughput. Paper presented at the 16th IEEE International Conference on Networks. New Delhi, India.

Ahmadi, S. (2009). An overview of next-generation mobile WiMAX technology. IEEE Communications Magazine, 47(6), 84–98. doi:10.1109/MCOM.2009.5116805

Akbari, A., Hoshyar, R., & Tafazolli, R. (2010). Energy-efficient resource allocation in wireless OFDMA systems. Istanbul, Turkey: Institute of Electrical and Electronics Engineers PIMRC. doi:10.1109/PIMRC.2010.5671913

Akyildiz, I. F., Gutierrez-Estevez, D. M., & Reyes, E. C. (2010). The evolution to 4G cellular systems: LTE Advanced. Physical Communication, 3(4), 217–244. doi:10.1016/j.phycom.2010.08.001

Alcatel (2006). WiMAX, making ubiquitous high-speed data services a reality.

Alcatel-Lucent. (2007). R1-072924: Incremental CQI feedback scheme and simulation results. 3GPP.

Alcatel-Lucent. (2008a). Alcatel-Lucent expands 3G WCDMA/ HSPA portfolio with new distributed base station that offers increased deployment flexibility and lowers power requirements. Alcatel-Lucent Press Release. Retrieved from http://www.alcatel-lucent.com/wps/portal/NewsReleases/

Alcatel-Lucent. (2008b). Alcatel-Lucent unveils 3G CDMA/EV-DO distributed base station that offers greater deployment flexibility while lowering power requirements. Alcatel-Lucent Press Release. Retrieved from http://www.alcatel-lucent.com/wps/portal/NewsReleases/

Alcatel-Lucent. (2009). R1-090394: CQI and CSI feedback compression. 3GPP.

Algamali, M. H. M., Jianxin, W., & Alhamidi, R. A. (2009). Base station scheduler scheme of IEEE 802.16 mesh mode. Paper presented at the WRI International Conference on Communications and Mobile Computing CMC '09. Yunnan, China.

Al-Howaide, A. Z., Doulat, A. S., & Khamayseh, Y. M. (2011). Performance evaluation of different scheduling algorithms. In Wimax. International Journal of Computer Science, Engineering and Applications (IJCSEA). 1(5).81-94.

Ali, N. A., Dhrona, P., & Hassanein, H. S. (2008). A performance study of scheduling algorithms in point-to-multipoint WiMAX networks. In Proceedings of IEEE Conference on Local Computer Networks (LCN 2008). Montreal, Canada: IEEE.

Ali, N. A., Dhrona, P., & Hassanein, H. S. (2009). A performance study of scheduling algorithms in point-to-multipoint WiMAX networks. Computer Communications, 32, 511–521. doi:10.1016/j.comcom.2008.09.015

Ali-Yahiya, T., Sethom, K., & Pujolle, G. (2007). Seamless continuity of service across WLAN and WMAN networks: Challenges and performance evaluation.[IEEE.]. Proceedings of Broadband Convergence Networks, 2007, 1–12.

Alkhansari, M. G., & Gershman, A. B. (2004). Fast antenna subset selection in MIMO systems. Institute of Electrical and Electronics Engineers Transformation on Signal Processing, 52, 339–347.

Alkhawlani, M. M., & Alsalem, K. A. (2010). Radio network selection for tight-coupled wireless networks. In Proceedings of Informatics and Systems (INFOS), 2010 the 7th International Conference on Informatics and Systems (pp. 1-8). IEEE.

Alkhawlani, M., & Ayesh, A. (2008). Access network selection based on fuzzy logic and genetic algorithms. Advances in Artificial Intelligence, 8(1), 1. doi:10.1155/2008/793058

Al-Naffouri, T. Y., Islam, K. M. Z., & Al-Dhahir, N. (2010). A model reduction approach for OFDM channel estimation under high mobility conditions. IEEE Transactions on Signal Processing, 58(4). doi:10.1109/TSP.2009.2039732

Alonso-Zarate, J., Kartsakli, E., Katz, M., Alonso, L., & Verikoukis, C. (2013). Multi-radio cooperative ARQ in wireless cellular networks: A MAC layer perspective. Telecommunication Systems, 52(3), 375–385.

Alouini, M. S., & Gesbert, D. (2004). How much feedback is multi-user diversity really worth? Paris: Institute of Electrical and Electronics Engineers ICC.

Al-Shurman, M., & Al-Mistarihi, A. Q. (2010). Network address assignment in mobile ad hoc networks. In Proceedings of 2010 International Congress on Ultra Modern Telecommunications and Control Systems and workshops (ICUMT). ICUMT.

Amirijoo, M., Frenger, P., Gunnarsson, F., Kallin, H., Moe, J., & Zetterberg, K. (2008). Neighbor cell relation list and physical cell identity self-organization in LTE. [IEEE.]. Proceedings of Communications Workshops, 2008, 37–41.

Andrews, J. G., Ghosh, A., & Muhamed, R. (2007). Fundamentals of WiMAX: Understanding broadband wireless networking. Prentice Hall.

Andrews, M., Kumaran, K., Ramanan, K., Stolyar, A., Vijayakaumar, R., & Whiting, P. (2004). Scheduling in a queuing system with asynchronously varying service rates. Probability in the Engineering and Informational Sciences, 18, 191–217. doi:10.1017/S0269964804182041

Andrews, M., Kumaran, K., Ramanan, K., Stolyar, A., Whiting, P., & Vijayakumar, R. (2001). Providing quality of service over a shared wireless link. IEEE Communications Magazine, 150–154. doi:10.1109/35.900644

Asheralieva, A., Khan, J. Y., & Mahata, K. (2011). Performance analysis of VoIP services on the LTE network. In Proceedings of Australasian Telecommunication Networks and Applications Conference, (pp. 1-6). doi:10.1109/ATNAC.2011.6096638

Astély, D., Dahlman, E., Furuskär, A., Jading, Y., Lindström, M., & Parkvall, S. (2009). LTE: The evolution of mobile broadband. IEEE Communications Magazine, 47(4), 44–51. doi:10.1109/MCOM.2009.4907406

Baek, C. W., Song, S., Cheon, C., Kim, Y. K., & Kwon, Y. (2001). 2-D mechanical beam steering antenna fabricated using MEMS technology. In Microwave symposium digest (Vol. 1, pp. 211–214). IEEE.

Baek, C. W., Song, S., Park, J. H., Lee, S., Kim, J. M., Choi, W., & Kwon, Y. (2003). A V-band micromachined 2-D beam-steering antenna driven by magnetic force with polymer based hinges. IEEE Transactions on Microwave Theory and Techniques, 51(1), 325–331. doi:10.1109/TMTT.2002.806516

Baek, S. Y., Hong, Y.-J., & Sung, D. K. (2009). Adaptive transmission scheme for mixed multicast and unicast traffic in cellular systems. IEEE Transactions on Vehicular Technology, 58(6), 2899–2907. doi:10.1109/TVT.2008.2010515

Balanis, C. A., & Ioannides, P. I. (2007). Introduction to smart antennas. Synthesis Lectures on Antennas, 2(1), 1–175. doi:10.2200/S00079ED1V01Y200612ANT005

Ball, C. F., Treml, F., Gaube, X., & Klein, A. (2005). Performance analysis of temporary removal scheduling applied to mobile WiMAX scenarios in tight frequency reuse. In Proceedings of the 16th Annual IEEE International Symposium on Personal Indoor and Mobile Radio Communications. IEEE.

Ball, C. F., Treml, F., Ivanov, K., & Humburg, E. (2006). Performance evaluation of IEEE802.16 WiMAX scenarios with fixed and mobile subscribers in tight reuse. Eur Trans Telecommun, 17(1), 203–218. doi:10.1002/ett.1102

Baltersee, J. (1998). Smart antennas and space-time processing. Aachen University of Technology, Institute for Integrated Signal Processing Systems.

Barbero, L. G., & Thompson, J. S. (2006). Performance analysis of a fixed-complexity sphere decoder in high-dimensional MIMO systems. In Proc. IEEE ICASSP 06. IEEE.

Bari, F., & Leung, V. C. M. (2009). Use of non-monotonic utility in multi-attribute network selection. In Wireless technology (pp. 21–39). New York: Springer. doi:10.1007/978-0-387-71787-6_2

Barker, N. S., & Rebeiz, G. M. (1998a). Distributed MEMS true-time delay phase shifter and wide-band switches. IEEE Microwave Guided Wave Letters, 1881–1890.

Barker, S., & Rebeiz, G. M. (1998b). Distributed MEMS true-time delay phase shifters and wide-band switches. IEEE Transactions on Microwave Theory and Techniques, 46(11), 1881–1890. doi:10.1109/22.734503

Barriac, G., & Madhow, U. (2006). Space-time precoding for mean and covariance feedback: Application to wideband OFDM. Institute of Electrical and Electronics Engineers Trans Communication, 54, 96–10.

Basukala, R., Ramli, H., Sandrasegaran, K., & Chen, L. (2010). Impact of CQI feedback rate/delay on scheduling video streaming services in LTE downlink. In Proceedings of 12th IEEE International Conference on Communication. Nanjing, China: IEEE.

Belghith, A., & Nuaymi, L. (2008). Design and implementation of a QoS-included WiMAX module for NS-2 simulator. Paper presented at the First International Conference on Simulation Tools and Techniques for Communications Networks and Systems, SIMUTools 2008. Marseille, France.

Bello, P. A. (1963). Characterization of randomly time-variant linear channels. IEEE Transactions on Communications Systems, 11, 360–393. doi:10.1109/TCOM.1963.1088793 doi:10.1109/TCOM.1963.1088793

Bellofiore, S. (2002). Smart antenna systems for mobile platforms. (Ph.D. dissertation). Arizona State University, Phoenix, AZ.

Ben-Jye, C., Yan-Ling, C., & Chien-Ming, C. (2007). Adaptive hierarchical polling and cost-based call admission control in IEEE 802.16 WiMAX networks. Paper presented at the Wireless Communications and Networking Conference. New York, NY.

Bhat, P., Nagata, S., Campoy, L., Berberana, I., Derham, T., & Guangyi, L. et al. (2012). LTE-advanced: An operator perspective. IEEE Communications Magazine, 50(2), 104–114. doi:10.1109/MCOM.2012.6146489

Bingham, N. H., Goldie, C. M., & Teugels, J. L. (1989). Regular variation. In Encyclopedia of mathematics and its applications. Cambridge, UK: Cambridge University Press.

Blum, R. S., Winters, J. H., & Sollenberger, N. R. (2002). On the capacity of cellular systems with MIMO. Institute of Electrical and Electronics Engineers Communications Letters, 6(6), 242–244.

Blume, O., Eckhardt, H., Klein, S., Kuehn, E., & Wajda, W. M. (2010). Energy savings in mobile networks based on adaptation to traffic statistics. Bell Labs Technical Journal, 15, 77–94. doi:10.1002/bltj.20442

Bo, R., Yi, Q., Kejie, L., Hsiao-Hwa, C., & Guizani, M. (2008). Call admission control optimization in WiMAX networks. IEEE Transactions on Vehicular Technology, 57(4), 2509–2522. doi:10.1109/TVT.2007.912595

Bontu, C., & Illidge, E. (2009). DRX mechanism for power saving in LTE. IEEE Communications Magazine, 47(6), 48–55. doi:10.1109/MCOM.2009.5116800

Borin, J. F., & da Fonseca, N. L. S. (2007). Uplink scheduling with quality of service in IEEE 802.16 networks. In Proceedings of the 50th Annual IEEE Global Telecommunications Conference (GLOBECOM '07), (pp. 2503–2508). Washington, DC: IEEE.

Brueninghaus, K., Astely, D., Salzer, T., Visuri, S., Alexiou, A., Karger, S., et al. (2005). Link performance models for system level simulations of broadband radio access systems. In Proceedings of IEEE International Symposium on Personal, Indoor and Mobile Radio Communications (pp. 2306–2311). Berlin: IEEE.

Bryzek, J., Peterson, K., & McCulley, W. (1994). Micro-machines on the march. IEEE Spectrum, 31(5), 20–31. doi:10.1109/6.278394

Bustillo, J. M., Howe, R. T., & Muller, R. S. (1998). Surface micromachining for microelectromechanical systems. Proceedings of the IEEE, 86(8), 1552–1574. doi:10.1109/5.704260

Cable Television Laboratories, Inc. (2009). PacketCableTM 1.5 specifications, audio/video codecs. Retrieved from http://www.cablelabs.com/specifications/PKT-SP-CODEC1.5-I02-070412.pdf

Caire, G., & Shamai, S. (2003). On the achievable throughput of a multiantenna Gaussian broadcast channel. IEEE Transactions on Information Theory, 49(7), 1691–1706. doi:10.1109/TIT.2003.813523

Caire, G., & Shamai, S. (2003). On the achievable throughput of multi-antenna Gaussian broadcast channel. Institute of Electrical and Electronics Engineers Transaction on Information Theory, 49, 1691–1706. doi:10.1109/TIT.2003.813523

Çalhan, A., & Çeken, C. (2010). An adaptive neuro-fuzzy based vertical handoff decision algorithm for wireless heterogeneous networks. In Proceedings of Personal Indoor and Mobile Radio Communications (PIMRC), (pp. 2271-2276). IEEE.

Çalhan, A., & Çeken, C. (2012). An optimum vertical handoff decision algorithm based on adaptive fuzzy logic and genetic algorithm. Wireless Personal Communications, 64(4), 647–664. doi:10.1007/s11277-010-0210-6

Carmona-Sánchez, A. (2008). Planificación mediante ATOLL de red WiMax móvil para los centros de la Universidad de Sevilla. Proyecto de fin de carrera. Escuela Técnica Superior de Ingenieros, Universidad de Sevilla.

Casner, S., & Jacobson, V. (1999). Compressing IP/UDP/RTP headers for low-speed serial links. Cisco Systems, RFC 2508. Retrieved from http://www.ietf.org/rfc/rfc2508.txt

Cetiner, B. A., Qian, J. Y., Chang, H. P., Bachman, M., Li, G. P., & De Flaviis, F. (2003). Monolithic integration of RF MEMS switches with a diversity antenna on PCB substrate. IEEE Transactions on Microwave Theory and Techniques, 51(1), 332–335. doi:10.1109/TMTT.2002.806521

Chambers, D. (2008). Femtocell primer. Retrieved from www.lulu.com

Chammakhi Msadaa, I., Camara, D., Filali, F., (2010). Mobility management in WiMAX networks. In Tang, Seok-Yee, Muller, Peter, Sharif, Hamid (Eds.). WiMAX Security and Quality of Service: An End-to-End Perspective. John Wiley & Sons. 221-250.

Chang, J., Lu, I. T., & Li, Y. (2011). Efficient adaptive double codebook based CSI prediction for SU/MU MIMO OFDM systems. Houston, TX: Institute of Electrical and Electronics Engineers Globecom.

Chang, Z., & Ristaniemi, T. (2012). Reducing power consumption via collaborative OFDMA mobile clusters. In Proceedings of IEEE Workshop on Computer-Aided Modeling Analysis and Design of Communication Links and Networks(CAMAD'12). Barcelona, Spain: IEEE.

Chang, Z., & Ristaniemi, T. (2013). Efficient use of multicast and unicast in collaborative OFDMA mobile clusters. In Proc. of 77th IEEE Vehicular Technology Conference. Dresden, Germany: IEEE.

Chang, Z., & Ristaniemi, T. (2013). Energy efficiency of collaborative OFDMA mobile clusters. In Proceedings of IEEE CCNC'13. IEEE.

Changhee, J., & Shroff, N. B. (2009). Performance of random access scheduling schemes in multi-hop wireless networks. Institute of Electrical and Electronics Engineers / Association for Computing Machinery Transactions on Networking, 17.

Chapa López, J. (2009). Análisis del comportamiento dinámico de redes inlámbricas de banda ancha fijas basadas en el estándar IEEE 802.16. (Master's thesis). Universidad Nacional Autónoma de México, Mexico City, Mexico.

Charilas, D. E., & Panagopoulos, A. D. (2010). Multi-access radio network environment. IEEE Vehicular Technology Magazine, 5(4), 40–49. doi:10.1109/MVT.2010.939107

Charilas, D. E., Markaki, O. I., Psarras, J., & Constantinou, P. (2009). Application of fuzzy AHP and ELECTRE to network selection. In Mobile lightweight wireless systems (pp. 63–73). Berlin: Springer. doi:10.1007/978-3-642-03819-8_7

Charilas, D., Markaki, O., Nikitopoulos, D., & Theologou, M. (2008). Packet-switched network selection with the highest QoS in 4G networks. Computer Networks, 52(1), 248–258. doi:10.1016/j.comnet.2007.09.005

Chauvel, D., Haese, N., Rolland, P. A., Collard, D., & Fujita, H. (1997). A micro-machined microwave antenna integrated with its electrostatic spatial scanning. In Proceedings Tenth Annual International Workshop (pp. 84-89). IEEE.

Chen, C., Lee, J., Wu, C., & Kuo, C. (2009). Fairness and QoS guarantees of WiMAX OFDMA scheduling with fuzzy controls. EURASIP Journal on Wireless Communications and Networking. doi:10.1155/2009/512507

Chen, J., Berry, R., & Honig, M. (2008). Limited feedback schemes for downlink OFDMA based on sub-channel groups. IEEE Journal on Selected Areas in Communications, 1451–1461. doi:10.1109/JSAC.2008.081011

Chen, J., Jiao, W., & Guo, Q. (2005). An integrated QoS control architecture for IEEE 802.16 broadband wireless access systems. In Proceedings of Global Telecommunications Conference, GLOBECOM'05. ACM.

Chen, T., Zhang, H., Zhao, Z., & Chen, X. (2010). Towards green wireless access networks. In Proceedings from CHINACOM'10: The 5th International ICST Conference on Communications and Networking in China. Beijing, China: CHINACOM.

Chen, Y., Alouini, M. S., Tang, L., & Khan, F. (2012). Analytical evaluation of adaptive-modulation-based opportunistic cognitive radio in nakagami-m fading channels. IEEE Transactions on Vehicular Technology, 61.

Chiaraviglio, L., Ciullo, D., Meo, M., & Marsan, M. A. (2008). Energy-aware UMTS access networks. In Proceedings from WPMC'08: The 11th International Symposium on Wireless Personal Multimedia Communications. Lapland, Finland: WPMC.

Chiaraviglio, L., Ciullo, D., Meo, M., & Marsan, M. A. (2009). Energy-efficient management of UMTS access networks. In Proceedings from ICT'09: The 21st International Teletraffic Congress. Paris, France: ICT.

Chi-Ming, L., & Shuoh Ren, T. (2010). Provisioning an end to end QoS for VoIP over WiMAX network. Paper presented at the International Computer Symposium (ICS). Taipei, Taiwan.

China Mobile Research Institute. (2010). C-RAN: The road towards green RAN. C-RAN.

Cho, Y. S. Kim Jaekwon, Yang W. Y., Kang C. G. (2010). MIMO-OFDM wireless communications with MATLAB. John Wiley & Sons

Choi, L. U., Ivrlac, M. T., Steinbach, E., & Nossek, J. A. (2005). Analysis of distortion due to packet loss in streaming video transmission over wireless communication links. In Proceedings of International Conference on Image Processing (IEEE ICIP 2005), (pp. 89-92). Genoa, Italy: IEEE.

Choi, W., & Andrews, J. G. (2007). Downlink performance and capacity of distributed antenna systems in a multicell environment. IEEE Transactions on Wireless Communications, 6(1), 69–73. doi:10.1109/TWC.2007.05207

Choi, W., Andrews, J. G., & Yi, C. (2005). The capacity of multicellular distributed antenna networks. In Proceedings of the International Conference on Wireless Networks, Communications and Mobile Computing, (pp. 1337-1342). Maui, HI: IEEE.

Choi, Y., & Bahk, S. (2008). Partial channel feedback schemes maximizing overall efficiency in wireless networks. IEEE Transactions on Wireless Communications, 1306–1314. doi:10.1109/TWC.2008.060863

Chu, F.-S., Chen, K.-C., & Fettweis, G. (2012). Green resource allocation to minimize receiving energy in OFDMA cellular systems. IEEE Communications Letters, 16(3), 372–375. doi:10.1109/LCOMM.2012.010512.2339

Chuck, D., Chen, K. Y., & Chang, J. M. (2010). A comprehensive analysis of bandwidth request mechanisms in IEEE 802.16 networks. IEEE Transactions on Vehicular Technology, 59(4), 2046–2056. doi:10.1109/TVT.2010.2040642

Cicconetti, C. et al. (2006). Quality of service support in IEEE 802.16 networks. IEEE Network, 20(2), 50–55. doi:10.1109/MNET.2006.1607896

Cisco Systems. (2003). Understanding delay in packet voice networks. Retrieved from http://www.cisco.com/warp/public/788/voip/delaydetails.pdf

Cisco. (2013, February 6). Cisco visual networking index: Global mobile data, forecast update 2012- 2017. Retrieved from http://www.cisco.com/en/US/solutions/collateral/ns341/ns525/ns537/ns705/ns827/white_paper_c11-520862.html

Clark, M. V., Willis, T. M., Greenstein, L. J., Rustako, A. J., Ercegt, V., & Roman, R. S. (2001). Distributed versus centralized antenna arrays in broadband wireless networks. In Proceedings of the IEEE Vehicular Technology Conference-Spring (VTC-Spring2001), (pp. 33-37). Rhodes, Greece: IEEE.

Cohen, L. (1995). Time-frequency analysis. Englewood Cliffs, NJ: Prentice-Hall.

Conway, J. H., & Sloane, N. J. A. (1998). Sphere packings, lattices and groups (3rd ed.). New York: Springer-Verlag.

Correia, L. M., Fledderus, E., Meijerink, E., Perera, R., Serrador, A., Turke, U., et al. (2001). Identification of relevant parameters for traffic modelling and interference estimation.

Correia, L., Zeller, D., Blume, O., Ferling, D., Jading, Y., & Godor, I. et al. (2012). Challenges and enabling technologies for energy aware mobile radio networks. IEEE Communications Magazine, 48, 66–72. doi:10.1109/MCOM.2010.5621969

COST-Action-231. (1999). Digital mobile radio towards future generatio systems. European Communities.

CPRI Specification V2.0. (2004). Common public radio interface (CPRI). Interface Specification. CPRI.

Curtis, S. (2012a, June 6). Small cells and WiFi to carry 60% of mobile traffic by 2016. Techworld. Retrieved from http://news.techworld.com/networking/3362145/small-cells-and-wifi-to-carry-60-of-mobile-traffic-by-2016/

Curtis, S. (2012b, September 26). Virgin media business to offer small cells as a service. Techworld. Retrieved from http://news.techworld.com/networking/3400674/virgin-media-business-to-offer-small-cells-as-a-service/

Daewon, L., Hanbyul, S., Clerckx, B., & Hardouin, E. (2012). Coordinated multipoint transmission and reception in LTE-advanced: deployment scenarios and operational challenges. IEEE Communications Magazine, 50(2), 148–155. doi:10.1109/MCOM.2012.6146494

Dahlman, E., Parkvall, S., Skold, J., & Beming, P. (2007). 3G evolution HSPA and LTE for mobile broadband. London: Academic Press. Retrieved from http://www.elsevier.com/books/3g-evolution/dahlman/978-0-12-372533-2

Dai, L., Zhou, S., & Yao, Y. (2002). Capacity with MRC-based macrodiversity in CDMA distributed antenna systems. In Proccedings of IEEE Globecom 2002 (pp. 987–991). Taipei, Taiwan: IEEE.

Dai, L., Zhou, S., & Yao, Y. (2005). Capacity analysis in CDMA distributed antenna systems. IEEE Transactions on Wireless Communications, 4(6), 2613–2620. doi:10.1109/TWC.2005.858011

Damen, M. O., Gamal, H. E., & Caire, G. (2003). On maximum likelihood detection and the search for the closest lattice point. IEEE Transactions on Information Theory, 49(10), 2389–2402. doi:10.1109/TIT.2003.817444

Daneshmand, M., Fouladi, S., Mansour, R. R., Lisi, M., & Stajcer, T. (2009). Thermally actuated latching RF MEMS switch and its characteristics. IEEE Transactions on Microwave Theory and Techniques, 57(12), 3229–3238. doi:10.1109/TMTT.2009.2033866

Daniel, K., Rohde, S., Subik, S., & Wietfeld, C. (2009). Performance evaluation for mobile WiMAX handover with a continuous scanning algorithm. Paper presented at the IEEE Mobile WiMAX Symposium MWS '09. New York, NY.

Das, S., & Schniter, P. (2007). Max-SINR ISI/ICI-shaping multicarrier communication over the doubly dispersive channel. IEEE Transactions on Signal Processing, 55, 5782–5795. doi:10.1109/TSP.2007.901660 doi:10.1109/TSP.2007.901660

Datla, D., Chen, X., Newman, T. R., Reed, J. H., & Bose, T. (2009). Power efficiency in wireless network distributed computing. In Proc. of 69th IEEE Vehicular Technology Conference. Barcelona, Spain: IEEE.

Datla, D., Volos, H. I., Newman, T. R., Reed, J. H., & Bose, T. (2012). Wireless distributed computing in cognitive radio networks. Ad Hoc Networks, 10(5), 845–857. doi:10.1016/j.adhoc.2011.04.002

David, S. I., Man, L., & Renaud, C. (2006). QoS and QoE management in UMTS cellular networks. West Sussex, UK: John Willey & Sons Ltd.

de Miranda Rios, V., de Lira Gondim, P. R., & de Castro Monteiro, C. (2012). Use of fuzzy logic for networks selection in heterogeneous wireless environment. In Proceedings of Advanced Communication Technology (ICACT), 2012 14th International Conference on (pp. 798-803). IEEE.

Delicado, J., Delicado, F. M., & Orozco-Barbosa, L. (2012). RPSF: A new QoS bandwidth request mechanism for the IEEE 802.16. J Telecommun Syst. doi:10.1007/s11235-010-9392-1

Dhawan, S. (2007). Analogy of promising wireless technology on different frequencies: Bluetooth, WiFi and WiMAX. 2nd International Conference on Wireless Broadband and Ultra Wideband Communications (AusWireless 2007).

Djahel, S., Zhang, Z., Nait-Abdesselam, F., & Murphy, J. (2012). Fast and efficient countermeasure for MAC layer misbehaviour in MANETs. IEEE Wireless Communications Letters, 1(5), 540–543. doi:10.1109/WCL.2012.080112.120367

Donthi, S., & Mehta, N. (2011). Joint performance analysis of channel quality indicator feedback schemes and frequency-domain scheduling for LTE. IEEE Transactions on Vehicular Technology, 3096–3109. doi:10.1109/TVT.2011.2159034

Doumi, T., Dolan, M. F., Tatesh, S., Casati, A., Tsirtsis, G., Anchan, K., & Flore, D. (2013). LTE for public safety networks. IEEE Communications Magazine, 51(2), 106–112. doi:10.1109/MCOM.2013.6461193

Du, Y. J., Bao, J. F., & Jiang, J. W. (2013). A new design of multi-bit RF MEMS distributed phase shifters for phase error reduction. Microsystem Technologies, 19(2), 237–244. doi:10.1007/s00542-012-1649-z

EDX (2007). WiMAX uplink and downlink design considerations.

Eklund, C., Marks, R. B., Stanwood, K. L., & Wang, S. (2002). IEEE standard 802.16: A technical overview of the WirelessMAN/sup TM/air interface for broadband wireless access. IEEE Communications Magazine, 40(6), 98–107. doi:10.1109/MCOM.2002.1007415

Ekström, H., Furuskär, A., Karlsson, J., Meyer, M., Parkvall, S., Torsner, J., & Wahlqvist, M. (2006). Technical solutions for the 3G long-term evolution. IEEE Communications Magazine, 44(3), 38–45. doi:10.1109/MCOM.2006.1607864

Elbuken, C., Topaloglu, N., Nieva, P. M., Yavuz, M., & Huissoon, J. P. (2009). Modeling and analysis of a 2-DOF bidirectional electro-thermal microactuator. Microsystem Technologies, 15(5), 713–722. doi:10.1007/s00542-009-0789-2

Elliott, R. (2002). A measure of fairness of service for scheduling algorithms in multiuser systems. In Proceedings of Institute of Electrical and Electronics Engineers Canadian Conference Electrical Comparison. Engineer. (CCECE02). CCECE.

Erceg, V. G. L., Tjandra, S., Parkoff, S., Gupta, A., Kulic, B., Julius, A., & Bianchi, R. (1998). An empirically-based path loss model for wireless channels in suburban environments. Paper presented at the Global Telecommunications Conference. Sydney, Australia.

Ericsson. (2008). R1-080887: CQI measurement methodology. 3GPP.

Ericsson. (2013, January 16). LTE release 12 – Taking another step toward the networked society, white paper. Retrieved from http://www.ericsson.com/news/130116-wp-lte-release-12_244129229_c

Erik, D., Stefan, P. L., Johan, S., & Per, B. (2007). 3G evolution, HSPA and LTE mobile broadband. Burlington, UK: Academic Press Elsevier.

Esmailpour, A., & Nasser, N. (2009). Packet scheduling scheme with quality of service support for mobile WiMAX networks. In Proceedings of IEEE WLN (pp. 1040–1045). IEEE.

Esmailpour, A., & Nasser, N. (2011). Dynamic QoS-based bandwidth allocation framework for broadband wireless networks. Institute of Electrical and Electronics Engineers Transactions on Vehicular Technology, 60.

Etemad, K. (2008). Overview of mobile WiMAX technology and evolution. IEEE Communications Magazine, 46(10), 31–40. doi:10.1109/MCOM.2008.4644117

Etemad, K., & Lai, M. (2011). WiMAX technology and network evolution. New York: Wiley.

ETSI TS 136 321 V10.7.0. (2013). LTE, evolved universal terrestrial radio access (E-UTRA), medium access control (MAC) protocol specification (3GPP. TS 36.321 version 10.7.0 release 10). Retrieved from http://www.etsi.org/deliver/etsi_ts/136300_136399/136321/10.07.00_60/ts_136321v100700p.pdf

ETSI. ES 200 800 v.1.3.1. (2001). Digital video broadcasting: Interaction channel for cable TV distribution systems (CATV). Retrieved from http://www.etsi.org/deliver/etsi_es/200800_200899/200800/01.03.01_60/es_200800v010301p.pdf

European Telecommunications Standards Institute. (2011). 3GPP TS 36.213: Technical specification group radio access network (E-UTRA), physical layer procedures, V10.1.0. Author.

Fattah, H., & Leung, C. (2002). An overview of scheduling algorithms in wireless multimedia networks. IEEE Wireless Communications, 9(5), 76–83. doi:10.1109/MWC.2002.1043857

Fernández-Bolaños, M., Vasylchenko, A., Dainesi, P., Brebels, S., De Raedt, W., Vandenbosch, G. A. E., & Ionescu, A. M. (2010). Dipole antenna and distributed MEMS phase shifter fully integrated in a single wafer process for beam steering applications. Microelectronic Engineering, 87(5), 1290–1293. doi:10.1016/j.mee.2009.10.009

Figueira, J., Mousseau, V., & Roy, B. (2005). ELECTRE methods. In Multiple criteria decision analysis: State of the art surveys (pp. 133–153). New York: Springer.

Floren, F., Edfors, O., & Molin, B. A. (2003). The effect of feedback quantization on the through-put of a multiuser diversity scheme. Paper presented at the Institute of Electrical and Electronics Engineers Global Telecommunication Conference (GlOBE-COM, 2003). San Francisco, CA.

Forsberg, D., Horn, G., Moeller, W., & Niemi, V. (2010). LTE security. London: John Wiley & Sons. doi:10.1002/9780470973271

Foschini, G. J. (1996). Layered space-time architecture for wireless communication in a fading environment when using multi-element antennas. Bell Labs Technical Journal, 1(2), 41–59. doi:10.1002/bltj.2015

Foschini, G. J. (2002). Layered space-time architecture for wireless communication in a fading environment when using multi-element antennas. Bell Labs Technical Journal., 1(2), 41–59. doi:10.1002/bltj.2015

Fraile, R., Lazaro, O., & Cardona, N. (2003). Two dimensional shadowing model. COST 273.

Franceschetti, M., Migliore, M. D., & Minero, P. (2009). The capacity of wireless networks: information-theoretic and physical limits. IEEE Transactions on Information Theory, 55(8), 3413–3424. doi:10.1109/TIT.2009.2023705

Freescale. (2008). Long term evolution protocol overview, whitepaper. Freescale Semiconductor.

Fridman, A., Weber, S., Graff, C., Breen, D. E., Dandekar, K. R., & Kam, M. (2012). OMAN: A mobile ad hoc network design system. IEEE Transactions on Mobile Computing, 1179–1191. doi:10.1109/TMC.2011.176

Fusco, G., Buddhikotl, M., Gupta, H., & Venkatesan, S. (2011). Finding green spots and turning the spectrum dial: Novel techniques for green mobile wireless networks. In Proceedings from DySPAN'11: IEEE Symposium on New Frontiers in Dynamic Spectrum Access Networks. Aachen, Germany: IEEE.

Gakhar, K., Gravey, A., & Leroy, A. (2205). IROISE: A new QoS architecture for IEEE 802.16 and IEEE 802.11e interworking. In Proceedings of the 2nd International Conference on Broadband Networks (BROADNETS'05) (pp. 607-612). Berlin: Springer.

Galih, S., Adiono, T., & Kurniawan, A. (2010). Low complexity MMSE channel estimation by weight matrix elements sampling for downlink OFDMA mobile WiMAX System. Int. Jor. of Computer Science and Network Security.

Ganapathy, H., & Caramanis, C. (2012). Queue-based subcarrier grouping for feedback reduction in OFDMA systems. In Proceedings of IEEE Infocom (pp. 1098–1106). IEEE. doi:10.1109/INFCOM.2012.6195466

Gao, X., Wang, W., Xia, X. G., Au, E. K. S., & You, X. H. (2011). Cyclic prefixed OQAM-OFDM and its application to single-carrier FDMA. IEEE Transactions on Communications, 59, 1467–1480. doi:10.1109/TCOMM.2011.031611.100045 doi:10.1109/TCOMM.2011.031611.100045

Gesbert, D., Kountouris, M., Heath, R. W., Jr., Chae, C., & Salzer, T. (2007). From single user to multiuser communications: Shifting the MIMO paradigm. IEEE Signal Processing Magazine, 24(5), 36–36. doi:10.1109/MSP.2007.904815

Ghosh, A., & Ratasuk, R. (2011). Essentials of LTE and LTE-A. Cambridge, UK: Cambridge University Press. doi:10.1017/CBO9780511997082

Ghosh, A., Ratasuk, R., Mondal, B., & Mangalvedhe, N. (2010). LTE-advanced: Next-generation wireless broadband technology. IEEE Wireless Communications, 17(3), 10–22. doi:10.1109/MWC.2010.5490974

Global Action Plan. (2007). An inefficient truth, global action plan. Retrieved from http://www.globalactionplan.org.uk/

Goldberger, J., & Leshem, A. (2011). MIMO detection for high-order QAM based on a Gaussian tree approximation. IEEE Transactions on Information Theory, 57(8), 4973–4982. doi:10.1109/TIT.2011.2159037

Goldsmith, A. (2005). Wireless communications. New York, NY: Cambridge University Press. doi:10.1017/CBO9780511841224

Gong, J., Zhou, S., Niu, Z., & Yang, P. (2010). Traffic-aware base station sleeping in dense cellular networks. In Proceedings from IWQoS'10: The 18th International Workshop on Quality of Service. Beijing, China: IWQoS.

González, G. D., García-Lozano, M., Corvino, V., Ruiz, S., & Olmos, J. (2010). Performance evaluation of downlink interference coordination techniques in LTE networks. In Proceedings of IEEE Vehicular Technology Conference (VTC). Ottawa, Canada: IEEE.

González, G. D., García-Lozano, M., Ruiz, S., & Olmos, J. (2012). An analytical view of static intercell interference coordination techniques in OFDMA networks. In Proceedings of IEEE Wireless Communications and Networking Conference (WCNC). Paris: IEEE.

González, G. D., García-Lozano, M., Ruiz, S., & Olmos, J. (2012). On the need for dynamic downlink intercell interference coordination for realistic LTE deployments. Wireless Communications and Mobile Computing. doi:10.1002/wcm.2191

Gopalan, A., Caramanis, C., & Shakkottai, S. (2012). On wireless scheduling with partial channel-state information. IEEE Transactions on Information Theory, 403–420. doi:10.1109/TIT.2011.2169543

Gore, D. A., & Paulraj, A. J. (2002). MIMO antenna subset selection with space-time coding. Istanbul, Turkey: Institute of Electrical and Electronics Engineers Transformation on Signal Processing. doi:10.1109/TSP.2002.803337

Gore, D., Nabar, R., & Paulraj, A. (2000). Selecting an optimal set of transmit antennas in wireless systems. Istanbul, Turkey: Institute of Electrical and Electronics Engineers ICASSP.

GPP TSG-RAN TR25. 814. Version 7.0.0. (2006). Physical layer aspects for evolved UTRA. Author.

Gray, R. M. (2006). Toeplitz and circulant mareices: A review. Foundation and Trends in Communication and Information Theory, 2(3), 155–239.

Guan, Q., Yu, F.R., Shengming, J., Leung, V.C.M., & Mehrvar, H. (2012). Topology control in mobile ad hoc networks with cooperative communications. IEEE Wireless Communications, 74-79. doi: 10.1109/MWC.2012.6189416

Gupta, M., Jha, S., Koc, A., & Vannithamby, R. (2013, February). Energy impact of emerging mobile internet applications on LTE networks: Issues and solutions. IEEE Communications Magazine. doi:10.1109/MCOM.2013.6461191

Gür, G., & Alagöz, F. (2011). Green wireless communications via cognitive dimension: An overview. IEEE Network, 25(2), 50–56. doi:10.1109/MNET.2011.5730528

Gutierrez, I., Bader, F., & Pijoan, J. L. (2008). Prioritization function for packet scheduling in OFDMA systems. Paper presented at the Wireless Internet Conference. Brussels, Belgium.

Hadisusanto, Y., Thiele, L., & Jungnickel, V. (2008). Distributed base station cooperation via block-diagonalization and dual-decomposition. In Proceedings of IEEE Globecom 2008. New Orleans, LA: IEEE.

Haipeng, L. E. I., Mingliang, A. Z., Yongyu, C., & Dacheng, Y. (2008). Adaptive connection admission control algorithm for LTE systems. In Proceedings of IEEE Vehicular Technology Coference VTC (pp. 2336-2340). IEEE.

Hall, J., & Mars, P. (1998). Satisfying QoS with a learning based scheduling algorithm. Durham, NC: School of Engineering, University of Durham. doi:10.1109/IWQOS.1998.675236

Haloka, S., Chen, T., Lehtomaki, J., & Koskela, T. (2010). Device-to- device (D2D) communication in cellular network- performance analysis of optimal and practical communication mode selection. In Proc. of 2010 IEEE Wireless Communications and Networking Conference. Sydney, Australia: IEEE.

Hämäläinen, S., Sanneck, H., & Sartori, C. (Eds.). (2012). LTE Self-Organising Networks (SON), Network Management Automation for Operational Efficiency. Wiley.

Han, F. M., & Zhang, X. D. (2007). Hexagonal multicarrier modulation: A robust transmission scheme for time-frequency dispersive channels. IEEE Transactions on Signal Processing, 55, 1955–1961. doi:10.1109/TSP.2006.890884 doi:10.1109/TSP.2006.890884

Han, F. M., & Zhang, X. D. (2009). MLSD for hexagonal multicarrier transmission with time-frequency localized pulses. IEEE Transactions on Vehicular Technology, 58, 1598–1604. doi:10.1109/TVT.2008.927032 doi:10.1109/TVT.2008.927032

Han, F. M., & Zhang, X. D. (2010). Asymptotic equivalence of two multicarrier transmission schemes in terms of robustness against time-frequency dispersive channels. IEEE Transactions on Vehicular Technology, 59, 1598–1604.

Harri, H., & Antti, T. (2009). LTE for UMTS OFDMA and SC-FDMA based radio access. West Sussex, UK: John Wiley and Sons Ltd.

Hasegawa, R., Shirakabe, M., Esmailzadeh, R., & Nakagawa, M. (2003). Downlink performance of a CDMA system with distributed base station. In Proceedings of the IEEE Vehicular Technology Conference-Fall (VTC-Fall 2003), (pp. 882-886). Orlando, FL: IEEE.

Hata, M. (1980). Empirical formula for propagation loss in land mobile radio services. IEEE Transactions on Vehicular Technology, 29(3), 317–325. doi:10.1109/T-VT.1980.23859

He, X. J., Lv, Z. Q., Liu, B., & Li, Z. H. (2012). High-isolation lateral RF MEMS capacitive switch based on HfO2 dielectric for high frequency applications. Sensors and Actuators. A, Physical. doi:10.1016/j.sna.2012.03.013

Hebb, D. O. (1949). The organization of behaviour. New York: John Wiley & Sons.

Hien, Q. N., & Erik, L. G. (2012). EVD-based channel estimation for multicell multiuser MIMO with very large antenna arrays. Paper presented at the International Conference on Acoustics, Speed and Signal Processing (ICASSP). DOI: 10.1109/ICASSP.2012.6288608

Hien, Q. N., Erik, L. G., & Marzetta, T. L. (2011). Uplink power efficiency of multiuser MIMO with very large antennas arrays. Paper presented at Forty-Ninth Annual Allerton Conference. DOI: 10.1109/Allerton.2011.6120314

Highsmith, W. R. (2002). An investigation into distributed base station design for LMDS systems. In Proceedings IEEE Southeastcon 2002, (pp. 162-165). Columbia, SC: IEEE.

Himayat, H., Talwar, S., Rao, A., & Soni, R. (2010). Interference management for 4G cellular standards. IEEE Communications Magazine, 48(8), 86–92. doi:10.1109/MCOM.2010.5534591

Hitachi Ltd. (2012). R1-122699: CQI estimation for CoMP. 3GPP.

Hlel, E. K., Cherif, S., Tlili, F., & Siala, M. (2005). Improved estimation of time varying and frequency selective channel for OFDM systems. Paper presented at ICECS. Tunisia.

Hochwald, B. M., Sweldens, W. (2000). Differential unitary space–time modulation. IEEE Transactions on Communications. 48(12).2041-2052.

Hollander, F. (2008). Large deviations. Washington, DC: American Mathematical Soc.

Holma, H., & Toskala, A. (2011). LTE for UMTS evolution to LTE-advanced (2nd ed.). London: Academic Press. doi:10.1002/9781119992943

Hongxia, Z., & Jufeng, D. (2009). A simple compensation algorithm for VoIP services in IEEE 802.16e system. Paper presented at 11th International Conference on Advanced Communication Technology. Korea.

Hoshyar, R., Shariat, M., & Tafazolli, R. (2010). Subcarrier and power allocation with multiple power constraints in orthogonal frequency-division multiple access systems. Institute of Electrical and Electronics Engineers Communications Letters, 14.

Hossain, E., Kim, D. I., & Bhargava, V. K. (2011). Cooperative cellular wireless networks. New York: Cambridge University. doi:10.1017/CBO9780511667008

Hoydis, J., Stephan, B. T., & Debbah, D. (2013). Massive MIMO in the UL/DL of celluar networks: How many antennas do we need? IEEE Journal on Selected Areas in Communications, 31(2), 160–171. doi:10.1109/JSAC.2013.130205

Hoyhtya, M., Palola, M., Matinmikko, M., & Katz, M. (2011). Cognitive engine: Design aspects for mobile clouds. In Proceedings of CogART 2011. CogART.

HTC. (2012). R1-122323: CQI definition and feedback reduction mechanism for CoMP. 3GPP.

Huawei, HiSilicon. (2011). R1-110021: Issues for aperiodic and periodic CSI reporting. 3GPP.

Huawei. (2011). Improving energy efficiency, lowering CO_2 emissions and TCO. Huawei Technologies Co., Ltd.

Huawei. (2011). R1-110015: Remaining issues in aperiodic CQI-only PUSCH. 3GPP.

Huff, G. H., & Bernhard, J. T. (2006). Integration of packaged RF MEMS switches with radiation pattern reconfigurable square spiral microstrip antennas. IEEE Transactions on Antennas and Propagation, 54(2), 464–469. doi:10.1109/TAP.2005.863409

Hughes, B. L., & Sweldens, W. (2000). Differential space–time modulation. IEEE Transactions on Information Theory, 46(7), 2567–2578. doi:10.1109/18.887864

Hui, L., & Guoqing, L. (2005). OFDMA-based broadband wireless networks: Design and optimization. Hoboken, NJ: John Willey & Sons.

Hur, S. H., & Rao, B. (2012). Sum rate analysis of a reduced feedback OFDMA downlink system employing joint scheduling and diversity. IEEE Transactions on Signal Processing, 862–876. doi:10.1109/TSP.2011.2173335

Hussain, M. A. R., et al. (2009). Comparative study of scheduling algorithms in WiMAX. In Proceedings of National Conference on Recent Developments in Computing and its Applications (NCRDCA '09). New Delhi, India: NCRDCA.

Hutchings, D. A., El-Shenawee, M., & Tung, S. (n.d.). Electromagnetic characterization of broadband MEMS antenna. Academic Press.

IEEE 802.11ac Specifications. (2012). Washington, DC: IEEE.

IEEE 802.16 Working Group. (2004). IEEE standard for local and metropolitan area networks –Part 16: Air interface for fixed broadband wireless access systems. Author.

IEEE 802.16 Working Group. (2013). The IEEE 802.16 working group on broadband wireless access standards. Retrieved from http://www.wirelessman.org/

IEEE Broadband Wireless Access Working Group. (2008). C802.16m-08/119: Link performance abstraction for ML receivers based on RBIR metrics. IEEE.

IEEE Standard (2004b). 802.16-2004.Part 16: Air interface for fixed broadband wireless access system.

IEEE Standard. (2009) Standard for Local and Metropolitan Area Networks- Part 21: Media Independent Handover. IEEE Std 802.21-2008. doi: 10.1109/IEEESTD.2009.4769367

IEEE Standards (2004a). IEEE Standard for local and metropolitan area networks, air interface for fixed broadband wireless access systems.

IEEE Standards (2005). IEEE Standard for local and metropolitan area networks. Air interface for fixed broadband wireless access systems. Amendment 1: Management information base.

IEEE Standards (2006). 802.16e-2005 and IEEE Std 802.16-2004/Cor1-2005-IEEE Standard for local and metropolitan area networks. Part 16: Air interface for fixed and mobile broadband wireless access systems. Amendment 2: Physical and medium access control layers for combined fixed and mobile operation in licensed bands and corrigendum 1.

IEEE Std. 802.16m. (2011). IEEE standard for local and metropolitan area networks part 16: Air interface for broadband wireless access systems, amendment 3: Advanced air interface. doi:10.1109/IEEESTD.2011.5765736

Indrasinghe, S., Pereira, R., & Haggerty, J. (2010). Efficient address management for mobile ad hoc networks. In Proceedings of International Conference on Broadband, Wireless Computing, Communication and Applications. Academic Press.

INTEL (2007). Mobile broadband brought to you by WiMAX.

Intel Corporation. (2012). R1-122628: Periodic and aperiodic CSI feedback modes for DL CoMP. 3GPP.

Irmer, R., Droste, H., Marsch, P., Grieger, M., Fettweis, G., & Brueck, S. et al. (2011). Coordinated multipoint: Concepts, performance, and field trial results. IEEE Communications Magazine, 102–111. doi:10.1109/MCOM.2011.5706317

ITU-R. (2008). M.2135: Guidelines for evaluation of radio interface technologies for IMT-advanced. ITU-R.

ITU-T. Rec. G.711. (1988). Pulse code modulation (PCM) of voice frequencies. Retrieved from http://www.itu.int/rec/T-REC-G.711-198811-I/en

ITU-T. Rec. G.723.1. (2006). Dual rate speech coder for multimedia communications transmitting at 5.3 and 6.3 kbit/s. Retrieved from http://www.itu.int/rec/T-REC-G.723.1-200605-I/en

ITU-T. Rec. G.726, 40, 32, 24, 16 kbit/s. (1990). Adaptive differential pulse code modulation (ADPCM). Retrieved from http://www.itu.int/rec/T-REC-G.726-199012-I/en

ITU-T. Rec. G.728. (1992). Coding of spech at 16 kbit/s using low-delay code excited linear prediction. Retrieved from http://www.itu.int/rec/T-REC-G.728-201206-I/en

ITU-T. Rec. G.729. (2007). Coding of speech at 8 kbit/s using conjugate-structure algebraic-code-excited linear prediction (CS-ACELP). Retrieved from http://www.itu.int/rec/T-REC-G.729-201206-I/en

ITU-T. Rec. H.323. (2009). Packet-based multimedia communications systems. Retrieved from http://www.itu.int/rec/T-REC-H.323-200912-I/en

Jafar, S. A., & Goldsmith, A. J. (2004). Transmitter optimization and optimality of beamforming for multiple antenna systems with imperfect feedback. Institute of Electrical and Electronics Engineers Transformation Wireless Communication, 3(4), 1165–1175.

Jain, A., Verma, A. K. (n.d.) Comparative study of scheduling algorithm for WiMAX.

Jalden, J., & Elia, P. (2011). Sphere decoding complexity exponent for decoding full rate codes over the quasi-static MIMO channel. IEEE Transactions on Information Theory. PMID:22287795

Jalden, J., & Ottersten, B. (2005). On the limits of sphere decoding. In Proc. ISIT 2005. ISIT.

Jalden, J., Barbero, L. G., Ottersten, B., & Thompson, J. S. (2007). Full diversity detection in MIMO systems with a fixed-complexity sphere decoder. In Proc. IEEE ICASSP 2007. IEEE.

Jalden, J., Barbero, L. G., Ottersten, B., & Thompson, J. S. (2009). The error probability of the fixed-complexity sphere decoder. IEEE Transactions on Signal Processing, 57(7), 2711–2720. doi:10.1109/TSP.2009.2017574

Jani, P., Niko, K. H., Martti, M., & Mika, R. (2008). Mixed traffic packet scheduling in UTRAN long term evaluation downlink. Paper presented at Indoor nas Radio Mobile Communication IEEE 19th International Symposium. New York, NY.

Jardosh, A. P., Iannaccone, G., Papagiannaki, K., & Vinnakota, B. (2007). Towards an energy-star WLAN infrastructure. In Proceedings from HotMobile'07: The 8th IEEE Workshop on Mobile Computing Systems and Applications. Tucson, AZ: IEEE.

Jau-Yang, C., & Yu-Chen, L. (2012). Dynamically alternating power saving scheme for IEEE 802.16e mobile broadband wireless access systems. Journal of Communications and Networks, 14(2), 179–187. doi:10.1109/JCN.2012.6253066

Jindal, N., & Ramprashad, S. (2011). Optimizing CSI feedback for MU-MIMO: Tradeoffs in channel correlation, user diversity and MU-MIMO efficiency. Budapest: IEEE. doi:10.1109/VETECS.2011.5956557

Jinning, A. J. I., & Nicholson, P. L. S. (1987). Artificial intelligence in communication networks. Paper presented at the Conference on Computing Systems and Information Technology. New York, NY.

Jorguseski, L., Le, T. M. H., Fledderus, E. R., & Prasad, R. (2008). Downlink resource allocation for evolved UTRAN and WiMAX cellular systems. In Proceedings of IEEE Personal, Indoor, and Mobile Radio Communications Conference (PIMRC 2008). Cannes, France: IEEE.

Jose, J., Ashikhmin, A., Marzetta, T. L., & Vishwanath, S. (2009). Pilot contamination problem in multi-cell TDD systems. Paper presented at ISIT. Seoul, Korea. DOI: 10.1109/ISIT.2009.5205814

Jun, S., Na, Y., An, L., & Haige, X. (2009). Opportunistic scheduling for heterogeneous services in downlink OFDMA system. In Proceedings of IEEE Computer Society (pp. 260-264). IEEE.

Jung, B. Y., Choi, M. S., Youn, H. Y., & Song, O. (2010). Vertical handover based on the prediction of mobility of mobile node. In Proceedings of Pervasive Computing and Communications Workshops (PERCOM Workshops), 2010 8th IEEE International Conference on (pp. 534-539). IEEE.

Jung, P., & Wunder, G. (2007). The WSSUS pulse design problem in multicarrier transmission. IEEE Transactions on Communications, 55, 1918–1928. doi:10.1109/TCOMM.2007.906426 doi:10.1109/TCOMM.2007.906426

Kaarthick, B., Yeshwenth, V. J., Nagarajan, N., & Rajeev. (2009). Investigating the performance of various vocoders for a fair scheduling algorithm in WiMAX. In Proceedings of the First Asian Himalayas International Conference on Internet, (pp. 1-5). doi:10.1109/AHICI.2009.5340356

Kaleem, F., Mehbodniya, A., Yen, K. K., & Adachi, F. (2013). A fuzzy pre-processing module for optimizing the access network selection in wireless networks. In Proceedings of Advances in Fuzzy Systems. Academic Press.

Kalikivayi, S., Misra, I. S., & Saha, K. (2008). Bandwidth and delay guaranteed call admission control scheme for QOS provisioning in IEEE 802.16e mobile WiMAX. Paper presented at the Global Telecommunications Conference. New York, NY.

Kang, M., & Kim, K. S. (2012). Performance analysis and optimization of best-m feedback for OFDMA systems. Institute of Electrical and Electronics Engineers Communications Letters, 16.

Kang, N. W., Cheon, C., & Jung, H. K. (2002). Feasibility study on beam-forming technique with 1-D mechanical beam steering antenna using niching genetic algorithm. IEEE Microwave and Wireless Components Letters, 12(12), 494–496. doi:10.1109/LMWC.2002.805954

Karakaya, B., Arslan, H., & Ali Cirpan, H. (2008). Channel estimation for LTE uplink in high doppler spread. WCNC. doi:10.1109/WCNC.2008.203

Karim, A. et al. (2010). Modeling and resource allocation for mobile video over WiMAX broadband wireless networks. IEEE Journal on Selected Areas in Communications, 28(3), 354–365. doi:10.1109/JSAC.2010.100407

Kassar, M., Kervella, B., & Pujolle, G. (2007). Architecture of an intelligent inter-system handover management scheme In Proceedings of Future Generation Communication and Networking (FGCN 2007) (Vol. 1, pp. 332-337). IEEE.

Kassar, M., Kervella, B., & Pujolle, G. (2008). An overview of vertical handover decision strategies in heterogeneous wireless networks. Computer Communications, 31(10), 2607–2620. doi:10.1016/j.comcom.2008.01.044

Kassim, H., & Baba, M. D. (2011). Performance analysis of fixed and mobile WiMax networks using NCTUns tools. Paper presented at the Control and System Graduate Research Colloquium (ICSGRC). Malaysia.

Keller, T., & Hanzol, L. (2000). Adaptive modulation techniques for duplez OFDM transmission. Institute of Electrical and Electronics Engineers Transaction on Vehicular Technology, 49(5), 1893–1906.

Khabbazian, M., & Bhargava, V. (2009). Efficient broadcasting in mobile ad hoc networks. IEEE Transactions on Mobile Computing, 8(2). doi:10.1109/TMC.2008.94

Khalil, A., & Ksentini, A. (2007). Classification of the uplink scheduling algorithms in IEEE 802.16. In Proceedings of International Workshop on Dynamic Networking (IWDYN' 07). IWDYN.

Khalil, A., & Ksentini, A. (2007). Classification of the uplink scheduling algorithms in IEEE 802.16. IRISIA.

Khan, F. (2009). LTE for 4G mobile broadband air interface technologies and performance. New York: Cambridge University. doi:10.1017/CBO9780511810336

Khan, M. A. S. et al. (2010). Performance evaluation and enhancement of uplink scheduling algorithms in point to multipoint WiMAX networks. European Journal of ScientificResearch, 42(3), 491–506.

Khazaai, J. J., & Qu, H. (2012). Electro-thermal MEMS switch with latching mechanism: Design and characterization. IEEE Sensors Journal, 12(9), 2830–2838. doi:10.1109/JSEN.2012.2194736

Khoshnevis, A., & Sabharwal, A. (2004). On diversity and multiplexing gain of multiple antenna systems with transmitter channel information. In Proc. Allerton Conference on Communication, Control and Computing. Academic Press.

Khozeimeh, F., & Haykin, S. (2010). Self-organizing dynamic spectrum management for cognitive networks. In Proceedings of Communication Networks and Services Research Conference (pp. 1-7). Montreal, Canada: CNSR.

Kian, C. B., Simon, A., & Angela, D. (2008). Joint time-frequency domain proportional fair scheduler with HARQ for 3GPP LTE systems. In Proceedings of IEEE Vehicular Technology Coference VTC (pp.1-5). Calgary, Canada: IEEE.

Kim, S., & Lee, J. (2012). To cooperate or not to cooperate: System throughput and fairness perspective. Institute of Electrical and Electronics Engineers Journal on Selected Areas in Communications, 30.

Kingsbury, N. (2005). Approximation formulae for the Gaussian error integral. Retrieved from http://cnx.org/content/m11067/2.4/

Kolios, P., Friderikos, V., & Papadaki, K. (2010). A practical approach to energy efficient communications in mobile wireless networks. Journal of Mobile Networks and Applications, 17(2), 267–280. doi:10.1007/s11036-011-0337-z

Kumar, S., Monghal, G., Nin, J., Ordas, I., Pedersen, K., & Mogensen, P. (2009). Autonomous inter cell interference avoidance under fractional load for downlink long term evolution. In Proceedings of IEEE Vehicular Technology Conference (VTC). Barcelona: IEEE.

Kumbasar, V., & Kucur, O. (2007). ICI reduction in OFDM systems by using improved sinc power pulse. Digital Signal Processing, 17, 997–1006. doi:10.1016/j.dsp.2007.03.010 doi:10.1016/j.dsp.2007.03.010

Kumbuza, X., & Ventura, N. (2006). Using the global positioning system (GPS) to add intelligence to wireless handover in WLAN. In Proceedings of Electro/Information Technology, 2006 IEEE International Conference on (pp. 23-26). IEEE.

Kuo, Y., Yang, T., & Huang, G. W. (2008). The use of grey relational analysis in solving multiple attribute decision-making problems. Computers & Industrial Engineering, 55(1), 80–93. doi:10.1016/j.cie.2007.12.002

Kwon, T., Lee, H., Choi, S., Kim, J., Cho, D.-H., & Cho, S. et al. (2005). Design and implementation of a simulator based on a cross-layer protocol between MAC and PHY layers in a WiBro compatible IEEE802.16e OFDMA system. IEEE Communications Magazine, 43(12), 136–146. doi:10.1109/MCOM.2005.1561931

Lakshminarayanan, B., & Weller, T. M. (2006). Design and modeling of 4-bit slow-wave MEMS phase shifters. IEEE Transactions on Microwave Theory and Techniques, 54(1), 120–127. doi:10.1109/TMTT.2005.860332

Latiff, A. A., & Fisal, N. (2007). Power reduction quadrant based directional routing protocol in mobile ad hoc network. In Proceedings of the 2007 IEEE International Conference on Telecommunication and Malaysia International Conference on Communications. IEEE.

Leandros, T., & Anthony, E. (1993). Dynamic server allocation to parallel queues with randomly varying connectivity. IEEE Transactions on Information Theory, 39, 466–478. doi:10.1109/18.212277

Lee, H., Kim, H.-D., & Cho, D.-H. (2008). Extended-rtPS+ considering characteristics of VoIP codecs in mobile WiMAX. In Proceedings of the IEEE 19th International Symposium on Personal, Indoor and Mobile Radio Communications, (pp. 1-5). IEEE. doi:10.1109/PIMRC.2008.4699724

Lee, J.-S., De Simone, F., Ebrahimi, T., Ramzan, N., & Izquierdo, E. (2012). Quality assessment of multidimensional video scalability. IEEE Communications Magazine, 50(4), 38–46. doi:10.1109/MCOM.2012.6178832

Lee, M. H. (2012). Jacket matrices: Constructions and its applications for fast cooperative wireless signal processing. LAP Lambert Publishing. Retrieved from http://www.amazon.com/Jacket-Matrices-Construction-Application-Cooperative/dp/3659291455

Lee, M. H., Manev, N. L., & Zhang, X. D. (2008). Jacket transforms eigenvalue decomposition. Applied Mathematics and Computation, 198(2), 858–864.

Lee, M. H., Matalgah, M. M., & Song, W. (2010). Fast method for precoding and decoding of distributive multi-input multi-output channels in relay-based decode-and-forward cooperative wireless network. IET Communications, 4(2), 144–153. doi:10.1049/iet-com.2008.0712

Lee, M. H., Zhang, X. D., Song, W., & Xia, X. G. (2012). Fast reciprocal jacket transform with many parameters. IEEE Transactions on Circuits and Systems, 59(7), 1472–1481. doi:10.1109/TCSI.2011.2177013

Lee, P., Jeong, J., Saxena, N., & Shin, J. (2009). Dynamic reservation scheme of physical cell identity for 3GPP LTE femtocell systems. Journal of Information Processing Systems, 5(4), 219. doi:10.3745/JIPS.2009.5.4.207

Lee, S. J., Tcha, Y., Seo, S.-Y., & Lee, S.-C. (2011). Efficient use of multicast and unicast channels for multicast services transmission. IEEE Transactions on Communications, 59(5), 1264–1267. doi:10.1109/TCOMM.2011.020811.090200

Leke, A., & Cioffi, J. M. (1997). A maximum rate loading algorithm for discrete multi-tone 8 modulation systems. proce. Institute of Electrical and Electronics Engineers Global Telecommunication Conference, 3(1), 514-158.

Lera, A., Molinaro, A., & Pizzi, S. (2007). Channel-aware scheduling for QoS and fairness provisioning in IEEE 802.16/WiMAX broadband wireless access systems. IEEE Network, 21(5), 34–41. doi:10.1109/MNET.2007.4305171

Leroux, P., Roy, S., & Chouinard, J.-Y. (2008). A multi-agent protocol to manage interference in a distributed base station system. In Proceedings of the International Conference on Advanced Technologies for Communications (ATC 2008), (pp. 421-426). Hanoi, Vietnam: ATC.

Li, I., Xin, W., Hanqi, Z., & Morgera, S. D. (2009). Integrating retransmission diversity with real-time scheduling over wireless links. Baltimore, MD: CISS. doi:10.1109/CISS.2009.5054752

Li, Z., Mopidevi, H., Kaynar, O., & Cetiner, B. A. (2012). Beam-steering antenna based on parasitic layer. Electronics Letters, 48(2), 59–60. doi:10.1049/el.2011.2787

Lihua, W., Wenchao, M., & Zihua, G. (2007). A cross-layer packet scheduling and sub channel allocation scheme in 802.16e OFDMA system. In Proceedings of Wireless Communications and Networking Conference, (pp. 1865–1870). IEEE.

Lim, S., Yu, C., & Das, C. (2009). RandomCast: An energy-efficient communication scheme for mobile ad hoc networks. IEEE Transactions on Mobile Computing, 8(8).

Lin, G., Lundheim, L., & Holte, N. (2008). Optimal pulses robust to carrier frequency offset for OFDM/QAM systems. IEEE Communications Letters, 12, 161–163. doi:10.1109/LCOMM.2008.071680 doi:10.1109/LCOMM.2008.071680

Lin, Y., & Shao, L. (2010). Wireless network cloud: Architecture and system requirements. IBM Journal of Research and Development, 54(1), 4:1-4:12.

Liou, R.-H., & Lin, Y.-B. (2013). An investigation on LTE mobility management. IEEE Transactions on Mobile Computing, 12(1). doi:10.1109/TMC.2011.255

Liu, A. Q. (2010). RF MEMS switches and integrated switching circuits (Vol. 5). Berlin: Springer. doi:10.1007/978-0-387-46262-2

Liu, Q. et al. (2006). A cross-layer scheduling algorithm with QoS support in wireless networks. IEEE Transactions on Vehicular Technology, 55(3), 839–847. doi:10.1109/TVT.2006.873832

Liu, Y., Li, W., Zhang, H., & Lu, W. (2010a). Graph based automatic centralized PCI assignment in LTE. In Proceedings of Computers and Communications (ISCC), 2010 IEEE Symposium on (pp. 919-921). IEEE.

Liu, Y., Li, W., Zhang, H., & Yu, L. (2010b). Distributed PCI assignment in LTE based on consultation mechanism. In Proceedings of Wireless Communications Networking and Mobile Computing (WiCOM), 2010 6th International Conference on (pp. 1-4). IEEE.

Lorincz, J., Capone, A., & Begusic, D. (2011). Optimized network management for energy savings of wireless access networks. Computer Networks, 55, 514–540. doi:10.1016/j.comnet.2010.09.013

LTE-Advanced. (2011). LTE, evolved universal terrestrial radio access (E-UTRA), physical channels and modulation (3GPP. TS 36.211 version 10.3.0 Release 10), ETSI, TS 36.211 version 10.3.0. Retrieved from http://www.etsi.org/deliver/etsi_ts/136200_136299/136211/10.03.00_60/ts_136211v100300p.pdf

Lu, J., & Ma, M. (2011). Cross-layer MAC protocol and holistic opportunistic scheduling with adaptive power control for QoS in WiMAX. J Wireless Pers Commun., 61, 19–40. doi:10.1007/s11277-010-9996-5

Lu, S., Cai, Y., Zhang, L., Li, J., Skov, P., Wang, C., & He, Z. (2009). Channel-aware frequency domain packet scheduling for MBMS in LTE. In Proceedings of the IEEE Vehicular Technology Conference-Spring (VTC–Spring 2009). Barcelona, Spain: IEEE.

Lu, T., & Zhu, J. (2013). Genetic algorithm for energy-efficient QoS multicast routing. IEEE Communications Letters, 17(1). doi:10.1109/LCOMM.2012.112012.121467

Lunttila, T., Lindholm, J., Pajukoski, K., Tiirola, E., & Toskala, A. (2007). EUTRAN uplink performance. In Proceedings of International Symposium on Wireless Pervasive Computing (ISWPC 2007), (pp. 515-519). San Juan, Puerto Rico: ISWPC.

Lutkepohl, H. (1996). Handbook of matrices. Chichester, UK: Wiley.

Ma, M., & Lu, J. (2009). QoS provisioning mechanism in WiMAX. In M. Ma (Ed.), Current technology developments of WiMAX systems. Berlin: Springer. doi:10.1007/978-1-4020-9300-5_5

Ma, M., Jiao, B., & Lee, C. Y. (2008). A dual-window technique for enhancing robustness of OFDM against frequency offset. IEEE Communications Letters, 12, 17–19. doi:10.1109/LCOMM.2008.071226 doi:10.1109/LCOMM.2008.071226

Maeder, A. (2009). IEEE 802.16m for IMT-advanced: The next step in WirelessMAN evolution. Retrieved from http://www3.informatik.uniwuerzburg.de/euroview/2009/data/slides/Session1-Maeder-slides-handout.pdf

Marques, F. R., Wanstedt, S., Porto, F. R., & Freitas, W. C. (2010). Scheduling for improving system capacity in multiservice 3GPP LTE. Journal of Electrical and Computer Engineering.

Márquez-Barja, J., Calafate, C. T., Cano, J. C., & Manzoni, P. (2011). An overview of vertical handover techniques: Algorithms, protocols and tools. Computer Communications, 34(8), 985–997. doi:10.1016/j.comcom.2010.11.010

Marsan, M. A., Chiaraviglio, L., Ciullo, D., & Meo, M. (2009). Optimal energy savings in cellular access networks. In Proceedings from ICC Workshops '09: The IEEE International Conference on Communications Workshops. Dresden, Germany: IEEE.

Marsan, M. A., Chiaraviglio, L., Ciullo, D., & Meo, M. (2010). A simple analytical model for the energy-efficient activation of access points in dense WLANSs. In Proceedings from e-Energy'10: The 1st International Conference on Energy-Efficient Computing and Networking. New York, NY: e-Energy.

Marsan, M. A., Chiaraviglio, L., Ciullo, D., & Meo, M. (2011). Switch off transients in cellular access networks with sleep modes. In Proceedings from ICC Workshops'11: The IEEE International Conference on Communications Workshops. Kyoto, Japan: IEEE.

Martin-Sacristan, D., Monserrat, J. F., Cabrejas Penuelas, J., Calabuig, D., Garrigas, S., & Cardona, N. (2009). On the way towards fourth generation mobile: 3GPP LTE and LTE-advanced. EURASIP Journal on Wireless Communications and Networking, 4.

Marzetta, T. L. (1999). BLAST training: Estimating channel characteristics for high capacity space-time wireless. Paper presented at 37th Annual Allerton Conf. Commnications, Control, and Computing. Retrieved from ftp://cm.bell-labs.com/cm/ms/who/hochwald/papers/training/training.pdf

Marzetta, T. L. (2006). How much training is required for multiuser MIMO? Paper presented at Fortieth Asilomar Conference on Signals, Systems, & Computers. Pacific Grove, CA. DOI: 10.1109/ACSSC.2006.354768

Marzetta, T. L. (2010). Noncooperative cellular wireless with unlimited numbers of base station antennas. IEEE Transactions on Wireless Communications, 9(11), 3590–3600. doi:10.1109/TWC.2010.092810.091092

Marzetta, T. L., & Alexei, A. (2010). Beyond LTE: Hundreds of base station antennas! Paper presented at IEEE Communication Theory Workshop. Retrieved from http://www.ieee-ctw.org/2010/mon/Marzetta.pdf

Matthaiou, M., McKay, M. R., Smith, P. J., & Nossek, J. A. (2010). On the condition number distribution of complex Wishart matrices. IEEE Transactions on Communications, 58(6), 1705–1717. doi:10.1109/TCOMM.2010.06.090328

Matthias, P. (2002). Mobile fading channels. West Sussex, UK: John Wiley & Sons, Ltd.

Mecking, M. (2002). Resource allocation for fading multiple-access channels with partial channel state information. In Proceedings of IEEE International Conference on Communications. New York: IEEE.

Meng, G., Shen, Y. H., & Yuan, Z. G. (2009). Maximum Doppler spread estimation by tracking the delay-subspace for LOFDM systems in doubly dispersive fading channels. In Proc. 2009 IEEE Int. Conf. Wireless Communications and Signal Processing. IEEE.

Meng, G., Shen, Y. H., & Yuan, Z. G. (2011). Cyclostationarity-based and super-imposed pilot-aided maximum doppler spread estimation for LOFDM systems in doubly-dispersive channels. Frequenz, 65, 93–101.

Meng, G., Shen, Y.H., & Xu, K. (2011). A low complexity frequency domain pilot time domain doubly average channel estimation for LOFDM systems. Przeglad Elektrotechniczny, 270-274.

Milanovic, J., Rimac-Drlje, S., & Bejuk, K. (2007). Comparison of propagation models accuracy for WiMAX. Paper presented at the 4th IEEE International Conference on Electronics, Circuits and Systems. Morocco.

Milanovic, J., Rimac-Drlje, S., & Majerski, I. (2010). Radio wave propagation mechanisms and empirical models for fixed wireless access systems. Tehnicki Vjesnik, 17(1), 43–53.

Mirzajani, H., Nasiri, M., & Ghavifekr, H. B. (2012). A new design of MEMS-based wideband frequency reconfigurable microstrip patch antenna. In Proceedings of Mechatronics and its Applications (ISMA), 2012 8th International Symposium on (pp. 1-6). IEEE.

Misra, S., Banerjee, B., & Wolfinger, B. E. (2012). A learning automata-based uplink scheduler for supporting real-time multimedia interactive traffic in IEEE 802.16 WiMAX networks. ComCom. doi:10.1016/j.comcom.2012.06.016

Mobile Operators Could Save $560m+ in OPEX Annually, According to New Arieso Study. (2011, June 15). Retrieved from http://www.fiercemobilecontent.com/node/18332/print

Mohanan, V., Budiarto, R., & Zainon, W. M. N. W. (2012). Holistic network selection for wireless mobile nodes in a 4G environment. In Proceedings of Communications (APCC), 2012 18th Asia-Pacific Conference on (pp. 53-58). IEEE.

Molisch, A. (2010). Wireless communication (2nd ed.). New York: Wiley and Sons.

Molisch, A. F., Win, M. Z., & Winters, J. H. (2003). Reduced –complexity transmits/ receives diversity system. Institute of Electrical and Electronics Engineers Transformation on Signal Processing, 51(11), 2729–2738.

Moseley, R. W., Yeatman, E. M., Holmes, A. S., Syms, R. R. A., Finlay, A. P., & Boniface, P. (2006). Laterally actuated, low voltage, 3-port RF MEMS switch.[IEEE.]. Proceedings of Micro Electro Mechanical Systems, 2006, 878–881.

Motorola. (2005). R1-051334: CQI feedback scheme for EUTRA. 3GPP.

Motorola. (2007). Long term evolution (LTE), overview of LTE air–Interface, technical white paper. Retrieved from http://www.motorola.com/web/Business/Solutions/Industry%20Solutions/Service%20Providers/Wireless%20Operators/LTE/_Document/Static%20Files/6993_MotDoc_New.pdf

Motorola. (2007). Node B specification sheet. Retrieved from http://www.motorola.com

Motorola. (2010). R1-103187: LTE-A dynamic aperiodic SRS - Triggering, duration, timing, and carrier aggregation. 3GPP.

Motorola. (2010). Real-world LTE performance for public safety. Retrieved from http://www.motorola.com/web/Business/US-EN/NGPS/pdf/Real_World_LTE_Performance_for_Public_Safety_White_Paper.pdf

Motorola. (2011). Barricaded suspect incident analysis: Enhancing critical incident response with public safety LTE. Retrieved from http://www.motorola.com/web/Business/_Documents/Application%20Briefs/Static%20Files/Motorola_Barricaded_Suspect_Analysis.pdf

Muldavin, J. B., & Rebeiz, G. M. (2000a). High-isolation CPW MEMS shunt switches: 1: Modeling. IEEE Transactions on Microwave Theory and Techniques, 48(6), 1045–1052. doi:10.1109/22.904743

Muldavin, J. B., & Rebeiz, G. M. (2000b). High-isolation CPW MEMS shunt switches: 2: Design. IEEE Transactions on Microwave Theory and Techniques, 48(6), 1053–1056. doi:10.1109/22.904744

Myung, H. G., & Goodman, D. J. (2008). Single carrier FDMA: A new air interface for long term evolution. Chichester, UK: John Wiley and Sons. doi:10.1002/9780470758717

Naja, R., Helou, M. E., & Tohmé, S. (2012). WiMAX double movable boundary scheme in the vehicle to infrastructure communication scenario. J Wireless Pers Commun. doi:10.1007/s11277-011-0389-1

Namuduri, K., & Rendse, R. (2012). Analytical estimation of path duration in mobile ad hoc networks. IEEE Sensors Journal, 1828–1835. doi:10.1109/JSEN.2011.2176927

Narasimhan, R. (2003). Spatial multiplexing with transmit antenna and constellation selection for correlated MIMO fading channels. IEEE Transactions on Signal Processing, 51(11), 2829–2838. doi:10.1109/TSP.2003.818205

Naruephiphat, W., & Charnsripinyo, C. (2009). Routing algorithm for balancing network lifetime and reliable packet delivery in mobile ad hoc networks. In Proceedings of Ubiquitous, Automatic and Trusted Computing, UIC-ATC 2009, Symposium and Workshop. UIC-ATC.

Nasiri, M., Mirzajani, H., Atashzaban, E., & Ghavifekr, H. B. (2013). Design and simulation of a novel micromachined frequency reconfigurable microstrip patch antenna. Wireless Personal Communications, 1–24.

NEC Group. (2009). R1-090303: Correction to RHO definition for CQI calculation. 3GPP.

Neely, M. J., Modiano, E., & Rohrs, C. E. (2003). Power allocation and routing in multi-beam satellites with time varying channels. Institute of Electrical and Electronics Engineers Trans. Networking, 11(1), 138–152. doi:10.1109/TNET.2002.808401

Ng, D. K. (1994). Grey system and grey relational model. ACM SIGICE Bulletin, 20(2), 2–9. doi:10.1145/190690.190691

Nokia Siemens Networks. (2007). R1-073662: CQI per PRB versus per group of best PRBs. 3GPP.

Nordquist, C. D., Baker, M. S., Kraus, G. M., Czaplewski, D. A., & Patrizi, G. A. (2009). Poly-silicon based latching RF MEMS switch. IEEE Microwave and Wireless Components Letters, 19(6), 380–382. doi:10.1109/LMWC.2009.2020025

Nuaymi, L. (2007). WiMAX: Technology for broadband wireless access. John Wiley & Sons. doi:10.1002/9780470319055

Oberhammer, J., & Stemme, G. (2006). Active opening force and passive contact force electrostatic switches for soft metal contact materials. Journal of Microelectromechanical Systems, 15(5), 1235–1242. doi:10.1109/JMEMS.2006.882810

Oh, E., & Krishnamachari, B. (2007). Energy savings through dynamic base station switching in cellular wireless access networks. In Proceedings from GLOBECOM'10: The IEEE Global Telecommunications Conference. Miami, FL: IEEE.

Okumura, Y., Ohmori, E., Kawano, T., & Fukuda, K. (1968). Field strength and its variability in VHF and UHF land-mobile radio service. Rev. Elec. Commun. Lab, 16(9), 825–873.

Olmos, J., Serra, A., Ruiz, S., García-Lozano, M., & González, G. D. (2009). Exponential effective SIR metric for LTE downlink. In Proceedings of IEEE International Symposium on Personal, Indoor and Mobile Radio Communications (PIMRC) (pp. 900-904). Tokyo, Japan: IEEE.

Olson, D. L. (2004). Comparison of weights in TOPSIS models. Mathematical and Computer Modelling, 40(7), 721–727. doi:10.1016/j.mcm.2004.10.003

Ortiz, L., Rangel, V., Gomez, J., Aquino, R., & Lopez-Guerrero, M. (2011). Performance optimization of mobile WiMAX netwoks for VoIP stream. In Proceedings of the 11th International Conference on Knowledge in Telecommunication Technologies and Optics, (pp. 165-169). Szczyrk, Poland: KTTO.

Ou, Y.-F., Ma, Z., Liu, T., & Wang, Y. (2011). Perceptual quality assessment of video considering both frame rate and quantization artifacts. IEEE Transactions on Circuits and Systems for Video Technology, 21(3), 286–298. doi:10.1109/TCSVT.2010.2087833

Ouyang, M., & Ying, L. (2009). On scheduling in multi-channel wireless downlink networks with limited feedback. In Proceedings of 47th Annual Allerton Conference on Communication (pp. 455–461). Monticello.

Pal Singh, J., Bambos, N., Srinivasan, B., & Clawin, D. (2002). Wireless LAN performance under varied stress conditions in vehicular traffic scenarios. In Proceedings of Vehicular Technology Conference, 2002 (Vol. 2, pp. 743-747). IEEE.

Palei, W., Liu, A. Q., Yu, A. B., Alphones, A., & Lee, Y. H. (2005). Optimization of design and fabrication for micromachined true time delay (TTD) phase shifters. Sensors and Actuators. A, Physical, 119(2), 446–454. doi:10.1016/j.sna.2004.10.006

Panasonic, HTC. (2010b). R1-103761: Aperiodic CQI reporting for carrier aggregation. 3GPP.

Panasonic. (2009). R1-090250: HARQ protocol handling of CQI-only reports. 3GPP. Panasonic, HTC. (2010a). R1-101262: Aperiodic CQI reporting for carrier aggregation. 3GPP.

Parekh, A., & Gallager, R. (1993). A generalized processor sharing approach to flow control in integrated services networks: The single node case. IEEE/ACM Transactions on Networking, 1, 344–357. doi:10.1109/90.234856

Parimal, P., Srikrshna, B., & Aravind, R. (2005). A sub-carrier allocation algorithm for OFDMA using buffer and channel state information. In Proceedings of Vehicular Technology Conference. IEEE.

Parkvall, S., Furuskar, A., & Dahlman, E. (2011, February). Evolution of LTE toward IMT-advanced. IEEE Communications Magazine. doi:10.1109/MCOM.2011.5706315

Parsons, J. J., & Oja, D. (2008). Conceptos de computación: Nuevas perspectivas. México: CENGAGE Learning.

Paulraj, A., Nabar, R., & Gore, D. (2003). Introduction to space-time wireless communications. Cambridge, UK: Cambridge University Press.

Paulraj, A., Nabar, R., & Gore, D. (2008). Introduction to space-time wireless communication. Cambridge University Press.

Pedersen, K. I., Monghal, G. I., & Kovács, Z. (2007). Frequency domain scheduling for OFDMA with limited and noisy channel feedback. Baltimore, MD: IEEE VTC. doi:10.1109/VETECF.2007.378

Pederson, M. V., & Fitzek, F. H. P. (2012). Mobile clouds: The new content sharing platform. Proceedings of the IEEE, 100, 1400–1403. doi:10.1109/JPROC.2012.2189806

Peebles, P. (2002). Probability, random variables, and random signal principles. New York: McGraw Hill.

Pelcat, M. et al. (2013). Physical layer multi-core prototyping. Lecture Notes in Electrical Engineering, 171. doi:10.1007/978-1-4471-4210-2_4

Pesola, J., Pönkänen, S., & Markopoulos, A. (2004). Location-aided handover in heterogeneous wireless networks. Wireless Personal Communications, 30(2-4), 195–205. doi:10.1023/B:WIRE.0000049399.43650.9f

Petridou, S. G., Sarigiannidis, P. G., Papadimitriou, G. I., & Pomportsis, A. S. (2007). Clustering based scheduling: A new approach to the design of scheduling algorithms for WDM star networks. In Proceedings of Communication and Vehicular Technology in the Benilux (pp. 1–5). Delft, The Netherlands: Academic Press. doi:10.1109/SCVT.2007.4436255

Piro, G., Grieco, L., Boggia, G., Capozzi, F., & Camarda, P. (2011). Simulating LTE cellular system: An open-source framework. IEEE Transactions on Vehicular Technology, 60(2), 498–513. doi:10.1109/TVT.2010.2091660

Pringle, L. N., Harms, P. H., Blalock, S. P., Kiesel, G. N., Kuster, E. J., Friederich, P. G., & Smith, G. S. (2004). A reconfigurable aperture antenna based on switched links between electrically small metallic patches. IEEE Transactions on Antennas and Propagation, 52(6), 1434–1445. doi:10.1109/TAP.2004.825648

Proakis, J. G. (1995). Digital communications (4th ed.). New York: McGraw-Hill International.

Qian, R., Qi, Y., Peng, T., & Wang, W. (2011). Scale effects oriented MIMO detector. In Proc. IEEE PIMRC 2011. IEEE.

Qian, R., Qi, Y., Peng, T., & Wang, W. (2012). Exploiting scalar effects of MIMO detection in cloud base-station: Feasible scheme and universal significance. In Proc. IEEE Globecom Workshops (GC Wkshps) 2012. IEEE.

Qian, R., Qi, Y., Peng, T., & Wang, W. (2013). On the scale effects oriented MIMO detector: Diversity order, worst-case unit complexity and scale effects. Signal Processing, 93(1), 277–287. doi:10.1016/j.sigpro.2012.08.006

Qian, R., Qi, Y., Peng, T., & Wang, W. (2013a). Scale effect analysis of early- termination fixed-complexity. EURASIP Journal on Advances in Signal Processing. doi:10.1186/1687-6180-2013-125

Qiu, X., & Chawla, K. (1999). On the performance of adaptive modulation in cellular systems. IEEE Transactions on Communications, 47(6), 884–895. doi:10.1109/26.771345

Qualcomm Europe. (2007). R1-072731: Scheduling requests using CQI. 3GPP.

Qualcomm. (2012). R1-122777: CQI definition for downlink CoMP. 3GPP.

Qui, J., Lang, J. H., Slocum, A. H., & Strumpler, R. (2003). A high-current electrothermal bistable MEMS relay.[IEEE.]. Proceedings of Micro Electro Mechanical Systems, 2003, 64–67.

Radwan, A., & Rodriguez, J. (2012). Energy saving in multi-standard mobile terminals through short-range cooperation. EURASIP Journal on Wireless Communications and Networking, 159. doi:10.1186/1687-1499-2012-159

Rahman, F. M., & Gregory, M. A. (2011a). Quadrant based intelligent energy controlled multicast algorithm for mobile ad hoc networks. In Proceedings of 13th International Conference on Advanced Communication Technology (ICACT), (pp. 1298 – 1303). Phoenix Park, Korea: ICACT.

Rahman, F. M., & Gregory, M. A. (2011b). 4-N intelligent MANET routing algorithm. In Proceedings of Telecommunication Networks and Applications Conference (ATNAC). Melbourne, Australia: ATNAC. doi: 10.1109/ATNAC.2011.6096664

Rahman, F. M., & Gregory, M. A. (2012). IP address associate 4-N intelligent MANET routing algorithm utilizing LTE cellular technology. In Proceedings of Telecommunication Networks and Applications Conference (ATNAC). Brisbane, Australia: ATNAC. doi: 10.1109/ATNAC.2012.6398077

Ramalingam, N., & Wang, Z. (2008). MIMO transmitter optimization with mean and covariance feedback for low SNR. New Orleans, LA: Institute of Electrical and Electronics Engineers GLOBECOM. doi:10.1109/GLOCOM.2008.ECP.840

Rangel Licea, V. (2009). Modelado de redes WiMAX. Retrieved from http://goo.gl/CBNa27

Rangel, V. (2002). Performance evaluation and optimisation of the DVB/DAVIC cable modem protocol. Retrieved from http://ethos.bl.uk/OrderDetails.do?uin=uk.bl.ethos.251309

Rashwan, A. H., Hesham, B. M. E., & Ali, H. H. (2009). Comparative assessments for different WiMAX scheduling algorithms. World Congress on Engineering and Computer Science- WCECS 2009. 1.

Rath, H. K., Bhorkar, A., & Sharma, V. (2006). An opportunistic DRR (O-DRR) uplink scheduling scheme for IEEE 802.16-based broadband wireless networks. Paper presented at the IETE International Conference on Next Generation Networks (ICNGN). Mumbai, India.

Rebeiz, G. M. (2003). RF MEMS theory, design and technology. Hoboken, NJ: Wiley.

Rodrigo, D., Damgaci, Y., Unlu, M., Cetiner, B. A., Romeu, J., & Jofre, L. (2011). Antenna reconfigurability based on a novel parasitic pixel layer. In Proceedings of the 5th European Conference on Antennas and Propagation (EUCAP) (pp. 3497-3500). IEEE.

Roh, W., & Paulraj, A. (2002). Outage performance of the distributed antenna systems in a composite fading channel. In Proceedings of the IEEE Vehicular Technology Conference-Fall (VTC-Fall 2002), (pp. 1520 - 1524). Vancouver, Canada: IEEE.

Rumney, M. (2009). LTE and the evolution to 4G wireless: Design and measurement challenges. Agilent Technologies Publication.

Rusek, F., Daniel, P., Buon, K. L., Erik, L. G., Marzetta, T. L., Edfors, O., & Tufvesson, F. (2013). Scaling up MIMO: Opportunities and challenges with very large arrays. IEEE Signal Processing Magazine, 30(1), 40–60. doi:10.1109/MSP.2011.2178495

Saaty, T. L. (1990). How to make a decision: The analytic hierarchy process. European Journal of Operational Research, 48(1), 9–26. doi:10.1016/0377-2217(90)90057-I

Saaty, T. L., & Alexander, J. M. (1989). Conflict resolution: The analytic hierarchy approach. New York: Praeger.

Sadri, Y., & Khanmohamadi, S. (2010). An intelligent scheduling system using fuzzy logic controller for management of services in WiMAX networks. The Journal of Supercomputing. doi: doi:10.1007/s11227-010-0523-y

Sadri, Y., & Khanmohammadi, S. (2013). A QoS aware dynamic scheduling scheme using fuzzy inference system for IEEE 802.16 networks. Wireless Personal Communications. doi:10.1007/s11277-013-1138-4

Safak, A., & Preveze, B. (2008). Analysis of delay factors for voice over WiMAX. Paper presented at the 23rd International Symposium on Computer and Information Sciences. Turkey.

Saha, S., & Mukhopadhyay, A. K. (2011). THMIP-A novel mobility management scheme using fluid flow model. 2nd International Conference on Emerging Trends and Applications in Computer Science, (NCETACS - 2011).

Saha, S., & Mukhopadhyay, A. K. (2012). Mobility management issues for next generation wireless networks. In Abawajy, Pathan, J. M., Rahman, Pathan, M. A., Deris, M. (Eds.). Network and Traffic Engineering in Emerging Distributed Computing Applications. Information Science Reference. 247-274.

Saleh, A. A. M., Rustako, A. J., & Roman, R. S. (1987). Distributed antennas for indoor radio communications. IEEE Transactions on Communications, 35(12), 1245–1251. doi:10.1109/TCOM.1987.1096716

Salem, M., Adinoyi, A., Rahman, M., Yanikomeroglu, H., Falconer, D., & Kim, Y.-D. et al. (2010). An overview of radio resource management in relay-enhanced OFDMA-based networks. IEEE Communications Surveys and Tutorials, 12(3), 422–438. doi:10.1109/SURV.2010.032210.00071

Samdanis, K., Kutscher, D., & Brunner, M. (2010). Self-organized energy efficient cellular networks. In Proceedings from PIMRC'10: The 21st IEEE International Symposium on Personal Indoor and Mobile Radio Communications. Istanbul, Turkey: IEEE.

Samdanis, K., Taleb, T., Kutscher, D., & Brunner, M. (2011). Self organized network management functions for energy efficient cellular urban infrastructures. Journal of Mobile Networks and Applications, 17(1), 119–131. doi:10.1007/s11036-011-0293-7

Samsung. (2010). R1-102186: Aperiodic CQI activation in CA. 3GPP.

Samsung. (2011). R1-110078: Simultaneous PUSCH and PUCCH transmissions in case of aperiodic CSI. 3GPP.

Sanayei, S., & Nosratinia, A. (2005). Exploiting multiuser diversity with only 1- bit feedback. Paper presented at the Institute of Electrical and Electronics Engineers Wireless Communication Networking Conference. New Orleans, LA.

Sanayei, S., & Nosratinia, A. (2007). Opportunistic downlink transmission with limited feedback. Institute of Electrical and Electronics Engineers Transactions on Information Theory, 53.

Sanjay, S., & Alexander, L. S. (2000). Scheduling for multiple flows sharing a time-varying channel: The exponential rule. Bell Labs, Lucent Technologies.

Savitha, K., & Chandrasekar, C. (2011). Vertical handover decision schemes using SAW and WPM for network selection in heterogeneous wireless networks. arXiv preprint arXiv:1109.4490.

Sayenko, A., Alanen, O., & Hamalainen, T. (2008). ARQ aware scheduling for the IEEE 802.16 base station. In Proc. IEEE Int. Conf. Communications. Beijing, China: IEEE.

Schuh, R. E., & Sommer, M. (2002). WCDMA coverage and capacity analysis for active and passive distributed antenna systems. In Proceedings of the IEEE Vehicular Technology Conference-Spring (VTC – Spring 2002), (pp. 434-438). Birmingham, AL: IEEE.

Schurgers, C., Aberthorne, O., & Srivastava, M. (2011). Modulation scaling for energy aware communication systems. In Proceedings of International Symposium on Low Power Electronics and Design. Fukuoka, Japan: Academic Press.

Seethaler, D., & Bolcskei, H. (2010). Performance and complexity analysis of infinity-norm sphere-decoding. IEEE Transactions on Information Theory, 56(3), 1085–1105. doi:10.1109/TIT.2009.2039034

Seethaler, D., Jalden, J., Studer, C., & Bolcskei, H. (2011). On the complexity distribution of sphere decoding. IEEE Transactions on Information Theory, 57(9), 5754–5768. doi:10.1109/TIT.2011.2162177

Senturia, S. D. (2001). Microsystem design (Vol. 3). Boston: Kluwer Academic Publishers.

Sesia, S., Toufic, I., & Baker, M. (2011). LTE - The UMTS long term evolution: From theory to practice. Chippenhan, UK: John Wiley & Sons. doi:10.1002/9780470978504

Sesia, S., Toufik, I., & Baker, M. (2009). LTE the UMTS long term evolution: From theory to practice. New York: John Wiley and Sons. doi:10.1002/9780470742891

Sezgin, A. Jorswieck, E., & Charafeddine, M. (2008). Interaction between scheduling and user locations in an OSTBC coded downlink system. Siegel, Germany: ITG-SCC.

Sharif, M., & Hassibi, B. (2005). On the capacity of MIMO broadcast channel with partial side information. Institute of Electrical and Electronics Engineers Transaction on Inform Theory, 51(2).

Sharp, I. (2013, April). Delivering public safety communications with LTE 3GPP. Retrieved from http://www.3gpp.org/Public-Safety

Sharp. (2009). R1-092103: Control overhead analysis on aperiodic PUSCH. 3GPP.

Sheu, T. L., & Huang, K. C. (2011). Adaptive bandwidth allocation model for multiple traffic classes in IEEE 802.16 worldwide interoperability for microwave access networks. IET Communications, 5(1), 90–98. doi:10.1049/iet-com.2010.0005

Shrivastava, S., & Vannithamby, R. (2009). Performance analysis of persistent scheduling for VoIP in WiMAX networks. In Proceedings of the IEEE 10th Annual Wireless and Microwave Technology Conference, (pp. 1-5). IEEE. doi:10.1109/WAMICON.2009.5207296

Sibille, A., Oestges, C., & Zanella, A. (2010). MIMO: From theory to implementation. Academic Press.

Simon, M. K., & Alouini, M. S. (2004). Digital communication over fading channels. New York: Wiley and Sons. doi:10.1002/0471715220

Siohan, P., Siclet, C., & Lacaille, N. (2002). Analysis and design of OFDM/OQAM systems based on filterbank theory. IEEE Transactions on Signal Processing, 50, 1170–1183. doi:10.1109/78.995073 doi:10.1109/78.995073

Sleep Mode for Mobile Base Stations Cuts Jamaican Operators' Carbon Footprint. (2013, February 26). Retrieved from http://www.gsma.com/publicpolicy/sleep-mode-for-mobile-base-stations-cuts-jamaican-operators-carbon-footprint

So, J. (2007). A downlink performance analysis of VoIP services over an IEEE 802.16e OFDMA system. IEEE Communications Letters, 11, 155–157. doi:10.1109/LCOMM.2007.061565

So, J. (2008). Performance analysis of VoIP services in the IEEE 802.16e OFDMA system with inband signaling. IEEE Transactions on Vehicular Technology, 57(3), 1876–1886. doi:10.1109/TVT.2007.909261

So, J. (2009). Performance analysis of a semi-fixed mapping scheme for VoIP services in wireless OFDMA systems. In Proceedings of the Fifth International Conference on Wireless and Mobile Communications, (pp. 13-17). doi:10.1109/ICWMC.2009.10

Sohn, H., Yoo, H., De Neve, W., Kim, C. S., & Ro, Y. M. (2010). Full-reference video quality metric for fully scalable and mobile SVC content. IEEE Transactions on Broadcasting, 56(3), 269–280. doi:10.1109/TBC.2010.2050628

So-in, C., Jain, R., & Tamimi, A. (2010). Scheduling in IEEE 802.16e mobile WiMAX networks: Key issues and a survey. IEEE Journal on Selected Areas in Communications, 27(2), 156–151. doi:10.1109/JSAC.2009.090207

Song, J., & Trajkovic, L. (2005). Modeling and performance analysis of public safety wireless networks. In Proceedings of 24th IEEE International Performace, Computing and Communications Conference (IPCCC 2005), (pp. 567-572). Phoenix, AZ: IEEE.

Song, J., Li, J., & Li, C. (2009). A cross-layer scheduling algorithm based on genetic algorithm. In Proceeding of the Seventh Annual Communication Networks and Services Research Conference. Moncton.

Song, L., & Shen, J. (2011). Evolved cellular network planning and optimization for UMTS and LTE. Boca Raton, FL: CRC Taylor & Francis Group.

Song, Q., & Jamalipour, A. (2005). A network selection mechanism for next generation networks. In Proceedings of Communications, 2005 (Vol. 2, pp. 1418–1422). IEEE.

Sorensen, T., Mogensen, P., & Frederiksen, F. (2005). Extension of the ITU channel models for wideband (OFDM) systems. In Proceedings of IEEE Vehicular Technology Conference (pp. 392–396). Dallas, TX: IEEE.

Sreng, V., Yanikomeroglu, H., & Falconer, D. (2002). Capacity enhancement through two-hop relaying in cellular radio systems. In Proceedings of IEEE Wireless Communications and Networking Conference (WCNC 2002), (pp. 881-885). Orlando, FL: IEEE.

Srinivasan, R., & Hamiti, S. (Eds.). (2009). IEEE 802.16m system description document (SDD): IEEE 802.16 task group m. Retrieved from http://www.ieee802.org/16/tgm/docs/80216m-09_0034r2.zip

Srivastava, J., Cooley, R., Deshpande, M., & Tan, P. N. (2000). Web usage mining: Discovery and application of usage patterns from web data. ACM SIGKDD Explorations, 1, 12–23. doi:10.1145/846183.846188

Standard, L. T. E. (2009). Evolved universal terrestrial radio access (EUTRA), physical channels and modulation (release 8). Retrieved from http://www.etsi.org/deliver/etsi_ts/136200_136299/136211/08.08.00_60/ts_136211v080800p.pdf

Stefania, S., Issam, T., & Matthew, B. (2009). The UMTS long term evolution forum theory to practice. Hoboken, NJ: John Willey & Sons Ltd.

Stevens-Navarro, E., & Wong, V. W. S. (2006). Comparison between vertical handoff decision algorithms for heterogeneous wireless networks. In Proceedings of Vehicular Technology Conference, 2006 (Vol. 2, pp. 947-951). IEEE.

Strohmer, T., & Beaver, S. (2003). Optimal OFDM design for time-frequency dispersive channels. IEEE Transactions on Communications, 51, 1111–1122. doi:10.1109/TCOMM.2003.814200 doi:10.1109/TCOMM.2003.814200

Su, J., Fan, B., Zheng, K., & Wang, W. (2007). A hierarchical selective CQI feedback scheme for 3GPP long-term evolution system. In Proceedings of International Symposium on Microwave, Antenna, Propagation and EMC Technologies for Wireless Communications (pp. 5–8). Beijing, China: Academic Press.

Suliman, F. E. M., Elhassan, N. M., & Ibrahim, T. A. (2012). Frequency offset estimation and cell search algorithms for OFDMA based mobile WiMAX. Paper presented at the 14th International Conference on Advanced Communication Technology (ICACT). Korea.

Sundaram, A., Maddela, M., Ramadoss, R., & Feldner, L. M. (2008). MEMS-based electronically steerable antenna array fabricated using PCB technology. Journal of Microelectromechanical Systems, 17(2), 356–362. doi:10.1109/JMEMS.2008.916291

Taghipoor, M., Tavassoli, G., & Hosseini, V. (2010). Guarantee QoS in WiMAX networks with learning automata. Paper presented at ITNG 2010. Las Vegas, NV.

Taherzadeh, M., & Khandani, A. K. (2010). On the limitations of the naïve lattice decoding. IEEE Transactions on Information Theory, 56(10), 4820–4826. doi:10.1109/TIT.2010.2059630

Tajer, A., & Wang, X. (2010). Multiuser diversity gain in cognitive networks. IEEE/ACM Transactions on Networking, 18(6), 1766–1779. doi:10.1109/TNET.2010.2048038

Tanenbaum, A. S., & Steen, M. V. (2007). Distributed systems: Principles paradigms (2nd ed.). Academic Press.

Tao, J., Weidong, X., Hsiao-Hwa, C., & Qiang, N. (2007). Multicast broadcast services support in OFDMA-based WiMAX systems. IEEE Communications Magazine, 45(8), 78–86. doi:10.1109/MCOM.2007.4290318

Tarhini, C., & Chahed, T. (2008). Density-based admission control in IEEE802.16e mobile WiMAX. Paper presented at the Wireless Days, 2008. New York, NY.

Tarokh, V., Seshadri, N., Calderbank, A. R. (1998). Space-time codes for high data rate wireless communication: performance criterion and code construction. IEEE Transactions on Information Theory. 44(2).744 – 765.

Teixeira, M. A., & Guardieiro, P. R. (2012). Scheduling mechanisms. In R. C. Hincapie, & J. E. Sierra (Eds.), Quality of service and resource allocation in WiMAX. InTech.

Telefonica – Focusing on Climate Change Pays Off For Everyone. (2010, September 8). Retrieved from https://idc-insights-community.com/groups/it_agenda/sustainability/telefonica-focusing-on-climate-change-pays-off-for

Texas Instruments. (2008). R1-080207: CQI reporting procedure for E-UTRA. 3GPP.

Texas Instruments. (2008). R1-080208: Differential CQI definition for E-UTRA. 3GPP.

Ting, P., Wen, C., & Chen, J. (2007). An efficient CSI feedback scheme for MIMO-OFDM wireless systems. Institute of Electrical and Electronics Engineers Transformations on Wireless Communications, 6.

Topalli, K., Civi, O. A., Demir, S., Koc, S., & Akin, T. (2008). A monolithic phased array using 3-bit distributed RF MEMS phase shifters. IEEE Transactions on Microwave Theory and Techniques, 56(2), 270–277. doi:10.1109/TMTT.2007.914377

Toskala, A. (2012). 3GPP TSG RAN workshop on Rel-12 and onwards: Samsung RWS-120002. Retrieved from http://www.3gpp.org/Future-Radio-in-3GPP-300-attend

Toskala, A., & Tiirola, E. (2006). UTRAN long term evaluation in 3GPP. In Proceedings of IEEE Personal Indoor and Mobile Radio Communications Conference (pp. 1-5). Helsinki, Finland: IEEE.

Tran, T. T., Shin, Y., & Shin, O. S. (2012). Overview of enabling technologies for 3GPP LTE-advanced. EURASIP Journal on Wireless Communications and Networking, (1): 1–12.

Trivellato, M., Tomasin, S., & Benvenuto, N. (2009). On channel quantization and feedback strategies for multiuser MIMO-OFDM downlink systems. Institute of Electrical and Electronics Engineers Transactions on Communications, 57.

Tsai, T., Jiang, C., & Wang, C. (2006). CAC and packet scheduling using token bucket for IEEE 802.16networks. The Journal of Communication, 1(2), 30–37.

Tse, D., & Viswanath, P. (2005). Fundamentals of wireless communications. Cambridge, UK: Cambridge University Press. Retrieved from http://www.eecs.berkeley.edu/~dtse/book.html

Tse, D., & Viswanath, P. (2005). Fundamentals of wireless communication. Cambridge, UK: Cambridge University Press. doi:10.1017/CBO9780511807213

Uysal, E., Prabhakar, B., & ElGamal, A. (2002). Energy efficient packet transmission over a wireless link. Association for Computing Machinery/Institute of Electrical and Electronics Engineers Transactions on Networking, (10).

Vanderveen, M. C. (1997). Estimation of parametric channel models in wireless communications networks. (Ph.D. dissertation). Stanford University, Department of Scientific Computing and Computational Mathematics, Palo Alto, CA.

Varadan, V. K., Jose, K. A., Varadan, V. V., Hughes, R., & Kelly, J. F. (1995). A novel microwave planar phase shifter. Microwave Journal, 38(4), 244–255.

Varadan, V. K., Vinoy, K. J., & Jose, K. A. (2003). RF MEMS and their applications. Hoboken, NJ: Wiley.

Varanese, N., Vicario, J., & Spagnolini, U. (2012). On the asymptotic throughput of OFDMA systems with best-M CQI feedback. IEEE Wireless Communications Letters, 145–148.

Varona, J., Tecpoyotl-Torres, M., Escobedo-Alatorre, J., & Hamoui, A. A. (2008). Design and fabrication of a MEMS thermal actuator for 3D optical switching applications. In Proceedings of IEEE/LEOS Summer Topical Meetings, (pp. 31-32). IEEE.

Venturino, L., Prasad, N., & Wang, X. (2009). Coordinated scheduling and power allocation in downlink multicell OFDMA networks. IEEE Transactions on Vehicular Technology, 2835–2848. doi:10.1109/TVT.2009.2013233

Vetrivelan, N., & Reddy, A. V. (2010). Modelling and analysing a novel restricted angle scenario model in MANET. In Proceedings of IEEE Regional Conference 10 (TENCON 2010). IEEE.

Video Quality Experts Group (VQEG). (2003). Final report on the validation of objective models of video quality assessment. Author.

Vijaykumar, H., & Ravichandran, M. (2011). Efficient location management of mobile node in wireless mobile ad hoc network. In Proceedings of the National Conference on Innovations in Emerging Technology, (pp. 77-84). Academic Press.

Vinella, D., & Polignano, M. (2009). Discontinuous reception and transmission (DRX/DTX) strategies in long term evolution (LTE) for voice-over-IP (VoIP) traffic under both full-dynamic and semi-persistent packet scheduling policies. (Thesis Dissertation). Aalborg University, Aalborg, Denmark.

Vishwanath, P., & Tse, D. (2003). Sum capacity of a vector Gaussian broadcast channel and uplink-downlink duality. IEEE Transactions on Information Theory, 49(8), 1912–1921. doi:10.1109/TIT.2003.814483

Vishwanath, S., Jindal, N., & Goldsmith, A. (2003). Duality, achievable rates, and sum-rate capacity of Gaussian MIMO broadcast channels. IEEE Transactions on Information Theory, 49(10), 2058–2068. doi:10.1109/TIT.2003.817421

Visotsky, E., & Madhow, U. (2000). Space-time transmit precoding with imperfect feedback. Istanbul, Turkey: ISIT.

Viswanath, P., Tse, D.N.C., & Iaroia, R. (2002). Opportunistic beam forming using dumb antenna. Institute of Electrical and Electronics Engineers transactions on information theory, 48(6), 1277-1294.

Viterbo, E., & Boutros, J. (1999). A universal lattice code decoder for fading channels. IEEE Transactions on Information Theory, 45(5), 1639–1642. doi:10.1109/18.771234

Vodafone India Switches off AC at Towers to Cut Energy Costs, and Carbon Emissions. (2013, March 20). Retrieved from http://articles.economictimes.indiatimes.com/2013-03-20/news/37872443_1_indus-towers-telecom-towers-vodafone-india

Walfisch, J., & Bertoni, H. L. (1988). A theoretical model of UHF propagation in urban environments. IEEE Transactions on Antennas and Propagation, 36(12), 1788–1796. doi:10.1109/8.14401

Wan, K., & Hwangjun, S. (2010). A novel combined packet scheduling and call admission control for video streaming over WiMAX network. Paper presented at the GLOBECOM Workshops (GC Wkshps). New York, NY.

Wang, H., Wang, Z., & Feng, G., L.V. H., Chen, X., & Zhu, Q. (2012). Intelligent access selection in cognitive networks: A fuzzy neural network approach. Journal of Computer Information Systems, 8(21), 8877–8884.

Wang, J., Ativanichayaphong, T., Huang, W. D., Cai, Y., Davis, A., Chiao, M., & Chiao, J. C. (2008). A distributed MEMS phase shifter on a low-resistivity silicon substrate. Sensors and Actuators. A, Physical, 144(1), 207–212. doi:10.1016/j.sna.2007.12.027

Wang, S.-Y., Chen, H.-Y., & Chuang, S.-W. (2010). NCTUns tool for IEEE 802.16j mobile WiMAX relay network simulations. Academic Press.

Website, G. P. P. (2013a). 3GPP TS 36.211: Evolved universal terrestrial radio access (E-UTRA), physical channels and modulation, V11.2.0. Author.

Website, G. P. P. (2013b). 3GPP TS 36.212: Evolved universal terrestrial radio access (E-UTRA), multiplexing and channel coding, V11.2.0. Author.

Wengerter, C., Ohlhorst, J., & vonElbwart, A. G. E. (2005). Fairness and throughput analysis for generalized proportional fair frequency scheduling in OFDMA. In Proceedings of the 61st IEEE Vehicular Technology Conference (VTC '05), (vol. 3, pp. 1903–1907). Stockholm, Sweden: IEEE.

Werner, K., & Jansson, M. (2009). Estimating MIMO channel covariances from training data under the Kronecker model. Signal Processing, 89(1), 1–13.

Wikipedia. (2013). Retrieved from http://en.wikipedia.org/wiki/Economies of scale

Williams, K. R., & Muller, R. S. (1996). Etch rates for micromachining processing. Journal of Microelectromechanical Systems, 5(4), 256–269. doi:10.1109/84.546406

WiMAX Forum. (2006a). Mobile WiMAX – Part 1: A technical overview and performance evaluation.

WiMaX Forum. (2006b). WiMaX end-to-end network systems architecture; Stage 2, Release 1: architecture tenets, network reference architecture, reference points.

WiMAX Forum. (2006c). WiMAX end-to-end network systems architecture; Stage 3, Release 1: detailed protocols and procedures.

WiMAX Forum. (2007). Deployment of mobile WiMAX™ networks by operators with existing 2G & 3G networks.

WiMAX Forum. (2008). WiMAX system evaluation methodology V2.1. Retrieved from http://www.wimax-forum.org/technology/documents/

WiMAX Forum. (2009). Network architecture (Stage 2: Architecture tenets, reference model and reference points).1(Release 1.0 Version 4).

WiMAX Forum. (2010). Proxy mobile IPv4. 3gpp2 RFC 5563

WiMax Forum. (2010). WiMax and the IEEE 802.16m air interface standard. Author.

Winters, J. H. (1983). Switched diversity with feedback for dpsk mobile radio systems. Institute of Electrical and Electronics Engineers Transformations on Vehicular Technology, 32(1), 134–150.

Winters, J. H. (1998). Smart antennas for wireless systems. IEEE Personal Communications, 5(1), 23–27. doi:10.1109/98.656155

Wong, C., Cheng, R., Lataief, K., & Murch, R. (1999). Multiuser OFDM with adaptive subcarrier, bit, and power allocation. Institute of Electrical and Electronics Engineers Journal on Selected Areas in Communications, 17(10), 1747–1758. doi:10.1109/49.793310

Wongthavarawat, K., & Ganz, A. (2003). Packet scheduling for QoS support in IEEE 802.16 broadband wireless access systems. International Journal of Communication Systems, 16(1), 81–96. doi:10.1002/dac.581

Woten, D. A., El-Shenawee, M., & Tung, S. (2009). Planar broadband dual-linearly polarized MEMS steerable antenna. In Proceedings of Antennas and Propagation Society International Symposium, 2009 (pp. 1-4). IEEE.

Wu, J. S., Yang, S. F., & Hwang, B. J. (2009). A terminal-controlled vertical handover decision scheme in IEEE 802.21-enabled heterogeneous wireless networks. International Journal of Communication Systems, 22(7), 819–834. doi:10.1002/dac.996

Wu, J., & Xiao, C. (2007). Performance analysis of wireless systems with doubly selective rayleigh fading. IEEE Transactions on Vehicular Technology, 56, 721–730. doi:10.1109/TVT.2007.891438 doi:10.1109/TVT.2007.891438

Wu, J., Zheng, Y. R., Letaief, K. B., & Xiao, C. (2005). Matched filter bound of wireless systems over frequency selective channels with receiver timing phase offset. In Proc. IEEE Global Telecommun. Conf. (GLOBECOM05), (pp. 3758-3762). IEEE.

Wu, J., Zheng, Y. R., Letaief, K. B., & Xiao, C. (2007). On the error performance of wireless systems with frequency selective fading and receiver timing phase offset. IEEE Transactions on Wireless Communications, 6, 720–729. doi:10.1109/TWC.2007.05417 doi:10.1109/TWC.2007.05417

Wu, T., Rui, L., Xiong, A., & Guo, S. (2010). An automation PCI allocation method for eNodeB and home eNodeB cell. In Proceedings of Wireless Communications Networking and Mobile Computing (WiCOM), 2010 6th International Conference on (pp. 1-4). IEEE.

Xiang, H. J., & Shi, Z. F. (2009). Static analysis for functionally graded piezoelectric actuators or sensors under a combined electro-thermal load. European Journal of Mechanics. A, Solids, 28(2), 338–346. doi:10.1016/j.euromechsol.2008.06.007

Xu, K., & Shen, Y. H. (2009). Effects of carrier frequency offset, timing offset, and channel spread factor on the performance of hexagonal multicarrier modulation systems. EURASIP Journal on Wireless Communications and Networking, 1–8.

Xu, K., Lv, Z., Xu, Y., & Zhang, D. (2013). Max-SINR based timing synchronization scheme in hexagonal multicarrier transmission. Wireless Personal Communications, 68, 1789–1805. doi:10.1007/s11277-012-0550-5 doi:10.1007/s11277-012-0550-5

Xu, K., Xu, Y. Y., Xia, X. C., & Zhang, D. M. (2012). On Max-SINR receiver for hexagonal multicarrier transmission over doubly dispersive channel. In Proc. 2012 IEEE Global Telecommun. Conf. (GLOBECOM12), (pp. 3673 - 3678). IEEE.

Xu, K., Xu, Y., & Zhang, D. (2011). SINR analysis of hexagonal multicarrier transmission systems in the presence of insufficient synchronization for doubly dispersive channel. Frequenz, 65, 149–157. doi:10.1515/freq.2011.020 doi:10.1515/freq.2011.020

Xu, K., Xu, Y., Zhang, D., & Ma, W. (2013). On max-SINR receiver for HMT over doubly dispersive channel. IEEE Transactions on Vehicular Technology, 62, 2381–2387. doi:10.1109/TVT.2013.2239674 doi:10.1109/TVT.2013.2239674

Xue, Y., Yin, C., Yue, W., & Liu, D. (2009). A QoS-aware resource allocation scheme with limited feedback in downlink OFDMA systems. In Proceedings of International Conference on Wireless Communications, Networking and Mobile Computing. Beijing: Academic Press.

Yaacoub, E., & Dawy, Z. (2012). Resource allocation in uplink OFDMA wireless systems: Optimal solutions and practical implementations. Hoboken, NJ: John Wiley and Sons / IEEE Press. doi:10.1002/9781118189627

Yaacoub, E., & Kubbar, O. (2012). Energy-efficient device-to-device communications in LTE public safety networks. In Proceedings of Globecom Workshops 2012 (International Workshop on Green Internet of Things), (pp. 391-395). Anaheim, CA: ACM.

Yaacoub, E., & Kubbar, O. (2012). On the performance of distributed base stations in LTE public safety networks. In Proceedings of IEEE International Wireless Communications and Mobile Computing Conference (IWCMC 2012), (pp. 927-932). Limassol, Cyprus: IEEE.

Yan, D. (2002). Mechanical design and modeling of MEMS thermal actuators for RF applications. (Doctoral dissertation). University of Waterloo.

Yang, S. F., Wu, J. S., & Huang, H. H. (2008). A vertical media-independent handover decision algorithm across Wi-Fi™ and WiMAX™ networks.[IEEE.]. Proceedings of Wireless and Optical Communications Networks, 2008, 1–5.

Yang, S., Yeo, C. K., & Lee, B. S. (2012). Toward reliable data delivery for highly dynamic mobile ad hoc networks. IEEE Transactions on Mobile Computing, 11(1).

Yang, X., Yin, J., & Yuan, S. (2009). Location-aided opportunistic routing for mobile ad hoc networks. In Proceedings of 5th International Conference on Wireless Communications, Networking and Mobile Computing. Academic Press.

Yarali, A., & Rahman, S. (2008). WiMAX broadband wireless access technology: Services, architecture and deployment models. Canadian Conference on Electrical and Computer Engineering, CCECE 2008. 77-82.

Yin, H., Gesbert, D., Filippou, M., & Liu, Y. (2013). A coordinated approach to channel estimation in large-scale multiple- antenna systems. IEEE Journal on Selected Areas in Communications, 31(2), 264–273. doi:10.1109/JSAC.2013.130214

Yonis, A. Z., Abdullah, M. F. L., & Ghanim, M. F. (2012). Effective carrier aggregation on the LTE-advanced systems. International Journal of Advanced Science and Technology, 41, 15–26.

Yu, K., Wang, X., & Zhang, L. (2009). Uplink performance analysis of VoIP services in TDD-OFDMA WiMAX networks. In Proceedings of the Fourth International Conference on Communications and Networking in China (pp. 1-5). doi:10.1109/CHINACOM.2009.5339799

Yusoff, R., & Baba, M. D. (2011). Performance analysis of transparent and non-transparent relays in MMR WiMAX networks. Paper presented at the 2011 IEEE Symposium on Industrial Electronics & Applications. Malaysia.

Yusoff, R., Baba, M. D., & Ibrahim, M. (2011). Weighted QoS admission control for IEEE 802.16j WiMAX networks. Paper presented at the Computer Applications and Industrial Electronics (ICCAIE). New York, NY.

Zaka, K., & Ahmed, N. Ibrar-ul-Haq, M., Irfan Anis, M., & Faria, B. (2009). Performance analysis and throughput optimization in IEEE 802.16 WiMax standard. Paper presented at the First Asian Himalayas International Conference on Internet. Nepal.

Ze-qun, H., Song-Nan, B., & Jung, J. (2009). A MIH services based application-driven vertical handoff scheme for wireless networks. In Proceedings of INC, IMS and IDC, 2009 (pp. 1428-1431). IEEE.

Zhang, H., Hong, P., & Xue, K. (2012). Uplink performance of LTE-based multi-hop cellular network with out-of-band relaying. In Proceedings of IEEE Consumer Communications and Networking Conference (CCNC), (pp. 817 – 821). IEEE.

Zhang, J., & Andrews, J. G. (2007). Cellular communication with randomly placed distributed antennas. In Proceedings of IEEE Globecom, (pp. 1400-1404). Washington, DC: IEEE.

Zhang, J., & Andrews, J. G. (2008). Distributed antenna systems with randomness. IEEE Transactions on Wireless Communications, 7(9), 3636–3646. doi:10.1109/TWC.2008.070425

Zhang, J., & De la Roche, G. (2010). Femtocells: Technologies and deployment. New York: Wiley. doi:10.1002/9780470686812

Zhang, W. (2004). Handover decision using fuzzy MADM in heterogeneous networks. In Proceedings of Wireless Communications and Networking Conference, 2004 (Vol. 2, pp. 653-658). IEEE.

Zhang, X. M., Wang, E. B., Xia, J. J., & Sung, D. K. (2013). A neighbour coverage-based probabilistic rebroadcast for reduced routing overhead in mobile ad hoc networks. IEEE Transactions on Mobile Computing, 12(3).

Zhang, X., & Zhou, X. (2013). LTE-advanced air interface technology. Boca Raton, FL: CRC Press Taylor & Francis Group.

Zhang, X., Lv, Z., & Wang, W. (2008). Performance analysis of multiuser diversity in MIMO systems with antenna selection. IEEE Transactions on Wireless Communications, 7(1), 5297–5311.

Zhang, Y., & Chen, H. (2007). Mobile WiMAX: Toward broadband wireless metropolitan area networks. Boston: Auerbach Publications. doi:10.1201/9780849326400

Zhao, X., & Yang, X. (2012). Downlink ergodic capacity analysis for wireless networks with cooperative distributed antenna systems. In Proceedings of IEEE International Conference on Communications (ICC 2012), (pp. 5911-5915). Ottawa, Canada: IEEE.

Zhen, K., Yu-Kwong, & Jianzhou, W. (2009). A low complexity QoS aware proportional fair multicarrier scheduling algorithm for OFDM systems. Vehiculer Transaction on IEEE Technology, 58, 2225-2235.

Zhou, S., Gong, J., Yang, Z., Niu, Z., & Yang, P. (2009). Green mobile access network with dynamic base station energy saving. In Proceeding from MobiCom'09: The 15th Annual International Conference on Mobile Computing and Networking. Beijing, China: ACM.

Zorba, N., Perez-Neira, A.I., Foglar A., & Verikoukis, C. (2009). Cross layer QoS guarantees in multiuser WLAN systems. Springer Wireless Personal Communications, 51.

About the Contributors

Raúl Aquino Santos graduated from the University of Colima with a BE in Electrical Engineering and received his MS degree in Telecommunications from the Centre for Scientific Research and Higher Education in Ensenada, Mexico, in 1990. He holds a PhD from the Department of Electrical and Electronic Engineering of the University of Sheffield, England. Since 2005, he has been with the College of Telematics, at the University of Colima, where he is currently a Research-Professor in telecommunications networks. His current research interests include wireless and sensor networks.

Victor Rangel Licea received the B.Eng (Hons) degree in Computer Engineering at the Engineering Faculty from the National Autonomous University of Mexico (UNAM) in 1996, the M.Sc in Telematics at the University of Sheffield, UK, in 1998, and the Ph.D. in performance analysis and traffic scheduling in cable networks in 2002, from the University of Sheffield. Since 2002, he has been with the School of Engineering, UNAM, where he is currently a Research-Professor in telecommunications networks. His research focuses on fixed, mesh, and mobile broadband wireless access networks, QoS over IP, traffic shaping, scheduling, handoff procedures, and performance optimization for IEEE 802.16 (wimax)-based networks. He has published more than 40 research papers in journals and international conferences, as well as directed more than 35 research master and bachelor theses. He currently has 1 Ph.D. student, 1 post-doc student, and 8 master students. Dr. Rangel has participated in the Technical Program Committee (TPC) and as a reviewer in more than 10 international conferences. He is a member of the National Research System (SNI).

Arthur Edwards Block received his Masters degree in Education from the University of Houston in 1985. He has been a Researcher-Professor at the University of Colima since 1985, where he has served in various capacities. He has been with the School of Telematics since 1998. His primary areas of research are Computer-Assisted Language Learning (CALL), distance learning, collaborative learning, multimodal learning, and mobile learning. The primary focus of his research is presently in the area of mobile collaborative learning.

* * *

Luis Alonso earned his PhD in the Department of Signal Theory and Communications of the UPC, and he reached the PhD degree in 2001. In 2006, he obtained a permanent tenured position in the University, becoming an Associate Professor within the Radio Communications Research Group. In 2009, he co-founded the Wireless Communications and Technologies Research Group (WiComTec), to which currently belongs. He participates in several research programs, networks of excellence, COST actions, and integrated projects funded by the European Union and the Spanish Government, always working on the design and analysis of different mechanisms and techniques to improve wireless communications systems. He has been collaborating with some telecommunications companies as Telefónica, Alcatel, Abertis, and Sener, working as a consultant for several research projects. He is external audit expert for TUV Rheinland. He is currently the Project Coordinator of two European Projects (Marie Curie ITN and IAPP), funded by the European Union, and he has been the Project Coordinator of other three European Projects (Marie Curie Actions ToK, IEF, and IAPP) as well. He has been the Scientist in Charge of a project carried out in coordination with ADIF, which is the Spanish Railway Infrastructure Administrator, related to wireless communications in the high-speed railway transportation system. He has also been the Scientist in Charge of one three-year Research Project funded by the Spanish Ministry of Science and Technology. He is author of more than 30 research papers in international journals and magazines, 1 book, 12 chapters in books, and more than 100 papers in international congresses and symposiums. His current research interests are still within the field of medium access protocols, radio resource management, cross-layer optimization, cooperative transmissions, cognitive radio, network coding, and QoS features for all kind of wireless communications systems.

Omar Álvarez Cárdenas was born in Colima on November 4th 1969. He graduated in 1993 as a Communications and Electronic Engineer at the University of Colima. In 1999, he completed his Master of Science in Telematics at the University of Colima. Actually is a research-professor at the School of Telematics with research interest in wireless communications, wireless sensor networks, metro ethernet networks, quality of service, modeling and simulating networks, and mobile computing.

Angelos Antonopoulos received his PhD degree from the Signal Theory and Communications (TSC) Department of the Technical University of Catalonia (UPC) in December 2012, while he holds an MSc degree from the Information and Communication Systems Engineering Department (ICSDE) of the University of the Aegean (2007). Since 2008, he has been involved in several national and European projects (ICARUS, CO2Green, Green-T, Greenet, etc.). He is currently working at the Smart Energy Efficient Communication Technologies (SMARTECH) area of the Telecommunications Technological Centre of Catalonia (CTTC) and his main research interests include MAC protocols, RRM algorithms, network coding, and energy-efficient network planning.

Habib Badri Ghavifekr received the B.S. degree from Tabriz University, Iran, and continued his study in Germany and received the M.S. degree (Diploma Engineer) from Technical University of Berlin, in 1995, both in electrical engineering. Immediately after that, he joined the Institute for Microperipheric at the Technical University of Berlin (nowadays BeCAP: Berliner Center for Advanced Packaging) as a scientific assistant and in 1998 the Fraunhofer Institute for Reliability and Microintegration (FhG-IZM) as a research assistant. In 2003, he received his PhD in electrical engineering from Technical University of Berlin. Since 2005, he is an assistant professor at Sahand University of Technology, Tabriz, Iran. His research interests are microsystem technologies, microelectronic packaging, MEMS, and electronic measurement systems for industrial applications.

Alexandra Bousia received her B.S. and M.S. degree in Computer and Communication Engineering from the Department of Computer and Communication Engineering in University of Thessaly, in 2008 and 2009, respectively. She is currently working towards the PhD degree in Wireless Communications at the Technical University of Catalonia (UPC), and she is working as a Marie Curie researched in the same department. Since 2011, she has been involved in several national and European research funded projects (Greenet, CO2Green, Green-T, Geocom). Her research interests include wireless networks, MAC protocols, energy efficient communication protocols and RRM algorithms.

Zheng Chang received the B.Eng. Degree from Jilin University, Changchun, China, in 2007, and M.Sc. (Communications Engineering) from Helsinki University of Technology (Now Aalto University), Espoo, Finland, in 2009. During 2008-2009, he was with the Department of Communications and Networking, Helsinki University of Technology. Since August 2010, he has been a Ph.D. student of University of Jyväskylä, Jyväskylä, Finland. Currently, he is also working in Magister Solutions Ltd. His research interests include signal processing, radio resource allocation for wireless systems, green communications, and WLAN.

Yue Chen, BS, MS, PhD, MIET, MIEEE, joined the Networks group at QMUL in 2000 and continued as a member of staff in 2003 after obtaining her PhD in wireless communications. She is a senior lecturer and has been involved in a numerous number of research activities, including the IST project SHUFFLE. Her current research interests include intelligent radio resource management for wireless networks, MAC and network layer protocol design, scheduling and load balancing optimization, CoMP, cognitive radio, LTE-A networks, machine-to-machine communications, and intelligent transport system.

Zaher Dawy received the B.E. degree in computer and communications engineering from the American University of Beirut (AUB), Beirut, Lebanon, in 1998, and the M.E. and Dr.-Ing. degrees in communications engineering from Munich University of Technology (TUM), Munich, Germany, in 2000 and 2004, respectively. Since September 2004, he has been with the Department of Electrical and Computer Engineering, AUB, where he is currently an Associate Professor. His research and teaching interests include distributed and cooperative communications, cellular technologies, radio network planning and optimization, radio resource management, context-aware mobile computing, mobile solutions for smart cities, computational genomics, and bioinformatics. Dr. Dawy is an Associate Editor for *IEEE Communications Surveys and Tutorials* and an Executive Editor for *Wiley Transactions on Emerging Telecommunications Technologies*.

Arthur Edwards received his master's degree in Education from the University of Houston in 1985. He has been a researcher-professor at the University of Colima since 1985, where he has served in various capacities. He has been with the School of Telematics since 1998. His primary areas of research are Computer Assisted Language Learning (CALL), distance learning, collaborative learning, multimodal leaning and mobile learning. The primary focus of his research is presently in the area of mobile collaborative learning.

Laura Victoria Escamilla del Río was born in Guadalajara, Jalisco, México in 1985, currently lives in Villa de Álvarez, Colima, México. She graduated in 2010 as a Telematic´s Engineer at the University of Colima, where she is now studying a Master in Computer Science. Currently, she is developing projects related to control system in domotics environments and wireless communications networks.

Juan Michel Garcia Díaz was born in Guadalajara, Jalisco, Mexico, on January 12, 1986, and currently lives in Villa de Alvarez, Colima, Mexico. He graduated in 2008 as a Computer Systems Engineer at the University of Colima, where he is now studying the Master of Computer Science. He is currently developing projects related to vehicular networks and multimodal interfaces. He is also interested in wireless communications networks.

Mario García-Lozano received his M.Sc. and Ph.D. in Telecommunications Engineering from the Universitat Politècnica de Catalunya (UPC, Barcelona-TECH), Spain, in 2001 and 2009, respectively. From 1999 to 2002, he was a member of the technical staff at Retevision, Spain, where he worked on the radio planning of LMDS networks. In 2002, he joined the Department of Signal Theory and Communications at UPC, where he currently lectures as a tenured associate professor. He has actively participated in several research projects funded by the European Union and the Spanish government. He has also worked as a consultant in projects funded by private telecommunication companies and institutions. His research activities are focused in the field of radio network planning and radio resource management issues both for cellular and broadcasting networks.

David González was born in Chitré, Herrera, Republic of Panama. He received his BS in Electronics and Communications Engineering degree from the University of Panamá in 2002. From 2002 to 2005, he worked as Telecommunication Engineer at Cable Onda, a cable TV operator in Panamá, where he was involved in the integration of VoIP services. During this period, he also participated at Universidad Tecnológica de Panamá as part-time assistant professor. In 2007, he received his MS degree (with emphasis in cellular networks) from the Universitat Politècnica de Catalunya (UPC), where he is currently working toward his Ph.D. degree in the Department of Signal Theory and Communications. David has participated in the European COST Actions 2100 and IC1004. His research interests include intercell interference coordination and radio resource management for OFDMA cellular networks.

Mark A. Gregory was born in Melbourne, Australia, and received a PhD and a Master of Engineering from RMIT University, Melbourne, Australia, in 2008 and 1992, respectively, and a Bachelor of Engineering (Electrical) from University of New South Wales, Sydney, Australia, in 1984. He is a Senior Lecturer in the School of Electrical and Computer Engineering, RMIT University, Melbourne, Australia. He is a retired Army officer who spent four years working on major defense projects and a director of an engineering consultancy. Dr. Gregory is a Fellow of the Institute of Engineers Australia, a Senior Member of the Institute of Electrical and Electronics Engineers Inc. and his research interests include cyber-security, fiber network design and operation, wireless networks, and technical risk. Dr. Gregory received an Australian Learning and Teaching Council Citation in 2009.

Elli Kartsakli received her PhD in Wireless Telecommunications from the Technical University of Catalonia (BarcelonaTECH) in February 2012. She holds a degree in Electrical and Computer Engineering from the National Technical University of Athens, Greece (2003), and an MSc in Mobile and Satellite Communications from the University of Surrey, UK (2004). Since 2009, she has participated in several national and European projects. Her research interests include wireless networking, channel access protocols and energy efficient communication protocols.

Kok Keong (Michael) Chai, BEng, MSc, PhD, MIEEE, joined Queen Mary, University of London (QMUL), UK, as a Joint Programme Lecturer in 2008. His research field is in the areas of next generation wireless networks with particular focus on intelligent radio resource management for next generation wireless networks, machine-to-machine communications, and Internet of things in intelligent transport systems. The innovations in his work include QoS-aware packet scheduling in OFDMA-Based LTE-A Networks, efficient ad hoc routing protocols for vehicular networks, and dynamic radio resource allocation for vehicular networks.

Md. Abdul Latif Sarker received the B.S. (Hons) and M.S. Degrees in Applied Physics, Electronics, and Communication Engineering from Islamic University in Bangladesh in 2003 and 2004, respectively. He is currently doing research towards the Ph.D. degree of Electronic Engineering as a researcher at the Institute of Information and Communication at Chonbuk National University, Republic of Korea, since 2010. His research interests include the areas of MIMO-LTE Advanced, Jacket Matrices, Digital Signal Processing (DSP) and Field Programmable Gate Array (FPGA).

Moon Ho Lee is a professor and former chair of the Department of Electronics Engineering at Chonbuk National University, Korea. He received the Ph.D. degree from Chonnam National University, Korea, in 1984, and from the University of Tokyo, Japan, in 1990, both Electrical Engineering. He was in the University of Minnesota, USA, from 1985 to 1986, as a post-doctor. He was conferred an honorary doctorate from the Bulgarian Academy of Sciences in 2010. He has been working in Namyang MBC broadcasting with chief engineer from 1970 to 1980; after that he joined to Chonbuk National University as a Professor. Dr. Lee has made significant original contributions in the areas of mobile communication code design, channel coding, and multi-dimensional source, and channel coding. He has authored 40 books, 160 SCI papers in international journals, and 260 papers in domestic journals, and delivered 410 papers at international conferences. Dr. Lee is a member of the National Academy of Engineering in Korea and a Foreign Fellow of the Bulgarian Academy of Sciences. He is the inventor of Jacket Matrix.

Mohammad Faiz Liew Abdullah received BSc (Hons) in Electrical Engineering (Communication) in 1997, Dip Education in 1999, and MEng by research in Optical Fiber Communication in 2000 from University of Technology Malaysia (UTM). He completed his PhD in August 2007 from The University of Warwick, United Kingdom, in Wireless Optical Communication Engineering. He started his career as a lecturer at Polytechnic Seberang Prai (PSP) in 1999, and was transferred to UTHM in 2000 (formerly known as PLSP). At present, he is Assist Professor in the Department of Communication Engineering, Faculty of Electrical and Electronic Engineering, University Tun Hussein Onn Malaysia (UTHM). He had 12-years' experience of teaching in higher education, which involved the subjects optical fiber communication, advanced optical communication, advanced digital signal processing, etc. His research area of interest are wireless and optical communication and robotic in communication.

Wenfeng Ma was born in 1974. He received the B.S. degree, M.S. degree, and Ph.D. degree from PLA University of Science and Technology, Nanjing, China, in 1996, 1998, and 2003, respectively. He is an associate professor with the Nanjing Institute of Communication Engineering, China. His research interests include new generation wireless mobile communication system, radio resource management, and network coding in wireless communication.

Margarita Glenda Mayoral Baldivia was born in Colima, México, on July 6th. She graduated in Degree in Computer, and in 1998, she completed his Master of Science in Telematics at the University of Colima. Currently, she is a Research-Professor at School of Telematics with research interest in security network, wireless communications. She is Main Contact of Program Networking Academy de Cisco.

Hadi Mirzajani received his B.Sc. degree in Electronic Engineering from Azad University of Tabriz, Tabriz, Iran, in 2010. Immediately after that, he joined the microsystems research group at Electrical Engineering department in Sahand University of Technology, Tabriz, Iran, as a Master of Science student. In that period, he was involved in designing numerous RF MEMS devices and components for wireless communication applications under supervision of Dr. Habib Badri Ghavifekr. After graduation from M.Sc. in September 2012, he continued his studies as a PhD candidate. He is now pursuing his PhD degree in Electronic Engineering with the focus on Radio Frequency Microelectromechanical Systems Technology under supervision of Dr. Habib Badri Ghavifekr in microsystems research group at Electrical Engineering department in Sahand University of Technology. He is the author and coauthor of numerous journal and conference papers in the fields of microsystems and microelectromechanical systems technology. He is also the reviewer of a number of journals and conferences in his fields of interest. His main research interests include RF MEMS/NEMS technology, micro/nanofabrication, MEMS-enabled reconfigurable antennas, smart and miniaturized antennas, and radio frequency integrated circuits.

Asish K. Mukhopadhyay is M.Tech (ECE) from IIT Kharagpur and Ph.D(Engg) from Jadavpur University, Kolkata. He is the Director of Bengal Institute of Tech and Management, Santiniketan, and the Chairman, Computer Society of India, Durgapur Chapter. With more than 38 years of experience in teaching, research, administration, he served institutions like IIT Kharagpur, NERIST Itanagar, CEMK, Kolaghat, NiT, Kolkata, BCREC, Durgapur, BCETW, Durgapur, holding various positions such as Principal, Dean, HoD, etc. His current area of research includes next generation wireless and mobile networks. He has about 65 research publications in national/international journals and conference proceedings and delivered many key note/theme lectures in conferences. He is honorary Life Fellow of ACEEE, Life Fellow of the Institution of Engineers (I), Sr. Member, IEEE, Sr. Life Member, CSI; Life Member of ISTE, SSI, and IETE.

Esmaeil Najafi Aghdam was born in Zonouz, Iran, in 1964. He received the B.E. degree from University of Sistan and Baluchestan, Zahedan, Iran, in 1990, and the M.S. degree from Amir-Kabir University of Technology, Tehran, Iran, in 1994, both in electronic engineering. In 1995, he joined the Department of Electrical Engineering at Sahand University of Technology, Tabriz, Iran, as a Lecturer. In 2002, he started his PhD program dealing with a high-performance bandpass Delta Sigma ADC. The research program was directed by Prof. P. Benabes at SUPELEC, France. Since 2006, he is an Assistant Professor at Sahand University of Technology. His current research interests include mixed mode electronic circuits, Delta Sigma Converters, RF design, Ultrasonic circuits and Electronic measurement.

Mohammadhossein Norouzibeirami received B.Sc. degree in Computer Engineering in 2005 from PNU bonab University and M.Sc. degree in Computer Software Engineering in 2008 from Islamic Azad University (IAU) Qazvin branch, Iran. He is a Faculty member at IAU Osku branch since 2008. His research interests are algorithm, resource allocation, data mining, and fuzzy logic.

Rehana Kausar, BEng, MSc, PhD, MIEEE, MIMAP, joined Queen Mary University of London in 2009 as a research student and teacher assistant. She had two MSc degrees, in Physics and Data Communications and Networks, with distinction. Her interests are Radio Resource Management in the next generation wireless networks, in particular cross-layer design adaptive scheduling architectures based on 3GPP specifications, mainly Release 8 and 10. The innovations in her work are QoS-aware packet scheduling architecture, service-specific queue-sorting algorithms, and an intelligent time domain scheduling algorithm for a fair resource allocation in terms of throughput and packet drop rate in LTE-Advanced networks.

Kyeong J. Kim received the M.S. Degree from the Korea Advanced Institute of Science and Technology (KAIST) in 1991, and the M.S. and Ph.D. degrees in electrical and computer engineering from the University of California, Santa Barbara, in 2000. After receiving his degrees, he joined the Nokia Research Center in Dallas as a senior research engineer. From 2005 to 2009, he worked with the Nokia Corporation in Dallas as an L1 specialist. His research has focused on the transceiver design, resource management, and scheduling in the cooperative wireless communication systems. Now he is working with Mitsubishi Electronic Research Laboratories (MERL) in Cambridge, MA, USA.

Anup Kumar Bhattacharjee completed B.E. (E&TC) in 1983, M.E.Tel.E. in 1985 from Jadavpur University. He completed Ph.D. (Engg.) in 1989. He has more than 25 years of teaching and research experience. He has published more than 150 research papers in various international journals and conferences of repute. He guided 6 PhD students successfully. His areas of interests are Antenna, EM Theory, Radar Engg., Microwave Circuits, Microwave Devices, and Satellite Communication.

Farukh M. Rahman, with 8 years of experience in Telecommunication Industry, has a combined resource of academic knowledge and relevant industry experience. He completed his Bachelor of Electrical and Electronic Engineering from IUT, Bangladesh, in 2001. Then he completed his Masters of Engineering in Information Technology from RMIT University, Australia, in the year 2005. Since then, he is working with the leading telecommunication companies of Australia and performed various roles within network and IT operations, escalated project and incident management, etc. Currently, he is working as a member of a large-scale program of work under National Broadband Network migration for Special Services. Farukh has sheer interest towards innovative researches and is currently pursuing PhD in Communication Engineering. His area of research is developing an optimum routing technique for MANET within LTE cellular network and already achieved few IEEE publications.

Tapani Ristaniemi received his M.Sc. in 1995 (Mathematics), Ph.Lic. in 1997 (Applied Mathematics) and Ph.D. in 2000 (Wireless Communications), all from the University of Jyväskylä, Jyväskylä, Finland. In 2001, he was appointed as Professor in the Department of Mathematical Information Technology, University of Jyväskylä. In 2004, he moved to the Department of Communications Engineering, Tampere University of Technology, Tampere, Finland, where he was appointed as Professor in Wireless Communications. In 2006, he moved back to University of Jyväskylä to take up his appointment as Professor in Computer Science. He is an Adjunct Professor of Tampere University of Technology. In 2013, he was a Visiting Professor in the School of Electrical and Electronic Engineering, Nanyang Technological University, Singapore. He has authored or co-authored over 150 publications in journals, conference proceedings and invited sessions. He served as a Guest Editor of *IEEE Wireless Communications* in 2011 and currently he is an Editorial Board Member of *Wireless Networks* and *International Journal of Communication Systems*. His research interests are in the areas of brain and communication signal processing and wireless communication systems research. Besides academic activities, Professor Ristaniemi is also active in the industry. In 2005, he co-founded a start-up Magister Solutions Ltd. in Finland, specialized in wireless system R&D for telecom and space industries in Europe. Currently, he serves as a consultant and a Member of the Board of Directors.

Silvia Ruiz Boqué received her MSc and PhD degrees in telecommunication engineering from the Universitat Politècnica de Catalunya (UPC), Spain, in 1986 and 1989, respectively. She is responsible of the Wireless Communications and Technologies Research Team (WiComTec, UPC) specialized in radio network planning and optimization field, where she has many international publications and books that are fruit of the collaboration in several European projects and COST Actions.

Yasser Sadri received B.Sc. degree in Computer Engineering in 2004 and M.Sc. degree in Computer Software Engineering in 2010 from Islamic Azad University (IAU) Shabestar branch, Iran. He is a main member of IAU Young Researchers club since 2003. He also has worked as an assistant to mechanize information system in zakarya hospital, Tabriz. Yasser is a Lecturer at IAU since 2010. His research interests are scheduling methods, resource allocation, next generation wireless networks, WiMAX networks, artificial intelligence, and fuzzy systems.

Sajal Saha is currently working as Assistant professor in the department of computer application, Narula Institute of Technology, Kolkata, India, since August 2004. He received his ME degree in Information Technology from West Bengal University of Technology (2007), MCA degree from Sikkim Manipal Institute of Technology, Sikkim (2004) and BSc (Physics) degree from Calcutta University (2001). His current research area includes Overlay based heterogeneous networks, Mobile IP route optimization, Remote Sensing, and GIS. Shri Saha is the recipient of Silver medal for securing 2nd position in ME examination. He has nine years of professional experience in educational and research field. He contributed significantly in the area of Mobile computing for the last five years. He published 20 papers in refereed international and national journals and conferences of repute. Total citation count of all his papers are 12 until now and h-index: 2. He authored a book titled *GIS and Remote Sensing: Applications in Flood Damage Assessment* published by Lap Lambert Academic Publishing, Germany.

Christos Verikoukis received degree in Physics and M.Sc. in Telecommunications Engineering from the Aristotle University of Thessaloniki in 1994 and 1997, respectively. He got his PhD from the Technical University of Catalonia in 2000. Since February 2004, he is a senior research associate in Telecommunications Technological Centre of Catalonia (CTTC). Before joining CTTC, he was research associate and projects coordinator in the Southeastern Europe Telecommunications & Informatics Research Institute in Greece. He has been involved in several European (FP5 IST, FP6 IST & Marie-Curie, FP7 ICT & People, EUREKA) and national (in Spain and in Greece) research funded projects, while in some of them he has served at the Project or the Technical Manager. He has published over 100 journal and conference papers, 10 chapters in different books, and 2 books. His research interests include MAC protocols, RRM algorithms, cross-layer techniques, and cooperative and cognitive communications for wireless systems.

Kui Xu was born in China. He received the B.S. degree, M.S., degree and Ph.D. degree from PLA University of Science and Technology, Nanjing, China, in 2004, 2006, and 2009. He is currently a lecturer in the Wireless Communications Department, Institution of Communications Engineering, PLAUST. His research interests include multicarrier modulation, synchronization, signal processing in communications, network coding, and blind source separation. He received the 2010 ten excellent doctor degree dissertation award of PLAUST.

Youyun Xu was born in 1966. He graduated from Shanghai Jiao Tong University with a Ph.D. degree in information and communication engineering in 1999. He is currently a professor with the Nanjing Institute of Communication Engineering, China. He is also a part-time professor with the Institute of Wireless Communication Technology of Shanghai Jiao Tong University (SJTU), China. He has more than 20 years of professional experience of teaching and researching in communication theory and engineering. Now, his research interests are focusing on new generation wireless mobile communication systems (IMT-advanced and related), advanced channel coding and modulation techniques, multi-user information theory and radio resource management, wireless sensor networks, cognitive radio networks, etc. He is a senior member of IEEE, and a senior member of the Chinese Institute of Electronics.

Elias Yaacoub received the B.E. degree in Electrical Engineering from the Lebanese University in 2002, the M.E. degree in Computer and Communications Engineering from the American University of Beirut (AUB) in 2005, and the PhD degree in Electrical and Computer Engineering from AUB in 2010. He worked as a Research Assistant in the American University of Beirut from 2004 to 2005, and in the Munich University of Technology in Spring 2005. From 2005 to 2007, he worked as a Telecommunications Engineer with Dar Al-Handasah, Shair, and Partners. Since November 2010, he is a Research Scientist at the QU Wireless Innovations Center (QUWIC), rebranded to QMIC (Qatar Mobility Innovations Center) in July 2012. His research interests include wireless communications, antenna theory, sensor networks, energy efficiency in wireless networks, video streaming over wireless networks, and bioinformatics.

Dongmei Zhang was born in 1972. She received her B.E. and M.E. degrees in communication engineering in 1993 and 2005, respectively. She is an associate professor with the Nanjing Institute of Communication Engineering, China. Her research interests include new generation wireless mobile communication system, radio resource management, and network coding in wireless communication.

Nizar Zorba holds a BSc in Electrical Engineering from JUST University (Jordan, 2002), a MSc in Data Communications by the University of Zaragoza (Spain, 2004), an MBA by the University of Zaragoza (Spain, 2005), and a PhD in Signal Processing for Communications by UPC-Barcelona (Spain, 2007). He is currently a research scientist at QMIC. He led and participated in more than 20 research projects (European, Qatari, and Spanish funded). He is author of 6 patents, 2 books, 5 book chapters and more than 80 peer-reviewed journals and international conferences. His research interests are QoS/QoE in wireless systems, energy efficiency, and resource optimization in WLAN and LTE systems.

Aws Zuheer Yonis has strong expertise in wireless access technologies and mobile communications such as LTE, LTE-Advanced, WiMAX, and applications to communication systems. His educational attainments are B.Eng. from Technical College of Mosul in Iraq, MSc. and PhD. from Faculty of Electrical and Electronic Engineering at University Tun Hussein Onn Malaysia in Malaysia. He became an engineer at college of electronic engineering at university of Mosul, Iraq, in 2006. He has published a book and many papers in international journals and conferences. He is member of IEEE, IAENG, SCIEI, SIE, CBEES, SDIWC, IACSIT, and Syndicate of Iraqi Engineers.

Index